S0-AQL-582

FREUD'S WOMEN

LISA APPIGNANESI
JOHN FORRESTER

OTHER

Other Press
New York

Library of Congress Cataloging-in-Publication Data

Appignanesi, Lisa.
 Freud's women / Lisa Appignanesi and John Forrester.
  p. cm.
 Originally published: New York : Basic Books, c1992.
 Includes bibliographical references and index.
 ISBN 1-892746-94-8 (pbk.)
  1. Freud, Sigmund, 1856-1939—Relations with women. 2. Freud, Sigmund, 1856-1939—Views on women. 3. Women and psychoanalysis—History. 4. Women psychoanalysts—History. I. Forrester, John. II. Title.

 BF109.F74 A86 2001
 150.19'52'082—dc21

                                                    2001053095

CONTENTS

ILLUSTRATIONS

Sigmund Freud and Martha Bernays, wedding photograph, 1886 (*courtesy A.W. Freud et al.*)

Sophie and Anna Freud, 1901 (*courtesy A.W. Freud et al.*)

Sigmund Freud with Anna in the Dolomites, 1913 (*courtesy A.W. Freud et al.*)

Amalie Freud, Martha Freud, Sigmund Freud and Minna Bernays, Altaussee, 1905 (*courtesy A.W. Freud et al.*)

Bertha Pappenheim – 'Anna O.'

Aurelia Kronich – 'Katharina', c. 1893 (*courtesy Peter J. Swales*)

Emma Eckstein, 1895 (*courtesy A.W. Freud et al.*)

Third International Psychoanalytical Congress, Weimar, 1911 (*courtesy A.W. Freud et al.*)

Loë Kann (*courtesy Vincent Brome*)

Lou Andreas-Salomé (*courtesy A.W. Freud et al.*)

Sigmund Freud and Anna at The Hague Congress, 1920 (*courtesy A.W. Freud et al.*)

Sigmund Freud and Anna in Maresfield Gardens, spring 1939 (*photo by and courtesy of Marcel Sternberger*)

Dorothy Burlingham and Anna Freud in Maresfield Gardens, 1979 (*photo by and courtesy of Michael John Burlingham*)

Eva Rosenfeld with her daughter Maedi and friend, c. 1922 (*courtesy Victor Ross*)

Ruth Mack Brunswick with her daughter Mathilda, named after Freud's daughter, c. 1930 (*courtesy A.W. Freud et al.*)

Marie Bonaparte with her children, Eugénie and Peter, c. 1913 (*courtesy A.W. Freud et al.*)

Joan Riviere with her daughter Diana, c. 1913 (*courtesy Archives of the British Psycho-Analytical Society and the Archives Committee*)

Helene Deutsch in 1936 (*courtesy Paul Roazen*)

PREFACE

In analysing one of his own dreams in *The Interpretation of Dreams*, Freud alludes to Rider Haggard's *She*: 'A strange book, but full of hidden meaning,' where 'the eternal feminine, the immortality of our emotions' is explored; and where the guide on 'an adventurous road that had scarcely ever been trodden before, leading into an undiscovered region' is a woman. *She* becomes for Freud here an allegory of his own dream book, his charting of the perilous royal road to the undiscovered region of the unconscious and its 'ultimate explanations' – the science of psychoanalysis. Freud's guide, too, we can infer, is a woman. Indeed, women – whether family, patients or friends – were to serve as Freud's guides and much besides throughout his life. And after his death, they have continued to be at once vexed and fascinated at the mirror he held up to them, as well as his reflection within it.

Writing *Freud's Women* has been something of an adventure for us too, though hardly so perilous a journey as that in quest of *She*. Alongside the intrinsic excitement of the trajectory, there has been the challenge of co-authorship. We knew from the start that the Freud in our title was to act as a possessive adjective. How *prepossessing* a one was an open question. What we were certain of was that the women were to have centre stage. The parts played by Freud's male teachers, his complex relationships with friends such as Wilhelm Fliess, Carl Jung and Otto Rank, how he gained – and lost – his disciples have been described and interpreted elsewhere; our work does not pit the women against the men, nor does it compare them.

When it came to dividing up the material, it seemed logical, because of our different areas of expertise, that the male member of the team would engage with those women whom we know primarily through Freud's eyes – his family, his dreams and patients, as well as his ideas on femininity – while the female member would engage with those remarkable figures who were the first women analysts, translators and writers close to Freud. In the event, this proved to be largely the way things turned out, though, given the amount of discussion and mutual editing, every part of the book now bears a double imprint.

The advantage of writing in common is the constant and continual exposure to the critical eye that the solitary author often only receives after the fact. There were, inevitably, fierce debates between us, not only over content and points of interpretation, but also over style and, oh yes, even footnotes. None the less, the 'boggy ground and the chasm' – to quote Freud on *She* again – are now traversed and charted; we live to tell the tale. In retrospect, we cannot imagine how this book could have come to be without the stimulus of double parenting.

Our task was potentially an interminable one, since so many women play a part in the history of psychoanalysis – and its debate on femininity has run and run. So we decided to limit our narrative to those women who had some continuing direct contact with Freud. As a result, we do not deal separately either with Karen Horney or Melanie Klein, for instance – though, of course, they figure in these pages. Nor do we intend this book to assess the respective contributions of men and of women to psychoanalysis.

Our acknowledgments could be as interminable as our material. We are indebted to all those who have been here before us, devoting separate studies to individual figures or probing a specific aspect of the histories we tell. Their names figure in text and bibliography. We also owe thanks to a great many people who have personally helped us: Michael Molnar of the Freud Museum, London; Victor Ross, Eva Rosenfeld's son, whose personal reminiscences of the Freud family were a great stimulus; Peter Swales; Sonu Shamdasani; Juliet Mitchell; Riccardo Steiner; Marina Warner; John Kerr (to whom we are grateful for making available to us a copy of his dissertation on Jung, Freud and Sabina Spielrein, together with additional chapters soon to be published in his detailed study, *A Dangerous Method*); Adam Phillips; Paul Roazen; Jacqueline Rose; Andrew Paskauskas; Anthony Stadlen; Jill Duncan of the Archives of the Institute of Psycho-analysis, London; Tom Roberts, Archivist at Sigmund Freud Copyrights, Wivenhoe, Essex; Teresa Brennan; John Deathridge (for his knowledge of the history of opera); Monica Holmes; Athol Hughes for her help on Joan Riviere. Hilary Laurie, our editor at Weidenfeld & Nicolson, has been ever patient and supportive, and our copy-editor, Linda Osband, a boon when we could no longer catch each other's slips.

We owe particular debts to Josh and Katrina, two long-suffering children, and their grandmother, who could all do with a rest from women and from Freud. And finally a too rarely voiced acknowledgment to each other, since we couldn't have done it without the mutual battles and the mutual encouragement.

Lisa Appignanesi
John Forrester
London & Cambridge, 1 March 1992

TEXT
ACKNOWLEDGMENTS

We would like to thank A.W. Freud et al., by arrangement with Mark Paterson & Associates, and The Estate of Anna Freud, by arrangement with Mark Paterson & Associates, for permission to quote unpublished material to be found in the Freud Archive, Library of Congress, Washington DC, The Anna Freud Bequest, Library of Congress, Washington DC, the Freud Museum, London, and Sigmund Freud Copyrights, Wivenhoe, Essex.

We would like to thank the Beinecke Rare Book and Manuscript Library, Yale University, for permission to quote from H.D.'s letters to Kenneth Macpherson and Bryher, and from her poem 'The Master'.

We are grateful to the following for permission to quote from published works:

Allen & Unwin for the following works from *The Standard Edition of the Complete Psychological Works of Sigmund Freud*, ed. James Strachey: *The Interpretation of Dreams* (vol. IV); *Delusion and Dream in Jensen's 'Gradiva'* (vol. IX); 'Leonardo da Vinci and a Memory of his Childhood' (vol. XI); *Introductory Lectures on Psycho-analysis* (vol. XVI).

The Atheneum Press, New York, for M.J. Burlingham, *The Last Tiffany*, 1989.

Baillière Tindall for Ernest Jones, *Papers on Psycho-analysis*, 5th edn (London: Baillière, Tindall & Cox, 1950).

Jonathan Cape for Simone de Beauvoir, *The Second Sex* (London: Jonathan Cape, 1953).

Harvard University Press for *The Complete Correspondence of Sigmund Freud and Ernest Jones, 1908–1939*, ed. R. Andrew Paskauskas (Cambridge, Mass., and London: Harvard University Press, 1993).

The Hogarth Press for Freud, *Collected Papers*; Freud and Breuer, *Studies on Hysteria; Letters of Sigmund Freud, 1873–1939*, ed. Ernst L. Freud, trans. Tania and James Stern (London: The Hogarth Press, 1970); *Sigmund Freud and Lou Andreas-Salomé. Letters*, ed. Ernst Pfeiffer, trans. William and Elaine Robson-Scott (London: The Hogarth Press and the Institute of Psycho-analysis, 1972); Ernest Jones, *Sigmund Freud. Life and Work* (London: The Hogarth

Press, 1953–7), vols I–III; Robert Fliess (ed.), *The Psycho-Analytic Reader* (London: The Hogarth Press, 1950); *Elisabeth Young-Bruehl (ed.), Freud on Women* (London: The Hogarth Press, 1990).

Indiana University Press for Susan Stanford Friedman, *Psyche Reborn: The Emergence of H.D.* (Bloomington, IN.: Indiana University Press, 1981).

H. Karnac (Books) Ltd and the Melanie Klein Trust for Joan Riviere, *The Inner World and Joan Riviere. Collected Papers 1920–1958*, ed. with a biographical chapter by Athol Hughes, foreword by Hanna Segal (London and New York: Karnac Books, 1991).

W.W. Norton & Company, Inc., for Helene Deutsch, *Confrontations with Myself* (New York: Norton, 1973).

Peter Owen Publishers, London, for Maryse Choisy, *Sigmund Freud. A New Appraisal* (London: Peter Owen, 1963).

Quartet Books Ltd for Lou Andreas-Salomé, *The Freud Journal* (London: Quartet, 1987).

Paul Roazen for Paul Roazen, *Helene Deutsch: A Psychoanalyst's Life* (New York: Anchor Press Doubleday, 1985).

Routledge for Aldo Carotenuto, *A Secret Symmetry: Sabina Spielrein between Jung and Freud* (1980); trans. Arno Pomerans, John Shepley and Krishna Winston (1982; 2nd edn with additional material, London: Routledge & Kegan Paul, 1984).

Sigmund Freud Copyrights, The Institute of Psycho-Analysis and The Hogarth Press for *The Standard Edition of the Complete Psychological Works of Sigmund Freud*, trans. and ed. by James Strachey in collaboration with Anna Freud, assisted by Alix Strachey and Alan Tyson (London: The Hogarth Press and the Institute of Psycho-analysis, 1953–74).

Tavistock/Routledge for Pearl King and Riccardo Steiner (eds), *The Freud–Klein Controversies 1941–45* (London and New York: Tavistock/Routledge, 1990).

Wayne State University Press for Martin Grotjahn, 'Sigmund Freud and the Art of Letter Writing', in Ruitenbeek, Hendrick M., *Freud As We Knew Him* (Detroit, Mich.: Wayne State University Press, 1973).

FREUD ON TRIAL

To write about the women who peopled Freud's life – his family, patients, friends, the early pioneers of psychoanalysis – and his ideas of the feminine is to be shadowed by the sense that Freud is on trial. The charges against him, where his views and understanding of women are concerned, have grown longer and heavier with the century. Perhaps the least damaging of these is the allegation that Freud was merely a conservative Victorian patriarch who saw woman's primary place as being that of reproductive servant of the species or, at idealized best, as a civilizing and nurturing angel, 'an adored sweetheart in youth, and a beloved wife in maturity'.

To be part of one's epoch may not be a first-degree offence, but to universalize time-trapped prejudices may. Freud stands accused of having transformed his subtle misogyny into a model of the world in which women can only be failed men, anatomically deprived as they are of the phallus which predestines men to power and rule. Submitting patients to his penetrative gaze and colonizing intelligence, Freud launched a theory which turned all women who deviated from the model, or who self-assertively strove for equal rights, into suitable cases for treatment – or simply suitable cases for a dose of 'penis normalis', which would also have the auspicious side-effect of allowing them to achieve biological happiness in the form of a baby. Then, too, he failed sufficiently to value the brilliance of his female disciples, using them as mere pawns, go-betweens in the developing circle of psychoanalysis where male authority was predominant, where the Oedipal saga was repeatedly played out in the truncated form of the father-son struggle for recognition. Even more personally damning for a scientist of supposed integrity, Freud is said to have falsified his patients' evidence, metamorphosing their own accounts of real childhood abuse into the register of fantasy, throwing over his early seduction theory for a more palatable – to us at least – version of events in which Oedipal desire shapes memory.

The case for the prosecution, even in this pastiche version, is convincing; with varying emphases it shadows psychoanalysis from its very inception. As early as 1931, Freud was defending his views on femininity against future and

existing critics, who included the redoubtable Karen Horney and the normally
ultra-orthodox Ernest Jones:

It is to be anticipated that men analysts with feminist views, as well as our women
analysts, will disagree with what I have said here. They will hardly fail to object that
such notions spring from the 'masculinity complex' of the male and are designed to
justify on theoretical grounds his innate inclination to disparage and suppress women.
But this sort of psychoanalytic argumentation reminds us here, as it does so often,
of Dostoevsky's famous 'knife that cuts both ways'. The opponents of those who
argue in this way will on their side think it quite natural that the female sex would
refuse to accept a view which appears to contradict their eagerly coveted equality
with men.

Freud's defence, here, thrusts one into the whirlpool of psychoanalytic
motivation where any attempt at 'objective' assessment or argument is
unavoidably suspect. It may no longer be, if it ever was, an altogether persuasive
rejoinder. None the less, it signals Freud's alertness to the prosecutors' charges
and makes one wary of arriving at too simple a verdict on a man whose
intelligence was so attuned to the workings of blind prejudice.

The case for Freud's defence has been both helped and hindered by his
discerning and respectful biographer, Ernest Jones. Writing about Freud's
attitude to women, Jones effectively created the grid upon which much
subsequent thinking has been based:

It would certainly be going too far to say that he regarded the male sex as the Lords
of Creation, for there was no tinge of arrogance or superiority in his nature, but it
might perhaps be fair to describe his view of the female sex as having as their main
function to be ministering angels to the needs and comforts of men. His letters and
his love choice make it plain that he had only one type of sexual object in his mind,
a gentle feminine one. While women might belong to the weaker sex, however, he
regarded them as finer and ethically nobler than men; there are indications that he
wished to absorb some of these qualities from them. There is little doubt that Freud
found the psychology of women more enigmatic than that of men. He said once to
Marie Bonaparte: 'The great question that has never been answered and which I
have not yet been able to answer, despite my thirty years of research into the feminine
soul, is "*Was will das Weib*? [What does Woman want?]"'

Freud was also interested in another type of woman, of a more intellectual and
perhaps masculine cast. Such women several times played a part in his life, accessory
to his men friends though of a finer calibre, but they had no erotic attraction for
him. The most important of them were first of all his sister-in-law, Minna Bernays,
then in chronological order: Emma Eckstein, Loë Kann, Lou Andreas-Salomé, Joan
Riviere, Marie Bonaparte.

Jones gives us a Freud as conventional in his tastes as he is in his turn-of-
the-century mystification of women, that 'dark continent' which he, the
intrepid psychic explorer, was only beginning to chart. But by channelling
Freud's women into two types, the 'gentle feminine' love object and the
'intellectual', 'masculine' friend, still mere accessory to the male, he abets our

desire for simple polarities and blinds us to the reality of variation. Even to Martha, his love choice, that supposedly supreme example of the weaker sex, Freud wrote: 'between ourselves – you write so intelligently and to the point that I am just a little afraid of you. I think it all goes to show once more how quickly women outdistance men.' Then, too, many of Freud's patients, those hysterics whom he was so keenly interested in, fit neither of Jones's two categories. Nor did Freud conceive of all of his women friends, such as Loë Kann and Lou Andreas-Salomé, to take just two from Jones's list, as being 'masculine'. As for erotic attraction, the matter is hardly as cut and dried as Jones leads one to believe.

In the sphere of opinion and prejudice, Freud's views on women were as erratic as anyone else's. He could fire off the dismissive quip: 'A woman who feels restless consults a physician or goes shopping', but he was equally able to observe during the Nazi occupation of Vienna that 'The women are the most capable' and that 'In general women hold up better than men.' During the Vienna Psycho-Analytical Society discussions of 1906 on the 'Natural Position of Women', he is quoted as having said: 'A woman cannot earn a living and raise children at the same time. Women as a group profit nothing by the modern feminist movement; at best a few individuals profit.' In answer to formal questioning in 1905 as an expert witness on the question of divorce law reform, his view was unequivocal: 'Equality of the sexes is impossible because of their different roles in the process of reproduction.' At the same time, he was strongly in favour of more liberal divorce laws and advocated 'the granting of a greater measure of sexual freedom'. Sexual freedom and the supposed equality of the sexes had little if nothing to do with one another in his eyes.

Yet he was generally liberal when it came to the question of women's access to the professions and certainly to psychoanalysis. When the members of the Society were reviewing their by-laws in 1910 and Isidor Sadger opposed the admission of women, Freud declared that he would 'see it as a serious inconsistency if we were to exclude women on principle'. And in a 1926 letter to his close friends Hans and Jeanne Lampl de Groot, we see him congratulating them on the birth of a daughter, rather than the son they seem to have desired, in these humorous, but none the less telling, words: 'I ... am even inclined to think that with today's attitude towards the sexes it doesn't make a great difference whether the baby is manifestly male or female. Especially as a clear predominance in one direction can be compensated to your liking by the result of future experiments.'

The jury will of necessity have to be out for a long time deliberating their verdict on Freud's attitude to women. Its deliberations are certainly not aided by the fact that access to some of the primary evidence in the Freud Archive in Washington is restricted – in the name of some scarcely tenable and idealized notion of professional propriety – until 2113. But the difficulty of the case is further compounded: if Freud the man's views were often conservative, the thrust of Freud the psychoanalyst's practice was certainly revolutionary.

The interpreting Freud, perhaps because of that very need to idealize women which Jones points to, listened acutely to his female patients and heard – beyond tics, paralyses, phobias, losses of voice – what they said, however disruptive this content may have been to current opinion. It was this thoroughly unconventional Freud who dignified women's intimate, secret confessions into a public sexual discourse – a discourse which for the first time gives non-judgmental voice to women's sexual feelings and testifies to the equal strength of women's sexuality. This interpreting Freud was a severe critic of modern sexual morality, who showed how the restrictive concept of marriage damaged women in particular: while men have recourse to a 'double sexual morality', 'women, when they are subjected to the disillusionments of marriage, fall ill of severe neuroses which permanently darken their lives.' This, too, is the Freud who pointed to the untenable conflict between marital duty and extra-marital desire:

The cure for nervous illnesses arising from marriage would be marital unfaithfulness. But the more strictly a woman has been brought up and the more sternly she has submitted to the demands of civilization, the more she is afraid of taking this way out; and in the conflict between her desires and her sense of duty, she once more seeks refuge in a neurosis. Nothing protects her virtue as securely as an illness.

While the theorizing Freud may talk of childbirth as the fulfilment of women's sexual destiny, the interpreting Freud carefully notes the conflicts women experience, discovering hidden perverse desires without the merest shudder of moral disapproval. He writes of a patient who dreamed her children dead:

Like so many young married women, she had been far from pleased when she became pregnant; and more than once she had allowed herself to wish that the child in her womb might die. Indeed, in a fit of rage after a violent scene with her husband, she had beaten with her fists on her body so as to hit the child inside it. Thus the dead child was in fact the fulfilment of a wish, but of a wish that had been put aside fifteen years earlier.

One of the most unsettling, and repeatedly forgotten, of Freud's aims in his theory of sexuality was to teach that the socially respected and universally esteemed figure of the mother was once the most desired sexual object of all. Freud had nothing interesting to say about the caring, nurturing and nursing functions of the mother. What he pointed to, quite aware of its 'sacrilegious' implications, was the 'unending source of sexual excitation and satisfaction' the mother's care afforded, especially 'since the person in charge of him, who, after all, is as a rule his mother, herself regards him with feelings that are derived from her own sexual life: she strokes him, kisses him, rocks him and quite clearly treats him as a substitute for a complete sexual object'. The nursing couple, which was to be transformed into a haven of asexual, good enough maternal care and preoccupation in later psychoanalysis, is, for Freud, the original template, the prototype of all the later sexual satisfactions.

Indeed, he was to argue that the most fulfilling of all sexual relations for a woman was that she could have with her child – though, he added, to make the satisfaction complete, the child should bring with it a penis. Similarly, adult men in their later erotic lives cannot escape the original sexual mother: 'anyone who is to be really free and happy in love must have surmounted his respect for women and have come to terms with the idea of incest with his mother or sister.' What could be more iconoclastic than replacing the sinless virgin Mary and her son Christ with Jocasta, unknowing mother of her son Oedipus's children, whose pleasure in her own and his sexualities no one has ever doubted?

At the beginnings of psychoanalysis we find the respectful attitude of sympathetic understanding with which Freud approached his patients, even if, as with Dora, other factors were in part to annul this understanding. But for there to be understanding, there must be something given to understand. And in the early pioneering days of psychoanalysis, those who entered so generously into the contract of the doctor-patient relationship were primarily women patients. This book, alongside its exploration of Freud's relationships to women, examines the foundation of psychoanalysis from the point of view of those early women patients. It assesses the contribution they made to the science Freud founded on the evidence they made available to him. Without Emmy von N., Katharina, Elisabeth von R., Dora – those anonymous cases who come to life through Freud's masterly literary gifts – it is almost impossible to think of Freud as Freud or psychoanalysis as psychoanalysis. From this vantage-point, psychoanalysis, like feminism, emerges as a response to the 'hysterical' women whose condition was emblematic of a collective malaise, and in turn a response to the untenable place of women in the late nineteenth century.

If psychoanalysis is, in this respect, a 'cure' for the very illness out of which it arises, then it is hardly surprising that the profession which Freud invented should be one in which the cross-over from patient to analyst was not an eccentric exception. Indeed, psychoanalysis is perhaps the only profession which enshrines in its rites of passage the movement from the patient's experience – daily confession on the couch – to the practitioner's status of competence and expertise. A significant number of Freud's women 'patients' made that cross-over: Emma Eckstein, Sabina Spielrein, Lou Andreas-Salomé, Helene Deutsch, Joan Riviere, Jeanne Lampl de Groot, Ruth Mack Brunswick, Princess Marie Bonaparte, Eva Rosenfeld and Anna Freud herself. Even this partial list, dating from a time when women's access to the professions was surrounded by difficulty, suggests that there is more than a grain of truth to the contention that psychoanalysis is a women's profession. 'Women always make the best psychoanalysts – until they fall in love, and then they make the best patients,' says the psychoanalyst in Alfred Hitchcock's *Spellbound*, though one would be tempted to reverse the order of Hitchcock's line and suggest that it is the best patients who make the best analysts.

Certainly there are more great women theoreticians and practitioners in psychoanalysis than in any comparable profession. In the history of British analysis alone, the roll-call is formidable: Melanie Klein, Anna Freud, Ella

Freeman Sharpe, Joan Riviere, Susan Isaacs, Paula Heimann, Marjorie Brierley, Marian Milner and Hanna Segal, to name only the most salient. In the light of the ever-growing influence of Klein's and D.W.Winnicott's theories, which concentrate so exclusively on fantasy and environmental relations of the child to the mother, it has become an implicit assumption that the mother imago in the transference will almost always be the core of analysis. It could even be seriously proposed that only a woman analyst can effectively analyse either male or female patients, although professional propriety and psychoanalytic logic demand that the maternal transference can be as easily evoked with an anatomically male analyst as with a female.

The percentage of women in the profession of psychoanalysis has been consistently higher than in any other. In 1940, 40 per cent of the analysts in Britain were women; the rest of the international psychoanalytic movement reached 30 per cent in the 1930s. Between 1920 and 1980, an average of 27 per cent of analysts in Europe were women, while in the USA, where a medical degree was necessary, the average percentage was none the less as high as 17 per cent. This compares with 4–7 per cent of women in medicine and 1–5 per cent in law for the same period.

These figures alone should make us question the standard historiographic treatment of psychoanalysis both by feminist and male historians which would see women analysts as mere pawns in a boys' game of institutional power struggles; or by overemphasizing the construction of theory at the expense of professional practice overlook women's significant contribution. It would be difficult to see women as powerful and independent as Lou Andreas-Salomé or Marie Bonaparte as pawns in anybody's game. To scrutinize psychoanalytic history with spectacles predisposed to find another story of male professionals vying with each other for power or for symbolic blood will certainly reveal that story. But other, more interesting stories may thereby remain obscured: stories of how diverse women came to make the difficult profession of psychoanalysis their own; and of how psychoanalysis, itself, took on specific qualities because of the theoretical advances and significant numbers of women analysts.

It should not be assumed that this kind of alternative women-oriented historiography will necessarily reveal women bringing their supposedly traditional virtues to the task of pacifying and accommodating the rivalrous feuds of male colleagues. The bitter fights over Freud's legacy in the British Psycho-Analytical Society shortly after Freud's death quickly undermine such a notion: here an institutional and theoretical debate was fought largely between women, and fought in tones and manoeuvres as pugnacious and malicious as any male contest. A history that recognizes women is not necessarily a history of the power of women's virtues, even if, in the British Society's fights, it was the fluently diplomatic Sylvia Payne who finally drew up the 'Gentlemen's Agreement' between Melanie Klein and Anna Freud that allowed the British Society to survive intact.

Why has psychoanalysis historically been so significantly a women's profession? A multiplicity of reasons can be cited: the coincidence of a new profession with an epoch in which women began to engage in careers, in which the first feminist movement won victories for women's access to education and the public sphere; the easier access to a profession whose social organization was familial and proceeded along lines of filiation; the intimacy of psychoanalytic practice, its unique flair for dignifying what might otherwise pass as mere gossip into a gateway to the unconscious; the focus of psychoanalysis on the family and sexuality, those spheres of emotional work which have traditionally been women's.

In the following pages we explore the lives, the work and the ideas of the women who, through their contact with Freud, played a part in the invention and history of psychoanalysis. If in the first instance these women were members of his family, that is only fitting, for it was the crucible of family relations that forged the Freud who would later find the truths of our lives in the distortions we inevitably create of our early familial experience. Yet it was only in the analytic encounter with his patients that Freud found out those truths, about himself and about others. Amongst those who became followers of Freud's ideas we find, from very early on, distinctive and original women disciples. Their stories, the optic they give us on Freud and the nature of their relations with the Professor form a significant portion of our study.

A single book dealing with such a rich, historical mine must needs set itself boundaries: spurred by our title, we have used the figure of Freud himself to set those boundaries. Many women whose contribution to psychoanalysis has been great find only passing mention in these pages, for the simple reason that their actual contact with Freud was minimal. But since it was largely Freud's women followers who made him focus on female sexuality, and women of more recent generations who have placed his ideas on femininity on trial, either as prosecutors or defence counsel, we have devoted a final section to the battle over Freud's theoretical legacy.

So, enter the mother.

Part I

THE
FREUD FAMILY
ROMANCE

THE YOUNG FREUD

Throughout his life Freud oscillated between recognizing the mother as the alpha and omega of human existence and passing over her in silence. 'For each of us,' he wrote in 1913, 'destiny takes the form of a woman (or of several).' In both Freud's inner life and psychoanalytic work – ruled by the logic of repetition and recapturing – these female figures of destiny can never quite escape being figures of the mother. What is unique about Freud is that this mother is a *sexual* being.

In 1912, when Sophie, the second of his three daughters, was preparing to be married, Freud wrote a short paper entitled 'The Theme of the Three Caskets', which announced his entry, at the age of fifty-six, into old age. In the heroic mode he adopted in this paper, Freud identified not only with Oedipus – the Oedipus who had killed his father, married his mother and dragged out his old age leaning on his faithful daughter, as Freud later was to lean on Anna, calling her his Antigone – but also with Shakespeare's King Lear. In Freud's reading, Lear had flouted the 'necessary ordering of human life' by asking for love from his daughters as if they were his wives, asking for love from them in the same unconditionally selfish way that a baby demands love from its mother. Lear, an old, dying man, 'is not willing to renounce the love of women; he insists on hearing how much he is loved.' In the final scene, when Lear carries his daughter Cordelia's dead body on to the stage, the natural order has been inverted. Lear has refused to be a dying father, and the retribution of the fates is to invert the mythological representation in which it is a young virgin, a Valkyrie, who carries the dead hero from the battlefield. Instead,

what is represented here are the three inevitable relations that a man has to a woman – the woman who bears him, the woman who is his mate and the woman who destroys him; ... they are the three forms taken by the figure of the mother in the course of a man's life – the mother herself, the beloved one who is chosen after her pattern, and lastly the Mother Earth who receives him once more. But it is in vain that an old man yearns for the love of woman as he had it first from his mother;

the third of the Fates alone, the silent Goddess of Death, will take him into her arms.

Mother; beloved; daughter-death: this moving allegory of the masculine condition was certainly already, in 1912, an accurate portrayal of Freud's relations with women, and it seems like an uncannily accurate premonition, if not an oracle, of his future relations with women in the twenty-seven years the 'old man' Freud was to remain alive.

Yet before a man grows old and is required to face death, he may have the illusion of occupying the position of power and authority that Freud granted to the father in his vision of human history:

In the beginnings of the human family, we assume, all females belonged to the father; the daughters were his sexual objects no less than their mothers. Enough of that attitude has been retained in actual life of the present day; in the unconscious these ancient wishes remain in all their force.

When men masquerade, as Freud himself was wont to, as the all-powerful father, there is a consequence that many have remarked on. The power and authority of the father place the mother entirely in his shade. Yet it is the mother who is the object of the child's positive and passionate desires, his or her *incestuous* desires. Late in life, Freud was to refer to everything attaching to this early mother as 'so grey with age and shadowy and almost impossible to revivify'. And an infirm man of seventy-seven, he was to reflect that *King Lear*'s bleak depiction of the old man's relations with his daughters, pointing inexorably towards the necessity for resignation in the face of death, is not the whole story:

Is it not curious, by the way, that in the play that deals with the father's relations to his three daughters there is no mention whatever of the mother, and after all there must have been one. This is one of the traits that gives the tragedy a rather harsh note of inhumanity.

Freud's mother had died some four years before he wrote this letter. On that occasion, Freud said to his close friend and colleague, Sándor Ferenczi, 'I was not free to die as long as she was alive, and now I am.' Perhaps the freedom her death gave him allowed him to see more clearly the inhumanity of a dramatic universe in which the real mother appears only in the guise of Death. In 1912, Freud had been able to discover this most powerful of all images of the mother, that of Death, in the daughters, who come between the old man and his death.

In *The Interpretation of Dreams*, the only dream from Freud's childhood to be found represents his mother's death. It was also the last dream of his own to figure in the book. Was it almost an oversight that he left his childhood relation to his mother to the end of his book on dreams? Or was it the climax, the triumphant conclusion, wherein he finally took full possession of his mother, as that anxiety dream indicated he wished to?

I saw *my beloved mother, with a peculiarly peaceful, sleeping expression on her features, being carried into the room by two (or three) people with birds' beaks and laid upon the bed.* I awoke in tears and screaming, and interrupted my parents' sleep.

Freud traced the anxiety of this dream to repression of 'an obscure and evidently sexual craving'; the nine-year-old boy's sadistic conception of sexual intercourse had became intertwined with the vision of the dying face of his mother's father, seen a few days before the dream, fusing into the conviction that sexuality leads to the death of the loved one. By analysing the dream and publishing his book on dreams, Freud overcame the barrier against incest – his father's prediction that 'The boy will come to nothing' – and took symbolic possession of his beloved mother. In this sense, the body of knowledge Freud discovered and made his own, psychoanalysis, discovered in the wake of his father's death in 1896, was always, but secretly, the body of his mother.

The secrecy that surrounds Freud's relationship to his mother was akin to the secrecy that surrounded his sexual life with his wife. Intimately self-revealing as he was when he needed to persuade his readers of the truths he had discovered in himself and others, Freud was also extremely self-concealing and private; and in no area of his inner life was he more discreet and self-protective than in that tabernacle of his childhood, his mother.

That the experiences of early childhood are formative is not unique to Freud's teachings, although he advanced that claim in a vigorous and more comprehensive form than any other thinker; but no other thinker found the heart of the tragic destiny of a human life to lie in childhood. We might say that, for Freud, once the age of reason beloved of the Jesuits has been reached, the die has been cast, the dice have been rolled and the bets have been laid, won and lost. The rest is very much up to the uncontrollable hazards of external fate. One's internal fate has already been decided in childhood, and it is the meeting, the intertwining, of external chance and internal destiny that gives content to the drama of the individual life.

Yet the recovery of this all-important period of one's life then confronts the fact that we have no reliable data on which to judge the course of early childhood: it is irredeemably subject to the amnesia that covers nearly all of our infancy. The only glimpses of the prehistoric epochs we are allowed come through fragments and shards of memory. And these, Freud argued, are tendentious clues, not so much to pure, unalloyed memory, to historical accuracy, but to the sea-changes wrought by earlier or subsequent waves of desire and disgust, love and shame, moments of intellectual triumph and moral cowardice.

It may indeed be questioned whether we have any memories at all *from* our childhood: memories *relating to* our childhood may be all that we possess. Our childhood memories show us our earliest years not as they were but as they appeared at the later periods when the memories were aroused. In these periods of arousal, the childhood memories did not, as people are accustomed to say, *emerge*; they were *formed* at that time.

It was an examination of his very earliest memory of childhood that prompted Freud to write these words. He remembered a green meadow covered in yellow flowers sloping down from a cottage, in front of which his nurse and a peasant woman are chatting, while he and his two playmates, another boy and a girl, are picking flowers in the grass.

The little girl has the best bunch; and, as though by mutual agreement, we – the two boys – fall on her and snatch away her flowers. She runs up the meadow in tears and as a consolation the peasant-woman gives her a big piece of black bread. Hardly have we seen this than we throw the flowers away, hurry to the cottage and ask to be given some bread too. And we are in fact given some; the peasant-woman cuts the loaf with a long knife. In my memory the bread tastes quite delicious – and at that point the scene breaks off.

The idyllic scene evoked here – the green meadow, the children playing, the Proustian moment of access to a world of sensual excess, colours, tastes – can only open momentarily, and only be kept open by the work of writing. Analysed, the memory does not lead Freud to the idyllic world of his early childhood, but rather to the more tempestuous world of his adolescence, to which we will come shortly. However, the atmosphere of the memory – of the bliss it was to be alive in that morn – is sustained whenever Freud (and his biographers) returned to the scene of the memory, to Pribor in Moravia, his birthplace: 'deeply buried within me there still lives the happy child of Freiberg, the first-born son of a youthful mother, who received his first indelible impressions from this air, from this soil.'

It is striking that Freud's youthful mother is absent from that idyllic scene, as she was to be from so many of the other public depictions of his inner life.

Mothers and Sisters

Sigismund, as he was named until he shortened it to Sigmund in his teens, was born on 6 May 1856. His youthful mother, Amalie Nathansohn, had married Freud's father Jakob in 1855. The family she married into was one that was already extensive and close-knit, and she was to help it remain so. She was born in 1835 and lived in Brody in north-east Galicia, but moved to Vienna with her parents when she was still a child and had vivid memories of the 1848 revolution, in which Jewish university students played a leading role. She was, according to one of her grandsons, a 'typical Jewess, of Ashkenasi origin': she was 'not what we would call a "lady", had a lively temper and was impatient, self-willed, sharp-witted and highly intelligent.' Another grandchild thought her vain, energetic, strong-willed, efficient, competent and egotistical: 'my somewhat shrill and domineering grandmother'. Despite some prolonged ill-health in her middle years, including a 'serious tuberculosis of the lung' which prompted Freud to worry about how to keep her alive a little longer, her strong will saw her through to the ripe age of ninety-five. Dutiful son that he always remained, in later life Freud visited her every Sunday, without fail.

She was the third of Jakob Freud's wives. His first, Sally Kanner, died in

1852, leaving two sons, Emanuel born in 1832 and Philipp born in 1836. His second, Rebecca, is a mysterious figure. She only surfaced from historical oblivion thanks to a mixture of old-fashioned historical detective work and new-fangled psychoanalytic deduction from traces Freud left in his dream-texts; we know nothing of her save for one entry in the civic register of the Jewish population for 1852: Rebecca, aged thirty-two. It has been suggested, somewhat implausibly, that, because she did not give Jakob the child expected of a Jewish marriage, she committed suicide. Freud's father could only have been married to her for about a year, and the family memories of Freud and his siblings bore no conscious traces of her.

In one of his writings, Freud endorsed Lichtenberg's aphorism: 'An astronomer knows whether the moon is inhabited or not with about as much certainty as he knows who was his father, but not with so much certainty as he knows who was his mother.' Yet in his own case, as the dreams he analysed in *The Interpretation of Dreams* reveal, uncertainty pervades maternal and paternal provenances alike. We see Freud restlessly enquiring into the marriages his father had contracted in the years just before little Sigismund's own birth – as if the complications and the secrecy surrounding the disappearances of his father's wives put maternity as well as paternity in doubt. Freud as a small child was equally if not more perplexed by the presence in his home of two brothers who were the same age as his mother, and who seemed more suitable candidates as fathers than the true father of them all. On both the male and the female side, the small child had few if any certainties to cling to: no wonder he identified with the riddle-solving Oedipus.

Freud and his biographer Jones helped paint the portrait of a pretty young mother, proud of her first-born son who was her 'indisputable favourite'. Freud also depicted the great happiness a woman achieves when her 'most powerful feminine wish', her wish for a penis-baby from her father, is fulfilled by the birth of a son; the mother 'is only brought unlimited satisfaction by her relation to a son; this is altogether the most perfect, the most free from ambivalence of all human relationships.' Was it also his own mother, dead only two years earlier as he wrote, that Freud had in mind when he described how 'a mother can transfer to her son the ambition which she has been obliged to suppress in herself, and she can expect from him the satisfaction of all that has been left over in her of her masculinity complex'? Perhaps it was this transference that Freud respected so much that his idealization of his mother expressed itself directly in his attempt to preserve for her sake her idealized image of him: the best possible son for the best possible mother. It was also his duty, he felt, perhaps a burdensome one, to sustain his mother's vitality, indeed her very life. In 1925, when she celebrated her ninetieth birthday, Freud wrote to his nephew in Manchester: 'We had made a secret of all the losses in the family: my daughter Sophie, her second son Heinele, Teddy [Theodor Freud, son of SF's sister Marie, drowned on 10 April 1923, aged eighteen] in Berlin, Eli Bernays and your parents. She knows the death of Caecilia (Mausi). We had to use many precautions not to be discovered and so I did not give notice of the event before the term.' The worst-case scenario was always that she lose her beloved Sigi: this was unthinkable. When she finally died in 1930, he confessed how much freer he now felt: 'superficially I feel only two things: the growth in personal freedom I have acquired, since it was always an abhorrent thought that she would learn of my death, and secondly the satisfaction that she has at last the deliverance to which she had acquired the right in so long a life.' It was almost as if his mother, in dying, gave him permission to die. When Freud felt the time had come for him to die, he reminded his physician, Max Schur, of his long-standing promise to help him. But he added: 'Talk it over with Anna, and if she thinks it's right, then make an end of it.' A woman, rather than a doctor or a priest, would always be for Freud the 'silent Goddess of Death'. Now, it was Anna – his Cordelia, the last of the three Fates who cuts the thread of life – into whose arms he entrusted himself.

The certainty and satisfactions Freud might have sought in his relationship to his mother were complicated by the presence of the old nurse employed by his half-brother and his wife, Emanuel and Maria Freud, who probably looked after their two small children, John and Pauline, and Sigmund. The nurse's identity is still unclear: she was either Monika Zajic, a woman of about forty, a member of the family in whose house the Freuds lived, or Resi Wittek, who certainly accompanied Jakob, Amalie and Sigmund Freud when they took the cure at Roznau in June 1857. Freud unearthed and reconstructed his nurse's existence in 1897, during his self-analysis: 'an ugly, elderly but clever woman, who told me a great deal about God Almighty and hell and instilled in me a high opinion of my own capacities'. 'Moreover, she washed me in reddish water in which she had previously washed herself' – as if his nanny forged a link for him between menstruation and his own potency, his own capacity for knowledge. No doubt the high opinion of his own capacities she gave him was also closely linked with its opposite: 'she was my teacher in sexual matters and complained because I was so clumsy and unable to do anything.' So, for Freud in the late 1890s, embarked on his search for the secret of hysteria in sexuality, his self-analysis revealed to him a wise woman – a witch, perhaps, a seductress – as the point of origin of his own vocation and knowledge.

This 'elderly woman, very shrewd indeed', who was 'old and ugly, but very sharp and efficient', was dismissed from the Freuds' employment for theft, at the same time as the birth of Sigmund's sister Anna, two and a half years his junior. The two events were linked in his memory, and their investigation and untangling was one of the milestones in his self-analysis:

if the old woman disappeared from my life so suddenly, it must be possible to demonstrate the impression this made on me. Where is it then? Thereupon a scene occurred to me which in the course of twenty-five years has occasionally emerged in my conscious memory without my understanding it. My mother was nowhere to be found; I was crying in despair. My brother Philipp (twenty years older than I) unlocked a wardrobe [Kasten] for me, and when I did not find my mother inside it either, I cried even more until, slender and beautiful, she came in through the door.

... When I missed my mother, I was afraid she had vanished from me, just as the old woman had a short time before. So I must have heard that the old woman had been locked up and therefore must have believed that my mother had been locked up too – or rather, had been 'boxed up' [*eingekastelt*]. ... The fact that I turned to him in particular proves that I was well aware of his share in the disappearance of the nurse.

But Freud's own dreams indicated that it was not only Philipp who was initially responsible for his nurse's disappearance: Freud, too, felt responsible, since he reconstructed a plot between himself and his nurse in which he stole silver coins from his mother and gave them to her. On asking his mother about this incident from his childhood, Freud received clarification: it was the old nurse who was the thief, not Sigmund on her behalf, and it was Sigmund who was the victim of the theft. Philipp himself fetched the policeman to apprehend her, and she received a ten months' jail sentence.

Freud's rediscovery of his nurse and the perplexity in which he, at the age of two and a half, was placed by her disappearance was to leave him with an acute sensitivity to the theme of two mothers; as Peter Gay notes: 'Like some figures who were to engross his fantasy life later – Leonardo, Moses, to say nothing of Oedipus – the young Freud enjoyed the loving ministrations of two mothers.' In his original dream, the two mothers are in conflict, one stealing from the other. In his essay on Leonardo da Vinci, he accentuated the crucial importance of Leonardo's early life being structured by his natural mother having to give up the young Leonardo to the new wife of his father:

He had had two mothers: first, his true mother Caterina, from whom he was torn away when he was between three and five, and then a young and tender step-mother, his father's wife, Donna Albiera. By his combining this fact about his childhood with the one mentioned above, and by his condensing them into a composite unity, the design of 'St Anne with Two Others' took shape for him. ... The artist seems to have used the blissful smile of St Anne [corresponding to Caterina] to disavow and to cloak the envy which the unfortunate woman felt when she was forced to give up her son to her better-born rival, as she had once given up his father as well.

This sense of the conflict between women over children also informs the extraordinary reading of the judgment of Solomon that Freud gave in passing in *Group Psychology and the Analysis of the Ego*: 'If one woman's child is dead, the other shall not have a live one either. The bereaved woman is recognized by this wish.' The usual interpretation of the judgment of Solomon is that the real mother of the child is recognized by her willingness to give up the child to another so long as the child is not cut in two. Freud was obliged also to see the other side of the coin: that the woman who has lost her child is so consumed by envy for the woman who still has a live child that she is prepared to see the child killed rather than let another woman have a live child. In this perception of the power of envy, is there not yet another echo of Freud's sympathy and identification with the ugly, forty-year-old, childless nurse, 'the old woman who provided me at such an early age with the means for living and surviving'? In the struggle over the little silver coins between the young Sigismund's mother and his nurse, it would seem that his sympathies were on both sides, on the side of the mother with means and the nurse without, and that, whatever the true facts might have been, he felt guilty about having been responsible for her disappearance.

Freud's two mothers were by no means an exceptional inheritance to carry into adult life. The social patterns of late nineteenth-century, petit-bourgeois and bourgeois family life entailed that wet nurses, nannies, governesses and servant girls were there to provide a 'downstairs' to 'upstairs' life. This nether world was often richer in emotional, and almost uniformly in sexual, experience, both for boys and girls, than the upstairs world of duty, virtue and purity. The figure of the seduced and seducing governess and nursemaid appears with remarkable regularity in Freud's case histories, from Miss Lucy R., through Dora to the late papers on female sexuality. One should never forget that the later Freudian schema of mother, father and child was always realized and derived from a more complex social reality, where liminal figures, such as the nursemaid and governess, could play the crucial role, just as Sigmund's nanny was to play the crucial role in his self-analysis of his early years.

Responsible as Freud may have felt about his nurse's disappearance, the person he fingered as the actual guilty party was Philipp, who, he noted in 1924, 'had taken his father's place as the child's rival'. So what was the young boy feeling guilty about? The short answer is: his aggressive desires towards the true perpetrator of the crime. But who was the true perpetrator of the crime? This was quite a problem for the small boy to solve: was it Philipp, who had sent his nurse away? Was it his father? The confusion between generations in the Freud household – a confusion added to by the fact that the Zajìcs owned and shared the house in which all the Freuds lived – set the boy a problem: who was paired off with whom? Jakob and the nurse were of an age, as were Philipp and Amalie; why, then, did Jakob share a bed with Amalie? Why then did Philipp get rid of the nurse? And who was responsible for this extremely unwelcome addition to the family, the new-born baby?

In 1932, Freud insisted that 'it is a remarkable fact that a child, even with an age difference of 11 months, is not too young to take notice of what is happening' when a second child is born to its mother. When the children are very close in age, the reproach against the mother that she did not give the first-born enough milk 'acquires a real basis'. There is surely a distinctive allusion to his own childhood here: Freud's brother Julius was born when he was eleven months old, but died eight months later. During his self-analysis, Freud uncovered memories of having 'greeted my one-year-younger brother (who died after a few months) with adverse wishes and genuine childhood jealousy.'

Yet a few months later Freud wrote: 'I have no knowledge of the birth of a sister, who is two and a half years younger than I am; my departure [from Pribor], my first sight of the railway and the long carriage-drive before it – none of these has left a trace in my memory.' We have already seen how his claim to have no knowledge of her birth should be treated with caution; he remembered the fear that his mother had been boxed up and removed, like his nurse, and he remembered his relief at seeing his mother reappear 'slender and beautiful' once again. Apparently little Sigismund's jealousy of his male sibling was recoverable through analysis, but the event of his sister's birth was still covered over by these other memories. This sister, Anna, was Jakob Freud's favourite daughter, his pet. Like Sigmund, she was born in Pribor, before 'the original catastrophe' of the family's departure from the idyllic countryside to Vienna, sometime in 1859. The intense dislike of the new-born sibling that Sigmund evinced at her birth continued to colour their relations. By the time Sigmund was eight, four more sisters had followed Anna: Rosa, Marie (Mitzi), Pauline (Pauli) and Adolfine (Dolfi); his only brother was born when he was ten, and some sense can be had of his privileges as eldest son in this close-knit Jewish family from the fact that at the Family Council his choice of a name, Alexander, was accepted.

The two boys undoubtedly had special privileges, not only from being the eldest and the youngest, but from the fact of being boys. Sigmund was an 'attentive but somewhat authoritarian brother.... When she was fifteen, his sister Anna remembered, he frowned on her reading Balzac and Dumas as too risqué'. No doubt he approved more of a book from the Freud family library that still survives: the *Magazin des Adolescents* of 1825, in which moral homilies about love and the correct way for young ladies to behave are embedded in the dialogues of Mademoiselle Bonne, Miss Frivole and so forth. The book was probably read not only by the girls, since it is inscribed with all the brothers' and sisters' names (including 'Sigismund' and 'Alexander'). He also had his sister's piano evicted from their cramped living quarters since its noise disturbed his reading and working. Certainly there was no question but that the boys would study and enter professions, whilst the girls would prepare for marriage and their own families. Which is what came to pass. Sigmund chose medicine, Alexander economics, becoming a professor at the Export Academy. The two brothers worked as the pillars, supporting those females in the family who were not yet married, and this arrangement lasted throughout their lives. In the early 1880s, Sigmund's letters worried over the uncertain futures of his sisters, and grieved over the emaciation their poverty led to, which his pittance of an income could not prevent. His sense of obligation is well captured in a letter he wrote to his wife, Martha, in 1884: 'Could you imagine me having 1000 Gulden in the drawer and letting Rosa and Dolfi go hungry? At least half of it I would give to them....' The sense of obligation never disappeared; Alexander and Sigmund would have regular private talks about any serious financial problems of their mother and sisters, and in 1938, because they were both leaving Vienna, they provided some £8,000 in capital to keep their four elderly, widowed or unmarried sisters in Vienna, where they had decided, or were obliged, to remain for the rest of their lives. The four sisters were murdered by the Nazis four years later.

Before their marriages (Dolfi was the only one to remain single) the girls took on tasks appropriate to their station and poverty, some refined, some not so refined: for instance, Rosa was a lady's companion for a while and Pauli accompanied Anna's children to the USA in the early 1890s. Sigmund would occasionally take his unmarried sisters on outings, such as the two-day hike he took his 'poor little sister' Dolfi on for a birthday treat in 1885.

Anna was the first of the family to marry. Quite typically Sigmund's young friends courted and mused over her, including his closest friend for a long period in his teens, Eduard Silberstein. In October 1883, she married Eli Bernays, Sigmund's future wife's older brother. Sigmund had early on singled out Eli as an obstacle to his total possession of Martha, so that the cross-marrying fraternal foursome were soon somewhat estranged. Later, at Sigmund's behest, the estrangement became complete, in part because of Eli's infidelities and the illegitimate children to whom he gave money. When Anna's first child Judith was born in 1886, Sigmund encountered and frostily greeted Eli making a visit to the Freud household and took the opportunity of his absence to visit his sister and congratulate her. In 1892, Eli and Anna migrated to the USA, with help from the rest of the family, including Sigmund. They took their youngest child, Edward, but left their two daughters in Vienna for a year – Judith with the grandparents and Lucy with Sigmund and Martha. Eli prospered in America and in later years, when they were reconciled, Sigmund always bestowed, in Homeric fashion, the epithets 'rich' or 'made lots of money' on him and his family. With good reason, since he became one of those wealthy Americans upon whom Freud's own income, the psychoanalytic movement and so much else in Vienna depended after the First World War: in 1920, he gave a million crowns to help found the Tivoli Children's Home in Vienna, of which Freud was a committee member. When Eli died, Anna inherited both wealth and epithet; her being 'well off' was always mentioned when her name came up.

The branches of the growing Freud family kept in contact, despite the Atlantic. Eli, Anna and their four children visited Europe in 1900; on that occasion Freud kept a rather disdainful distance from them. When their son Edward visited the Freuds' summer house in Karlsbad in 1913 at the age of twenty-two, Anna, Freud's youngest daughter, fell in love with him and thought of marrying him. In 1980, when they met up again, she told him the story, and, 'nodding at his wife, Doris Fleischman Bernays, feminist and counsel on public relations in partnership with her husband, she said with a smile, "You did better with her." To which Mr Bernays replied, also with a smile, "If I had married you, it would have been double incest."' One senses that the Freud family were close enough for daughter Anna, for one, not to have been too bothered about committing incest by marrying her two-fold cousin.

Sigmund's favourite sister was Rosa, four years his junior. He participated actively in her education and wrote to her regularly, when he was out of Vienna, or when she was visiting their half-brothers in Manchester in 1884–5. Their closeness extended to their sharing 'a nicely developed tendency towards neurasthenia', the only family neurotic symptoms that Freud, writing in 1886, could detect. She was, in his and many other's eyes, the beautiful sister. 'As a widow, well on in her sixties, she could still command love from young men, something about which she was very proud and not in the least discreet.' As did her sisters, Rosa engaged in the traditional clothes-making for the single Sigmund; he wrote from Paris in 1885: 'Rosa writes that she is terribly busy – my winter coat, my shirts and boots!' For a time she was engaged to Brust, a friend of Freud's, but she eventually married Heinrich Graf, of whom the bride's protective elder brother approved: 'he is an excellent man and has no motive other than long-standing affection'. The wedding was one of the very few Freud could bring himself to attend. The Grafs soon moved in to the flat above the Freuds at Berggasse 19.

Rosa had two children: Herman, born in July 1897, and Cäcilie (Mausi), born in October 1898. The young Freuds and Rosa's children spent time in and out of each other's flats. Both died in young adulthood: Herman was the only one of the close Freud family to die in battle in the war, in 1917; Cäcilie committed suicide on finding she was pregnant in August 1922. Freud wrote to Jones: 'I am not feeling very strong and am deeply shaken by the death of my best niece, a dear girl of 23, who took Veronal last week while alone at Vienna.' The pregnancy was hushed up, so much so that Anna Freud, then twenty-six, who at times had been close to her, was not aware of the true reason for her cousin's suicide until she read Ernest Jones's biography of her father in the 1950s. This loss, together with her husband's earlier death in 1908, over which she grieved intensely, cast a deep shadow over Rosa.

The other sisters' lives were no easier. As a young woman, Mitzi was obliged to work as a maid or governess in Paris for a while, from where she sent her mother money, but failed to learn any French. She married her cousin, Moritz Freud, and had children, but saw two of them die in young adulthood. Teddy drowned in Berlin in 1923, at the age of eighteen. Martha, the youngest, married Jakob Seidmann, a journalist; later she called herself Tom, dressed as a man, became a talented illustrator of children's books, but was always a complicated, restless woman. She committed suicide in 1930, a year after her husband had killed himself. Pauli, Freud's youngest sister, born when Sigmund was eight, moved to New York and married Valentin Winternitz, who had emigrated to America in 1887. Freud never met Winternitz, but it did not prevent him contemplating 'petitioning' him in late 1899, almost certainly as to the possibility of emigrating because of the difficulties of his practice in Vienna and his lack of renown. However, Winternitz died suddenly, aged forty-one, in May 1900. Eli asked Freud to supervise Pauli's return to Europe; she settled in Berlin – for a time the Freud 'family headquarters' – with help from both her husband's and the Freud family. Her only child Rosi, born in 1896, led a troubled life, suffering a schizophrenic episode in 1913.

Like so many Jewish families of the period, the Freuds' lives were always intertwined. Freud recounts bumping into his sister Rosa and Heinrich Graf one summer in Venice, journeying with them, then meeting up with his sister Anna and her family, and a day later his brother Alexander arriving unexpectedly. So it is not surprising, then, that Freud reported that the American children 'look just like my own'. The group of widowed sisters remained especially close to one another, to their mother and to their brothers' families, often spending summers together in one large family group in Ischl or another of the regular run of Viennese resorts. Either by fate, chance or brotherly persuasion, the unmarried Dolfi took on a traditional daughterly role, nursing Freud's father on his death-bed and taking care of their mother in her old age. Dolfi, Freud reflected, 'the sweetest and best of my sisters, has such a great capacity for deep feeling and alas an all-too-fine sensitiveness.' When the commanding Amalie died in 1930, Dolfi, nearly seventy herself, was in dire straits; yet again, the family rallied round, and her spirits revived when two of her widowed sisters came to live with her. Mutual support was perennial in the Freud family. And if Sigmund in the beginning was the respected male, adored by his sisters and mother, then he managed so to construct his life that, in old age, the pattern was replicated and he was once again surrounded by the love of women, friends and followers, in addition to the core triad of wife, sister-in-law and youngest daughter.

First Love

The privacy and the cloak of discretion so common to many people's early years of sexual maturity has not been pierced in Freud's case to any substantial degree. We know of one recorded instance of Freud 'in love' before his protracted wooing and long marriage with Martha Bernays, the beloved one who is chosen after the pattern of the mother. From this brief first encounter, which he made public by attributing the remembered story to an anonymous interlocutor as part of his self-analysis, Freud teased out some salient insights into the fluidity of fantasy and memory.

Freud's 'first calf-love' was for the daughter of some friends of the family he stayed with when he twice returned to his birthplace in the summers of 1871 and 1872, probably having accompanied his mother on her visit to a Moravian spa near Freiburg. In his self-analysis, published at the age of forty-two, the memory of this first adolescent love lay interestingly concealed behind his earliest childhood memory: playing at the age of three with his nephew and niece, John and Pauline. Probing behind the screen of this childhood memory, Freud arrived at the memory from his sixteenth year: the moment of his return to the scene of his early childhood idyll and his passion there for Gisela Fluss, the twelve-year-old sister of the friend with whom he was staying: this 'half-naive, half-cultured young lady'. Characteristically, Freud kept his passionate feelings for the girl secret, blaming on his return the 'nonsensical Hamlet in me, my diffidence' for not talking to her. And when she left, 'I passed many hours in solitary walks through the lovely woods that I had found once more and spent my time building castles in the air. These, strangely enough, were not concerned with the future but sought to improve the past.' If only his family had never left the small town where he was born, then he would have grown up, strong and healthy, in the country, would have followed his father's profession and married the girl he had known for all those years! The analyst Freud was later well aware that the idyll of the pastoral life played a strong part in precipitating this love at first sight. 'I never felt really comfortable in the town. I believe now that I was never free from a longing for the beautiful woods near our home.'

Freud's screen memory concealed not only this pastoral youthful infatuation, but also the project that his father and half-brother Emanuel concocted of weaning him from his intellectual pursuits, settling him in business in Manchester and arranging a marriage between him and his niece, Pauline – the little girl whose flowers he had seized and who had been rewarded with bread. The childhood memory expressed two different memories or fantasies from his adolescence: if only he hadn't moved from Freiberg, he would have married Gisela, whom he could have 'deflowered' as he had done Pauline; improbably, Freiberg and Manchester are thus fused as symbols of a more comfortable life ('bread') in which his sensual passions ('flowers') would be gratified.

It was not to be. The upshot of Freud's first love for Gisela was for him to enter into a period of self-conscious and self-ironizing superiority to females and to affairs of the heart. In correspondence with Gisela's brother, Freud coined the nickname 'Ichthyosaura' for her, playing on her name ('Fluss' means 'river') and her being a creature become altogether alien to him. The ironic mode then dominates, with Freud composing an epic poem to his fishy 'principle', the code-name for girls the boys were using some three years later, when Gisela got married. As Freud vowed to turn away from the past, he also vowed to renounce this excessively playful fantasizing about the opposite sex: 'Let no one seek a principle save in the present, not in the alluvium or diluvium, nowhere save among the children of man, not in the gruesome primeval past.' Women may have fascinated him, but the desire to pursue them was sublimated into the desire to pursue knowledge. When making his first trip to Trieste at Easter 1876, where he was working as a student on the gonadic structure of eels in the Zoological Experimental Station, he remarked: 'on my first day in Trieste, I felt that the city was inhabited by none but Italian goddesses, and I was filled with apprehension, but when I stepped expectantly into the streets on the second day, I could discover no more of these.' Two weeks earlier he had reported on his encounter with the goddesses on his first walk in Trieste in a more comical and pseudo-scientific vein:

The people, finally, are very ugly, with few exceptions. ... The cats are beautiful and friendly, but the women are especially distinctive. Most of them ... have the typical Italian figure, slim, tall, slender-faced, with longish nose, dark eyebrows, and small raised upper lip. So much for the anatomical features. Physiologically, all that I know about them is that they like to go for walks. ... Unfortunately, they are not beautiful in our German sense, but I remember that on my first day I discovered lovely specimens among the new type which I have not encountered since.

While in Trieste, he dissected 400 eels, the descendants of ichthyosauri, in search of the elusive male gonads, but 'all the eels I have cut open are of the tenderer sex.'

Freud's flight from women was more than a simple youthful flight from

all members of the 'fishy' sex. The letters recounting his infatuation with
Gisela Fluss also expounded on the manifold virtues of her mother, her
intelligence, her culture, her versatility, her constant cheerfulness, her gentleness
with her children, her cordial show of hospitality. It was the mother, who
'cared for me as for her own child', then, as much if not more than the
daughter, who fired Freud's imagination, and even he recognized it at the
time: 'it seems that I have transferred my esteem for the mother to friendship
for the daughter. ... I am full of admiration for this woman whom none of
her children can fully match.'

   'Caring for someone as their own child' reminds us of the 1910 paper in
which Freud first coined the term the Oedipus complex, describing the rescue
fantasies in which the child in gratitude gives the mother 'another life, that
of a child which has the greatest resemblance to himself. The son shows his
gratitude by wishing to have by his mother a son who is like himself.'
Gratitude to a superior maternal figure was quite explicitly the grounds of
Freud's admiration for Frau Fluss:

I slept upstairs that night, and got up the next morning well and without toothache.
She asked me how I had slept. Badly, I replied, I didn't sleep a wink. Or so it seemed
to me. Smiling, she said, I came to see you twice during the night, and you never
noticed. I felt ashamed. I cannot possibly deserve all the kindness and goodness she
has been showing me. She fully appreciates that I need encouragement before I speak
or bestir myself, and she never fails to give it. That's how her superiority shows
itself: as she directs so I speak and come out of my shell.

Discoverer of the Oedipus complex that he was to be, at sixteen the young
Freud was already aware of this generational fluidity in the fantasies of love,
whereby he might love both mother and daughter. After all, the slippage
between generations in his own family meant that he was never sure if Philipp
or Jakob was the man who held the key to the maternal secrets. The fluidity
between generations was also to be celebrated in Freud's last paper on
'Femininity', where he described how a man's love and a woman's are a phase
apart psychologically. 'It is in this identification [with her own mother] too
that she acquires her attractiveness to a man, whose Oedipus attachment to
his mother it kindles into passion.' Freud's first love quite clearly required
kindling by the melding of mother and daughter. Ernest Jones went so far
as to suggest that this uncertainty about the proper ordering of generations
underlay Freud's independence and determination to find things out for
himself, and thus perhaps his most consequential character-trait.

   The question of the proper ordering of family relations was even more
clear-cut in the other romantic proposal to preoccupy Freud's adolescent
dreams: the project that he marry his niece Pauline, and become an English
textile merchant. While visiting his relatives in Manchester in 1875, when he
was nineteen, for the first time his scientific preoccupations – his defence
against this incestuous plan – began to shift away from the theoretical and
philosophical zoology and evolutionary biology he was up to then enthusiastic
about towards the plan to become a doctor who helped people, who might

be of practical use. 'The theoretical (scientific) alternative to the emigration and marriage plan thus constituted a defense against incest, and the actual subject of his future research, the sexuality of sea creatures, has the character of a psychic compromise between desire and defense.' But Freud showed no interest in marrying Pauline. Indeed, a dream about sea creatures which he included in *The Interpretation of Dreams* recognizes that the parental plan involved 'bringing in sex where it did not belong'. With Gisela Fluss, Freud found himself entangled with a sexual triangle involving a mother and a daughter; with Pauline, he found himself entangled in the incest to which his complex family structure lent itself more easily than most. Freud, characteristically, rapidly evaded getting involved in either scene. With the first of these fleeting brushes with passion, with Gisela, Freud turned away from law and politics, his first, and more belligerent, career choices, to a new interest, which would be 'no empty flirtation', but the humble devotion of a scientist to mother nature; with the second turning away, from Pauline and the project of incest, he began to take seriously the project of medicine, with the mastery that the idea of cure implies. On both occasions, he had turned away from women and had buried himself in the pursuit of knowledge.

Alongside this story of successive waves of sexual repression is the related story of the moderation of his youthful aggressive enthusiasm for the generals of antiquity, for Alexander, Hannibal and Massena, into support for the equally pugilistically minded English philosophers and scientists, Huxley and Tyndall, and then to the more compassionate benefactors, the imperial scientific helpers of humanity, the Kochs and Pasteurs. We should, however, underestimate neither Freud's aggressive tendencies, which he would later see as a universal part of human sexuality, nor the aggressive conception of sexual relations which his fantasies gave rise to: the 'gross sexual aggression' alluded to in the grabbing of the flowers from little Pauline. It is not going too far to say that the defloration fantasy is the crux, the authentically Freudian sexual fantasy.

In one of his pseudonymous appearances as a patient, the mature Freud muses: 'Taking flowers away from a girl means to deflower her. ... The most seductive part of the whole subject for a young scapegrace is the picture of the marriage night. (What does he care about what comes afterwards?) But that picture cannot venture out into the light of day. ...' The analyst Freud comments: 'It is precisely the coarse sensual element in the phantasy which explains why it does not develop into a *conscious* phantasy but must be content to find its way allusively and under a flowery disguise into a childhood scene. ... Can you imagine a greater contrast to these designs for gross sexual aggression than childish pranks?'

The only other childish prank that Freud remembered from his childhood, this time when he was five, also had this destructive sexually aggressive aspect:

It had once amused my father to hand over a book with *coloured plates* (an account of a journey through Persia) to me and my eldest sister to destroy. Not easy to justify from the educational point of view! ... the picture of the two of us blissfully pulling the book to pieces (leaf by leaf, like an *artichoke* [Freud's favourite flower], I found myself saying) was almost the only plastic memory that I retained from that period of my life.

As a student, buying and possessing expensive monographs became Freud's *'favourite hobby'*. His lack of guilt over the expense incurred stemmed from his pride that this hobby was innocuous when compared to others young men indulge in.

In 1898, Freud had a new hobby: tearing up dreams. The monograph on dreams he was writing appeared in his dream as a botanical monograph. He had torn up coloured plates in childhood; as a student he had dissected bodies and collected expensive monographs with coloured plates. Now he tore up dreams and the lives hidden inside them, association by association, leaf by leaf. The botanical dream casts Freud's new hobby in the floral, the natural register, from stories about men forgetting to bring their wives flowers, to preoccupations with a patient called *Flora* (whose family name was probably *Rosa*nes); the dream tells Freud: 'I may allow myself to do this.' By *this*, Freud now means not only sexual violation, but also the writing of his dream book out of the analysis, the defloration, of his patient's dreams, their coloured plates. Perhaps it is worth pointing out that the sexual fantasy underlying Freud's taste for monographs and his interpretation of dreams is one which violently opens up women, laying bare their secrets, rather than one which invades and destroys.

From an early age, Freud's love of flowers was well known to his family: 'he would roam the forest and woods near Vienna with his friends, bringing back rare plants and flower specimens.' His later passion for collecting mushrooms and the family hikes when they all competed to find the best fungi also supplied him with one of his most mysterious and often quoted analogies, one which continues the botanical register in which he had cast dreams. The dream-wish 'grows up, like a mushroom out of its mycelium', but this origin of the dream resists all attempts at complete interpretation: 'This is the dream's navel, the spot where it reaches down into the unknown.' This point that resists the deflowering interpreter is an unmistakable allusion to the mystery of femininity, the 'dark continent': the navel is the unerasable mark of our former connection to the mother.

Later, when an old man, his birthdays would occasion a veritable flood of orchids into the flat in Vienna. In 1936, the Vienna Psycho-Analytical Society's celebration of his eightieth birthday included a young girl bearing alpine flowers to the old man, who took her aside to tell her how touched he was. His followers certainly knew how to respond to the unconscious 'language of flowers' that he spoke so well and for so long.

We might even take the picture of John and Sigmund depriving little Pauline of her flowers as the allegory of the analyses, the tearing apart, of their female patients that the two doctors, Josef Breuer and Freud, were to publish in *Studies on Hysteria*. The very perception of the 'remarkably well-stocked memory' of the hysteric – with its 'striking gaps ... as though her life was chopped in pieces', and the need to fill in these gaps as the aim of a complete analysis – may owe something to the defloration fantasy. As we will see, Katharina the *Alpenkind*, with her story of her attempted violation by her father, was to capture the pastoral imagination of her doctor, the lover of alpine flowers. Freud would always remain most at home with fragments, pieces; his preferred methods would always be dissecting, analysing, separating what was mixed up or without cleft, cutting through concealing veils and opening up what was hidden.

Beyond Freud's repudiation of the defloration fantasy embodied in his memory of his childhood, we can catch a glimpse of another element of the 'peculiar idioticon' of Freud's unconscious: the theme of the three women. In that memory, three females appear: the nanny/nurse, the infant-virgin, and the peasant woman with a knife. It is, perhaps, far fetched to identify these immediately with the three fates, the one who sews, the one who measures, the one who cuts. But we have already seen how fundamental to man's relation to woman Freud was to find this theme.

In 1875, at the age of nineteen, set on his course towards medicine, the young Freud was not, as far as we know, to be touched again by the passions of love until 1882, when he met Martha Bernays. With a hint of self-pity for his absorption in his scientific work, he had proclaimed while researching in Trieste: 'Few small children appear on the streets. Those I have seen look very precocious, and already temper their beauty with face powder. Since it is not allowed to dissect human beings, I really have nothing to do with them.' And he quite probably did have nothing more to do with them until 1882. There are and were rumours: Martha's relative John was curious as to whether Freud kept a mistress in Paris while he was visiting him in 1885; Bruno Bettelheim's uncle, Karl Bettelheim, told him of visiting brothels with Sigmund Freud. When Marie Bonaparte asked Freud if he was a virgin when he married, he answered, 'No.' All in all, Jones's judicious remark about Freud's premarital sexual life seems to stand: 'It is pretty certain that the emotion [of love] did not touch him again till ten years later, when he met his future wife. ... Even any physical experiences were probably few and far between.'

The young Freud was certainly abstemious and repressed when we compare him not only with contemporaries like Arthur Schnitzler, whose diary of his youth in Vienna records new affairs, crushes, amorous scrapes and catastrophes on an almost daily basis, but also with his close friends. In 1884, he described to Martha the trajectory of his one-time closest friend Silberstein:

When he was still very young, Anna was his first love, then he had a liaison with Fanny, in between he was in love with every girl he met, and now he is with none [having married for money]. I was in love with none and am now with one. ... Today he is about to gather together again his old boon companions ... but I am on duty, and in any case my thoughts are not in the past, but elsewhere.

Sloughing off the past was, perhaps aptly for a man who made a science of memory, something Freud engaged in with periodic glee, as he regularly burnt his papers and letters. The first turning-point was his meeting Martha Bernays in April 1882. Then, he celebrated a second turning-point with another bonfire when once and for all he committed himself – on account of his yearning to be married as soon as possible – to the humble practice of medicine: 'Everything, moreover, that lies beyond the great turning-point in my life, beyond our love and my choice of profession, died long ago and must not be deprived of a worthy funeral.'

Martha Bernays: 'A Little World of Happiness'

Martha Bernays was born on 26 July 1861. She came from a distinguished Jewish family: her grandfather, Isaac Bernays (1792–1849), was the conservative Chief Rabbi of Hamburg, presiding reluctantly over the liberalization of the relations between the Jewish and non-Jewish communities. He had three sons, Michael, Jakob and Berman. Michael renounced his faith and became Professor of Languages at the University of Munich; Jakob taught Latin and Greek at the University of Heidelberg and, in 1857 (reprinted 1880), published *The Foundations of Aristotle's Lost Essay on the Tragic Effect*, whose novel interpretation of the concept of catharsis as the 'elimination of affects' almost certainly influenced Freud's, Breuer's and Bertha Pappenheim's theories in the early 1880s. The third son, Berman, born in 1826, Martha's father, a merchant, moved to Vienna in 1869 when Martha was eight and became Secretary to the well-known economist Lorenz von Stein; the move, according to Peter Swales, followed Berman's release from prison after his conviction the previous year on charges of criminal fraud. He died on 9 December 1879, leaving two daughters, Martha and Minna, and one surviving son, Eli, who took over his post as Secretary and, some two years later, took on Sigmund Freud's brother Alexander as an assistant.

The distinction of her family played some part in Freud's wooing of Martha: 'finding a respected name and a warm atmosphere in her home was decisive in my choice of a wife'. Martha's mother, Emmeline, *née* Philipp (13 May 1830–26 October 1910), was an even-tempered, intelligent and well-educated woman who came from a Swedish family. Taking on the tones of his father's hostility to religion, Martin Freud described his grandmother as a 'typical Jewess, of Sephardic origin', who adhered to orthodox Jewish practices. In February 1880, two months after the sudden death of her husband, Emmeline appointed Siegmund Pappenheim as the legal guardian of her son and two daughters; he fell ill that summer and died the next April. It is not clear how the Freuds and the Bernays met, but the families were certainly friendly and it was probably friendship between the daughters of the two families that led to Martha and her sister Minna visiting.

At that time, Freud, having finally taken his MD examination in 1881, was working as a demonstrator in Ernst Brücke's Physiological Institute. He later described this period of his life in *The Interpretation of Dreams*:

In an indistinct part of the background of one of my laboratory dreams I was of an age which placed me precisely in the gloomiest and most unsuccessful year of my medical career. I was still without a post and had no idea how I could earn my living; but at the same time I suddenly discovered that I had a choice open to me between several women whom I might marry!

In 1885, Freud reminded Martha of their first meeting:

Do you believe in omens? Since I learned that the first sight of a little girl sitting at a well-known long table talking so cleverly while peeling an apple with her delicate fingers could disconcert me so lastingly, I have actually become quite superstitious. Do you remember, you unsuspecting worm?

Instead of burying himself with his books in his room on that evening in April 1882, Freud had joined the circle round the family table. Within a few weeks, he was sending the twenty-one-year-old Martha Bernays a red rose; they had their first private talk while out walking on 31 May. On 15 June, Freud wrote her the first of what would eventually amount to several thousand love letters; her answer was 'a tender handshake under the table'. Two days later, he proposed to her; she accepted him, and they became unofficially and secretly engaged – secretly because Freud believed that he, as a student without means or prospects, and with firmly irreligious views, would be unacceptable to Martha's family. They were to marry over four years later, on 14 September 1886.

Martha had had the conventional education of young women of her time; familiar with the German classics and those of world literature in translation, she remained an avid reader (but only in the evenings, when her duties permitted) to the end of her life. Possessed of slender grace and strong features, Freud, although he proclaimed himself rather insensitive to beauty, found her 'sweet, generous and reasonable', with an inner peace and serenity. Once married, her domestic authority was for fifty years unquestioned, even by the Nazis, as her son Martin remembered: 'SS troops trampled through his flat, pulling open wardrobe and cupboard doors until stopped by mother, who behaved with incredible fortitude' and told a soldier who was rifling the linen precisely what she thought of such 'shocking behavior in a lady's house, and ordered him to stop at once'. On Freud's death, Oskar Pfister paid tribute to the family she had created and sustained, remembering back to his first visit in April 1909: 'In your house one felt as in a sunny spring garden, heard the gay song of larks and blackbirds, saw bright flower-beds, and had a premonition of the rich blessing of summer.'

Freud had an absolute and unconditional conception of love and demanded the same from Martha, as we learn from the voluminous but, up to the present, one-sided correspondence which kept them close during the long years of their engagement. Whilst he found happiness and fulfilment in the state of being in love and being loved, the egotistical and exclusive possession of the loved one he required meant that Martha was often reacting against the excessive demands he made on her. The story of their courtship is one of a balance struck between his jealousy and despair, Martha's surprise at what her jealous lover could drive himself to, and her reactively diplomatic but quite determined refusal to give up her rights and her independence.

From the start of the engagement she was convinced of Freud's love, and only under exceptional stress would the anguish of the long wait make her doubt his love or their eventual happiness. The greatest threat to their relationship was her fiancé's own tempestuous changes of mood and jealousy; he was tempting fate when he wittily wrote, in 1884: 'Yesterday I was very grumpy; you should have been here so as to wish you weren't.' Was it deep uncertainty about either his own or Martha's capacity to love, was it his vigilant and unceasing desire to plumb the depths of the other, to dissect her to the bone, or was it his adherence to a rigid and traditional code of relations between the sexes which made him so labile? Whichever, or all three, it was certainly Martha's ability to cope with Freud's changes of mood and the extreme demands he made on her that showed her strength of character. Freud was a tyrannical, jealous lover, intent on possessing her exclusively, repeating his childhood desire to eliminate all rivals from the field and recapture the original and singular adoring relation to his mother. 'I must admit to myself that I do have a tyrannical streak in my nature. ... I find it terribly difficult to subordinate myself.' Having had letter paper printed in which an M and an S were intertwined, Freud noted: 'the tyrannical temperament that makes little girls afraid of me could not be subdued. I wanted exclusiveness, and since I had attained it in great and important matters, I strove to achieve it in small and symbolic ones'; the paper 'renders every page useless for intercourse save between Marty and me.' From early on in their engagement, Freud treated anyone else who claimed responsibility for Martha as an enemy. Often enough the feeling would be clothed in wit and humour; in the very first days he wrote: 'I feel so much like a knight errant on a pilgrimage to his beloved princess who is being kept prisoner by her wicked uncle.' Or his struggle with his feelings of exclusive possession would occasion some acute reflections: 'what mattered was whether she loved several people, not whether several or everyone loved her.' But the seriousness and explicitness of his claim on her was, from the early days of their engagement, in no doubt:

From now on you are but a guest in your family. ... For has it not been laid down since time immemorial that the woman shall leave father and mother and follow the man she has chosen? You must not take it too hard, Marty, you cannot fight against it; no matter how much they love you I will not leave you to anyone, and no one deserves you; no one else's love compares with mine.

Towards the end of the engagement, when they had come through so much together, and the chief obstacles for his rivalry had been disposed of, he would find new causes for jealousy: 'Do you know that I really hate this whole trousseaux business – and why? It strikes me as a very worthy object for jealousy. Understand?' Even their future marriage could be seen as a threat to his unstable place in her heart: 'once one is married ... one lives rather with each other for some third thing, and for the husband dangerous rivals soon appear: household and nursery.'

But in the early days, Freud had more immediate rivals than babies and bed-linen: Martha's family and her past admirers. He threw a jealous fit over her friendship with a cousin Max, requiring her to distance herself from him and call him Herr Meyer. A friend of his, Fritz Wahle, had also been close to Martha; Sigmund required her to distance herself from him as well: he had stormy meetings with Fritz, at which both men shed tears and letters were torn up. Sigmund was convinced that Fritz was in love with Martha; Fritz wanted to retain his intimacy with her, was very upset at Sigmund's desire for exclusive possession, but insisted that he was not in love with her. Sigmund wrote Martha a little disquisition on the stubborn fact of ambivalence, some twenty-five years before Eugen Bleuler was to coin the term:

The solution of the puzzle is this: only in logic are contradictions unable to co-exist; in feelings they quite happily continue alongside each other. To argue like Fritz is to deny one half of life. Least of all must one deny the possibility of such contradictions in feeling with artists, people who have no occasion to submit their inner life to the strict control of reason.

All this took place less than a month after they had become secretly engaged. To sort out the argument, Sigmund travelled to Wandsbek, near Hamburg, where Martha was staying. He suggested, probably as a test of her feelings, a probationary engagement of one year. Her reply was 'Nonsense.'

Eli Bernays was staying with the Freuds at this time, and was helping Sigmund conduct his courtship, by lending him clothes and helping him out with money. But within a few months, he, himself, was the object of a new jealous campaign, over Alexander Freud's unpaid assistantship to him. When, in December 1882, Eli announced his engagement to Anna, Freud's sister, the foursome made it up, and Eli and Anna's public happiness prompted Sigmund and Martha to announce their engagement. But within a couple of months Eli had done something of which Sigmund strongly disapproved, which Ernest Jones felt obliged not to disclose in his biography seventy years later. When Sigmund's ultimata went unheeded, diplomatic relations were broken off. His campaign was clearly directed against all those close to Martha, particularly her family. He made this quite explicit, on the occasion of another jealous outburst a couple of years later: 'You have only an Either-Or. If you can't be fond enough of me to renounce for my sake your family, then you must lose me, wreck your life and not get much yourself out of your family.'

The chief object of his jealousy became Martha's mother, Emmeline; it was her 'heartlessness and caprice' which Freud held responsible for the Bernays family's permanent return to Hamburg in June 1883 – a move which prevented the impecunious engaged couple from seeing each other for long periods:

there is no denying that she is taking a line against us all, like an old man. Because her charm and vitality have lasted so long, she still demands in return her full share of life – not the share of old age – and expects to be the centre, the ruler, an end in herself. Every *man* who has grown old honourably wants the same, only in a woman one is not used to it … it is simply the claim of age, the lack of consideration of energetic old age, an expression of the eternal conflict between age and youth which exists in every family. . . .

And at the smallest sign that Emmeline was making too great a claim on Martha, he would advance his own, self-consciously egotistical counter-claim: 'I know you have not misunderstood my efforts to make you my own as intimately as possible, and if this be egotistical, love after all cannot be anything but egotistical.'

If one of the tasks he was asking of Martha was to detach herself from her mother and her family, so as to give him the exclusive possession he demanded, he was himself being transformed in a less public and tempestuous way. This change could still be signalled on the level of jealousy and possession: 'I think brain anatomy is the only legitimate rival you have or ever will have.' In becoming engaged, Freud was giving up the dreams of a lonely existence devoted to the pursuit of a great scientific discovery: by 1885, he could write that he had 'now overcome the love for science in so far as it stood between us, and that I want nothing but you.' Once, when, in a moment of despondency, Martha confessed to the foreboding that he would abandon her and marry a professor's daughter, thus securing both his financial security and his advancement in science, he responded forcefully, warning her how she, instead of yearning to sacrifice herself to her only rival, science, should be less good-natured, more jealous, in the face of this rival: 'Don't you realise that this very science could become our bitterest enemy, that the irresistible temptation to devote one's life without remuneration or recognition to the solving of problems unconnected with our personal situation, could postpone or even destroy our chances of sharing life – if I, yes, if I were to go and lose my head over it?' In Paris, this foreboding of hers struck a chord with Freud when he met the daughter of his admired teacher, Jean-Martin Charcot, and he, half-humorously, adopted the fantasy for her benefit, rendering it into his own dialect, that of the 'conquistador':

Now just suppose that I were not in love already and were something of an adventurer; it would be a strong temptation to court her, for nothing is more dangerous than a young girl bearing the features of a man whom one admires. Then I would become a laughing stock, be thrown out, and would be the richer from the experience of a beautiful adventure. It is better as it is, after all.

He portrayed himself as having formerly been destitute save for his talent and ambition, which had now been given up and replaced by his love for Martha; now

I prefer to do without my ambition, make less noise in the world and have less success rather than injure my nervous system. For the rest of my time in the hospital I will live like the Goys, modestly, learning the ordinary things without striving after discoveries or reaching to the depths. What we shall need for our independence can be attained by honest steady work without gigantic striving.

And towards the end of their engagement, when he was studying in Paris, the grand ideas that Charcot inspired in him had the perverse effect of making him want to give up the idea of solving the great problems of the world: 'My ambition would be satisfied by a long life spent learning to understand something of the world, and my plans for the future are that we get married, love each other and work with the object of enjoying life together instead of exerting every ounce of my energy trying to pass the post first, like a racehorse.'

Freud thus conceived of himself as having formerly been ambitious and that this ambition had become absorbed into the new realism that Martha embodied for him. In recommending his much loved *Don Quixote* to her, despite its coarseness and sensual brutality, he asked:

Don't you find it very touching to read how a great person, himself an idealist, makes fun of his ideals? Before we were so fortunate as to apprehend the deep truths in our love we were all noble knights passing through the world caught in a dream, misinterpreting the simplest things, magnifying commonplaces into something noble and rare, and thereby cutting a sad figure. Therefore we men always read with respect about what we once were and in part still remain.

Here already, in August 1883, is the authentic voice of the later Freud, respectful of dreams and ideals, the scales taken from his eyes by love, finding their roots in the simple and the everyday, and aware that our past illusions still live on in us, even when we recognize them as illusions. The adventurer, the conquistador who was intent on overpowering Martha, was also always in danger of seeing through his own ideals and illusions, and finding that he was not a Cortés but rather a Don Quixote – someone equally human and tragic, but now also ridiculous.

The later Freud was to show how Quixote was as great an adventurer as his earlier swashbuckling models. The ripping apart of self-glorifying illusions – such as his own identification with generals and conquerors – and the jealous vigilance over his own motives and desires were to be the initial forms of Freud's own psychoanalytic findings. Later, those discoveries were to be seen, in his and many others' eyes, as no less glorious conquests: victory over the unruly passions of the soul.

But in his courtship Freud, the later great disillusionist, found his own grandiose illusions dissipated by his love for Martha. In their place, he elaborated a naïve and sentimental domestic idyll, their 'little world of happiness', filled with beds, mirrors, a clock, an armchair, linen tied with pretty ribbons, hats with artificial flowers 'and an enormous bunch of keys – which must make a rattling noise':

we are certain to achieve what we are striving for – a little home into which sorrow may find its way, but never privation, a being-together throughout all the vicissitudes of life, a quiet contentment that will prevent us from ever having to ask what is the point of living. I know after all how sweet you are, how you can turn a house into a paradise, how you will share in my interests, how gay and painstaking you will be. I will let you rule the house as much as you wish, and you will reward me with your sweet love and by rising above all those weaknesses for which women are so often despised.

Yet equally a part of his transformation from lofty idealist, from pure scientist, was a more subtle transformation that Martha effected in his attitude to her. Over the long, difficult and tumultuous years of their engagement, she was able to moderate the defloration fantasy that, together with his desire to recreate his early adored relation to his own mother, exclusive of all later siblings, underpinned his need for exclusive possession of her. This aggressive fantasy was closely linked for Freud to the requirement for absolute honesty which ruled his demands on Martha, and would, in later years, rule the very conception of analysis: 'I have always been frank with you, haven't I? I haven't made use of the licence usually granted to a person of the other sex – of showing you my best side. For a long, long time I have criticised you and picked you to pieces, and the result of it all is that I want nothing but to have you and have you just as you are.' This aggressive urge for truth – 'I cannot flatter; I can, it is true, be mistaken' – was what Martha managed to resist and to moderate. She found ways to be both honest and yet not give in to his requirement that she love him and only him. Perhaps she learned early that his bouts of zealous honesty, so often turned into emotional blackmail, would be followed by self-recrimination and outpourings of affection and contrition. Freud had a need for her to be both subservient, in the sense of absorbing and living entirely by his values, and herself: 'it would be a ghastly loss for us both if I were compelled to decide to love you as a dear girl, yet not as an equal, someone from whom I would have to hide my thoughts and opinions – in short, the truth.' At the very beginning of their engagement, he had realized how tyrannical his requirement for honesty was already becoming: 'I have been trying to smash her frankness so that she should reserve her opinion until she is sure of mine.' And when she did resist and demonstrate her independence, his reaction was not always a placid one: 'you write so intelligently and to the point that I am just a little afraid of you. I think it all goes to show once more how quickly women outdistance men. Well, I am not going to lose anything by it.'

Freud continued to demand that she love unconditionally, without quali-fication, on his terms: 'I don't want you to love for qualities you assume in me, in fact not for any qualities; you must love me as irrationally as other people love, just because I love you and you don't have to be ashamed of it.' Yet six months later, in June 1884, when they had not seen each other for a year, he was to write the most telling account of how Martha had resisted his bullying veracity:

I really think I have always loved you much more than you me, or – more correctly: until we were separated you hadn't surmounted the *primum falsum* of our love – as a logician would call it – i.e. that I forced myself upon you and you accepted me without any great affection. I know it has finally changed.... Do you remember how you often used to tell me that I had a talent for repeatedly provoking your resistance? How we were always fighting, and you would never give in to me? We were two people who diverged in every detail of life and who were yet determined to love each other, and did love each other. And then ... you admitted that I had no influence over you. I found you so fully matured and every corner in you occupied, and you were hard and reserved and I had no power over you. This resistance of yours only made you the more precious to me, but at the same time I was very unhappy....

That Freud provoked resistance in Martha is the clearest indication of how rampant the deflowering drive in Freud was and was to remain, when he came to 'confront' his neurotic patients. That she found a way to mollify the assault on her values and her person, and to oblige him to realize that a victory over her would have been a defeat for himself, is a measure of her tact and strength of character. At the beginning, he wanted her to be independent of her family, but only in order for her to become permanently identified, united, fused with him; in this, he failed to see how contradictory was his project of bullying someone else into independence. It was Martha's achievement to find genuine independence of both family and Freud, without sacrificing her relations with either. But the storms continued until virtually their wedding day; at one point, Freud demanded (again) that she break off all relations with her brother Eli or else cease corresponding with him. Even then, she found a compromise, but confessed 'that for the first and only time she had felt herself destitute of any love'.

The blind love of veracity was to be a theme throughout Freud's life and work, tempered at times, but capable of bursting through in his defiant relish for being in opposition: 'even at school I was always the bold oppositionist, always on hand when an extreme had to be defended and usually ready to atone for it'. His love of splendid isolation, his taste for the hostility of Ibsen's 'compact majority', implied his identification with Dr Stockmann, *the enemy of the people*, the naïve physician who values truth above all other considerations, and who is blind to all the other consequences of his actions. His militaristic bent, the conquistador, the 'extremely daring and fearless human being' who lay beneath his reserved exterior, could find expression in his love of truth. He even decided to adopt and cultivate uprightness and honesty as his distinctive bedside manner; the refrain persisted in his dipping his hand into the Bocca della Verità on his first visit to Rome in 1901 and vowing to return. By 1910, however, writing to Ferenczi about sexual honesty in marriage, he had become more pragmatic: 'Truth is only the absolute goal of science, but love is a goal of life quite independent of it and conflicts between the two great powers are very well conceivable. I do not see any necessity for regularly subordinating one to the other as a matter of principle.' None the less, as his attitude to *Moses and Monotheism* or to telepathy in the 1930s indicated, new circumstances could easily revive the rash and unruly veracity which Martha had been one of the first to confront.

So that 'breakthrough to woman' which Freud was to see as a turning-point for many of his male patients was one that he had achieved in the course of his falling in love with Martha and the slow reorientation of his life that necessarily followed. It soon became clear that if he wanted to marry, he would have to turn away from pure science, from Brücke's Physiological Institute, and prepare himself for medical practice; what counted were material prospects. Freud still hoped to make a great discovery, which would make his name and guarantee a post or sufficient patients. He cast this way and that, pinning his hopes on his gold-staining microscopy technique, then on his espousal of the virtues of cocaine as an analgesic. These discoveries were to prove fragile though; he fell back on the slow, hard grind of acquiring experience and a solid reputation.

Within six weeks of meeting Martha, Freud had joined the General Hospital, where he stayed for three years, trying to live on his paltry stipend there, taking on the odd patient, mostly referred from Breuer, to gain experience and earn extra gulden. From May 1883 on, he worked for a considerable time on the psychiatric wards, both male and female: admitting the patients, writing up two-page symptom- and character-sketches, prescribing their treatments, which were usually chemical, and occasionally referring the more acute patients to asylums for the insane. At the beginning of 1884, he wrote to Martha: 'Today I put my case histories in order at last and started on the study of a nervous case; thus begins a new era!' In May of that year, Hermann Nothnagel, one of his superiors, warned him that 'you can build up a practice only if the general practitioners send you patients for electrical treatment.' By the end of 1884, he had a brass plate on his door, and, in early 1895, he cast aside his hopes of the great scientific 'breakthrough' and prepared himself for the more humble profession of practising physician.

At some point in 1885, he seized upon specializing in children's nervous diseases as one way to make his mark and his name when he was to set up his practice. In 1886, working briefly in Berlin while on his way back to Vienna from Paris, he wrote to Martha:

What appeals to me ... are the children in the clinic, who on account of their small format and because they are usually well washed l find more attractive material than the large editions of patients. As long as their brains are free of disease, these little creatures are really charming and so touching when they suffer. I think I would find my way about in a children's practice in no time.

On his return to Vienna in April 1886, he took on a part-time appointment, which he was to hold until 1896, at the newly reformed children's hospital, which, its director Max Kassowitz claimed, was now 'the first public hospital for children'. There about 100 children were seen a week. Freud worked twice a week and had unlimited access to children who provided a large amount of clinical material, without interference by seniors. He wrote up nearly ninety of these little patients as case histories in his two monographs on children's paralyses.

The plans and years of the slow acquisition of experience and knowledge were all geared to the day when he could open a medical practice that would offer sufficient income for Martha and he to get married. The obstacle, from the beginning to the end, was money: 'Oh, my darling Marty, how poor we are! Suppose we were to tell the world we are planning to share life and they were to ask us: What is your dowry? – Nothing but our love for each other ... nothing but two poor human creatures who love one another to distraction.'

In 1882, the immediate reason for keeping their engagement secret was to
avoid the wrath of her family when they learned that she was intending to
marry someone without money or prospects. From the first day, the financial
arrangements were settled: Martha would be the banker, Sigmund would give
her all the money and then ask her to send some to him when he needed it.
As the years passed, the money calculations became more detailed, the dialect
of contract and account, of debt and credit, became more prominent – even
the postal kisses were entered into an account ledger. Yet, not surprisingly,
the question of money could prove divisive, and they both played on the
incipient inequality and resentment that could build up. When Sigmund heard
of a legacy or a gift that might come Martha's way, he would immediately
joke about his financial dependency on her:

Woe to the day you become so rich that I, like a character in a bad novel, have to
ask you politely whether you wish to continue to be my betrothed as I don't want
to stand in the way of your happiness, etc.... I give you the solemn promise that I
will marry you even if you don't get the 1500 Marks. If necessary, I will marry you
with 150,000,000 Marks.

He was thus betraying some unease at being reminded of the situation that
his friend Silberstein had been placed in, of marrying money without love, of
finding financial independence at the cost of a loveless marriage and hypocritical servitude to a rich wife. In contrast to Silberstein, it was he, Sigmund,
and not Martha, who was rich, rich because, in the traditional metaphor, she
was the possession he acquired through marriage, 'a jewel that I have pawned
and that I am going to redeem as soon as I am rich.'

The truth was that Freud had no prospects; indeed, he was being given
money and was borrowing from generous friends and was still not making
ends meet, whilst Martha *did* have a dowry, albeit a small one, and was being
promised wedding gifts by relatives, some of whom were making considerable
financial sacrifices to do so. Yet the money never seemed enough to set up
house with. Freud's attitude here is complex, embodying several contradictory
sentiments. He conceived of their engagement as having been a heroic gesture
of independence and declaration of the triumph of love over material and
social adversity; this view fitted in well with his penchant for seeing himself
in opposition. Their recklessness – as Emmeline Bernays called it in a letter
trying to postpone their imminent marriage in 1886 – amidst their poverty
allowed Sigmund to co-opt Martha into the heroic and defiant stance he liked
to adopt towards the world:

we shall serve as a model for future generations of lovers, and only because we had
the courage to get fond of each other without asking anyone's permission.... So we
are like the people who walk on a tight rope or climb poles whom any audience
applauds, although the same audience would be very unhappy to see their own sons
and daughters doing the same thing instead of using a convenient ladder or staying
comfortably below.

Or, as he had put it two years earlier, 'to take up science as a poverty-stricken man, then as a poverty-stricken man to capture a poor girl – but this must continue to be my way of life: risking a lot, hoping a lot, working a lot. To average bourgeois common sense I have been lost long ago.' Being given money would remove them from this morally comfortable position. Despite Freud's counsel to Martha that 'only the poor have difficulty in accepting presents, never the rich', his loathing of passive dependency and being cared for can be fairly judged from the eruption of irritation when, in early 1884, he was laid up with sciatica for some weeks: 'I seem like a woman in her lying-in, and I curse at times over the unrestrained love.'

As well as being proud, Freud also resented the cost of marrying a poor woman, the cost of his independent choice, the fact that everything he achieved came the hard way, love, marriage and happiness being no exception to this rule. There is some confusion in the evidence concerning Martha's dowry. A series of later dreams of Freud's centred around the claim that he was proud that his wife had brought no dowry to the marriage; indeed, the one completely analysed dream that Freud wanted to include in the dream book, only to have it censored by the first psychoanalytic reader, Wilhelm Fliess, pursued this theme. Yet Martha's dowry, inadequate as it might seem given their pressing needs, was intact, if somewhat dispersed, when they came to planning their wedding in the final months. Their getting married depended almost entirely on the sum she brought with her.

This fact of Freud remembering that she brought no dowry, in effect remembering the past as he had written to her in August in 1882 – 'What is your dowry? – Nothing but our love for each other' – undoubtedly has a deep significance. Martha's dowry is linked in with Freud's long-term relation to women and money. We have already seen how Freud had lost his loved nanny when a hoard of shiny coins was discovered in her possession, coins that little Sigismund believed were his because he remembered stealing them from, or being given them by, his mother.

She made me steal zehners to give them to her. There is a long chain from these first silver zehners to the heap of paper ten-florin notes which I saw in the dream as Martha's weekly housekeeping money. The dream could be summed up as 'bad treatment'. Just as the old woman got money from me for her bad treatment, so today I get money for the bad treatment of my patients.

He was convinced that he was as guilty as his nurse. But his mother (and Philipp, no doubt) had established to their satisfaction that the nurse was the guilty one; she had used the innocent boy to her own thieving ends. Pre-Freudians, perhaps they assumed that the guilty party had to be an adult.

Taking what his mother said on trust, Freud corrected the dream interpretation from which he constructed the scene of the purloined coins: 'the dream picture was a memory of my taking money from the mother of a doctor – that is, wrongfully. The correct interpretation is: I = she, and the mother of the doctor equals my mother.' Freud's 'mistaken' interpretation of the dream arose, then, from not knowing that he was identified with his nurse. But, thus clarified, the dream portrayed his nurse as wrongfully taking money from his mother. And with this new interpretation it is not so much Freud who is in the wrong when he takes money from mothers and other women patients, but by implication Martha, to whom he gives this money.

The choice of scenarios is an unenviable one : if he is the thief, not only does he steal from his mother, but he is the cause of his innocent and beloved nurse's dismissal – a scene very like the self-confessed core of Rousseau's autobiographical *Confessions*, in which Rousseau stole a ribbon and let Marion the servant-girl, for whose love he stole it, be convicted of the crime and ignominiously dismissed from service. But if the nurse were the thief, then he becomes an innocent victim, abused by women who steal from him his means and his birthright. The twin themes of his guilt or his victimization are repeated in his recalling how his nurse both 'provided me at such an early age with the means for living and going on living', through, he implies, her having been 'my teacher in sexual matters'; and, in this way, she laid the foundation for 'neurotic impotence' since she 'complained because I was clumsy and unable to do anything.'

The theme can be summed up in the following question : 'What did he owe women ?' And the question subdivides : 'Is he in debt because of what they *gave* him or is he in debt for what he *stole* from them ?' Naturally, in his later professional life the question of theft is not so stark. There is taking money under false pretences, for his 'bad treatment' of them (not curing his patients when he had led them to believe he could) ; there is also the taking of money from women whom he should treat for free. In the dreams of the 1890s, the ancient figures of his nurse and his mother merged with the women in his adult life : his family, his friends and his patients. Indeed, he later described his memory in the following way : 'she used to insist on my dutifully handing over to her the small coins I received as presents – a detail which can itself claim to have the value of a screen memory for later experiences.'

What were these later experiences ? His dream had revolved around the ethics of taking money from his patient, Flora Rosanes, the wife of his old friend, Ignaz, and giving this money to Martha for the house-keeping. This scene repeated his imagined version of the childhood scene : he was giving the money his mother gave him to his nurse. The question – 'Who is the thief ? Me or the nurse ?' – Freud had answered on analogy with his bad feelings about taking his patient's money. Yet structurally speaking, making the nurse rather than himself the wrongdoer entailed that it was Martha and not he who was in the wrong in taking this money. She was in the wrong in *demanding* the money for their house from him. His later dreams would tell him that *he* was the one who had had to pay for the marriage, not his wife's family : 'it was the fault of my *fiancée* that I was not already famous at that youthful age' by exploiting cocaine as a local anaesthetic, he wrote in 1925, but hastened to add, 'I bore my *fiancée* no grudge.' Somewhere here was Freud's wish not to have to accept money from his wife's family, as if he would thereby be repeating the theft of the shiny zehners of his childhood. And maybe his judgment was being interfered with by thoughts of how much easier it *might* have been if he had married someone other than Martha, since at one point he had 'had the opportunity of marrying someone with a dowry of 100,000 gulden' – a mysterious rich girl about whom we know nothing more.

The dream of 'Company at table d'hôte' made a closely intertwined point clearly:

Frau E. L.'s speech in the dream, 'You've always had such beautiful eyes', can only have meant: 'People have always done everything for you for love; you have always had everything *without paying for it.*' The truth is, of course, just the contrary: I have always paid dearly for whatever advantage I have had from other people ... in the dream thoughts the chief emphasis is laid on a wish for once to enjoy unselfish love, love which 'costs nothing'.

What Freud had never had without paying for it in some way, this dream implied, was sexual satisfaction. That was never free. And the model for every possible sexual satisfaction was his marriage – that, also, was paid for by him. Late in life, this theme of the necessary sacrifice could be linked with the idea of life as a detour:

After forty-one years of medical activity, my self-knowledge tells me that I have not really been a true physician. I became a physician through an enforced deflection from my original intention, and the triumph of my life lies in this: that I have once again found my initial direction after a great detour.

This 'enforced deflection' was the requirement to earn sufficient money to support himself, his wife and his family: it was the very existence of Martha (and the financial needs symbolized by the word 'dowry') which obliged him to take this detour. The triumph of his life, then, was to have overcome the cost of his marriage to Martha. This is what was at stake when Freud remembered Martha as not having a dowry. Perhaps he should have told himself one of those 'shiny' jokes he would later collect, treasure and make his own: 'A wife is expensive but you have her for a long time.'

Over sixty years later, in the late 1940s, Martha recalled the agony of their engagement in a rather different tone from Freud's glorification of their independence and bravery:

It was such a torture! Today youth is more courageous: they marry and they go to college, and somehow it works out. How shocked everybody was when the first rent of Dr Freud's office and apartment was paid with the little sum I brought with me as my dowry.

Freud opened his practice on Easter Day, 1886. Over the next few months, he agonized over the income and outgoings, as the practice slowly gained momentum. Freud still had 1,000 gulden left over from the Paneth donation, one of the 'semi-unselfish capitalists' Freud liked to paint as the sole instrument of their marriage; Martha brought 1,800 gulden, of which 1,200 would go on the trousseau, and then, late in the day, another 2,000 was given to her in gifts. Part of the dowry had been invested by Eli, and Freud raged and stormed at Martha for entrusting it to him; he then grew suspicious that Eli had in effect embezzled it from his sister Anna's dowry. Eventually, the money was returned to Martha, with Sigmund and Martha not quite over the threshold of an 'irreparable rupture'. In August, Sigmund was on army manoeuvres doing his statutory military service. From there, he returned to Vienna for a change of clothing. At that late date, he found that he was short of cash – a patient had failed to pay his bill and the army was paying him less than he had expected – and he was forced to borrow money from Minna Bernays for the fare to Wandsbek. The civil marriage took place on 13 September 1886; the next day, bowing to the legal necessity of having a religious ceremony, they were married privately by a rabbi in Martha's mother's home. Immediately afterwards they departed for their honeymoon in Lübeck.

2

'NOT A BAD SOLUTION OF THE MARRIAGE PROBLEM'

Martha and Sigmund Freud were to live together for fifty-three years. Strangely enough, we know more about the inner turmoil of their engagement, at least from Freud's point of view, than we do about their marriage. Very few of the many letters and papers Sigmund and Martha left have emerged from the closed vaults to which daughter Anna and her like-mindedly secretive collaborators at the Freud Archive have confined them – as if source material on the Freud family were incriminating loot to be stashed in an anonymous Swiss bank account.

Once married, it is remarkable how silent Freud was, even to his closest friends such as Wilhelm Fliess, about his relations with Martha. Some sense of the jealous reserve with which Freud guarded their marriage can be had from the tone, quasi-ironic, quasi-patronizing, of his evaluation of it in a letter to his future son-in-law, Max Halberstadt, in 1912: 'I have really got along very well with my wife. I am thankful to her above all for her many noble qualities, for the children who have turned out so well, and for the fact that she has neither been very abnormal nor very often ill.' And to Marie Bonaparte in 1936, there is the same tone: 'It was really not a bad solution of the marriage problem, and she is still today tender, healthy, and active.' The marriage was to be judged by its fruits and by the most basic goods in life: children, health, common affection. How intimate they were we will never know, even if it makes sense, and it is by no means clear that it does, to ask such a question of a marriage. Certainly there is the mysterious and, to the twentieth-century ear, almost bizarre description that Freud gave in the dream book of a woman whom he would 'not have liked to have as a patient, since I had noticed that she was bashful in my presence and I could not think she would make an amenable patient. ... The person in question was, of course, my own wife.'

Martha became what Freud had wanted her to be and become: 'an adored sweetheart in youth, and a beloved wife in maturity.' She was an admirable manager of the home, and within months of their marriage was scolding Sigmund for his messy disruption of the domestic order she imposed, so he could, willingly, ironically and with affection, describe himself to Minna as henpecked. Where possible, Martha appeased those friends and relations that the more irascible and impulsive Sigmund affronted, and imported into the running of the home the North German virtue, so alien to the easy-going Viennese, of punctuality – a virtue that Sigmund also enshrined in the hourly sessions of his psychoanalytic practice. Her domestic authority was unquestioned; when, in 1920, their daughter Anna wanted to change some rooms around, Sigmund wrote to her: 'I cannot force her [Martha], have always let her have her way in the house.' Though not quite always: in his seventies, Sigmund became very attached to a series of dogs, gifts from his female friends and admirers; Martha's disapproval of his penchant for spoiling them with food from the dinner table never abated. Outside the house, in Sigmund's public world, Martha had no place; as she once told a relative: 'I shun any kind of publicity. I believe in the proverb that the best wife is the one about whom the least is said.' When she was eighty-seven after Freud's death, her humility and her pride in her lack of 'obtrusiveness' without any sign of self-denigration shine through in her touching self-description as 'old mother Freud: an old grandmama who still toddles around between children and children's children.' She herself would have taken it as a tribute that there is remarkably little to say about Martha Freud.

In the late 1940s, she wrote to a granddaughter: 'I wish for you to be as fortunate in your marriage as I have been in mine. For during the fifty-three years I was married to your grandfather, there was never an unfriendly look or a harsh word between us.' More expressively, she replied to Ludwig Binswanger's letter of condolence on Sigmund's death:

How good, dear Dr, that you knew him when he was still in the prime of his life, for in the end he suffered terribly, so that even those who would have most liked to keep him forever had to wish for his release! And yet how terribly difficult it is to have to do without him. To continue to live without so much kindness and wisdom beside one! It is small comfort for me to know that in the fifty-three years of our married life not one angry word fell between us, and that I always sought as much as possible to remove from his path the misery of everyday life. Now my life has lost all content and meaning.

The one reported row in those fifty-three years was a dispute over the correct way to cook mushrooms.

Yet there was one long-standing conflict, whose non-resolution gives a sense of the success of their marriage. Whereas Sigmund came from a Jewish family that, under the influence of the Enlightenment-inspired movement of the early and mid-nineteenth century, had dispensed with virtually all religious rituals and habits, with the sole exception of the Seder, Martha's family still preserved her grandfather's conservative Jewish resistance to this movement. Freud was acutely aware of this and, in a tribute to her family's traditions during their engagement, had diplomatically, but forcefully, written: 'And as for us, this is what I believe: even if the form wherein the old Jews were happy no longer offers us any shelter, something of the core, of the essence of this meaningful and life-affirming Judaism will not be absent from our home.' None the less, when they established that home, Sigmund forbade Martha lighting the candles on Friday night; a cousin clearly remembered Martha telling her 'how not being allowed to light the Sabbath lights on the first Friday night after her marriage was one of the most upsetting experiences of her life.' The atmosphere of the home was from then on resolutely secular. Their son Martin remembered: 'Our festivals were Christmas, with presents under a candle-lit tree, and Easter, with gaily painted Easter eggs. I had never been in a synagogue, nor to my knowledge had my brothers or sisters.' The feud had not been definitively won, though. Martha obviously still bridled under Freud's tyranny, and he still chided her about her attachment to religious traditions; when he was in Rome in 1907, he visited the catacombs and wrote to Martha: 'In the Jewish [catacombs] the inscriptions are Greek, the candelabrum – I think it's called Menorah – can be seen on many tablets.' Feigning not to know the Hebrew name for the 'candelabrum' is another playful dig in Martha's ritually inclined ribs. By 1938, the feud had been going for fifty years, but was still not settled, according to their visitor, Isaiah Berlin: 'Martha joked at Freud's monstrous stubbornness which prevented her from performing the ritual, while he firmly maintained that the practice was foolish and superstitious.' After Sigmund's death, Martha began lighting the candles every Friday night.

During their engagement, Martha and Sigmund established a pattern of authority and submission which was to endure. She learned the hard way that his bark was worse than his bite, and that he was most effusively affectionate and most considerately pliable following a storm, one of his bitter, tyrannical stands on principle. As Jones so wittily put it, 'she was to have her own way provided it was his, but when it came to the point he usually deferred to her.' But theirs was a marriage which was almost a caricature of the by then traditional division of labour. Freud earned the money, gave her a weekly house-keeping allowance, and often kept from her the financial worries he had as his practice fluctuated. Martha managed the complex domestic arrangements of house, servants and children. In the early decades of their marriage, Martha would take the children and the household away from Vienna for nearly four summer months, to the lake or mountain resorts, to somewhere with 'Alpine roses right down to the road, the small green lake, glorious woods all around, with strawberries, flowers, and mushrooms as well.' There the family would play and jostle with the children of the family circle of friends from Vienna – the Breuers, Hammerschlags, Schwabs, Schiffs and the Kassowitzes. Freud would stay on in Vienna, visiting occasionally, but keeping his practice going save for a month or six weeks off, and these he would often use for travels to the south, to his beloved Italy. Martha did not enjoy the frenetic pace of his holidays and, apart from her responsibilities to the children, did not wish to accompany him.

As we will see, Freud was a man who could cultivate and sustain, perhaps even thirsted after and required, intense intellectual relations with women, but his wife was not one of these. She was, none the less, Freud reflected, 'fundamentally quite ambitious' and, therefore, 'very satisfied' by all the celebrations for his seventieth birthday in 1926. And earlier, in 1900, when Freud and Martha went to hear Georg Brandes, 'Martha, in whom ambition is a very important trait, persuaded me to send a copy of the dream book to his hotel' – a curious echo of Freud's gift of Brandes's book *Moderne Geiste* (*Modern Thinkers*) to her on a special occasion in October 1883. But in later years, Freud's disciples were shocked and surprised to learn how little Martha knew of or cared for psychoanalysis. René Laforgue recounts how, during one of his trips to Vienna,

she asked my advice about a problem, a tic which troubled a little boy of her acquaintance. I told her of my astonishment at her addressing herself to me and not to her husband. She replied with her customary frankness, 'Do you really think one can employ psychoanalysis with children? I must admit that if I did not realize how seriously my husband takes his treatments, I should think that psychoanalysis is a form of pornography.'

Of course, the target of this – quite probably – feigned innocence was as much her daughter Anna, the 'child analyst', as her husband. Theodor Reik remembered her saying of a hysterical woman, 'She'll get over it if she'll use her will.' But one could easily imagine Sigmund, less pious in his psychoanalytic orthodoxy than his followers, saying such a thing. Certainly Martha cultivated her ignorance of her husband's work as part of their agreed-upon division of labour. Her trust in his work was unshakable because it rested on trust in his person. This may have made things easier for Freud at home, since he would hear no doubts of the wisdom of his unorthodox methods of treatment from his wife. Martha would never have said to Sigmund what the wife of Wilhelm Stekel, one of Freud's earliest followers, said to her husband when he started to treat patients psychoanalytically as opposed to medically: 'I can't go along with you in this matter, it's like a swindle.'

Freud's often severe ethical condemnations of friends and colleagues hinged on bad faith, breaking of trust, lack of candour and hypocrisy. When in 1910 Fritz Wittels was proposing to publish a novel which was a barely disguised attack on his former intimate, Karl Kraus, Freud insisted to him: 'He was your friend. When a friendship is broken, regardless of the reason, one has to keep silence.' Wittels went ahead and published, even though, while lampooning Kraus in public, he was writing him affectionate letters of reconciliation in private. Freud broke with Wittels over this instance of hypocrisy, which Wittels excused as 'ambivalence', asserting his right to act according to his feelings. In 1929, nearly twenty years later, Freud's memory of the incident was implacably clear and his attitude still unswervingly severe: 'this refusal of a cultural correction of an impulsive attitude seemed to be incompatible with the duties of the analyst to the public.' But Freud was to become with age remarkably tolerant of sexual and ethical extravagances: 'ethics are a kind of highway code for traffic among mankind'. Martha's morality was more conventional but also more pragmatic, focusing on responsibilities and the pain caused to others; for instance, she could never forgive their family friend Stefan Zweig for leaving his wife for a younger woman, and commiserated with his abandoned wife over this with unremitting hostility to the by then extremely unhappy Zweig. But in her youth, she had forgiven her brother Eli his marital infidelities and had also been tolerant of her intimate friend Elise, who had 'married before her wedding'. On hearing about Elise, her fiancé Sigmund had ordered her to break off relations with 'the poor girl who looks for a man no matter where', declaring, 'I am not worrying about the question of decency ... but about the utter weakness and lack of principle'. Perhaps Freud was correct when he had, a year before this incident, in 1884, reluctantly recognized how independently minded and almost indifferent to his coercive entreaties Martha was.

On returning from their honeymoon, Sigmund and Martha set up house in a four-room apartment in Maria Theresienstrasse 8, on the site of the Ringtheater which had burnt down with large loss of life in December 1881. Their first child was born on 16 October 1887 and was named Mathilde, after Breuer's wife, who had been supplying Martha with advice and baby clothes from early on in the pregnancy. The respect and gratitude Sigmund felt for his wife he transmitted to her mother and sister:

I have now lived with her for 13 months and I have never ceased to congratulate myself on having been so bold as to propose to her before I really knew her; ever since then I have treasured the priceless possession I acquired in her, but I have never seen her so magnificent in her simplicity and goodness as on this critical occasion which after all doesn't permit any pretences.

But there were other tones, of irony and humour permeated by familiar deeper themes, of Freud's dowry being squeezed between mother and 'nurse', when he reported on his four-day-old daughter's health: 'So far two offers for her little hand have been received. ... The decision, however, is still outstanding, and so is the dowry. I actually owned a gold coin, as a start for the dowry, but let myself be inveigled into giving it to the midwife.'

Two boys were also born in their first home, Martin in 1889 and Oliver in 1891. In that year they moved to Berggasse 19, in search of more space for their growing family. Sigmund chose the new apartment without Martha having seen it; she was dissatisfied with his choice, thought the neighbourhood a poor one, the stone stairs dark, steep and dangerous, and the accommodation insufficient. Perhaps Freud appreciated the symbolic location of the apartment, on a long street whose character changed markedly as one moved up the hill: at the foot was a poor Jewish quarter, with a market; at the top of the hill, the street opened out on to the university, in a quarter where the bourgeois, professional classes, who were to become Freud's patients, lived.

In Berggasse 19, Martha bore three more children: Ernst in 1892, Sophie in 1893 and Anna in 1895. The sons were named after heroes of Freud's: Jean-Martin Charcot, Oliver Cromwell and Ernst Brücke; of the daughters' names, there will be more to say later. The birth of the second girl Sophie once again stimulated Freud's dowry complex into life: 'She is small, but behaves very intelligently, as though she had already learnt in her mother's

womb that she must find some other compensation here for her dowerlessness.' In August 1893, with five children aged five, three, two, sixteen
months and four months, Freud wrote to Fliess from the top of his favourite
mountain to cancel a trip they had been planning together. He now intended
to spend more time with Martha, who had uncharacteristically joined him and
'expressed the wish to spend several days with me up here ... and I felt
obliged to afford her this pleasure.'

The events at home had shown her how difficult it is to make arrangements for
leaving the children, and for the past six years, since child followed child, there has
been little room for change and relaxation in her life. I do not believe I can deny
her this wish. You can imagine what is behind it; gratitude, a feeling of coming back
to life again of the woman who for the time being does not have to expect a child
for the year because we are now living in abstinence; and you know the reasons for
this as well.

Martha had help with her brood, usually having two servants. Later a governess
took care of the three elder children, while the *Kinderfrau* Josefine looked after
the three youngest, in particular her favourite Anna. Martha's sister, Minna,
often used to help out for months on end, and then, in late 1896, Minna
moved in permanently. She was to live with the Freuds for the rest of her
life.

Minna Bernays: 'My Closest Confidante'

Born on 18 June 1865, Minna was nearly four years younger than Martha.
Always close, the girls were none the less very different. Where Martha was
small and delicate, 'sharp-witted but very seldom sharp-tongued', Minna was
large, stately, self-confident, energetic and opinionated. Some months before
Sigmund's courtship of Martha began, Minna had become engaged to one of
his close friends, Ignaz Schönberg. One afternoon, in those early days of the
courtship between Martha and Sigmund, while they were out walking with
her mother, he asked so many questions of Martha that 'when she got home
she told her young sister Minna about it all and added: "What do you make
of it?" She got the rather damping answer: "It is very kind of Herr Doctor
to take so much interest in *us*."' On that point, Minna was to prove both
wrong and right; as we have seen, Sigmund's highest priority was to detach
Martha from her family, in order to have exclusive possession of her; but
one of the ways he found to achieve this was to make a firm and, as it turned
out, a life-long ally of Minna.

The tone was set early; just before he was to visit the Bernays in Wandsbek,
after a separation of fourteen months, he wrote to Minna: 'Woe to them
who try to spoil so much as one hour of my stay with their friendly intentions!
Should you hear or know of anyone dying to meet me, please help me to
scare him away. In return we will often take you with us and be very nice to
you.' Minna was to act as lookout: an integral part of the threesome when
seen from the outside world, but excluded from the twosome's desires for

union. Minna was not only the lookout, keeping both friends and family – notably Martha's mother – at bay, but also an accomplice in detaching Martha from too great a subservience to her mother's dominating and wilful character; as Jones put it, Freud employed Minna to accomplish a 'clever bit of weaning'. Freud adroitly made use of the two sisters' different characters, as expressed in their different feelings for and attitudes towards their mother. To Martha he wrote: 'You don't love her very much and are as considerate as possible to her; Minna loves her, but doesn't spare her.'

There is also no doubt that, from the start, Sigmund and Minna got on very well. They wrote regularly to one another and she was included in the exchange of books and ideas that stocked the prolonged engagement. On one occasion Sigmund remarked to Martha how he and Minna shared 'wild, passionate natures', whereas Ignaz and Martha were 'thoroughly good people'. 'That is why we get on better in a criss-cross arrangement; why two similar people like Minna and myself don't suit each other specially; why the two good-natured ones don't attract each other.'

In 1884, Schönberg's health began to deteriorate ominously, and by 1885 Freud had examined him and declared to Martha that he was now lost, his tuberculosis out of control. Schönberg broke off his engagement to Minna, an act with which Freud strongly disagreed. 'Minna', Freud wrote to Martha, 'won't want to do anything but stand by Schönberg as long as there is such a person. And you wouldn't behave differently, wouldn't leave me before I died, if it looked as though I were going to die. And I certainly wouldn't give up what is most precious to me as long as I am alive.' The key argument, which, one suspects, not only had great consequences for Minna's life, but also touched her feelings deeply, was that 'he ought not to see her as someone else's wife if he remains alive' – a mild version of suttee, in which the young woman's hopes of marriage are effectively sacrificed on the sick-bed of her fiancé.

if serious illness made it impossible for us to marry, we two would behave differently. I have been looking upon you for a long time as my own, and I would never set you free; I would accept the fact that you suffered with and about me, and I doubt that you, my little woman, would do otherwise. A human being is so miserable when all he wants is to stay alive.

But in the end, Freud's concern was with the living, not the dead or the dying: 'Tell Minna from me that whenever we entertain friends, there will always be a place laid for her.' When Schönberg died in early 1886, Freud wrote to Minna from Paris:

try to regain something of your lost youth during which one is meant to do nothing but grow and develop, give your emotions a long rest and live for a while quietly with the two of us who are closest to you. ... I advise you to burn your letters while it is still winter, clear your head of all this, and think what a long life we still have ahead of us, and what wonderful and extraordinary things may still happen to our little circle.

It was firmly in the Freud circle that Minna was to live her life. She became a lady's companion for a while in the 1880s, then a governess in Brno where a rich aunt lived. She visited the Freuds often during the first seven years of the marriage, when her sister was pregnant for most of the time and was more and more burdened with the upkeep of a large household teeming with young children. A few days before Anna was born late in 1895, Minna arrived for a stay of several months. In March 1896, she 'accepted a position' in Frankfurt, but by the end of the year was back with the Freuds in Vienna, this time permanently. Martha certainly welcomed the help with her six children. In the summer after Minna moved in, Martha and Sigmund journeyed together in Tuscany and Umbria – their first holiday alone together since their honeymoon. Minna was thirty-four when she moved in and had for a long time been resigned to never marrying.

If Martha, the appeaser, would always pour oil on troubled waters, Minna all her life had a sharp, witty tongue. If Martha had always held aloof from engagement with Freud's intellectual and clinical concerns, Minna became his close confidante – indeed, in 1894 he called her 'my closest confidante'. Looking back, he remembered only Fliess and Minna believing in his theories during the 1890s; on publication of *The Interpretation of Dreams*, he relayed to his increasingly estranged friend Fliess her warnings about the reception to be expected, as if she were its co-author: 'Minna quotes the Countesses Wallenstein and Terczky after their reception at the Viennese court: we can expect further ostracism.' She came to share not only Sigmund's intellectual concerns but also his tastes in energetic travelling holidays, often joining him for his exhausting journeys through Italian cities and ruins, after the family had been left in a tranquil summer spot. When Freud was on holiday with Ferenczi in 1910, he complained in a letter to Carl Jung how passive and feminine Ferenczi was, letting everything be done for him; he was probably thinking of Minna when he added: 'These trips arouse a great longing for a real woman.'

Minna was the great talker of the older generation of the Freuds; Paula Fichtl, the Freuds' maid from the 1920s on, remembered Martha as silent and Minna as constantly talking. She certainly had equal rights within the family and would sometimes introduce herself on the telephone as Frau Professor Freud. However, her health was not wonderful, and she often gave Freud cause for concern, both because of the financial responsibility and because she had become very dear to him. In the autumn of 1900, Minna spent some weeks in Merano, a favourite resort in the Tyrolian Alps for the invalided and ill bourgeoisie of the Austro-Hungarian Empire. She was nursing a chronic inflammation of the lungs that had already given reason for disquiet in her teens, when she had been sent to recover in Sicily. It was now compounded by other symptoms, cardiac and intestinal. She returned to Vienna to a long period of ill-health, a colonic ulcer and a slow recovery.

The Minna Affair: Freud's Other Woman?

Minna's illnesses have a bearing on a controversial claim, namely that she and Freud engaged on an affair. In an interview late in his life, Jung revealed that Minna herself had confessed this to him on the first occasion he met her at Berggasse 19; there are, as Peter Gay has pointed out, internal contradictions in Jung's retrospective account. More complicatedly, there is other evidence that the emotional truth of that first meeting between Jung and the Freud family was distinctly clouded by Jung feeling obliged to confess, falsely as it then turned out, to being strongly attracted to Freud's daughter (probably Mathilde or Sophie). More recently, Peter Swales has argued that Minna's long stay in Merano was for the purposes of an abortion. But even more recently published letters indicate that the primary purpose of Minna's stay was for her lung condition; although this of course does not preclude her also having had an abortion, it does make the case for it less plausible.

Swales's intricate and bold argument hangs on an additional claim. In *The Psychopathology of Everyday Life* of 1901, Freud analysed the motives for the forgetting of the word 'aliquis' in a line of Vergil, attributing the forgetting to an anonymous young man. Swales argues that, like the anonymous interlocutor of 'Screen Memories', the young man is a disguised version of Freud himself. Swales's case in this respect is convincing; it was Freud himself who was anxiously awaiting a woman's menstrual blood to flow, just as the faithful await the miracle of the liquefaction of the blood of St Januarius each year in Naples. However, there is no positive reason to suppose that it was *Minna*'s period that Freud was anxiously awaiting; there is substantial evidence, though, that from 1893 on Sigmund and *Martha* were often anxiously awaiting the flow of blood that would mean that their collection of 'brats' was not to become even more sizeable.

Speculation over the Minna affair has been stimulated in part by the view that Freud's sexual relationship with his wife atrophied within a relatively few years of their marriage and the birth of their six children. Almost certainly, concern over his wife's health and the undesirability of having more children affected their sexual relationship in the 1890s. Freud's contemporaneous concern with the noxious effects of various forms of contraception and of sexual abstinence was surely a reflection of their difficulties with contraception and abstinence. And his great interest in Fliess's theories of the masculine and feminine biological cycles and their underlying biochemistry included the hope that his Berlin friend, the Kepler of biology as he once called him, would find the secret of sexual reproduction and supply Sigmund, Martha and many others with a non-noxious method of contraception. The writer, Janet Malcolm, has remarked that 'if Freud had continued his own efforts in this direction, he would have become the inventor of a better condom, not the founder of psychoanalysis'. Though Malcolm's comment highlights Freud's marital dilemmas, it is perhaps more fittingly applied to Fliess, whose biological speculations in this direction provoked Freud's admiration somewhat more than his collaboration.

The Freuds were certainly living in abstinence in 1893; by 1895, however, this was no longer the case, and Martha's sixth pregnancy caused them some consternation. A couple of years later, Freud mentioned how sex was of no more use to him, but he also remarked on how he would have periods of sexual quiescence, implying periods of non-quiescence as well. He attempted to explain these using Fliess's theories of biological cycles. In 1900, in a resigned but perky tone, he reviewed the regimen which preserved his cheerful mood: 'You know how limited my pleasures are. I am not allowed to smoke anything decent; alcohol does nothing for me; I am done begetting children; and I am cut off from contact with people. So I vegetate harmlessly. ...'

Vegetate for the rest of his life Freud did not; but it appears unlikely that he gave the carnal side of his nature free rein with anyone. In 1910, he mentioned to Jung how 'my Indian summer of eroticism that we spoke of on our trip has withered lamentably under the pressure of work. I am resigned to being old and no longer even think continually of growing old.' This posture of accepting with resignation his old age had obviously communicated itself to Emma, Jung's wife. In 1911, she wrote to Freud, exhorting him to a less resigned and pessimistic view of his own life, and reminding him of what he had told her when they had met two months previously in September:' 'My marriage has been amortized long since, now there is nothing more to do than – die.' But four years earlier, writing to Jung, Freud had, half-disapprovingly, half-jokingly, resurrected one of the old dichotomies – science vs. love – which had been so important to him when courting Martha: '[Max] Eitingon ... seems to have taken up with some woman again. Such practice is a deterrent from theory. When I have wholly overcome my libido (in the common sense), I shall start on a "Love life of Mankind".' This is not the talk of a man who has quite yet given up his love life, nor the talk of a man who wishes to. One might almost say that Freud submitted to his sexual desires in the same cheerfully pessimistic spirit with which he would later submit to his cancer.

On Thursday, 8 July 1915, when he was nearly sixty, Freud wrote a letter to J.J. Putnam in America about his ethical ideals, mentioning in passing sexual ethics: 'Sexual morality as defined by society, in its most extreme form that of America, strikes me as very contemptible. I stand for an infinitely freer sexual life, although I myself have made very little use of such freedom. Only so far as I considered myself entitled to.' That night, Freud had a dream: 'Martha comes towards me, I am supposed to write something down for her – write into a notebook, I take out my pencil. ... It becomes very indistinct.' One of his associations to this dream, he later noted, 'has to do with successful coitus Wednesday morning.' The links are intriguing: is the writing in the dream, writing which is also coitus, a response to Martha's demand for sexual relations? Or did the demand stem from elsewhere? Was Freud prey to what Jones and he called somewhat lightly a 'J.J.P. complex' – a complex of incestuous attraction to a youngest daughter that J.J. Putnam had covertly analysed in one of his psychoanalytic papers? Certainly Freud's were not the only dreams to respond to Putnam at this time. His daughter

Anna was translating Putnam's work and was beginning to make psychoanalytic demands of her father.

In his later years, Freud's reputation as a pansexualist, the notorious father of the libido, gave many people expectations of meeting a degenerate roué. When the French poetess Comtesse Anna de Noailles met Freud, she was outraged: 'Surely,' she exclaimed, '*he* never wrote his "sexy" books. What a terrible man! I am sure he has never been unfaithful to his wife. It's quite abnormal and scandalous!' However, the Comtesse was quite wrong about Freud's lack of susceptibility to charming and seductive women. When separated from Martha during their engagement, Freud had, when attending a dance at Breuer's, shown himself to respond to feminine youthful beauty, albeit with the pain of the alien rather than with the pleasure of the fortunate: 'I am ashamed to say that on such occasions I am very envious.... The occasion itself was very pleasant: there were mostly girls of from fifteen to eighteen, and some very pretty ones. I fitted in no better than the cholera would have.' And a few months before their marriage when he had started to see his own patients, he reported to Martha, in a spirit of playful pre-Freudian superstition, how the presence of a beautiful and interesting woman in his consulting-room had twice caused the photograph of Martha to fall off the writing table.

Given the evidence, and the overall picture of Freud's sexual life that can be put together, the story of the affair with Minna will remain simply an interesting rumour. But there is a truth about Freud contained in that rumour: Minna belonged to that category of woman to whom Freud was fundamentally attracted, those with 'wild, passionate natures', who were also intellectual and 'masculine', to use that curious but unavoidable phrase that he – and they – so often employed. Freud certainly knew what sort of woman he wished for a wife, and made sure that he got her. But over the years his intimate friendships were with women from this other category, who did not conform to his 'ideal of womanhood': the 'adored sweetheart in youth' who becomes the 'beloved wife in maturity'. Minna was one of the many throughout his life who showed him that this ideal not only did not cover many women, but also did not touch on many of the things he in reality wanted from or found in women. And she showed him this from within his own family over a period of many years. What is most striking about Freud's relationships with women, especially when compared with those with men, is how very rarely they would end in the bitterness and permanent distance that overtook so many of his male friendships, from Breuer and Fliess to Jung and Ferenczi. Mistrust, betrayal and disillusion rarely if ever provoked the break up of these feminine friendships.

If Minna is the first in a line of masculine intellectual women, as Jones and others after Freud have argued, it becomes clear that, amidst the patients and the friends of a very different cast and personality, Martha was the only incarnation of Freud's 'feminine' ideal. It should not be forgotten how much of our insight into his traditionalist idealization of the feminine woman stem from love letters written at a young age to a woman he was seeking to conquer. How much weight should we attach to these love letters? How do we weigh them against the relationships forged with his early patients, who were so important for Freud's practice and theory, and with whom he also had complex and intimate friendships? Are we not left with only Martha as the sole and single truly 'feminine' woman in Freud's life? And once we have extended the category of the 'masculine intellectual woman' that far, Martha, too, should be included – Martha who, before their marriage, was certainly strong-minded and intelligent in her responses to Freud. The mystery then becomes: why did Freud need to erect for himself this citadel-like category of the conventional feminine woman, and transform Martha into such a woman? Was it because he could sustain in this way a particular masculine self-image: the adventurous conquistador, the vigorous deflowerer, the clinical dissector? The feminine woman who can be the object of such fantasies – the conquered, deflowered and dissected woman – is also revealed as the foil or the balm to such fantasies. The fantasy that the delicate object of such care is passive and helpless is sustained by the deeper, more sadistic fantasy that she has been *made* passive and helpless by the conquering virile despoiler; the despoiler makes good on his own destructive acts by caring for the delicate flower he has crushed. The roles of doctor and lover can even be fused in such acts of reparation: 'A robust woman who in case of need can single-handed throw her husband and servants out of doors was never my ideal, however much there is to be said for the value of a woman being in perfect health. What I have always found attractive is someone delicate whom I could take care of.'

What Freud's years of experiences with his hysterical women patients were to teach him was that caring for a woman did not necessarily imply that she be passive and helpless, or that her distress and vulnerability exclude moral courage and intelligence. One cannot help wondering if the conventional image of the sweet, domestic angel which Freud required of a woman, and demanded of his wife, did not, through the years of marriage, that crucible of sexual disillusion, come to be seen as an illusion. Martha may have been a woman whom Freud made conform to this illusion, and it is easy to speculate that she had to bear the cross of his illusion, and to be crucified on that cross, because of the special and unapproachable relationship between Freud and his mother. That Martha was obliged to become the sole living example of the conventional feminine woman may have helped Freud to discover that all the other women were not like that at all – including, first and foremost, his own mother. Freud did, after all, as we shall later see, rediscover his own incestuous feelings for his mother in his relations to a ninety-two-year-old patient of his. In other words, did Freud's fidelity to his own idealization of Martha allow him to recognize that no *other* women conformed to this ideal?

Daughters

Freud was everything you might expect from a conventional bourgeois Jewish father of his time and place: affectionate, stern, caring, at times somewhat distant and remote, preoccupied with his work. The family always came first in his conception of his duties, and thus of his fears: 'My psychic constitution urgently requires the acquisition and the spending of money for my family as fulfillment of my father complex that I know so well.' Freud seems to have tried to live by the dictum he set down, somewhat severely, for Martha during their engagement in 1882: 'One must not be mean with affection; what is spent of the funds is renewed by the spending itself.' There are many stories of his generosity, to his children, to his friends and their children, and to comparative strangers. Many of these stories indicate how Freud bound people to him with his generosity, whilst – perhaps by – leaving them entirely free of obligation.

None of his children openly rebelled against his paternal authority. Yet that did not mean that he escaped the 'endless cares' which he thought inevitably accompanied the 'infinite joy' of parenthood. As we have already seen, his three daughters came to have a deep, almost mythic significance for him, as he identified them with the three daughters of King Lear and the three fates. Yet in their characters and personal histories, they required three different and very specific responses to the crises that define every life. Given Freud's preoccupation with supporting his family and the unresolved question of his balance of credit and debt to women, symbolized by the dowry, the enmeshing of Freud in his daughters' destinies manifested itself, not unsurprisingly, in the epochal question of their marriages.

The life of his first-born Mathilde was to be deeply marred by illness. In 1893, according to Jones, she had almost died of diphtheria; in 1897, she suffered from septic diphtheria: 'I was ready to give up for lost my Mathilde'. With the care of Oscar Rie, she recovered, and a few months later Freud was reporting to Fliess: 'Mathilde has a short childhood, is growing rapidly, is becoming completely feminine in character and appearance, and also shows the first signs of puberty.' As eldest sibling and sister, she grew up to be good-natured, protective and sensible, the younger children often turning to her for help and protection, and usually receiving it. In 1905, Mathilde suffered an attack of appendicitis. Freud's old friend Ignaz Rosanes wanted to try a new method of ligature of the blood vessels following the operation. The vessels opened a few hours later and Mathilde almost died of internal bleeding. For some time she was on the verge of death in a sanatorium with fever; yet again Freud 'had already given up hope of her recovery.' And when she did recover, he indulged in a characteristically 'Freudian slip', impulsively hurling a slipper at the wall so that a beautiful little marble Venus fell on the floor and broke: 'My attack of destructive fury served therefore to express a feeling of gratitude to fate and allowed me to perform a *"sacrificial act"* – rather as if I had made a vow to sacrifice something or other as a thank-offering if she recovered her health! The choice of the Venus of Medici for this sacrifice was clearly only a gallant act of homage towards the convalescent.' She eventually regained her health, but had to have further minor operations to remove cysts resulting from the first surgery. Two years later another fever made her father suspect peritonitis.

She convalesced in the family spa of Merano, obviously very low in spirits as well as in considerable pain, at a time when her mother Martha was preoccupied with her own seventy-eight-year-old mother's ailing health. Freud wrote Mathilde a letter in reply to her plea for help, reassuring her about her chances of a full recovery. He chose this moment when her low self-esteem had made her open up to him to reassure her that her secret fear that she was not good-looking enough to attract a man was perfectly groundless,

first of all because you seem quite attractive enough to me, and secondly because I know that in reality it is no longer physical beauty which decides the fate of a girl, but the impression of her whole personality. ... The more intelligent among young men are sure to know what to look for in a wife – gentleness, cheerfulness, and the talent to make their life easier and more beautiful.

Freud was very aware that Mathilde was concerned with her marriage prospects; and there is ample evidence that the venerable tradition of securing alliances and the lineage through a well-placed marriage of his daughter had a hold over him as well.

Freud was often to blur the distinction between matchmaker and psycho-analyst; it seems that he could not resist trying to play matchmaker in order to secure disciples firmly wedded to his movement by marrying them to his daughters, who, after all, were part of his person, and who he half-wished would remain so. Over thirty years previously, he had himself joked with Martha about marrying his own master Charcot's daughter, thus gratifying erotic and professional ambitions with one stroke. During these years when the question of the twenty-year-old Mathilde's marriage prospects were uppermost in her mind, the meetings with the younger men who were to become his first disciples would often raise, at least in the form of unconscious fantasy and dream wishes, the question of their attraction to the master's daughter. Ludwig Binswanger recalled:

I myself dreamed of the entrance to his house at No. 19, Berggasse, which was then being remodeled, and of the old chandelier swathed in a shabby covering to protect it from the plastering. Freud's interpretation of this dream, which I found rather unconvincing – he recalled it thirty years later when my wife and I visited him on the occasion of his eightieth birthday – was that it indicated a wish to marry his oldest daughter but, at the same time, contained the repudiation of this wish, since it actually said that – I remember Freud's words – 'You won't marry into a house with such a shabby chandelier.'

Meeting Freud for the first time on the same occasion as Binswanger's visit in early March 1907, Jung too later confessed – perhaps not altogether truthfully – to having taken a fancy to one of Freud's daughters. Over the summer of 1908, Freud was hoping that Sándor Ferenczi's visit to the Freud family on holiday at Berchtesgaden would lead to his engagement to Mathilde.

Mathilde spent six months during 1908 recuperating in Merano. While there, she met Robert Hollitscher, a businessman twelve years older than her; they became engaged in October 1908. They married on 7 February 1909 and lived in Vienna, close to the Freuds. Thirteen months later, 'brave as always', she had to undergo another serious operation. Two years of good health followed. In 1912, misfortune overtook her again. Freud and Ferenczi had been planning to visit Ernest and Loë Kann Jones in London that summer; it was to have been only Freud's second visit in over thirty years to the England he much admired. Despite the doubts that the botched appendicitis operation had sown, Mathilde became pregnant in the early summer of 1912. But the pregnancy provoked her old troubles; a high fever and irritation of the old scars made an abortion necessary. Her father cancelled his holiday plans to be with her. However, he did manage to slip off to his beloved Rome two weeks later. Once the pregnancy had been terminated, Mathilde recovered rapidly, but she was never to have children.

In the years after her marriage, Mathilde visited her parents' home frequently, usually having lunch there; by 1922 Freud could describe her marriage as having become 'frozen into an egoism à deux'. After her sister's Sophie's death in 1920, she and Robert looked after the younger of her children, Heinele, and were completely enchanted with their little adopted son, as was Freud himself: 'I myself was aware of never having loved a human being, certainly never a child, so much.' When Heinele died suddenly, of miliary tuberculosis, in 1923, Freud was devastated; so must Mathilde have been. Mathilde continued to be fully integrated with her father's circle, becoming a very close friend of Ruth Mack Brunswick, who named her daughter after her. And her father continued to be the munificent patriarch to her and Robert, supporting them on and off as he did all his children, particularly during the bleak years of the Depression: 'Robert [Hollitscher] does not make a penny in his business and Max [Halberstadt] is struggling wearily against the collapse of Hamburg life. They live by the allowance I can give them.'

In 1925, Freud described Mathilde as 'a chronic invalid [who] behaves in a marvellous normal way'. In her later life, Mathilde turned the Freud women's family passion for weaving and knitting into an occupation, running a boutique specializing in hand-made, hand-woven clothes. She and Robert – by all accounts a gloomy, rather misanthropic man – emigrated with the Freuds to England in 1938. Mathilde, who, unlike her sister Anna and her friend Dorothy Burlingham, was always exquisitely dressed, took over a boutique specializing in cocktail dresses, *Robes belles* in Baker Street, which she ran until she retired in the 1960s. Robert died in 1959. Mathilde, whose life had been distorted from her childhood by life-threatening illnesses, lived on to the ripe age of ninety-one.

Sophie Freud was born in 1893, the fifth of the Freud children. She was Freud's Sunday child, his 'ray of sunshine'; 'the loveliest part' of his sister Rosa's wedding, he reported to Fliess in 1896, 'was our Sopherl – with curled hair and a wreath of forget-me-nots on her head.' Anna, the sixth and last Freud child, always felt that Sophie was the favourite girl, and the edge of antagonism and jealousy was reciprocated. None of the sisters had an academically oriented education; Freud did not envisage them as intending to pursue professional careers. Certainly Sophie, growing up as the 'pretty one', seemed eager to adopt her allotted role as wife and mother as quickly as she could. When she was nineteen, she became engaged to Max Halberstadt, a thirty-year-old photographer in the Bernays family circle in Hamburg, where she had gone for a few weeks' holiday. She arrived home, 'gay, radiant, determined', and informed her parents of the fait accompli, rather than, as would have been more customary, introducing Max and then asking their permission. Freud took his 'superfluity' in good part, but he immediately set out to ensure that, while recognizing the rights of the young man and bowing to the inevitable as he watched his 'little daughter suddenly turn into a loving woman', he gained a new member of the Freud clan rather than altogether losing his daughter. His considerable skills in managing triangles were exercised elegantly in his overture to his future son-in-law:

Since our wishes have always been for our daughters to feel free to follow their hearts in the choice of a husband, as our eldest daughter has actually done, we have every reason to be satisfied with this event. But we are parents after all, burdened with all the delusions that accompany this condition, feel obliged to assert our importance, and we would therefore like to set eyes on the energetic young man whose determination has infected our child before we declare a solemn Yes and Amen.

There were other serious matters to discuss, amongst them 'the financial foundations of your marriage ceremony'. Once again, Freud was confronted with the question of a dowry.

Freud painted a flattering portrait of Max in the letters he wrote to him – 'a serious, loving, clear-headed and intelligent husband'; while he dashed off to Mathilde an only slightly less complimentary version – 'evidently a very reliable, serious, tender, refined and yet not weak human being'. Yet he felt impelled to moderate Sophie's expectation that her parents would uncon-ditionally acquiesce in her happiness, and to gain her assistance in the formal exchanges appropriate to a father giving away his daughter. The figure of King Lear was beginning to cast its shadow.

Sophie was no longer with Max in Hamburg, but was with Aunt Minna on the Adriatic coast; Martha and Sigmund had decamped to Karlsbad. Max came alone to Karlsbad to meet and pay his respects to his future parents-in-law. Freud, as he had threatened, wanted to discuss with him the weighty question of the dowry. The parents cunningly conferred their official approval on the engagement by joining with Max in sending a telegram to Sophie: 'Mama Papa Max congratulate you.' Sophie took offence, perhaps at Max's sudden complicity with her parents. She had obviously enjoyed her moment of headstrong independence, while at the same time demanding immediate and unqualified enthusiasm for her choice from her parents and Aunt Minna.

Freud interpreted her attack of pique as in part due to her 'having ignored us so completely when you decided to get engaged.... The degree of your remorse may be judged by the fact that you even succeeded in upsetting your Aunt, normally so imperturbable.'

Freud's *coup de théâtre* was left for the end of this letter to his daughter:

And now I must tell you that I played a little trick on [Max] as he went away. He had paid behind our backs his bill for the wretched attic room, which was the only thing we could get for him, and so I showed him a little knitted purse which I carry with me for foreign money and pretended that it was an old piece of needlework of yours, and asked him to keep it. This purse, however, contained the 6.80 Kr., which he had paid to Frau Schubert. Now you can explain the whole thing to him and disown the needlework.

With this little trick, Freud had found a way of obliging Max to accept his hospitality. Max could not, of course, refuse a purse, such a symbolically redolent object, that his beloved had made and given to her father. The gift of the purse was an intimate and weighty exchange, standing for Freud's, the father's, gift of his daughter to the husband. Freud had managed to weave together the act of giving away his daughter with the act of ensuring that the financial transactions associated with marriage were properly observed.

But in writing to Sophie about the purse – after all, he could have written to Max himself to tell him of the little deception, after the deed had been done – Freud was asking her to collude with him in passing the gift off as being nothing intimate, in no sense symbolic of a paternal act of 'renunciation'. And he thus delegated to Sophie the role of paternal messenger ensuring that she explain his actions to Max: how Max had been deceived into thinking he was being given something precious to Freud that symbolized his daughter, when what was really occurring was not only the reassertion of the proper financial relations between father and prospective son-in-law, but also the reassertion of Freud's authority as Sophie's father.

As if he had had a premonition of Sophie's hasty engagement, Freud had written a sketch of 'The Theme of the Three Caskets' in a letter to Ferenczi of 23 June 1912. It did not take much foresight to realize that, with Mathilde married in 1909, the beautiful Sophie would soon do the same and leave home, leaving Anna to 'make do for six children all by herself'. The year following Sophie's engagement was the only period in Freud's life that Anna could remember him being depressed. Sophie married Max in January 1913. Freud was undoubtedly preoccupied with the loss of his daughter; Ferenczi interpreted his 'Sophie-Complex' for him, exhorting him not to take it so hard. But there may have been other reasons for Freud's disquiet. According to a letter from Hans Lampl to Anna Freud written in 1956, Sophie had a therapeutic abortion in the spring of 1913, probably performed by Dr Rudi Kaufmann. Freud might well have feared that both his older daughters would now be childless – another cause for the depression that lay heavily over him.

But Sophie conceived again later in 1913 and gave birth to Ernst, the first of the Freuds' grandchildren, on 11 March 1914: 'around 3 o'clock a little boy as first grandchild! Very remarkable! An elderly feeling, respect before the wonders of sexuality!' Sophie and Max were living in Hamburg and having difficulty making ends meet. Freud visited them in September 1914, as the war began in earnest; he noted with obvious approval how Sophie was raising her son in accordance with the psychoanalytic precepts not of her father, but of Hermine Hug-Hellmuth, the first child analyst. A second son was born in 1918: Heinz, known to all as Heinele. In 1919, Sophie became pregnant again, but now disaster struck.

The influenza epidemic which swept the world after the end of the war was particularly virulent in starving Germany and Austria. On 26 January 1920, Freud wrote to his mother in his usual protective way:

I have some sad news for you today. Yesterday morning our dear lovely Sophie died from galloping influenza and pneumonia. We learned of it at noon from a telephone conversation with Minna at Reichenhall. Oli and Ernst have left Berlin to be with Max. Robert and Mathilde are leaving on the 29th to try and assist the poor bereaved man. Martha is too upset; one couldn't let her undertake the journey, and in any case she wouldn't have found Sophie alive. She is the first of our children we have to outlive.... I hope you will take it calmly; tragedy after all has to be accepted. But to mourn this splendid, vital girl who was so happy with her husband and children, is of course permissible.

Sophie's death was the first in the series of bitter losses and injuries Freud was to suffer in the next few years. He carried on writing to his friends, whilst numb with the injury of her death. The phrases he used to describe it were always bleak and controlled, if never as matter of fact as in the moment of writing to his own mother. To Ferenczi: 'For years I was prepared for the loss of my sons; now comes that of my daughter. Since I am the deepest of unbelievers, I have no one to accuse and know that there is no place where one can lodge an accusation ... way deep down I sense the feeling of a deep narcissistic injury I shall not get over.' And to Pfister:

Sophie leaves two sons, one of 6, the other 13 months, and an inconsolable husband who will have to pay dearly for the happiness of these seven years.... I work as much as I can, and am thankful for the diversion. The loss of a child seems to be a serious, narcissistic injury; what is known as mourning will probably follow only later.

But was it ever possible for Freud to mourn the loss of his daughter? Sophie's son died three years later in 1923, making a double blow that was impossible to bear. When Ludwig Binswanger's son died of tubercular meningitis in 1926, Freud wrote to him of Sophie's death: 'But that I bore remarkably well. It was the year 1920, one was worn down from the misery of war, prepared for years to hear that one had lost a son or even three sons. Thus, resignation to fate was well prepared.' Heinele, on the other hand, had stood 'for all my children and other grandchildren, and since then, since Heinele's death, I no longer care for my grandchildren, but also take no pleasure in life. This is also the secret of the indifference – people have called it bravery – toward the danger to my own life [his own cancer].'

Sophie's first-born, Freud's first grandchild, appeared in *Beyond the Pleasure Principle* (1920) as the little boy who masters the loss of his mother in play. His endlessly repeated game with a wooden reel on a piece of string, which he would throw away from him, uttering an expressive '*o-o-o-o*' [*fort* (gone)] and then pull back with a joyful '*da*' [there], revealed to Freud the primary compulsion to repeat, behind which he perceived the concept of the death drive introduced in that work. In observing his grandchild, Freud had been able to imagine himself playing a game in the space created by the absence of the mother. He had collaborated with Sophie, as they tried to ascertain the meaning of the little boy's game of *fort/da*. The grandfather, through his daughter, gained access to the grandchild's game, grandfather shifting easily into the shoes of his grandchild, his daughter becoming mother. Through the child, he replayed the loss of the mother. When the work was completed and published, Sophie was gone. Her sons stayed briefly with their father; then they were looked after for a while by her two sisters, Mathilde and Anna.

Freud would sometimes talk of his loss to his patients; he might share it with them if they had experienced something similar. Hilda Doolittle had been pregnant at the end of the First World War and had almost lost her child through influenza and pneumonia. In one session, she spoke of that terrible time, the last year of the war. 'He said he had reason to remember the epidemic, as he lost his favourite daughter. "She is here," he said, and he showed me a tiny locket that he wore, fastened to his watch-chain.'

The third of Freud's three daughters was Anna, child of psychoanalysis and its inheritor. If her sisters were destined by their father for conventional marriage and motherhood, the messages Anna received were far more ambiguous. As the third and youngest daughter, she could easily have taken on the traditional role of looking after her aging parents by not marrying. In the event, that conventional role was radically expanded. Anna not only looked after her aging father, but she protected, nursed and succoured his most precious child of all: psychoanalysis. How much of the genealogy of psychoanalysis that eventually ran from Freud to Anna depended on the father–daughter relationship? How different would the history of psychoanalysis have been if Anna had been born, as Freud thought she would be, Wilhelm? Was it necessary for the lineages of power to pass through the daughter's line?

But before any such questions can be asked, Freud's most precious child had to see the light of day.

Part II

INVENTING PSYCHOANALYSIS

3

THE FIRST PATIENTS

In 1885, Freud was triumphant when he was awarded a travel grant to spend some months at the Salpêtrière in Paris working under Jean-Martin Charcot. Freud's stay during 1885–6 was the turning-point in his professional development. There he encountered 'a successful and self-sufficient scientific community: it had a central senior figure with a paradigmatic medical theory, periodical organs and professional organizations of its own, and a carefully placed network of students across the country.' Freud was to become the well-placed representative in Vienna of the Charcot scientific community.

The Salpêtrière, founded originally as a part of the Great Confinement of the late seventeenth century to imprison prostitutes, debauched girls and female adulterers, had become an asylum in the nineteenth century: a vast pathological museum and custodial village, where some five to eight thousand women – 1 per cent of the entire population of Paris – were housed. In 1862, Charcot, then aged thirty-seven, was appointed its Head Physician; over the next ten years, he made for himself an international medical and scientific reputation with clinical neurological studies of enduring character. In the 1870s, following his colleagues' reorganization of the various wings of the hospital with a view to separating the mad from the epileptics and the hysterics, Charcot turned his attention to these last and attempted to distinguish them nosologically from the epileptics. His scientific reputation may have been built on the complex and delicate diagnostic skills he had employed to bring order to what became the classical neurological symptom-pictures, but his widespread fame was based on his dramatic and public display of the taming of hysteria from the early 1870s to the mid-1880s.

Building on Paul Briquet's work of 1859, which already stressed that hysteria was a disease of the nervous system, to be found in both sexes, Charcot showed hysteria to be a far more stable clinical entity than its centuries-old reputation for protean indefiniteness and chameleon-like dupery gave reason to think. Despite its name, hysteria had not always been regarded as essentially linked to the uterus, the disease of the wandering womb. In the mid-eighteenth century, William Cullen had described the hysterical condition as one of the neuroses, a term he coined to imply that its seat lay not in the uterus but in the nervous system, whose general significance was being advocated by the Edinburgh school, of which he was the leader. Whilst the uterine theory did make a come-back in the early nineteenth century, shortly after the noun 'hysteria' came into use, after 1859 Briquet and Charcot reaffirmed the neurological theory as part of their attempts for greater professional recognition for psychiatry and neurology. Hysteria for Charcot was resolutely somatic : an organic disorder of the higher nervous system, with unknown or diffuse ('functional') anatomical and physiological localization. With this secure physical symptom-picture, hysteria became more widely recognized ; indeed, it grew into a standard diagnosis in the general practitioner's repertoire, resulting in wider and wider sections of the population becoming medicalized.

As Michel Foucault said of this period: 'there was a battle of hysteria. ... Hysteria was the ensemble of phenomena of struggle which unfolded around this new medical apparatus of clinical neurology.' The symptom-picture of hysteria had previously been extremely diverse: sensations of suffocation and strangulation, paroxysmic fits and convulsions, violent expressions of emotion, loss of sensation, hypersensitivity and coughing. For most of its history the diagnosis of hysteria had been very closely linked to women – from the Greek wandering womb theory to its application in the defence and secularization of the witch-hunts of the early seventeenth century. Charcot became famous for his strict delineation of a sequence of four stages of the hysterical crisis or attack: the aura; the attack properly speaking (with screaming, pallor, loss of consciousness and muscular rigidity); the clonic or 'clownish' phase (large movements, contortions and theatrical gestures imitating the expression of grand passions); and the final phase of resolution (sobbing, tears and laughter). But alongside the dramatic enactment of this precise sequence of trances and convulsions, with all their overtones of erotic excess, were the quieter and more stable symptoms: local paralyses and contractures, together with local anaesthesias and hyperaesthesias (pains), which he called the stigmata of hysteria. The religious overtones of Charcot's choice of terms were part of his Republican, anti-clerical agenda for the reinterpretation of the ecstasies of religious states of mind and body, including the witches and devil's dances of the Middle Ages.

These stable diagnostic markers had the precise somatic stamp of the neurologist all over them, and it was these that were most commonly found in the hundreds of cases on the wards in the Salpêtrière : 79 per cent of all cases displayed the localized stigmata, 76 per cent visual abnormalities (particularly narrowing of the visual field, or sometimes hysterical blindness), in contrast with only 12 per cent whose symptom-picture included the grand attack, the hallmark of the dramatic presentation of patients to large crowds with which Charcot's public reputation was associated ; 37 per cent of all patients displayed no convulsive phenomena at all. Resolutely bodily in its reform of the hysteria diagnosis, this symptom-picture – a medley of pains and paralyses, loss of sensitivity, localized and chronic bodily ailments – was the disease-picture of ordinary hysteria that Freud and many other doctors in the last two decades of the nineteenth century came to expect and to find. In 1841–2, only 1 per cent of women admitted to the Salpêtrière were diagnosed as hysterical; in 1882–3, the figure rose to 17.8 per cent. Charcot had made a strenuous attempt not only to separate hysteria from epilepsy, but also from neurasthenia, nymphomania, general nervousness and insanity; he had rescued hysteria from psychiatry and reclaimed it for neurology and general internal medicine. In the process, hysteria became the classic fashionable disease of the *belle époque*.

Charcot's twice weekly lectures enacted the drama of the encounter between master and hysteric, made infinitely more so by his use of the method of hypnosis. Hypnosis, like hysteria, also required Charcot's vociferous advocacy to attain respectability. Throughout the nineteenth century, mesmerism and animal magnetism had aroused medical and political controversy, whether through their use in psychiatry, in general medicine for miracle cures over which the medical profession had no automatic control, or in pioneering anaesthetic surgery.

Charcot worked to wrest hypnosis from its dangerous position on the fringes of science, but only for the purposes of experimental reproduction, isolation and control of the major symptoms of hysteria. This theatre of the body was extremely well prepared behind the scenes, in the newly created laboratories and photographic studios of Charcot's expanding scientific empire within the Salpêtrière. The laboratories served to introduce the newly won prestige of the experimental method into clinical medicine; the photographs, now justly infamous and endlessly reprinted, served literally to fix and stabilize the clinical gaze, the relationship between scientific doctor and docilely complicit patient – between the voyeuristic and erotic, sometimes even amorous, attention of the male doctor and the virtuoso clinical performer, who knew, for the most part, on which side her bread was buttered.

'It is repeatedly said that Charcot and his co-workers were victims of the hysterics. It would be more true to say that they were victims of the scientistic ideology of the nineteenth century.' But maybe the doctors, their science and the hysterics were all accomplices in a complex game of give and take, whose microsocial habitat was the Salpêtrière for the period of Charcot's ascendancy, from the early 1870s to his death in 1893. For with his death, Charcot's work crumbled to nothing. The very diagnosis of hysteria was rejected within ten years by his pupils. The epidemic that had swept not only the decadent cosmopolitan capitals of Europe and America but had been found in small provincial towns and hospitals was spent by the First World War. Ernest Jones reflected in his autobiography:

For some reason that we do not yet understand, conversion hysteria was far commoner in those days than after the First World War. Paralyses and anaesthesia were to be seen in every hospital, and most infirmaries could produce patients with astasia-abasia who had been bedridden for perhaps twenty or thirty years. Hysterical convulsions were similarly frequent, and apart from those seen in hospital I often enough had to minister to girls in convulsions met with on a stroll through the town.

It is not only doctors and psychoanalysts who have been perplexed by the disappearance of hysteria. Some historians suggest that it has been redescribed, being assimilated into the new psychiatric categories, such as schizophrenia. Others, however, see in hysteria's waning corroboration of the complex social system of relationships, of social roles and demands, that gave rise to the epidemic in the first place. It is not so much that doctors first invented hysteria and then dispensed with it when it no longer served their purposes; rather, it was a collaborative invention, of doctors, fathers, husbands, families – and patients.

Many doctors, untouched by Charcot's professional scepticism and attempt to break the link between hysteria and the female sex, painted a portrait of the hysteric's symptoms as the pathological version of the weaknesses and failings to which the entire female sex were condemned. The volatility of the symptoms reflected the volatility of women; the exaggerated emotionality reflected the more important place emotions had in the inner life of women. Whereas in the early eighteenth century, hysteria had been linked to sexual restraint and asceticism, by the second half of the nineteenth century the hysteric's excess of sexuality was the more dominant theme. And she could be a pathological intensification of either the prostitute and nymphomaniac, with inflamed sexual passions enticing the same from men, or of the fragile, pure flower, whose disease stemmed directly from the virtue that made her man's ideal. Treacherous and deceitful, hysteria could be read as the perfect allegory of the feminine vices visible in its imitating, counterfeit symptoms. Excessive and uncontrollable, hysteria rendered public the hidden lusts, perverted religious passions and over-sensitivities of the weaker sex. All were made visible in the *Iconographie photographique de la Salpêtrière*, which, despite the neurological protestations of the master, was fanned by the evident erotic fascination of his young assistant doctors for the pathological types methodically displayed, arranged – by hypnosis – for the twenty minutes it took to take the photographs.

Doctors could not only paint a portrait of the pathological sensibilities that gave rise to hysteria. They could also describe the unique challenge the hysteric posed to the doctor. And the challenge continued. As recently as the 1950s, a psychiatrist suggested that 'if after five minutes with a patient, you find yourselves gripping the arms of your chair, then the patient is a hysteric'. At times, the nineteenth-century medical portraits are in themselves shrilly hysterical and acutely insightful warnings of the powers the hysteric may unleash on the unsuspecting and rational man of science. How humiliating he finds it when his medical skill is entirely inadequate in the face of her chronic ever-changing symptoms! How compromised he finds himself when, in dignifying her illness with the name 'hysteria', he has involuntarily created a bond with her, set against the family whom his moral and social, if not his medical, instincts heartily support in their struggle with the malingering or morally self-indulgent patient! A few doctors perceived the complexity of the relations they established with their hysterical patients. In fact, the relationship with the hysteric was the practice ground for many declarations of the proper course of conduct for doctors, the occasion for many belated confessions of the virtues and marks of noble character the doctor must possess to succeed in his trade.

The finest analysis of the subtle relations between doctor and patient has been offered by Carroll Smith-Rosenberg, who points to the entirely contradictory qualities required of bourgeois women as the source of the conflicts made manifest in hysteria: on the one hand, the pure and virtuous, delicate virginal object of esteem, love and protection; on the other, the pain-bearing, self-denying keeper of hearth and home. Like Freud's analysis, Smith-Rosenberg portrays the woman's sick role as a compromise between escape from this unresolvable conflict and protest against her untenable position. It is a passive form of resistance against the system of social expectations organized round her sex, both the product and the indictment of that culture. And disruptive hysteria certainly was: instead of a house centred around a warm, loving hearth, there is an invalid, absent from her duties, requiring constant attention in a darkened bedroom at the back of the house.

No longer did she devote herself to the needs of others, acting as self-sacrificing wife, mother, or daughter: through her hysteria she could and in fact did force others to assume those functions. Household activities were reoriented to answer the hysterical woman's importunate needs. Children were hushed, rooms darkened, entertaining suspended, a devoted nurse recruited. Fortunes might be spent on medical bills or for drugs and operations. Worry and concern bowed the husband's shoulders; his home had suddenly become a hospital and he a nurse. Through her illness, the bedridden woman came to dominate her family to an extent that would have been considered inappropriate – indeed, shrewish – in a healthy woman.

The doctor as often as not played rival to the husband, and father to an ailing daughter. Smith-Rosenberg speculates that it was the doctors' alertness – not necessarily entirely conscious – to the sexual and familial ambiguities that elicited their many strident and suspicious homilies: 'The physician had, by his alertness to deception and self-indulgence and by his therapeutic skills, to prevent the hysterical woman from using her disease to avoid her feminine duties – and from making him an unwitting accomplice in her deviant role.' Describing the woman who has discovered in childhood that illness gives her the attention she is otherwise deprived of, Freud shows how she makes use of illness in 'her marriage with an inconsiderate husband, who may subjugate her will, mercilessly exploit her capacity for work, and lavish neither his affection nor his money upon her':

Her state of ill-health will have every appearance of being objective and involuntary – the very doctor who treats her will bear witness to the fact; and for that reason she will not need to feel any conscious self-reproaches at making such successful use of a means which she had found effective in childhood.

Freud's first ten years of practice taught him much about the complex games of power, complicity, sympathy and erotic ambiguity that prolonged treatment of hysterics involved. Where other physicians saw the hysteric as intractable and self-assertive, Freud saw resistance. The longest chapter in

Breuer and Freud's *Studies on Hysteria* of 1895, Freud's chapter on psycho-therapy, is in part a guide to physicians wishing to join and win the battle of wills with the hysteric, a battle which, in terms of the resources of tact and courage required of the doctor, was the equal of that required of any other of life's great struggles. And, despite the covert battle of wills, the doctor will find himself endowed by his patient with unlimited power and influence, and with the absolute authority of a parent over a child.

Feminist historians have not always focused this subtly on the unprecedented complexity of doctor–patient relations in the great encounter of the hysteric and the specialist in nervous diseases. The first wave of feminist historiography of hysteria painted the hysteric simply as victim. Due to larger changes in social organization, the position of women became more ambiguous, more of a weak point; male doctors responded with a heightened misogyny, which found its expression in moral distaste for the hysteric, gynaecological theories of her condition and surgical intervention on her genitals. The label hysteric was a self-serving stereotype that legitimized the increasingly endangered status quo in a period of rising demands for equality and independence from women's groups. The male authorities tacitly colluded, urged on by sexual fear and hostility. The hysteric was a victim, a front-line casualty of the intensified war of men on their womenfolk's aspirations and protests.

A somewhat different account has been given by Elaine Showalter in terms of the 'lack of autonomy and powerlessness' that the shell-shocked, unmanned soldiers of the First World War shared with the hysterics of twenty years previously. The hysteric of the home and the hysteric of the trenches thus, through their common symptoms, shared in a passive, distorted protest against the demands made on them by patriarchal culture. Their bodily symptoms were a covert form of protest: 'the "protofeminism" of hysterical protest'. As Dianne Hunter puts it: 'feminism is transformed hysteria, or more precisely, that hysteria is feminism lacking a social network in the outer world'. Putting the accent more on sexual identity than on social power, Jane Gallop reflects: 'If feminism is the calling into question of constraining sexual identities, then the hysteric may be a proto-feminist.'

Showalter describes feminism and hysteria as two sides of the same coin, or two ends of a continuum; she thus points to similar forces at work within both feminism and hysteria. One of the most important of these may be the sexual conservatism of so much feminist activity. Feminism had very strong links with the hygiene and eugenics movements of the late nineteenth and early twentieth centuries; major political campaigns linked up with older temperance and social purity movements, so that feminist women came to embody the ideals of sexual purity that men fell so far short of. The sexual depravities and exploitation of men endangered the species; it was women's duty to protest against their immorality and biological irresponsibility. The first patient of psychoanalysis, Bertha Pappenheim, is a classic example of such a feminist, calling on women to require men to conform to the moral loftiness which the ideal of womanhood represents and demands. Often, it was the feminists who became the embodiment of the ideals of sexual asceticism. Espousing these values could, Freud would observe with many of his early patients in the 1890s, give rise to the conflicts which could only be resolved by the creation of symptoms. Or, as Jan Goldstein puts it: 'Fin-de-siècle hysteria, it appears, was a protest made by women who had so thoroughly accepted that value system that they could neither admit their discontent to themselves nor avow it publicly in the more readily comprehensible language of words.'

Yet the epidemic of hysteria may not be so readily explicable in terms of an unresolvable conflict of values. As recent research reveals, far from being a disease confined to heavy-curtained drawing-rooms and frustrated bourgeois women, hysteria was equally prevalent in the working classes. Nearly all of Charcot's celebrated hysterics, and nearly all of the less celebrated ordinary hysterics admitted to the Salpêtrière, were lower-class women who, as Goldstein puts it, 'lived outside the framework of a bourgeois value system'. The trope of contrasting the neurotic, sexually inhibited middle-class women with the honest and expressive, animal sexuality of the lower classes was to make its way into Freud's cases in the *Studies on Hysteria*, and would continue in his later work. Whether such a contrast is borne out by recent epidemiological and social historical studies is now very much in doubt. What is more intriguing as a plausible historical explanation for the rise and fall of hysteria, both in time and within different sections of a population, is the possibility that psychoanalysis killed off hysteria, in a process of 'psychological gentrification'. Charcot's neurological views of hysteria were accepted and received wide dissemination in the last two decades of the nineteenth century. But his followers and others proceeded to draw out the psychological implications, particularly those concerning the traumatic genesis of symptoms, of his model. A psychology of hysteria succeeded his neurology, just as a psychology of aphasia succeeded the 'brain mythology' of the 1870s and 1880s. Freud was an active party to both transformations. Such a hypothesis suggests that the introduction of psychological terms to the patient culture made the path of conversion, of speaking through the body, unavailable from then on. The hypothesis has been applied to different countries at different times, for instance in the 1970s to the psychiatric wards in Freud's old hospital, the Vienna General, where southern European immigrants displayed numerous old-fashioned hysterical symptoms, whereas indigenous Austrians no longer were capable of producing such symptoms. The links between psychoanalysis and hysteria may be closer even than their fateful historical conjunction.

The erotic excess of the hysteric was a commonplace; but the erotic content of the relationship with the doctor was also brought to awareness, not least by the women writers – Charlotte Perkins Gilman, Alice James, Eleanor Marx, Virginia Woolf – whose illness-ravaged lives have created the third category of the grand hysteric, to place alongside Charcot's medical performers and Freud's secret story-tellers. The erotic relationship between doctor and patient was to be the territory that Freud made very much his own, that field within the greater uncharted map of hysteria where he chose, or was chosen, to display what an earlier doctor had evoked as required of the doctor confronting the hysteric: 'the nerve and the tact that will make him equal to the great emergencies of life'. Yet he could write in the *Studies* of his attitude to hysteria in the early years of his practice: 'I had come fresh from the school of Charcot, and I regarded the linking of hysteria with the topic of sexuality as a sort of insult – just as the women patients themselves do.'

The final, and ironic, twist in the story of Charcot's influence on Freud was to have left him a legacy of gender *indeterminacy* in his view of hysteria. On his return from Paris in 1886, Freud lectured to the Vienna Society of Physicians on male hysteria, to which Charcot had devoted an inordinate number of his own lectures, in an attempt both to drain the old uterine etiology of hysteria of the last of its force, and to focus attention on the somatics of the disease, rather than on the 'masculine' or 'feminine' passions that gave rise to it. Charcot's views on the causality of hysteria were twofold: firstly – and here he made common cause with the dominant French psychiatric thinking of his time – that the disposition to hysteria was largely determined by degenerate heredity; secondly, that the onset of hysteria was often found in a traumatic shock to the nervous system. Charcot's investigations of hysteria in males and in children aided him in confirming the hereditarian theory: male hysterics very often acquired their disposition from their hysterical mothers or other female relatives, as did the children.

So this was Freud's conceptual baggage on his return to Vienna to set up his private practice as a nerve specialist. Despite his 1886 lecture on male hysteria – a declaration of his discipleship to his French master, but not altogether news to his sceptical audience – he did not pursue its study. All the hysterics described, or even mentioned in passing, in *Studies on Hysteria* were women. There remains the question whether his later concept of bisexuality, which he thought to be especially prominent in hysteria, owed something to the vigorousness with which Charcot loosened up the link between femininity and hysteria by studying male hysteria in such clinical detail.

Freud's development in the late 1880s and 1890s is the story of a growing distance from the Salpêtrière orthodoxy. He took up sides against Charcot on the significance to be attached to psychology over and against physiology in the description of hysteria – following Hippolyte Bernheim, his later teacher on hypnosis, on this point. As Charcot's translator, one might have expected Freud to remain close to the master's views; but he, like many other of Charcot's pupils in the late 1880s and 1890s, criticized more and more of the doctrines. On the very public and unseemly debate over hypnotism, between the school of the Salpêtrière and the school of Nancy (Ambroise Liébeault and Bernheim), Freud joined Bernheim in his critique of Charcot, and became his translator as well as his rival's. But he finally found Bernheim's enthusiastic espousal of the equation of hypnotism with suggestion too simplistic and question-begging. These debates and Freud's reactions to them revealed his growing familiarity with the very different demands of psychotherapeutic practice. Returning home to Vienna, Freud had nothing distinctively Charcotian to offer in the way of therapy, since Charcot had advocated hypnotism as an artificial analogue of hysteria, not as a therapy. Freud also needed to have at his command methods that could pass for efficacious techniques. He was at first eclectic, as the *Studies on Hysteria* show, using electrotherapy, hydrotherapy, massage, the Weir Mitchell rest-cure. In this respect, he was no different from other Viennese specialists in the nervous diseases, like Moritz Benedikt, Moritz Rosenthal, Johannes Schulz, Wilhelm Winternitz, who since the 1860s had been advocating and practising this potpourri of methods.

In contrast to Charcot, the Nancy school, particularly Liébeault, and its vigorous advocacy of hypnotism, was far more in the tradition of charismatic healers. To them, every one of their own considerable therapeutic successes was due simply to suggestion. This was a great deal to offer doctors in search of guaranteed cures. By the end of 1887, Freud was becoming an enthusiast for the cures effected by hypnotic suggestion. He spent some weeks in the summer of 1889 with the Nancy school. The attitude of complete medical authority, embodied by Charcot in relation to knowledge and pedagogy, and then recommended for the purposes of therapy and cure by the Nancy school, became his starting-point in the early days of his struggling practice. For a brief time, he was a great public enthusiast of hypnotism. But it did not take many years for him to discover that things were not quite so simple – that, for instance, hypnosis only worked well when the issue was an unimportant one. And his patients played a large part in disabusing him of the power of hypnotism and medical charisma.

Amongst the other doctrines of Charcot's Freud rejected outright was that of hereditarian degeneration. Every finely written detail of the upstanding and admirable moral characters of his hysterics was, Freud thought, a nail in the coffin of the degeneration theory. In its place he elaborated his theory of the toxicity of sexual malpractices and the seduction theory; his later theory of infantile sexuality also explicitly set itself against the implied therapeutic pessimism of the hereditarian doctrine. But the concept of trauma was to be developed in new and fruitful ways, as first he investigated the specific content of the traumas he found operative in hysteria, and then the mechanisms by which memories become traumatic: the mechanisms of repression and defence.

Once he had established his practice, Freud was to have new teachers and collaborators to offset the influence of his French masters: his patients, his own grand hysterics. At the back of his mind was the story of Anna O., which Breuer had told him in 1882 and 1883. But, as *Studies on Hysteria* demonstrates, he needed his own, first-hand experience before he could make proper use of Breuer's remarkable case. That experience was by no means a matter of calm and considered accumulation. The experience of treating hysterics was unsteadying, challenging, unnerving. The effort to construct a theory was quite clearly for Freud an attempt to cope with these difficult, sometimes distressing relationships. In the late 1890s, Freud's theories became grand systems, colossal structures, breathtaking speculative leaps. But the spur to theory was the slow but steady development of the talking cure: his hysterics insisted on having a very large say in what he would, within ten years of leaving Paris, call psychoanalysis.

It was the case of Anna von Lieben, whom Freud called his 'teacher' and whom he had treated jointly with Breuer, that prompted them, in 1892, to write a 'Preliminary Communication' together. It was published in January 1893 and formed the first of the four sections of the book, *Studies on Hysteria*, that the two authors then agreed to write. The second section consisted of five case histories, one by Breuer (Anna O.) and four by Freud. The third section, 'Theoretical', was written by Breuer; the fourth, 'The Psychotherapy of Hysteria', by Freud, who finished it in early 1895. The book appeared, after what had been a difficult period of gestation that cost Freud Breuer's friendship, in May 1895.

As James Strachey so astutely remarks, *Studies on Hysteria* 'is the story of the *discovery* of a succession of obstacles that have to be overcome.' There is the hint, masked by its jocularity, of Freud's disquiet at what actual treatment of patients required when he wrote to Fliess in 1888: 'visiting and talking people into or out of things – which is what my occupation consists in – robs me of the best time for work.' Each of the patients whose treatments were recounted in the volume presented the authors with difficulties and impasses. Yet each of the patients showed Breuer and Freud the way out of those impasses. It took the doctor to recognize the impasse as part of the therapeutic process. But it often took the ingenuity or the assertiveness of the patient to reveal the next step forward – indeed, it was often entirely up to them to *take* the next step forward. Frau Emmy von N. insisted on talking about what *she* wanted to talk about and was unresponsive to suggestion; Lucy R. could not be hypnotized, so Freud was obliged to develop the pressure technique – pressing on her forehead and releasing, which would inevitably produce the next association. And he was obliged to analyse *every* symptom with Elisabeth von R.

The following sections tell the stories of the five women whose case histories appeared in the *Studies*, together with Freud's 'teacher', whom, for reasons of discretion, Freud did not write up as a separate case history. When Freud's record of his encounters with the hysterics is placed alongside the records of the real lives of these women, the tension between biography and psychoanalysis is particularly revealing.

Anna O.: The First Patient

The patient, whose life became known to me to an extent to which one person's life is seldom known to another, had never been in love; and in all the enormous number of hallucinations which occurred during her illness that element of mental life never emerged.

Freud always insisted that psychoanalysis had been discovered by someone other than himself. That person was Josef Breuer, his mentor and colleague, and psychoanalysis was born in Breuer's treatment of Anna O. – Bertha

Pappenheim. Freud knew of her case within a few months of Breuer finishing her treatment in June 1882. In the early 1890s, Freud persuaded Breuer to write up the story of Bertha's treatment as the first of a series which became the *Studies on Hysteria*. There Breuer told the story of the complex collaboration between himself and his patient, which resulted in her invention of the 'talking cure', what Breuer and Freud at first called the 'cathartic cure'. Much of the credit for this invention must go to Bertha herself; in his later accounts Freud conscientiously paid tribute to both Bertha and Breuer.

From his early conversations with Breuer, and then with Martha, at the time his fiancée, the issue which was to make Bertha's treatment so important to Freud was raised: the response of the doctor to the sexuality of the patient. Yet sexuality never entered Breuer's account of Bertha's case: it was only after the fact that Martha and Freud reconstructed Bertha's relations with Breuer. And over the years Freud reconstructed the story time and again. Historians of psychoanalysis have added crucial new elements to this reconstruction, in the form of previously undiscovered documents and case notes; they have also viewed Bertha Pappenheim's treatment with the hindsight her later distinguished life has given us.

In writing about this first psychoanalytic patient, then, there are two stories to tell: first, the story of Bertha Pappenheim – her early life, her illness, her treatment by Breuer, her recovery and her later career; and second, the story of Anna O. – what Freud made of the story Breuer told him and how her case became the founding myth of psychoanalysis. Nothing, indeed, could be more characteristic of a myth than Freud's wildly implausible gesture of disclaiming responsibility for founding psychoanalysis by repeatedly acknowledging his debt to Breuer and this first patient. But myth here does not mean, as it so often does when 'history' and 'myth' are contrasted, an illusion, a self-serving mask of a deliberately hidden truth. Rather myth here signifies the structure which permits the story of the origin, the birth of psychoanalysis, to be told.

Bertha Pappenheim was born into a family who were considered to be millionaires. Her grandfather had acquired a large fortune through marriage and had made profitable use of it in the Pressburg ghetto in founding the grain-dealing family business around 1800. Her father, Siegmund, continued the business in Pressburg and then in Vienna, where the family moved when the Pressburg ghetto was opened up in the early 1840s. Bertha's mother, Recha, came from the Goldschmidt family of Frankfurt, which included the poet, Heine. Her parents' arranged marriage took place in 1848. Bertha was born on 27 February 1859, the third of four children. Bored and miserable in the confines of her wealthy, respectable and orthodox Jewish home; deprived by both family traditions and state restrictions of a secular secondary education beyond the Catholic private school – more like a finishing school for governesses – she attended; over-protected by her parents, whose other two daughters had died in childhood; possibly envious of her younger brother, who was able to escape from the closed family world and enter university.

eventually studying law, she began to generate systematic daydreaming, her private theatre. When, in July 1880, while on holiday in the mountain resort of Ischl, her father fell ill of peripleuritis, Bertha and her mother undertook to nurse him. As a consequence the twenty-one-year-old young woman also fell ill of what was to become a classic and complex case of hysteria.

The first visible and permanent symptom was a cough. The family doctor, Josef Breuer, was called for in late November and soon realized that this was a case of severe psychical disturbance. Over the incubation period, from the time of nursing her father to December, Bertha had generated a variety of paralyses and anaesthesias; what is more, 'two entirely distinct states of consciousness were present which alternated very frequently and without warning and which became more and more differentiated in the course of the illness.' By 10 December, Bertha had taken permanently to her bed.

The symptoms Breuer now confronted consisted of hallucinations that her hair and ribbons were black snakes, contractures of various limbs, and a gradual falling away of language, as it degraded in syntax and grammar, till she became almost completely deprived of words.

And now for the first time the psychical mechanism of the disorder became clear. As I knew, she had felt very much offended over something and had determined not to speak about it. When I guessed this and obliged her to talk about it, the inhibition, which had made any other kind of utterance impossible as well, disappeared.

She could now talk, but only in English! Then, when she was feeling most at ease, she would speak French and Italian, but could not remember the periods when she spoke only English. Gradually, in the early spring of 1881, she improved and rose from her bed on 1 April.

On 5 April, Bertha's father died. Her condition took another turn for the worse. She now had difficulty seeing and recognizing people: Breuer was the only person she always recognized when he entered the room. She generally refused food, but allowed Breuer to feed her. Breuer asked Krafft-Ebing for his opinion on the case; during the consultation, Bertha could not see him, until he blew smoke in her face. In her anger and anxiety, she struck Breuer; it took a long time to calm her down. When Breuer returned a few days later, he found her condition had deteriorated: she had not eaten and she was consumed by terrifying hallucinations, which she was now commenting upon aloud.

Breuer next took advantage of a peculiarity of her daily rhythms. Bertha was in a somnolent state in the afternoon, but spontaneously came into a state of deep hypnosis, which she called 'clouds', in the evening.

If during this she was able to narrate the hallucinations she had in the course of the day, she would wake up clear in mind, calm and cheerful. ... It was a truly remarkable contrast: in the day-time the irresponsible patient pursued by hallucinations, and at night the girl with her mind completely clear.

But her condition deteriorated and, on 7 June 1881, Breuer had her removed – against her will, though she was not taken by surprise – to a country house near the sanatorium run by Emil Fries and Hermann Breslauer in Inzersdorf near Vienna. Before and after this removal, she was suicidal, refusing food and unable to sleep. Then she grew calmer again.

Both Breuer and her family had noticed that in her hypnotic evening state, she would often act out some imagined scene, accompanied by muttered words. If someone repeated these words, she would animatedly pick them up and spin stories from them: sad and charming stories, fairy-stories. Telling the story would calm her. With her father's death, and the violation of her hallucinatory state by Krafft-Ebing, these stories turned blacker and became terrifying hallucinations. Complete mental relief would come when, 'shaking with fear and horror, she had reproduced these frightful images and given verbal utterance to them.'

Bertha had invented the 'talking cure', this 'chimney-sweeping' as she described it. It now became the regular procedure she and Breuer adopted when he visited her. Because of his intermittent visits,

I was obliged to overcome her unwillingness [to tell the stories] by urging and pleading and using devices such as repeating a formula with which she was in the habit of introducing her stories. But she would never begin to talk until she had satisfied herself of my identity by carefully feeling my hands.

During the time she spent in the country sanatorium, however, Bertha's nights became unbearable and Breuer resorted to giving her chloral. She settled in and became friends with the resident doctor, Breslauer.

She derived much benefit from a Newfoundland dog which was given to her and of which she was passionately fond. On one occasion, though, her pet made an attack on a cat, and it was splendid to see the way in which the frail girl seized a whip in her left hand and beat off the huge beast with it to rescue his victim. Later, she looked after some poor, sick people, and this helped her greatly.

Breuer went on holiday. When he returned, he found that Bertha was in a very poor, demoralized state. He decided that she needed some intensive story-telling work, so he brought her to Vienna for a week, where he worked evening after evening with her, hearing three to five stories each time. It was at this point that he noticed that a given symptom, relating to a specific event or to the 'spontaneous products of her imagination', would disappear the moment she had finished telling the story of its first appearance, irrespective of the time lapse since the symptom was formed. Breuer now set out progressively and systematically to eliminate her original symptoms, alongside his primary task of eliminating acute psychic stimuli.

The surge of improvements of the late summer, however, did not last. On returning to Vienna in the autumn, and especially towards Christmas, Bertha was once more often agitated, gloomy and irritable. Breuer considered and then decided against sending her away to the Bellevue Sanatorium, Kreuzlingen, on Lake Constance. A completely new mental phenomenon now presented itself, in many ways the most astonishing Bertha was to reveal to him. Her two different consciousnesses, the normal one during the day and her evening hypnosis state, persisted, but in the hypnotic state she lived in the winter of 1880–1 and had completely forgotten all subsequent events, except the death of her father, whereas 'in the first she lived, like the rest of us, in the winter of 1881–2'. The veracity of the memories she inhabited was checked against the diary her mother had kept of the previous year. This re-living continued until the termination of Breuer's treatment of her, in June 1882. Moods from the 1881 consciousness would permeate the 1882 consciousness, but could only be brought into the open as lived, talkable detail in the 1881 evening consciousness. Not only was Breuer dealing with contemporary events and the distressing events of the self-same day of the previous year, but he was now also investigating with Bertha the inner events of the incubation period of late 1880, from which all the hysterical phenomena stemmed. The abre-action, as Breuer would later call it, of the memories underlying these symptoms seemed to lead to the definitive disappearance of the symptom. The cathartic method had been invented:

Each individual symptom in this complicated case was taken separately in hand; all the occasions on which it had appeared were described in reverse order, starting before the time when the patient became bed-ridden and going back to the event which had led to its first appearance. When this had been described the symptom was permanently removed.

All this work required much time. To speed it, Breuer resorted to artificial hypnotism, rather than simply making use of Bertha's spontaneous evening 'clouds', so as to gain access to these pathogenic memories. The work involved an extremely detailed ransacking of Bertha's past experiences, usually ending up with an event involving her father. For instance, one symptom, not hearing when someone came in, was traced back through 108 separate detailed instances, each of which had to be recounted in the exact chronological order of their occurrence. And the symptoms were reinforced as she talked them away: 'during the analysis of her not being able to hear she was so deaf that for part of the time I was obliged to communicate with her in writing.' Using this technique, Breuer revived her memories of the night in July 1880 when, sitting beside her father's sick-bed waiting for the surgeon to arrive, Bertha had experienced her first snake hallucination and was overcome with paralysis. Bertha had decided to finish the treatment on 7 June 1882, the anniversary of the day she had been removed to the country chalet for treatment – 'without deceit, but by force', as Breuer put it in his unpublished manuscript. On that day, the room was rearranged to resemble her father's sick-room and she reproduced the terrifying snake hallucination. With this dramatic scene, Breuer recounted, she was once again free to speak German and free from all the disturbances she had previously exhibited. But, he added, she took some time to regain her mental balance entirely; since then, however, she had enjoyed complete health.

What Breuer did not say in his case history was how the treatment had not come to such an idyllic end, but had, over the prior few months, run somewhat out of his control. Bertha had become addicted to the chloral she was prescribed for her sleep, had undergone severe intermittent convulsions linked to her level of drug use, and was suffering from facial pain so acute that it necessitated injections of morphine, to which she was also, in June 1882, addicted. In mid-1882, Breuer wrote to Robert Binswanger, the physician in charge of the Bellevue Sanatorium at Kreuzlingen, where Bertha was subsequently sent for a cure: 'I am not engaged in breaking her of this addiction since, despite her good will, when I am with her I am powerless to cope with her agitated state.' It was clear that Breuer felt unable to go on with her treatment. After Bertha had spent three weeks with her mother visiting family in Karlsruhe, she was brought to the Kreuzlingen sanatorium, where she stayed until October 1882: she had deteriorated again. Her German was still sketchy, her neuralgia was severe and her addictions not yet given up. It is plausible that Breuer thought her neuralgia was not psychogenic and, therefore, not part of the brief for his cathartic cure. Bertha's mother was not of this opinion and made quite plain to Binswanger the treatment she recommended: 'the sum of previous experiences serves to suggest that this neuralgia is not a wholly independent condition but is closely connected with her psychic processes. ... After recounting everything which she reproduced whilst in a kind of dreamlike state of mind about past times and events she invariably experienced tangible relief.' But the Kreuzlingen doctors preferred their own methods: exercise, baths and isolation from the family.

Despite being in poor shape on leaving Kreuzlingen for her aunt's in Karlsruhe at the end of October 1882, Bertha registered to train as a nurse at the Baden Women's Union, though she did not complete the three-month theoretical course. She returned to Vienna in January 1883, but on three occasions from 1883 to 1887 spent a number of months in the Inzersdorf Sanatorium. In August 1883, Breuer confided to Freud that Bertha was 'quite deranged'; but by January 1884 he reported to Binswanger that she was 'in good health, no pains or other troubles'. Yet over the next few years she was still struggling for health. Freud could well have heard of her progress in 1887 not only from Martha but from Karl Bettelheim, an old friend of Breuer's and of Freud's, who treated her at Inzersdorf in 1887.

The character traits that Breuer had already remarked on in Bertha in his notes of the early 1880s – energy, tenacity, obstinacy, a powerful intellect, will-power, determination, sensitivity to injustice, an instinct to help the sick and the poor – solidified over the years. In 1888, Bertha moved to Frankfurt am Main. She immersed herself in literary activities to start with, turning her story-telling gift, so important to the foundation of psychoanalysis, to use in a little book of children's stories, whose tenor is very much that of the stories with which Breuer heard her initiate the talking cure. In 1890, she published a book of short stories, *In the Second-Hand Shop*, under the pseudonym P. Berthold. The predominant mood of these stories, which deal with the loss of familial bliss and the strength of children's love, is one of pathetic melancholy. In one story, an abandoned husband finds his long-lost daughter and recovers his spirits and love of life.

Bertha's later vocation is already evident in these stories. She was to become a tireless fighter against injustice, struggling to overcome the poverty and misery around her and the blindness of the daughters of the bourgeoisie to its existence.

These children, who grew up with veiled eyes, do not know the relationship between poverty, illness, and crime. They only know poverty in the shape of begging in the streets or in theatrical presentations, illness as something disgusting, and crime as a sin before which one has to make the sign of the cross in the moral sense.

Bertha's stories also reveal her desire to have as many children as possible in order to fulfil her deep longing to be the embodiment of mother love.

In the early 1890s, Bertha began to recover her repressed Jewish identity (which Breuer's case history was to eliminate entirely) through her commitment to active social work: first in the soup kitchens for Jewish immigrants from eastern Europe, then in a small Jewish nursery school, in sewing classes and in a girls' club. In Frankfurt, like many other women in the Goldschmidt family, she engaged in charitable work with orphans and, more unusually, became actively involved in the basic practical jobs. In 1895, she accepted a position as the deputy housemother in a Jewish orphanage for girls, a position which became permanent in 1897; she held it until 1907. In 1898, she began what was to be a prolific career as a journalist and pamphleteer with an article on the education of young, middle-class women, which advocated their preparation for independent life and knowledge of the real world, not the protected world of their comfortable families. In 1899, she translated Mary Wollstonecraft's *Vindication of the Rights of Women* into German, an appropriate parallel to Freud's earlier translation of J. S. Mill's *The Emancipation of Women*, and wrote a play entitled *A Woman's Right*, which stressed the political, economic and sexual exploitation of women. Here the two male characters, one a rake, the other a bourgeois husband, are both revealed as exploiters and seducers of women. The wife, having found out the truth about the husband, decides not to leave him because of the children, but from that moment on claims her 'woman's right' and refuses to have sexual relations with him. The somewhat mawkish and melancholic failure of relations between men and women in her early stories is here transformed into the exposure of and struggle against man's unscrupulous sexual exploitation of women. Bertha had become a fully fledged feminist – a parallel career open to many of Freud's 'hysteric' patients.

In 1900, she wrote *The Jewish Problem in Galicia*, exposing how poor education led girls to poverty and vice. Her research meant extensive travel in eastern Europe and Russia, then the Middle East, investigating prostitution and white slavery in eastern Europe. At the same time, she founded a society, Care by Women, and began on what she later called her *Sisyphus Work*, bringing the problems of prostitution and slavery to the attention of the western Jews. The enormous influx of poor refugees and women in need from eastern Europe prompted her to found the *Jüdischer Frauenbund* (JFB) (Jewish Women's Union), following the Berlin convention of the International Council of Women in 1904. She became its first President, and remained President and its source of inspiration and energy until her retirement in 1924, a leader unashamed to seek out followers whom she 'could infect with one's own will, and ... make them fit to be helpers.' In 1907, she resigned from her post as housemother in the orphanage and founded a home for girls at risk and illegitimate children at Neu-Isenberg.

One of her colleagues characterized her tellingly:

A volcano lived in this woman ... she only fought about things that were directly involved in her goals. ... She felt ... the tragedy of these battles. ... Her fight against the abuse of women was almost a physically felt pain for her. ... Thus the passionate nature of her battle against white slavery.

Well into the Weimar 1920s, Bertha conceived of the JFB as based on non-professional, scantily rewarded philanthropy. And throughout that period, she aimed to reconcile her and her helpers' German, Jewish and female affiliations. The organization was pitted against the assimilation of Jews and against the decline of religion; yet Bertha was also hostile to the contemporary Zionist movement, regarding it as abandoning the cultural tasks of the majority of Jews, but also as hostile to women, the family, motherhood and the orthodox Jewish faith. Bertha never mentioned regretting not having married, though she often repeated that love had passed her by and that life had left her isolated, as this poem so well expresses:

> Love did not come to me –
> So I live like the plants,
> In the cellar, without light.
>
> Love did not come to me –
> So I sound like a violin
> With a broken bow.
>
> Love did not come to me –
> So I bury myself in work
> And, chastened, live for duty.
>
> Love did not come to me –
> So I like to think of death
> As a friendly face.

She conceived of her professional functions as fundamentally those of a surrogate mother:

Motherliness is the primary feeling of a woman, it can be delightfully experienced even by one who has remained untouched. ... Women who have to miss the happiness of real personal motherhood may have an opportunity for spiritual motherhood, if they follow the silent paths of caring for children and young people who have been neglected or abandoned by their natural mothers.

The JFB became the institutional embodiment of this conception of mother-hood, encompassing her advocacy of equal opportunities for women, her conviction of the sacredness of the family and the primary responsibility of woman lying in her roles as wife and mother. She asked of the woman/mother precisely what she asked of herself: to be everything, including even, perhaps, the father. She had become the 'successful hysteric'.

In her later years, Bertha kept her treatment by Breuer private. Even so, some people recognized her in Anna O. when the case history was published in 1895. Her desire for privacy and a clean break from her early adulthood probably led her to destroy all her papers dating from before 1890. In later life, her view of psychoanalysis was of a piece with her distrust of professional social workers. Freud (and Breuer) may have made much of her as the first patient of psychoanalysis, as the figurehead of the psychoanalytic ship, but she herself had little, if any, time for psychoanalysis. The energetic and influential life Bertha made for herself seemed remarkably detached from the cathartic episode of her early womanhood. The woman who had gone to a Catholic school which had been so deficient compared with the education she should ideally have had, and then invented the talking cure, would later rank confession and psychoanalysis together, as if they were crutches which only the weak might need: 'Psychoanalysis in the hands of the physician is what confession is in the hands of the Catholic priest. It depends on its user and its use, whether it becomes a beneficial tool or a two-edged sword.' What we cannot know is whether her cure with Breuer established the basis for her later active life or whether it hindered her emergence in the late 1890s as the 'first social worker in modern Germany' – as she has been called, despite her hostility to social work as a profession. Anna O. appears as unrelated to Bertha Pappenheim as does the caterpillar to the butterfly. Whether Bertha's cathartic cure was her cocoon will never, now, be established.

What we do know is that Bertha's cure was the cocoon of psychoanalysis. There is a disconcerting parallel here. Just as there is an inexplicable discontinuity, in time and in personality, between, on the one hand, Anna O.'s illness, her treatment by Breuer and her slow recovery in the 1880s, and, on the other, the emergence of the powerful and healthy Bertha Pappenheim in the 1890s, so there is a sharp discontinuity between Breuer's experimental cure of his patient in the early 1880s and the emergence of Freud's psychoanalysis in the mid-1890s. The rupture in Bertha Pappenheim's life is mirrored in the two-stage prehistory of psychoanalysis.

Freud came to hear some of the details of Breuer's treatment of Bertha from him in November 1882, and again in more personal detail, when the two men were drawing ever closer, in the summer of 1883. He reported these two conversations to Martha, despite Breuer's admonition to keep them from her until they were married. And it was to be his brooding over the significance of the case, and his chivvying of Breuer to make the treatment public, which would lead, thirteen years later, to the publication of *Studies on Hysteria*.

Breuer was not the only contact Freud had with the Pappenheims. In certain respects, Martha had a greater stake in hearing Breuer's story than Freud. In February 1880, two months after the sudden death of Martha's father, her mother Emmeline appointed Bertha's father as the legal guardian of her son and two daughters. So when Bertha was reacting so strongly to her own father's serious illness later that year, and to his death early in the next, Martha was also mourning the joint loss of her guardian and father. A common cultural reference that Breuer, Bertha and her mother probably shared, and which may have had a significant part in their invention of the cathartic cure, was the revival, stimulated by Martha's uncle, Jakob Bernays, of a medicalized version of the Aristotelian cathartic theory of tragedy, very much the fashion in Vienna in the early 1880s: the purifying (Aristotle's 'cathartic') function of tragedy was seen to be directly curative of the body. It is also likely that Martha followed the news of Bertha's illness independently of Freud and Breuer, both in Vienna and later in Kreuzlingen, through her friend, Emma Ruben, wife of Wilhelm Pappenheim, Bertha's first cousin, who lived in Vienna, following her marriage around 1880. Bertha was to remain a friend of Martha's well into the 1880s and 1890s, appearing at her *Kaffeeklatsch*, and in odd references in letters, throughout that period. Bertha had visited Martha on at least two occasions in early 1887; in that year, Martha wrote to her mother that Bertha was well during the day but still suffered from hallucinatory states in the evenings. So, although Bertha's relations with Breuer may well later have been restricted owing to the still mysterious events that led to the interruption of her treatment, she remained, as did so many other patients of both Breuer and Freud, firmly integrated into the tight circle of friends and relations.

The mythical cast the story of Anna O. has taken on in the history of psychoanalysis finds its crux in the way Bertha's treatment may have been terminated. Our knowledge of this termination comes from an account of Freud's, in a letter to Zweig, written almost fifty years to the day after the event. According to this account, Breuer had told Freud the following version:

On the evening of the day when all her symptoms had been disposed of, he was summoned to the patient again, found her confused and writhing in abdominal cramps. Asked what was wrong with her, she replied: 'Now Dr B.'s child is coming!' ... Seized by conventional horror he took flight and abandoned the patient to a colleague. For months afterwards she struggled to regain her health in a sanatorium.

Once told to Freud at some point early on in their friendship, Breuer never spoke of the episode again. Nor did he include it in his case history. Recent scholarship has steered clear of endorsing this version of the end of Bertha's treatment by Breuer, because there is no other source, published or unpublished, which backs it up. The most probable date for Freud's most intimate conversation on the subject of Bertha's treatment, and therefore the most probable source for this story, is August 1883. That something had indeed happened in Bertha's treatment which had disturbed Breuer is clear from the letters Freud and Martha exchanged in October and November 1883 – and it was definitely something sexual:

a colleague [at the sanatorium] is completely enchanted by the girl [Bertha], by her provocative appearance in spite of her grey hair, by her wit and her cleverness. I believe that if he as a psychiatrist did not know so well what a burden the inclination to a hysterical illness can be, he would have fallen in love with her.

Martha's reply indicated not only that she was more interested than Freud in looking at things from her friend Bertha's point of view, but also that she was intrigued by this series of doctors, first Breuer, then Freud's psychiatrist friend, who found themselves fascinated by Bertha:

It has often been on the tip of my tongue to ask you why Breuer gave up Bertha. I could well imagine that those somewhat removed from it were wrong to say that he had withdrawn because he realised that he was unable to do anything for her. It is curious that no man other than her physician of the moment got close to poor Bertha, that is when she was healthy she already [had the power] to turn the head of the most sensible of men – what a misfortune for the girl. You will laugh at me, dearest, I so vividly put myself in the place of the silent Frau Mathilde [Breuer] that I could scarcely sleep last night.

Martha knew that something unspeakable must have happened to end so abruptly Breuer's treatment of Bertha. And she obviously suspected that the something was erotic and had given rise to hurt feelings on Frau Breuer's part. But whereas Martha had placed herself in both Bertha's and Mathilde's positions, thereby making the scene of jealousy between Breuer's wife and his patient quite clear, Freud overlooked her concern for the two women and focused attention back on themselves:

My beloved little angel, you were right to expect that I would laugh at you. I do so with great gusto. Are you really so vain as to believe that people are going to contest your right to your lover or later to your husband? Oh no, he remains entirely yours, and your only comfort will have to be that he himself would not wish it any other way. To suffer Frau Mathilde's fate, one has to be the wife of Breuer, isn't that so?

Freud stresses that *he* is not like Breuer, and complications with patients like Breuer's with Bertha will never affect *him*. It is almost as if he is saying that, unlike the charming Breuer, no woman other than Martha could fall in love with him. Freud at this time appeared to have no inkling that the relationship between Bertha and Breuer could be of any special *medical*, as opposed to *extra-marital*, interest; Martha at this time was more genuinely enquiring than he about the strange passions that circulate between doctor and patient.

In 1932, Freud said of Bertha's exclamation 'Dr B.'s child is coming!': 'At this moment he held in his hand the key that would have opened "the doors to the Mothers", but he let it drop.' Yet what had concerned both Freud and Martha in 1883 was more like a key to the *fathers*: a key to the sexual responses of male doctors to their patients. When Breuer came to write up Bertha's case and supplement it with the chapter on theory that he wrote for *Studies on Hysteria* in 1895, he did not comment on Bertha's sexuality – indeed, he emphasized its absence: 'The element of sexuality was astonishingly undeveloped in her. The patient, whose life became known to me to an extent to which one person's life is seldom known to another, had never been in love.' Yet in his unpublished case notes of thirteen years before, which Freud had never seen, he had linked this absence of sexuality to her intimacy with her father: 'At all events, she has never been in love to the extent that this has replaced her relationship to her father; it has itself, rather, been replaced by that relationship.' In his theoretical discus,ion in 1895, he would even go so far as to give a tragic dimension to the situation of well-brought up young girls in his society: 'The young girl senses in Eros the terrible power which governs and decides her destiny and she is frightened by it. All the greater, then, is her inclination to look away and to repress from her consciousness the thing that frightens her.' Breuer's awareness of the importance of sexuality also led him to castigate his medical colleagues for their ignorance about feminine sexuality:

It is a most unfortunate thing that clinical medicine ignores one of the most pathogenic factors or at least only hints at it delicately. This is certainly a subject in which the acquired knowledge of experienced physicians should be communicated to their juniors, who as a rule blindly overlook sexuality – at all events so far as their patients are concerned.

Young doctors overlook the factor of sexuality precisely because, Breuer implies, they are blinded by the presence of their *own* sexuality. But his awareness of this dimension had not prevented him falling victim to a sexual crisis from which he himself had turned away, one in which he was suddenly implicated, whether we take that crisis to have primarily been his wife's chronic jealousy – which we can regard as probable given the correspondence between Sigmund and Martha – or being confronted with Bertha's scene of childbirth.

Did Bertha actually say: 'Now Dr B.'s child is coming!'? Dora Breuer, the daughter born during Anna O.'s treatment, had corroborated at least part of Freud's reconstruction of the end of Bertha's treatment by asking her father about it before he died in 1925. None the less, Freud and his biographer Ernest Jones further added to the mythical aura that Bertha's treatment had already acquired by implicating Dora Breuer's birth in Bertha's story. Freud told Stefan Zweig that Dora was 'born shortly after the above-mentioned treatment, not without significance for the deeper connections!'; Jones's biography of Freud asserted that the day after Bertha's exclamation Breuer had left Vienna with his wife for a second honeymoon, which resulted in the conception of a daughter, Dora. As Henri F. Ellenberger has established, this story is not true: Dora Breuer was born on 11 March 1882, three months *before* the supposed scene of Bertha's hysterical childbirth, not nine months after it. So what was the source of the connection between Bertha's exclamation about Dr B.'s baby and the story of Dora Breuer's birth?

We can venture a speculative explanation of how this phrase concerning Dr B.'s baby became linked to Dora Breuer's birth – and in this way show why it so unnerved Breuer. Breuer recounted how Bertha's 're-living of the previous year continued right up until the illness came to a definitive conclusion in June 1882.' If on 7 June 1882 she was reliving the events of 7 June 1881, she might well have been reliving Breuer's (and his wife's) experiences of that day: 7 June 1881 is almost exactly nine months before Dora Breuer's birthday. With her cry 'Now Dr B.'s child is coming!', 'she recognised (and wanted her doctor to know that she recognised) that events in his personal life as well as in her own had taken place at the time, 7 June 1881'. The 'now' of the baby that is coming was the 'now' of 1881, not 1882.

So at that moment in the double chronology, Bertha's birth announcement may have been intended by her and correctly, if reluctantly, interpreted by Breuer as being a repetition of the conception of his own daughter. Bertha's choosing this date, this anniversary, for her demonstration of her repressed sexuality became interpreted by Breuer as a sign of an unacceptable intertwining of his personal with his professional life. He would have suddenly realized that Bertha was keeping a very close watch on his personal life, on his wife and their children. She was now nursing him, we might say, had cast him in the role of father, but in a way that kept open the ambiguity that she might one day nurse his baby, Dr B.'s baby, as well as the father.

We might even guess that Breuer did not even perceive that his wife was jealous of Bertha until Bertha revealed her identification with his wife, by mimicking the moment of conception from the previous year. Suddenly Breuer *identified* with his wife: 'if she is pregnant then I (my wife) would be jealous, which is indeed how she feels. Now I see it!' It was when Bertha seemed to invade his own marriage, through her uncanny recollection of the scene of the conception of his daughter, that Breuer took fright. His wife's silence could now be interpreted: the silence of the wronged woman, who is too proud to make her claim in speech, since any words will go beyond what should be said. That is the true significance of Breuer confessing to Freud in July 1883 that he called his wife Cordelia. And if his wife is Cordelia, who is he but Lear, who could not recognize honest love when it was staring him in the face, but needed excessive and unnatural demonstration of this love?

All this was later described by Freud as 'the presence of a strong unanalysed positive transference of an unmistakably sexual nature', or 'the girl had suddenly developed a condition of "transference love"'. These descriptions jump the gun somewhat on what was a rather confused and complex situation involving Bertha and Breuer. But it was this perception of the mystery of Breuer's relation with Bertha that sustained Freud in the face of his own experiences with his female patients. Freud came to believe that what he experienced with his patients was a repetition of what Breuer had experienced with Bertha: the transference, in all its 'universal' significance. And there was a hint of rebuke for Breuer in his tone when he told the story of his first brush with the erotic in his patients:

I was engaged in relieving ... the suffering of one of my most acquiescent patients ... by tracing back her attacks of pain to their origins. As she woke up on one occasion, she threw her arms round my neck. The unexpected entrance of a servant relieved us from a painful discussion, but from that time onwards there was a tacit understanding between us that the hypnotic treatment should be discontinued. I was modest enough not to attribute the event to my own irresistible personal attraction, and I felt that I had now grasped the nature of the mysterious element that was at work behind hypnotism. In order to exclude it, or at all events to isolate it, it was necessary to abandon hypnotism.

Freud surmised that Breuer had dropped Bertha when he encountered something similar with her. Freud pressed on, being 'modest enough not to attribute the event to my own irresistible personal attraction'. Here there is considerable continuity between the youthful Freud's perception of himself as lacking in superficial charm, the quality that draws people instantly to one, and his response to an incident like this in the consulting-room. He had written to Martha during their engagement:

I consider it a great misfortune that Nature has not granted me that indefinite something which attracts people. I believe it is this lack more than any other which has deprived me of a rosy existence. It has taken me so long to win my friends. I have had to struggle so long for my precious girl, and each time I meet someone I realise that an impulse, which defies analysis, leads that person to underestimate me. This may be a question of expression or temperament or some other secret of Nature, but whatever it may be it affects one deeply.

In contrast, in Freud's eyes Breuer was a man of immediate charm, which did not dim with deeper acquaintance. Even his verdict on Breuer in the late 1890s, after they had fallen out, consistently bore out this judgment, with its implicit contrast to himself. To Freud, Breuer was the epitome of the medical charmer who worked his many cures by sleepwalking. Breuer was too *successful* a doctor to have discovered the transference: 'through a lucky deal, not through knowledge or ability, he won the game of life and made his fortune.' Breuer was the most successful general practitioner in Vienna, a 'personal friend, a stimulating conversationalist and a doctor, all in one person.' As his obituarist put it, Breuer had 'exemplary relations with his patients, his quiet manner ... radiated optimism and was itself often a healing influence.' His patients would not care from whence his success came. To Freud, smitten with the thirst for knowledge and understanding, Breuer's 'unabated need to do good', even the remarkable 'absence of so much badness', and his very therapeutic success became a symbol of his failure to follow the thread his Ariadne, Bertha Pappenheim, had put in his hands. To Freud would go the task of repeating, over and over again, now on a mythical scale, the successes and failures that Bertha and Breuer had achieved. And he would turn out to be every bit as good, and on occasion as erratic, as the sleepwalking Breuer at cultivating and managing the now explicit erotic relations with his female patients.

And, finally, there is nothing better suited to become the myth of origin than the story of a birth. Freud founded psychoanalysis on the view that he was only repeating this original giving birth, which was Breuer's, yet what was being given birth to Breuer refused to recognize as his baby. He hid the baby, one might say, just as Moses's mother hid her baby. Breuer's baby consisted of the words: 'Now Dr B.'s child is coming!', which he hid only for Freud to 'rediscover'. One detects the mythical narrative structuring of Freud's letter to Zweig in the opening phrase: 'On the evening of the day when all her symptoms had been disposed of....' This fictional moment, when *all* her symptoms had been disposed of, when she is cured of *all* her troubles and pains – when she has become a new person: this is the moment when Breuer is confronted by the baby coming, proving that Breuer has not created psychoanalysis, but only allowed it to come into the world, separate from him. In Freud's account, Breuer declines to be the midwife to his patient's fantasied baby, he declines to be what the psychoanalyst would later always be: the midwife to desire. But the mythical baby does come into the world as a whole person, rather like Freud's description of his own daughter Anna's entry into the world as a 'nice, complete little woman'. This revised version, which for years became the authorized version, of the end of Anna O.'s treatment includes all the crucial elements which distinguish psychoanalysis: repression, sexuality, transference. This is Freud's myth of the origin of psychoanalysis, in which Anna O. plays the part of the mother, Breuer plays the part of the father, and Freud *subsequently* plays the part that Breuer turned down: that of the midwife.

So what was Bertha's, as opposed to Anna O.'s, significance in the history of psychoanalysis? Was she strictly an opportunity – the first occasion on which theory could master a new tract of experience; the invasion of yet one more territory of private life by the new mental professionals, albeit in the unlikely guise of the ever-caring Breuer and his more suspicious and tricksy young colleague? And does Bertha end up, as Mary Jacobus argues, 'marginal to a history not her own; first on the stand as a historical witness, she testifies at a trial which is really a trial of strength between men and which, because man-to-man, excludes her'? Certainly there was eventually rivalry, and certainly Bertha's story *had to become* mythical for psychoanalysis to be born. But there still lingers the conviction that without this specific woman, and without patients as talented as she was at guiding doctors, at taking control of their treatment, at beguiling the doctors, at seducing and fooling doctors into the traps of error, fiction and truth, there would not have been psychoanalysis. Himself sympathetic to the activity of the patient, Sándor Ferenczi put the case for psychoanalysis being as much the patient's as the doctor's responsibility: 'An inspired patient and her understanding physician shared in the discovery of the [cathartic] fore-runner of psycho-analysis.' Bertha may indeed have been 'unconscious' and embalmed in her case history, but the mysterious dialectic in her life between the distressed, young and fascinating bourgeois woman and the determined, feminist philanthropist resists consigning her too easily to being only the prop in a boys' own story.

Cäcilie M.: Freud's Teacher

In 1897, writing to Fliess, Freud called Anna von Lieben, the woman he would rename Cäcilie M., his '*Lehrmeisterin*', his teacher. Earlier, in 1892, he had invoked her in a somewhat less complimentary way, but none the less one indicative of her centrality to his work: his 'prima donna'. By the end of his life, in a letter to a relative of Anna's, Freud was referring to her as his 'former patient and teacher'. Amongst his early patients, Anna had the distinction of being in treatment for far longer than any other mentioned between 1887 or 1888 and the autumn of 1893. And it was she who gave Freud his first personal experience of the possible effectiveness of a talking cure, as well as teaching him much about the nature of hysteria. What Freud's account of her case makes clear is that a talented patient needs to exist for a talented doctor to emerge. The talking cure is a collaborative act.

Anna von Lieben, born Baroness Anna von Todesco in 1847, was the second of four children of Baron von Todes~~ ~~d Sophie (née Gomperz). Backed by old money, the family had becom. industrialists and bankers in the nineteenth century and were ennobled for their charitable donations in founding schools. Sophie von Todesco was a socie v hostess, particularly in the 1860s. Anna grew up in luxury at the Villa Todesco, where she precociously displayed her gifts in painting, music and poetry. However, from about 1862 on, when she was fifteen, Anna was often ill: a cold developed into an illness of the womb and ovaries, from which pathological symptoms arose, including her first hysterical attacks. During this period, she was cared for by her Gomperz grandmother and her aunt, also a Gomperz, Josephine von Wertheimstein. Anna adored Josephine, who was another of the great Viennese hostesses of the 1870s and 1880s, entertaining her family and her friends. Josephine's salon was also famous for its nervous illnesses. She herself received a miraculous cure for her own nervous breakdown from Theodor Meynert, later Freud's teacher in psychiatry, whose methods were quite the obverse of Freud's. As Arthur Schnitzler noted: 'He tried to convince patients with delusions that they could not possibly have them.'

From 1866 to 1868, when she entered her twenties, Anna lived in England with her sister, who had married an English baron. For most of 1867 she was confined to bed. Her writings of the time are full of her fantasies of being outside, of being free. It is plausible that she was in some turmoil over a marriage her parents had brokered on her behalf, to a noble and rich man, whom she refused. She returned to the Continent in 1868 and spent the summer at the spas, particularly at Franzensbad, which specialized in female maladies. She stayed there for most of 1869, in the company of Elise von Sichrovsky, who was to marry Theodor Gomperz in August 1869. On 31 December 1870, Leopold, Baron von Lieben, a Jewish banker of thirty-five, proposed to her; Anna accepted him. In 1872, they were married and took up residence in the Palais Todesco on Vienna's Ring, though they also spent much time at their villa at Bruhl. Between 1873 and 1875, Anna gave birth to two daughters and a son; then in 1878 a second son, Robert, was born. Anna seemed only to be free from neurotic illnesses when pregnant.

At home within her family, she developed eccentric and domineering habits. A creature of the night, Anna existed on caviar and champagne; had a professional chessplayer waiting outside her room all night; roused her children from their beds to be with her on occasion and ignored them entirely on others. In 1882, she became addicted to morphine. Despite her eccentricities and her addiction, she was never hospitalized or placed in a sanatorium, though some of her posthumously published poems reveal a fear that she might be.

When Freud began treating Anna in 1887 or 1888, he made contact through her once again with one of the men who had most influenced his intellectual development in the 1870s: Franz Brentano. It turns out that Brentano too had acquired an interest in hypnotism. So the welcome that Freud received from the noble von Liebens could in part have stemmed from Brentano's benign influence.

In 1880, Ida von Lieben, Leopold's sister, had become engaged to Brentano. Brentano was a Catholic priest who had, several years before, resigned his university position at Würzburg on account of his opposition to the new doctrine of papal infallibility. He took up a Chair in Vienna in 1874. As a student, Freud had attended Brentano's lectures on metaphysics, on Mill's *Utilitarianism* in 1874, and on philosophical psychology and logic in 1875, with further courses in his third year; in all he took six courses with him. Already in early 1875, Freud had developed a close, personal relationship with this 'remarkable man (a believer, a teleologist (!) and a Darwinian and a damned clever fellow, a genius in fact), who is, in many respects, an ideal human being'. Under Brentano's influence Freud had decided to take his Ph.D. in philosophy and zoology, a project he later discarded (or at least indefinitely postponed); Brentano was certainly a key factor in his repudiation of materialism and his shift away from the scientific reductionism of the Helmholtz school. In 1879, Theodor Gomperz asked for Brentano's help in finding a translator for a volume in the complete edition of John Stuart Mill's writings that he was preparing, to replace the translator who had suddenly died. Brentano immediately named Freud, who polished off the translation in the autumn and winter of 1879–80, while doing his tedious year of military service.

Brentano's desire to marry had involved him in a new and equally celebrated public struggle for his personal beliefs and desires. He wanted to marry Ida, 'one of the most noble daughters of Vienna', but the reactionary interpretation of an old Austrian law made such a marriage illegal for a former priest. Brentano once again resigned his Chair at the University of Vienna, acquired Saxon citizenship and married in Leipzig on 16 September 1880. He returned to Vienna to resume lecturing – now as only a simple lecturer (*Privatdozent*). Earlier the same year, on 8 February, Brentano had visited Breslau to see a Dr R. P. Heidenhain, who was using Hansen's hypnotic techniques for research (the Hansen whose performances Freud had witnessed, probably in January and February 1880, and which, in 1925, he was to credit with having given 'scientific support' to the conviction of the genuineness of hypnosis). While in Breslau, Brentano suggested that Heidenhain's unmarried sister should come to Vienna and look after the Auspitz household, which she did in July 1881; she also supervised the education of the Auspitz and von Lieben children. In other words, the sister of a famous hypnotist, a colleague of the Hansen whose shows so impressed the young Freud and convinced him of the seriousness of hypnotism, was educating Anna von Lieben's children late in the 1880s under the aegis of a prestigious old friend of Freud's. One cannot imagine that the intelligent and enquiring Anna was ignorant of the various phenomena of hypnosis. The link between the Brentanos and the Liebens grew even closer in 1888, when the von Liebens moved into the same apartment house as the Brentanos and Ida Brentano took a large share in the care required by Anna, her sister-in-law.

The young Dr Freud's practice and home was some five minutes walk away from this house. It is feasible that Freud was called in to treat Anna's facial neuralgias as early as 1887, on the recommendation probably of Breuer, the von Liebens' family doctor, who continued to treat Anna alongside Freud. 'Indeed, it was the study of this remarkable case, jointly with Breuer, that led directly to the publication of our "Preliminary Communication".' Sometime in 1888 Freud began to use hypnotism on Anna, following a short, second visit to Charcot, and by 1889 he was using the hypnotic technique almost daily. Anna interrupted her treatment with Freud in 1889 to visit Paris, possibly to see Charcot; in July, she accompanied Freud when he went to Nancy to study with Bernheim, with the aim of 'perfecting my hypnotic technique'. 'Thinking it would be instructive, I had persuaded one of my patients to follow me to Nancy. This patient was a uniquely gifted hysteric, a woman of good birth, who had been handed over to me because no one knew what to do with her.' By 1889, Freud already viewed Anna as one of his success stories. 'By hypnotic influence I had made it possible for her to lead a tolerable existence and I was always able to take her out of the misery of her condition. But she always relapsed again after a short time, and in my ignorance I attributed this to the fact that her hypnosis had never reached the stage of somnabulism with amnesia.' So, despite Freud's success at hypnotizing Anna, this was never enough. And it was on her that Freud first tried out the rudimentary technique of free association that Bernheim's method of breaking down post-hypnotic amnesia inspired in him: if one can break down an artificial amnesia, why cannot one try to break down 'natural' amnesias, with the patient in the normal waking state, without hypnosis?

Although we know little of the details of the relationship between Freud and Anna, it is plausible that Anna, his 'teacher', led Freud towards engaging in the talking cure with her. When he first started treating her in 1887 and 1888, he was still learning his trade; it is clear that he changed his therapeutic methods over the years of his work with her. Responsibility for those changes was inevitably something of a joint affair.

At some point in his treatment of her, Anna came upon a long forgotten memory, and from then on for nearly three years she lived through all the forgotten traumas of her life, accompanied by a cacophony of suffering and old symptoms. In this way, she finally resolved her 'hysterical psychosis for the payment of old debts', debts as old as thirty-three years previously (that is, back into her pre-pubertal childhood, before her first illness at the age of fifteen). 'The only way of relieving her was to give her an opportunity of talking off under hypnosis the particular reminiscence that was tormenting her at the moment, together with all its accompanying load of feelings and their physical expression.' As she worked   ith Freud, her old debts became Freud's new ones: 'a highly intelligent woman, to whom I am indebted for much help in gaining an understanding of hysterical symptoms'.

Over the years, Freud made literally hundreds of observations of her standard cycles: of inexplicable moods, followed by a variety of hysterical symptoms (hallucinations, pains, spasms, declamatory speeches), followed by the emergence in hallucinatory form of an experience from her past which explained the symptoms of the present attack. One of her many symptoms was a violent facial neuralgia which appeared suddenly two or three times a year, lasted for from five to ten days, resisted any kind of treatment – even the cruel expedient of extracting most of her teeth – and then ceased abruptly. Freud managed to prohibit her from having these pains, and then sought under hypnosis for the traumatic scene that underlay the symptom:

She described a conversation which she had had with [her husband] and a remark of his which she had felt as a bitter insult. Suddenly she put her hand to her ch ' gave a loud cry of pain and said: 'It was like a slap in the face.' With this her   ... and her attack were both at an end.

Analysing a string of such insults which had ended up as the facial neuralgia led Freud and Anna back to the original, the first scene, in the early months of her pregnancy: 'She saw a painful sight which was accompanied by feelings of self-reproach, and this led her to force back another set of thoughts. Thus it was a case of conflict and defence.' The conflict attached itself to the toothache from which she was at the time suffering, which, from then on, could be evoked whenever Anna's mental conflicts became insupportable. In this way, the neuralgia was a symbolization of her thoughts: she had converted these into the physical symptom. Anna displayed a panoply of such symbolizations: the violent pain in her right heel, stemming from the fear that she might not 'find herself on the right footing' with a group of strangers; a penetrating pain between her eyes, arising from the 'penetrating' look her grandmother had given her when she was fifteen.

Freud recognized that Anna von Lieben was 'a woman who possessed quite unusual gifts, particularly artistic ones, and whose highly developed sense of form was revealed in some poems of great perfection.' The respect and admiration must have been mutual, since Anna included in her book of poems one entitled 'Case History', which was quite clearly her version of the therapy Freud and she had devised together:

> Youth that was buried too early
> Must have life once again,
> Once again to gulp breath,
> In order to sink away forever.

Whilst recognizing her great culture, Freud did not want to attribute the creativity of her symptoms entirely to her artistic gifts. 'In taking a verbal expression literally and in feeling the "stab in the heart" or the "slap in the face" after some slighting remark as a real event, the hysteric is not taking liberties with words ... hysteria is right in restoring the original meaning of the words in depicting its unusually strong innervations.' Anna may well have taught Freud that bodily symptoms and hallucinations are poetic creations, but the creative act is not one to be ascribed solely to the individual patient. The poetry and creativity of Anna von Lieben was a clue to the universal poetry of all neurotics. And Freud was Anna's student, not her impresario or artistic patron.

Anna von Lieben died on 31 October 1900, at the age of fifty-three, of a sudden heart attack, a myocardial degeneration. She had kept a diary of her analysis with Freud. Unfortunately, this was destroyed by one of the doctors who, from 1893 on, followed Freud in the treatment of her chronic hysterical symptoms, her twilight states. Intriguingly, at least two of these doctors married into Anna's family while treating her: one, Paul Karplus, a colleague of Breuer's and brother of one of Freud's students in the academic year 1894–5, married her daughter Valerie; the other, Josef Winter, married into the Auspitz wing. Whether, as is rumoured, Freud and Anna were mutually infatuated in some way is undecidable; whether it was Anna who, on awakening from hypnosis, threw her arms around his neck and, at least in retrospect, showed him the erotic basis of hypnosis and a first hint at transference, is not altogether clear. But given the repeated intertwining of the position of personal physician and suitor in her family – a signal of the intricacy of relations between wealthy, cultured patients and their doctors – it seems inevitable that Anna was one of the patients who drew Freud on to the track of sexuality. Freud was to encounter a similar set of complexities in his treatment in the early 1890s of another powerful and independent woman: Fanny Moser.

Emmy von N.: Freud's First Case History

Breuer's Anna O. opened the section on 'Case Histories' in the *Studies on Hysteria*; four cases of Freud's followed, the first of which was that of Emmy von N. Freud treated Emmy von N. first in 1889 and was thoroughly committed at the beginning to using the full weight of suggestion that the hypnotic state yielded to the doctor. His experience with her obliged him to turn to a more subtle conception of the relationship between doctor and patient.

Fanny Moser, *née* Sulzer-Wart, was born in 1848. She came of a German Swiss family, knighted by German kings, although her father preferred peasant life to that of the aristocracy. Fanny had thirteen brothers and sisters, the eldest born in 1832, the youngest six years after her. As she grew up, the illnesses and deaths in her family constituted a veritable mare's nest of traumatic memories. Four of her siblings died as infants before she was born. Two of her siblings died as infants, another at the age of thirteen, when Fanny was aged between two and six; a sister at fifteen, when Fanny was eighteen; and a brother, probably the one she mentioned to Freud as addicted to morphine, at thirty-three, when she was twenty. Only four of the children were still alive when Freud treated her. Her brother, six years younger than her, succeeded to their father's estate and lived there; later on, he was the only relative with whom she had close contact. When she was fifteen, Fanny found her mother lying on the floor smitten by a stroke; when she was nineteen, she came home and found her dead.

Four years later, she met and married her husband – a famous and extremely prosperous manufacturer of watches and railway carriages, some forty years older than her, who had been a friend of the family. The couple's courtship started when Fanny was travelling on a train and broke her glasses, the glasses which to many would have been a sign of her non-marriageability. The sixty-five-year-old Heinrich Moser sitting opposite felt impelled to assist her. The children of her husband's first marriage, older than Fanny, treated her as an intruder. None the less, the marriage seemed a happy one and two daughters, Fanny and Mentona, were born in 1872 and 1874. Fanny's husband died of a heart attack a few days after the birth of her second daughter. Fanny was then twenty-six. Following his death, the children of the first marriage accused Fanny of having poisoned him. An exhumation found no evidence of murder, but his relatives kept up their campaign against her and the rumours persisted, fuelled by the disappearance of crucial legal documents. They were still extant and persuasive to members of the family into the 1960s, including her younger daughter who died in East Berlin in 1971.

As in the classic detective stories, the basis of the rumour was obvious: Fanny and her daughters inherited the most valuable part of her husband's enormous fortune. She was now one of the richest women in Europe, but her name was, at least in many circles, so surrounded by scandal that, when she visited health resorts and spas, she sometimes forbade her children to tell people their name. When Fanny attempted to gain access to a court, the rumours and scandal forced her away. Instead, she became a salon hostess, an admired eccentric, a philanthropist and patron of arts, a woman of extravagant lifestyle and opinions, much respected by the artists and scientists whom she entertained – the geologist Albert Heim, the neuropsychiatrists Auguste Forel, Eugen Bleuler and Otto Wetterstrand, and the philosopher Ludwig Klages amongst them. In 1887, she moved into a *Schloss* on a Swiss lake, where she resided for the rest of her life, modelling her ménage on German feudal lines and entertaining a court of guests and residents.

In the spring of 1889, Fanny made the journey to Vienna for medical treatment. Since her husband's death, she had been constantly ill, with varying degrees of severity. In 1888–9, she was suffering from depression and insomnia, and was tormented by pains, tics and hallucinations. Meeting Breuer in Vienna, a 'chance remark' of his enabled her to extricate herself from her treatment by Freud's distinguished 'medical predecessor', whom she had come to value little. Probably on Breuer's recommendation, she then turned to Freud.

In contrast with his rather brief clinical remarks about Anna von Lieben, Freud's account of his treatment of Fanny Moser was his first extensive case history. In the *Studies on Hysteria*, he renamed her Frau Emmy von N. His account indicates that right from the start he was exceptionally eager to try out his newest ideas on her, including Breuer's technique of investigation: her 'symptoms and personality interested me so greatly that I devoted a large part of my time to her and determined to do all I could for her recovery.' He continued: 'What she told me was perfectly coherent and revealed an unusual degree of education and intelligence.' This patient's interest in receiving a cure from her doctor was certainly met more than half way by the doctor's interest in her exceptional qualifications as a patient. Freud became aware that Fanny could be put into a somnabulistic state easily – something he had failed to achieve with Anna von Lieben; he described her somnabulistic states as exhibiting 'an uninhibited unfolding of her mental powers and of a full command over her store of memories.' It was this that decided him to employ Breuer's technique of investigation with her. The account he gave of his treatment of her leaves no doubt of the closeness of understanding and collaborative enthusiasm which existed between them.

One of the curious features of the case history is the fact that Freud, in this *first* self-consciously analytic case of those published in 1895 in *Studies on Hysteria*, simply reproduced his notes from the period of treatment and presented these as an adequate account. Interestingly, these notes, made each evening after seeing Fanny, not only give a full picture of the treatment, but they also excel in that literary as opposed to scientific quality, that 'detailed description of mental processes', which Freud had purportedly resigned himself to being obliged to adopt. This first case is fully the literary and rhetorical equal of any later case history, in particular that other famous case history, of some seventeen years later, in which Freud chose this same didactic, virtuoso, seemingly so honest and vulnerable mode of presentation: the Rat Man. However, this first case history also displays to us the masterful authoritarian postures that Freud thought it necessary to adopt to secure a cure with hypnosis. It is rather shocking, and certainly ironic, to see Freud the hypnotist blithely wiping away his patient's memories, as if he is on the road to discovering behaviour therapy rather than psychoanalysis. Yet he is also explicit about what he learned from Fanny: the importance of talking, as opposed to hypnosis. And implicit is his eventual realization that it was family secrets, and secrets his patient kept from him, which proved central to her illness. Of course, displaying these youthful errors in this way was also an apt rhetorical manoeuvre: it demonstrated how far he had progressed in his dealings with patients since these very early days. Like Breuer with Bertha Pappenheim, Freud had to be shown by his patient how to allow her to find her talking cure. He may have known about Breuer's treatment of Bertha, but he did not fully act on that example until his own patients required him to.

The first thing Freud recommended for Fanny was 'that she should separate from the two girls [her daughters of seventeen and fifteen] into a nursing home, where I could see her every day.' Fanny agreed 'without raising the slightest objection.' Freud added, as if to apologize for this show of medical authority and to indicate the minimal isolation he put her under: 'She was not forbidden to see her children, to read, or to deal with her correspondence.' This cure by isolation, as the French school called it, was a fundamental strategy for therapeutic practitioners at the time, and doctors like Charcot who employed it were well aware that the patient agreeing to be placed in a medically controlled environment not only underscored the doctor's authority, but also cleared the way for future exercise of that authority by eliminating the interference of the family. Freud would later give a particular inflection to this view, by coming to regard a patient's family as being necessarily, at some point in the course of the treatment, the enemies of a patient's analysis. Here, however, his motives were less clear. The effects of this separation of Fanny from her daughters were none the less to be considerable. Perhaps by chance, Freud had hit on the crucial tormenting element in Fanny's life: the question of her relations with her daughters.

Fanny did suffer from self-reproaches when she agreed to Freud limiting her daughters' visits to her. But once he had cut her off from her daughters and secured his medical pre-eminence, the treatment was under way. Fanny's body collaborated in Freud's plan of isolating her so that only he had influence over her, in particular by erupting in a flurry of symptoms whenever the resident house-physician entered her room – by starting, by making a clacking sound, by grimaces and tics. To start with, he prescribed warm baths and massages twice a day (except when she had her period). Most importantly, he began to use hypnosis. He discovered what a susceptible patient she was and started the work of dissipating her fears of animals under hypnosis. He also discovered the unresolved distressing affects attaching to the past events which had originally provoked the sadnesses, pains, resentments, disgust and fears: traumatic memories, often of the death of her siblings and family, of people being taken off to insane asylums where they were maltreated, of being forced in childhood to eat food that disgusted her, of the period when she was nursing her morphine-addicted brother, and, most importantly, the period surrounding the birth of her second daughter and the death four days later of her husband.

A rhythm developed from the start: in her normal waking state, Fanny would tell him things, or display symptoms, which he would then investigate or try to eliminate once he had put her into the hypnotic state. Yet from very early on, their conversations in the normal state, particularly while he was massaging her, would encroach on the topics supposedly reserved for the hypnotic state, so that she was constructing, 'apparently unconstrained and guided by chance', a supplement to the hypnosis. Fanny was demonstrating to Freud the technique of free association. She was beginning to wrest control of the rhythm of the treatment away from the Charcotian hypnotist, despite her isolation in the nursing home. Similarly, she made it clear to Freud that if he interrupted her stories and tried to get rid of them without hearing all the details, she would return to them on some other occasion; 'her unruly nature', as he put it, 'rebelled, both in her waking state and in artificial sleep, against any constraint'. She made the new rules of the game quite explicit to him: 'She then said in a definitely grumbling tone that I was not to keep on asking her where this and that came from, but to let her tell me what she had to say. I fell in with this.'

Following her rhythm, allowing her lively memory to dictate whether they would have something to work on or not, Freud ended up in a situation where 'her hypnoses soon ceased to produce material.' Since her condition had improved so markedly, so that she felt better than at any time since her husband's death, Freud allowed her to return home to Switzerland. But the improvement in her symptoms did not last. While Fanny was in the nursing home under Freud's supervision in May and June 1889, her elder daughter Fanny had developed symptoms not unlike her mother's, and had also required gynaecological attention, which she had received from a doctor, probably Rudolf Chrobak, whom Freud had recommended to her mother. Recurrence of the trouble when the family returned to Switzerland led to a severe nervous illness, and her mother was now blaming herself as well as Freud and the other doctors for this unfortunate turn of events. 'By an act of will as it were', she relapsed. She turned to another doctor in another sanatorium, but her condition worsened until a woman friend secretly abducted her away. In 1890 she returned to Freud for further treatment.

The renewed work proceeded well, eliminating the traumatic incidents that had taken place since the year before, including an incident that hinted at an erotic dimension to Fanny's inner life. The after-effects of her stormy battles with the physician at the sanatorium were particularly prominent. The final incident in her brief treatment on this second visit to Vienna proved very instructive to Freud in his growing dissatisfaction with suggestive hypnotism, and is equally instructive to us in indicating how authoritative he felt he should be as a doctor.

Freud discovered that Fanny was eating very little and drinking no water. He immediately brought his will to bear in an effort to get her to eat and drink, but to no avail: 'the furious look she cast at me convinced me that she was in open rebellion and that the situation was very grave.' In his effort to have his way, Freud put their future relationship on the line: he threatened to leave if she did not accept within twenty-four hours that it was her fear, rather than her constitution, which made it impossible for her to eat and drink normally. Give up your symptom, or give up your masterly doctor! His threat worked; the next day, she was 'docile and submissive', adding, however, '"but only because you say so."' But Freud already knew that 'a promise like this, based only on her obedience to me, never met with any success, any more than did the many general injunctions which I laid upon her'. So he immediately put her under hypnosis and investigated the psychical history of the origin of the symptom – her reasons for not eating and drinking. He discovered a whole chain of memories relating to disgust at mealtimes: for instance, how her severe mother had forced her to eat up the food she had been given long after mealtimes, when the fat was congealed on it. 'The therapeutic effect of these discoveries under hypnosis was immediate and lasting.' Freud had succeeded where Fanny's mother had failed. 'Growing stout' and drinking water became the index of Freud's success in the letters she wrote him after she had left Vienna.

It was the experience of getting essentially nowhere with Fanny's anorexia when he attempted, as he had been taught by Bernheim, to gain control over her with suggestion that prompted grave doubts in him about the power of suggestion. By wanting, in fact needing, to tell him all the details of the traumatic memories and incidents, Fanny was putting a brake on his authoritarian tendencies, but was also showing him the clear superiority of 'psychical analysis' – of the discovery of the memories of disgusting incidents – in comparison with suggestion.

Freud, however, was by no means free of the impulse to demonstrate his power over Fanny. Certainly, at the beginning of the treatment, he conceived of himself as active and authoritative : Fanny 'entertained' him with pictures, with incidents. His therapy then consisted in 'wiping away', 'expunging', 'wiping out' and 'prohibiting' her pathogenic memories, to the point where he regarded it as a victory when she could no longer recall them, even under hypnosis. Then, too, throughout the treatment he continued to give her lessons in hygienic mental management, for example : 'there is a whole multitude of indifferent, small things lying between what is good and what is evil – things about which no one need reproach himself.' Sometimes he even tried shaming her out of her symptoms ; or on one occasion of frightening her out of her fear. He grew to realize only gradually and never completely that these lessons were often worse than useless. Nor could he resist playing all sorts of tricks on her to convince himself and her of the efficacy of hypnosis. Indeed, the final pages of the case history recount three such tricks, which show Freud to have been very keen to demonstrate the stupidity, cruder hypnotic skills and less amicable effectiveness of the other doctors who had tended to Fanny. He was using his patient to make fun of other doctors ; but it was certainly at Fanny's expense, as Breuer quickly pointed out to Freud.

Freud saw Fanny one more time after her second visit to Vienna, when in the spring of 1891 she asked him to visit her at her castle in Switzerland and give her his opinion on her elder daughter's nervous condition. Fanny also manifested a new symptom, a phobia about trains, which Freud, in his self-confident way, took to be designed to prevent her travelling to Vienna for treatment with him, a proto-transference interpretation. It was at this time that he played another trick on Fanny, one which had a sensible aim, but was equally manipulative of her, and in a quite specifically personal way. He put her into hypnosis in order to deal with the phobic inhibition, whereupon

she expressed a fear that in future she was likely to be less obedient under hypnosis than before. I determined to convince her of the contrary. I wrote a few words on a piece of paper, handed it to her and said : 'At lunch today you will pour me a glass of red wine, just as you did yesterday. As I raise the glass to my lips you will say : "Oh, please pour me out a glass, too", and when I reach for the bottle, you will say : "No thank you, I don't think I will after all." You will then put your hand in your bag, draw out the piece of paper and find those same words written on it.' This was in the morning. A few hours later the little episode took place exactly as I had pre-arranged it, and so naturally that none of the many people present noticed anything. When she asked me for the wine she showed visible signs of an internal struggle – for she never drank wine – and after she had refused the drink with obvious relief, she put her hand in her bag and drew out the piece of paper on which appeared the last words she had spoken. She shook her head and stared at me in astonishment.

It is on this note that Freud left Fanny: having reasserted both the powers of suggestion and the intimacy of his relationship with her 'so naturally that none of the many people present noticed anything.' And he knew that her avoidance of drinking wine was a worthy adversary in such a contest of wills; when Fanny died, her obituaries noted that amongst the many philanthropic causes she supported she was especially devoted to the temperance movement.

Yet even Freud had forgotten one of the post-hypnotic time-bombs he had implanted in Fanny, one which, at her own request in 1890, had given him exclusive hypnotic rights over her, so that she would not come under the control of a doctor who was antipathetic to her. In the summer of 1893, Fanny wrote to Freud asking for his permission for her to be hypnotized by another doctor. 'I accordingly renounced my exclusive prerogative in writing.'

The narrative account of Freud's treatment of Fanny ends on this knowing note, with Freud seemingly still in control, at a distance, and also ironically aware how much the power of suggestion places him in the role of an ex-lover. Indeed, in 1890, the same year as he treated Fanny for the second time, he had published an article which lauded hypnosis precisely because of the way it mimicked and drew on the most profound emotional resources of human relations:

outside hypnosis and in real life, credulity such as the subject has in relation to his hypnotist is shown only by a child towards his beloved parents, and that an attitude of similar subjection on the part of one person towards another has only one parallel, though a complete one – namely in certain love-relationships where there is extreme devotion. A combination of exclusive attachment and credulous obedience is in general among the characteristics of love.

Yet the case history and Fanny's later life provides some grounds for doubting how justified Freud's knowingness was. In a note added to the 1925 *Gesammelte Schriften* edition of the case history, Freud wrote that 'no analyst can read this case history to-day without a smile of pity.' He then attempted to rectify the inadequacies of the account by pointing to the factor underlying the whole case, which he had only discovered at the time of his final visit to Fanny's castle:

When … I spent a few days as Frau Emmy's guest in her country house, there was a stranger present at one of the meals who clearly tried to make himself agreeable. After his departure my hostess asked me how I had liked him and added as it were in passing: 'Only imagine, the man wants to marry me!' When I took this in connection with some other remarks which she had made, but to which I had not paid sufficient attention, I was led to conclude that *she was longing at that time to be married again but found an obstacle to the realization of her purpose in the existence of her two daughters, who were the heiresses of their father's fortune.*

This longing, this wish which in retrospect constituted the 'immediate aetiology of the illness', ties together three themes: sexuality, daughters, inheritance. It is the conflict involving these that Freud implies he was blind to at the time. Other evidence about Fanny's life indicates that he was correct about her sexual needs. As Ola Andersson established, Fanny's energetic salon life in the *Schloss* to which she had moved in 1887 also included her taking a succession of lovers, frequently the personal physicians whom she had live in the house. She was discreet about these affairs and impressed many with her moral earnestness, but her daughters were not alone in knowing of these affairs. People in the neighbourhood remembered her particularly for her erotic extravagance.

What is curious is the slow, almost reluctant way in which Freud began to realize that, despite the close understanding they had developed, his view of Fanny was at best partial, since she had an immense capacity for keeping secrets. She kept hidden from Freud for some while the extent of her social and intellectual connections: 'She described her life on her estate and her contacts with prominent men … and I really found it extremely hard to reconcile activities of this kind with the picture of such a severely neurotic woman.' When Freud visited her castle in 1891, he discovered that 'her dislike … of saying anything about herself was so great, that, as I noticed to my astonishment … none of the daily visitors to her house recognized that she was ill or were aware that I was her doctor.' On this visit, Freud sized up her well-organized life:

During the several days which I spent in her house I came for the first time to realize the whole extent of her duties, occupations and intellectual interests. I also met the house physician [*Hausarzt*], who had not too many complaints to make about the lady; so she had to some degree come to terms [*ausgesöhnt*] with the profession.

Freud was obviously an admirer of Fanny Moser's, on seeing her in situ. But he had always been such an admirer, right from the start of his relationship with her, as comments throughout the case history indicate.

Frau Emmy von N. gave us [Breuer and myself] an example of how hysteria is compatible with an unblemished character and a well-governed mode of life. The woman we came to know was an admirable one. The moral seriousness with which she viewed her duties, her intelligence and energy, which were no less than a man's, and her high degree of education and love of truth impressed both of us greatly; while her benevolent care for the welfare of all her dependents, her humility of mind and the refinement of her manners revealed her qualities as a true lady as well.

Yet he also ascribed her disposition to neurosis to these very fine qualities; she appeared to Freud as one of those fine women who fall ill of their virtues, including that ambiguous virtue, 'the natural helplessness of a woman':

[h]er feelings were very intense; she was of a vehement nature, capable of the

strongest passions ... since her husband's death, she had lived in complete mental solitude; her persecution by her relatives had made her suspicious of friends and she was jealously on guard against anyone acquiring too much influence over her actions. The circle of her duties was very wide, and she performed the whole of the mental work which they imposed on her by herself, without a friend or confidant, almost isolated from her family and handicapped by her conscientiousness, her tendency to tormenting herself and often, too, by the natural helplessness of a woman.

Such an attitude of respect and of almost awed admiration probably encouraged Freud to overlook signs that there were other sides to Fanny. To start with, he came 'fresh from the school of Charcot, and I regarded the linking of hysteria with the topic of sexuality as a sort of insult – just as the women patients themselves do'. In retrospect, he realized that not only had he not sought out, but he had been given no hint by Fanny, even under deep hypnosis, of the sexual side of her life; he evoked a picture of himself as having luxuriated in being treated by Fanny like a well-brought-up boy, who is too young to know of such things: 'what I was allowed to hear was no doubt an *editio in usum delphini* of her life-story.' The Delphin edition of the Latin classics was an expurgated version prepared for the use of the Dauphin, son of Louis XIV. In using this metaphor, Freud was, not entirely inappropriately, painting himself as a young and innocent man, sequestered in a castle and deprived of knowing what the adults did when he was not present. He continued:

I cannot help suspecting that this woman who was so passionate and so capable of strong feelings had not won her victory over her sexual needs without severe struggles, and that at times her attempts at suppressing this most powerful of all instincts had exposed her to severe mental exhaustion. She once admitted to me that she had not married again because, in view of her large fortune, she could not credit the disinterestedness of her suitors and because she would have reproached herself for damaging the prospects of her two children by a new marriage.

Freud was so impressed by the moral character of his patient that he assumed that she had indeed 'won her victory over her sexual needs'; in his discussion of her case, he went to the other extreme from that of Charcot, finding the cause of her neurosis in this Pyrrhic victory: 'It is necessary, I think, to adduce a *neurotic* factor to account for this persistence [of her symptoms] – the fact that the patient had been living for years in a state of sexual abstinence.'

We do not know when Fanny started her succession of affairs with her live-in lovers. They may well have begun after the end of her analysis with Freud, though it would almost certainly be over-emphasizing the importance of Freud to speculate that they were instigated by that brief episode. But we might allow ourselves the speculation that it was precisely because he was located as the object of a potential sexual liaison – a liaison between the aristocratic, abstinent widow and the considerate and authoritative physician – that Freud would so readily assume his patients to be abstinent, and desiring *because* they were abstinent, once he began to think that his patients' symptoms were generated by sexual desire. Faced with a desiring woman, he too quickly infers she is sexually abstinent, as if desire only flows from abstinence. Such an assumption is linked to another that he was later to be instrumental in questioning: that innocence implies lack of desire, and that desire implies the loss of innocence.

What might have come to Freud's consciousness first was his awareness of and sympathy for the moral struggles associated with abstinence. Certainly, Freud failed to perceive that Fanny was quite capable of finding a satisfactory compromise between the pressure of her sexual needs, the pain of her symptoms and her duty towards her dependents, chiefly her daughters – a compromise that did not require abstinence. By avoiding marriage, she safeguarded the inheritance of her daughters, and in Freud's eyes, then, her moral superiority stemmed from her placing her daughters' interests in the inheritance above her own sexual needs. But conforming to the noble self-denying ideal that Freud painted was not the only way of safeguarding her daughters' inheritance.

It is in keeping with the family drama Freud had reconstructed that he next heard from the family some twenty-five years later, consulted as an expert legal witness over that inheritance. In 1918, the elder daughter asked him for a report on her mother's mental condition. Fanny, now seventy, had fallen in love with a man much younger than herself, whom she wanted, after having resisted all this time, to marry. Eventually, and despite, rather than because of, the protestations of her entourage, she realized that he did not love her and that he was in the process of defrauding her. The elder daughter wished to deprive her mother of legal authority over her estate and, as Freud wrote, 'was intending to take legal proceedings against her mother, whom she represented as a cruel and ruthless tyrant. It seems that she had broken off relations with both her children and refused to assist them in their financial difficulties.'

Freud, the doctor whose first medical act in 1889 had been to separate the mother from her daughters, had never had a high opinion of the daughters while he was treating their mother. He had quickly come to view the elder daughter's nervous symptoms as manifestations of a 'pathological disposition which was to manifest itself a year later in a character-change', severely professional language which he refrained from applying to her mother without considerable respectful and admiring qualification. And when in 1891 he was invited by Fanny to give his opinion of the daughter at her *Schloss*, he found that 'she exhibited unbridled ambitions which were out of all proportion to the poverty of her gifts, and she became disobedient and even violent towards her mother ... I formed an unfavourable impression of the psychological change that had occurred in the girl....' What news of Fanny that Freud heard via the grapevine pointed the accusing finger at this daughter: 'her daughter's deplorable condition, which caused her every kind of distress and agitation, did eventually undermine her health.'

Others in Fanny's circle described the daughter as 'beautiful and intelligent and the pride of her mother'. But a break between mother and daughter followed the daughter's determination to receive a scientific education. Was Freud in 1891 being called in to adjudicate as pathological this desire of the daughter? Were these 'unbridled ambitions' the nineteen year old's desire to be a doctor? There is an historical inconsistency here, since the younger daughter Mentona remembered her mother as giving the elder daughter permission to study medicine on the basis of Freud's advice; it is even possible that the opening up of access to education and interests in the wider, masculine world was sufficient in itself to cure the daughter of her symptoms, as is documented in other cases. Whatever the course of events, even Freud might have felt twenty years later that his original judgment against the daughter had been hasty and unduly biased, when he noted that the daughter on whom he had pronounced such an unfavourable prognosis 'had obtained a doctor's degree and was married'. However, his 1918 reply to this medical colleague, this litigious daughter, shows the strength of his loyalty to Fanny Moser and his high estimate of her character – his fidelity, one might almost say – after nearly thirty years:

Your mother's behaviour towards you and your sister is far from being as enigmatical to me at it is to you. I can offer you the simple solution that she loved her children just as tenderly as she also hated them bitterly (what we term ambivalence), and that this was so already then – in Vienna. By nature your mother was a highly estimable, serious, and morally austere woman who was guided by the strictest sense of duty – it is [quite?] possible that this noble character was ruined by the unsolved conflicts of her life.

There was no question of Freud, thirty years on, siding with the daughters against the mother; his responsibility still lay with his ex-patient. The elder daughter, the addressee of this letter, was, he implied, still one of those unsolved conflicts. And she was still one of those conflicts, not only because she was a daughter, but also because she was a doctor. As Freud intimated in his case history, and as we can infer from our additional information about her style of life, Fanny's relations with the medical profession were always fraught and passionate.

A few years later at a Scientific Congress I met a prominent physician from Frau Emmy's part of the country. [She] had gone through the same performance with him – and with many other doctors – as she had with me. Her condition had become very bad; she had rewarded his hypnotic treatment of her by making a remarkable recovery, but had then suddenly quarrelled with him, left him, and once more set her illness going to its full extent. It was a genuine instance of the 'compulsion to repeat'.

Her daughter may well have been implicated in this compulsion, despite her having become a doctor precisely in part to recover, we might speculate, the love and attention her mother bestowed elsewhere and in secret. By 1895, Freud might well have had this reconstruction of Fanny's behaviour in mind when he wrote to Fliess: 'There are two kinds of women patients: one kind who are as loyal to their doctor as to their husband, and the other kind who change their doctors as often as their lovers.'

If we draw up the inventory of this early analytic episode, we are struck by Freud's attentiveness to the doctor–patient relationship, even when he is abusing it with his tricks and his pride in the shaman-like power granted him over his patients. What we fail to find is an equal attention granted to Fanny's relations with her daughters. A few days after beginning Fanny's treatment, Freud had asked her under hypnosis what event in her life had produced the most lasting effect on her. She replied, her husband's death. He encouraged her to describe the event in full detail, which she did. Without a break, she went from describing her husband's death into a litany of grievances against the baby whom she blamed for his death, the younger daughter: how she had been odd for a long time, how she screamed and didn't sleep, how she developed an incurable paralysis, how she had had visions at the age of four, how she had for a long time thought her an imbecile, how she had encephalitis and inflammation of the spinal cord ... At this point Freud had interrupted. He pointed out that this same girl was now a normal girl in the bloom of health. 'I made it impossible for her to see any of these melancholy things again, not only by wiping out her memories of them in their *plastic* form but by removing her whole recollection of them, as though they had never been present in her mind.' Freud came to regret this hasty act, not only because he later discovered that interrupting her in this overbearing manner only postponed his having to hear her out, but also because 'when I saw Frau Emmy again in a relatively good state of health, she complained that there were a number of most important moments in her life of which she had only the vaguest memory. ... I had to be careful not to tell her the cause of this particular instance of amnesia.'

Yet any regret at this tampering with her sense of the past he might feel was tempered by his belief that this wiping out of her memories of her husband's death, of her early resentments against her daughter and of her conviction that there was something seriously wrong with her was the reason for her good health. The unsolved conflicts of her life, over her sexuality and her daughters, arose precisely because she represented her situation to Freud (or he represented her as representing it to him) as being an insoluble dilemma of the form '*either* sexual satisfaction *or* dutiful care of my daughters'. All these conflicts were concentrated in a pure form in this, the most important event of her life, the birth of her daughter and the death of her husband. And it was precisely this event whose details Freud had not even let her finish recounting and had then conveniently – for him – wiped away.

Once Fanny had broken with her young lover in 1918, she lived for another six years, suffering for much of the time from the delusion that she was destitute, that she would not be able to buy her next meal, even though some millions of her fortune remained after her lover had plundered it. When she died, the prominence of her obituary owed much to her extravagant philanthropy and to her generosity to individual artists and other talented persons in need.

The story of Fanny's daughters – the two daughters whose relevance for the mother's saga was so early on deliberately excluded by Freud – is a telling fable. The elder, Fanny, who became a doctor and then a research zoologist, published authoritative monographs on the development of the lung in vertebrates. However, following a series of spectacularly impressive occult experiences which broke down her scepticism, she devoted the second part of her scientific career to investigating parapsychology and reports of ghosts. She died in Zurich in 1953. The younger daughter, Mentona, rebelled directly against the stifling comfort and privilege of her upbringing. In 1903, she published a pamphlet entitled 'The Upbringing of Women of the Upper Classes: Considerations and Recommendations', a vehement attack on the education given to girls from rich families. Taking Florence Nightingale as a model, she urged young girls to seize control of their own lives, to educate themselves about the social world and the nature of poverty. She became involved in social work as a radical and a militant, joining the Swiss Communist Party in 1919 and moving to the USSR in 1926, where she founded a home for abandoned children in 1928. Later she moved to East Berlin, where she lived to her death at the age of ninety-six. All we know of her personal life is that she married, had two children and was later divorced. Thus, between them, the two daughters' careers symbolized two very different paths open to the generation that followed their stifled neurotic mothers: the path of assimilation to the masculine professional and scientific world, and the path of feminist protest, of struggle and of dedicated social work. Freud's later career was to bring him into close contact with women following both paths, of whom the classic instance is Helene Deutsch; but psychoanalysis itself was to provide Deutsch and others of these women with an ideal means of leaving the values and neuroses of their mothers behind.

Katharina: An Idyllic Case

The Alpine inn-keeper's daughter, Aurelia Kronich, was a very different sort of patient from the wealthy salon hostesses, Fanny Moser and Anna von Lieben. It is hardly surprising then that Freud was elated to find that his theories applied perfectly to her as well: 'it was a nice case for me'. So nice that Freud thought fit to include it as one of the four case histories he contributed to the *Studies on Hysteria*. Thus it was that this inn-keeper's daughter, whom Freud conversed with on top of a 6,000-foot mountain one August day in 1893, became a demonstration of the radical new therapy and theory of hysteria he and Breuer were putting forward. The elegance of the case history, so much more like a novella than any other case, must have been part of what persuaded Freud to include it.

Yet in the writing of the case history, Freud's virtuosity in matching the polish of fictional prose incorporated one startlingly anomalous fictional element of its own. The chief protagonists of the case history were portrayed as being Katharina, as Freud christened his patient, and her uncle and aunt's family, whereas in reality Katharina's seducer was her father, not her uncle, and it was her parents' marriage that fell apart as a result of the events that also led to Katharina's neurosis. In 1924, in a footnote added to the edition of the *Studies* prepared for inclusion in his *Gesammelte Schriften*, Freud disowned this fictionalizing of Katharina's family structure with the dry comment: 'From the point of view of understanding the case, a distortion of this kind is not, of course, a matter of such indifference as would be shifting the scene from one mountain to another.' In 1895, however, it was the idyllic mountain backdrop and the enviable simplicity of his explanation for Aurelia's symptoms that most impressed Freud. The Freud of 1924 had a considered view of what was and was not indifferent; but we are tempted to infer that, for the Freud of 1895, it was not a matter of great significance that the sexual transgressions and precocious sexual disgust of the inn-keeper's servant resulted from the seductions of her father rather than her uncle.

The story of Freud and Aurelia begins with Freud climbing, with his friend Oscar Rie, to the newly opened Ottohaus, an inn on the Rax mountain some fifty kilometres from Vienna. At the inn, the young girl who had served them lunch told Freud that her nerves were bad and how, as so often with Freud's cases, she had been failed by one of his medical colleagues. The self-description of her symptoms allowed Freud to diagnose her as suffering from recurrent anxiety attacks, or, more correctly, from a hysterical attack the content of which was anxiety, together with a hallucination of an unknown face. Freud describes himself as pondering whether to take the plunge and analyse her, but it is clear that he relished the prospect of trying out his theories on this untutored girl of eighteen. He had a very clear idea of what might lie behind her attacks: 'I had found often enough that in girls anxiety was a consequence of the horror by which a virginal mind is overcome when it is faced for the first time with the world of sexuality.'

The words he used to communicate this hunch to the girl are interesting for what they tell us about Freud's sense of propriety: 'you must have seen or heard something that very much embarrassed you, and that you'd much rather not have seen.' This overture worked most efficiently: the girl told him about an incident some two years before when she was sixteen. She had been searching for her cousin Barbara, who was supposed to make some visiting gentlemen their lunch, and had found her in her father's room, on the bed. He was lying on top of her. This was the moment when 'everything went blank, my eyelids were forced together and there was a hammering and buzzing in my head.'

Three days later, Aurelia took to her bed and was sick without stopping for three days. Freud, according to his rule of thumb, translated this being sick as meaning disgust. He put this to her; she agreed, but could not work out why she was disgusted. Freud had no idea either, but told her to 'say whatever occurred to her, in the confident expectation that she would think of precisely what I needed to explain the case.' She then recounted how she had told her mother about what she had seen; how there had been terrible scenes between her parents, and her mother had eventually moved out with the children into the inn they were presently occupying. She then produced two further sets of memories. The first was of her father having 'made sexual advances to her, herself, when she was only fourteen years old.' '[F]rom the way in which she reported having defended herself it seems to follow that she did not clearly recognize the attack as a sexual one. When I asked her if she knew what he was trying to do to her, she replied: "Not at the time."' The second was of goings on between her father and Barbara, which she had noticed but which had not aroused her suspicions.

With the recounting of these older memories, Aurelia was transformed: 'The sulky, unhappy face had grown lively, her eyes were bright, she was lightened and exalted.' And Freud also was satisfied: he understood clearly what had happened to her:

So when she had finished her confession I said to her: 'I know now what it was you thought when you looked into the room. You thought: "Now he's doing with her what he wanted to do with me that night and those other times." That was what you were disgusted at, because you remembered the feeling when you woke up in the night and felt his body.'

'It could well be,' she replied, 'that that was what I was disgusted at and that was what I thought.'

Yet Freud was not quite satisfied:

'Tell me just one thing. What part of his body was it that you felt that night?' But she gave me no more definite answer. She smiled in an embarrassed way, as though she had been found out, like someone who is obliged to admit that we had now got to the bottom of everything, where there is not much more to be said. I could imagine what the tactile sensation was which she had later learnt to interpret; her facial expression seemed to me to be saying that she presumed that I was thinking along the right lines, but I could not penetrate further; as it is I owed her a debt of gratitude for having made it so much easier for me to talk to her than to the prudish ladies of my city practice, who regard what is natural as shameful [naturalia turpia].

The anxiety was now satisfactorily explained, but the hallucinated face was still an enigma. Aurelia now told Freud that it was her father's enraged face, enraged as he had become since the break-up of the marriage for which he blamed her. And Aurelia was certainly still haunted by at least this piece of paternal forcefulness, since she had told Freud 'it's my fault they were divorced' as she started to recount her memory of discovering her father in bed with her cousin. Indeed, this hallucinated face was the ghost of the marriage, her way of keeping the marriage alive, perhaps. Freud saw it as having been generated after Aurelia had told her mother about her father's earlier attempts to make love to her. Her mother had replied in a rather callous way: 'We'll keep that in reserve. If he causes trouble in the Court, we'll say that too.' As Freud put it, this face had become a mnemic symbol, the product of the period when her own state ceased to interest her mother, who was entirely preoccupied with the dispute. It was Aurelia who had provoked the open hostility between her parents, and it was Aurelia who was being held in store as further ammunition in the fight her mother was caught up in waging with her father. We now know that the case never came to court and that her parents never did divorce, although they remained permanently estranged and separated, and that the father paid considerable sums to his wife. It would seem that the mother was successful, whether or not she actually used Aurelia against him.

Yet Freud was not concerned with the dynamics of the family, the disruption this caused for Aurelia, nor with the guilt she felt at being the cause of the marriage's break-up. He had decided from the beginning that Aurelia's attacks stemmed from her being confronted with the world of sexuality; and he did not just mean finding out the facts of life. Being faced with sexuality meant that her own body, her own desires, were implicated. That Freud did mean this is clarified by the footnote he added to the case in 1924, when he revealed that it was not, as he had originally written in 1895, Aurelia's uncle who had attempted to make love to her, but Aurelia's father. There he wrote: 'The girl fell ill, therefore, as a result of sexual temptations which originated from her own father.' Freud's view in 1893, in accordance with the 'Preliminary Communication', was that hysterics suffer from reminiscences. In private, he had tightened up this generalization: hysterics can *only* suffer from reminiscences; only a memory can produce neurotic symptoms. And he was now tightening this up still further: only *sexual* incidents can form the basis of what will become a traumatic memory; any non-sexual incidents can only figure as auxiliary moments. Other events and emotions, such as the young girl's being upset over the upheaval in her own and her parents' lives, or over her own responsibility in the break-up of her parents' marriage, could not by themselves create hysterical symptoms. Only a sexual memory that was revived, that returned from repression, stirred by later events could count as the cause of these symptoms. Thus, the father's assaults on Aurelia when she was fourteen, together with her witnessing the goings-on between her cousin and her father, were the traumatic moments that became effective when they were revived by her coming upon her father lying on top of her cousin in the bedroom. This brief but crystal-clear case supported the view that Freud was now becoming convinced of.

In every analysis of a case of hysteria based on sexual traumas we find that impressions from the pre-sexual epoch which produced no effect on the child attain traumatic power at a later date as memories, when the young girl or married woman has acquired an understanding of sexual life.

For Freud, a present-day experience could never be pathogenic, no matter how distressing it was. Only memories could create neuroses. And here he was, on top of an Austrian mountain far from the noxious environment of city and of civilization, with an *Alpenkind*, who showed him that even here memories of family life could provide a fertile ground for neurosis.

Freud's discretion in toning down the incestuous dimension of his case history of Aurelia, by making her seducer her uncle, not her father, led to distortions of the family structure that can now, Aurelia having been identified by the recent detective work of Peter Swales, Gerhard Fichtner and Albrecht Hirschmüller, be undone. Aurelia, born on 9 January 1875, was the second of the five children of Julius and Gertrude (*née* Göschl) Kronich. Her parents had worked in Vienna, in a number of different occupations, including running a coffee stall, in the 1870s. Then, in 1884–5, they took up the tenancy of the Hotel zum Baumgartner, located two-thirds of the way up the Schneeberg, and made good use of the father's interest and skill in mountain climbing, and the mother's family tradition of cooking and inn-keeping. With a certain business acumen, they soon became 'a show-business family' in a 'highly visible world of Alpine-folkloric make-believe'. The hotel acquired an excellent reputation and the family prospered, as the Schneeberg and the Rax, its twin just across the valley, became the popular resort of the Viennese, amongst whom the Freuds and many in their circle were to be counted; they could now, with the building of the Semmering railway, gain easy access to them in their search for the Alpine idyll of clean air, mountain walking and respite from the summer heat. In early 1893, a new mountain lodge was opened on the Rax, and, in her need to get free of her philandering husband, Gertrude Kronich secured its tenancy as of 1 April and moved there with all her children. This hotel, the Ottohaus, was the scene of Aurelia's consultation with Freud, across the valley from the scene of her father's infidelities with Barbara Göschl, the cousin who had moved in with the family in 1890 or 1891, when she was twenty-five. After the family rows following on Aurelia's confiding to her mother what she had seen, her father and Barbara lived as husband and wife in the old Baumgartnerhaus, where Barbara gave birth to two children, in 1896 and 1897. Aurelia turned down one, quite well-off suitor sometime in 1894 or 1895, but fell in love with Julius Öhm, a local forest manager; they married on 26 September 1895 and moved to the estates of Julius's employer 300 miles away in Hungary. Their first child was born in 1896, and five others followed over the period from 1897 to 1905. Whilst her marriage was happy, Aurelia felt isolated in Hungary. She returned each summer to the Ottohaus on the Rax, which was taken over by her brother in 1903, and she died there, suddenly, on 3 September 1929 of a heart attack probably brought on by an excess of morphine the local doctor prescribed for her extreme pain.

That Sigmund Freud had entered into the family mythology, despite Aurelia keeping quiet about both her father's sexual assaults and her brief mountain-top consultation with Freud, is proved by an improbable story Aurelia's daughter, Gisela, recounted, having heard it from her grandmother Gertrude. Gisela, at the time five or six, was living at the Baumgartnerhaus with her grandmother, who had taken over the tenancy again, when her husband left in 1903. Gisela was overtaken by a great fever and awful pains in her stomach, and Freud, who happened to be touring in the vicinity, acted as her doctor, spending forty-eight hours at her bedside. What is less mythological is the consultation that Aurelia's son had with Freud in 1919 or 1920; invalided out of the army following a grenade explosion during the war, he was placed in a private asylum in Döbling by Freud. Certainly these stories indicate that

Freud had his place in Aurelia's family romance, just as Aurelia found her place as perhaps the most romantic of all Freud's case histories: the *Alpenkind* whom Freud cured in an afternoon's chat overlooking the scene of the crime. She may also have owed her place in *Studies on Hysteria* not only to the virtues of her crystal-clear case, but also to the literary brilliance which this parallel evocation of the screen-memory of his childhood, in which the young Sigismund and his nephew robbed the little Pauline of the beautiful flowers she had picked from an Alpine meadow, inspired in her physician.

Elisabeth von R.: 'The First Full-Length Analysis'

An 'unhappy story of this proud girl with her longing for love' is how Freud described the case of Ilona Weiss, to whom he gave the pseudonym Fräulein Elisabeth von R. He was called in to see this young woman because of the chronic pains she suffered from in her legs and an attendant difficulty she had in walking. Together with a physician colleague – probably Breuer – Freud entered into what he called a preliminary period of treatment: they suspected that her condition would respond to psychical treatment, but did not want to overlook organic causes of her pains. The four weeks of 'pretence treatment' consisted in kneading and electrical stimulation of her muscles, while 'my colleague was preparing the ground for psychical treatment', to which, when it was proposed to her, she readily assented. Even before the psychical treatment had begun, however, Freud had perceived an erotic dimension to her leg pains: 'Her face assumed a peculiar expression, one of pleasure rather than of pain; she cried out – somewhat, I could not help thinking, as with a voluptuous tickling – her face flushed, she threw back her head, closed her eyes, her trunk bent backward.' It was, in addition, the indefiniteness of her pain, despite her being 'a highly intelligent person', and her reluctance to complain about her chronic condition, that encouraged Freud in thinking that he was dealing with a hysterical pain, in other words that there were traumatic memories and affects associated with them encased in her muscular pain. All these signs made Freud reasonably convinced that the unhappy young lady was nursing a secret behind a mask of stoical indifference. He was determined to tear away the mask and reveal it. The process of tearing away the mask proceeded systematically: Freud did without hypnosis and developed a regular method for the elucidation of her symptoms. It was this advance that justified him in calling Ilona's treatment 'the first full-length analysis of a hysteria undertaken by me'.

The youngest of three daughters of a well-born Hungarian family, Ilona had a very close relationship with her father,

who used to say that this daughter of his took the place of a son and a friend with whom he could exchange thoughts. Although the girl's mind found intellectual stimulation from this relationship with her father, he did not fail to observe that her mental constitution was on that account departing from the ideal which people like to see realized in a girl. He jokingly called her 'cheeky' and 'cock-sure', and warned her against being too positive in her judgements and against her habit of regardlessly telling people the truth, and he often said she would find it hard to get a husband. She was in fact greatly discontented with being a girl. She was full of ambitious plans.

Ilona wanted to study and was indignant at having her desires curtailed by marriage; instead, she turned in on her family and 'nourished herself on her pride in her father and in the prestige and social position of her family'. A few years before Freud saw Ilona, her father had fallen ill of a chronic and fatal heart ailment: it was Ilona who nursed him to the end. Her pains in her legs began at this time, though it was not until two years after he died that she became incapable of walking.

A year after his death, her eldest sister married a man who showed little consideration for the family. Not long after, her other sister entered into an arranged marriage, but this time the new brother-in-law seemed to Ilona to be a model of what she, distrustful of the institution of marriage and the sacrifices it required of women, hoped for in a husband. Ilona became very attached to their first-born child. However, her mother fell ill and, in the summer months when all three families hoped for her recovery in their idyllic communal summer resort, Ilona's pains increased considerably. 'From this time on Elisabeth [Ilona] was the invalid of the family.' She took a course of treatment at a spa, but was then called urgently to her middle sister, who, pregnant again, was acutely ill. When she arrived, she found her sister dead of heart disease aggravated by the pregnancy.

In her pain at this new loss, Ilona as well as her mother turned against the widowed brother-in-law, in part blaming this man for endangering his wife's life with a rapid second pregnancy. He in turn drew apart from his deceased wife's family, and Ilona suspected, without firm evidence, that he was making unreasonable financial demands on them. Such was the situation in which she came to Freud. He painted her predicament in sombre colours:

Unreconciled to her fate, embittered by the failure of all her little schemes for re-establishing the family's former glories, with those she loved dead or gone away or estranged, unready to take refuge in the love of some unknown man – she had lived for eighteen months in almost complete seclusion, with nothing to occupy her but the care of her mother and her own pains.

It looked as if this high-spirited and independent-minded girl had been dealt a bad hand in the game of life, and that the doctor could not hope to rectify this; she expected nothing either from her physical or her psychical treatment, and Freud was inclined to agree with her that he could help neither with her pains nor with the hardships of her life:

If we put greater misfortunes on one side and enter into a girl's feelings, we cannot refrain from deep human sympathy with Fräulein Elisabeth. ... As far as the physician was concerned, the patient's confession was at first sight a great disappointment. ... During this first period of her treatment she never failed to repeat that she was still feeling ill, and that her pains were as bad as ever; and, when she looked at me as she said this with sly look of satisfaction at my discomfiture, I could not help being reminded of old Herr von R.'s judgement about his favourite daughter – that she was often 'cheeky' and 'ill-behaved'. But I was obliged to admit that she was in the right.

At this point in Ilona's treatment, then, Freud had reached exactly the same point he was to reach later in the case of Dora, when she was to tell him about the transactions and complex jugglings to which she had been made party. As Jacques Lacan put it in his commentary on the 'Dora' case:

he is faced with the question, which is moreover classical in the first stage of a treatment: 'This is all perfectly correct and true, isn't it? What do you want to change in it?' To which Freud's reply is: ... 'Look at your own involvement,' he tells her, 'in the disorder which you bemoan.'

In every case, there is a crucial moment (or moments) when Freud turns the patient's narrative against her in the interests of discovering how it is not only the cruel hands of fate and family that have made her story one of hardship and victimization, but how she has implicated herself in the construction of her tale. Freud was never one to think of his patients as mere victims of circumstance. With Ilona, this consisted in Freud stating his unshaken conviction that he would eventually find the deeper determinants of her symptoms, and, as we will see, in his conviction that an erotic conflict would figure as such a determinant. No matter how convincing the seeming ineluctable character of the events that had led her to this predicament, they must press on – quite literally:

I carried this out by instructing the patient to report to me faithfully whatever appeared before her inner eye or passed through her memory at the moment of the pressure [of his hand on her head]. She remained silent for a long time and then, on my insistence, admitted that she had thought of an evening on which a young man had seen her home after a party. ...

This was the secret Freud was looking for: her hopes of this young man, her warm feelings towards him and the gradual fading of her hopes, 'this disappointment in her first love'.

It was therefore in this relationship and in the scene [of her return from the party to her father's sick-bed] that I could look for the causes of her first hysterical pains. The contrast between the blissful feelings she had allowed herself to enjoy on that occasion and the worsening of her father's state which had met her on her return home constituted a conflict, a situation of incompatibility. The outcome of this conflict was that the erotic idea was repressed from association and the affect attaching to that idea was used to intensify or revive a physical pain which was present simultaneously or shortly before.

Despite Freud's assurance, there is a hint here of him clutching at a straw. He eagerly seized on this erotic conflict as the cause of her pain; yet her pains did not disappear, nor did the story quite make sense to Freud himself. None the less, following his conviction that her secret lay in an erotic conflict of this sort, a second and more fruitful period of the treatment opened. Her pains 'joined in the conversation', responding to the eliciting of her memories.

Freud actively incited her memories by 'getting her into situations' which would evoke emotional memories: going to parties where she would meet her first love, visiting her sister's grave. And her pains were gradually alleviated, as they worked through her distressing memories of her father's final sickness. Using the pressure technique and employing the coming and going of her pains as indicators of their progress, Freud acquired an absolute conviction that each and every one of her leg pains could be resolved through eliciting her memories. In this way, her condition markedly improved, but her pains remained and Freud still did not know their true origin. Obviously the erotic conflict over her young man was not the final answer; Freud began to suspect another, deeper conflict, also of an erotic nature.

One day while I was working with the patient, I heard a man's footsteps in the next room and a pleasant voice which seemed to be asking some question. My patient thereupon got up and asked that we might break off for the day: she had heard her brother-in-law arrive and enquire for her. Up to that point she had been free from pain, but after the interruption her facial expression and gait betrayed the sudden emergence of severe pains. My suspicion was strengthened by this and I determined to precipitate the decisive explanation.

Freud now uncovered how, at the period of the visit to the summer resort just before her sister had died, Ilona had become increasingly despondent about her life, how 'she was now overcome by a sense of her weakness as a woman and by a longing for love in which, to quote her own words, her frozen nature began to melt.' That summer she had spent happy moments getting to know her sister's husband and dreaming on walks of 'finding a husband who would know how to capture her heart like this brother-in-law of hers.' This was the moment when her leg pains suddenly became so acute that she could no longer walk. Then there was the awful journey to her sick sister's bedside, on which she was plagued by increasing pains, only to find her sister dead in an oppressively silent house:

At that moment of dreadful certainty that her beloved sister was dead without bidding them farewell and without her having eased her last days with her care – at that very moment another thought had shot through Elisabeth's mind, and now forced itself irresistibly upon her once more, like a flash of lightning in the dark: 'Now he is free again and I can be his wife.'

Freud was triumphant; he knew now that the erotic conflict was not simply one of ordinary disappointment, but one of a conflict engaging 'her whole moral being'. 'She succeeded in sparing herself the painful conviction that she loved her sister's husband, by inducing physical pains in herself instead.' He now proceeded to convince her, in a decidedly forceful, almost brutal, manner, that this was the only solution that made sense of her history.

She cried aloud when I put the situation drily before her with the words: 'So for a long time you had been in love with your brother-in-law.' She complained at this moment of the most frightful pains, and made one last desperate effort to reject the explanation: it was not true, I had talked her into it, it *could* not be true, she was incapable of such wickedness, she could never forgive herself for it. It was easy to prove to her that what she herself had told me admitted of no other interpretation.

Convinced that he had made the decisive breakthrough of her defences, Freud now conducted his quasi-military campaign on two fronts. The first of these he would later call working-through: going over all the little incidents in her past which could now be given their true significance – reconstructing the history that had been submerged into her physical pain:

On his first visit to the house he [the future brother-in-law] had taken her for the girl he was to marry and had greeted her before her elder but somewhat insignificant-looking sister. One evening they were carrying on such a lively conversation together and seemed to be getting on so well that his fiancée had interrupted them half-seriously with the remark: 'The truth is, you two would have suited each other splendidly.'

His conclusion was that 'her tender feeling for her brother-in-law had been dormant in her for a long time, perhaps even from the beginning of her acquaintance with him, and had lain concealed all that time behind the mask of mere sisterly affection.'

But Freud conducted his campaign on another front as well: 'taking a friendly interest in her present circumstances'. Here he displayed fewer of the talents of the story-teller and problem-solver, more those of the family solicitor and matchmaker. He negotiated with Ilona's mother, clearing away the charges of blackmail that had been laid at the brother-in-law's door, and attempted to persuade the mother to tell her daughter everything concerning these family questions, including, no doubt, those about money, and to take up the role of confessor, the procedure which Ilona had grown accustomed to with Freud. Next Freud turned to the question of finding a suitable match for his patient: 'I was also, of course, anxious to learn what chance there was that the girl's wish, of which she was now conscious, would come true.' Here his negotiations with Ilona's mother proved less fruitful. The mother had also guessed her daughter's fondness for her widowed son-in-law, but she and the family advisers were, for several reasons, reluctant to organize a match between them. Having informed Ilona of his various dealings, both satisfactory and unsatisfactory, with her mother, they brought the analysis to an end. Some weeks later, Freud heard from the mother how Ilona resented Freud's sharing of her secret with her mother and refused to discuss things openly with her. Her pains returned. Yet Freud was convinced of his solution and 'that everything would come right'. Within months, he seemed to be proved right. Ilona was in good health and communicating sporadically with him. He obviously relished the happy end to this poignant little tale from the *belle époque*:

In the spring of 1894 I heard that she was going to a private ball for which I was able to get an invitation, and I did not allow the opportunity to escape me of seeing my former patient whirl past me in a lively dance. Since then, by her own inclination, she has married someone unknown to me.

Freud paints a fine picture of the patient who could not walk whirling past her physician, perhaps acknowledging him with a happy and gracious wave as she swept by. And he is also content that her satisfactory final docking in the harbour of marriage was not the result of the matchmaking of her mother nor even that of her analyst. Instead, it was, apparently, solely the achievement of this gifted, ambitious, moral girl with her 'excessive demand for love which, to begin with, found satisfaction in her family', but who was possessed of an 'independence of her nature which went beyond the feminine ideal and found expression in a considerable amount of obstinacy, pugnacity and reserve.' Perhaps the obstinacy, pugnacity and reserve were still shining through when she recollected, in talking many years later with her daughter, how Freud was 'just a young, bearded nerve specialist they sent me to', who had tried 'to persuade me that I was in love with my brother-in-law, but that wasn't really so.' Such a divergence of view over the 'true' history of a patient's passions was to become characteristic of Freud's case histories and their subjects' own recollections. It remains an open and delicate question who was better placed to judge her past accurately: the doctor who treated her at the lowest moment of her life, obliging her to go over those painful scenes to which he attached such great importance, and who then wrote her up as a case history a few years later? Or the wife and mother, recalling her past from the vantage-point of the mature tranquillity of a happy marriage, and passing down the story of her youth for the edification of her daughter? It was the Rat Man who later quoted Nietzsche to Freud: '"I did this," says my Memory. "I cannot have done this," says my Pride and remains inexorable. In the end – Memory yields.' It was surely appropriate that the immediate occasion for him telling Freud this saying was a fictional story, from Sudermann's novel *Geschwister* (*Sisters*), in which a woman, as she sat by her sister's sick-bed, feels a wish that the sister should die so that she herself might marry her husband. The woman thereupon committed suicide, thinking that she was not fit to live after being guilty of such baseness. Freud could pride himself in this, 'the first full-length analysis of a hysteria undertaken by me', on having helped Ilona Weiss avoid such an ending to her story.

Lucy R.: A 'Small Tale of Trouble'

Freud's treatment of the thirty year-old English governess he baptized with the name Miss Lucy R. was a relatively brief and informal investigation into her human predicament. How had 'this small tale of trouble', with which he was quite obviously in great sympathy, become converted into a set of neurotic symptoms? In a few short sessions, Freud's sympathy with the difficulties of Lucy's life was channelled into an energetic enquiry and solution of the puzzle of her symptoms: her tiredness and lassitude, the hallucination of the smell of burnt pudding and later of cigar smoke. Freud's warmth towards Lucy was converted into pride and self-satisfaction at the tidy, elegant and definitive restoration of her health and vigour that in the end was achieved.

Miss Lucy R. was an English governess who looked after the two children of a widowed director of a factory some way from Freud's office in Vienna. He saw her on consultation for brief periods at infrequent but regular intervals. He made extremely half-hearted and quickly abandoned attempts to employ hypnosis with her. At about the time he treated her towards the end of 1892, Freud had decided to avoid the word 'hypnotism' and many of the rituals associated with it, if not the idea that he could use some kind of abnormal physiological state to effect a change in the balance of mental forces and hence a cure in his patients. Almost certainly, Lucy came to him from a course of treatment with his friend Fliess for her recurrent suppurative rhinitis – a condition that Freud shared with her throughout the 1890s, or at least during the period of his greatest intimacy with Fliess. After Fliess's successful treatment of her, she had been left with a residual symptom: a subjective sensation of the smell of burnt pudding. This was the most obvious of her symptoms, and it was the one that Freud treated as a hysterical symptom, to be traced back to a definite traumatic scene. To do so, he employed that persistent questioning, that acuteness in matters of the heart and that sympathy which were now becoming his customary method of work.

Miss Lucy R.'s analysis consisted in Freud uncovering three scenes which embodied two different conflicts. The first scene was the one that gave rise to the hallucination of the burnt pudding: when she was with her two charges, the director's children, supervising their cooking of a pudding, they had teasingly withheld from her a newly arrived letter from her mother in Glasgow. She took this as an expression of their affection for her: they did not want her to leave to return home to her mother, which she was thinking of doing. In the excitement of the scene, the pudding burnt. The conflict between her affection for the children and her wish to depart because she was no longer being treated properly by the other servants and the director became symbolized by the smell of the pudding, facilitated by her chronic nasal problems.

But why was this so acute a conflict?

'Was there something particular, apart from their fondness for you, which attached you to the children?'

'Yes. Their mother was a distant relation of my mother's, and I had promised her on her death-bed that I would devote myself with all my power to the children, that I would not leave them and that I would take their mother's place with them. In giving notice I had broken this promise.'

Freud, however, was not content with this answer. He pressed her, suspecting a further motive to do with the live director rather than his dead wife, convinced already that she was secretly in love with her employer. Here, for the first time, we see a feature of Freud's relations to his female patients which was to recur with Dora and others: his conviction that the core of their conflict consisted in their secret love for a man, an authority figure. In being so convinced of this, Freud was to pass over the female figures who, although dead or distant, might well have exercised a hold as strong as that of the live man.

I said to her: 'I cannot think that these are all the reasons for your feelings about the children. I believe that really you are in love with your employer, the Director, though perhaps without being aware of it yourself, and that you have a secret hope of taking their mother's place in actual fact. ...'

She answered in her usual laconic fashion: 'Yes, I think that's true. ... I'm not unreasonably prudish. We're not responsible for our feelings, anyhow. It was distressing to me only because he is my employer and I am in his service and live in his house. I don't feel the same complete independence towards him that I could towards anyone else.'

Lucy had begun to entertain hopes of a reciprocated love and eventual marriage when the director had talked intimately to her about how much he depended on her for looking after his orphaned children.

With this discussion, the hallucinated smell of burnt pudding began to disappear, but was gradually replaced by a similar smell of cigar smoke. Pressing Lucy, Freud discovered two new scenes symbolized by this smell: on both occasions visitors to the house had transgressed the director's rule that visitors should not kiss his children, and on one of these occasions the director had vented his fury on the governess. 'The scene had crushed her hopes.' With the discovery of this scene of disillusionment, when she realized how the director's feelings for her were in no sense special, the hallucinatory smell dissipated, and two days later her spirits were entirely transformed from despondency to sunny happiness. Freud asked her: '"And are you still in love with your employer?" – "Yes, I certainly am, but that makes no difference. After all, one can think and feel in private what one wishes."'

Certainly Freud had pin-pointed one of Lucy's conflicts: between her love for the director and her more realistic perception of his indifference to her. Yet the current conflict had also involved her desire to leave her position as governess and her sense of being bound by her promise to the dead mother. That promise to 'take the mother's place with' the children had effectively committed her to winning the director's admiration and respect as if she were the mother herself. Perhaps her conflict had started with this obligation to take over the dead mother's place, and then manifested itself as her unrequited love for the live father. To offer this interpretation of her situation is, of course, to structure her inner world according to the classic Oedipal model, a model which Freud was some years off from formulating. Certainly cases such as this one would eventually serve Freud as an excellent example of 'this common phantasy in girls ... which derives from the Oedipus complex, of the mistress of the house disappearing and the master taking the newcomer as his wife in her place'; this fantasy of the newcomer or the servant girl would serve Freud in understanding Ibsen's Rebecca West in his brilliant if controversial reading of *Rosmersholm* just as it served in understanding Miss Lucy R.

Yet this proto-Oedipal model allows us to see how Freud was eager, perhaps too eager, to picture Miss Lucy R. as 'an over-mature girl [*überreifes*] with a need to be loved, whose affections had been too hastily aroused through a misunderstanding', as he described her in the final chapter of the *Studies*. There may well have been equally important hidden themes of rivalry and inhibition at taking over the position of the mother. Certainly Freud's cure of her lassitude and wretchedness, as well as the hallucinations of smell, restored her to a state of mind in which she no longer felt the need to return to her own mother's side, and was able once again to fulfil her obligation of taking the place of the children's mother. But there are different ways of describing this outcome. Did Freud reconcile her to her position as down-trodden and exploited woman, wasting her life away being the servant? Or did he help her to break through her inhibition, the inhibition of the Oedipal daughter, so that she could fulfil her promise to the dying wife and take her place? Whichever is the truer, Freud achieved this by concentrating all his attention on Lucy's libidinal relation to her employer, leaving to one side the connected, but only implicit, question of the dead mother.

4

THE DREAM OF
PSYCHOANALYSIS

If the scenes of Charcot hypnotizing the hysteric and of Breuer aiding Bertha Pappenheim to re-enact her forgotten injuries were to be the original theatre of psychoanalysis, it was only when Freud placed this theatre, this other scene, within the dream that it became recognizably and uniquely Freud's. There is one dream that records this transposition and programmatically shows us how Freud's dream of psychoanalysis was to unfold: the dream of Irma's injection, dreamt two nights before his wife's thirty-fourth birthday, on 23/24 July, 1895:

A large hall — numerous guests, whom we were receiving. — Among them was Irma. I at once took her on one side, as though to answer her letter and to reproach her for not having accepted my 'solution' yet. I said to her: 'If you still get pains, it's really only your fault.' She replied: 'If you only knew what pains I've got now in my throat and stomach and abdomen — it's choking me' — I was alarmed and looked at her. She looked pale and puffy. I thought to myself that after all I must be missing some organic trouble. I took her to the window and looked down her throat, and she showed signs of recalcitrance, like women with artificial dentures. I thought to myself that there was really no need for her to do that. — She then opened her mouth properly and on the right I found a big white patch; at another place I saw extensive whitish grey scabs upon some remarkable curly structures which were evidently modelled on the turbinal bones of the nose. — I at once called in Dr M., and he repeated the examination and confirmed it. ... Dr M. looked quite different from usual; he was very pale, he walked with a limp and his chin was clean-shaven. ... My friend Otto was now standing beside her as well, and my friend Leopold was percussing her through her bodice and saying: 'She has a dull area low down on the left.' He also indicated that a portion of the skin on the left shoulder was infiltrated. (I noticed this, just as he did, in spite of her dress.) ... M. said: 'There's no doubt it's an infection, but no matter; dysentery will supervene and the toxin will be eliminated.' ... We were directly aware, too, of the origin of the infection. Not long before, when she was feeling unwell, my friend Otto had given her an injection of a preparation of propyl, propyls ... propionic acid ... trimethylamin (and I saw before me the formula for this printed in heavy type). ... Injections of that sort ought not to be made so thoughtlessly. ... And probably the syringe had not been clean.

In *The Interpretation of Dreams*, Freud uses this dream as the specimen dream, the dream by which he will introduce the main thesis of the book: dreams are the fulfilment of a wish. What is the wish represented as fulfilled by this dream? It 'acquitted' Freud 'of the responsibility for Irma's condition by showing that it was due to other factors': Otto, Leopold and Dr M. were all responsible, through their ignorance or their oversights, for the medical fiasco that the dream enacts. The dream was thus 'in the nature of a self-justification, a plea on behalf of my own rights'; it was an exculpation achieved firstly by deriding the incompetence and ignorance of other doctors, and implicitly by referring to special circumstances that meant that it really was only Irma's fault, or the fault of nobody: fate rather than fault.

In his associations to the dream, Freud discovered that Irma was only one patient among many. Indeed, the dream is a prolonged meditation on the question of what makes a good patient. Irma was, in fact, a real patient, and the difficulties Freud had with her were by no means straightforward, though they may well have been common. In the associations, once we have been introduced to the cast of female patients, we are led to further medical themes: there is Irma's friend; there are Drs M., Otto and Leopold; and there is Freud's friend in Berlin who advises him on scientific matters, and who provided him with a chemical formula that appears towards the end of the dream: trimethylamin. Irma has led him to uncover a series of self-reproaches; but for each dream-element that alludes to a self-reproach, there is an answering dream-element, which wipes out – and more – the imputed moral or professional fault. Thus, corresponding to the recalcitrant Irma, there is her friend, who, if she were to undergo Freud's analysis, would quickly produce the evidence confirming Freud's theories of the aetiology of the neuroses. To the criticisms that Dr M. lays against Freud's extravagant hypotheses, there is the response provided by the Berlin friend who, the day before, had supplied Freud with encouragement and scientific facts that promised to aid him in his work. The structure of these self-reproaches is thus the following:

$$
\text{Freud} \begin{cases} \text{- - - - - Element representing reproach} \\ \\ \text{- - - - - Element representing justification} \end{cases}
$$

Each element is paired off: the dream is a list of self-justifications closely linked to a list of self-recriminations. The logic is that of the talion, with self-justification cancelling out self-recrimination. And the wish-fulfilment of the dream is embodied in the representational 'triumph' of the self-justificatory elements.

The dream is populated by two sorts of character: there are female patients, and there are male doctors; there are characters representing a self-reproach, and there are characters representing self-justification. We know the identities of nearly all the characters in the dream. Dr M. is Josef Breuer, Freud's friend and medical mentor; Otto is Oscar Rie, Freud's close friend and family doctor; Leopold is Ludwig Rosenstein, another friend and medical colleague; the friend in Berlin who told Freud about trimethylamin is Wilhelm Fliess.

Not a single person cited either in the dream or in Freud's associations falls outside the two categories of doctor and patient; even Freud's brother, who lends Breuer his pallor and clean-shaven chin, appears in the associations because 'we had news a few days earlier that he was walking with a limp owing to an arthritic affection of his hip.' So the dream repeats the scene of Freud's treatment of a female hysteric and his calling in Breuer for an opinion on the case. The scene of the dream is thus a recapitulation of the scene of the origin of psychoanalysis itself: the examination of a female patient by Freud and Breuer.

However, alongside this collaboration between Freud and Breuer there lay another medical collaboration, clearly referred to in the dream, but not revealed in Freud's published version of the dream: Freud's and Fliess's joint treatment of Emma Eckstein. It is an important story, not, we will conclude, the only important story hidden inside this dream, but essential to tell. The scene of Freud's treatment of Emma is one of the primal scenes of psychoanalysis.

Emma started receiving treatment from Freud sometime in the early 1890s. We do not know what her symptoms were, but she became a special patient, remembered long after by the Freud children. The crucial period of her treatment extended from 1895 to 1897, overlapping with Freud's espousal of the seduction theory and his discovery of the meaning of dreams.

In December 1894, Fliess visited Freud in Vienna, examined Emma and recommended that he operate on her nose, in order to alleviate certain of her symptoms, ones possibly connected, in the doctor's view, with masturbation. Fliess returned to Vienna in early February, operated on Emma and left. Freud reported on her post-operative progress on 4 March: the patient was not doing well. She had excessive secretion of pus, a bone chip had been expelled and a rather noxious smell emanated from her nose. Four days later, on 8 March, Freud gave Fliess the sudden upsetting news that Emma's condition had worsened to the point where Freud had hurriedly called in a surgeon, Rosanes, who, in attempting to halt the increased flow of blood from her nose, had discovered that a half-metre of gauze had been left by Fliess in her nasal cavity during his operation on her. Extracting the gauze led to a massive haemorrhage, in which the patient almost lost her life. After the haemorrhage was stemmed, Freud had had to go into the next room to be sick; he'd been given liquid courage by the doctor's wife (also a prospective patient of Freud's), only to be rebuked on his return with Emma's words: 'So this is the strong sex.'

'So we had done her an injustice; she was not at all abnormal.' The letters of the next few weeks were full of the worryingly shaky progress Emma then made; Freud was distraught and worried by the life-threatening episode which a purportedly harmless operation had caused. But once Emma's life was no longer in danger, by the end of May, Freud began tentatively to entertain once again hypotheses concerning the psychic origins of her bleeding. Freud's accounts of these events to Fliess at times hinted at the grossness of the surgical error Fliess had committed, an error in which Freud's complicity could be mooted, if not demonstrated. Fliess was always extremely sensitive to any aspersions being cast on his professional competence; at one point in the proceedings, he wanted a 'testimonial certificate' from one of the surgeons in Vienna 'exonerating' him from any responsibility for the 'mishap'. Freud was 'offended' by this idea: if he, Freud, still had the highest estimation of his friend's medical wisdom, that should suffice, no matter what others may think. Freud found himself in the uncomfortable position of go-between: between Fliess and Emma, and between Fliess and the other doctors who had taken over the case in this dire, potentially fatal emergency. Freud was sometimes the spokesman for Fliess, defending his knowledge and skill, while not denying the actual facts of the medical matter; to Fliess, he was the spokesman for the other doctors, with their in the main muted, though sometimes acerbic – or so we can infer – criticisms of Fliess's competence; and he was also Emma's spokesman, manfully assuring Fliess that she still had complete faith in the two doctors: 'It does speak well for her that she did not change her attitude towards either of us; she honours your memory beyond the undesired accident.' By the end of April the crisis was over: Emma made her recovery and continued in analysis with Freud, thus confirming her fidelity to at least the geographically closer of her two doctors.

Freud's dream of July 1895 includes many allusions to the Emma episode, amongst them the detailed examination of Irma's throat, modelled on Emma's nose, and Freud's alarm at the unsuspected and uncomprehended pain of his patient. Almost certainly, this violation of an innocent woman evoked the scene of violation, of defloration we know to have been so active in Freud's fantasy world: two men maltreating an innocent girl. If this fantasy was awoken, then the pressure on Freud for exculpation was even greater: not only did he need to exculpate his profession, but he also needed to exculpate his sex.

If, behind Irma, we find Emma, then the exculpation that is most urgent is that of Fliess, whose surgical error had almost cost Emma her life. Freud identifies with his Berlin friend and thus absolves both himself and his friend from medically irresponsible behaviour. This is undoubtedly part of what is going on, but it is not the whole story; it would be misleading to make Irma, and behind her Emma, only intermediaries, or victims, in a story which is essentially a tale of two doctors: Freud's trust in Fliess, his exculpation of him, his idealization of his medical knowledge (and of medical knowledge in general, his own included), his transference to him and his gradual disillusionment with the sage of Berlin. Such a story eliminates the feminine in favour of Freud's relationship to the male friends, colleagues and authorities. And this elimination of the feminine actually conceals a more important elimination: that of the patient. It was the relationship to his patients that made Freud, in Cornelius Castoriadis's words, someone to remember.

Sex and the Ideal Patient

To restore the dimension of the feminine to Freud's dream, we should turn away for a moment from the Emma episode and consider the three women who figure in the dream and its associations: Irma, then her 'intimate woman friend of whom I had a very high opinion', and a third woman, whom Freud would 'not have liked to have as a patient, since I had noticed that she was bashful in my presence and I could not think she would make an amenable patient. ... The person in question was, of course, my own wife.' In these associations, Freud was measuring these potential women patients according to a standard, an '*Ideal*' as he puts it in the German text, of the amenable patient; instead of opening their mouths and telling more, they were reserved, bashful, recalcitrant and shy. In short, these patients would display resistance. The doctor-patient relationship that Freud depicts here is wholly couched in terms of recalcitrance, unwillingness, resistance; it is entirely in conformity with the description he had given a few months earlier, in the chapter on therapy in *Studies on Hysteria*, of the physically muscular and laborious work of overcoming resistance:

We force our way into the internal strata, overcoming resistances all the time ... we experiment how far we can advance with our present means and the knowledge we have acquired ... we are constantly making up arrears. ... By this method we at last reach a point at which we can stop working in strata and can penetrate by a main path straight to the nucleus of the pathogenic organization. With this the struggle is won, though not yet ended. ... But now the patient helps us energetically. Her resistance is for the most part broken.

So in the dream, Freud is giving us a glimpse of his more subjective reactions to the resistance of his patients: he found them 'foolish because she had not accepted my solution', whereas the 'wise' patient is one who 'would have yielded sooner'. On the one hand he admires and respects a woman who suffers from hysterical choking but shows herself 'strong enough to master her condition without outside help'; yet if she were to become his patient, he would wish her to yield, to be pliable, to be wise and intelligent in giving herself over entirely to him, to be deflowered, no less, to put it in terms of Freud's fundamental fantasies.

The symbol of this picture of the recalcitrant patient is the false teeth and the disillusionment they lead to:

at a first glance, the governess had seemed a picture of youthful beauty, but when it came to opening her mouth she had taken measures to conceal her plates. This led to recollections of other medical examinations and of little secrets revealed in the course of them – to the satisfaction of neither party.

But the false teeth also made him think of his wife Martha; almost certainly he was reminded of an incident during their engagement when Martha tried to conceal her tooth trouble from her fiancé with what Freud called, when he detected it, 'one of those subterfuges' of hers, which 'kept annoying me for almost two years'. These little tricks, deceptions and dishonesties intensely infuriated Freud, the lover of truth and openness at all costs: 'I would rather think of you with false teeth in your mouth than one dishonest word.' In the dream of Irma's injection, he is reflecting that it is because a beautiful woman patient has false teeth in her mouth that she displays the lack of honesty which eventually leads to disappointment on both sides. For her, the disappointment arises because eventually the truth will out; for him, the disappointment comes not from the discovery of falsity at the heart of beauty, but from the deceptions and evasions with which his vain, recalcitrant patients attempt to evade him. Yet again, Freud the lover of truth, the tyrant of honesty, sallies forth, requiring the same ideal standards of his female patients as he had of his fiancée. We shall see that, by an irony of history, Freud's love of truth was to cost him the friendship of the woman he admired most in this dream, precisely because of the moral strength for which he admired her.

There is a wavering, however, in Freud's view of his patients; at times his associations lump these three women together as all foolishly recalcitrant to treatment – it is as if he is saying 'all women resist, all women are the same.' At other times, his associations unfavourably compare the recalcitrant and bashful Irma with the patient he admires: 'women are all the same save one, the ideal....' But however recalcitrant they were, Freud had already mapped out in early 1895 the strategy for overcoming his patients' resistance: 'The interest shown in her by the physician, the understanding of her which he allows her to feel and the hope of recovery he holds out to her – all these will decide the patient to yield up her secret.' Besides being critical of the patients who make his job difficult, who obstinately cling to their hysterias, Freud was also a therapeutic optimist, aiming to cure nervous disorders, unlike the doctors he derides for their ignorance of hysteria in the dream. He held out hope of a full recovery to his patients. So it was as much Freud as his patients who were disappointed by lack of progress. He might well blame his patients (and the other doctors who behaved so absurdly and had no faith in him), but he was the idealist; he was, as he had been ten years previously, with the new drug cocaine, the champion of a new therapy. We might go so far as to say that it is insofar as Freud promised her something, something that was 'too much', that he experiences her as recalcitrant; his promise meant that not only did she have high expectations, but so did he. And such high expectations would be immediately converted into a sense of disappointment, even of frustration, when his 'solution' was not accepted, turned out not to be what she wanted, what she was expecting, what she had been promised.

In his search for exculpation in the dream, Freud paints the portrait of the good patient, the ideal patient who would accept his solution. What was the solution he offered Irma that neither she nor Breuer would accept? There was no doubt that Freud thought that she was a hysteric, but he also toyed with alternatives.

My patient Irma was a young widow; if I wanted to find an excuse for the failure of my treatment in her case, what I could best appeal to would no doubt be this fact of her widowhood, which her friends would be so glad to see changed. And how strangely, I thought to myself, a dream like this is put together! The other woman, whom I had as a patient in the dream instead of Irma, was also a young widow.

Freud followed a similar line of thought when talking of friend Otto: 'he has a habit of making presents on every possible occasion. It was to be hoped, I thought to myself, that some day he would find a wife to cure him of the habit.' These two passages, both indicating how Freud conceived of marriage as a straightforward therapy for the neuroses, is quite close to the surface of Freud's account: widows and bachelors, each with their neurotic traits – compulsive giving, persistent pains – will be transformed by sexual satisfaction. In the background of these thoughts, no doubt, is Fliess's recent marriage to a member of the Freud circle in Vienna. As if Freud would be more successful as a marriage-broker than a psychotherapist.

In his paper on anxiety neurosis, published early in 1895, Freud had maintained that in acquired, as opposed to hereditary, cases of anxiety neurosis, 'influences from *sexual life* are the operative aetiological factors'. Thus virginal anxiety could be found in girls 'by their first encounter with the problem of sex', in newly married women who gain no pleasure from the sexual act, and in women whose husbands' potency was impaired or who practised coitus interruptus or reservatus:

it is easy to convince oneself that they depend simply on whether the woman obtains satisfaction in coitus or not. ... She is saved from the neurosis if the husband who is afflicted with ejaculatio praecox is able immediately to repeat coitus with better success. ... If, on the other hand, [in coitus interruptus] the husband waits for his wife's satisfaction, the coitus amounts to a normal one for *her*; but *he* will fall ill of an anxiety neurosis.

Self-evidently, then, Freud added, 'anxiety neurosis also occurs as anxiety in *widows* and intentionally *abstinent women*'. Characteristically, Freud showed special sympathy for abstinent women when he remarked:

where abstinence is concerned there is in the case of women no doubt the further matter of intentional repression of the sexual circle of ideas, to which an abstinent woman, in her struggle against temptation, must often make up her mind. The horror which, at the time of the menopause, an ageing woman feels at her unduly increased libido may act in a similar sense.

These findings about the origins of anxiety show Freud in a thoroughly modern sexological guise he was not often later to adopt: the writer of marriage manuals, with their detailed attention to the good sexual life, and in particular the rhythms of sexual excitement and satisfaction in the woman.

It is against this background of scientific convictions and preoccupations that Freud's thoughts about Irma's widowhood should be seen. He was not responsible for her condition because she was either holding something back from him, being recalcitrant, or she was neurotic because she was a widow. And he could not be held responsible for that, no matter how much he would wish her to get married again. With such patients, Freud had at the start of his medical practice – when he attended a joint consultation with Chrobak –

been told how the doctor should conduct himself. Chrobak's patient's meaningless anxiety could only be assuaged by information about her physician's exact whereabouts at all hours of the day. During the consultation, Chrobak told Freud that this patient was still a virgin, despite eighteen years of marriage, and that in cases like these the doctor cannot hope for a cure, but must protect the husband's reputation, this 'domestic misfortune', with his own. When people talk about the doctor's inability to cure such a patient, all the doctor can do is keep silent. In such cases, Chrobak went on, the only cure was the repeated dosage of a *'penis normalis'*.

So the wish to cure sexually abstinent patients could be realized quite simply: Freud could give his patients sexual satisfaction. This, we should remember, is a *medical* solution to a problem of his *medical* practice, but it does have as a necessary consequence that the role of the doctor and the role of the lover are combined together. Freud had started his account of the Irma dream by pointing out that the confusion between social roles played an important part in the dream:

During the summer of 1895 I had been giving psycho-analytic treatment to a young lady who was on very friendly terms with me and my family. It will be readily understood that a mixed relationship such as this may be a source of many disturbed feelings in a physician and particularly in a psychotherapist. While the physician's personal interest is greater, his authority is less; any failure would bring a threat to the old-established friendship with the patient's family.

To understand the significance of this confusion between professional and personal life, we have to look yet further into the identities of the dream's principal protagonists. It turns out that re-analysing, for Freud's benefit, the dream of Irma's injection has been a favourite blood sport amongst Freudians ever since it was published; Freud himself responded to one such wild interpretation with some crucial information about the true identities of the figures in the dream. In January 1908, Karl Abraham wrote to Freud:

I should like to know whether the incomplete interpretation of 'Irma's injection' dream ... is intentional. I find that trimethylamin leads to the most important part, to sexual allusions which become more distinct in the last lines. After all, everything points to the suspicion of syphilitic infection in the patient.

Freud replied the next day:

Syphilis is *not* the subject-matter. ... Sexual megalomania is hidden behind it, the three women, Mathilde, Sophie and Anna, are my daughters' three godmothers, and I have them all! There would be one simple therapy for widowhood, of course. All sorts of intimate things, naturally!

With these short sentences, three of the main themes of the dream are brought together: the sexual, the familial and the medico-therapeutic. We have already ascertained that Freud's 'one simple therapy for widowhood' is synonymous with a more nakedly sexual desire. Even though Freud broke off an association about examining his patients undressed with the words, 'frankly,

I had no desire to let myself go any deeper at this point', the question of a sexual relation to his patients shines through the text, and he could not but have been aware of it. But once we fill in the identities of the three women patients we discover a more complex familial theme, since the women patients whom Freud possesses in the dream turn out to have also been his daughters' godmothers. It is not just the sexual desire of a doctor for his attractive women patients, nor even the desire to assuage their sexual frustration that Freud found in his own dream; he discovered sexual desires in a close family network, desires whose realization would amount to incest.

The Three Godmothers

Irma herself is Anna Hammerschlag-Lichtheim; her friend is Sophie Schwab-Paneth; the third woman, who for most of the dream was identified with Martha, is Mathilde Breuer. These are the three women whom Freud has in this dream – these are certainly, in his imagination, Freud's women. They are the women after whom his three daughters were named.

Anna Hammerschlag was the daughter of Samuel Hammerschlag, who had been Freud's Hebrew teacher at school; in the 1880s, Freud spoke of 'the deep-seated sympathy which has existed between myself and the dear old Jewish teacher ever since my school days.' Together with Breuer, Hammerschlag was the most intimate, reliable and 'paternally solicitous' of Freud's patrons and advisers: 'He has been touchingly fond of me for years: there is such a secret sympathy between us that we can talk intimately together ... he always regards me as his son.' Long before she was married, Freud singled out his teacher's daughter Anna as 'an admirable girl' whom he prized as a friend for, and a good influence on, his sisters. In 1885, she married Rudolf Lichtheim of Breslau, the son of Ludwig Lichtheim, a long-standing friend of Breuer's, eminent neurologist and proponent of a schema which Freud was to criticize in his book on aphasia, and with whom Breuer's eldest son Robert later worked as a young doctor. On her marriage, Freud obviously wished to keep his family in touch with her, since he urged his fiancée to write her a congratulatory postcard. However, Anna's husband died within a year. She eventually worked as a schoolteacher. In the late 1880s, the Freuds rented summer villas at Reichenau, alongside the Breuers, Hammerschlags, Schwabs, Schiffs, Kassowitzes. On 30 April 1893, Paul Hammerschlag, Anna's brother, married Josef and Mathilde Breuer's daughter, Bertha. The Hammerschlags and Breuers lived in the same block of flats, first of all in Brandstätte, then from 1912 in Neustifftgasse. Anna herself was a good friend of Martha Freud's, as Freud indicated when he mentioned how Anna was on 'very friendly terms with me and my family'. The cast of the dream of Irma's injection, both the male doctors and the female patients, is quite clearly a sizeable portion of the 'close Jewish milieu inhabited by Freud'.

Sophie Schwab-Paneth also came from this milieu. Sophie's mother was one of the three sisters Frau Hammerschlag, Frau Schwab and Frau Altschule. So Sophie was Hammerschlag's niece, and Anna's cousin and intimate friend.

Sophie became engaged to a medical colleague of Freud's, Josef Paneth, and in April 1884 she and Josef gave Freud a capital sum of 1,500 gulden, the interest on which was specifically intended to finance Freud's trips to see Martha in Wandsbek. Sigmund quite accurately told Martha that 'it really sounds like a chapter out of Dickens', and he felt indebted to Sophie in particular, since the money evidently came more from her side of the family than from his. But even at that date, Freud suspected that Sophie would soon be a widow, on account of Paneth's tuberculosis; he was to die in 1890. Sophie and Josef were married in May 1884 – it was one of the few marriage ceremonies Freud attended, and he wrote Martha a malicious sixteen-page letter mocking it. When Sigmund and Martha's first child Mathilde was born in 1887, duly named after the first of the godmothers, all three godmothers-to-be, Mathilde Breuer, Sophie Paneth and Anna Lichtheim, were in and out of the house. Sophie even offered her son Ludwig's hand in marriage to the four-day-old lady.

Sophie figured in both *Studies on Hysteria* and in the dream of Irma's injection; on both occasions Freud admired her as someone 'with no less strength of character than intelligence'. In the *Studies*, he described her as 'a highly-gifted lady who suffers from slight nervous states and whose whole character bears evidence of hysteria, though she has never had to seek medical help or been unable to carry on her duties'. Her sense of shame at the violent effect produced in her by her reminiscences was a major factor in preventing her from divulging more about them to her friends. She had nursed on their death-beds three or four of those she loved and staged chronologically exact 'annual festivals of remembrance' for her loved ones, when she would weep over their mental images and re-enact the last stages of the final illnesses.

Freud's analysis of his own '*non vixit*' dream in *The Interpretation of Dreams* was also a rumination on Josef Paneth's brief career as an ambitious young demonstrator in the Vienna Physiological Institute, cut short by his early death. The very act of publishing the analysis was an enactment of the repressed unconscious wishes that Freud attributed to Paneth in the dream: 'sacrificing to my ambition people whom I greatly value', either by wishing them dead or through his inveterate indiscretion – 'the reproach that I was unable to keep a secret.' Both Paneth and Freud had worked in Brücke's laboratory, where promotion was slow. Freud's associations employed Paneth's impatience with his superior's disinclination to move on, an impatience redoubled by Paneth's certainty that he could not expect to live long, so that his grumbles were sometimes so ambiguously coloured that they sounded like death-wishes – to represent his own urgent desire for a vacancy to fill. 'Wherever there is rank and promotion the way lies open for wishes that call for suppression.' And, building on this story about Paneth's callous wish for another man's elimination so that he could step into his shoes, Freud revealed his own thoughts: 'How many people I've followed to the grave already! But I'm still alive. I've survived them all; I'm left in possession of the field.'

None the less, there was a counterpoint to these murderous, egoistic wishes: 'No one is irreplaceable! ... all those we have lost come back!' And, strangely enough, in the elegiac climax of this dream that celebrated the death of his friends and their eternal recycling in the form of *revenants*, Freud once again evoked, only to consign once again to fond memory, the women, Mathilde, Sophie and Anna, who had given their names to his children:

I had insisted on [my children's] names being chosen, not according to the fashion of the moment, but in memory of people I have been fond of. Their names made the children into *revenants*. And after all, I reflected, was not having children our only path to immortality?

Undoubtedly the '*non vixit*' dream analysis reveals most about Freud's relationships with his male friends; but we still catch glimpses of his sexual megalomania in the phrases describing how the deaths of friends and colleagues leave him 'in possession of the field'. Perhaps Sophie recognized herself in the dream of Irma's injection and divined more than she should have of its underlying wishes. Be that as it may, she was certainly the first person to respond to the publication of *The Interpretation of Dreams*: 'The book has just been sent out. The first tangible reaction was the termination of the friendship of a dear friend, who felt hurt by the mention of her husband in the *non vixit* dream.' This woman whom Freud admired for her independence of spirit, who commemorated the death of her loved ones in such a full and distinctive manner, was deeply offended by Freud's using her husband's death to show how nobody was irreplaceable; perhaps she felt that he had been more indiscreet than he should have in sacrificing, if not the living, then at least their memory, to his ambition, his dream book.

The three women, Freud told Abraham, are 'Mathilde, Sophie and Anna ... my daughters' three godmothers, and I have them all!' Where is Mathilde Breuer to be found in the dream? The name Mathilde figures as a direct association to Breuer repeating Freud's examination of Irma, but it does so in connection with Mathilde S., a long-standing patient of Freud's admitted to Svetlin Hospital in Vienna with the diagnosis of severe mania and erotic delusions concerning him, whose unexpected toxic reaction to the sulphonal he prescribed for her led to her death. He had turned at that time to Breuer for help, but to no avail. Three years later in 1893, when his six-year-old daughter Mathilde contracted diphtheria, Freud feared that she would die; 'it struck me now almost like an act of retribution on the part of destiny. It was as though the replacement of one person by another was to be continued in another sense: this Mathilde for that Mathilde, an eye for an eye and a tooth for a tooth.' What had saved her was her request for a strawberry; although it was not the strawberry season, a renowned shop came up with one. When she ate it, it provoked a coughing fit which immediately cleared the obstruction in her throat; the next day she was well on the way to recovery.

The Irma dream is rife with these identifications, and Mathilde Breuer may well have appeared in connection with Dr M. as well as through her obvious connection with erotically obsessed Mathilde S. and the story of Mathilde Freud's near-fatal illness. Born Mathilde Altmann, youngest daughter of wine merchant Solomon Altmann, thus coming from the class of propertied tradespeople, she married Josef Breuer in 1868, when she was twenty-two. Breuer was still working at the hospital and had to get special dispensation to continue as assistant to Johann Oppolzer; the faculty wanted him to live every other night in hospital, but Breuer refused, thus endangering his academic career. Eventually he got his dispensation when he offered to live close to the hospital, and the newly married couple set up home, with Breuer's widowed father. Between 1869 and 1876, Mathilde bore four children: Robert, Bertha, Margarethe (Gretel) and Johannes. The last child, Dora, was born in 1882, during Breuer's treatment of Bertha Pappenheim.

Mathilde was a strikingly beautiful, somewhat shy and reserved woman. In an intimate conversation where they talked moral insanity, strange case histories, including Bertha Pappenheim's, and families, Breuer told Freud about his wife and Freud told Breuer how intimate he and Martha already were. The two men then discovered that they called their women by the same nickname, Cordelia, because, Breuer said, Mathilde is incapable of displaying affection to others, even including her own father. Ever since he had met her in early 1875, when he was a student of eighteen, Freud had always been a great admirer of hers, and she of him, in those balmy days of his friendship with her husband, when he could write to Martha: 'They are both dear, good, and understanding friends. We talked till 1 a.m. She always insists on my taking a small apartment before long and hanging out a sign, just a sign, a beautiful sign.' Two years after he wrote this letter, it was indeed Mathilde Breuer who insisted on hanging the sign outside Freud's first consulting-room in April 1886.

The end of Freud's friendship with Breuer meant a more general breaking off of relations between the two families; Freud remained acutely sensitive to any signs of his friends or family undergoing 'Breuerisation'. Josef's death in 1925 led to a healing of the wounds, with Robert Breuer's assurance to Freud that Josef had throughout the years always followed his work with interest. The following year, Mathilde, by now eighty, congratulated Freud on his seventieth birthday, to which Freud replied:

The lines in which you congratulate me on my seventieth birthday moved me most deeply. Your black-edged letter brought back like a flash of lightning everything from the moment when, glancing through the door of the consulting-room, I first saw you sitting at the table with your barely two-year-old daughter, through all the years when I could almost count myself as one of your family, and then all the changing events of my life since. Please accept from me in remembrance of this past my most deferential thanks.

In the Irma dream, Freud had already placed Mathilde in the company of two widows, as if he wanted her as an accomplice in his expunging of Breuer's medical competence and influence. Is it insofar as they are widows that Freud desires to have these friends, these patients? Perhaps. But these three women are something more than patients who are also friends that Freud sees regularly and has done for years. They are also, as he says in so many words to Abraham, those three women best calculated to represent his daughters in a dream. He has them all, not only all three of them, but all of the *roles* they play: insofar as they are patients, he cures them; insofar as they are patients who are widows, he 'cures' them of the sexual abstinence that is their misfortune; insofar as they represent daughters, he 'has' them. It is not sexual megalomania in the sense of quantity that is most striking in this dream, but the different sorts of women who are possessed. Not three, so much, as patient, widow, godmother, friend – and daughter. What part are we to assign to Freud's daughters in this seminal dream of psychoanalysis? To discover this, we must investigate the theory of hysteria which Freud was advancing in this period.

The Seduction Theory

The good patient would tell him more, where the recalcitrant patient was reluctant. What Freud expected his hysterics to tell him were stories of their sexual seduction in childhood. In the course of his treatments during the early 1890s, patients would recall experiences of sexual seduction, ranging from simple advances by word or gesture to actual sexual assault, provoking fright. In the views he then developed, seduction was the necessary condition for repression: instead of referring to some hereditary hysterical disposition,

the place of this indefinite hysterical disposition can now be taken, wholly or in part, by the posthumous operation of a sexual trauma in childhood. 'Repression' of the memory of a distressing sexual experience which occurs in maturer years is only possible for those in whom that experience can activate the memory-trace of a trauma in childhood.

As he had put it several weeks after the dream of Irma's injection, 'I am on the scent of the following strict precondition for hysteria, namely, that a primary sexual experience (before puberty), accompanied by revulsion and fright, must have taken place; for obsessional neurosis, that it must have happened, accompanied by *pleasure*.'

The seduction theory was both a record of what Freud heard from his patients and a part of the general psychology that he felt was needed to explain pathological defence. From the beginning, he insisted that the condition for pathological defence was a peculiar relation to memory of presexual sexual shocks. He could also distinguish between events remembered with unpleasure and hence leading to a conflict and thus to hysteria, and events remembered with pleasure but accompanied by a reproach, leading to obsessional neurosis. Throughout 1896, he concentrated on the different consequences flowing from the chronological timing of the events and the details of the scenes: 'hysteria is not repudiated sexuality but rather *repudiated perversion*' on the part of the seducer, the father; but one trend in the patient's mind does not repudiate but rather yearns for this seducer, 'the prehistoric, unforgettable other person who is never equalled by anyone later.' The miniature case histories he sent Fliess filled in how the details of these seductions were connected to the symptoms of later years, implicating the 'oral sexual system', showing how the bestial character of symptoms stemmed from the perversions of the seducers (smell, urine, faeces, blood). Freud seemed not only to be reaching back into the prehistoric past of his patients' lives, but into earlier epochs in history, when medieval torturers and their victims performed similar acts of seduction and violence. And the note of amazement at the veracity and clarity of his discoveries is always there:

I was able to trace back, with certainty, a hysteria that developed in the context of a periodic mild depression to a seduction, which occurred for the first time at 11 months, and hear again the words that were exchanged between two adults at the time! It is as though it comes from a phonograph.

At the same time as he explored a blood-curdling medieval fantasmagoria, he was scouting out the little domestic tragedies contained in the ruthless sexual exploitation by bourgeois men and boys of servant girls and the repressed desires such a domestic sexual economy lodged in the respectable young girls and women of the households, an economy which he was to explore in greatest detail in his case history of 'Dora'. However, beginning early in 1897, he also began to explore a new source for the content of symptoms: 'hysterical fantasies which regularly, as I see it, go back to things that children overhear at an early age and understand only subsequently.' These fantasies are 'protective structures, sublimations of the facts, embellishments of them, and at the same time serve for self-relief. Their accidental origin is perhaps from masturbation fantasies.'

Fiction, dreams, fantasies and then another similar mental activity begin to hold Freud's attention – romances: the romance of illegitimacy, of prostitution, and then the 'romance' of the death of the parents – 'the wish that they should die'. More and more, the language of wishing takes over:

At later stages the defence against libido has made room for itself in the Ucs. [unconscious] as well. Wish fulfillment must meet the requirements of this unconscious defence. This happens if the symptom is able to operate as a punishment. ... The motives of *libido* and of *wish fulfillment as a punishment* then come together.

The importance of the veracity of the memories of seduction began to decrease, firstly as Freud recognized that repression acted on the memory of *impulses* derived from the primal scenes, and secondly as fiction became as active in producing symptoms as the fragmentary kernels of fact were. The three elements in play were 'memory fragments, *impulses* (derived from memories) and *protective fictions*'. And it is the fantasies, the 'unconscious fictions', that are formed *in place of* memories that now possess the necessary prerequisite for pathological defence: namely that they have not been subject to a *prior* defence.

What we are faced with are falsifications of memory and fantasies – the latter relating to the past or future. I know roughly the rules in accordance with which these structures are put together and the reasons why they are stronger than genuine memories.

Here, in 1897, Freud found various interests of his connecting together;

he knew how to deal with the causes and structures of fantasies because they were directly analogous to dreams. Just as he had discovered the importance of wishing in analysing the dream of Irma's injection, he now rediscovered the importance of *motive* in the construction of symptoms. 'Remembering is never a motive but only a way, a method. The first motive for the formation of symptoms is, chronologically, libido. Thus symptoms, like dreams, are *the fulfillment of a wish.*'

The language of seduction and the language of wishing were closely entangled, in the same way as fantasy and reality moved closer together, now that they were both on an equal footing:

Where does the material for creating the [family] romance – adultery, illegitimate child, and the like – come from? Usually from the lower social circles of servant girls. Such things are so common among them that one is never at a loss for material, and it is especially apt to occur if the seductress was a person in service. In all analyses one therefore hears the same story twice: once as a fantasy about the mother; the second time as a real memory of the maid.

This splitting, or doubling, of the female characters was to re-emerge in Freud's work later, with the distinction between the idealized, desexualized mother and the debased woman of easy virtue.

In 1897, with the link between neurosis and the dream established in the common structure of wishful fantasy, Freud had started to write his dream book. The slowly developing themes of the supremacy of wishing over reality and the indifference between fiction and fact led Freud to a crisis-point in the late summer of 1897: the disavowal of the seduction theory. Freud gave four arguments for his abandonment of the theory that neurosis always had as its cause a scene of seduction in childhood: disappointment that the analyses were never completed, despite having revealed these scenes of seduction; surprise that his analyses always pointed to the father as seducer and that the necessary level of perverse seductions of children in the population to generate all the hysterias was a most improbable one; 'the certain insight that there are no indications of reality in the unconscious, so that one cannot distinguish between truth and fiction that has been cathected with affect. (Accordingly, there would remain the solution that the sexual fantasy invariably seizes upon the theme of the parents.)'; and finally the observation that even in psychosis the naked scene of seduction does not force its way through to consciousness. The development of his thought had, over the previous few months, led him gradually but inexorably to this recognition; in September 1897, he felt it as a sudden loss.

In reaction, he turned inwards, to his self-analysis, 'the most essential thing I have at present,' one 'which I consider indispensable for the clarification of the whole problem'. This was the moment at which Freud discovered his old nursemaid, not his father, as his 'prime originator', his seducer. The form the seduction took is difficult to judge, but it was certainly in the register of phallic self-esteem: she 'instilled in me a high opinion of my own capacities' and 'provided me at such an early age with the means for living and going on living.' In reconstructing his memories of her through analysis of his dreams, Freud came upon one of those 'horrible perverse details' he found so inexplicable – and therefore so convincing of its factual truth – in his patients' stories: 'she washed me in reddish water in which she had previously washed herself.' Very soon, he uncovered his memories of fearing his mother was gone for good – the way the old nurse had disappeared – when she was confined giving birth to Anna. The culprit was again not his father, but his half-brother Philipp, who he feared had locked up his mother the way he had got his nurse locked up.

Within the series of dreams of the first half of October 1897 that enabled Freud to rediscover his old nurse was one concerned with her rough treatment of him. In the dream, Freud's 'habits' (of smoking) and his 'lack of cleanliness', together with his exhibitionistic desires, were the object of an old and ugly maidservant's castigation; Freud must have reconstructed a scene from his childhood in which his old nurse punished him for exhibiting and making a mess of himself. Yet the reference to the maidservant – Freud's use of her to stand in for his old nurse – pointed to his next step in the self-analysis. For the maidservant looked after a ninety-year-old lady named Therese Franckel, whom Freud had for years been visiting twice a day. His dreams were leading him to the discovery of his nurse, but they were also indicating the figure who was behind the maidservant: the old lady.

Freud had been visiting Therese Franckel for a number of years in a strictly medical (rather than psychotherapeutic) capacity, and the simple actions he performed on each occasion were always the same. In the morning, he would drop eye-lotion into her eye and give her a morphine injection. On one of his visits, the automatic sequence of actions was inverted: instead of eye-drops, he put morphine in her eye. Then, in great fear, he realized what he had done and immediately reassured himself that the slip was not a serious one, but he reflected that if he had given her an injection of eye-drops it would have been extremely serious. Yet again an improper injection loomed large in Freud's inner life.

On analysing his blunder – and it was one of the first such blunders that he treated as a meaningful act – he thought of the phrase '*sich an der Alten vergreifen*' ('to do violence to the old woman'). The day before, a young male patient of Freud's had told him of a dream of having sexual intercourse with his mother. Freud was reflecting, fresh from his rejection of the seduction theory, yet tinkering all the while with its elements, that a dream such as this passed over the difference in ages between the son and the mother, just as the Oedipus legend made nothing of the difference in age between Oedipus and Jocasta. It thus illustrated the way elements from different epochs were combined: 'in being in love with one's mother one is never concerned with her as she is in the present but with her youthful mnemic image carried over from one's childhood.'

While absorbed in thoughts of this kind I came to my patient, who is over ninety, and I must have been on the way to grasping the universal human application of the

Oedipus myth as correlated with the Fate which is revealed in the oracles; for at that point I did violence to or committed a blunder on 'the old woman'.

What was the Fate that was revealed in Freud's oracle? You too wish to violate your mother – this myth has a universal application which no one, not even you, can escape. To prove it, just at the moment when he was reflecting that it did not matter if the mother was extremely old in reality, Freud did violence to the old woman.

The old woman and her maidservant offered Freud a convenient point of transference for the two mothers of his childhood. When the nurse appeared in his dreams, he turned to his real mother for the truth about the historic past, just as he took a step beyond the dream of the maidservant to a real violation of the old lady who lay behind her. The old lady and his mother were closely twinned – so closely that, for several years in the 1890s, he had only two duties to perform on Sunday, one familial, the other medical. He would visit his old widowed mother twice that day, and he would visit the old lady twice to give her the injection. To his blunder with this old lady, then, Freud owed what he called 'a single idea of general value' – an idea that would grow into a vision far grander than the seduction theory:

I have found, in my own case too, being in love with my mother and jealousy of my father, and I now consider it a universal event in early childhood.... (Similar to the invention of parentage in paranoia....) If this is so, we can understand the gripping power of *Oedipus rex*.... Everyone in the audience was once a budding Oedipus in fantasy and each recoils in horror from the dream fulfillment here transplanted into reality, with the full quantity of repression which separates his infantile state from his present one.

It would be another thirteen years before Freud coined the term Oedipus complex, but here was certainly the germ of one of the most fundamental of all his concepts. The break with the seduction theory is summed up in the final quoted phrase, where he juxtaposes the dream-fulfilment world of the infantile state with the present reality created by repression. As he put it some eighteen months later, in his most succinct, his starkest formulation: 'Reality – wish fulfilment – it is from these opposites that our mental life springs.' It is around the axis formed by these opposites that *The Interpretation of Dreams* revolves.

Emma Eckstein and the Wish Theory of the Psyche

At each of the stages of development of Freud's theory of wish-fulfilment, Emma Eckstein played a part. The first hint of the importance that wishing would take on for Freud came in March 1895, in the same letter as the first report on the seriousness of Emma's condition:

a small analogy to Emma E.'s dream psychosis that we witnessed. Rudi Kaufmann, a very intelligent nephew of Breuer's and also a medical man, is a late riser. He has his maidservant wake him, and then is very reluctant to obey her. One morning she woke him again and, since he did not want to listen to her, called him by his name, 'Mr Rudi.' Thereupon the sleeper hallucinated a hospital chart (compare the Rudolfinerhaus) with the name 'Rudolf Kaufmann' on it and said to himself, 'So R. K. is already in the hospital; then I do not need to go there,' and went on sleeping!

Here in this quasi-clinical, almost anecdotal observation, we see the germ of the idea that dreams and pathological mental states are both wish-fulfilments; but it is not developed explicitly in this clinical vein for some time.

In the early 1890s, Freud traced back pathological defence to the incompatibility between an idea and the ego, with the ensuing attempt by the ego to rid itself, through repression, of the threatening idea: the girl who blamed herself because she thought, while nursing her sick father, of a young man who had made an erotic impression on her; the governess who felt her love for her employer to be incompatible with her pride. Unruly wishes may give rise to such incompatibility, but so might other mental processes. The alcoholic who cannot bear to recognize that his addiction has made him impotent is refusing to recognize reality because of the pain it would bring him. The examples seem to cry out for the concept of wish-fulfilment: 'the mother who has fallen ill from the loss of her baby, and now rocks a piece of wood unceasingly in her arms, or the jilted bride who, arrayed in her wedding-dress, has for years been waiting for her bridegroom.' These delusional states were probably close to the dream psychosis that Fliess and Freud, early in 1895, observed in Emma, which he interpreted as due to the power of a wish; he could then see Rudi's simple dream as a brief psychotic episode. The student who sees his name on the hospital chart and the mother who rocks the piece of wood are both in the grip of a powerful wish.

Instead of developing a clinical theory of the importance of wishes, Freud, late in 1895, wrote the *Project for a Scientific Psychology*, a grand speculative model of the mind, based in part on a deductive and mechanistic account of the simple elements of the brain. This developed the concept of wish at a highly theoretical level. Over the next few years, we find developing, unevenly but side by side, two accounts of wishing, one a deductive account, based on the postulated properties of the psychic apparatus, and the other a 'clinical' view of wishes far more akin to the everyday, ordinary language notion. Freud expressed the theoretical line, developed in the *Project* and then in the final chapter of *The Interpretation of Dreams*, most clearly as follows: 'Thought is after all nothing but a substitute for a hallucinatory wish; and it is self-evident that dreams must be wish-fulfilments, since nothing but a wish can set our mental apparatus at work.' The clinical argument, on the other hand, included the discovery that dreams are wish-fulfilments and that neurotic symptoms are *also* wish-fulfilments, *on the analogy with dreams*. Freud had to rediscover this crucial analogy on several occasions – in May 1897, as we have seen, when he linked wish-fulfilment to the libidinal motives for symptom-formation; and then again in February 1899:

Not only dreams are wish fulfilments, so are hysterical attacks. This is true of hysterical symptoms, but probably applies to every product of neurosis, for I recognized it long ago in acute delusional insanity. Reality – wish fulfilment – it is from these opposites that our mental life springs.

The example of acute delusional insanity Freud had in mind was quite probably Emma Eckstein's dream psychosis. When he had observed it back in late 1894 or early 1895, he had immediately made the connection between symptoms and dreams, the connection which was so crucial to his psychology in general, but most of all to the theory of wish-fulfilment.

Why did the concept of the dream as wish-fulfilment take so long to come to its eventual pre-eminent position in Freud's thought? The answer is to be found in the tenacity with which he held to the seduction theory in the period 1895–7. Emma Eckstein's dream psychosis and the dream of Irma's injection may have taught him the importance of wish-fulfilment, but the seduction theory focused his attention on what the temporal conditions for pathological defence were (the prematurity of sexual awakening, the linking of a scene from the presexual era with later sexual desires) at the expense of the simple question: why is the patient thinking this distressing thought in the first place?

But there was another area of Freud's work where wishes began to assume significance: the discovery of the transference.

In one of my patients the origin of a particular hysterical symptom lay in a wish, which she had had many years earlier and had at once relegated to the unconscious, that the man she was talking to at the time might boldly take the initiative and give her a kiss. On one occasion, at the end of a session, a similar wish came up in her about me. She was horrified at it, spent a sleepless night, and at the next session, though she did not refuse to be treated, was quite useless for work. After I had discovered the obstacle and removed it, the work proceeded further; and lo and behold! the wish that had so much frightened the patient made its appearance as the next of her pathogenic recollections and the one which was demanded by the immediate logical context.

This account of the technique of psychotherapy was written in early 1895, just when Freud was treating Emma both analytically and clearing up the mess left by Fliess's bungled operation; the patient who desired a kiss from him may well have been Emma. The aplomb with which Freud dealt with such a desire on the part of a patient, an aplomb he later prided himself on in comparing his response to Breuer's flight from the desiring hysterical patient, was secured by regarding the mental image of Dr Freud kissing his patient as quite definitely the patient's affair. This image had nothing to do with him; this image was strictly a consequence of the patient's *wish*. If Freud hadn't been quite clear that the patient was *wishing* this, and that is why she imagined the man taking the initiative and kissing her, then he would have found himself implicated in the kissing scene. In other words, being clear that the patient was *wishing* this, allowed him to be sure it was the *patient*, not the *analyst*, who produced the transference phenomenon.

Hence the recognition of the transference required that Freud perceive that an important section of the 'ideas' that hysterics repressed were wishes rather than any other sort of mental act (e.g. reproach for an action suffered, etc.). The concepts of transference and wish form a couple, an interdependent pair of concepts: it is implausible to think that one could have one without the other. The crucial importance of the concept of wish-fulfilment in Freud's thought is derived from the concept of transference and the daily practice of dealing with it, more than the abstract demands of his theoretical schema. What we thus see in the early months of 1895 is the emergence of the concept of wish: in the context of Emma's dream psychosis, then of simple wish-fulfilling dreams, of transference wishes in which Freud was implicated by Emma and other patients in imagined erotic scenes, and then, in the summer of that year, in the general thesis that all dreams are wish-fulfilments, and the general theory that the operations of the mind are only ever set in motion because of wishful states. Emma herself supplied him with the clinical material to back up this account: a symptom of not being able to go into shops alone traceable to two scenes, one before puberty, one after. On the first occasion, she had been sexually assaulted in a shop by the shopkeeper; on the second, she had fled from the shop because she thought the assistants were laughing at her. The sexual release on the second occasion unconsciously awakened her memory of the first occasion, transforming the libido into anxiety that she did not understand, because she could not remember the first occasion. Hence her flight. 'Now this case is typical of repression in hysteria. We invariably find that a memory is repressed which has only become a trauma by *deferred action*. The cause of this state of things is the retardation of puberty as compared with the rest of the individual's development.'

Here we see how Freud's espousal of the seduction theory was working against the advance of the wish theory of neuroses and hence of dreams. Emma's case was crystal-clear in terms of her attempted 'seduction' by the shopkeeper. But a year after Emma had nearly bled to death because of Fliess's error, Freud was finding a history of bleeding in her case, turning the dramatic events of her 'bleeding scene' to psychoanalytic use. In other words, he took Emma's response to that scene as evidence of her transference, and reconstructed her prehistoric wishes from the new material:

I know only that she bled out of *longing*. She has always been a bleeder, when cutting herself and in similar circumstances; as a child she suffered from severe nosebleeds; during the years when she was not yet menstruating, she had headaches which were interpreted to her as malingering and which in truth had been generated by suggestion; for this reason she joyously welcomed her severe menstrual bleeding as proof that her illness was genuine, a proof that was also recognized as such by others. She described a scene from the age of fifteen, in which she suddenly began to bleed from the nose when she had the wish to be treated by a certain young doctor who was present (and who also appeared in the dream). When she saw how affected I was by her first hemorrhage while she was in the hands of Rosanes, she experienced this as the realization of an old wish to be loved in her illness, and in spite of the danger during the succeeding hours she felt happy as never before. Then, in the sanatorium, she became restless during the night because of an unconscious wish [*unbewusste*

Sehnsuchtsabsicht] to entice me to go there; since I did not come during the night, she renewed the bleedings, as an unfailing means of rearousing my affection.

So Freud shows how this terrible accident had been employed by Emma's unconscious wishes to her advantage. What is remarkable is the sureness of touch he displays in wending his way towards using the traumatic bleeding scene for the purposes of advancing Emma's *analysis*. And it is here, again, in the context of a transference interpretation, that we find him employing the term 'wish'.

Several months later, Freud discovered one of Emma's childhood memories. Its tone was that of the medieval fantasy-horror, one which Freud now perceived as so analogous to his patients' stories, just as Charcot had linked the symptoms of the hysteric with the grand religious bodily seizures of the Middle Ages. In this memory, Freud had found another scene of seduction, of violation. Yet, in contrast to Emma's memory of the shopkeeper's assault, or to the reality of Fliess's bloody violation of her, it was by now completely ambiguous to what extent this was a real seduction, a real event:

Why are the confessions [of those possessed by the devil] under torture so like the communications made by my patients in psychic treatment? ... Eckstein has a scene where the diabolus sticks needles into her fingers and then places a candy on each drop of blood. As far as the blood is concerned, you are completely without blame! A counterpart to this: fear of needles and pointed objects from the second psychic period. In regard to cruelty in general: fear of injuring someone with a knife or otherwise.

A week later, there was a new scene:

Imagine, I obtained a scene about the circumcision of a girl. The cutting off of a piece of the labium minor (which is even shorter today), sucking up the blood, after which the child was given a piece of the skin to eat. This child, at age 13, once claimed that she could swallow a part of an earthworm and proceeded to do it. An operation you once performed was affected by a hemophilia that originated in this way.

Emma's longing, her eager collaboration in her analysis, gave Freud much precious material; she had the ability to provoke him emotionally – 'So this is the strong sex!' – and to contribute substantial changes and fundamental new elements to his theories: the wish theory of psychosis and dreams; the transferential reconstruction of her early pleasures in menstruation and its prehistory in her battles with her family; fantastic scenes from her inner life, in the no-man's land between fantasy and memory, resonating with the sadistic acts and fantasies of a former historical epoch. And she showed Freud how his ideas and techniques would finally make their way in the world. Not through publications, books and lectures, but along the prolonged and painful path by which his unhappy and neurotic patients would themselves become analysts. Just as Freud entered his self-analysis, discovering that he could only help his patients when he made himself a patient, when he attempted to heal his own neurosis, it was as if the inverted mirroring process was taking place in Emma: she got up off the couch and started to treat other neurotic patients.

By the end of 1897, Emma Eckstein had once again made her mark in the history of psychoanalysis, by taking her own patients and working with them according to Freud's technique, providing Freud with support he much appreciated: 'Eckstein deliberately treated her patient in such a manner as not to give her the slightest hint of what would emerge from the unconscious and in the process obtained from her, among other things, the identical scenes with the father. Incidentally, the young girl is doing very well.'

Emma Eckstein was born in Vienna on 28 January 1865 to a well-known bourgeois family. The child of Albert (born 1825) and Amalia (née Wehle, in 1836) Eckstein, she had five sisters and two brothers. Her father was an inventor who owned a parchment factory; one of her brothers was Gustav Eckstein (1875–1916), a social democrat and associate of Karl Kautsky, the leader of the Socialist Party; and a sister, Therese Schlesinger, a socialist, was one of the first women members of parliament. Emma never married, living with her mother for many years. When she started her treatment with Freud, she was nearly thirty; as we have seen, the treatment lasted something in the region of three years – one of the most protracted and detailed of Freud's early cases. There is also some evidence that she had a further analysis with him sometime around 1910. Emma certainly became a follower of Freud's, but less in psychoanalysis than in the area of sexual and social hygiene. A two-page article on education that she wrote in 1899 was rather strict and authoritarian in tone, and denied that sexuality was a part of childhood. It is as if she assented to the account of her past that Freud gave in 1895, and left to one side the question of the torturing fantasies he discussed in 1897. In late 1902, she was working on a pamphlet, which was eventually published in 1904 as *The Question of Sexuality in the Raising of Children.* During 1903, she was discussing it with Freud and borrowing books from him, as we learn from their correspondence of the period. He commented, somewhat critically, on the earlier draft of the pamphlet, but was warmly approving of the final version, which, alluding to its pedagogical tone, he nicknamed 'the light of the world'.

Much of her pamphlet was devoted to the dangers of masturbation in childhood, calling for a much wider recognition of its prevalence and seriousness, and for the need for official education about its dangers. It is with the healthy part of the child, she argued, that one must ally in order to combat the practice of this secret and solitary vice, whose temptations she described with the passion of personal experience. In particular, she focused in on how daydreams, those 'parasitic plants', invaded the life of young girls. In this respect, she was describing a characteristic feature of the girlhood not only of herself, but of many others of her era who would enter psychoanalysis, from Bertha Pappenheim to Anna Freud. But she also drew on her own psychotherapeutic experience when she described treating an eighteen year old who reluctantly revealed how she was convinced that one could get pregnant from dancing, from massage or from a kiss; this revelation Emma confessed to seeing at first as the product of a diseased imagination, until she realized how universal and representative of the imaginings of young girls it was. Emma's tone and approach was to be repeated when Hermine Hug-Hellmuth published *A Young Girl's Diary* in 1919, in which one finds similar beliefs and fears; by then these were entirely familiar to psychoanalysts, but they still had the capacity to shock a wider public, just as they had at first shocked Emma.

Emma had become friendly not only with Freud, but with other members of his family, in particular Minna; from 1895 on, Freud's tone in his letters was chatty and familiar, telling her how the children were, why she should go off to the mountains to practise winter sports for her health, and urging her to get in touch to fix up another meeting when he had to cancel at the last moment. But, as we would expect from the stormy course of Freud's treatment of Emma in the 1890s, the relationship did not always run smoothly. Unfinished business from those earlier days was still very much on the agenda in Freud's letter to Emma of November 1905, a reply to the angry and hurt letter she had sent him when he declined to take her back into treatment:

That you could be so misled, could so misunderstand the freedom to say anything in the treatment, and attribute to me the intention of offending [you] when I relied on my unshakeable trust in your friendship and your love of truth in order to permit you to obtain insight into a delicate but nevertheless usual and expectable transference – that, it is true, did not shake my opinion of you, but it did again instill in me respect for the elemental femaleness with which I constantly have to struggle. [All he meant was] that it is impossible for me to let the discontinuation of treatment (the interruption, I hope) be explained with the pretext that I regard your pains as organic.

Freud continued that it would be closer to the truth to say that they had had a quarrel, or she could not accept something he had asserted, or she simply wanted time to think things over. Yet he could not resist offering her an analytic interpretation, clearly referring back to his working of the transference during her treatment:

May I at the end draw your attention to a small contradiction which is in fact at the bottom of your being angry. At one time I am supposed to have offended you by denying you the qualities that would attract a man; the other time I must have offended you by explaining to you how it happened that in our relationship love did not appear. Can both injuries really be comprehended from the same standpoint? I hope you will soon tell me: No (which, after all, you like to say)....

Whilst it is difficult to interpret this letter – and this is a difficulty characteristic of many of Freud's letters to former patients, in which he slips into talking in an intimate code that was clearly developed in the course of their private and long drawn-out sessions – it seems probable that Freud is asking Emma to recognize that, while she had hoped Freud would fall in love with her, the conditions for a man falling in love with her are different from those governing an analyst falling in love. Analysts are not like ordinary men, he seems to be saying. She may have made herself unattractive to men, but that is irrelevant to the question of *his* falling in love with her.

Emma's anger at Freud, and his response in terms of her transference, her unrequited love, was probably quite a familiar experience for him, even by 1905. Certainly what he wrote in 1915 about analytic relationships with certain 'elemental' women fits his handling of this episode with Emma like a glove:

There is, it is true, one class of women with whom this attempt to preserve the erotic transference for the purposes of analytic work without satisfying it will not succeed. These are women of elemental passionateness who tolerate no surrogates. They are children of nature who refuse to accept the psychical in place of the material, who, in the poet's words, are accessible only to 'the logic of soup, with dumplings for arguments'. With such people one has the choice between returning their love or else bringing down upon oneself the full enmity of a woman scorned. In neither case can one safeguard the interests of the treatment. One has to withdraw, unsuccessful; and all one can do is to turn the problem over in one's mind of how it is that a capacity for neurosis is joined with such an intractable need for love.

Freud's letter to Emma of November 1905 is also evidence that the question 'organic or psychic?', the question that was so much a part of the dream of Irma's injection, continued to plague his relations with her, but also with himself. It was ultimately to be the cause of their parting. One of Freud's early followers was Dr Dora Teleky, a member of another comfortable Viennese family and the second wife of the son of Freud's mentor, Ernst Brücke. She had been one of only three auditors of Freud's lecture course at the University in 1900 and, in 1903 and 1904, was the first woman to register officially for Freud's courses. Teleky was a good friend of Emma's and her family. In 1910 or thereabouts, Teleky claimed to find an ulcer or a collection of pus on Emma's abdomen; she operated and removed it, or perhaps only pretended to do so. Emma, who at this stage seemed to want to find an organic base to her pain, felt briefly better. Freud was angry at the radical interference by another doctor – perhaps too angry, since it brought back shades of the Fliess episode. He is reported to have said that Emma would now never get better: 'Well, that's the end of Emma, that dooms her from now on, nobody can cure her neurosis.' It seems that in the event he was right. Emma took to her couch and remained a partial invalid until she died on 30 July 1924 of a cerebral haemorrhage.

Some years later, Freud referred to an Eckstein again in his writings, this time to her brother Friedrich, 'a friend of mine, whose insatiable craving for knowledge has led him to make the most unusual experiments and has ended by giving him encyclopaedic knowledge'. Friedrich

has assured me that through the practices of Yoga, by withdrawing from the world, by fixing the attention on bodily functions and by peculiar methods of breathing, one can in fact evolve new sensations and coenaesthesias in oneself, which he regards as regressions to primordial states of mind which have long ago been overlaid. He sees in them a physiological basis, as it were, of much of the wisdom of mysticism.

Once again, an Eckstein had something to teach Freud about the relation between the mind and the body, and he treated this distinctly unFreudian sort of knowledge with more tolerance and seeming openmindedness than one might have expected. Perhaps Emma had managed to teach him some caution.

The last direct communication from Freud to Emma that we possess is a letter he wrote on 4 August 1906, telling her in an intimate and chatty tone about a mutual friend whose life was no longer in danger and about his holiday activities. He had been prompted to write to her, he said in opening the letter, by a dream about her.

The Three Daughters

We now know how appropriate it was for Freud to communicate with Emma on account of a dream: she was one of the crucial female figures merged with the figure of Anna Hammerschlag-Lichtheim in the dream of Irma's injection. But we have not as yet considered the three female figures who lie behind all the others: the three daughters. Straight off we know there is something wrong about Freud's interpretation of his dream to Abraham: he implies that the three godmothers are included in the dream because of their relation to his daughters. But one of those daughters had not as yet been born, when he dreamed the dream – although she was the true object of the dream insofar as the dream centred on his wife's pregnant condition, and insofar as the dream was a prophetic metaphor for the birth of psychoanalysis. With the analysis of the dream, Freud could legitimately say, 'Here, on July 24, 1895, the secret of the dream revealed itself to Dr Sigm. Freud.' But it would be equally true to say that the dream announced the birth of psychoanalysis, by cloaking its birth in the figure of the baby to be born four and a half months later.

Or is it the other way round? Did the birth of psychoanalysis cloak the birth of that baby, that Anna named after the figure of Anna in the dream, the Anna who would devote her life to psychoanalysis, would take on the cloak of her father after he was dead and, as Elisabeth Young-Bruehl so movingly describes, lives her last days snuggled inside his cloak. There is a lot of confusion about children and women in this dream, and it was to continue. As Freud became ever more convinced of the seduction theory, it became ever more plausible to interpret Irma's injection as revealing his own sexual desires for his daughters. 'I have them all' – not only the widowed young women friends, but the daughters they symbolized. Such dreams continued to dog Freud as he wrestled with the seduction theory.

Recently I dreamed of overaffectionate feelings for Mathilde, only she was called Hella; and afterward I again saw 'Hella' before me, printed in heavy type. Solution: Hella is the name of an American niece whose picture we have been sent.

Mathilde could be called Hella because she recently shed bitter tears over the defeats of the Greeks. She is enthralled by the mythology of ancient Hellas and naturally regards all Hellenes as heroes. The dream of course shows the fulfillment of my wish to catch a *Pater* as the originator of neurosis and thus puts an end to my ever-recurring doubts.

The ambiguity of this dream is striking. To prove his seduction theory is right, Freud has an erotic dream about his daughter: he sacrifices himself to science by taking on the mantle of the father who seduces his daughters. He confirms his theory by besmirching his own character. Of course, the dream would bear a different reading if Freud, in his heart of hearts, did not really believe in his theory. Upholding the theory keeps at a distance the fear that the dream reveals a 'real' desire for Mathilde. So it is clear how the seduction theory itself has become an alibi; the theory itself now embodies an exculpation: Freud *qua* father is not responsible for this erotic wish for his daughter, any more than Freud *qua* man is responsible for Irma's pains or the erotic, transferential desires of his patients. Erotic thoughts about his daughter stem from *other* people's perverse impulses, those perverse patients of his with whose mental processes he *identifies* in order to construct the theory of their neuroses. It is always the patient who is responsible for these wishes in the transference, with Freud the analyst following on afterwards, in their wake. But the seduction theory works the opposite way round: it is always the father (as opposed to the patient) who is responsible for the introduction of the erotic into the parent–child relationship. Soon, however, Freud's double exculpation (in his work with patients, the transference; in his theories, the responsibility of the father) was to fall more into line: it is the child in the patient who transfers erotic wishes to the analyst, repeating without knowing it ancient erotic wishes from his or her childhood. So the demise of the seduction theory represents the victory of one part of Freud's theory over the other: it represents the victory of the reality of transference over the reality of infantile sexual memories.

Freud's self-control in his sexual life was matched by his control over his dream-life. Wild dreams, incomprehensible dreams revealed themselves as steps forward in the elaboration of his theory. 'Hella' sounds the same as '*heller*', meaning 'clearer': Freud's dream was also a desire to see more clearly, to see the girl more clearly perhaps as well. And who is Hella? Hella was his niece in America, his sister Anna's third daughter, born in 1893. Again, the third daughter … Yet nieces also had a special place in Freud's past. His original niece was Pauline, his near-contemporary, whom he and John had treated so badly as children, robbing her of her flowers. Maybe there was another reason why Freud baulked at publishing the idea of fathers seducing daughters; the disguise he usually chose, that it was the uncle not the father, recalled his own original active assault on his niece. When he talked of uncles seducing nieces, he had as his paradigm himself, aged three, seducing his niece aged two and a half!

It would be too risky, it seems, to admit that the father could be a seducer, and even eventually that he desires to have a daughter *in order* to seduce her. That he wishes to become an analyst in order to exercise – by means of hypnosis, suggestion, transference, interpretation bearing upon the sexual economy, upon proscribed sexual representations – a *lasting seduction upon the hysteric.*

As Freud retracted the seduction theory, the theme of the father seducing his daughters receded. He was attempting to find, in his relationships to his female patients, a middle way between the absolute authority of the hypnotist and the figure of the seducer – the figure which appeared once his failure as such an authority was revealed to him by his patients' refusal to conform to his truths. Yet the theme of the three women persisted. In September 1898, a dream evoked 'three women who had brought the greatest happiness and sorrow' into a man's life and, behind them, the 'three Fates who spin the destiny of man, and I knew that one of the three women – the inn-hostess in the dream [who was making Knödel] – was the mother who gives life, and furthermore (as in my own case) gives the living creature its first nourishment. Love and hunger, I reflected, meet at a woman's breast.' But the childhood memory evoked by this 'dream of the three fates' also located the mother as the harbinger of death, presaging the three women, each versions of the mother, each versions of death, evoked as we have seen in 'The Theme of the Three Caskets':

When I was six years old and was given my first lessons by my mother, I was expected to believe that we were all made of earth and must therefore return to earth. This did not suit me and I expressed doubts of the doctrine. My mother thereupon rubbed the palms of her hands together – just as she did in making dumplings, except that there was no dough between them – and showed me the blackish scales of *epidermis* produced by the friction as a proof that we were made of earth.

And, in between the woman who gives life and the woman who reveals death, in the short span of life we have, there is no time to lose. *Carpe diem*, the dream tells Freud: 'One should never neglect an opportunity, but always take what one can even when it involves doing a small wrong. One should never neglect an opportunity, since life is short and death inevitable.'

The theme of permitting himself something, some sexual pleasure, is the same, running from the dream of Irma's injection through the dream of the three fates, and continuing in the dream that repeated Irma's injection for *On Dreams*, the abbreviated version of *The Interpretation of Dreams* that Freud wrote in late 1900:

Company at table or table d'hôte ... spinach was being eaten ... Frau E. L. was sitting beside me; she was turning her whole attention to me and laid her hand on my knee in an intimate manner. I removed her hand unresponsively. She then said: 'But you've always had such beautiful eyes.' ... I then had an indistinct picture of two eyes, as though it were a drawing or like the outline of a pair of spectacles. ...

Frau E. L., like Irma, is an old family friend, but, this time, one whom Freud has not seen for a long time. Her real identity is, almost certainly, Bertha Breuer, Josef and Mathilde's eldest daughter, who in 1893 married Paul, Anna Hammerschlag's brother. Freud advertises his indifference to this woman, both in the dream and in the associations: 'a person with whom I have hardly at any time been on friendly terms, nor, so far as I know, have I ever wished to have any closer relations with her.' Behind her is the figure of Minna Bernays, who now concentrates in herself the figure of patient, of friend, of family and of equivocal erotic object. '[I]n the dream thoughts the chief emphasis is laid on a wish for once to enjoy unselfish love, love which "costs nothing".' The intertwining of these thoughts has led some historians to speculate that the secret hidden behind this dream is Freud's supposed affair with Minna. It is as plausible to suggest another speculation, of greater weight, but equally unprovable: that Freud had *analysed* Minna. To gauge the weight of this speculation, one only has to reflect that it is at least plausible that Freud analysed Minna; whereas it is utterly implausible that he analysed Martha.

The dream of *Company at table or table d'hôte* is centred on the idea of what has to be paid for love, and the debts we necessarily incur in our friendships and relations in life. In this repetition of the Irma dream, it is a woman, Minna, who replaces Fliess, the intellectual confidant and friend, as well as standing in for the three women whom Freud possesses. Freud's growing 'independence' from his male colleagues can be gauged from this and by the fact that, whereas colleagues and patients were opposed to one another in the Irma dream, in the dream of *Company at table or table d'hôte* the colleague and the patient have become one, just as Emma Eckstein became both colleague and patient.

Freud's debt to his female patients was clear in *The Interpretation of Dreams* and throughout the 1890s. It would seem he was one of those men who was more prickly about the debts he had to male patrons and teachers than to these women. In the dream of Irma's injection, he still looks to Fliess for support in his battle with his other medical colleagues for full possession of the patients. By 1900, after his self-analysis, Freud no longer needed so acutely what he would later call the homosexual relation to men: a passive relation to an admired friend and patron. History would have its revenge on his behalf. In the dream, all the medical colleagues criticize him, and disparage and ridicule his treatment of his patients. Each of those medical colleagues became the butt of Freud's derision for not being his follower. And each was to suffer the fate of seeing his children follow Freud. Oscar Rie, always lukewarm about Freud's findings, despite being Freud's close friend and family doctor, eventually did marry, as Freud had hoped he would in associating to the dream, and then had two daughters: Marianne, later married to Ernst Kris, who became a psychoanalyst, and Margarethe, who was analysed by Freud and later married the analyst Herman Nunberg. Leopold Rosenberg's daughter Anny, later Katan, also became an analyst and was analysed by her childhood friend and enemy, Anna Freud. Although none of Breuer's children became analysts, in October 1895 Freud could refer to Robert, Breuer's twenty-six-year-old son, as 'my only follower in Vienna'. Fliess himself had a son, Robert, who became an analyst and the editor of a volume with the scintillatingly appropriate title *The Psychoanalytic Reader* – exactly the role his father had been the first to create, and a role which was his only lasting claim to fame. Family networks would always be the core of psychoanalysis, ever since that July night in 1895 when Freud's dream of the sexual possession of three women fulfilled his desire for professional, familial and filial ascendancy.

Freud's dream came true. He succeeded in capturing the hearts and minds of the children, whose status in the dream as hidden objects of desire is so ambiguous ('I have them all'). And they, by displacement in the form of his friends' children, would be the vindication and guarantee of immortality that Freud sought ('was not having children our only path to immortality?'). And he also succeeded by building psychoanalysis out of not only his desires for his patients, but also out of their resistances.

If Irma's injection portrayed a dialectic between the bad and the ideal patient, by 1900 Freud had no need of the ideal patient. He knew now that patients are all the same. To be a patient is to be in a state of resistance to the analyst. If he had any doubts on that matter, his next patient was to prove the supreme test case.

5

DORA:
AN EXEMPLARY
FAILURE

If there is one woman who sums up for many what is both fascinating and repellent, most subtle and most bullying in Freud's relationships with women, then that woman is Dora. Dora was brought to Freud by her father for treatment in 1900 for '*tussis nervosa*, aphonia, depression and *taedium vitae*'. Her treatment formed the basis for Freud's longest case history of a women patient, one who has since captured the sympathy of many of Freud's readers, but latterly above all of feminists. 'The core example of the protesting force of women', 'a resistant heroine' for Hélène Cixous, the French theorist, Dora's case history has become an 'urtext in the history of woman'. She has become the symbol of that character-type of the nineteenth century, the hysterical woman, symbol of the 'silent revolt against male power over women's bodies and women's language'. The story of Dora provides a paradigm case for catching patriarchy with its pants down, of tracing how 'sexual union is understood accurately as a power relation' and is irrevocably cast in the terms of dominance and submission. Dora is a feminist before her time, 'the one who resists the system, the one who cannot stand that the family and society are founded on the body of women, on bodies despised, rejected, bodies that are humiliating once they have been used.'

'To that must be added that in Dora there is a very beautiful feminine homosexuality, a love for woman that is astounding', a homosexuality that she triumphantly kept secret from Freud, as she led him away from her secret love for a woman, allowing him to concentrate his energies and intelligence on a busy masculine network of deceiving and humiliating relationships. Her rapid departure from Freud's treatment is viewed as her triumph, and perhaps her only way out of being recoded back into the normalizing and Oedipal ways with which Freud was unconsciously complicit.

Michel Foucault was the first to see in Dora a champion of those to whom the sexuality of men was 'foreign' and 'violating': 'Dora was cured, not despite the interruption of her analysis, but because in taking the decision to interrupt it, she fully and completely took on herself the solitude of which her existence up till then had only been the wayward wandering.' Yet the way in which

Dora walked out on Freud is not unambiguously the victory of her desire for self-determining solitude, it is not necessarily a 'proto-feminist political vote'. Some feminists feel relief when Dora is finally done with Freud's tricksy games, so much an extension of the games her own family sucked her into playing; but her departure may not have been so much 'the incarnation of the revolt of women forced to silence, but rather a declaration of defeat'. For Dora to have truly succeeded, we would have to see her finding the promised land that can be glimpsed through her story, regaining the 'adorable, white body' of her loved one, and her own feminine, silent body, the feminine enjoyment that lies beyond the phallic world of Oedipal triangles, 'the (m)Other Woman whom Dora adores'.

Ida Bauer, to give Dora back her real name, was born on 1 November 1882, at Berggasse 32, down the street from the flat the Freuds lived in from 1891 on, where she underwent her analysis. She was the second of two children of her parents, Philipp and Katharina. Katharina (*née* Gerber), or Käthe as she was usually known, was some eight years younger than her husband, to whom she had been engaged at the age of seventeen and married at nineteen. She came from the mountain town of Königinhof (today Dvur Kralové in north central Czechoslovakia) and spoke Czech as a child. In later years, she missed her family and would often return to visit them, with or without her husband and children – yet another symbol of the distance between her and her husband and children which was so characteristic of her later life.

Ida's father, the third of four children, was born in 1853, in Pollerskirchen, Bohemia, of a Jewish family in the textile trade. In the late 1850s or early 1860s, the family moved to Vienna. The striking similarities between his and Freud's backgrounds ended with Philipp going into the family business, rather than to university, and making a marriage which combined the resources of two family textile businesses. Philipp became a successful industrial manufacturer of cloth, owning two factories in what is now Czechoslovakia, at Warnsdorf and Nachod.

Certainly well-off, the family lived unpretentiously, in the style of those cultured Jewish families who had left the ghettos with the mid-nineteenth-century reforms and espoused to their very bones the cause of liberalism and the value of art and learning. A charming, friendly, intellectually alive man, of considerable perspicacity, shrewdness and obstinacy, Philipp also had a gift for deviousness and for seeing the world through his own, peculiarly tinted spectacles. His life was a story of a struggle with many bodily ailments and illness. Blind in one eye from birth, he had, like many young men of his class, entered marriage infected with syphilis. In 1888, when Ida was six, he was diagnosed as having tuberculosis. On medical advice, the family moved to Merano, the spa where female members of Freud's own family, amongst them Minna and Anna, would often spend long periods, nursing their illnesses and convalescing. Ida grew up in this town of wealthy transients from the age of six to 1898, when she was nearly sixteen. In those ten years, Philipp recovered markedly from his tuberculosis, and during this time Ida performed many of the nursing duties his condition necessitated. But in 1892 Philipp suffered a detached retina in his one good eye and became effectively blind. Then, as Ida's brother, Otto, was later to write in a letter to Karl Kautsky, 'the miracle happened; when the functioning eye was affected by the detached retina, the other eye, considered blind until then, adapted to the service demanded of it; after about three months, it could read and write. ... [This was] the most impressive experience of my childhood.'

It was at this time, Freud surmised, that Philipp's wife learnt of his syphilitic history from Ida's paternal aunt. From the estrangement to which this knowledge led, the mother emerged possessed by a cleanliness compulsion and the constant fear of contamination, which Ida described to Freud; Otto's friends were astounded by the unreasonable demands his mother made upon her family. The single major point of contact between Ida and her mother that Freud was to detect was in their shared preoccupation with the contamination that sexuality entails: the fear of venereal disease, the disgust at the white vaginal discharge, or 'catarrh' as the women called it, that both of them suffered from, sharing the view that it was Philipp who had loaded this bodily burden on both of them. In addition, Ida would often accompany her mother to spas, where she would seek relief from her vaginal and bowel complaints.

Philipp, Ida and her brother all agreed to treat Käthe as the collective cross they had to bear, and she seems to have absented herself, through her cleaning and preoccupation with contamination, from engagement with any of them. Freud agreed to fall in with Ida's contemptuous dismissal of her mother, effectively ignoring any significance her mother might have had in her life; this uncharacteristic compliance of his with Ida's view of reality is less surprising when we observe that the mother is generally given scant treatment in Freud's patients' histories.

Within two years of his miraculous recovery from blindness, in 1894, Philipp was struck down by another serious illness, when his syphilis entered its tertiary stage and a meningeal inflammation caused some paralysis and mental disturbance. A new friend of the family's in Merano, a commercial traveller by the name of Hans Zellenka, recommended that Philipp consult Freud in Vienna, which he did with some success for his illness. During this third period of illness, Zellenka's wife, who was herself often in poor health, nursed Philipp, in place both of Ida and of the increasingly withdrawn Käthe. It soon became clear to all that Philipp and his nurse, 'this young and beautiful woman', as Ida later described her, were embarked on a 'common love-affair'. Yet Ida herself also grew close to the Zellenkas, whom Freud renamed Herr and Frau K. in his case history. She became 'almost a mother' to their two children, one of whom, Klara, suffered from a congenital heart defect. She conveniently kept the children from interrupting the discreet *rendezvous* of her father and his lover. And Ida also became intimate friends with Frau Zellenka, to the point where, on the joint summer holidays the families would take, Ida shared a bed with her, and Herr Zellenka was evicted from the marital chamber.

Ida was sent to a convent school in Merano, the Kloster der Englischer Fräulein, and was unable, because of her sex, to go on to a Gymnasium like her brother. She was also under the tutelage of a series of governesses, who were, as we will later see, to play a significant part in her view of the relations between men and women. In 1890, when she was eight, she had the first attack of what Freud would later call her '*petite hystérie*': an attack of dyspnoea – difficulty in breathing – which necessitated a rest for six months. In 1894, at the age of twelve, at the same time as her father was stricken with tertiary syphilis and grew close to Frau Zellenka, Ida was sick again, with migraine, loss of voice and chronic coughs. In the early summer of 1898, Philipp brought her to Freud for a consultation, but nothing came of it, as the symptoms soon faded of their own accord. But that same summer saw a change in Ida's attitude to her father's friendships with the Zellenkas. Having suddenly and inexplicably cut short her stay at the Zellenkas' lakeside villa, Ida informed her mother that Herr Zellenka had propositioned her while they were walking beside the lake. Philipp and Käthe called Herr Zellenka to account, and he denied any such proposal. He also cast doubt on Ida's pure-mindedness, backing this up with information about Ida's salacious reading habits and interests with which his wife had supplied him.

This incident took place when Ida was fifteen, although Freud described her as sixteen, having displaced by one year her ages throughout his case history. Later that year, the Bauers left Merano for good, settling briefly at Reichenberg near Philipp's factories, but then later that year moving to Vienna. The movements of the Zellenkas appeared to be co-ordinated with those of the wealthier Bauers, so that Philipp and his lover were never apart for long. In the two years after the scene at the lake in June 1898, Ida turned against the Zellenkas, pressing her father to break off all relations with both of them, but particularly with the wife. Her father refused to do so. Ida's affection for her father disappeared and her relations with her mother grew even worse: she stopped eating and wrote a suicide note, which her parents found. In the middle of an argument with her father about the Zellenkas, she lost consciousness and was seized with convulsions of which she remembered nothing. Philipp resolved to take her to Freud, 'to try and bring her to reason' and to cure her of her depression, irritability and attempts to blackmail her parents with threats of suicide.

Freud enthusiastically greeted Ida as a patient who would provide him with a suitable test of his theories of hysteria, his technique of analysis and of the interpretation of dreams. The picklock he took to Ida's case was his claim that 'sexuality is the key to the problem of the psychoneuroses. ... No one who disdains the key will ever be able to unlock the door.' But he wished also to demonstrate how 'dream-interpretation is woven into the history of a treatment and how it can become the means of filling in amnesias and elucidating symptoms.' So he constructed his case history in three parts: Part I described 'the clinical picture', starting with Ida's father's account of her illness and why he had brought her to Freud. Parts II and III gave a heavily annotated record of the interpretation of two of Ida's dreams, whose analyses had in part led to the findings sketched in Part I, and in part extended that clinical history further. The second dream in particular revealed new material, largely because the end of its interpretation coincided with the end of Ida's analysis. On the third day of their exploration of the dream she announced and acted upon her intention to leave Freud.

The significance of the scene by the lake to Ida was not lost even on her father as he introduced Freud to the circumstances of his daughter's illness. At first glance, this scene, this 'insult to her honour', was a perfect candidate for the traumatic incident which Breuer's and Freud's earliest theories had required in hysteria; what is more, it was an unambiguously sexual scene. Ida must have quickly placed considerable trust in Freud – or, alternatively, found out pretty quickly what sort of stories would keep him happy and on her side – because she soon told him of a second, earlier incident, 'secret till her confession during the treatment'. When she was thirteen or fourteen, Herr Zellenka had stage-managed a scene in which he could be alone with her and had suddenly 'clasped the girl to him and pressed a kiss upon her lips.' Ida's reaction had been a violent feeling of disgust. Yet she told no one about it. With this second traumatic incident, so reminiscent of many other pairs of incidents, starting with Emma Eckstein's twinned scenes in shops, Freud would have had the ingredients for an account of Ida's hysteria, if he still maintained the traumatic theory. Yet instead he asserted that Ida's reaction of disgust on the first occasion was in itself hysterical, and reconstructed her having felt Herr Zellenka's erect penis against her body.

Instead of the genital sensation which would certainly have been felt by a healthy girl in such circumstances, Dora was overcome by the unpleasurable feeling which is proper to the tract of mucous membrane at the entrance to the alimentary canal – that is by disgust.

Many later writers – including Erik Erikson, Steven Marcus and Peter Gay – have felt obliged to protest at Freud demanding of Ida, at the age of thirteen or fourteen, the healthy awakening of her throbbing clitoris as it responds to the erect member pressed against her, instead of her disgust, displaced upwards towards what would become the locus of so much of their mutual investigation, the mouth. However, this passage makes clear that Freud viewed her throughout as having 'had the capacities for sexual response of a grown woman.' More to the point, he uniformly regarded the response of disgust as an agent of repression, no different from any other of the agents of 'civilized sexual morality', such as shame or guilt, or of the tyrannical super-ego whose claims to respect he was to undercut so mercilessly in the name of a freer sexual life. In viewing her violent feeling of disgust as pathological, he was 'affirming the positive nature of female sexuality' and was being the 'advocate of nature, sexuality, openness, and candor'.

Yet it is also equally true that the Freud who is so certain of the pathology of her response is the Freud whose psychoanalytic knowledge is a violation of her psychosexual privacy, the Freud whose interpretations are like erect, violating members requiring her assent, even if it comes in a form which he, at least, regards as satisfactory, that of her vigorous *dissent*. This Freud is re-enacting in his conversations with Ida the sexual advances of Herr Zellenka. Out of self-defence, perhaps, Ida slipped away at this point, declining to follow up Freud's pursuit of Herr Zellenka's forgotten erect member, instead continually reproaching her father and dwelling, with much pain, on her father's love affair with Frau Zellenka: '*here there were no gaps to be found in her memory*'.

Ida unfolds the story of this family affair, showing Freud how everyone had been sacrificed, or assigned their role, in a merry-go-round designed to ensure the tranquillity of Philipp and Frau Zellenka's pursuit of their mutual pleasure and company. Even Käthe Bauer told Ida that she owed her husband's life to the other woman's good offices, because Frau Zellenka had, she was led to believe, persuaded him to desist from suicide for the sake of the children. Here Ida's insight was merciless, seeing the story of suicide as a typically extravagant one invented by lovers intent on securing themselves elbow-room. And she could also see how Frau Zellenka's poor health now depended entirely on her husband's presence, the proverbial headache systematically employed. As she retailed for Freud her bitter knowledge of the tricks others played on each other, how they arranged things 'to get the greatest possible pleasure from an adulterous situation', she was supplying him with the weapons he would use against her to explain her own predicament.

Ida was overcome by the feeling that 'she had been handed over to Herr K. as the price of his tolerating the relations between her father and his wife; and her rage at her father's making such a use of her was visible behind her affection for him.' Freud found himself obliged to agree, yet was also embarrassed and reluctant to do so. After all, if he were to agree with Ida's indictment of her family and its hangers-on, agree that it was their manipulation of her which caused her malaise, why should he not talk to Philipp Bauer on Ida's behalf, convince him of the truth of her accusation against Herr Zellenka and show him the justice of Ida's demand that he terminate the family's friendship with the Zellenkas?

It is this course of action that Freud declined to follow, fearing that Ida would have won a victory which was just the mirror image of the father's and the Zellenkas' manipulations. He declined to be manipulated by her into acting as her agent. Instead, he went on the offensive. Rather than agreeing with her, commiserating with her or becoming incensed on her behalf, he unsettled the reassurance she gained from analysing and describing the moral disorder surrounding her. He turned her reproaches against her father and Frau Zellenka on herself. Hadn't she been entirely complicit in overlooking the attentions of Herr Zellenka? Hadn't she done more than overlook the lovers' meetings of her father and Frau Zellenka? Hadn't she often enough aided and abetted in them? Hadn't she explained away the warnings of her independently minded governess about the moral unseemliness of these comings and goings by attributing these to the spite of a jealous woman whose good relations with Ida were only a mask worn to catch the eye of her employer, Philipp Bauer, whose love she sought? And hadn't she drawn this conclusion about her governess's love for her father by observing how the governess was kind to Ida when he was present and ignored her entirely when he was not? Hadn't Ida behaved in exactly the same way as this governess when she so promptly stepped into the shoes of Frau Zellenka, often preoccupied elsewhere, and cared for and taught the Zellenkas' children, discussing them at length with Herr Zellenka and becoming their mother?

Ida's complicity in her father's relations with Frau Zellenka, and her readiness to take over Frau Zellenka's maternal functions, persuaded Freud to inform her that 'she had all these years been in love with Herr K.' Yet he immediately recognized that, if this were the case, Ida's refusal of his proposal by the lake was inexplicable. Most of the rest of the analysis was devoted to discovering why she had refused him. His solution was to show how so many of her symptoms expressed a revival of her old affection for her father, summoned up so as to suppress her longing and love for Herr Zellenka and to save her pride. Ida, Freud pointed out, was behaving towards her father like a 'jealous wife', putting herself in both her mother's and Frau Zellenka's place: 'she was in love with him.' Thus the episodic character of her cough, though copied from the similarly episodic poor health that Herr Zellenka's departures and returns to Merano induced in his wife, expressed a longing for Herr Zellenka. Here, however, the model was that of a sexual relation she inferred took place between her impotent father and his lover: oral intercourse, a woman sucking a penis, itself modelled on the sucking at the breast of a child. As was first pointed out by Lacan, followed by others, Freud was too ready here to place Ida in a quasi-feminine role of nurse to a man's penis, too ready to insert the erect penis into a scene where it probably does not belong, overlooking the more plausible fantasy of Ida identifying with the impotent man who gives and receives satisfaction in sucking a woman's genitals.

As was to prove increasingly the case, Freud was so intent on explaining Ida's repudiation of Herr Zellenka that he overlooked Ida's more secret love for Frau Zellenka. But Freud was the first to notice his own oversight. At the end of Part I of the case history, he apologized for having to spoil the tidy and elegant story of Ida's inner life as he had told it up to then. The medical scientist's obligation to truth, that same obligation that required him to breach medical discretion, now demanded that he disclose a further complication: Ida's love for Frau Zellenka.

Through yet another incident in which Freud could only explain the sudden cooling of Ida's friendship for a cousin by postulating her jealousy of the cousin's intimacy with Frau Zellenka, he heard of Ida's long-standing intimacy with the beautiful, older woman, how they talked of every imaginable subject together, including the failings of her husband. Freud's central interpretation was again put under scrutiny: 'How Dora managed to fall in love with the man about whom her beloved friend had so many bad things to say is an interesting psychological problem.' The denial by Herr Zellenka of the scene by the lake to which he had added the perfidious opinion of Frau Zellenka 'that she [Ida] took no interest in anything but sexual matters' now emerged as doubly wounding to Ida: 'Frau K. had not loved her for her own sake but on account of her father. Frau K. had sacrificed her without a moment's hesitation so that her relations with her father might not be disturbed.' Despite all this Freud persisted in asserting Ida's love for Herr Zellenka to be the centrally suppressed feature of her mental life, though now placing alongside it her need 'to conceal her love for Frau K., which was in a deeper sense unconscious.'

Ida had had the first dream that Freud concentrated his skills upon the night after the scene by the lake. Its components, depicting a house on fire, her father standing beside her bed and her mother wanting to save her jewel-case from the burning house, were taken apart and analysed. At first sight, the dream expressed her intention to leave the Zellenkas' villa, where she was vulnerable to the improper attentions of Herr Zellenka, as he threatened to exercise his rights and invade the bedroom – *his* bedroom as he called it – which Ida was sharing with his wife. Behind this intention, Freud found the 'temptation to show herself willing to yield to the man', against which 'she summoned up an infantile affection for her father so that it might protect her against her present affection for a stranger.' The father standing beside her bed was called on to protect her against the fire of sexual desire, which threatened to ruin, by wetting them with disgusting sexuality, her jewel-case, her genitals. In attempting to understand her disgust for sexuality, Freud probed her amnesia of early masturbation, linked to her bed-wetting in late childhood, and her first hysterical symptoms: these had been sympathetic identifications with her father's physical exertions in intercourse, compounded by her self-reproaches for her 'catarrh', her vaginal discharge, which she linked to the 'frivolous and untrustworthy' sexuality of men, as her governess viewed it. Thus her symptoms might well express an identification with and excitement in her father's sexuality, but they were also an attempt to escape contamination, escape heterosexual contact.

Ida's second dream signalled the impending end of her treatment. Consciously, Freud suspected nothing of this, even though the first dream had, in the very fact of its being dreamed again two years after the scene by the lake, contained a warning that Ida once more felt erotically threatened and intended to leave the place of danger. This time she would leave alone, without calling on her father for help.

None the less Ida's dream did conscientiously address the questions Freud had highlighted for her: why did she delay telling her parents about the scene by the lake? And why did she then suddenly tell them about it? This second dream was more complex than the first; in it, Ida was walking about in a strange town, found a letter from her mother saying her father was dead, and began her journey back, via the station, through a thick wood, where she refused to be accompanied by a man whose help she had asked, till she returned home to find her mother and the others already at the cemetery. The associations revealed Ida's identification with a young suitor of hers, an engineer living in Germany, who would have to wait to secure his own future before he could press his suit. Going on alone reminded her of her visit to the Dresden art gallery, where she had spent two hours sitting alone admiring the famous Sistine Madonna. In depicting herself alternately as a young man far from home, or alone and identified with a virgin mother, she was enacting a fantasy of revenge on her father.

The next stage of the interpretation confirmed this vengeful craving: Freud discovered in the dream a picture of the defloration of the female genitals, in the clever puns on medical terms he attributed to Ida, turning the woods and nymphs glimpsed in a painting into pubic hair and vulva, her own vulva into which the young engineer would one day plunge, this betrayal with a man other than her father fulfilling the desire for revenge in another way. Ida even managed to pun on her family name, the name of her father: *kalter Bauer* means to ejaculate, usually ejaculate from nocturnal emission or from masturbation. A new piece of the dream came to consciousness: '*she went calmly to her room, and began reading a big book*'. From this dream-element emerged the story of her attack of appendicitis, shortly after her aunt's death, which Freud, with no opposition from Ida, interpreted as a 'phantasy of *childbirth*' once he had calculated that the attack took place nine months after the sce· by the lake.

The day after this piece of dream interpretation Ida announced to Freud that this was her last session. '"When did you come to this decision?" – "A fortnight ago, I think." – "That sounds just like a maidservant or a governess – a fortnight's notice." – "There was a governess who gave notice with the K.'s, when I was on my visit to them that time at L—, by the lake." – "Really? You have never told me about her. Tell me."' With the story of the governess, Freud finally discovered all the motives he was in search of: the reasons for Ida's delay in telling her parents, for having then told them, and hence the reason why she was in analysis with Freud, as well as why she was terminating the analysis.

The governess had been seduced and abandoned by Herr Zellenka, and had *told her parents* what had happened; they had said that she must leave the house immediately, but she had *delayed* giving her notice, in the hope that Herr Zellenka would return to her again. Now Freud had enough detail about the actual events beside the lake to give Ida his definitive account of that scene. When Herr Zellenka had begun to make his proposal to Ida, he said: 'You know I get nothing out of my wife', the very words which, so the governess had told Ida, he had used in seducing her as well. At that moment, Ida had slapped him in the face and hurried away. So, Freud argued, she had not been offended by his suggestion, but rather 'actuated by jealousy and revenge'. At that moment, Freud suggested, Ida had asked herself: 'Does he dare to treat me like a governess, like a servant?' 'Wounded pride added to jealousy and to the conscious motives of common sense – it was too much.'

So both the very idea of telling her parents and the idea of delaying taking such decisive action had been borrowed from the governess's story; she had indeed waited a fortnight, from 30 June to 14 July, before she had informed her mother. Similarly, Freud interpreted the delay as giving Herr Zellenka time to renew his proposal. Ida assented to this interpretation, somewhat to

Freud's surprise, and, in her last recorded contribution to the analysis, told him how seriously the Zellenkas had talked of divorce over the years, although, as was so often the case with their timing, they never both wanted a divorce at the same moment. Freud pressed Ida to admit that she was still awaiting a renewal of his proposal, just as her mother had been engaged at the age of seventeen and waited two years for her husband, and that the real reason for her bitterness at his denials of the scene by the lake and the slanders of Ida's character was because she had thought his proposal a serious one, which she hoped he would renew. Taking his cue from Ida's awareness of the apparent readiness of the Zellenkas to divorce, Freud proposed a truly Schnitzlerian solution to Ida:

Your father's relations with Frau K. – and it was probably only for this reason that you lent them your support for so long – made it certain that her consent to a divorce could be obtained; and you can get anything you like out of your father. Indeed, if your temptation at L— had had a different upshot, this would have been the only possible solution for all the parties concerned. And I think that is why you regretted the actual event so deeply and emended it in the phantasy which made its appearance in the shape of the appendicitis.

At the end of this session of 31 December 1900, Ida warmly bade Freud good-bye. In retrospect, Freud underlined how vengeful Ida's last dream had been and how much a vengeful act her departure from him was. By going it alone, Ida was spitefully abandoning her father. With her suicide letter, referred to in the dream through her mother's letter informing her of her father's death, she took revenge on both her parents. Her revenge against Herr Zellenka was expressed in the dream-thought: 'Since you have treated me like a servant, I shall take no more notice of you, I shall go my own way by myself, and not marry.' In the tones of a wounded lover, of the failed seducer, Freud reflected: 'Her breaking off so unexpectedly, just when my hopes of a successful termination of the treatment were at their highest, and her thus bringing those hopes to nothing – this was an unmistakeable act of vengeance on her part.' 'For how could the patient take a more effective revenge than by demonstrating upon her own person the helplessness and incapacity of the physician?' She left him musing whether he should have acted a part with her, shown her more affection, just as he mused whether Herr Zellenka would have conquered her neurosis where Freud had failed, if only he had pressed his suit 'with a passion which left room for no doubts', leading to a 'triumph of the girl's affection for him over all her internal difficulties.' If Ida's aim was to take revenge, then she had found a vulnerable target in Freud. Here was a lesson for Freud, a lesson not only in the laws of the heart, but in the dramatic uses to which his patients put psychoanalysis.

Ida left Freud reflecting on the mistakes he had made. He classed them under two headings: the transference and the secret love for Frau Zellenka. At the beginning of the case history Freud declared: 'the factor of "transference" ... did not come up for discussion during the short treatment.' At the end he considered how his failure to perceive Ida's transference to him had led to the unexpected curtailment of the treatment, reassuring himself that the transference between Philipp and himself was minimized since he had always avoided the 'secrecy and roundabout ways' of Ida's father. But he had missed spotting that her first dream was a warning that she was in a dangerous situation and was making plans to leave, and thus missed noticing that he was now unknowingly acting the part of Herr Zellenka, owing to 'the unknown quantity in me which reminded Dora of Herr K.' What in Freud reminded Ida of Herr Zellenka? 'I suspect that it had to do with money, or with jealousy of another patient who had kept up relations with my family after her recovery.' What might these connections have been? Did Ida see something in common between Herr Zellenka's job as a commercial traveller and Freud's job as a psychotherapist? Or were there covert financial arrange-ments between Philipp Bauer and Herr Zellenka, in which the rich industrialist paid fees to the younger man, just as Ida's father paid fees to Freud in an attempt to keep Ida from upsetting the delicate family *complot*? We do not know. Nor do we know which patient in Freud's circle knew Ida and could elicit her jealousy – yet her very mention encourages us to suspect a further network of complex relations modelled upon, or in parallel with, the family relations mapped out in such detail in Freud's case history.

The drift of Freud's remarks on transference leads us to see him as trapped in the role of a virile male upon whom Ida is determined to wreak a revenge that is aimed at all men. It should be said that Freud was none too bothered about playing this role; he certainly seemed to prefer the role of Herr Zellenka to that of Ida's impotent, invalid father. The other 'omission' to which he himself pointed as the 'fault in my technique' was intertwined in a complex way with his vision of the transference to a virile male. We have already seen how Freud appended to Part I, the Clinical Picture, the 'further complication' of the 'homosexual current' finding expression in Ida's love for Frau Zellenka. Again, as he winds up the case, Freud finds himself obliged to append reflections on this 'homosexual (gynaecophilic) love for Frau K.', 'the strongest unconscious current in her mental life.' Freud located the heart of this homosexual relationship in the sexual knowledge that Ida possessed, fruit of the intimate conversations and mutual reading the young married woman and the girl spent so much time engaged in. Freud kicked himself for not noticing how remarkable was the extent of her knowledge, and how carefully she concealed the sources of this knowledge.

I ought to have attacked this riddle and looked for the motive of such an extraordinary piece of repression. If I had done this, the second dream would have given me my answer. The remorseless craving for revenge expressed in that dream was suited as nothing else was to conceal the current of feeling that ran contrary to it – the magnanimity with which she forgave the treachery of the friend she loved and concealed from every one the fact that it was this friend who had herself revealed to her the knowledge which had later been the ground of the accusations against her.

This secretive magnanimity is perhaps the most striking expression of what Cixous called Ida's 'very beautiful feminine homosexuality'. It is this magnanimity which Freud detects beneath a cruel, sadistic and vengeful dream. One suspects that for Freud at this time, no cruel impulse, no matter how strong or malicious, was as forceful as erotic longings; in every dream the unconscious wish being expressed would show itself not to be cruel or vengeful but rather libidinal. He should have looked beneath the second dream for the positive erotic desire expressed in it, just as he had already detected in the first dream, beneath the intention to flee danger and the call for help from her father, her 'temptation to show herself willing to yield to the man'. He only had the analytic generosity to discover the deepest, the homosexual, current in Ida's life once she had gone, once her presence no longer enticed him into concentrating, to the exclusion of much else, on what she wanted from Herr Zellenka.

Why did Freud neglect the importance of Frau Zellenka until it was too late, until Ida had wreaked her vengeance? The answer to this question intertwines the two mistakes Freud discussed: the transference and the homosexual current – but not only on Ida's side; Freud's own certainly came into play.

Freud wrote his case history of Dora during the last declining phase of his friendship with Wilhelm Fliess, the long-time intimate male friend which a 'possibly feminine' side of him demanded. That feminine side was in the process of being repudiated just when he wrote the 'Dora' case history. At the heart of the painful process of repudiation and estrangement was the fate of the one idea that Fliess had transmitted to Freud which was to be crucial to all his later work: the concept of bisexuality. In his dying friendship with Fliess, in the idea of the inherent bisexual character of human beings and in his relations with Ida, the theme of the repudiation of femininity – his own, but also others' – was at work. The case of Dora counterposes the official scientific and masculine discourses of Fliess – his simple certitudes about masturbation and the simple surgical alleviation of its noxious effects – with the duplicitous oral pleasures of women, their secretive feminine conversations about sexuality. Freud's attempted repudiation of the secretive femininity represented by Frau Zellenka was to be the last gasp of his attachment to the scientific ideal represented by Fliess; from now on, Freud's psychoanalysis was to follow the circuitousness of the feminine way, eschewing for good the clean cuts of Fliessian surgical ideals.

In his conversations with Ida, it would seem that Freud was so intent on enacting the part of Herr Zellenka, the man he thought 'still quite young and of prepossessing appearance', that he did not bother to analyse the trans-ferential or counter-transferential part he was playing. We have already pointed out how Freud's reconstruction of the scene by the lake was also a re-enactment of that scene. Pressing himself on Ida, what did she feel – beneath his outer garb of civility, concern, acute comments and unexpected surprises – but the penetrating hardness of his theory? Like Ida's father, like Herr Zellenka, at least in wish if not in reality, Freud too has a mistress: his psychoanalytical science, embodying his own desire to know about female desire. In the field of knowledge, Freud is not quite as straightforward as he paints himself. One sign of that is the outburst at the opening of the case history, where he justifies his publishing an account of Ida's treatment by accusing those 'persons of delicacy, as well as those who were merely timid', who would refrain from such publication in the name of medical discretion, of 'a disgraceful piece of cowardice'. Such cowards do not recognize that their duty towards science, and through science to all other patients, is far more compelling than the ethical consequences that flow from perceiving that 'it is certain that the patients would never have spoken if it had occurred to them that their admissions might possibly be put to scientific uses; and it is equally certain that to ask them themselves for leave to publish their case would be quite unavailing.'

It is certainly ironic, but perhaps not an accident, that the key to Ida's erotic life lay in the mystery of her sexual knowledge, and that this was the key Freud failed to try. Was not Freud himself precisely the master of sexual knowledge? But *his* sexual knowledge was scientific, and the opposite of Ida's excitedly secret intimate talk with the woman whom she loved in part precisely because she was the source of erotic knowledge. Whereas Ida's sexual knowledge was from the first eroticized, could not have been knowledge without being eroticized, Freud used the severest tones to combat the possibility of *his* knowledge being eroticized. He castigated those physicians who read his case histories 'as a *roman à clef* [*Schlusselroman*] designed for their private delectation'. He assured his medical readers – who may even 'envy either me or my patients the titillation that, according to their notions, such a method must afford' – that their indignation at the sexual details that are discussed in psychoanalysis is entirely misplaced. Analysis is analogous to the requirements of gynaecologists for complete exposure, and, provided one is 'dry and direct' and 'call[s] bodily organs and processes by their technical names', patients themselves will often assure Freud that his 'treatment is far more respectable than Mr X.'s conversation!' In this assurance, as Neil Hertz has pointed out, 'what is thrust aside is the possibility of the doctor's deriving pleasure from these oral exchanges'. Freud's scientific conversation and knowledge refuses the pleasure that he discovered too late was one of Ida's principal, although necessarily secret, erotic pleasures, the oral eroticism of conversation. The danger for Freud is that his treatment will become equivalent to 'oral sexual intercourse between two women'.

Freud was alert to the importance of sources of sexual knowledge, but his concern not to corrupt an innocent girl, or interfere with his study of what he himself considered to be a quasi-experimental subject, misled him. Early on in the analysis, on hearing of the scene when Herr Zellenka kissed Ida and pressed his body against hers, he

questioned the patient very cautiously as to whether she knew anything of the physical signs of excitement in a man's body. Her answer, as touching the present, was 'Yes', but, as touching the time of the episode, 'I think not'. From the very beginning I took the greatest pains with this patient not to introduce her to any fresh facts in the region of sexual knowledge; and I did this, not from any conscientious motives, but because I was anxious to subject my assumptions to a rigorous test in this case. ... But the question of *where* her knowledge came from was a riddle which her memories were unable to solve. She had forgotten the source of all her information on this subject.

His own assumption, of course, was the principle we have already seen in action in his dealings with Ida, namely that her capacities for sexual response were those of a grown woman – after all, is that not one of the consequences of Freud's discovery of infantile sexuality? – and that she possessed the *knowledge* to exercise or repudiate those capacities.

There is never any danger of corrupting an inexperienced girl. For where there is no knowledge of sexual processes even in the unconscious, no hysterical symptom will arise; and where hysteria is found there can be no longer any question of 'innocence of mind' in the sense in which parents and educators use the phrase.

Fending off the charge of corrupting his patients, of giving them nothing but unseemly suggestions, is also preventing that 'thoroughgoing epistemological promiscuity in which the lines would blur between what Dora knew and what Freud knew'. On those occasions when he did pursue the question of Ida's sexual knowledge, Freud pinpointed two probable sources: her governess, and the fervent and secretive reading of encyclopaedias, the book that Freud regarded as such a significant addition to Ida's second dream. Ida had recovered her memory of reading the big book in her dream after Freud had interpreted her walk through a wood with nymphs in the background as being a fantasy of the female genitals and their defloration, a fantasy built out of esoteric medical terms for the genitals: '*Vorhof* [vestibulum]' and '*Nymphae* [labia minora]'. In his understandable haste to pursue Ida's association to the big book, which led him quickly to the interpretation of her appendicitis as a fantasy of childbirth, Freud neglected to note how Ida had employed precisely *his* 'dry and direct technical names' to depict erotic fulfilment. Ida was taking her revenge here, but in an ironic mode, by showing Freud, the verbally acrobatic interpreter of dreams, how his medical terms, the language of medical books and impotent doctors, were as easily eroticized as any other. If Freud had been alert, he would have learnt the lesson she was teaching him: psychoanalysis could as easily be a hothouse for the eroticization of language, for taking pleasure in knowledge, as an enclave protected from it.

The model for this erotic conversation was Ida's intimate friendship with Frau Zellenka: the scene of two women talking. Perhaps the most profound transference and counter-transference in Freud's analysis of Ida was the transposition of this scene to Freud's consulting-room. When he and Ida engaged in psychoanalysis, they were re-enacting the secret scene of the transfer of sexual knowledge of Ida and Frau Zellenka. Lurking behind Freud's footnotes about the homosexual current being the deepest stratum of Ida's unconscious, and the mystery of the sources of her sexual knowledge, was a realization, never made explicit, that psychoanalysis could be an eroticized conversation in which Freud played the part of a woman. It is clear that Freud was uncomfortable with, and at first unaware of, being cast as a woman in the transference. Certainly, as his later testimony demonstrates, he did not like playing the part of the mother in the transference, although it is clear that, at least by the 1930s, he had become aware of the maternal transference, aware of his personal discomfort with it, and also perhaps somewhat used to playing that part. None the less, we surmise that, from his early analyses on, including the case of Ida, he was *unconsciously* very much at ease playing the part of a woman. The surprising warmth Ida showed him when saying good-bye, the surprising extent of her trust in him from the beginning, despite the demonic fashion in which he pursued her with his interpretations, despite his dislike of her inability to surrender to her own erotic impulses, despite her endless reproachfulness, suggests that she may have found it quite easy to transfer the noble magnanimity she showed to the woman she loved, the secret source of her sexual knowledge, to Freud, her new source of sexual knowledge. In his way, Freud was not unlike Frau Zellenka: he accepted Ida's trust and, in the very act of writing the case history, betrayed her.

When he discussed the transference, Freud omitted to consider two roles he may have been playing, both of them those of women: the woman who is the object of love (Frau Zellenka), and the woman who is socially degraded, seduced and abandoned (the governess). In the case history two governesses figure: the first was Ida's own, an unmarried well-read woman of 'advanced views', 'with whom Dora had at first enjoyed the closest interchange of thought, until she discovered that she was being admired and fondly treated not for her own sake but for her father's; whereupon she had obliged the governess to leave.' Freud assumed that this woman, who 'read every sort of book on sexual life and similar subjects, and talked to the girl about them, at the same time asking her quite frankly not to mention their conversations to her parents', was Ida's source of sexual knowledge. In keeping with the concept of deferred action, the basic Freudian schema whereby it takes two traumatic scenes to create the entire symptomatic picture, this governess was the prototype for Frau Zellenka, both in their conversational and intellectual intimacy, and in Ida's sense of being betrayed for the sake of her father.

But it was the other governess who held the key to Ida's life history: the Zellenkas' governess, whose complaint to her own parents and whose delay in acting in the hope of Herr Zellenka pursuing his advances Ida repeated. If Ida had not identified with this governess, if she had not told her parents of Herr Zellenka's proposal, it is possible that things might have continued as they were: Philipp Bauer and Frau Zellenka preoccupied with their affair, Herr Zellenka paying his frequent courtesies to Ida, including sending flowers every day for a whole year and giving her valuable presents, to which everyone involved so assiduously turned a blind eye. But Ida's denunciation of Herr Zellenka broke the rules, violated the 'system of silent contracts, the contracts of general hypocrisy'. The Zellenkas closed ranks and ganged up on her. It was this betrayal by her friends, her lovers, that led to the dramatic change in Ida's view of the situation and to the symptoms that now protested against the arrangements in which she had thereto been complicit.

Ida's decision to go public was quite uncharacteristic: she had been perfectly

Ivone Adler
Ida Bower

content with the secret intimacies with her governess and Frau Zellenka; she understood the rules of secret pleasure, maybe even learned from them that women could only find their pleasures and could only survive if they entered into their own secret pacts. Freud commented that a 'normal girl, I am inclined to think, will deal with a situation of this kind by herself'. Even if we are somewhat sceptical, less certain than Freud, about what would count as normal in such a situation, Freud's opinion was probably accurate that such would have been 'normal' for her, in the sense of 'more characteristic', of Ida. It was her identification with the governess which launched her on to a new path of whistle-blowing and denunciation of hypocrisy and low morals. As if to underline to Freud that this other governess, seduced, abandoned, humiliated, living in hope, held the key to the case, Ida waited till the final session to inform him of her existence, and then closed that final session by leaving the new world of secret sexual knowledge Freud had created with her. In that final session, Ida *showed* and told Freud that the governess held the key: she demonstrated this by treating *him* as a governess, a family servant, whose services were no longer required. As if to underline his belated understanding that Ida's story was intimately bound up with those of the family servants, when Freud came to choose her pseudonym the only name that came to him was 'Dora', his sister Rosa's nursemaid. Her real name was Rosa, the same as her mistress', so to avoid confusion in the house she was rebaptized. '"Poor people," I remarked in pity, "they cannot even keep their own names!"' And it was not just the analogy of maids who lose their identities and patients who lose theirs in the process of analytic communication that led Freud to choose this name: 'it was a person employed in someone else's house, a governess, who exercised a decisive influence on my patient's story, and on the course of the treatment as well.'

Feminists, social historians and close readers of Freud have made us familiar with the crucial sexual role of the governess or nursemaid in bourgeois families in fin-de-siècle society. Freud's own little disquisition on 'The part played by servant girls' in the fantasies that make up the architecture of hysteria, written in a letter to Fliess in 1897, in broad strokes showed how

an immense load of guilt, with self-reproaches (for theft, abortion), is made possible by identification with these people of low morals who are so often remembered, in a sexual connection with father or brother, as worthless female material. And, as a result of the sublimation of these girls in fantasies, most improbable charges against other people are contained in the fantasies. Fear of prostitution (fear of being in the street alone), fear of a man hidden under the bed, and so on, also point in the direction of the servant girl. There is tragic justice in the circumstance that the family head's stooping to a maidservant is atoned for by his daughter's self-abasement.

As we have seen, Freud also discovered that his own 'teacher in sexual matters' was his old nurse. The theme is perennial. When he wrote about the daughter atoning for the father's misdeeds, he may have had Rosalia, a case from *Studies on Hysteria*, in mind, whose father

wounded [the family's] feelings more particularly by the way in which he showed an open sexual preference for the servants and nursemaids in the house; and the more the children grew up the more offensive this became. After her mother's death Rosalia became the protector of the multitude of children who were now orphaned and oppressed by their father. She took her duties seriously and fought through all the conflicts into which her position led her, though it required a great effort to suppress the hatred and contempt which she felt for her father.

Sexuality leaks, and sometimes bursts, into the family cell through the channel of the nurse, the governess, the maid. If the hysteric appears in two theatrical guises in Freud's cases, firstly as the sacrificed young woman who cares for those she secretly loves and hates (Bertha Pappenheim), then as the rebel determined not to be abused by the hidden hypocrisies and illicit passions of her milieu (Ida), then the maidservant is the link between these two figures. The maidservant is the other side of the coin of the hysteric. As we will later see, Freud's analysis of Ernest Jones's wife, Loë Kann, turned melodramatic when Jones slept with Loë's maid, 'the nicest case of *Übertragung* [transference] I ever saw.' In his late papers on female sexuality Freud reaffirms this model:

The part played in starting [masturbation in girls] by nursery hygiene is reflected in the very common phantasy which makes the mother or nurse into a seducer. ... Actual seduction, too, is common enough; it is initiated either by other children or by someone in charge of the child who wants to soothe it, or send it to sleep or make it dependent on them.

Ida was surely repudiating her own identification with the abandoned governess when she slapped Herr Zellenka and resolved to inform her parents; she refused to be seduced and abandoned. And her refusal carried over into her leaving Freud. But nor did Freud wish to be identified with the position of servant Ida placed him in, and his principal reason for refusing this identification may well have been the threat to his scientific knowledge: he did not wish the psychoanalyst to join the company of Ida's secret teachers, the governess and Frau Zellenka. He did not wish to recognize that he had entered into rivalry with Frau Zellenka and the governess; he did not want to have his latinate language of psychoanalysis defiled by proximity with the oral exchanges between these women.

Yet Freud displayed considerable eagerness to play another female part, this a traditional Jewish one that came naturally to his active analytic stance. For Ida, as for Ilona Weiss, he was quite ready to act as matchmaker. Philipp Bauer had brought his daughter to Freud so that he could cure her of her opposition to Philipp's affair and prevent her from committing suicide. Freud instead seemed intent on reorganizing the Bauers and the Zellenkas into a new marital arrangement. He insisted to Ida that she had taken seriously the possibility of Herr Zellenka divorcing his wife and marrying her, and in his *post hoc* reflections had quite clearly thought Herr Zellenka was serious in his pursuit of Ida. The probable knock-on effect of the Zellenkas' divorcing would have been the divorce of Ida's parents and Philipp's marriage to his lover. With such a double marriage as his suggested goal, Freud was in effect substituting Ida the daughter for Käthe the mother, inserting one woman into the system of exchanges only to exclude, as a sort of excretion of the marriage system, another. In other words, Freud's interpretations of the seriousness of Herr Zellenka's marriage proposal amounted to an Oedipal victory of daughter over mother. One cannot imagine that Freud was blind to this implication of his proposal. But the Oedipal rivalry was never directly addressed by Freud. His proposal was another of his invasive challenges to Ida's version both of the world and of her inner feelings for the actors in that world. Yet its invasiveness was at the same time a form of collusion, almost a shared dirty secret, with Ida, since Freud remained studiously silent, in a silence that speaks volumes, about the one actor who had seemingly withdrawn from all involvement in the bedhopping, but would be as affected by it as anyone: Ida's mother.

Freud next saw Ida Bauer fifteen months after the end of the analysis. Ida had read a newspaper report of Freud's appointment as Professor and, on 1 April 1902, came to consult him. She was, he ascertained to his own satisfaction, still running on governess's time, since her visit came a fortnight after the neuralgia this news had provoked had come on. She told Freud how she had been confused after the end of the analysis, but then an improvement had set in. Then, in May 1901, little Klara Zellenka had died. Ida had paid the Zellenkas a visit of condolence:

they received her as though nothing had happened in the last three years. She made it up with them, she took her revenge on them, and she brought her own business to a satisfactory conclusion. To the wife she said: 'I know you have an affair with my father'; and the other did not deny it. From the husband she drew an admission of the scene by the lake which he had disputed, and brought the news of the vindication home to her father. Since then she had not resumed her relations with the family.

However, an extraordinary incident, worthy of a fiction by Schnitzler or Pasternak, had, in October, brought on a six-week-long bout of aphonia.

She had come across [Herr Zellenka] in the street one day; they had met in a place where there was a great deal of traffic; he had stopped in front of her as though in bewilderment, and [in] losing all awareness of himself, had allowed himself to be knocked down by a carriage. She had been able to convince herself, however, that he escaped without serious injury.

The new neuralgia was, Freud thought, self-punishment at having taken her revenge on Herr Zellenka and on Dr Freud. Freud did not want to find out more; he had done with Ida Bauer. 'I do not know what kind of help she wanted from me,' he wrote, which was not surprising since he did not want to find out, after what she had done to him, 'but I promised to forgive her for having deprived me of the satisfaction of affording her a far more radical cure for her troubles.'

All this having been said, the question remains: why did Freud write up the story of an interrupted, perhaps even failed, treatment? And why did he then delay five years in publishing it? When Freud had begun his treatment of Ida in October 1900, he was triumphant and masterful about the prospect of the 'case that has smoothly opened to the existing collection of pick-locks.' Yet Ida's sudden departure on the last day of 1900 caught him unawares. His reaction was to set to writing her up. He finished the paper, 'the subtlest thing I have written so far', in three weeks. Something must have changed his opinion about it. Most probably he worried about the effect reading it would have on Ida. He placed it back in his desk drawer, withdrawing it from its planned publication.

What caused Freud to change his mind again? He tells us he waited till he heard news that 'a change has taken place in the patient's life of such a character as allows me to suppose that her own interest in the occurrences and psychological events which are to be related here may now have grown faint.' The news he heard was more than likely that of the birth of Ida's son, on 2 April 1905. The paper, the child, as it were, of Freud and Ida's relationship, his version of her appendicitis, could then be published: it appeared in October and November of the same year.

So Freud was also still running on governess's time. Just like Ida in that crucial period from 30 June to 14 July 1898, he had formed an intention to communicate Ida's story, which he then waited before carrying out. The period of time he waited was the time it took Ida to have a baby. In Freud's view, then, it suddenly became appropriate to publish the paper once the young woman's interest in the family conspiracy to which she had been party had been altogether replaced, not only by her marriage, which took place in December 1903, but by the birth of a child. With the birth of the child, Ida had been 'reclaimed once more by the realities of life'. She had finally become the 'mature young woman of very independent judgement, who had grown accustomed to laugh at the efforts of doctors, and in the end to renounce their help entirely' that Freud had perhaps not altogether accurately described her as when she was seventeen. The actual *publication* of Ida's story thus emerges as yet another clear sign of Freud's counter-transference, his idea of what girls and young women are for. Ida was another of the young women whom Freud hoped, indeed trusted, would be cured by marriage and the consequent creation, as he put it to Sabina Spielrein when she was considering analysis with Freud just as she was getting married, of 'someone else [i.e. a baby] ... who will have more rights than both the old and the new man put together. At this stage, it is best for analysis to take a back seat.' In giving birth, Ida had in Freud's eyes crossed the Rubicon that separates the girl from the woman.

Ida had married an engineer and composer, a man nine years older than herself. Her parents had misgivings about the marriage, but nevertheless Philipp took his son-in-law into the family business and supported his not altogether successful musical activities, to the point of hiring an orchestra on one occasion so that his son-in-law could hear his own music. Two months after her son was born in 1905, Ida converted to Christianity. In her married life, she became a frequenter of salons and upper-class circles. In 1915, her husband was called up into the army and returned from the front permanently handicapped, with a severe head and ear injury affecting his sense of balance and his memory. He died of heart disease in 1932.

In 1922, Ida consulted Dr Felix Deutsch, a follower of Freud's and also Freud's personal doctor in 1923. She complained of dizziness and ringing in her ears. He soon deduced from her pride at having being written up by Freud as a famous case that she was 'Dora'. In the paper Deutsch wrote about her some thirty-five years later – a paper so full of errors of fact that one must read it with considerable scepticism – he portrayed Ida as a woman disappointed in her marriage, denouncing men in general as selfish, demanding and ungiving. Having given her a physical examination, Deutsch swung into psychoanalytical mode, interpreting the ringing in her ears as linked to her relationship to her son, now seventeen, whose return from his nightly excursions she stayed awake listening for. She agreed and asked for another consultation, which was her last. However, Ida's brother Otto followed up her visit to Deutsch, greatly concerned about her health. On one point Deutsch's account appears trustworthy: Ida's marriage had turned out rather unsatisfactorily. The relations that sustained her were those with her brother and son.

Ida had always been close to her brother Otto, who had remained as aloof from the family conflicts as he could while growing up, accommodating his difficult mother and taking her side in family rows, but also advising Ida not to interfere with their father's affair with Frau Zellenka, since they should be glad that he had found a woman he could love. A year older than her, he had been brilliant and precocious, writing a play, *Napoleon*, at the age of nine, just when his sister suffered her first attack of what would later be called her hysterical symptoms. This was the period in her life that Freud saw as marking a divergence between her and her brother's development, when she changed from being a 'masculine', 'wild creature' to being 'feminine', 'quiet and well-behaved'. Otto had been much influenced in his youth by his uncle, Philipp's socialist brother. His experience at school in the brief period, just after Ida's scene by the lake, when the family lived in Reichenberg near Philipp's factories, persuaded him that he was 'morally obligated' to serve the working class because of the privileges, particularly the educational ones, that had been granted him. In 1907, having taken a degree in law, Otto published *The Nationalities Question and Social Democracy*, in which he attempted to resolve the tension in Marxist theory between national and cultural diversity and the egalitarian requirements of socialism. He also became full-time parliamentary secretary to the Austrian Social Democrat Party, working closely with its leader Viktor Adler. Adler and Otto Bauer, like Freud and Heinrich Braun, Adler's brother-in-law and Freud's close school friend, and like many another former inhabitant of Berggasse, all came from Bohemian–Jewish middle-class families.

In 1912, Käthe Bauer died of cancer of the colon; Philipp Bauer died less than a year later, of tuberculosis ('degeneration of the prostate'), having been nursed by both Ida and Otto. In 1914, at the age of thirty-three, Otto married Helene Landau, a woman ten years his senior, with three children; she had no more children with Otto. It is said that Otto consulted Freud some time shortly after his marriage: Freud advised him not to enter politics, but rather to be a teacher, a profession more suited to his temperament. Freud is said to have warned Otto: 'Do not try and make men happy, they do not wish happiness.' Captured by the Russians in the war, Otto was returned to Austria in 1917. In the socialist republic set up in 1918, he was assistant to Adler, and then, when Adler died in November 1918, his successor as Foreign Minister until July 1919, resigning when his proposals for the unification of Germany and Austria were rejected by the Allied Powers. It was Adler's inheritance that Otto, now leader, then attempted to preserve: a party vigorous enough to share power with the Christian Socialists for eighteen months, and to govern Vienna for the next sixteen years. Renowned for his speeches and his passionate attacks on opponents, Otto was also to become known for his indecision and his 'clear tendency to snatch defeat or at least stalemate from the jaws of victory'. He was more concerned by the bogies of pre-war imperial politics, the church and the aristocracy, or by the need to refute the example of Lenin, than by the rise of fascism; he cared more to act by constitutional means and defend individual rights than to aid his party to seize power when it was under unconstitutional and quasi-military threat. Of the siblings, it was Ida, the socialite bourgeois housewife, who was by nature a rebel, not Otto the socialist politician, who accommodated and acquiesced, both to his family as a youth and to the corrupt rules of Austrian politics as an adult.

In 1926, Otto fell in love with a beautiful and younger married woman, Hilda Schiller-Marmorket, a committed socialist; he would not divorce, although their affair lasted for the rest of his life. In the political crises of 1933 and 1934, Otto failed to rise to the threat represented by the suspension of parliament and the defeat of the socialist uprising. With his failure, the socialists were outlawed and he fled into four years of underground resistance in Brünn, Czechoslovakia. In May 1938, with the *Anschluss*, he fled to Paris, where he died of a heart attack in July. He was given a state funeral, socialist leaders from all over the world attending.

Ida's brother always had a large picture of his sister in his room, prominently displayed and in the place of honour, and she told Deutsch how, despite being leader of a political party, he visited her whenever she needed him – 'in contrast to her father, who had been unfaithful even to her mother.' In later years she looked to her son for the support Otto had previously given her, although he was less and less often in Vienna. A musician, like his father, Kurt was unlike him in being successful. Working first with Max Reinhardt in the mid 1920s, he then went to the Volksoper, and was assistant to Toscanini, along with Solti and Leinsdorf, at the Salzburg Festival: here he worked alongside another Freudian child, Herbert Graf, otherwise known as little Hans. Kurt stayed on to teach at the Salzburg Mozarteum. In 1937, he married and moved to Czechoslovakia. In 1938, he left Europe for the United States, taking a position in Chicago, where he remarried and became a US citizen. In 1943, he moved to San Francisco, where he was to spend the rest of his working life as Chorus Master, then Artistic Director and finally General Director of the San Francisco City Opera.

Ida was thus stranded in Vienna, without any close family, when the *Anschluss* took place in 1938. After great difficulties, and with assistance from her son, she finally managed to leave for Paris, and eventually New York, where she settled. The disease her mother died of, a cancer of the colon, was diagnosed too late; she succumbed to it in 1945 at the Mount Sinai Hospital.

As a result of Felix Deutsch's zealously orthodox follow-up to Freud's paper, some writers have assumed that Ida's life was a failure. Prey to numerous psychosomatic diseases, resentful and reproachful, the death of 'one of the most repulsive hysterics' Deutsch's informant had ever met was a blessing to those who were close to her. This account is distinctly unreliable. Certainly one fact which is known about Ida's later life would suggest a somewhat different personality, and gives one pause for thought. The newly invented game of contract bridge became hugely popular in Vienna between the two world wars. Playing and teaching bridge became the centre of Ida Bauer's life. In the private bridge circles of her world, she was a master, who would teach other middle-class women in their living-rooms. Her partner in this genteel but intellectually absorbing and challenging occupation was none other than Frau Zellenka. It is as if, across the years, they had finally dispensed with the superfluous men who had previously been their partners in their complex social games and contracts, yet they had retained their love of those games whose skill lies in the secret of mutual understanding of open yet coded communications within and across a foursome. Ida, adept at keeping her hand secret, also knew when and how to play it.

Freud might well have been impressed by Ida's fidelity to her friend Frau Zellenka; it certainly would have reinforced in him his belated conviction that Ida's secret love for her had been the deepest current in her mental life. He might also have thought of Ida's choice of occupation as a bridge master as an example of that rarest of all skills, successful sublimation.

Part III

A
WOMAN'S
PROFESSION

6

EARLY FRIENDS,
EARLY CASES,
EARLY FOLLOWERS

Yes, indeed, psychotherapy is as old as illness, and we doctors could not give it up if we wanted to, because the other party to our methods of healing – namely the patient – has not the slightest intention of doing without it.

Like many other charismatic men of his century, Freud moved up the social hierarchy through the good graces of women, many of whom were connected to one another if not by family ties, then certainly by that equally effective circuit of salon gossip. It is suitably symbolic of Freud's career and destiny that the famous couch, the one object forever associated with him, was given to him by a grateful patient, one Madame Benvenisti, sometime around 1900. As we have already seen, he had the luck, the talent or the good contacts to be employed as doctor and hypnotist by some rich and remarkable women. He may, as he implied to Marie Bonaparte in conversations in the 1920s, have gone through a bad patch in the late 1890s: 'I treated only poor people at the time, no princess!' His old school friend, the psychiatrist Julius Wagner-Jauregg, remembered him as 'a practitioner in neurology but without any patients'. To start with, Freud undoubtedly had to be eclectic: he could not baulk at taking on patients with a wide variety of complaints, and treating them in a variety of ways. Success, after all, depended solely on becoming 'a doctor in whom people can have confidence'. However, the patients we have records of were often distinguished, well-connected, well-born and, as Freud himself insisted, intelligent, high-minded and interesting to their doctor.

The famous poetess Elisabeth Glück, whose given name was Betty Paoli, was a patient of Breuer's, whom he had got to know via the Fleischl circle. Fleischl had used her as a subject in his experiments with hypnotism and catalepsy. At the age of twenty-two, she had published provocatively erotic poems written in a grand style, which had gained her a certain notoriety. She began consulting Freud in 1888 about her 'nervous illness' and he started her on a cure. Mathilde Schleicher, the twenty-seven-year-old daughter of the well-known Viennese painter Cölestin Schleicher, was treated by Freud and gave him a book in June 1889 as a token of gratitude and respect; he continued to treat her until at least October 1889. Another of Freud's very first patients, also from the most fashionable intellectual salons of the day, proved to be a woman to whom his debt would be considerable.

Elise Gomperz was the wife of Professor Theodor Gomperz, the man who had, on the basis of Brentano's recommendation, commissioned Freud's translation of Mill's *Essays* in 1879. The Gomperzes were one of the best-known and most cultured of Viennese Jewish families, whose circle very much overlapped with Freud's own: Chrobak was Elise's doctor during her pregnancies and childbirths, and was a close friend of the family, together with his wife Helene; Breuer was the Gomperzes' doctor for four decades.

Elise was born on 12 September 1848, the elder of the two daughters of the General Secretary to Kaiser-Ferdinands-Nordbahn, Heinrich Sichrovsky, who had in his youth, when serving in England in the early 1830s, been so impressed by the new railways that he had done all he could to bring them to Austria, in part with the support of the Rothschild banking house in Vienna. A slim girl, with an oval face, dark hair and brown eyes, Elise married Theodor Gomperz on 8 June 1869. Gomperz was thirty-seven at the time and, since the two families were close, had known Elise since she was a girl. He was the brother of Josephine Wertheimer, the close friend of Anna von Lieben, Freud's Frau Cäcilie M.

In August 1886, Theodor Gomperz wrote to his sister Josephine about Elise's state of nerves, 'the inheritance of a very old civilized race and of the urban life', and how they were giving him cause for concern. As early as the summer of 1886, Charcot had suggested to Theodor that she should start treatment with 'his pupil Freud'. Elise was certainly having regular hypnotic treatment from Freud in her own home in the early 1890s; her husband was at times very sceptical and followed the cure with concern. As he wrote to his son Heinrich in October 1892: 'Nothing new here, except that Freud was here yesterday and, because of the failure of the electrical treatment, has predicted a certain cure with hypnosis, which hasn't prevented Mama having suffered an equally severe attack, despite its having been delayed for a few hours. ...' Freud's treatment was at the very least – but perhaps at the very most – easing Elise's pains and helping her sleep. Three weeks later, Theodor was writing: 'Mama seems through hypnosis to be really on the way to a cure. Would only that the means of healing was not so uncanny and so little tried.' By January 1893, his tone was again sceptical:

I am very pleased to learn that ... you are starting to feel better, and regret only that you also consult Freud from a distance. ... Only and always ear-confession and hypnosis – from that we have seen no wonders; I could only ever see increasing deterioration. All reasonable people – Breuer and Freud here excepted – warn incessantly about the continuation of these until now more than fruitless experiments. ... It seems to me that hypnosis is like a newly discovered medicine whose dosage is not yet tried and tested, and that, like other and more directly effective therapies, has the not wholly appropriate effect of a poison. ...

In April 1893, Theodor was accusing hypnotic suggestion, this 'school for hallucination', of being responsible for Elise's hyperaesthesia; a year later, in February 1894, she was still seeking relief from Freud's hypnotic treatments. We know virtually nothing of what happened in these treatments. A patient such as Elise, who saw Freud within a few weeks of him setting up practice, fresh from Charcot and Paris, and terminated her treatment some eight years later, must have witnessed many changes of mind and attitude in her physician. In that time, Freud had abandoned hypnosis, had become an accomplished dream interpreter and convinced that the key to neurosis lay in the deeply buried traumatic memories of seductions. She would have herself experienced the failures, setbacks and naïve experiments in which Freud's odyssey of those years implicated those around him. It is also possible, however, that Theodor's distrust in the early 1890s of the hallucinatory poison of the treatment stemmed from its uncovering of family secrets which he and others would have preferred to stay buried, as Elise's son was many years later to discover.

Freud's link with the Gomperz family did not stop with the parental generation. While Elise's husband, Freud's former patron, had become a slightly apprehensive sceptic where Freud's professional abilities were concerned, his son Heinrich, born in 1873, was to prove a respectful and long-standing friend to Freud's theories, if by no means a self-avowed follower. In late 1899, Heinrich, also, like his father, an academic philosopher, corresponded with Freud about his dream book and entered into a quasi-analytic, quasi-scientific relationship with Freud, who offered to 'play the role of the "other"' in the application of 'the philosopher's unrelenting love of truth also to your inner life'. Freud reported on this 'very amusing' philosopher-student to Fliess: 'Supposedly he believes nothing whatsoever, but has all sorts of beautiful and witty ideas. ... His dreams constantly quote my dreams, which he then forgets, and so forth. Interpreting dreams appears to be more difficult for others than I had indicated.'

Heinrich later viewed 'the experiments' as a 'complete failure', because he knew everything already. But he remained in consistent contact with Freud for many years, supplying him with additional information about Plato's story in the *Symposium* of the division of the sexes from one original sexless whole; Freud thanked Heinrich and incorporated the material, 'partly in his [Heinrich's] own words', into a footnote added to the 1921 second edition of *Beyond the Pleasure Principle*. Freud thus repaid the compliment by making Heinrich's own thoughts effectively his own – a truly undecidable counterpart to his perception that Heinrich made Freud's thoughts his own and then forgot this fact. And then, in 1931, in a letter wishing Freud well on his seventy-fifth birthday, Heinrich repeated once again his habitual gesture of attributing to Freud knowledge which was *almost*, but not quite, always already his own: 'only recently did I come across letters you wrote to my mother in 1893, which I found in her bequest, and which enlightened me about a family secret, which I was in any event on the track of already.'

Elise played a part in Freud's appointment to a professorship in 1902. On Freud's return from his first visit to Rome – as momentous an occasion, given his fascination for the Eternal City, as his first love – she suggested that he attempt to reverse his failing professional fortunes by acquiring the social prestige of a professorship. She, as a Frau *Hofrat*, wife to a prestigious official professor at the university, offered to pull the strings to the best of her ability. Following the campaign plan she drew up with Freud, he called on Professor Exner and received renewed backing in his application to the Minister of Education from Krafft-Ebing and Nothnagel; all, however, would have come to nothing without Elise's intercessions on his behalf. And even this vigorous lobbying might have come to nothing if another patient of Freud's, Baroness Marie von Ferstel (*née* Thorsch), had not heard about the case, possibly from her friend Elise Gomperz: '[Marie] refused to rest until she had made the Minister's acquaintance at a party, managed to ingratiate herself with him and via a mutual lady friend made him promise to confer a professorship on the doctor who had cured her.' One promise was not enough. She approached him personally and offered him the gift of a picture for a new art gallery in exchange for Freud's Chair. The deal was done, though she could not deliver her aunt's *A Castle in Ruins* by Böcklin, but only a picture by Emil Orlik. The papers now moved very fast from the Ministry to the Court and back. Marie von Ferstel had the undoubtedly satisfying experience of arriving one day for her analytic session and, instead of telling Freud her dreams, fulfilling his by brandishing a letter the Minister had sent her informing her that the professorship would be granted shortly and exclaiming: 'I've done it!'

This was not the only largesse Freud received from Marie von Ferstel in the early years of the century. The daughter of a rich banker, she was the wife of a senior diplomat, who was the son of the famous Heinrich von Ferstel, architect of the Votivkirche, the University and notable Ringstrasse buildings. She came to Freud for treatment in September 1899, and continued on and off until at least the summer of 1903. She gave the Freuds tickets for *Don Giovanni* at the Salzburg Festival in August 1901 and opened her house to the Freud family. At Christmas, the children would dress up and call on her to receive their presents from under the tree. She also presented Freud with the deeds to a villa in a resort near Vienna, which Freud soon sold.

Conflict with her family over her enthusiasm for and generosity towards Freud followed. At some point in these years, she turned violently against him and vilified his reputation. There were other early patients who were neither grateful nor amenable to Freud's unconventional ideas and conception of the doctor-patient relationship. In 1899, Arthur Koestler's mother, who suffered from violent headaches, was referred to Freud by her sister, who ran a finishing-school and was impressed by her acquaintance with him. She saw him two or three times and then refused to see him again: 'He massaged my neck and asked me silly questions ... he was a disgusting man.'

Other patients were more appreciative and became very attached to Freud. Anna von Vest, a member of the Klagenfurt aristocracy, was an unmarried woman of forty-two when she started her treatment with Freud in 1903. Her legs had been paralyzed since her early twenties, when a Graz doctor had treated her hysterical symptoms by removing her ovaries. A series of sanatorium cures in Graz and Merano over the next twenty years were to no avail. Eventually, her doctor sent her to consult Freud in Vienna; she had to be carried from the train to the hotel, where Freud came twice to see her. After one week, according to her later account, she was able to visit him on foot by herself, and after a fortnight she was able to go to the theatre; Freud declared her 'redeemed' a year later and the analysis ended. The hidden cause of her illness, according to the analysis? 'An unhappy upbringing', a friend reported her as having said; 'she laid everything at her parents' door'. The 'conversations' revolved for the most part around sexuality and her jealousy of her younger sister.

Two years later, she had a slight relapse, but until she was fifty-five in 1916, twelve years after her analysis, she was basically healthy. Even as an invalid she had not neglected her great musical gifts. In 1904, after her cure, she settled in Vienna as an accomplished professional pianist and accompanist, moving in artistic circles and known in the best gossip columns for her scurrility and irony. From 1903 on, she and Freud exchanged a considerable number of letters, in the friendly and analytic way he had of keeping close to his patients; she had also become friendly with his family, and did favours for them, such as putting up Freud's son Ernst in 1914. During the war, she worked as a nurse in a Dutch military hospital. After the war and the death of her brother-in-law, she moved with her sister and mother to Klagenfurt. In 1925 she requested further analysis and this time Freud acceded, asking 'one Anna' (his daughter) to make way for 'another' in his analytic schedule. This time there was no miracle cure. Anna had become, in Freud's words, *'freudlos gezeugt'* – barren of joy; the analysis was brief and they ceased corresponding. Anna Freud, though, still kept in touch with Anna von Vest. When she was seventy-three, in 1934, she developed a small stomach growth and died of cancer the next year. A short while before her final illness, she had said that she had Professor Freud to thank for thirty years of health.

Freud's account – and it is surely an account of Anna von Vest, because the details fit so well – was published in his valediction to psychoanalytic therapy, 'Analysis Terminable and Interminable'. Freud chose to reconsider, without naming them, the cases of two patients of his, as if released from the obligation of discretion and, at the same time, weighed down by their recent deaths: one was Ferenczi, his intimate friend and colleague; the other was Anna von Vest, the patient he had treated 'in the earliest years of my work as an analyst', who

had been cut off from life since puberty by an inability to walk, owing to severe pains in the legs. ... An analysis lasting three-quarters of a year removed the trouble and restored to the patient, an excellent and worthy person, her right to a share in life. In the years following her recovery she was consistently unfortunate. There were disasters in her family, and financial losses, and, as she grew older, she saw every hope of happiness in love and marriage vanish. But the one-time invalid stood up to all this valiantly and was a support to her family in difficult times. I cannot remember whether it was twelve or fourteen years after the end of her analysis that, owing to profuse haemorrhages, she was obliged to undergo a gynaecological examination. A myoma was found, which made a complete hysterectomy advisable. From the time of this operation, the woman became ill once more. She fell in love with her surgeon, wallowed in masochistic phantasies about the fearful changes to her inside – phantasies with which she concealed her romance – and proved inaccessible to a further attempt at analysis. She remained abnormal to the end of her life.

Could I, or rather psychoanalysis, have prevented this unfortunate relapse, the rebirth of her neurosis following on from the accidental but uncanny repetition of the original surgical removal of her ovaries ? – this is what Freud was sadly asking himself in his last paper on psychoanalytic technique, written when he was eighty-one, two years after Anna von Vest's death.

With the acquisition in 1902 of the much prized title of professor, Freud's practice improved. Psychoanalysis became fashionable, if not respectable, for the wealthy. By the 1910s, many patients journeyed to Vienna specifically for treatment by him. In the early 1920s, daughter Anna was trying to protect Freud from taking on patients even in the summer, which he had previously kept a neurosis-free zone : 'just let all millionairesses stay crazy, they don't have anything else to do.' If Freud had Rastignac-like ambitions of making his way in society, then by the 1920s he could feel well satisfied with his progress.

Female Paranoia and the Vocation of the Analyst

There was one class of patient whom Freud was resigned to not being able to help, though these patients were of enormous assistance to his theoretical work.

In 1894, a young woman from the lower classes was referred to Freud by Breuer because she had developed unmistakable delusions of observation and persecution. It seemed to her that her neighbours pitied her, thinking that she had been jilted by a recently departed lodger and was pining for his return. They made frequent insinuations about the man in question and about her condition – all of which, she claimed, were untrue. Some time before the lodger's departure, she had told her older sister that on one occasion, when she had been tidying his bedroom, he had called her to his bed and put his penis in her hand. Now she denied all knowledge of that scene and experienced recurrent bouts of paranoia. Freud tried, unsuccessfully, to retrieve the scene by 'concentration hypnosis' and, as he already expected in cases of paranoia, saw the patient no more.

But her story provoked in him a veritable flurry of theorizing. What did the woman gain by not recognizing the reality of the sexual scene ? Freud hypothesized that she spared herself the self-reproach related to the experience of sexual excitement, by projecting the subject matter of the reproach outwards on to other people. Thus the unwanted judgment came from outside, not from within, and such external gossip and calumnies could easily be rejected. In other words, what was intolerable to the ego was projected on to the world. The mechanism of projection used by paranoiacs was simply an abuse of a normal mechanism, whereby we choose whether to attribute a mental event to an internal or external cause.

The march of theory did not stop there. Freud turned to the mechanism of substitution found in normal life, showing how it was abused in obsessions in the same way that the judgments distinguishing between inner and outer causation were abused in paranoia. With the deceptively simple key of projection revealed to him by the female patient who flatly denied her own sexual seduction, Freud took a roll call of psychiatric types, all revealing the mechanism of projection: the litigious paranoiac, who refuses to recognize his own guilt or unearned privilege; those nations who refuse to recognize their defeat in war and invent conspiracies of betrayal; the alcoholic who refuses to recognize how alcohol makes him impotent and so invents reasons for jealousy of the woman who must be the cause; the hypochondriac who insists he is being poisoned, rather than looking within for his own debility.

Take, for instance, a cook who has lost her looks, and who must accustom herself to the thought that she is permanently excluded from happiness in love. This is the right moment for the emergence of the gentleman from the house opposite, who clearly wants to marry her and who is giving her to understand as much in such a remarkably bashful but none the less unmistakeable fashion.

'In every case,' Freud concluded, 'the *delusional idea* is maintained with the same energy with which another, intolerably distressing, idea is fended off from the ego. Thus they love *their delusions as they love themselves*. That is the secret.'

The prognosis for paranoia was always poor. Freud entertained little hope of curing such patients. They would not stay in analysis for long since the treatment often exacerbated their symptoms: the analyst could well appear as one of their principal persecutors. So Freud's work with his paranoiacs had an edge of hasty disinterested enquiry, mixed with pity, for patients whose delusional symptoms were all too comprehensible to him, but who had stepped over the hazy line which marked off those who could be saved from those who were damned. A year after he had written his draft on paranoia, Freud published a brief case history of a woman, Frau P., who had become distrustful and uncommunicative, particularly in relation to her husband's relatives. The key to her case Freud found in the sexual relations she had had with her brother in childhood; she was now reproducing in distorted form, in hallucinations and in projected self-reproaches, the shameless and perverted sexual practices of her youth. Projection is the mechanism of defence: distrust of other people appears instead of self-reproach. What is most damaging in projection is the alteration of the ego that takes place as the patient attempts to master unwanted delusions and hallucinations, Freud now concluded. In later works, he would continue to investigate the underlying similarities between neuroses such as hysteria and psychoses such as paranoia, by emphasizing that in the beginning of a pathological process, the ego is detached from reality but then, as in the systematic delusions of full-blown paranoia, creates a new reality.

Female paranoia presented Freud with an unrivalled vision of the primary conditions for defence and neurosis. Yet the vision was granted as if in aspic, or through a glass museum case. The female paranoiac's defence of projection appeared always to be a defence against a sexual desire which could under no circumstances be acknowledged. Instead, the desire was planted in the outside world. Here, indeed, Freud could recognize himself: was he not the theorist who imputed sexual desires to others precisely where they most vigorously denied it?

Freud had the kinship of paranoia and psychoanalysis pointed out to him in a most brutal manner: by his intimate friend Wilhelm Fliess, in the closing moments of their friendship. 'The "thought reader" perceives nothing in the other, but merely projects his own thoughts' – this was how Fliess described Freud's analytic interpretations to him. To defend his own method, Freud often felt called upon to defend the veracity, or the kernel of truth, in the paranoiac's delusions – and would do so more than twenty years later, when describing a male paranoiac suffering from delusions of jealousy, as follows: 'His abnormality really reduced itself to this, that he watched his wife's unconscious mind much more closely and then regarded it as far more important than anyone else would have thought of doing.' What the paranoiac cannot see, however, is his own unconscious. 'The enmity which the persecuted paranoiac sees in others is the reflection of his own hostile impulses against them.'

So the psychoanalyst and the paranoiac both perceive the unconscious of others far more closely than anyone else, except the paranoiac perceives only what is a 'reflection' of his own unconscious – though no less accurately and faithfully for that. The paranoiac is the mirror image of the analyst, save that the analyst can tear himself away from the mirror and recognize that he has his own body, with its own desires, whereas the paranoiac can never allow himself to step outside of the mirror. The analyst is able to stop himself believing that, like Descartes's famous image of the madman, his body is made of glass. This kinship of the analyst and the paranoiac extended, as Fliess had so cruelly but somewhat blindly put it, to their characteristic mental operations: the analyst and the paranoiac could revolve undisturbed around one another, like double stars in the firmament of sexual defences, with the analyst forever interpreting, the patient forever projecting.

Freud's female paranoiacs revealed to him not only the kinship of their mental operations to that of the analyst, but also the quintessentially female wave of repression upon which, in the *Three Essays on the Theory of Sexuality*, he laid such emphasis in the transition from childhood to womanhood. When in 1907, very early on in their correspondence, Freud enlisted Jung in the attempt to understand paranoia, he sketched this primal scene of paranoia as follows:

The basic situation is this: a person (f[emale].) conceives a desire for intercourse with a man. It is repressed and reappears in the following form: people outside say she has this desire, which she denies. (Or else: the intercourse has taken place during the night against her will. But this is not the primary form.)

Female paranoia thus illustrates most starkly the cultural predicament of women who deny their own sexual desires, only to see them reappear in a threatening form from outside. Sexual activity will thenceforth consist in hot denials.

However, within a year Freud had rejected this view of the primal scene in paranoia and had discarded what he had learnt from Frau P. and the other female paranoiacs. The male paranoiacs took over. It is difficult not to see this transformation as resulting from Freud's relationships with his new disciples, who replaced the male friend for him; it was the retrospective mastering of his stormy relationship with Fliess that gave Freud the vital clue to a revised theory: paranoia arises from 'a detachment of libido from a homosexual component'. Where Fliess had surrendered to the homosexuality left unsatisfied at the end of their friendship by erecting a paranoia, Freud, on the other side of the mirror, had prevailed over it, turning it instead into analytic theory. As Freud wrote to Ferenczi in 1910: 'A piece of homosexual cathexis has been withdrawn and utilized for the enlargement of my own ego. I have succeeded where the paranoiac fails.' It was this idea that exercised Freud in the next few years, linking up with his new theory of narcissism, where the subject's own, necessarily homosexual, body supplies the model for the repressed scene of desire. Yet he was never to write more than a sketch of a case history of a male paranoiac whom he had treated. Whereas the female paranoiac had been and was to remain a recognizable and somewhat tragic figure in the Freudian array of pathological clinical types, he would only ever describe in detail the male paranoiac at second hand. Präsident Schreber's *Memoirs* served as the analytic material from which he expounded the theory that paranoia results from defence against the fundamental proposition 'I (a man) love him'. Leonardo da Vinci's biography twinned up with the Schreberian analysis to tell the narcissistic side of the story of male homosexuality denied.

What of the female paranoiac in this revised theory, centred on the homosexual scene of desire? There is almost a touch of remorse at having abandoned her in favour of a male model – one which he very rarely saw in his consulting-room – in Freud's immediate attempt in the 1907 letter to Jung to integrate his original model of the 1890s, Frau P., within the new homosexual template: 'My old analysis (1896) also showed that the pathological process began with the patient's estrangement from her husband's *sisters*.' But the sisters had not been prominent in the 1896 account, where he had simply written: 'She became uncommunicative and distrustful, showed aversion to meeting her husband's brothers and sisters.' After this brief, almost dutiful, flaring up of his old interest, the female paranoiac is ignored in favour of Schreber and those modelled after him.

Only in 1915 did Freud return to the question of how his earlier account of female paranoia could fit into his homosexual model. He tested it against the case of a young woman who had hired a lawyer to protect her against a man who had tempted her into a lover's rendezvous and was now threatening to blackmail her with photographs taken on that occasion by unseen witnesses. How could the Schreberian model be applied here? Where was the struggle against an intensification of the woman's homosexual trends? Where was the persecutor of the same sex that Freud's model required, herself standing in for someone the subject has loved in the past? This case did not present any hint of such a homosexual attachment; it conformed exactly to the model Freud had proposed in 1896 and again in 1907: 'The girl seemed to be defending herself against love for a man by directly transforming the lover into a persecutor: there was no sign of the influence of a woman.'

As if in deliberate remembrance of his own early narrative procedures and theoretical insights, Freud's account of the case, derived from two meetings with the young girl, is cast in the narrative form of two scenes. He reveals how the delusions of persecution arose not from her response to a single meeting with the man, but to two love scenes; her delusion did not arise simply from her relation to the man but required the intervention of a third party: a woman. The first meeting at the man's rooms had passed off without incident beyond their sexual intimacy, which had not extended to intercourse; in Freud's first meeting with the girl, she had not mentioned this first tryst with the man, because nothing untoward had occurred.

The day after their first meeting, the girl had seen the man talking to her elderly superior at the office in which they all worked – a woman with whom the girl had a close bond. The girl was convinced that the man and her superior had been talking about her erotic adventure, but also that the two of them had themselves been engaged in a love affair, of which she had hitherto been ignorant. The girl felt betrayed and naked, and remonstrated with her lover; he managed to pacify her and a short time later she felt confident enough to visit him for a second time. It was on this second occasion, as they were lying on the bed embracing, that she had heard a click which alarmed her and, on leaving the house, had seen two men on the staircase holding a box and whispering. It was these men that she immediately cast as the photographers, the click the noise of the shutter. Convinced of the man's betrayal of her, she approached the lawyer, asking him to protect her from the man.

The case was now open and shut. When this pretty, quiet and celibate young woman, who lived alone with her widowed mother, had seen her lover talking with her superior, a straightforward mother-substitute, she had placed the man in the position of the father. And this triangulation, this Oedipalization of the scene, allowed the homosexual motive of the delusion to emerge. 'The *original* persecutor – the agency whose influence the patient wishes to escape – is here again not a man but a woman.' Her love for her mother stood between her and her erotic satisfaction, disturbing her relations with men. Freud then felt called upon to expound generally on the mother's relation to the erotic development of girls:

Sigmund Freud and Martha Bernays, wedding photograph, 1886

Sophie and Anna Freud, 1901

Sigmund Freud with Anna in the Dolomites, 1913

Amalia Freud, Martha Freud, Sigmund Freud and Minna Bernays, Altaussee, 1905

Bertha Pappenheim – 'Anna O.'

Emma Eckstein, 1895

Third International Psychoanalytical Congress, Weimar, 1911

1 Sigmund Freud, 2 Otto Rank, 3 Ludwig Binswanger, 4 O. Rothenhäusler, 5 Jan Nelken, 6 R. Forster, 7 Ludwig Jekels, 8 A. A. Brill, 9 Edward Hirtschmann, 10 J. E. G. von Emden, 11 Alphonse Maeder, 12 Paul Federn, 13 Adolf Keller, 14 Alfred von Winterstein, 15 J. Marcinowski, 16 Isidor Sadger, 17 Oskar Pfister, 18 Max Eitingon, 19 Karl Abraham, 20 James J. Putnam, 21 Ernest Jones, 22 Wilhelm Stekel, 23 Paul Bjerre, 24 Eugen Bleuler, 25 Maria Moltzer, 26 Mira Gineburg 27 Lou Andreas-Salomé, 28 Beatrice Hinkle, 29 Emma Jung, 30 M. von Stack, 31 Antonia Wolff, 32 Martha Böddinghaus, 33 Franz Riklin, 34 Sandor Ferenczi, 35 C. G. Jung, 36 Leonhard Seif, 37 K. Landauer, 38 A. Stegmann, 39 W. Wittenberg, 40 Guido Brecher.

When a mother hinders or arrests a daughter's sexual activity, she is fulfilling a normal function whose lines are laid down by events in childhood, which has powerful, unconscious motives, and has received the sanction of society. It is the daughter's business to emancipate herself from this influence and to decide for herself on broad and rational grounds what her share of enjoyment or denial of sexual pleasure shall be. If in the attempt to emancipate herself she falls a victim to a neurosis it implies the presence of a mother-complex which is as a rule over-powerful, and is certainly unmastered. The conflict between this complex and the new direction taken by the libido is dealt with in the form of one neurosis or another, according to the subject's disposition. The manifestation of the neurotic reaction will always be determined, however, not by her present-day relation to her actual mother but by her infantile relations to her earliest image of her mother.

In being drawn erotically to the man, the girl needed to throw off the influence of her mother complex, her 'powerful emotional attachment to her mother'; she did so by means of projection. 'The mother thus became the hostile and malevolent watcher and persecutor.' With the click, which Freud interpreted as 'a knock or beat in her clitoris', she had taken the mother's place in an imagined scene of parental intercourse: instead of choosing her mother as a love-object, she identified with her mother regressively.

Thus Freud had saved his new account of the homosexual character of the paranoid defence. Yet the fact that no apparent sign of this underlying homosexual trend was visible still bothered him. The paranoid defence had itself made the advance from the original female object to a male – the persecutors had all been male: her lover and his two unknown accomplices. This advance was itself unusual; it was an indication of the strength of her erotic attraction to the man. The conflict Freud depicted was in truth a quite evenly balanced one: between the young woman's desire for sexual pleasure and her attachment to her mother. Freud made amends to his female paranoid patients by preserving the original scene of desire refused: a woman desiring intercourse which is repudiated and reappears in the outside, in the form of persecuting accusations. But the transformation from desire to persecution, from inside to outside, was entirely achieved by the intercession of a new and dominating figure: the interposition between the girl and her lover of the 'earliest image of the mother'. Yet she is only called upon when there is a surge forward of the desire for a man. It is still that desire for heterosexual intercourse that initiates the entire sequence of defences.

Une scène peut en cacher une autre: behind the scene of desire lay the bond to the powerful love for the mother. If Schreber's analysis had advertised the increasing emphasis on the all-powerful father in Freud's work during the 1910s, his successful attempt to recuperate his female paranoiacs to that model opened up an entirely new dimension of the pre-Oedipal mother. He would not call her such until the 1930s, after his own mother had died. But her first appearance in this 1915 paper showed he still could make use of that uncanny bond, which was not a transferential bond, with the female paranoiac.

Perhaps Freud's sense of needing to make amends to his female paranoiacs explains, at least in part, the curious incident Joan Riviere experienced in one of her sessions with him, recounted in Jones's biography:

During her analysis Freud spoke very angrily one morning of an English patient he had just seen who complained bitterly of monstrous, and indeed fantastic, ill-treatment she had suffered at the hands of an English analyst in Ipswich – of all places. Mrs Riviere's cool mind at once perceived that this was a cock-and-bull story, but she contented herself with remarking that there was no English analyst of the name mentioned, that there never had been an analyst in Ipswich nor indeed anywhere in England outside of London. That made no impression, and Freud continued his tirade against such scandalous behaviour. Shortly afterwards, however, he received a letter from Abraham saying he had recommended an English lady to consult him and that she was a wild paranoiac with a fondness for inventing incredible stories about doctors. So poor Abraham had been the wicked analyst in Ipswich!

This credulity and gullibility in the face of the female patient – in Jones's eyes so characteristic of Freud, and so much a necessary precondition for the development of psychoanalysis – was the inevitable accompaniment of the sympathetic attention Freud always found for those most inaccessible of patients, the female paranoiacs. With them, his curiosity in the kernel of truth to be found in all delusions and illusions was unencumbered by the expectation of therapeutic benefit, while at the same time his sympathy for any woman deprived, by whatever means, of sexual fulfilment could find adequate expression. The slightly cold disinterestedness that some of his patients noticed in him could then be exercised in the most profitable way, through maximizing his own gain in understanding.

Female Homosexuality: Between Betrayal and Indifference

A certain remoteness is the dominant tone of the only other detailed case history of a woman Freud published after 'Dora': the case of female homosexuality of 1920. The case of Dora could never be described as one in which the transference was absent, despite Freud saying he overlooked it at the time. In contrast, the young female homosexual appeared, like the paranoiac, to exclude the analyst, rather than to engage him in a complex and subtle series of manoeuvres. Whereas the paranoiac's world was too full of meaning, so that Freud was obliged, without too much regret, to understand her without living contact, as if through a glass window, the young homosexual girl neatly turned the tables on Freud. She co-operated actively with the treatment, but remained completely detached.

Once when I expounded to her a specially important part of the theory, one touching her nearly, she replied in an inimitable tone, 'How very interesting', as though she were a *grande dame* being taken over a museum and glancing through her lorgnon at objects to which she was completely indifferent.

If the girl's cool detachment and perspicacity mimicked those of the analyst,

Freud was a match for her at least on this score. All Freud had promised her father was that he would 'study the girl carefully for a few weeks or months'. As a result of this careful study, Freud was certain that he understood the psychogenesis of the girl's homosexuality: 'it was possible to trace its origin and development in the mind with complete certainty and almost without a gap'. Yet by his own admission, the analysis had never even got properly started; he depicted this analysis that wasn't an analysis with one of his typically striking analogies, one drawn from his own experience as a sufferer from travel anxiety: psychoanalysis is a two-stage journey – first one must make all the necessary preparations, acquiring tickets, planning the route and so forth, 'before, ticket in hand, one can at last go on to the platform and secure a seat in the train. ... But after all these preliminary exertions one is not yet there – indeed, one is not a single mile nearer to one's goal. For this to happen, one has to make the journey itself from one station to the other, and this part of the performance may well be compared with the second phase of the analysis.' The second phase of the young homosexual woman's journey never took place. Either she left Freud, or he left her – it is not exactly clear which – stranded on the station platform, ticket in hand, while the train pulled out. His view was that she had decided that she had no intention of getting on the train in his company. And so he washed his hands of her and handed her back to her parents.

The father of this attractive and intelligent eighteen year old had brought her to Freud for analysis on account of her all-consuming love for a mature woman of somewhat doubtful reputation – a *cocotte*, as the parents called their daughter's lady-love. Her father's suspicion, anger and rage had been to no avail when he learned of her attachment to the woman; the seriousness of her involvement, and the danger she was in, had become clear to him when his chance encounter with his daughter and her love in the street had provoked a serious attempt at suicide on the daughter's part – she threw herself over a wall on to a railway line. It was this obstinate determination that had led the father to the pass of bringing the girl to Freud in hope of a cure of her homosexuality.

Freud promised no cure, either to the father, the daughter or to his readers. Indeed, one of the most curious features of this paper is the lengthy digressions and defences devoted to repudiating charges that homosexuality stems either from biological or psychological degeneracy or from constitutional her-maphroditism – or even that there are good reasons for desiring not to be homosexual. Freud is worrying away in this paper at issues that, one would have thought, the first of his *Three essays* of 1905 had entirely disposed of. His coolness and lack of 'therapeutic' hope stemmed from positions he had adopted long before: that homosexuality is in no sense – other than the superficially conventional one – abnormal; both homosexuality and het-erosexuality depend equally upon a restriction in the choice of object. In his reflections in this paper, he put the psychoanalytic case in a particularly delicate and ironic way: 'In general, to undertake to convert a fully developed homosexual into a heterosexual does not offer much more prospect of success than the reverse, except that for good practical reasons the latter is never attempted.' But this sly dig at the arbitrary prejudices associated with socially acceptable sexual mores could not have been sufficient justification for demonstrating to the analytically educated something they already knew: that homosexuality was perfectly normal. The paper must, therefore, have had another aim than that of the defence of the rights and the pleasures of the homosexual.

What seems to have interested Freud in this case was the particularly striking manner in which the young woman's homosexuality had been determined in puberty. He went out of his way to assure the reader that she had no neurotic symptoms whatsoever and that her early childhood had been entirely normal. She had even followed a conventional path in early puberty, showing an early inclination to motherhood through her interest in young children. What was distinctive about her was how, at the age of sixteen, she had reacted to the birth of another brother. That this is the turning-point of the whole story is underlined by Freud's rhetorical flourish: 'The position of affairs which I shall now proceed to lay bare is not a product of my inventive powers; it is based on such trustworthy analytic evidence that I can claim objective validity for it.'

The birth of her baby brother transformed her from a girl with a maternal attitude into a homosexual attracted to mature women. What is more, she became a homosexual who adopted the characteristically masculine pattern of love: active adoration of the beloved, combined with a desire to rescue the loved one from her sexually disreputable life. What was astonishing was that the woman she loved was a substitute for her mother – somewhat disguised, since she was fused with her masculine ideal, her somewhat older brother, but fundamentally modelled on the mother. The mother's sudden and unwished for demonstration of her maternal fertility had elicited love from the daughter, rather than the rivalry one might expect.

Freud was quite perplexed by this unexpected reaction. Usually, in circumstances such as these, he wrote, when a mother and a daughter find themselves competing over who has the right to bear the child,

the daughters are apt to feel for their mothers a mixture of compassion, contempt and envy which does nothing to increase their tenderness for them. The girl we are considering had in any case altogether little cause to feel affection for her mother. The latter, still youthful herself, saw in her rapidly developing daughter an inconvenient competitor; she favoured the sons at her expense, limited her independence as much as possible, and kept an especially strict watch against any close relation between the girl and her father.

But, despite the girl's homosexuality being organized around her love for her mother, this scene of competition between mother and daughter was, Freud reassured his readers, the crucial scene of the family drama. What had been left out of account that, up to now, had made its outcome incomprehensible was the father's role. With the revival of her Oedipus complex at puberty:

She became keenly conscious of the wish to have a child, and a male one; that what she desired was her *father*'s child and an image of *him*, her consciousness was not allowed to know. And what happened next? It was not *she* who bore the child, but her unconsciously hated rival, her mother. Furiously resentful and embittered, she turned away from her father and from men altogether. After this first great reverse she forswore her womanhood and sought another goal for her libido.... After her disappointment, therefore, this girl had entirely repudiated her wish for a child, her love of men, and the feminine role in general. ... She changed into a man and took her mother in place of her father as the object of her love.

The scene was to become a familiar one in Freud's later writings on femininity, when he described the little girl's disappointment at not receiving the precious object she desired so much. But in that later scene, it is the *mother* who does not give the girl the precious object; it is this disappointment that prompts her to turn away, in hope, to the father. Here, with the young homosexual girl, she is disappointed by the father and turns from the treacherous *father* to the mother. And, at the same time, she adopts, by identification with the previously loved father, all the characteristics of the masculine active overvaluation of the object – the attitude that Freud would later describe as a 'masculinity complex' founded on the defiant and obstinate refusal to believe that she does not possess a penis.

In this case history written in 1920, Freud does add in penis envy as a supplementary factor to explain why this young girl, disappointed by her mother's triumphant fertility, is so ready to play the part of a man in love. He also describes how the daughter's homosexuality could pacify her mother, since by turning away from men she would retire in her rival's favour, leaving the field of men entirely to her. And in his final overview of the case, he inclines to the view that her homosexuality was, at bottom, 'probably a direct and unchanged continuation of an infantile fixation on her mother' – thus beginning to open up the exploration he had so long delayed, both in his case histories and in his theory, of the part played by relations in childhood with the mother. But the factor that fixes the girl in her defensive attitude of homosexuality is a more specific one – indeed, in Freud's eyes, the most idiosyncratic feature of the whole case: the father had reacted to his daughter's sudden passion for mature women with rage and extreme displeasure. This paternal rage was a wild passion, quite unlike his usual subdued and well-controlled relations to her. Discovering that her homosexual inclinations provoked a newly passionate relationship with her father, 'she realized how she could wound her father and take revenge on him. Henceforth she remained homosexual out of defiance against her father.'

Freud does not link this defiance and this sadistic attitude to her father to the anal-sadistic stage of infantile sexuality, but his terms of description clearly belong to that already well-established register of his. The father and the daughter have found each other again, but on the terrain of anal erotism. Freud's own attitude to the father is very revealing, however; he twice reiterates that this father was overly influenced by his wife as regards his relations with his daughter. It is the fact that he mentions this factor twice without spelling out the implications that should alert us to its importance, and specifically to its bearing on Freud's view of his own part in the case. The father's passionate disapproval of his daughter's homosexuality is thus highlighted as being the one emotional reaction to his daughter that is not under his wife's control, or at her instigation. The father had, to borrow one of Freud's favourite phrases, finally made a breakthrough to the daughter. And, through her obstinate love of mature women, the daughter did, after all, find a way to win her father back from her mother. This newly established bond between father and daughter is, however, an awkward, even hapless, one, since its register is primarily that of hate rather than love. Freud's own less than explicit pointers to its stable and mutual satisfactions betray his unease with such a paternally conditioned solution to the daughter's deep sense of betrayal.

Just as Freud had found himself playing a part he did not wish to with Dora, so he found himself in an unfortunate position with this other eighteen year old: unfortunate because he was being asked to take on the role of an enraged and disapproving father. He was being lied to and deceived by the girl, just as she had triumphantly deceived her father, and he found that he was expected to condemn her deceptions as well as her homosexuality. Freud's discomfort at being asked – implicitly, in the transference – to play this part led him to go out of his way to affirm how unreprehensible homosexuality is, and how much a part of analytic work, as well as of ordinary life, are betrayal, lies and self-deception.

I can imagine that to point out the existence of lying dreams of this kind, 'obliging' dreams, will arouse a positive storm of helpless indignation in some readers who call themselves analysts. 'What!' they will exclaim, 'the unconscious, the real centre of our mental life, the part of us that is so much nearer the divine than our poor consciousness – it too can lie! Then how can we still build on the interpretations of analysis and the accuracy of our findings!'

By concentrating *his* remarks upon the questions of homosexuality and of deception, Freud reveals *to us* what the paternal sensibilities of this girl were. This effort to show the gulf between himself and the father, between psychoanalysis and the father (who no doubt required absolute honesty of his daughter), only shows how little distance this girl and her analyst had travelled together down the analytic track.

She transferred to me the sweeping repudiation of men which had dominated her ever since the disappointment she had suffered from her father. Bitterness against men is as a rule easy to gratify upon the physician; it need not evoke any violent emotional manifestations, it simply expresses itself by rendering futile all his endeavours and by clinging to the illness. ... As soon, therefore, as I recognized the girl's attitude to her father, I broke off the treatment and advised her parents that if they set store by the therapeutic procedure it should be continued by a woman doctor.

Given what has already been pointed out, there is something not quite right about this account of the transference. Freud describes her transference as being one of repudiation of men, expressed specifically in rendering the physician's efforts futile. Her father's efforts to change her choice of object had, it is true, been entirely futile. But the very effort of trying to influence his daughter had transformed him from a man who was somewhat cowed by his wife into an independent agent, although not as yet a successful one. The girl, we can surmise, was happier with an active, if angry, father, than with a father who did only her mother's bidding. So Freud's description is rather narrowly conceived: she does not repudiate her father so much as stabilize her relations with him. Rather it is Freud who repudiates, by breaking off the treatment so abruptly. And perhaps he is even being somewhat vengeful in suggesting she consult a woman analyst, thus retiring in favour of a woman analyst the way she had retired in favour of her mother. Psychoanalysis is, he would often say, a cure through love: why not force the pace for this young homosexual woman by confronting her with a suitable object of love in the shape of a mature woman analyst? After all, he knows with certainty, he claims, what any analysis, even one conducted with a woman, would discover: what she really longs for is a baby from the father.

So in this case vignette, we find Freud playing the role of a father of whom he does not quite approve. He repeats the father's preoccupation with the everyday deceptions of the girl; he repeats the father's preoccupation with the girl's homosexuality. The girl's homosexual choice of object had been the one weapon which had proved successful in gaining her father's passionate attention. Freud painted the picture of an enraged father who would stop at nothing to transform his daughter from a homosexual to a heterosexual. And in the closing pages of the paper, he discusses a final solution to the stalemate of homosexuality: surgical intervention – as if the father could consummate his rediscovered sadistic love for his daughter in this brutal and irreversible way. Here Freud considers whether Steinach's recent remarkable experimental transformations of animals from males into females and vice versa offer hope of a biological 'therapy' for homosexuality by operating on the sex-glands. For homosexual women, he imagines the operation would require the removal of the 'hermaphroditic ovaries', but concludes that:

A female individual who has felt herself to be a man, and has loved in masculine fashion, will hardly let herself be forced into playing the part of a woman, when she must pay for this transformation, which is not in every way advantageous, by renouncing all hope of motherhood.

So Freud himself considers and rejects this surgical promise, refusing to identify himself with the Steinach-father who violates his daughter in order to make her into a proper woman.

Freud in this case was asked to play the part of the father, cut through all her lies and force her to be heterosexual – the Steinach position. Freud abdicates from this position of responsibility, this position infused with fantasies of paternal omnipotence: he defends the rights of homosexuals to be considered normal, he defends the rights of patients to lie and deceive. As so often, his evasion leaves him open to 'feminine' longings akin to fantasies of rape: he was always prone to the excesses of therapeutic optimism inspired in him by such intemperately masculine doctors. In the 1890s he had eagerly submitted to surgery at the hands of Wilhelm Fliess, whose conception of the fundamental bisexuality of human beings Freud made his own and which supplied the conceptual terrain upon which the plausibility of such surgical intervention in sexual life, both in the 1890s and the 1920s, was considered. And in November 1923, a few weeks after the operation on his cancer, Freud submitted to the Steinach operation of the ligature of the vas deferens, in the hope of regenerating his vital powers for the fight against the alien invader. Freud will not himself cut, but he will allow himself to be cut – he will, at times, of defensive necessity, take on this passive feminine position.

So, just as the homosexual woman was successful in regaining her father's attentions, so her requiring Freud to manoeuvre gingerly around the paternal transference amounted to another success of sorts. He wrote up this pre-liminary analysis of a few weeks' standing not, as he might have done, as an investigation of the malleability of the Oedipus complex in puberty, nor even as an investigation of retiring in favour of another person, but very much on the father's terms: as 'The Psychogenesis of a Case of Homosexuality in a Woman'.

The case also raises the question of what Freud thought a woman analyst could offer the girl that he, a man, could not. Is this question connected with the other paternal transference relationship that was probably preoccupying him at this time, that of his own daughter and patient, Anna, whom he would, not long after he wrote up this case, pass on to a woman analyst, Lou Andreas-Salomé? There is a simple answer to this question, an answer that has been proposed by many commentators: Freud did not find it easy to play the part of the mother in the transference. In addition, in a case such as this, when the paternal transference was both blocked with almost insuperable resistances, and yet probably less deep than the maternal transference, cutting one's losses and turning to a woman made pragmatic sense as well.

Yet Freud was not that distant from the mother's position in this case: like her, he was tolerant of the girl's homosexuality; like her, he was allowed to share in at least some of the secrets of the girl's deceptions of the father and in some of the plans and projects of the love affair. What is more interesting are the difficulties Freud encountered in playing the *father*'s role. As with Dora, Freud seemed perfectly at ease with this relatively benign maternal transference, yet seemed either not to notice, or to discount this fundamental basis of the relationship, treating it as of little significance. As with Dora, he insisted that the main terrain of the analysis must be the paternal transference: this was the territory he thought he should be occupying. Perhaps it was not his reluctance to provoke a maternal transference whose necessity he recognized, nor the absence of a propitious paternal transference, that prompted him to suggest calling upon a woman. It is just as likely that it was the constant discomfort of this *particular* paternal transference – which was tempting him into being intolerant of her sexual inclinations and into a cycle of anger and disappointment over her hypocrisy and her bad faith – that made the recourse to a woman analyst a release. Perhaps, too, a revenge.

The Analyst as Woman

Freud's triptych of pathological types had been established as early as 1894: the hysteric, the obsessional (and phobic) and the paranoiac. The first and third of these were encountered in their most accessible and engaging form in women; only the obsessional resolutely continued to embody and display the essence of the masculine. The immediate context of Freud's revisions of his theory of paranoia in 1907 and 1908 had been his coming to terms with the end of his friendship with Fliess, and the growing complexity of his relations with his disciples – particularly with Jung, the masculine type, his designated crown prince and heir, and Ferenczi, the feminine type, whose passive admiration elicited in Freud the desire for a real woman. Relations with men were high on Freud's agenda: the fruit of his own struggle with the intensity of these relations was his sense of conquering that piece of unruly homosexuality which had surfaced as paranoia in Fliess.

None the less, women were by no means excluded from these increasingly complex relationships between men; quite the reverse. Jung's initial overture to Freud, in 1906, had probably been sparked by his own erotic involvement with a young woman patient, Sabina Spielrein. Freud spent the summer of 1906 at the Hotel du Lac at Lavarone writing a little book; Jung was later to interpret the product of that scene of writing as one designed to give him pleasure. Jung's 'gift' of a woman was clearly situated in the dimension of transference and counter-transference, where the male doctors and the female patient struggled with their apportioned social roles and sexual imaginaries. Freud's gift – for he did send a copy of the book to Jung eager to have his comments on it – was more nuanced: he presented Jung with a portrait of the psychoanalyst as a *woman* in love. So, just at the moment when Freud was beginning to acquire male colleagues whom he could, at least at times, regard as on an equal footing with him, he interestingly portrayed the essence of the analytic profession as being a feminine one.

The book was entitled *Delusions and Dreams in Jensen's 'Gradiva'*. It gave a psychoanalytic reading of a recent novella, which tells the story of a young archaeologist, Norbert Hanold, from the north of Europe, who on a visit to Rome falls in love with a bas-relief of a Grecian girl with a particularly striking gait; he baptizes her 'Gradiva' – 'the woman who steps along'. Prompted by a nightmare, in which he sees her, untroubled, accept her death under the ashes of the eruption at Pompeii, he erects a system of delusions in which Gradiva inhabits both Pompeii and the contemporary, living world. Driven to Pompeii by his delusions, he imagines he has returned to the fateful day in 79 AD when Vesuvius erupted. Here he encounters his 'Gradiva' in the flesh.

Gradiva is not, in fact, an apparition. She is another German-speaking visitor from the north, indeed a childhood playmate from the archaeologist's own town. He, of course, does not recognize her and can only perceive her as the apparition of his Gradiva from the past. She understands his delusional state and quite deliberately initiates his 'cure', by 'entering into his delusion, the whole compass of which she elicited from him, without ever contradicting it', just as a real psychoanalytic cure must 'begin by taking up the same ground as the delusional structure and then investigating it as completely as possible.' 'This unusually clever girl, then, was determined to win her childhood's friend for her husband, after she had recognized that the young man's love for her was the motive force behind the delusion.' Pressing forward in her ruthless examination of her 'patient', it is at the moment when he strikes her living hand, supposedly to slap a fly resting there, that she declares: 'There's no doubt you're out of your mind, Norbert Hanold!' In recognizing that she knows his name, Hanold realizes that she is not a ghost from Pompeii. Then who is she? Zoe Bertgang, daughter of Richard Bertgang, Professor of Zoology.

Zoe now reveals to him how it is on the model of the prehistoric, that is childhood affection for Zoe, that his delusional love for the Pompeiian Gradiva was entirely built. His whole history of turning away from living sexuality, as represented by Zoe, towards the dead world of archaeology is uncovered, piece by piece. And, as is appropriate in turn-of-the-century love affairs, it is finally up to him to seize the initiative and kiss his newly found Gradiva, making his own 'the childhood friend who had been dug out of the ruins'.

The story has much value for Freud because the account of Norbert's delusions and the dreams interlaced with them conform so closely to the psychoanalytic theses of the repressed unconscious and its expression in compromise formations. Undoubtedly the manner in which archaeology is used as the guiding metaphor both for what is repressed and for the method by which the forgotten past still lives on in the present appealed strongly to Freud, who had likened analysis to archaeological investigations in the 1890s and would do so regularly throughout his writings.

However, it is in the final section of his little book that Freud discusses the most remarkable feature of Jensen's novella: the fact that the work of the physician and the process of the cure through love are one and the same thing. Norbert Hanold meets his physician in the very heart of his delusion: the ghost woman from 79 AD is also the girl from his home town, who sets out with determination, sympathy and intelligence to cure him of his illness. Is such a cure 'conceivable or even possible'? The answer is clear: it is quite conceivable, since Zoe's cure of Norbert is remarkably similar to a psychoanalyst's cure of a patient. What is more, the happy ending reveals exactly where psychoanalysis departs from a rationalistic conception of a cure accomplished by undoing repressions. If a critic were to view the 'cure' as having been accomplished simply by Norbert having been shown by Zoe the inner origin of all his delusional mental states, the engagement of Zoe and Norbert would appear as an arbitrary and structurally superfluous addition by the author, tacked on 'no doubt to the satisfaction of his female readers'.

Nothing is further from the truth, Freud argues, taking his cue from the 'female readers':

The process of cure is accomplished in a relapse into love, if we combine all the many components of the sexual instinct under the term 'love'; and such a relapse is indispensable, for the symptoms on account of which the treatment has been undertaken are nothing other than precipitates of earlier struggles connected with repression or the return of the repressed, and they can only be resolved and washed away by a fresh high tide of the same passions. Every psycho-analytic treatment is an attempt at liberating repressed love which has found a meagre outlet in the compromise of a symptom. Indeed, the agreement between such treatments and the process of cure described by the author of *Gradiva* reaches its climax in the further fact that in analytic psychotherapy too the re-awakened passion, whether it is love or hate, invariably chooses as its object the figure of the doctor.

The rational reconstruction or the systematic unearthing of the repressed past – the method Freud implies is anticipated by the 'male readers' – is the exact opposite of Zoe's cure of Norbert and of psychoanalysis. The passion locked up in the repressed memories not only must be, but always is, employed as the only means for the cure. What is more – and on this point *Gradiva* goes far beyond what is expected in medical treatment – the passion must be experienced by the curer as well as the afflicted.

Zoe only engages in the cure of Norbert because she herself is trapped in a hopeless love for her father, who, like Norbert, only has time for his intellectual work – in the father's case, his zoological specimens, named in the dead language of Latin. Zoe, his living daughter, but also given 'life' in a dead language, seeks to escape from her attachment to her father by gaining the love of Norbert, her old playmate. Her therapeutic activity is premised on perceiving that Norbert's delusions are distorted expressions of his love for her. 'It was only this knowledge which could decide her to devote herself to the treatment; it was only the certainty of being loved by him that could induce her to admit her love to him.'

So the happy ending is not at all an arbitrary supplement, designed only to please 'female readers'; it is the logical conclusion of the necessary prerequisites of this cure through love that is psychoanalysis. The 'female readers' are *right* to demand this happy ending; it is an essential part of the story. However, Freud wishes to draw the line at this point, by indicating how Zoe/Gradiva is, unfortunately, better placed than the practitioners of the medical technique discovered by Breuer and developed by Freud. Like the doctors, she too made conscious what is repressed and she too made explanation and cure coincide. However,

Gradiva was able to return the love which was making its way from the unconscious into consciousness, but the doctor cannot. Gradiva had herself been the object of the earlier, repressed love; her figure at once offered the liberated current of love a desirable aim. The doctor has been a stranger, and must endeavour to become a stranger once more after the cure; he is often at a loss what advice to give the patients he has cured as to how in real life they can use their recovered capacity to love. To indicate the expedients and substitutes of which the doctor therefore makes use to help him to approximate with more or less success to the model of a cure by love which has been shown us by our author – all this would take us much too far away from the task before us.

How, indeed, we may ask, does the psychoanalyst manage to carry through a cure by love when he cannot reciprocate, cannot offer his hand in marriage, as Zoe does to Norbert? The answer is, by employing a 'complicated technique' in place of love, a series of 'expedients and substitutes'. These compensate the analyst for not being able to adopt Zoe's position of being able to reciprocate in every way the patient's demands. Yet the analyst does quite knowingly adopt the position of the beloved woman; and, more importantly, Freud does not deny that the feeling of the patient for the analyst may well be reciprocated by the analyst. What the analyst cannot offer is reciprocity in social reality, outside the cure. Having a strong affective motive for wishing to cure the patient may well be as indispensable for the analyst as it was for Zoe Bertgang. As Freud was to say, when embarking on the cure through love of Loë Kann Jones: 'she is a highly intelligent, deeply neurotic, Jewess, whose disease history is easy to read. I will be pleased to be able to expend much Libido on her.' There is no doubt in Freud's mind that, like Zoe, the analyst must expend libido on his – or her – patient.

The 'female readers' were right. Only a cure through love is believable. Jensen's *Gradiva* portrays two men, the zoologist and the archaeologist, the father and the lover, totally locked into their work with the prehistoric dead, to the exclusion of the living, the erotic woman. It is only the siren call of the woman that can restore them to life. It is the age-old knowledge of woman, as expressed in their understanding of love as the supreme balm, that can recall them from their petrified self-absorption. Freud's psychoanalyst is entirely appropriately cast here as the active feminine principle of love, who will, to conform to the proprieties of a patriarchal society, appear on the surface as allowing herself to be loved, when it is she who has done all the work, the loving, that calls the man back from the dead desert of lovelessness. The cure through love is quintessentially the cure accomplished by a woman; psychoanalysis, as the reinvention of the cure through love, emerges as quintessentially a woman's profession, certainly a 'feminine' profession. This is the underlying message of Freud's *Delusions and Dreams in Jensen's 'Gradiva'*.

The casting of the analyst as the beloved woman who understands and reciprocates combines two themes: firstly, the debt that psychoanalysis owes to popular wisdom and ancient knowledge, forgotten and derided by modern science. It is this refrain one hears most clearly when Freud talks of the ancient and popular art of dream interpretation:

Science and the majority of educated people smile if they are set the task of interpreting a dream. Only the common people, who cling to superstitions and who on this point are carrying on the convictions of antiquity, continue to insist that dreams can be interpreted. The author of *The Interpretation of Dreams* has ventured, in the face of the reproaches of strict science, to become a partisan of antiquity and superstition.

Secondly, there is the debt psychoanalysis owes to women: that to the female hysterics *and* to the popular wisdom which goes under the derisory name of old wives' tales:

It may perhaps interest you to learn how anyone could have formed such an idea as that the act of birth is the source and prototype of the affect of anxiety. Speculation had a very small share in it; what I did, rather, was to borrow from the *naïve* popular mind. Long years ago, while I was sitting with a number of other young hospital doctors at our midday meal in an inn, a house physician from the midwifery department told us of a comic thing that had happened at the last examination for midwives. A candidate was asked what it meant if meconium (excreta) made its appearance at birth in the water coming away, and she promptly replied: 'It means the child's frightened.' She was laughed at and failed in the examination. But silently I took her side and began to suspect that this poor woman from the humbler classes had laid an unerring finger on an important correlation.

So woman, who initially figures in the history of psychoanalysis as the pliant and passive object of the doctor's science, is sometimes ceded her rights as mother and true originator, now the one in possession of Freud's 'collection of pick-locks'. She is supremely well qualified to sit in the analyst's chair.

A Woman's Profession

Women had been drawn to Freud's courses from the very beginning. One of the first to sit in was Emma Goldman, who in September 1895 had come to Vienna incognito from London. 'It was Freud who gave me my first understanding of homosexuality,' she recalled. In her later stormy career as an anarchist, her positive views on free love were more influenced by Edward Carpenter and Havelock Ellis than by Freud, whose psychoanalysis she came to regard as 'nothing but the old confessional'. None the less, she had her influence on the repertoire of memorable psychoanalytic images. In 1909, when Freud came to lecture at Clark University in the United States, she interrupted him very noisily from the back. He instantly returned the compliment and depicted the repressed as the member of an otherwise quiet and attentive audience who insists on chattering and shuffling his feet, is ejected and whose attempts at re-entering the room are now blocked by the men who stand with their chairs placed against the door.

Despite Freud having a number of other women students in the years that followed – Dora Teleky in 1903–4, Dr Aurelia Axter, Dr Else Friedland and Dr Gisela Kaminer in 1906–7, Dr Ada Hirsch, Dr Clara Honigsberg and Caroline Bum in 1908–9, and Emilie Pisko from 1906 to 1910 – it was not until 1910 that a woman was elected a member of the Vienna Psycho-Analytical Society. Indeed, up until 1910 it was not clear if a woman could be a member of the somewhat informally constituted Society. At a discussion in April 1910, Freud declared that he would 'see it as a serious inconsistency if we were to exclude women on principle.'

Shortly after, Dr Margarethe Hilferding was elected a member of the Society. Born Margarethe Hönigsberg in 1871, she studied medicine at the University of Vienna, where she met her future husband, Rudolph Hilferding, in the socialist student movement. They married in 1904 and had two sons, Karl Emil (1905–42) and Peter (later Milford, born 1908). Her husband, also trained as a doctor but dedicated to political activity and writing, became a founder of *Marx-Studien* and author of a fundamental work on Marxist economics, *Finance Capital* (1910). From 1906 on, he worked mainly in Berlin. During the war he was a doctor in the Austrian army, but in 1920 he became a German citizen and eventually Finance Minister in two different governments (1923 and again in 1928–9).

Throughout the early period of their marriage, Margarethe Hilferding remained in Vienna and worked as a doctor, allying herself closely with Adler's socialist-inclined group. At some point, probably in the 1910s, she and Rudolph divorced. She had no inner vocation for medicine, she once told the Psycho-Analytical Society, but her interest in science had been an attempt 'to secure herself against a relapse into her luxuriant fantasy life.' She gave only one paper to the Society during her brief membership, 'On the Basis of Mother Love', delivered on 11 January 1911.

It is perhaps not surprising that the first paper given to the Society by a woman should be concerned with the mother. And the general theme of the paper presaged what would become distinctive themes in some of the writings of later women analysts. Hilferding's paper opens by distinguishing between physiological and psychological maternal love. Her focus is on women who, disappointed by the birth of their child, lack the feeling of mother love. When that feeling finally takes them over, Hilferding notes, its arrival is to be attributed to psychological rather than physiological factors. Drawing on observations from other cultures as well as her own, she concludes that 'there is no innate mother love'. None the less, she wishes to qualify this conclusion in the light of psychoanalytic knowledge. Not every instance of mother love is 'psychological'. It is the physical involvement of mother and child that gives rise to mother love, in particular the sexual relationship between mother and child: 'during the period following delivery the child represents a natural sexual object for the mother.'

This sexual relationship begins before birth: fetal movements give pleasure to the mother, and it is the loss of this pleasure in birth that may give rise to aversion to the child. But Hilferding introduces another principle as well: the expectation that there is a close correspondence between the sexuality of the child and that of the mother:

if we assume an Oedipus complex in the child, it finds its origin in sexual excitation by way of the mother, the prerequisite for which is an equally erotic feeling on the mother's part. It follows, then, that at certain times the child does represent for the mother a natural sexual object; this period coincides with the infant's need for care.

After this period, the child must make way for the husband – or perhaps for the next child.

Later, with the birth of other children, what appears to be innate mother love is the revival of the experiences of care and nursing for the first child. And, Hilferding adds, the sexual relationship between mother and child may be disturbed by lack of sexual gratification from the husband, which may lead to women clinging for too long to the child as sexual object.

Freud's response to Hilferding's paper was rather unexpected: 'the way to find out something about mother love can be only through statistical examination – today we are in a position to say only what motives may come into play in it.' And he went on to praise Hilferding for what was not psychoanalytic in her paper: 'those explanations that she arrived at before she concerned herself with psychoanalysis are the ones that are the most estimable, being original and independent.' It was as if he were warning her not to adopt his psychoanalytic theory like a ready-made suit – because, as likely as not, it would not fit. Trust your own experience first, he seemed to be saying. But then again, Freud's response was of a piece, one could say, with attitudes which would become clearer as the psychoanalytic movement developed: in his heart of hearts, he seemed not to like followers, distrusting and resenting their implicit sycophancy; but he was certainly no happier with critics and opponents, who presented a vital danger to his life's work.

The drift of Freud's remarks on Hilferding's psychoanalytic arguments was to argue against the close intertwining, the harmonious symbiosis of mother and child's sexualities. What most generally affects the mother, he asserted, is that the sight of the child revives her own infantile sexuality: she envies and hates the child as she had envied and hated her siblings in childhood. In particular, much maltreatment of children arises because of infantile masturbation and parents' violent reactions to it. Freud is less sanguine, at least in this discussion, about the idyll of mutual sexual satisfaction between mother and child, referring instead to those young mothers 'who have experienced the harmful effect of modern literature and who use the yearning for a child as a subterfuge for their sexual cravings.'

Hilferding attended the Wednesday evening meetings of the Vienna Psycho-Analytical Society regularly throughout 1910 and 1911. When Wilhelm Stekel gave a paper on 'The Choice of a Profession and Neurosis' in November 1910, her remarks in the discussion expressed considerable indignation at Stekel's overlooking of the social restrictions on women in contemporary Vienna: 'neither the taking up of a profession nor the specific choice of one is free, least of all in the case of the woman; for her, indeed, only medicine and philosophy are possible.' She also took exception on her sex's behalf to a speculative attempt by Viktor Tausk to link female medical students and homosexual inclinations. But there is little surviving evidence of her theoretical views or even of whether she practised analysis: in one clinical vignette, she reported on having cured a seventeen-year-old factory girl's attack of vomiting through making pertinent remarks about her sister's pregnancy and the boyfriend she shared with her sister.

Over the spring of 1911, the conflict between Alfred Adler and Freud intensified, resulting in Adler's resignation in June. A further constitutional manoeuvre obliged the remaining Adlerians to resign from the Vienna Psycho-Analytical Society on 11 October 1911; Hilferding was one of the five who resigned then. After the First World War, she served for some years as the President of the Vienna Society for Individual Psychology, the Adlerian group. Little is known of her work in the inter-war years. She died in the Theresienstadt concentration camp at some point after 1942.

Hermine Hug-Hellmuth, 1871–1924

Hermine Hug-Hellmuth, the third woman after Hilferding and Sabina Spielrein to become a member of the Vienna Psycho-Analytical Society, is a figure whose exact place in the history of psychoanalysis has only recently become clear. Why it remained obscure for so long, given Hug-Hellmuth's status as the first child analyst, prompts speculation about the factors that promote and demote figures from prominent places in such histories. One of the few gentiles and even fewer women in the very early days of analysis, it is clear that Hug-Hellmuth's personally reclusive and unclubbable personality played its part. This was compounded by two major scandals: one which burst upon the life of this 'quiet, withdrawn' figure; another which caused her death. Scandals, in the days when the Viennese Society was struggling for respectability, were not calculated to endear their central characters to the movement. Equally crucial to Hug-Hellmuth's obscurity in psychoanalytic history was the very fact that she was the *first* child analyst. After her relatively early death, the figures in competitive ascendancy in child analysis, Anna Freud and Melanie Klein, had remarkably little to say about her work. They chose either to ignore her, for fear of too close an association, or to denigrate her not insubstantial achievements. Hug-Hellmuth's is a case not of patriarchal dismissal of a significant woman, but of female rivals partially obliterating a precursor.

Certainly Freud thought highly of Dr Phil. Hug-Hellmuth. As early as 1911, just after she had begun to attend Freud's Wednesday evenings, he was recommending a paper of hers to Jung for the *Jahrbuch*, the major psychoanalytical journal: 'I have received a splendid, really illuminating paper about colour audition from an intelligent lady Ph.D. It solves the riddle with the help of our psychoanalysis.' In a 1914 letter to Karl Abraham, describing his 'charming', 'decent, civilized' little grandson Ernst, he notes: 'Strict upbringing by an intelligent mother enlightened by Hug-Hellmuth has done him a great deal of good.' On a number of occasions, he cites several of the many dreams Hug-Hellmuth recorded, and further mentions her as a contributor to psychoanalytical periodicals. Perhaps more significantly, since this occurs after the scandal of Hug-Hellmuth's death, he mentions her in his 'Autobiographical Study' of 1925–6 as one of the key figures in the 'application of analysis to education' and to 'the prophylactic upbringing of healthy children', giving Melanie Klein and Anna Freud only a footnote in the same context. Freud may have been promoting Hug-Hellmuth's work posthumously in part to evade being seen promoting his daughter's work, or denigrating Melanie Klein's, but the means of evasion, if such it was, meant paying his respects to a woman now shrouded in scandal.

If Father Freud chose not to dismiss Hug-Hellmuth, Daughter Anna, at least in this one respect, did not follow in his footsteps. Perhaps because she was striving to make child analysis her own field, perhaps because there was a residual fear of identifying with a woman who, by all reports, was an unattractive precursor, Anna effectively dismissed Hug-Hellmuth. In her first book on the technique of child analysis of 1927, which bears a marked similarity in many key respects to Hug-Hellmuth's seminal paper in that field, the only acknowledgment she gave her was to say: 'Hermine Hug Hellmuth attempted to replace the knowledge obtained from an adult patient's free associations by playing with the child, seeing him in his own home, and trying to become familiar with all his intimate daily circumstances.' Certainly the fact that Anna's arch-rival, Melanie Klein, then chose indirectly to attack Anna's work by attacking Hug-Hellmuth on all those tenets that the Viennese women held in common cannot have endeared Hug-Hellmuth to Anna. As George MacLean and Ulrich Rappen point out in their recent careful study of Hug-Hellmuth and her work, fifty-four years after the older woman's death Anna was still keeping to the letter of Hug-Hellmuth's will, which asked that nothing ever be written about her or her work. An intriguing injunction in itself and one that Freud was amongst the first to break, it was certainly a convenient tool for Anna Freud in what was perhaps a necessary struggle to establish her ascendancy.

Hermine Hug-Hellmuth was born on 31 August 1871 to Ritter Hugo Hug von Hugenstein, a respected military man in the Hapsburg Empire, and Ludovika Achelpohl, who brought him a dowry that was much needed to restore the ailing family finances. After one child had been lost to the couple, Hugo brought his five-year-old illegitimate daughter, Antoine, into the marriage, legitimating her by officially declaring her age as two. Tragedy pursued the family. When Hermine was two, Hugo lost his newly inherited wealth in the stock market crash; a year later a second child was born and died within a month; and a year after that Hermine's mother contracted tuberculosis and lived as an invalid until her death when Hermine was twelve.

In the midst of all this, Hermine's father had an unusual eye to his daughters' education. They were still only children when, in 1876, he wrote a will providing money to support them 'in their intended training as teachers'. In the event, Hermine and Antoine fulfilled their father's desires more than adequately. Both obtained qualifications as primary and secondary schoolteachers and both obtained doctorates from the University of Vienna. In 1897, the very year that the University of Vienna first permitted the enrolment of women, Hermine registered as a 'special' student, returning again in 1904 as a 'regular' student, after more teaching and after having completed the necessary entrance qualification of a 'gymnasium' degree in Prague. In May 1909, she obtained her doctorate in physics, with a dissertation on 'Some physical and chemical properties of radioactive deposits at the anode and cathode'; her sister Antoine had obtained hers with a dissertation in philosophy on Novalis's fragments five years before and had already seen its publication.

Little is known about the relationship between the half-sisters in these years, except that they did on occasion share an apartment. The bare facts of Antoine Hug's story read like an outline for a Charlotte Brontë novel. A Ph.D. schoolteacher, at the age of forty-one she entered into an affair with Rudolf Rossi von Lichtenfels, the married former headmaster of a school where she had taught. They started a school together, Rudolf's wife serving as administrator and cook, and Antoine investing her legacy into the venture. However, the school soon failed. In 1906, Antoine had an illegitimate child by Rudolf, a boy who took his father's Christian name and the surname his mother used: Rudolf or Rolf Hug. The affair lasted until the boy was two; then Antoine was left to fend for herself, sometimes with her half-sister's help.

Where Antoine gave birth to a child, Hermine, now variously known as Hug or von Hug-Hellmuth, gave birth to child analysis. In 1907, Isidor Sadger, one of Freud's early and prolific, though it seems less-loved, followers, became the Hugs' family doctor. A friendship developed, the only male relationship Hug-Hellmuth's translators and editors could detect in her life. There is no information as to whether or not they were lovers, though certainly Sadger – the man who argued and voted against admitting female members to the Vienna Psycho-Analytical Society – became Hug-Hellmuth's analyst and introduced her to Freud and psychoanalytic writings. As her many papers, published in rapid succession from 1912 through the remaining twelve years of her life, testify, Hug-Hellmuth quickly began to use her teaching work as an observational terrain for psychoanalysis.

Another ready site for observation was her nephew Rolf, whose dreams, actions and childhood remarks are prominent throughout her papers. Though Hermine and Antoine rarely lived together after Rolf's birth, it is clear from the following anecdote that little fatherless Rolf cast Hermine in the paternal image:

At the age of six, my nephew who had been attached to me from the earliest age, stopped calling me 'aunt', deformed the name Hermine, first of all into Hermun and then transformed it into Herman; and when we told him this was a man's name, he replied, 'It doesn't matter, so you are a man.' 'But that's not possible, I am a woman.' – 'Yes, but for me, you're a man.'

Hug-Hellmuth's writings suggest that Antoine spoiled Rolf, over-compensating for an illegitimacy which replicated her own and for his lack of a father. Under the watchful eyes of the two women, the boy was, it seems, at first precocious. Then, after his mother's death in 1915 when he was nine, he was precociously delinquent. The fact that Hermine was not named as

Rolf's guardian in Antoine's will implies that there was some strain between the two sisters regarding the child – as there was, apparently, about politics, with Antoine cast as the radical. After his mother's death, Rolf was shuttled between fostering families and boarding-schools, his aunt sometimes acting as a source of finance and always acting as an observer. One of her late papers, 'The Libidinal Structure of Family Life' (1924), after describing infantile sexuality and the vagaries of the Oedipus complex and the family romance, comments specifically on the social cruelty inflicted on illegitimate children, whose protest against the 'unfairness and unkindness of society' often leads to delinquency. Delinquent Rolf stole, was expelled from various schools and eventually repaid his aunt for her 'paternity' and her observations with a violence unequalled in the history of psychoanalysis.

On 8 October 1913, Hug-Hellmuth was voted a member of the Vienna Psycho-Analytical Society, of which she proved a mainstay during the difficult war years. Three weeks later she gave the first of what were to be several papers to the Society, on topics ranging from children's games to a study of lesbianism. But that first paper to the group was an indication of what would be the main emphasis of her work: a discussion of the American educationalist, Stanley Hall. This cross-over between education and psychoanalysis was to be the subject of her first monograph, published in 1913 and translated into English by Stanley Hall's group in 1919 as *A Study of the Mental Life of the Child*. As in so much of her writing, Hug-Hellmuth is intent on showing how Freud's theories of infant sexuality, derived with the exception of Little Hans from the analysis of adults, are actually present in the real child. None the less, her interpretations and observations are organized within a framework of child development, which comes not from psychoanalysis but from the educational writers of her day, whose concern is with the social organization, education and pedagogic supervision of children. Hence in this monograph, she classifies the development of the child into three stages: the first nursing stage; the period of play which occurs between the ages of one to six; and the subsequent period of serious study. Play, she stresses, is crucial to the child's cognitive, imaginative and emotional development. Like Anna Freud after her and far more than Freud himself, Hug-Hellmuth is interested in tracing and ensuring the child's appropriate development. In her 1914 paper, 'Child Psychology and Pedagogy', she talks of 'the double goal of applying the psychoanalytic method to the infantile mental life ... "curing" and "educating" – improving the child's mental life in a therapeutic and educational sense', and of preparing 'for an era in which the psychoanalytic method executed with knowledge becomes a tool for education'.

After having worked as an analyst with children for over seven years, Hug-Hellmuth was prepared to define her 'Technique of Child-Analysis', first presented as a paper to the International Congress in The Hague in 1920, a Congress attended by both Anna Freud and Melanie Klein. It is here that we see how very close her ideas both of the aims and practice of child analysis are to what were to become Anna's. Once again, Hug-Hellmuth notes the double function of child analysis, at once 'curative and educative' since it consists not only 'in freeing the young creature from his suffering', but 'must also furnish him with moral and aesthetic values'. For Hug-Hellmuth, unlike Melanie Klein, but again like Anna, the child is a different being from the adult since her definitive mental structure is not yet formed, and is not ready for analysis until the age of six or seven. Like Anna, Hug-Hellmuth stresses the need for a preliminary phase in which the analyst engages the child's trust and gets to know the child's parents, when possible securing their co-operation. Then, too, in some measure, the analyst becomes a person that the child can identify with. In all this, Anna replicated Hug-Hellmuth.

Hug-Hellmuth's keenness to provide evidence for Freud's theories by finding their source in children's experience involved her in the first scandal by which she came to be remembered and therefore forgotten. In 1919, *A Young Girl's Diary*, a journal written by a young girl belonging to the upper middle class, and recording the life of Rita from the age of eleven to fourteen, was published anonymously by the *Internationaler Psychoanalytischer Verlag*. The sexual honesty of the *Diary*, and its revelation of a young girl's fantasies and sexual curiosities, were themselves startling enough to spark controversy and make the volume into an instant bestseller. But on top of that, there were rumours of a literary fraud: how could a young girl have written such things! It was only in 1922 when the book was into its third edition in German and its first in English, and speculation was rife about who Rita was, that Hug-Hellmuth, already thought by some to be the volume's author, came forward as its editor. In her preface to the new edition, she did little to combat the charges of fraud except quietly to note that the Rita of the book, who must needs remain anonymous, had given her the diary and had subsequently grown up, married and died. As proof of the volume's worth, she cited that ultimate authority, Freud, who had written to Hug-Hellmuth about the *Diary* in 1915:

The diary is a little gem. I really believe it has never before been possible to obtain such a clear and truthful view of the mental impulses that characterize the development of a girl in our social and cultural stratum during the years before puberty. We are shown how her feelings grow up out of a childish egoism till they reach social maturity; we learn what form is first assumed by her relations with her parents and with her brothers and sisters and how they gradually gain in seriousness and inward feelings; how friendships are made and broken; how her affection feels its way towards her first objects; and, above all, how the secret of sexual life begins to dawn on her indistinctly and then takes complete possession of the child's mind; how, in the consciousness of her secret knowledge, she at first suffers hurt, but little by little overcomes it. All of this is so charmingly, so naturally, and so gravely expressed in these artless notes that they cannot fail to arouse the greatest interest in educators and psychologists. ... It is your duty, I think, to publish the diary. My readers will be grateful to you for it.

One of the chief critics of the *Diary*'s authenticity was the British educational psychologist, Cyril Burt. In reviewing the *Diary* after its English publication, he underlined that the book's sophistication, both stylistically and in conceptual depth of understanding, could not be the work of a teenage girl. Accurate as it may have been in evoking real experience, the Diary was a fiction written by an older person recalling the past. Burt, as it later transpired, was of course himself something of an expert in literary fraud: articles under various women's names were found, after his death, to have been written by him.

The truth of the Diary's authorship remains an open question, despite the Vienna Psycho-Analytical Society's attempt to check out the narrative's factual basis by doing some intricate detective work. Whether Hug-Hellmuth had been given the Diary, or written a fiction based on her own teenage journals or simply recollections, is still unknown. Helene Deutsch's verdict on 'this classic picture of feminine adolescence' is perhaps as good as any: 'People said that this diary was a creation of her [Hug-Hellmuth's] fantasy, to which I would answer that if this was the case, Dr Hug-Hellmuth had both psychological insight and literary talent. ... The book is so true psychologically that it has become a gem of psychoanalytic literature.'

'Psychological insight' was certainly what Hug-Hellmuth was by 1920 widely recognized as possessing. The summer before the important Hague Congress, she was invited to lecture on child analysis and education at the Berlin Psychoanalytic Clinic – a series of lectures which must have proved provocative to the ambitious Melanie Klein, since in her autobiography she seems intent on denying Hug-Hellmuth's importance:

Dr Hug-Hellmuth was doing child analysis at this time in Vienna, but in a very restricted way. She completely avoided interpretations, though she used some play material and drawings, and I could never get an impression of what she was actually doing, nor was she analyzing children under six or seven years. I do not think it too conceited to say that I introduced into Berlin the beginnings of child analysis.

While in Berlin, Hug-Hellmuth stayed and grew friendly with Karen Horney, though their respective views on women were radically different: Hug-Hellmuth in her few writings on women was a somewhat reductionist, biological Freudian, taking penis envy as a given and stressing its ramifications in women's generalized envy of the favoured male. In 1922, Hug-Hellmuth took on the work of organizing the Vienna Society's out-patient arm, the Ambulatorium's teaching programme. Soon she was heading the Ambulatorium's educational services. Here, too, interestingly, in her teaching and organizational commitments to the more socially oriented facets of psychoanalytic activity, she was a precursor of Anna Freud. Late that year and into the next, she lectured again, this time to a general public at a centre for adult education. The material from these many lectures and Hug-Hellmuth's continuous analysis of children found its way into her final summary work, New Ways to the Understanding of Youth (1924), conceived of as a series of lectures for a broad body of care professionals and parents, 'teachers, educators, school physicians, kindergarten teachers and social workers'. With a wealth of clinical detail and an experienced teacher's lucidity, Hug-Hellmuth set out the basics of Freudian theory and its pertinence for a child's development, education and well-being.

This publication, which marked the high-point of Hug-Hellmuth's career as psychoanalyst and educator, coincided with the year of her death. On 9 September 1924, her regular daily help, Magdalena Kittner, and a locksmith broke into her locked ground-floor flat to find her dead on the sofa. She had been strangled. In the subsequent enquiry, her nephew Rolf confessed to the crime. He had climbed through her window just after midnight and woken her with his movements. She had screamed. A tussle ensued, in which he had tried to smother her with a pillow. When she had continued to scream, he had strangled her and then gagged her, finally carrying her on to the couch and placing a clean pillow under her head. He had then taken 2,600,000 kronen from her underwear as well as a gold watch, before making his way back out of the window.

In the many newspaper reports which followed and in the trial records, a picture of Hug-Hellmuth as a 'pedantic and fastidious' woman of few words and fewer friends emerged. Hug-Hellmuth, it was revealed from both Sadger's and her maid's depositions, had for some time been afraid of being murdered by her nephew, who stole from her and whose consistent demands for money over the years had grown increasingly violent. Despite this, earlier that year Hug-Hellmuth had given Sadger a copy of her will, which named Rolf as her sole beneficiary. At the trial Rolf painted himself as the victim of his aunt's erratic educational methods: warmth would be followed in the next moment by severity. By giving him so little money, he also claimed, she had forced him to lie and steal. Sadger's deposition told the story from Hug-Hellmuth's point of view: that of a woman who had tried to cope as best she could with a nephew whose criminality increased with the years and of whom she lived in escalating terror.

Eighteen-year-old Rolf was sentenced to twelve years in prison. On being freed after serving most of his term, Rolf visited a leading psychoanalyst, Paul Federn, and asked for compensation from the Vienna Psycho-Analytical Society, on the grounds that he had been used for psychoanalytic experimentation. Federn referred him to Eduard Hitschmann, who interpreted Rolf's demand as a demand for analysis. 'The analyst was of the opinion that a woman analyst would be best – she could in effect replace the deceased aunt! He suggested me,' writes Helene Deutsch. In the event, Rolf never appeared for a session, but instead trailed a frightened Helene through the streets. Her husband, without her knowledge, hired a detective to protect her, so that two male figures eventually followed Deutsch. And then Rolf vanished, never to be heard of again.

Two notices appeared in psychoanalytic journals following Hug-Hellmuth's murder. Siegfried Bernfeld, in a brief entry marking the event in the *International Journal of Psychoanalysis*, added: 'In a will made a few days before her death, she expressed a desire that no account of her life and work should appear in psychoanalytic publications.' Hug-Hellmuth, it would almost seem, had fully foreseen the manner of her death and, loyal to psychoanalysis, had left an injunction which would attempt to remove the tarnish of scandal from her profession. Like so many attempts at repression, the effect has been the obverse. The scandal has remained attached to her name, but her very real accomplishments have grown shadowy. It is almost premonitory of that future place in history that the only extant pictures of Hug-Hellmuth are a caricature and a newspaper illustration showing her corpse.

7

SABINA SPIELREIN AND LOË KANN: TWO ANALYTIC TRIANGLES

Sabina Spielrein

The first woman analyst, Emma Eckstein, began her connection with psycho-analysis as a patient, traversed a number of crises – for both her and her analyst – before herself turning to analytic practice. The first woman analyst to have a significant theoretical impact on psychoanalysis not only started as a patient but also emerged to become an analyst from a triangle involving Freud and his most important disciple, Jung. Late in life, recognizing how crucial his women patients had been to the development of his work, Jung wrote: 'I have had mainly women patients, who often entered into the work with extraordinary conscientiousness, understanding, and intelligence. It was essentially because of them that I was able to strike out on new paths in therapy.' The 'case' which more than any other forced Jung on to new paths was that of the remarkable woman, Sabina Spielrein, who was his first psychoanalytic patient. It is probable that the intensity of Jung's relationship to Spielrein was the immediate, if not the only, cause of his writing to Freud in 1906, thus initiating a triangular relationship which was to prove fateful both to the two men and to the history of psychoanalysis. Spielrein added a wholly new dimension of mutual knowledge to the relationship between the two men. She was the classic instance of a woman becoming the means of communication between Freud and another analyst.

The Jung–Spielrein–Freud triangle seems to lend itself to that view of the early history of psychoanalysis as a set of transactions between men, between leaders and followers, fathers and sons, members of the brother band or primal horde, in which women figure as units of exchange, goods for barter and sacrifice. Yet she was always an unknown quantity in their relation, never under either party's control, and remained so well beyond their falling out. Neither knew, in the end, just exactly what her significance for them had been; neither therefore could openly acknowledge her distinctive contribution to psychoanalytic thinking.

Sabina Spielrein was not only Jung's first analytic case. She was also his first analytic muse and mistress, in a relationship which moved unevenly between sexual and mystical registers. Some historians of Jung's development have seen her as the woman who revealed the function of the anima to him. Freud intervened in her and Jung's relations at a moment of crisis, called upon as the third party, at once arbiter and Jewish teacher – the person she turned to in distress when Jung's behaviour towards her and her family had become intolerable. Her significance in the early history of psychoanalysis did not cease with the resolution of the crises in her relationship with Jung. Far from it; with that resolution, she found emotional and intellectual independence from Jung, and became a firm and faithful follower of Freud's, delegated after the First World War to represent orthodox psychoanalysis in Geneva.

If one follows the Freud–Spielrein–Jung story from her point of view, one is struck by her capacity for making the most of the intellectual and professional environments in which she found herself, whether or not she was an element in other people's transactions. Her eventful and crisis-ridden formative years were spent in the Zurich of her love affair with Jung and psychoanalysis. And, it should not be forgotten, as Bettelheim emphasized, 'the most significant event in Sabina's young life was that, whatever happened during her treatment by Jung at the Burghölzli, it cured her.... However questionable Jung's behaviour was from a moral point of view ... somehow it met the prime obligation of the therapist toward his patient: to cure her.' But the rest of her life, whether in Vienna, Geneva or Moscow, tells an equally eventful story: of a woman of restless intellectual and emotional energy, with a capacity which never abated for intense relationships and for being alive to the right things at the right time. A passionate idealist, a woman of immense strength of character and resilience, Spielrein was the first woman psychoanalyst of significance, and she was until very recently almost entirely forgotten. Aldo Carotenuto and Mireille Cifali have done much to retrieve lost documents concerning her life; John Kerr's substantial study has allowed a firmer chronology of her early life and entry into psychoanalysis to be established.

She was born on 7 November 1885 in Rostov on Don, into a well-to-do, cosmopolitan, Russian Jewish family. Her father was a businessman, and her mother was a university graduate, who spent much time travelling and engaged in affairs, including competing for the attentions of men with her daughter as she grew up. Her mother was also determined that Sabina should know nothing of sexuality and, before her daughter was allowed to attend, succeeded in having the local Rostov Gymnasium curriculum altered to exclude biology.

As her concealed autobiographical analytic writings reveal, the task of creation was Sabina's great childhood preoccupation, leading her from digging in the earth to find the Americans on the other side of the world, to innumerable chemical experiments on mysterious liquids she kept in jars, expecting 'the big creation' to take place one day.

Once I asked an old woman in the neighbourhood if I could not have a child just like my mother. 'No,' she said, 'you are still too small to have a child; now you might be able to give birth to a kitten.' These joking words had their effect on me: I awaited the kitten and thought a lot about how I could give this kitten an intelligent soul like a person has if I were just very careful with its education.

Up to this point in her life, Sabina was fearless, like Siegfried, the god-defying Aryan hero who was later so obsessively to preoccupy her. Then, after one of her father's attempts to instil caution in her, 'one day I was overwhelmed by terror on seeing two little black kittens on the chest of drawers in the other room. It was an illusion, but so clear that to this very day I can still see those little creatures just sitting there quietly next to each other. "This is death," or "the plague," I thought. With one shudder, my period of anxiety started.' Reflecting on this experience later, Spielrein wrote:

I perceived the child as a dangerous, in itself deadly disease. Very often I hear women describe pregnancy and birth as a dangerous illness (infectious disease, plague, particularly bubonic plague), a malignant tumour, a growth. It appears to me that it is a common occurrence that a woman imagines the new being as something that grows at the expense of the old one. It is interesting that we react sometimes with lust, sometimes with anger, or at least with displeasure, to these images of destruction. In accordance with this, my fear of infectious diseases was the fear of a child, but not only that, it was my fear of the kidnapper, the seducer.

Commenting on her own 'case', Spielrein demonstrated how an interest in science develops from a craving for sexual knowledge.

In her early teens, before she had turned into a serious, somewhat withdrawn and insecure young woman, she had made up her mind, with her father's backing, to study medicine. In August 1904, she went to Zurich to enrol in the medical school. It is probable that her parents recognized that she needed treatment. Whatever the exact course of events, she suffered some kind of nervous breakdown or psychotic episode, and was admitted to the Burghölzli Hospital late in the summer of 1904. Its director, Eugen Bleuler, had made it the most respected and progressive hospital in Europe, a psychiatric asylum in the older sense of the word, for both patients and doctors, to which increasing numbers of young medical students from Europe and America were making their way to train. Sabina was put under the charge of the young Dr Carl Gustav Jung, a recently graduated and highly respected scion of Basel's social aristocracy. According to Jung, 'her condition had got so bad that she really did nothing else than alternate between deep depressions and fits of laughing, crying, and screaming. She could no longer look anyone in the face, kept her head bowed, and when anybody touched her stuck her tongue out with every sign of loathing.' Her treatment at the hospital allowed her to be formally discharged on 1 June 1905; she had already, in April 1905, enrolled in the University Medical School, where, true to her childhood passions, she was very enthusiastic about organic chemistry. She thus had the distinction of being the first hospitalized psychiatric patient to move seamlessly from ward, via psychotherapeutic treatment, to dissecting room and lecture hall, and finally to become a psychoanalyst.

Over the period 1904 to 1911, while she lived in Zurich, she was initially

Jung's psychiatric patient, then almost certainly the first patient he treated with a self-consciously psychoanalytic method. She was at the same time an important subject, and then collaborator, in his experimental researches in free association. She soon became his friend, intellectual and emotional intimate. In May 1908, she took her preliminary medical examination. In 1911, she submitted her medical dissertation and qualified.

Jung's formal psychoanalytic treatment of her took place soon after her admission to the hospital, in the autumn of 1904, thus lasting at most three months. It was combined with suggestion, and with the investigations the Burghölzli group were conducting into associations and reaction times, as they developed the theory of 'complexes' which the association experiments revealed. What Jung meant by psychoanalysis in 1904 was not very far removed from an extended association experiment, designed to probe the patient's complexes with stimulus words and questions. Jung's analysis probably focused primarily on the masochistic pleasures Sabina had experienced in childhood from her father beating her buttocks. At the same time, the analysis was didactic in character. Jung lent Sabina books on psychopathology, and she quickly developed into a colleague in scientific work – as was Jung's wife Emma, the two of them helping him prepare his *Habilitationsschrift* on reaction times in 1905. Spielrein later recalled, in a letter to Freud:

We had numerous discussions about it, and he said, 'Minds such as yours help advance science. You must become a psychiatrist.' I stress these things again and again so that you may see it was not just the usual doctor–patient relationship that brought us so close together. He was writing the paper while I was still in the mental hospital. . . . I spoke of the equality or intellectual independence of woman, whereupon he replied that I was an exception, but his wife was an ordinary woman and accordingly only interested in what interested her husband.

The implication that the equality of women scientists was an exception to the general rule of the subordination of women was a fact of everyday life in the laboratory of Freudianism that the Burghölzli became for a few years from 1905 on. 'No one could make a slip of any kind without immediately being called on to evoke free associations to explain it. It did not matter that women were present – wives and female voluntary interns – who might have curbed the frankness usually produced by free associations. The women were just as keen to discover the concealed mechanisms as their husbands.' Indeed, the women seemed to have a special aptitude for analysis, as Jung pointed out in an account of hospital life written for Freud in 1907: 'The women understand you by far the best and usually at once. Only the "psychologically" educated have blinkers before their eyes.' Wild analysis had spread like a contagion throughout the hospital, and Jung was aware of at least some of the dangers that such a democracy of the unconscious might entail: 'It is amusing to see how the female outpatients go about diagnosing each other's erotic complexes although they have no insight into their own. With uneducated patients the chief obstacle seems to be the atrociously crude transference.'

From the patient's point of view, the emotions stimulated by this interplay

of the unconscious between residents and medical staff alike were more
ambiguous and distressing. Spielrein's letters and diary reveal the entourage,
the troupe of young women patients and students gathered admiringly round
Jung, vying suspiciously with each other for his favours; by the time she wrote
the following entry she was a very experienced and somewhat disillusioned
campaigner: 'When I was out walking, I met Frl. Aptekmann. She was once
a patient of my friend's [Jung] and is now "one of the many". ... She loves
him and believes that he loves her. "Blessed is the one who can believe."'
So it was immensely reassuring for Sabina when Jung told her that it was 'as
if he had a necklace in which all his other admirers were pearls, and I – the
medallion.'

Sabina wrote out a retrospective version of the early unfolding of events
in her diary in 1910: 'We came to know each other, we became fond of each
other without noticing it was happening; it was too late for flight; several
times we sat "in tender embrace." Yes, it was a great deal!' It certainly was
a great deal for both of them, but from early on, it was almost as if Sabina
was to be Jung's offering in friendship to Freud. In September 1905 – that
is well before Jung had written to Freud for the first time in April 1906 –
he had prepared what was probably a referral note for Sabina to carry with
her on a projected visit to Vienna to see Freud. Here, he described her as a
'highly intelligent and gifted person of great sensitivity', although, he continued,
'Her character has a decidedly relentless and unreasonable aspect, and she
also lacks any sense of appropriateness and external manners, most of which
must, of course, be attributed to Russian peculiarities.'

In the event, Sabina never visited Vienna at this time, so the referral, in
which Jung would have used the patient as a living calling card, never reached
Freud. Once he *had* written to Freud, a vignette version of Sabina quickly
found its way into Jung's letters, an implicit appeal for help with this difficult
patient – shades of the scenario in which Breuer confessed to Freud the
emotional mess he was in with Bertha Pappenheim:

At the risk of boring you, I must abreact my most recent experience. I am currently
treating an hysteric with your method. Difficult case, a 20-year-old Russian girl student,
ill for 6 years.

First trauma between the 3rd and 4th year. Saw her father spanking her older
brother on bare bottom. Powerful impression. Couldn't help thinking afterwards that
she had defecated on her father's hand. From the 4th–7th year convulsive attempts
to defecate on her own feet, in the following manner: she sat on the floor with one
foot beneath her, pressed her heel against her anus and tried to defecate and at the
same time to prevent defecation. Often retained the stool for two weeks in this way!
Has no idea how she hit upon this peculiar business; says it was completely instinctive,
and accompanied by blissfully shuddersome feelings. Later this phenomenon was
superseded by vigorous masturbation.

I should be extremely grateful if you would tell me in a few words what you think
of this story.

Freud's reply was encouraging, but he was more interested in pursuing the connection between anal erotism and its associated character types, which did not exactly fit Sabina's wild and mystical character. Jung dropped his overture about his important patient for a while.

In the published anecdotes and case histories of this period, Sabina crops up on a number of occasions. In Jung's set-piece defence of Freud, 'The Freudian Theory of Hysteria' of September 1907, her case of 'psychotic hysteria' is a central case history, recounted along the lines he had described to Freud. In *The Psychology of Dementia Praecox* (1907), she figures again:

A certain young lady could not bear to see the dust beaten out of her cloak. This peculiar reaction could be traced back to her masochistic disposition. As a child her father frequently chastised her on the buttocks, thus causing sexual excitation. Consequently she reacted to anything remotely resembling chastisement with marked rage, which rapidly passed over into sexual excitement and masturbation. Once, when I said to her casually, 'Well, you have to obey,' she got into a state of marked sexual excitement.

In Jung's excited letter to Freud in July 1907, the erotic tension between Sabina and Jung is clear, Here Jung interpreted Sabina's wish to be a psychoanalyst who performs the perfect cure as also the desire for the analyst – that is herself identified with Jung – to fulfil his/her unfulfillable sexual-phallic wishes.

Jung found himself particularly drawn to Spielrein. A Jewish woman of high ideals in need of a holy cure, she made him feel like her saviour. This 'Jewess complex' dated back a long way for him. Jung first described himself this way in recounting a brief holiday infatuation to Freud in the spring of 1907, shortly after having met Freud for the first time; it was clearly a continuation of a quasi-analytic conversation the two men had been having about Jung's relations to Freud as a Jew as well as to Jewish women. Jung's first 'patient', his cousin Helene Preiswerk, whose mediumistic trances he had written up as his doctoral dissertation, had described herself as Jewish, although she was not; the first detailed study of a complex in a normal as opposed to a pathological subject, conducted by Jung and Franz Riklin in 1902–3, describes the love of a 'Christian doctor', probably Jung, for 'a Jewish girl'.

For Sabina, Jung was her first love and she struggled for many years to free herself from the hold he had over her. His 1906 sketch of his difficult Russian patient showed how her anal fixation gave rise to perverse fantasies in which disgust and horror were pre-eminent. Any stirrings of love would be quickly swamped by the activation of disgust. As if she were driven by the very force of her own name ('Spiel-rein' = 'play-pure'), Sabina's relation to Jung was ruled by this threat of disgust. Simultaneously, or perhaps as a consequence, her overwhelming need was to idealize Jung, to keep him on a pedestal. This register of disgust and idealization was one Sabina well understood, in herself and in Jung.

In the first few months of Jung's collaboration with Freud, Jung was less than whole-hearted in his belief in the sexual basis of the neuroses; his later repudiation of this feature of Freud's theories has often been linked back to these early misgivings. However, during 1907 and 1908, Jung became a fervent sexualist for a period, raising the sexual theory of the neuroses as a standard around which to gather the Freudian faithful and to separate the sheep from the goats – amongst whom was his chief and patron, Eugen Bleuler. Undoubtedly, his relationship with Spielrein reflected (or in turn instigated) this new and decisive turn. And in June 1908, Jung's lightning mutual analysis of the charismatic wild analyst Otto Gross – bohemian, anarchist and sexual libertarian – had a deep effect on his attitude to sexuality, and by implication to Spielrein:

Now he [Jung] arrives, beaming with pleasure, and tells me with strong emotion about Gross, about the great insight he has just received (i.e., about polygamy); he no longer wants to suppress his feeling for me, he admitted that I was his first, dearest woman friend, etc., etc. (his wife of course excepted), and that he wanted to tell me everything about himself.

It was not only Jung who was moving towards erotic expression of their intimacy. As her *Journal* shows, Sabina increasingly played the active part:

The complexity of the situation makes me adopt the unnatural position of the male, and you – the feminine role. I am very little inclined to give an absolute significance to what has been said; I altogether understand that you need to resist, but I also understand that resistances excite me. I am also very aware that if everything depended on me, I would resist desperately. ... Oh you! If only you knew how dear you are to me, without the least thought of the child.

The child Sabina is referring to here was – and was to become even more fully – the *leitmotiv* of their later passion and conflict. By 1908, Sabina was stating, simply and often, how haunted she was by the thought that she desired a child from Jung. The theme of the child had emerged gradually; they gave it the name 'Siegfried'. To her, Siegfried represented the mythical progeny of their idealized intimacy. She resisted Jung's pressure to interpret Siegfried as the physical child she desired from him; she viewed Siegfried as embodying the heroic destiny that awaited her, a girl for whom both her father and grandfather had appeared in dreams predicting great things. Jung succeeded in persuading Sabina of his interpretation. She could eventually accept the sexual interpretation, by viewing intercourse and childbirth as 'my heroic deed to sacrifice myself after all for this sacred love and create a hero'. Her diary in 1910 reveals her still agonizing over whether to have Jung's child – 'Siegfried, my baby son!'

Jung's interpretation of Siegfried as a baby placed him and Spielrein in the positions of Sieglinde and Siegmund, incestuous brother and sister, outcasts because of their passionate transgression of the sanctity of marriage. When she analysed the Siegfried motif in her 1911 paper on 'Destruction', Sabina emphasized the connection between Brünnhilde and Sieglinde, thus equating the child and the lover: 'she [Brünnhilde] loves what Sieglinde loves, namely Siegfried. Accordingly, she feels herself to be in Sieglinde's role; Sieglinde thus becomes her "wish personality" in terms of her sexuality. By saving Siegfried she saves her own wish-child.' Brünnhilde is a saviour type, rescuing her own love in its sacrifice, redeeming her own love through the mingling of her body with the fire that consumes Siegfried's body. 'For Wagner death is often nothing more than the destructive component of the instinct to become.' Reading between the lines here we recognize that Spielrein resisted Jung's interpretation of Siegfried as a 'real' baby not so much because it confronted her with the reality of her own sexual desires, but rather because the 'coital' interpretation failed to capture the tragic ambiguity of the fulfilment of sexual desire as simultaneously entailing the destruction of the subject. In the ultimate destruction that the sexual act requires, 'man wishes to annihilate himself, and woman wishes to be annihilated.'

However the question of the sexual consummation of their relationship is answered, Jung and Spielrein had been acting for some years as if they were engaged in an illicit affair. After Spielrein left the hospital they would meet in secret, in his office, her flat or in the countryside. This intimacy was by no means solely driven by the erotic; their sense of intellectual communion – Jung's feeling of his ideas being understood by the alert, perhaps prescient Spielrein – was ever-present. Jung would leave notes – interspersed with comments like: 'you have taken my unconscious into your hands with your saucy letters' – in her pigeon-hole, telling her where and when the next secret assignation would be. His letters in 1908 preached the virtues of 'freedom and independence', praising her for not 'being smothered in the banality of habit'. She is someone who is not 'bogged down in sentimentality, who uses her love to create freedom, not ties'. His feelings reached their peak of intensity in December 1908: he was now resigned to the lie of marriage, resigned to the higher virtue of committing this lie only once. Yet he ended this letter with a plea and a declaration: 'Return to me, in this moment of my need, some of the love and guilt and altruism which I was able to give you at the time of your illness. Now it is I who am ill.' The letter was written a few days after his wife Emma gave birth to Franz, the son he had longed for.

The son he now had – the Siegfried who was not Siegfried – provoked an almost psychotic state in Jung, implying for us that, as Spielrein was so often later on obliged by his evasion to insist, the Siegfried fantasy was a joint one. Certainly the birth of Franz caused a crisis in their relationship. Sometime in February 1909, Jung perhaps tried to brush Spielrein off in a callous way:

when he asked me how I pictured what would happen next (because of the 'consequences'), I said that first love has no desires, that I had nothing in mind ... now he claims he was too kind to me, that I want sexual involvement with him because of that, something he, of course, never wanted, etc. ... My ideal personage was destroyed, I was done for; I thought I wanted to kiss him and had no will to resist, since I no longer respected either him or myself. I stood there with a knife in my left hand and do not know what I intended to do with it; he grabbed my hand,

I resisted; I have no idea what happened then. Suddenly he went very pale and clapped his hand to his left temple: 'You struck me!'

Spielrein fled. Jung lived in fear that she would make public their relations at a delicate moment in his career: he was gradually terminating his work at the Burghölzli and was setting up a private practice as an acknowledged Freudian – in fact, as editor of the *Jahrbuch*, the most public of all Freudians – just when a wave of personal attacks on Freudians was under way.

But someone else – possibly Emma Jung – intervened, by writing anonymously to Sabina's parents, warning them about the danger their daughter was in. The parents asked Jung to explain himself. In reply, Jung asked the mother to pay him fees for his treatment of her daughter, to ensure that the doctor felt the 'necessary restraints' alongside the absolute frankness in sexual matters the treatment required:

I moved from being her doctor to being her friend when I ceased to push my own feelings into the background. I could drop my role as doctor the more easily because I did not feel professionally obligated, for I never charged a fee. ... Therefore I would suggest that if you wish me to adhere strictly to my role as doctor, you should pay me a fee as suitable recompense for my trouble. In that way you may be *absolutely certain* that I will respect my duty as a doctor *under all circumstances*.

As a friend of your daughter, on the other hand, one could have to leave matters to Fate. For no one can prevent two friends from doing as they wish.

Faced with what she could only interpret as a betrayal, Spielrein's response was, and was to remain, to protect Jung so as to protect herself. As she wrote some eighteen months later: 'the crucial thing for me is to see my ideal salvaged.' And the incident in which she had struck him, drawing blood, also convinced her that she needed to be delivered from the mess she and Jung were now in, compounded as it now was by Jung's high-handed treatment of her parents. With a fine sense of the appropriate, she eventually turned to Freud as an 'angel of deliverance', and also as if to a higher tribunal – a parental tribunal that Jung would be forced to recognize – for justice.

But Jung had beaten her to it. In March 1909, he had once again written to Freud about this – still anonymous – patient:

a complex is playing Old Harry with me: a woman patient, whom years ago I pulled out of a very sticky neurosis with unstinting effort, violated my confidence and my friendship in the most mortifying way imaginable. She has kicked up a vile scandal solely because I denied myself the pleasure of giving her a child. ... Meanwhile I have learnt an unspeakable amount of marital wisdom, for until now I had a totally inadequate idea of my polygamous components.

Freud had responded, reassuringly: 'To be slandered and scorched by the love with which we operate – such are the perils of our trade, which we are certainly not going to abandon on their account.'

Freud's immediate response to Spielrein's request in June 1909 for an interview in Vienna to talk over something urgent was to play for time while he got Jung's side of the story. Playing for time also meant playing dumb about what he had already heard from Jung of his relations with her. To Jung, he cast himself in the role of the old analytic hand:

Such experiences, though painful, are necessary and hard to avoid. Without them we cannot really know life and what we are dealing with. I myself have never been taken in quite so badly, but I have come very close to it a number of times and had *a narrow escape*. I believe that only grim necessities weighing on my work, and the fact that I was ten years older than yourself when I came to Ψa [Freud's abbreviation of psychoanalysis], have saved me from similar experiences. But no lasting harm is done. They help us to develop the thick skin we need and to dominate 'counter-transference', which is after all a permanent problem for us; they teach us to displace our own affects to best advantage. They are a *'blessing in disguise'*.

The way these women manage to charm us with every conceivable psychic perfection until they have attained their purpose is one of nature's greatest spectacles. Once that has been done or the contrary has become a certainty, the constellation changes amazingly.

This attitude of avuncular marvelling at the wiles of women as if they were the Eighth Wonder of the World was shaken the next day, when Spielrein enclosed with her letter some of Jung's love letters to her and informed Freud of her intimacy with Jung. Freud adopted another tack. No longer dumb, he was 'ever so wise and penetrating; I made it appear as though the most tenuous of clues had enabled me Sherlock Holmes-like to guess the situation.' He warned Spielrein that he was reluctant to set himself up as a judge, since he would be bound to want to listen to the other party as well. He suggested that she extricate herself from her predicament without the help of a third party: 'I would urge you to ask yourself whether the feelings that have outlived this close relationship are not best suppressed and eradicated, from your own psyche I mean, and without external intervention and the involvement of third persons.'

Freud's advice to Spielrein made out that he was dealing with difficulties arising in a stormy transference relationship between doctor and patient, relegating to a postscript any reference to the 'somewhat gushing effusions' of the 'young man'. No doubt mindful that he was addressing his favoured son, the future leader of psychoanalysis, the same assumption informed his exhortation to Jung to treat the episode as being all in the course of a day's work: 'In view of the kind of matter we work with, it will never be possible to avoid little laboratory explosions.' Jung was all contrition to Father Freud, thankful that he had not received what he had been fearfully expecting, a 'dressing-down more or less disguised in the mantle of brotherly love.'

Spielrein read Freud's letter very astutely: 'when I received your last letter, unfavourable though it was to me, tears came to my eyes: "He loves him! What if he could understand this!"' His advice to Spielrein had the effect he wished, since Jung could report to Freud a few days later that 'she has freed herself from the transference in the best and nicest way'. The freeing of her transference expressed itself in confronting Jung and laying down her terms: he must apologize to her parents, he must confess everything to Freud, and he must request Freud to acknowledge to her in writing the fact that Jung had confessed to him. Jung duly gave in on all fronts. He was now obliged to tell Freud of the letter he had written to Sabina's mother, which had up to then not been at issue:

I imputed all the other wishes and hopes [concerning the child, Siegfried] entirely to my patient without seeing the same thing in myself. When the situation had become so tense that the continued perseveration of the relationship could be rounded out only by sexual acts, I defended myself in a manner that cannot be justified morally. Caught in my delusion that I was the victim of the sexual wiles of my patient, I wrote to her mother that I was not the gratifier of her daughter's sexual desires but merely her doctor ... a piece of knavery which I very reluctantly confess to you as my father.

Spielrein now had Freud's ear, and he duly wrote her his own apology for having treated her as a patient and Jung as her doctor, whereas their relationship was more fundamentally that of man and woman – which could not but elicit some old-fashioned courteous flattery from him: 'I must ask your forgiveness. ... However, the fact that I was wrong and that the lapse has to be blamed on the man and not the woman, as my young friend himself admits, satisfies my need to hold women in high regard.'

In Freud's responses to Jung's confession about his involvement with Sabina and to Sabina's plea for him to recognize Jung's injustices against her, we already hear crystallized that tempting image of the elemental woman in amorous pursuit of her analyst whose dangers for the analyst Freud was to describe in his paper on transference-love in 1915: 'an incomparable magic emanates from a woman of high principles who confesses her passion'. There Freud vividly described the woman passionately in love with her male analyst, who will stop at nothing to gain her sexual end. The image of the temptress is clearly presaged in his reassuring aside to Jung, at the height of the Spielrein crisis: 'The way these women manage to charm us with every conceivable psychic perfection until they have attained their purpose is one of nature's greatest spectacles', echoing Jung's far more distasteful, tendentious and self-serving, but not fundamentally dissimilar, portrait of Sabina as, 'of course, systematically planning my seduction'. Freud came to recognize that Spielrein was not one of those 'women of elemental passionateness', 'who refuse to accept the psychical in place of the material, who, in the poet's words, are accessible only to "the logic of soup, with dumplings for arguments"', despite his own initial eagerness to save Jung's face by presuming she was one such. In this change of interpretative tack, we see Freud's pragmatic flexibility. To his credit, he quickly ceased to regard Spielrein as an example of nature's awesome seducers; yet we learn much about Freud in seeing him respond with such alacrity to Jung's invitation to view her in this light.

Spielrein now prepared a lengthy letter to Freud, virtually a file on her relationship with Jung, spelling out the chronology that put Jung's actions in a very poor light:

Four and a half years ago Dr Jung was my doctor, then he became my friend and finally my 'poet,' i.e., my beloved. Eventually he came to me and things went as they usually do with 'poetry.' He preached polygamy; his wife was supposed to have no objection, etc., etc. Now my mother receives an anonymous letter that minces no words, saying that she should rescue her daughter, since otherwise she would be ruined by Dr Jung.

However, the crisis was now over. Both parties had got what they wanted. Spielrein had made contact with Freud and had extorted the confession of wrongful treatment from Jung. Jung had escaped public shame and had received forgiveness and understanding from Freud. When Jung and Spielrein picked up their relationship a year later, they did so as 'the best of friends'. Ten years later, as they continued to correspond and reveal their inner lives to one another, he summed up her importance for him as follows:

The love of S. for J. made the latter aware of something he had previously only vaguely suspected, that is, of a power in the unconscious that shapes one's destiny, a power which later led him to things of the greatest importance. The relationship had to be 'sublimated' because otherwise it would have led him to delusion and madness (the concretization of the unconscious). Occasionally one must be unworthy, simply in order to be able to continue living.

Unworthy he certainly had been. Of exactly what, Spielrein was, finally, the only one to know.

Spielrein spent the summer of 1909 in Berlin. She was now working towards her final examinations, which she took in December 1910, passing her oral in January 1911. She submitted her dissertation, 'The Psychological Content of a Case of Schizophrenia', in September 1911. Bleuler and Jung made sure that it was published simultaneously in the *Jahrbuch*. Not only was it one of the first works to use Bleuler's newly coined term 'schizophrenia', but it also employed a novel method of testing psychoanalytic interpretations. Spielrein studied the delirious speech of a paranoiac woman patient, deciphering and interpreting it in terms of her own framework of dissolution and dissociation. She then checked her conclusions against the patient's file, which up to then she had not seen. And then she supplemented the analysis with mythological parallels, very much akin to Jung's contemporary work on mythological interpretation – as a result, preceding him in publishing on mythology by some months. For the first year of her work, from the spring of 1909 to the summer of 1910, Bleuler had supervised her. From then on till early 1911, Jung took over and they returned to their old intimacy, with the past tumultuous events continuing to reverberate for both of them.

We talked on and on. My friend [Jung] listened to me with rapture, then showed me his paper, not yet printed, and a letter to Prof. Freud and Freud's reply. He showed it to me because he was deeply stirred by the parallels in our thinking and feeling. He told me that seeing this worries him, because that is how I make him fall in love with me. ... 'So I am not one among the many, but one who is unique, for certainly no girl can understand him as I can, none could surprise him this way with an independently developed system of thought that is completely analogous to his own. He resisted, he did not want to love me. Now he must, because our souls are deeply akin, because even when we are apart our joint work unites us.' ... He urged me to write my new study on the death instinct. ...

Their relationship had now changed into a closer intellectual partnership, with tinges of competition and mutual suspicion. Whilst neither could resist the pleasures of flirting, Spielrein was displacing some of her passion into their work in common.

I greatly fear that my friend, who planned to mention my idea in his article in July, saying that I have rights of priority, may simply borrow the whole development of the idea. ... How could I esteem a person who lied, who stole my ideas, who was not my friend, but a petty, scheming rival? And love him? I do love him, after all.

The idea in question was truly an important one. It had been distinctively Spielrein's for some years, certainly since 1908 and her *Transformation Journal*. It became the core of the paper she prepared on completing her medical studies and moving to Vienna, published in the *Jahrbuch* in 1912: 'Destruction as the Cause of Coming into Being'; she read a portion of the paper to a critical and uncomprehending meeting of the Vienna Psycho-Analytical Society in November 1911, the invitation probably being linked to Theodor Reik's presentation two weeks previously 'On Death and Sexuality'. It was Spielrein who discussed the 'death instinct'; it was Reik who reflected on the fusion of Eros and Thanatos. Six weeks before she gave the paper, she was elected a member of the Vienna Psycho-Analytical Society, on 11 October 1911, the same day that Margarethe Hilferding, the first woman member, resigned in the course of the dispute with Adler. Spielrein was now the only woman in the Society. She was also by far the youngest of the first generation of women analysts to publish – only twenty-six when her first paper appeared, whereas Hilferding was forty when she resigned. Hug-Hellmuth, whose first paper was published later in 1912, was over forty, and Lou Andreas-Salomé, who turned fifty in 1911, was still to make contact with Freud.

The spoken version of her thesis that she presented to the Society began by explicitly addressing the question of the existence of a 'death instinct', as proposed by the Russian biologist and founder of immunology, Ilya Mechnikov. Her combination of metaphysical biology and the interpretation of mythology did not strike many chords with her audience, with the exception of Freud and Tausk. The written version, published a few months later, had the unenviable and perhaps unique fate of being a major influence on both Freud and Jung, whilst both denied that influence until belatedly recognizing that Spielrein had been on their same tracks all the time. Even then the Spielrein they recognized as their precursor was never quite Spielrein's Spielrein.

The written text had a distinctive and searching starting-point for her enquiry: why does the sexual drive give rise both to positive and pleasurable emotions and to negative ones, such as anxiety and disgust? These negative feelings are most apparent in girls and Spielrein in a transparently personal tone, depicts the poignantly feminine anxiety over the transience of the pleasure to be gained from the sacrifice involved in the sexual act:

One feels the enemy inside oneself, in one's own glowing love which forces one, with iron necessity, to do what one doesn't want to do: one feels the end, the fleetingness, from which one vainly tries to flee to distances unknown. 'Is that all?' one wants to ask. 'Is this the climax, and nothing further, nothing beyond?' What happens to the individual in the sexual act which could justify such a mood?

Spielrein was as Freudian as Freud in her conceptual assumptions: the psyche is to be described in the conflict between two fundamental forces or instincts. And she also structured psychic life around the themes of destruction, loss and sacrifice that she and Jung, both in their emotional relationship and their many discussions together, had explored over the years.

Destruction and transformation are inherent features of the sexual, the procreative drive. Where the ego, the exclusive channel for the self-preservative instincts, demands stasis, the instinct for propagation of the species may well ignore the demands of the ego, may bypass it entirely. However, the ego may recognize the requirements of these other drives welling up from the depths. It may welcome the damage that sexuality does to the individual; and it may welcome pain and pleasure equally. Sexual love is giving oneself up to the other, the antithesis of the ego; it is a phase in the drive for procreation, a dangerous phase, but one which becomes pleasurable because one dissolves oneself in the other who is so like oneself.

Spielrein was here combining the Freudian emphasis on the centrality of sexual passions with the speculations common to turn-of-the-century biology. The balance between destruction and transformation in normal life is the expression of the 'struggle between two antagonistic streams, that of the ego and that of the species', expressed in the self-preservative and procreative instincts. Thus 'destructive imagery arises as the response of the ego to the threat of dissolution inherent in the sexual instinct'; but it is also inherent in the sexual instinct, which can only be effective through destroying the adult form, that is, in the transformation of the old that brings something new into being.

As far back as early 1908, Spielrein had written of the two fundamental psychic principles as being the power of persistence of complexes and the instinct of transformation which works by attracting new meanings. This principle of transformation – similar to sublimation in many respects – subsumes sexual instinct, the instinct of species preservation. However, sexuality is antagonistic to the differentiated individual and is therefore experienced as destructive; something must be held back in copulation or it would become a rape-murder. It is the principle of transformation, then, that contains the seeds of both creation and destruction within it:

This demonic force, whose very essence is destruction (evil) and at the same time is the creative force, since out of the destruction (of two individuals) a new one arises. That is in fact the sexual drive, which is by nature a destructive drive, an exterminating drive for the individual, and for that reason, in my opinion, must overcome such great resistance in everyone.

It is characteristic of neurotics to emphasize the destructive component of the sexual drive at the expense of the exaltation of love. In the flight of psychotics from their objects, Spielrein found the irony of their assured self-destruction: 'Complete denial of all love-objects external to the self only leads to the achievement of oneself as the object of libido and results in the destruction of the self.'

Spielrein worked out the consequences of the twofold character of the sexual instinct in three different spheres: in biology, in psychological life, and in mythological products. Bridging the psychological and the mythological was Wagnerian love – 'the act of procreation consists in self-destruction'. She illustrated it in the mythological section with *The Flying Dutchman*, with *Tristan und Isolde* and, most importantly, with *Siegfried* and *Götterdämmerung*, alongside Adam and Eve and Talmudic fables. The inevitability of love leading to destruction of the self is the tragic heart of her account:

In love, the dissolution of the I in the lover is at the same time the strongest self-confirmation – the I lives anew in the person of the lover. Is love absent? Then the image of one's psychology or physiology being altered under the impact of a strange, alien power – as in the sexual act – is a destruction or death image. The drive for self-preservation is a simple drive consisting of only one positive; the drive for the preservation of the species, which has to dissolve the old in order to create the new, is in its nature ambivalent, consisting of one positive and one negative component.

It is such arguments that allow us to see Spielrein's thought as a grand metaphysical extension of her teacher Bleuler's conception of ambivalence as both intellectual (the contrary or negative element that necessarily accompanies a positive image) and affective (the constant mutual accompaniment of love and hate). But her arguments also allow us to see the reason for Freud's acute summary judgment of her paper: 'her destructive drive is not much to my liking, because I believe it is personally conditioned. She seems abnormally ambivalent.' And it was the same concept of the twin-sidedness of unconscious powers, beautifying and destroying, which Jung attributed to 'my pupil Dr Spielrein' in a note added to *Symbols and Transformation* in 1952.

Spielrein's paper explores the connection of this transforming principle, containing both creation and destruction, with the dialectic of the collective species-preserving sexual drive and self-preserving ego-individual drive. As Jung was also arguing in his parallel text, *Transformation and Symbols of the Libido*, which he and others later claimed had led to his break with Freud, the unconscious is collective, the conscious ego is individual; phylogenetic memories emerge in schizophrenia (not in hysteria), myths and dreams. But whereas Jung's collective unconscious was *opposed* to the individual sexual drive, Spielrein's unconscious is collective *because* it is sexual. It is the sexual drive that forces individuals to transcend and transform themselves, impelling them towards inevitable creativity, destruction and death.

Many members of the Vienna Psycho-Analytical Society read Spielrein's argument as concerning the sado-masochistic components of sexuality; indeed, there are echoes, perhaps unwitting, in Helene Deutsch's later descriptions of the maternal and masochistic, tenderly giving woman, of Spielrein's inventory of the costs of sexuality for the frail ego. Freud, himself, was as much preoccupied with her relations with Jung as with anything in her arguments:

Fräulein Spielrein read a chapter from her paper yesterday (almost wrote the *ihrer* [her] with a capital 'i'), and it was followed by an illuminating discussion. I have hit on a few objections to your [*Ihrer*] (this time I mean it) method of dealing with mythology, and I brought them up in the discussion with the little girl. I must say she is rather nice and I am beginning to understand. What troubles me most is that Frl. Spielrein wants to subordinate the psychological material to *bio*logical criteria; this dependence is no more acceptable than a dependency on philosophy, physiology or brain anatomy. *Ψa fara da se* [goes by itself].

Freud went on to use Spielrein's presentation to launch a substantial attack on Jung's method of analysing mythological material. In this letter he suggested that the story of Adam and Eve should be stood on its head: it was Adam who seduced Eve, who may have been in reality his mother, and not the other way round. Thereby Freud was also reminding Jung that he had been in the wrong in his relations with Spielrein. But even in admonishing Jung, Freud renewed the bond of male solidarity with his whimsical sketch of Spielrein: 'The little Spielrein girl has a very good head and I can corroborate the fact that she is very demanding.'

In assimilating Spielrein to Jung, Freud was doing her theoretical work an injustice. Little did he know how influential her ideas had been on Jung. Little, for that matter, did Jung want to know. As Jung finished writing his explosive and almost unreadable essay on *Transformation and Symbols*, and turned to editing Spielrein's paper for publication, he wrote another of his condescending and arrogant letters to her, where he confessed noticing for the first time the 'incredible parallels' between his work and hers. Spielrein's reply must have been angry and tough, for Jung answered: 'I meant this as a compliment – the priority is yours. The death wish was clearer to you than to me. Understandably! Consequently, I have expressed myself so differently that no one will think you have gotten it from me.' Their telepathy, their 'secret penetration of thoughts', their 'swallowing' up of each other, will be secret from everyone: it is 'not for the public'.

If Jung still hoped that Spielrein would be his secret representative at Freud's Viennese court he had misjudged her. She definitively turned from Jung towards Freud in February 1912, when Jung received, without noticing its significance, another paper of hers, 'A Contribution to the Understanding of the Child's Mind': a disguised Siegfried, in which she used her own childhood fantasies as the primary analytic material – including her exploration of the remarkably late date, while she was attending zoology lectures at the university in October 1905, that is, after her analysis with Jung, when she had learned the sexual facts of life. With this paper, she began to turn towards the analysis of children – with Freud's benediction, since it is probable that he had referred to her one of the three cases she discussed. Perhaps she was also aware that, as the only woman member of the Society in Vienna, this field would be wide open for her to make her own. However, she was never to be exclusively or even predominantly preoccupied by child analysis. As Freud's suspicion towards the woman he still regarded as Jung's disciple thawed, as he increased his subtle efforts to seduce her away from Jung, Spielrein summed up the analysis of one of her dreams: 'Now Prof. Freud is the one who causes me to glow; if Dr J. were also the director, his love would leave me cold.'

Both Freud and Jung underplayed Spielrein's influence on them, Jung because she knew more of his inner personal and conceptual development than anyone, and Freud because he associated her ideas with Jung and repudiated in advance any influence from so dangerous a source. Both only paid very belated tribute to her ideas, Freud in *Beyond the Pleasure Principle* and Jung in *Symbols and Transformation*; both distorted her ideas in the process. Freud wrote: 'A considerable portion of these speculations [concerning the death instinct and the possibility of a primary masochism] have been anticipated by Sabina Spielrein in an instructive and interesting paper which, however, is unfortunately not entirely clear to me. She there describes the sadistic components of the sexual instinct as "destructive".' In presenting her work in this fashion, Freud ignored the 'transformative' principle, perhaps seeing it as too akin to the prospective, future-oriented tendencies of Jung's interpretation of dreams and myth dating from the period of their break, in 1912–13, and after. Perhaps Freud was right to sense that Spielrein's emphasis on transformation was linked to Jung's heresies. However, although the prospective and the occult had been themes in Jung's earliest work, in 1902, it is highly probable that when he returned to them, in 1908 and 1909, he was doing so in part under Spielrein's influence. Her diaries of the period centred on her own distinctive concept of transformation, and it was this period when he was most closely involved with her.

In early 1912, Freud referred two non-paying patients to Spielrein and she eagerly entered into their analyses. Yet she was not happy in Vienna and was preparing to decamp to Berlin. Before she left, in late April 1912, she said good-bye to Freud, when they 'discussed certain intimate matters'. One of these was very probably her desire to enter analysis with Freud. Another, equally probably, was the place that Jung occupied in her inner world. Either on this occasion or sometime earlier in the autumn of 1911, she showed Freud her analysis of one of her Siegfried dreams, and he showed his approval of it. The remark that he added, which struck Spielrein with immense force and reverberated with her for years, was not entirely characteristic of his response to women asking him whether they should or should not have a child: '"You could have the child, you know, if you wanted it, but what a waste of your talents, etc." These simple words exerted a tremendous influence on me....' She had 'transferred' the Siegfried theme to Freud, and he had, in his own way, accepted the gift. Things would never be the same between her and Jung. Some years later, she wrote to Jung: 'Strange to say, I no longer dream of "Siegfried", and I think this has been the case since I showed Prof. Freud my analysis of the Siegfried dream.' Perhaps this was the most important moment in Spielrein's relations with Freud, which allowed her to wean herself from Jung, and perhaps even of the need to be close to Freud.

The next surprising twist in her story is told in a simple diary entry, written less than three months after her good-bye to Freud: 'On the 14th of June [1912] I married Dr Paul Scheftel. To be continued.' We know very little of Scheftel – he is barely mentioned in Sabina's later letters save that he was Jewish and that he had a progressive disease, which first drove him insane and eventually killed him sometime in the 1930s. Faithful to Jung, faithful to Freud, faithful by nature, Spielrein cared for him till the end. Yet if her nature required fidelity, her fate was to make her solitary and independent.

The 'tumultuous' events of marriage, in her diary, however, take second place to analysis: the entry in which she alluded to the events of her marriage night and her relations with her husband and his mother concludes with: 'At night – "Freud".' The project of analysis with Freud preoccupied her throughout the summer; Freud, however, was not of the same mind. As so often with his younger women patients, Freud viewed marriage as an alternative, probably a superior alternative, to analysis, rather than a pale substitute, an irrelevance or a flight.

We had agreed that you would let me know before 1 Oct. whether you still intend to drive out the tyrant by psychoanalysis with me. Today I would like to put in a word or two about that decision. I imagine that the man of whom you say so many nice things has rights as well. These would be badly prejudiced by treatment so soon after your marriage. Let him first try to see how far he can tie you to himself and make you forget your old dreams. Only what remnant he fails to clear up belongs properly to psychoanalysis. Meanwhile, it might happen that someone else will turn up who will have more rights than both the old and the new man put together. At this stage, it is best for analysis to take a back seat.

Freud had transformed the significance of Siegfried by pointing out that she could have the child if she wanted. He now gracefully and prudently, maybe even timorously, wished to retire, so as not to get enmeshed in a new version of Siegfried. With Jung become an apostate to be driven with all his works from the fold of the faithful, he had little time for Spielrein's fantasies of saviours bridging the gulf between Aryans and Jews. He pointed out to Spielrein: 'The Lord, in that anti-Semitic period, had him born from the superior Jewish race. But I know these are my prejudices.'

By the beginning of 1913, Spielrein was pregnant. It was a difficult pregnancy, reviving her Siegfried fantasies and her love for Jung. She struggled, and so did the foetus, as she almost miscarried. '[Siegfried] appeared once more in a dream during my pregnancy, when I was in danger of losing my baby. And that is of course why my reborn daughter is called "Renate". Perhaps my many dreams with sun symbolism are – Siegfried dreams!' She appealed to Freud for help. Where her involvement with Jung was concerned, he was not inclined to be as conciliatory as he had been in 1909: 'I imagine that you love Dr J. so deeply still because you have not brought to light the hatred he merits.' Corralling Spielrein to his cause now meant reminding her of her Jewishness: 'I am, as you know, cured of the last shred of my predilection for the Aryan cause, and would like to take it that if the child turns out to be a boy he will develop into a stalwart Zionist.' On hearing news of the girl's birth, Freud congratulated Sabina, still in vindictive military mode: 'It is far better that the child should be a "she". Now we can think again about the blond Siegfried and perhaps smash that idol before his time comes.'

Spielrein was living in Berlin – where two of her brothers had also settled – when the war broke out. She was working as an analyst and had made contact with Friedrich Krauss, Professor of Medicine at the University of Berlin. It is therefore possible that she was attached to the clinic at the Berlin Charité, where Krauss succeeded Ziehen as director. She attended the Berlin Society, without growing close to its head, Karl Abraham, and contributed a series of brief papers to the psychoanalytic journals: on the forgetting of names, on animal symbolism and a phobia in a boy, on menstrual dreams and on various expressions of the Oedipus complex in childhood. As these themes suggest, she had quite definitely sided with Freud against Jung in the institutional battles of 1913 and 1914. But with the war, it is probable that she elected as a Russian national to quit Berlin and go to Switzerland; first to Zurich, where she was in contact with Bleuler, then to Lausanne. She had had enough of psychoanalysis and said that she 'wanted to do something useful'; she therefore worked in a surgical clinic. And her inner life turned to her old love, music. She composed songs and took music lessons. In 1919, musical activity stopped and she returned to analytic work: she wrote to Freud asking if she could again be affiliated to the Vienna Society and, as a result of the loss of her family fortune during the Russian Revolution, she sought to earn money translating Jung's works into Russian. At about this time the Siegfried dreams returned and, from 1916 to 1919, she reopened her correspondence and friendship with Jung.

In these letters, she attempted to persuade Jung with a synthesis of his, Adler's and Freud's views, and to admonish him for refusing to recognize his debt towards and affinity with Freud:

You can understand Freud perfectly well if you wish to.... You should have the courage to recognize Freud in all his grandeur, even if you do not agree with him on every point, even if in the process you might have to credit Freud with many of your own accomplishments. Only then will you be completely free, and only then will you be the greater one. You will be amazed to see how markedly your entire personality and your new theory will gain in objectivity through this process.

Jung's replies were equally tough-minded: 'Freud's opinion is a sinful rape of the holy. It spreads darkness not light … only out of the deepest night is new light born. Siegfried is that spark. I lit in you a new light for time of darkness. Surround this inner light with devotion.' They also wrote more intimately, theory intertwining with subtle analysis of dreams and personal

revelations. Spielrein made no bones about the personal significance for her
of rejecting Jung's theories in favour of Freud's. Ironically, now it was she
who argued that Siegfried was a 'real' child:

where, in the course of analysis, does one find support for the assumption that
Siegfried is supposed to be not a real but an ideal child? I struggled with this question
for years until I succeeded in no longer regarding the symbols of the subconscious
from the prospective point of view and attributing to them only the meaning
of infantile desires. The struggle was very difficult for me, and the guilt resulting
from my missing my life goal so great that Siegfried almost took my baby daughter's
life.

The decisive way in which Spielrein managed her inner life in this correspondence enabled her to return to psychoanalysis, with Freud's financial
aid. However, Jung's image continued to pursue her for the next few years.
In a disguised autobiographical dream she published in 1922, she traces the
gradual diminishing of the force of his image; there, he appears as a 'syphilitic
Don Juan', whom she can finally forget.

Spielrein attended the International Psychoanalytic Congress at The Hague
in September 1920, delivering a paper, 'The Origin and Development of
Spoken Speech', that revealed a new and seminal line of enquiry. Her interest
in children had begun before the war, but now it took a novel form which
linked analysis to developmental psychology and linguistics. Her overall
framework, as ever dualistic, was the contrast between autistic and social
languages (singing, poetry). Speech, she stated, was an intermediary zone
between the pleasure and reality principles. She reviewed the theories of
language acquisition and put forward her hypotheses about the origin of the
words 'mama' and 'papa', examples of the process whereby first words arise
out of the act of sucking, imbued with magical, wishfulfilling qualities.

This line of enquiry was to have momentous consequences in the later
twentieth century, in the great debate between Jean Piaget and L. S. Vygotsky.
With her almost telepathic sense of burgeoning intellectual movements,
Spielrein now moved to Geneva, sent there by her analyst colleagues to
colonize a new city. She joined the Institut Jean-Jacques Rousseau, which had
been set up by Edouard Claparède in 1912 as a pedagogical laboratory at the
university. The Institut had regularly included lectures on psychotherapy for
its students; Théodore Flournoy, who was well acquainted with and sympathetic to Freud, had lectured on psychoanalysis in 1913. But psychoanalysis
was still controversial when Spielrein arrived in early 1921. Claparède gave
her a consulting-room and an official post as his assistant. She lectured, got
involved in the psychology laboratory, held consultations with children, became
active in the local psychoanalytic association and brought life to a smaller
group of more committed, psychoanalytically oriented psychologists for a
brief period before the Institut Jean-Jacques Rousseau was dissolved in 1922.
She offered didactic analyses to her colleagues, several of whom took her up
on her offer, including Pierre Bovet, Claparède, Charles Odier (who was, like
Spielrein, later to be sent out on an analytic colonizing mission, this time to

Paris), and last but not least the young and talented Piaget. Spielrein returned the compliment by following Piaget's courses in the early 1920s.

Born in 1896, Piaget had studied psychology with Alfred Binet in Paris and had had a training in clinical methods with Bleuler and Jung in Zurich. When he met Spielrein, he was very much following Freud's view that the pleasure principle governs the inner life of childen, studying their errors to expose the structure of cognitive development. He was in analysis with Spielrein for eight months in 1921; in later years, he concealed the identity of his analyst for a long time, indeed he never directly acknowledged that it was her. In 1978, Piaget described how he found it 'extraordinary to discover all my complexes', although he had been immune to his analyst's theory. Other accounts have it that once he understood that his eccentric mother was reappearing in his transference to the analyst, he said, '*J'ai compris,*' and walked out. Certainly he was a member of the Genevan analytic group at this time; Freud expected to hear reports on its activities from Piaget when he made the journey to Berlin to deliver a paper on 'The Symbolic Thought of the Child' at the International Psychoanalytic Congress of 1922. Throughout the 1920s, Piaget's works regularly drew on analytic case-material for illustrating his developing theories. Spielrein's paper about her daughter Renate's beliefs about the origin of human beings (if she fell down, she would break into two girls) was cited in Piaget's classic *The Child's Conception of the World*, originally published in 1926. Spielrein, however, was not averse to criticizing her analysand in print. She accused him of being overly Adlerian in his 'construction of the real in the child', preferring Freud and his 'sociogenic' focus – an uncanny fore-shadowing of her future colleague Vygotsky's famous criticism of Piaget. Yet she was researching in parallel with Piaget when in 1923 she published her 'Some Analogies between the Thoughts of the Child, of the Aphasic and Preconscious Thought', in which she analysed the monologue of a child as if it were an association experiment, and compared the results with an aphasic's description of performing a simple task.

In this Genevan period of the early 1920s, her most intellectually prolific, Spielrein had found other intellectual collaborators besides Piaget: the Genevan School of Linguistics under Charles Bally, editor and follower of its most distinguished representative, Ferdinand de Saussure (whose son Ferdinand was also a young analyst there). With Bally, she worked on grammatical structure and its relations to the forms of preconscious thought. One fruit of this collaboration was her paper delivered to the Berlin Congress on 'Time in Subliminal Psychic Life', later published in *Imago* in 1923. She argued that the developing thought of children and the structure of dreams show similar techniques for representing time: the future is represented by repeated action, the past – the most difficult time concept for the preconscious to apprehend – is only represented by spatial metaphors implying distance from the present. The same analogies also hold for the formation of compound verbs in a number of different languages. Here she was developing in a less metaphysical mode some preoccupations with how alien time was to the unconscious that had first been stated in her earlier work on 'Destruction' – themes that Freud had explicitly commented on approvingly and was to develop into his own pithy theses on the timelessness of the unconscious.

Despite her intellectual productivity in Geneva, and the faintest of hints in an analytic paper she published that she had had a passionate love affair with a younger man, Spielrein had never settled in. Her forte was obviously not empire-building, which other envoys of Freud were more successful at in Switzerland: Mira and Emil Oberholzer had, together with Pfister, founded the Société Suisse de Psychanalyse in Zurich on 24 March 1919. Mira Gineburg, as she was born in Poland in 1887, had had analysis with Freud, probably in 1922, and, despite her husband falling out with Freud over lay analysis, remained a faithful follower of Freud and a faithful friend to her fellow-Pole and analyst, Helene Deutsch.

Freud suggested to Spielrein that she move to Berlin and work in the Polyclinic there. She informed him that she was now planning to move to Moscow. In the last extant communication between them, he heartily approved of this decision, but could not resist adding a barbed comment that could also be a reminder to her to be her own woman and not to assume that her intimacy with her correspondents would ensure that the world would give her what she was seeking: 'I hope to hear from you soon, but would earnestly request that you write your address on the inside of your letter, which so few women are wont to do.'

It turned out to be a thriving time for psychoanalysis in Moscow, with two young researchers, A. R. Luria and Vygotsky, joining the Moscow Psycho-analytic Institute. As its secretary for a time, Luria gave periodic reports to the *International Journal of Psychoanalysis*, chronicling Spielrein's rapid involvement in a wide variety of activities: teaching, serving as a training analyst, working in a children's home (Psychoanalytic Clinic for Children) that she had founded, and running seminars on the psychoanalysis of children. In this latter area she took up a distinctive position, being opposed to Klein and to Hug-Hellmuth in their use of explanations in the analysis of children, which she regarded as suggestive influence. Her influence on her colleagues is difficult to map in detail; Kerr suggests that she 'jump-started Russian psychology into the twentieth century'. Here was a woman who was a personal friend and pupil of Bleuler and Jung, a colleague of Freud's and Piaget's, who could aid the young Vygotsky in his critique of Piaget's use of the Bleulerian concept of autistic thought, using the interpretative method of analysis of a child's monologue which Spielrein had developed from Jung's association exper-iments. Luria was also to take these same experiments further in his work on human conflict in the late 1920s.

We know very little of Spielrein's continuing life once she moved to the Soviet Union. Psychoanalysis was banned in 1936, the Moscow Society having been disbanded in the 1920s; she practised covertly as an analyst – and her name still appeared on a list of Russian analysts in 1937. In 1924, she moved back to her home town Rostov and taught at the local university. She had a second child, Eva; Renate, a talented musician, studied the cello in Moscow. Spielrein's three younger brothers died in the purges of the 1930s. When

Rostov was captured by the invading German army in November 1941, all the Jews of the city, including Spielrein and her two daughters, were taken to the synagogue and shot.

Loë Kann – 'a treasure of a woman'

If Jung's early relationship to Freud and psychoanalysis was inextricably bound up, in both its making and its unmaking, with Sabina Spielrein, then Loë Kann played a similar role in the forming of close, and eventually intimate, relations between Ernest Jones, the first major British proponent of psycho-analysis, and her analyst, Sigmund Freud. For Jones, this triangular nexus, in which a woman became the focus of tensions and delicate communication between the two men, repeated itself again twice: once with Anna Freud and later with Joan Riviere. On each occasion, things worked superficially to Jones's disadvantage, yet he was capable of making the best of the blows of fate that Freud seemed to have a hand in. He was to remain good, indeed life-long, friends with Loë Kann, Anna Freud and Joan Riviere, as well as with that supposed destroyer of sons, Sigmund Freud.

Whereas Sabina Spielrein was something of a calling card for Jung, his first psychoanalytic patient and a perceived threat to his marriage – a marriage he was determined never to let be destroyed – Loë Kann was Jones's wife, whom Freud analysed because Jones asked the favour of him. Reading between the lines, Freud perceived her as Jones's gift to him. Loë never even considered becoming an analyst, but she was Jones's wife and at times financial sponsor throughout the period when he was establishing himself in London, then in Canada, and then back again in London.

In the course of her relationship with Freud, we see something of the radical independence the interpreting Freud demanded of his patients; we also see, if one shifts the optic, the dependence on himself that he had them build, so that, at least for the duration of analysis, he became the central axis of their lives. We also observe how adept Freud was at negotiating analytic triangles – as if such analytic *ménages à trois* expedited the appearance and resolution of that more theoretical and universal triangle, that of Oedipus. And finally, we see how Freud, perhaps surprisingly given how concerned he is often painted to have been about binding his younger disciples to the Cause, was willing to risk his relationship with Jones to the ethical requirements demanded of him by his analysis of Loë. With hindsight, the risk was worth taking: Freud gained and retained the lifelong loyalty of both parties. Because of the newly available correspondence between Freud and Jones, most of which was conducted in English – on Freud's side in an English which was rusty and sometimes quaint – we can now have a more thorough insight into this particular analytic triangle. This is supplemented by the sporadic but extremely revealing letters Loë wrote to Freud, before, during and after her analysis with him.

Ernest Jones encountered psychoanalysis and Loë Kann at about the same time: in 1905. David Eder, a doctor colleague of Jones's who would also later be a founder member of the London Psycho-Analytic Society in 1913, played a significant part in both events. Unable to break into the regular career paths of London medical institutions, and already under a cloud because of a scandal in which he had been accused of indecent behaviour while medically examining a young girl – a charge from which he was completely cleared – Jones was at the time struggling to establish a Harley Street practice with his close friend Wilfred Trotter. Loë Kann was a Dutch woman from a Jewish family, settled in London out of love for the city. In his extensive correspondence with Freud, Jones once wrote: 'Now I have always been conscious of sexual attractions to patients; my wife was a patient of mine.' So it is possible that they met because Eder referred Loë Kann to Jones. Within a year of meeting, they were living as husband and wife: Jones had fallen into the habit of sharing Loë's flat.

Loë was wealthy and generous, a woman of some experience and decided spirit, with a passion for order and detail. She was also, however, a chronic invalid, having had several operations for renal stones by the time Jones met her. He was shocked to discover that she was using morphine to cope with the pain. Morphine, indeed, was to be a constant theme in their relationship, in her analysis and throughout her life.

By early 1908, Jones had spent time with the psychoanalytic group in Zurich centred on Bleuler and Jung, and was becoming more and more committed to psychoanalysis. In the second crisis that was decisively to influence his career, he was dismissed from the West End Hospital because of his strictly Freudian, but unchaperoned, enquiry into the sexual meanings of a young girl patient's arm paralysis. In fear for his career, Jones accepted the post of director of a new psychiatric clinic in Toronto, Canada, despite Loë's dislike of the prospect of moving to what she considered a puritanical and dull country, without cosmopolitan life and friends. Before setting off, Jones spent the early months of 1908 touring Europe: in Munich, he adopted a bohemian life-style, had a rapid analysis from Otto Gross and worked in Emil Kraepelin's Psychiatric Clinic. He attended the first International Psychoanalytic Congress at Salzburg in 1908, where he met Freud for the first time, and then spent time in Budapest and Paris.

In September 1908, he sailed for Canada, ahead of Loë, and went 'house hunting for my harem, which consists of a wife, two sisters and two servants, being at present in a rented furnished house.' The harem soon arrived and took over the organization of the *ménage*. Despite passing themselves off as married, rumours of Jones's and Loë's illegal status got around, and Jones had to make the first of a series of self-excusing and deceiving explanations of his moral conduct. His troubles with the 'incredibly developed prudery' of the Canadians over the next few years included an incident in which a patient accused him of having sexual intercourse with her 'to do her good', and a brush with a crusading woman doctor, the secretary of the local Purity League, who asked for Jones's dismissal and expulsion from the country. Jones tried paying off the patient – something he hid from Freud – but was eventually supported by the medical school and its administration in the conflict with his morally horrified accusers. The patient, however, attempted to shoot Jones. 'That alarmed my wife – aided perhaps by some unconscious motive, the nature of which you will have no difficulty in discerning – and she has insisted on the house and myself being guarded by detectives.'

Rumours of Jones's recommending masturbation and advising debauchery to young women who subsequently got pregnant were later compounded by two patients' husbands who persecuted Jones, one because his wife, following analysis, insisted on a divorce, the other because of the marital difficulties his wife's analysis had caused him. Loë, who had never been happy in Canada, was alarmed by these scandals and urged Jones to leave private practice; he confessed to Freud his fear that she might leave him because of his involvement with 'such dangerous work'. Throughout that year Loë battled with Jones's commitment to psychoanalysis, which she did not believe in. Jones travelled to Europe in the summer, attending the Weimar Psychoanalytic Congress, where he discussed with Freud his wife's health – her abdominal pains, her kidney stones, her morphine addiction – and 'offered me her treatment', as Freud was to put it some years later. Loë now proved surprisingly optimistic about the prospect of analysis with Freud:

Your opinion that there was a chance for her to get better carried very great weight, for she could hardly help living with me and not thinking highly of you. She said she would do anything, so long as she wasn't expected to believe things she couldn't believe (i.e. have ideas forced on her against her will). Rather to my surprise she was very definite on the point that she would rather be treated by you than by anyone else.

Loë's delayed entry into analysis was finally fixed for the autumn of 1912, which she and Jones were to spend in Europe. In preparation, she began to reduce her daily dosage of morphine. Over the summer, Freud began a process of courteous seduction, sending enticing messages to Loë via Jones; the ground for a positive transference was being well prepared. And the personal tone between Jones and Freud sharpened, as Freud caught wind of a sexual liaison Jones had, characteristically, suddenly got caught up in. Freud thought it a pity that Jones could 'not master such dangerous cravings, well aware at the same time of the course from which all these evils spring, taking away from you nearly all the blame but nothing of the dangers.' Jones on his side pointed out to Freud how his anxieties about his daughter Mathilde were perhaps condensed with anxieties about the future of his other daughter, psychoanalysis, in danger because of the increasingly open conflict with Jung. It was during that summer that Jones and Ferenczi cooked up the idea of 'a small group of men [who] could be thoroughly analysed by you, so that they could represent the pure theory unadulterated by personal complexes, and thus build an unofficial inner circle' – the idea that Freud quickly turned into the secret committee of seven close followers who would guard the faithful transmission of psychoanalysis.

Loë and Jones arrived in Vienna in September and took a small flat. Freud expressed the view that it would be better if Jones were out of the way during

Loë's analysis, so he spent the next three months travelling in Italy. Freud's initial opinion of Loë was highly favourable and was to remain so: 'she is a highly intelligent, deeply neurotic, Jewess, whose disease history is easy to read. I will be pleased to be able to expend much Libido on her.'

The introductory phase of the treatment lasted several weeks. It was an analysis in which letters played a significant part. Loë wrote to Jones asking him to tell her how the Professor's letters recorded her progress; and Freud's letters to Jones about this 'precious creature of the highest value' completed the circle of correspondence by underlining that Loë was 'gentle enough to let me read your [Jones's] letters'. Slowly, however, Freud's and Loë's accounts of the analysis began to diverge, and, in early November 1912, Loë had a severe attack of some kind, probably of abdominal pains, and let loose to Jones a volley of abuse concerning Freud, which Jones dutifully communicated to him:

She complains bitterly about you, that you do not trust her, do not believe her statements, and twist everything until she is quite confused in her mind. I suppose the resistance had previously been concealed in a woman's deceptive way, by her pretending to agree to conclusions that in her heart she did not accept. At all events, you probably have as much resistance to deal with now as will more than make up for its previous absence. She is beginning to feel the treatment as an attack on her personality.

This was just what Freud needed to get the analysis going. The grain of truth in Loë's outburst against Freud lay in 'my doubt expressed to her whether her pains are from the kidney or from the soul'. This question – are her pains organic or psychical? – became a permanent, never quite resolved theme of her analysis.

Then Freud's letters to Jones began to get less informative. And, to Jones's distress, Loë's letters virtually ceased, in explanation of which Freud warned Jones that 'she confessed yesterday, that she was a big liar when a child.' Jones now began to feel left out in the cold, reduced to hearing of his wife through Freud's letters, prompting him to the following *cri de coeur*:

From no patient have I received a more vivid impression of the terrific forces pent up in the unconscious than I have from my wife. It is as though a horrible abyss of unalterably black despair and hopelessness suddenly yawned in front of one, and one stands paralysed and helpless before an awful *Abgrund* [abyss]. Then it closes again, and a smiling surface appears to help one forget what one would willingly forget. I trust that you will get a look inside this volcano of emotion, and teach her how to make a better use of its fires.

Freud reported good progress in December: Loë's pains had disappeared, her morphia was being steadily reduced, and he was now contemplating confronting the 'chief point', her sexual anaesthesia. Jones might have heard something sinister when Freud told him at the end of December that 'you do not realise completely how well she is' – it is Freud who knows about Loë now, and notices how well she has become in Jones's absence. Certainly the cement between Freud and Loë was growing ever stronger: he is almost shame-faced in his confession of their intimacy: 'I could not help leading her over to my family for some moments Tuesday evening [Christmas Eve]'.

Jones now considered what sexual strategy he should adopt when he returned to Vienna for a week to see Loë. He asked for Freud's advice: 'I feel that the next month is an unfavourable occasion to test the anaesthesia matter, partly because it is unlikely to be overcome in such a short stay (don't you find that it often takes much time and practice?).' Then, as Freud told Jones on 1 January 1913, Loë's maid Lina appeared on the analytic stage: 'Lina had a second attack of pains, she nursing her. The nicest case of *Übertragung* [transference] I ever saw. The girl takes upon her the kidney stones, which have left the mistress.'

Freud's use of the term 'transference' indicated that he already sensed that Lina was fully implicated in the analysis. The crisis that now blew up entirely vindicated his use of such an analytically freighted term. There is a gap in the letters between Freud and Jones for a month here. During that time, Jones came to Vienna and, in accordance with the agreement that had been worked out between Freud, Loë and Jones, Loë and Jones probably avoided attempting sexual intercourse, although Jones had already in advance of the visit manufactured his own sense of rejection when he had written to Freud: 'I do not think I will make any overtures myself, but will be guided entirely by her feelings; I anticipate she will desire intercourse.' Whether or not he had sexual relations with Loë during his visit to Vienna, he certainly had sexual relations with Lina. Loë was very upset. As Freud later explained to Jones:

It was a tremendous shock at first. She got the old pains, not very strong though, raised the morphia at once to 4 from 1.2 and renounced treatment. You remember, she identified Ψa, your and my own person and so she had to break off with all three of them. Yet there was a thread left undamaged between her and myself. I got hold of it and persuaded her to go on not for your sake but in her own interest. She agreed and it came to be right. We are down to 0.8 at this time, no pains at all, resistance much diminished, her behaviour almost normal in the affair which was even more intricate than you can surmise, and she lends an attentive ear to everything Ψa can tell her. We did turn the accident to the side of profit, now analysis being no more an act of complaisance for you, it is meeting with a much better reception. At the end I will have to thank you for the dangerous experiment.

On 24 January, during this period of crisis following Jones's betrayal, Loë had written Freud a letter, an elegiac good-bye to analysis, in which Jones was not even mentioned. She expressed the desire to keep Freud as a a friend – 'I love you (only my kind of friendship-love [*meine Art von Freudschaft-Liebe*])' – and to find in him the father she had never recognized. Aware of the forthcoming marriage of Freud's daughter Sophie, she compared her own unhappy marriage, 'which was no marriage – is "*Heirat* [marriage]" masculine or feminine?', with what she is sure will be the happy marriage of Freud's daughter: happy because she is Freud's daughter.

although mine [father] never knowingly failed me, maybe I didn't encounter anything worth wishing for (probably my only conception of a father was as a double of the mother!) until the possibility of a father like you was clearly presented to me through your daughter's call: 'Papachen'. I now want to ask for a soft spot in your heart? After your daughter is married would you once advise me as a father would his daughter? What would you then advise me? I cannot promise that you wouldn't later rue it – but only that I would be grateful and would do my best – but to advise is always a risk. Till then –

In this premature good-bye to analysis, Loë asks Freud to exchange the role of analyst for that of friend; in passing, she mentions 'Jones II', a man who was evidently a recent young lover. And it was obviously thinking of him that prompted her to dismiss the problem of sexual anaesthesia which was so central to her relationship with Ernest by saying: 'I cannot believe that pleasure would be lacking in an act of sexual intercourse where love isn't lacking.'

Jones II, as she punningly called him, was a young American, Herbert Jones – whom she also referred to as Davy. It is almost certain that Ernest knew nothing consciously of his existence as yet. He was back in London and contrite over his relationship with Lina, which he tried to explain in a letter dated 30 January 1913:

The relation with Lina was an old affair (which explains the identification behind her hysterical attacks), and in Italy I was fully determined to break it off. But some devil of desire made me yield to the temptation. I do not feel very guilty about my relation to her, nor did it indicate any abnormality in myself, but something tells me from within that the continuation of it in Wien was dictated by a repressed spirit of hostility against my dear wife (as punishment for her anaesthesia), and you can imagine what heart-rending remorse that is causing me.

Freud, meanwhile, perhaps unconvinced that Jones's action in sleeping with Lina was anything other than 'mean and treacherous', was continuing Loë's analysis, and asked Jones to take on a new, caretaker role: 'stick to your work, do not break communication with her and hold on firmly, till I can step off the scene. There is more going on now than I can make you know, but it is unavoidable.' What Ernest did not and should not know about, quite probably, was the existence of Davy. Freud was now at the centre of the spider's web of Loë's relationships, thoroughly interwoven with the analysis; the way had become clear for a proper analysis, on her terms, not on Freud's or Jones's:

There is a change in her position against you *as well as against me*. She considers herself free as long as treatment lasts, and according to the rules of Ψa she has the right to do so. *I am glad she took up this position herself or I would have been obliged to force her into it.* I could not go on in the role of your friend as long as I am to act as her physician. I had to forget everything except this last. Now it has come natural to me, you know I am not working for you but for her delivery to the exclusion of every other aim.

Things had turned out in such a way that Loë was now in the only position in which a person can, Freud implied, conduct a proper analysis: free of obligations to others. And, Freud also implied, he would have had to force her into such freedom if external and internal events had not conspired to oblige her spontaneously to become free. Even with such a determined, defiant and often head-strong woman as Loë, the 'sense of duty' could, in his eyes, still drive her into illness, just as it does, he had asserted in 1908, so many women:

the cure for nervous illnesses arising from marriage would be marital unfaithfulness. But the more strictly a woman has been brought up and the more sternly she has submitted to the demands of civilization, the more she is afraid of taking this way out; and in the conflict between her desires and her sense of duty, she once more seeks refuge in a neurosis. Nothing protects her virtue as securely as an illness.

Psychoanalysis, as Jones's Canadian patients' husbands had found out, was clearly – necessarily – destructive of marriages constructed out of duty and obligation. Freud himself noted in 1917, having learned some hard lessons from Ida Bauer and other patients:

In psycho-analytic treatments the intervention of relatives is a positive danger ... they cannot be induced to keep at a distance from the whole business. ... It is not to be wondered at, indeed, if a husband looks with disfavour on a treatment in which, as he may rightly suspect, the whole catalogue of his sins will be brought to light. ... In the years before the war, when arrivals from many foreign countries made me independent of the favour or disfavour of my own city, I followed a rule of not taking on a patient for treatment unless he was *sui juris*, not dependent on anyone else in the essential relations of his life.

Arriving in Vienna as a married woman, superficially obligated to Jones and in part entering analysis for him, Loë Kann had now become such a patient: a woman independent of a man or anyone else. She now had the chance to use that freedom to take what she could from analysis.

Despite some tantalizingly missing letters in the Freud–Jones correspondence, which may have been made to 'disappear' or be accidentally missing, the course of the next few months is clear. Loë continued to cut down on her morphia; since Lina's counterfeits, she no longer had her old pains, but sporadically produced new ones. She left Vienna briefly in March, writing to Freud to tell him how happy she was with Davy Jones, how she had never felt as close to anyone as him, but that sexually her happiness still 'passes via the same byways – only through his [happiness] is it to be reached – if only the way were sometimes the same.' Jones was becoming resigned to losing Loë as Freud confessed the difficulties of 'standing in this way between two of my friends', although Jones did not as yet know of the existence of his eponymous rival. By the beginning of May, Freud knew for certain which way things were bound to go, as he wrote to Ferenczi: 'I still do not know how Jones will take it when he finds out that his wife, in consequence of the analysis, does not want to remain his wife anymore.' Jones, himself, was on his way to Budapest to begin an analysis with Ferenczi; and he had finally learned of Davy Jones's existence. Loë, still in analysis, and now in high spirits, was finding new friends amongst the analytic community, inviting

Freud, Hanns Sachs and Otto Rank to dine with her and Davy. Meanwhile, Freud was mending his fences with Jones, in elegiac mode:

You had a big share in my private thoughts all this year over, you know. I am indeed of opinion you have lost your wife more completely than you realise. She is a treasure of a woman, but of deep-going abnormality and I am not without misgivings about her physical health and her fate, when this business with Jones II comes to an unfavourable end, as might easily be. ... I had to work against my own interest. Your house in London, had the treatment come to another result, would have become a regular stopover for me and so have fulfilled one of my earliest wish-fancies.

Freud, of course, suspected that Jones must be feeling hostile towards him, and gently enquired about it. Jones confessed: 'my unconscious, with the logic peculiar to itself, had been blaming you for the loss first of my greatest friend (Trotter), then of my wife, i.e. the man and woman who were dearest to me.' But the analysts were now well in control: Freud quietly forbade Loë going to Budapest to visit Jones; Ferenczi urged Freud not to divulge their discussion of Jones's analysis to Loë. Ernest and Loë's separation was being very effectively managed.

But Freud's increasingly tender paternal feelings were also in need of protection, as he confessed to Ferenczi:

I have become extraordinarily fond of this Loë and brought out in her a very warm feeling filled with sexual inhibition as rarely before (thanks to age in all likelihood). Unfortunately, this child brings great sorrow to me, which you are not supposed to let him (E. J.) in on.

In one of his reports on her progress to Jones, he did feel able to reveal how 'one cannot be with Loë for very long before one becomes truly fond of her.'

Now, however, the organic side of her pains was coming to the fore. Her analysis was not yet complete. Nor was her relationship with Davy Jones anything like a cut and dried matter. He had left for America at the end of May, plunging her into despair and uncertainty as to whether there would be any future together. Loë had offered to pay for Ernest's expenses in getting established in London for the next three years. So, incongruously enough, Loë and Ernest returned to London in August and started setting up house together. Davy and his family arrived in London from America, well ahead of schedule. However, Loë's desperation persisted, bound up with her 'altruistic qualms about "spoiling a young life"' and her concern for her age and health. Surprisingly, and generously, the person who believed in her and Davy most was Ernest: 'I fancy it will go well with them, for she can do anything in the world when she loves.'

As Ernest prepared to leave London for the Munich Psychoanalytical Congress in September, coinciding with Davy's departure for eight months to America, Loë entrusted a package of letters to Freud to him, letters written over a period of four days. The emotional range of these letters highlights her fundamental joie de vivre, her quintessential charm, but also her desperation. In one, she confesses to uncertainty as to whether Davy will ever return to marry her: 'If he thinks in the right direction he'll come to Vienna in May to fetch me – if no ... well it can't be helped!' In counterpoint, scrawled along the side of the letter, she adds a postscript: 'Written on Davy's knee, so please excuse wobbly mess – he breathes too often & too deep.' Yet the next day, she draws up a suicide note addressed to Freud, a supplement to analysis:

I suppose that I ought to *own* up that what's kept me going these days is the *conviction* that I'll commit suicide after the visit from Ernest and Davy. ... My chief desire ... has been to get clear about my relations with Ernest, in that I could be fair at least. Now you tell me that I don't want to go into them, for fear it may do away with my hatred & so send me back to him. If I really wanted to go back to him – I can't see anything terrible in it. ... And even if I *don't* want to go back after the explanation, even if I still find myself sick & tired to go on with the job, – well I'd much rather die with things clear between us than like this. ... I *would* have lived for 7 years with Davy and then (at the worst) I could have killed myself with the satisfaction of having had those 7 years. I needed some stimulus like that, but now I have lost the taste for life.

On his return from Munich, Ernest reported to Freud that Loë was much better, was installing a stray kitten in their house, and had commandeered from Jones all the pharmacological means to cure its illnesses and kill it if necessary. Her furnishing of his – their – house became the first in a series of reasons why she had to delay returning to Vienna to restart analysis. Eventually Freud wrote her a scolding letter, to which she replied with spirited contradiction of his rebuke that she should be ashamed of herself:

As for being ashamed – I have never been ashamed in my life, thank God, and am far from it now. I have taken morphine and never tried to hide it from anyone, least of all from you. I have done all I could without it and taken the minimum dose I required. I am sorry to say that the smallest doses had no effect whatsoever. I have – therefore – nothing to be ashamed of, as you see.

Despite this disclaimer, it seems clear that Loë's struggles concerning analysis centred on her morphine habit. Eventually, at the end of November, she left London, saying good-bye to Ernest for the last time as a single woman. They were both deeply shaken and moved. At the other end of the railway tracks there was Freud, who had been impatiently waiting to see her since the end of September, ready to give her the presents he had acquired for her in Rome in September but not very pleased with her; he was quite prepared to give her a hard time: 'I know the former sweetness will be banished from our relations.' Soon he established how deplorable her condition was, how inaccessible she had become to analysis. However, she gave in and signed up for daily analysis in the beginning of 1914. To Jones, Freud had some equally short words to say about his personal life: 'But will you do me the personal favour of not making marriage the *next step* in your life, but to put a good deal of choosing and reflection into the matter.'

Davy Jones arrived in Vienna in January, and Loë once again became friendly to Freud and accessible to analysis. Freud sorted out to his and her mutual satisfactions the extent of the organic determination of her pains. And she opened up: 'As a nervous case she is very nice, all to be explained by her mother relation.' By the end of March, Freud had the story fully worked out and presented it to Jones:

I know (not she) that she intended to give her father a child, accumulating the contents of the alimentary channel to that purpose and grew wild raging at the mother, who made her 'miscarry', destroyed that child in formation by the daily enemas. The revulsion came after she had taken a husband (you know him) who fulfilled two important fatherly conditions ('helping the father' is one, 'showing his penis to the child' the other); she changed into her mother and ever since she and the mother are struggling within her soul.

This brief sketch of Loë's analytic history is a good example of how Freud rendered the reconstructed early history of a patient into the soon to be classic mould of the Oedipus complex. Loë's desire for a baby to give to her father is expressed in her later, adult precondition for loving a man: the desire to 'help the father'. 'Showing his penis to the child' is probably a compromise between Loë's infantile conception of faeces as a child and the equation of penis and baby: the man showing his penis 'to the child' thus restores her faith in the man having received the baby from her. Of course it may also quieten her anxiety: the man (still) has the penis; it has not been taken away (by mother, by the child). In defence against the infantile rage at her mother revived by her own supplanting of the mother in her relationship with 'a husband', she attempted to vacate the vulnerable and deprived position of the child by *becoming* the mother, the mother who has control over enemas, faeces, babies – and penises, no doubt. Freud's bracketed hint to Jones – 'you know him', the husband – could well have been a way of telling him: now you see that you were the husband who both fulfilled the preconditions for her loving, by allowing her to help you and by showing her your penis, but, as a consequence, you precipitated a chronic conflict in her, between the little girl in her who gives the baby/penis to the father/husband, and the mother in her (perhaps represented by some other person) who destroyed the gift of the child. The key unresolved question here is: to what extent did Freud regard her morphine addiction as a repetition of the maternal punishments, the daily enemas? And was it possible for Loë to sustain a relation to a man that did not involve revulsion at his automatic transformation into the punishing mother?

Jones's reply focused on an incident that was obviously well known to Loë's analyst, but which cast him in a different, more implicated role than Freud had suggested. Jones suspected that her long-standing hatred of him dated from the time of her miscarriage before they moved to Canada: 'what you say about the relation of the mother to the alimentary canal seems to accord with this view; after that date I became her mother. Is this right?' In their combined attempts to understand Loë, Freud and Jones were putting together a picture which Freud would summarize in his lecture on femininity some twenty years later:

If the girl has remained in her attachment to her father – that is, in the Oedipus complex – her choice is made according to the paternal type. Since, when she turned from her mother to her father, the hostility of her ambivalent relation remained with her mother, a choice of this kind should guarantee a happy marriage. But very often the outcome is of a kind that presents a general threat to such a settlement of the conflict due to ambivalence. The hostility that has been left behind follows in the train of the positive attachment and spreads over on to the new object. The woman's husband, who to begin with inherited from her father, becomes after a time her mother's heir as well. So it may easily happen that the second half of a woman's life may be filled by the struggle against her husband, just as the shorter first half was filled by her rebellion against her mother. When this reaction has been lived through, a second marriage may easily turn out very much more satisfying.

When he wrote the last two sentences, Freud may have had in mind Loë Kann's inner life, amongst others; what neater version of the sequence of rejected first husband and satisfying second husband could one find than Jones I and II?

Yet in mid-1914, the chief issue in the analysis still lay on the table, still was not successfully dealt with: Loë's morphia. Freud was pessimistic as he worked at the issue. So was Jones, as he discovered from Lina, whose transference with Loë was so successful that she was now his mistress and housekeeper in the flat in London, that Loë had deceived them all about the amount of morphia she had been taking; Jones added: 'Please do not speak of this, though I am sure it is true.' Freud's next letter to Jones told him of the *fait accompli*:

I have come back yesterday at night from Budapest, where we – Rank and I and Ferenczi as an interpreter – have helped Loë to become Mrs Herbert Jones. I am sure it must be hard for you and so it is for me when I remember the series of events from the evening in the Weimar coffeehouse when you offered me her treatment to the moments when I assisted to her wedding with another. It is a most remarkable chain of changes between persons and feelings of such [. . .] and the most striking points seem to me, that our relations have not been spoiled and that I have learned even to like the other man. As for her, I fully appreciate what I have heard from you as a first description of her person. She is charming, is a jewel as you call her in your noble-minded letter and she is too extraordinarily abnormal to make a worker's happiness. She must be judged for herself, measured by a standard fitted to her only self.

After the marriage, Loë returned immediately to analysis, now devoted principally to the battle with morphia, with Freud reluctant to believe his beloved Loë had deceived him, preferring to trust Loë rather than Lina. Rushing to wean her finally from morphia as the end of her analysis approached, Freud's efforts proved fruitless. As she finished, in early July

1914, she boosted her morphia intake to deal with increased pain. Freud was clearly disappointed at his lack of success.

Despite this failure, Freud's friendship with Loë was secure, secure enough to entrust his daughter Anna to her to take back to England in July 1914. When he suspected Ernest of amorous intentions vis-à-vis Anna, he warned his daughter off in no uncertain terms and suggested that she consult Loë on intimate sexual matters. The complex *ménage* thus still had life in it, as Anna dreamt not of the Jones whom Freud suspected of being always vulnerable to the 'devil of desire', but of the beautiful, charming and childless Loë. Even as he entertained Anna in late July 1914, Jones grumbled to her father that he had been indiscreet with Loë: 'She is trying hard to make mischief with Lina, whom she hates pretty strongly. Why did you tell her my remark about the morphia, which was meant only to give you a hint? Now she is cross with me over it.'

But no more letters were to arrive from Vienna, with Freud's explanation of his indiscretion. At the end of July, the First World War broke out. Perhaps the fact that war prevented Jones from ever receiving an explanation or apology from Freud explains why he thought fit to repeat the charge concerning Loë Kann, some forty years later, in his biography of Freud:

Freud was not a man who found it easy to keep someone else's secrets. ... I sent Freud some private information I thought he should have about a patient of mine [*sic*] he was treating – it was a question of surreptitious use of morphia – and told him it was important that the patient should not know of my communication. He wrote back assuring me he would keep the knowledge to himself, but it was not long before I received a furious letter from the patient complaining of my action.

Jones's view that Freud could not keep a secret went hand in hand with another weakness of his, one that was more ambiguous – his credulity and his obstinacy:

his resistiveness was a defence against the danger of being too readily influenced by others. With a patient he was treating before the war, whose life history I knew intimately, I would come across instance after instance where he was believing statements which I knew to be certainly untrue and also, incidentally, refusing to believe things that were as certainly true.

The old saga of Loë Kann's analysis with Freud supplied Jones with his best argument for this view of Freud's character. But one cannot help feeling that some old scores were still being settled in public here, just as Freud was to settle his old scores with Ferenczi and Anna von Vest in 'Analysis Terminable and Interminable'.

Loë's response to the declaration of war was idiosyncratic and entirely her own, as Jones noted: 'Loë is buying up large quantities of morphia to send to foreign armies, because when the supply of morphia runs short it will be given only to those likely to recover, while the hopeless must die in pain. Isn't she wonderful?' She and Davy also acquired an ambulance, which he drove while she looked after the men inside, the 'heavily wounded, who had been bombed out of hospital sometimes, and we armoured the ambulance to give them a feeling of protection when London was being bombed.' But her renal stones reappeared late in 1914, necessitating an operation. She grew fat while Davy developed chronic ill-health. At one point during the war, Loë decided that Davy's illness centred on his jealousy of Ernest, so she decided never to see Ernest again; she did not keep to her decision.

When the war ended, she wrote a long letter to Freud in which she characteristically cast her feelings about the war in terms of her intimates. She had come to hate all Germans, and to hate even Freud's soldier sons: it was either them or her beloved Davy. Her ambivalence betrayed itself in being loath to enter a 'German's' house:

I shall not nurse my hatred artificially: I'm willing to forget all I can, stuff it deep down in my unconscious (and don't you dare to dig it up with your Ψa) and I'm sure Time will help lots. But I'd feel an absolute skunk if I came to your house now, but I'd dearly love to see you and Anneri.

It was a difficult letter to write, since Freud was the one 'German' she tried to set aside from the class of hated Germans: 'I do hope you don't mind my sending this beastly brutal letter – *that's* what I resent: *having been made to feel like this*. Anyway – I have torn up 3 efforts and you'll understand! Like Heine's God: "c'est ton métier".' The Heine phrase had an echo for them both. She had quoted it in her first letter to Freud, before ever meeting him, when she was preparing to come to Vienna to start analysis. For Loë Kann, Freud was the nearest she would ever get to having a father-like god, whose profession was perfect understanding of her.

For this god, Loë came up with a decisive and charming solution to her reluctance at entering a 'Germanic' house. Jones told Freud about it in December 1919: 'Have you yet heard of her scheme for presenting you with a furnished house in the Hague (Kobus's [her brother], he having gone to live in Palestine), if you will consent to live there permanently?' Freud's reply to her renewing the friendship was characteristically courteous, although he was quizzical as to how she, as a Jew, could feel so much hatred. Freezing and half-starving in defeated Vienna, he still had the grace to enclose a gift of a small wooden box, inlaid with ivory. And she still found the bullying and coquettish spirit to deny his mortality:

It is all very well threatening me with your old age, but if you *dare* to leave this crazy world before we have met several times more, I'll pray God that all cigars in Heaven may be squashed and damp and rank! So there. I have been saving for you ever since the autumn of 1914 a large roll of cigar-holders (hundreds of 'em) which I hunted down (after many efforts) somewhere in Oxford. You told me they were the only good cigar case, and I enclose a sample to refresh your memory.

Her remarks about Ernest were nothing less than charmingly malicious: 'I wonder why he is such an incorrigible fibber (to put it politely!),' she mused, as she filled in on his latest antics as a self-important deceiver and snob, using his impending second marriage as the occasion for a bubbly, good-natured and utterly crushing character assassination of her former 'husband'.

Having failed to move Freud to The Hague, Loë and Davy Jones moved to the country for Davy's health, and Loë invited Freud to come and stay with their '2 dogs, 1 pet-cock, chickens, 1 donkey, 1 cat, 2 kittens & heaps of mosquitos & bumble bees.' Ernest described their *ménage* to Freud with a Loë-like eye for the ridiculous:

I must tell you the latest story of Loë. She replaced Trottie [the dog] by a more obvious symbol, a cock, who always slept in her bedroom. A time came when she had to go away for a while, so that he had to take his place with the hens in the fowl-coop. Lest, however, he should suffer from fear or loneliness in this unaccustomed environment she had her bed moved there also and slept there with him for the first two nights until he no longer found it strange. Of her health I have no news.

Loë and Davy moved back to London in 1923, since his health had not improved. In an undated letter to Freud, the last written by her that has survived, she opened with: 'You say that I've got to be angry before I write, so here goes.' The two topics that provoked her anger were: 1. Freud's 'horrid disease' – so that we can infer she is writing in 1923 or 1924; and 2. Anna's desire to pay off the Freud family's debt to Loë. Loë waxes lyrical in her anger at this insult to her friendship: '*we'd* accept money from *you* with absolute bliss, anytime we needed it, and you were willing to let us have it.' And she appends some pressed snowdrops to the letter, with the following, witty and ridiculing, bill:

COST of this little present (for future reference)
1. *Planted & cultivated* by Dame Nature: a free gift
2. *Manure*, supplied fresh daily, gratis from the birds
3. *Irrigation*, by God and our old dog, cost price
4. *Gathered by* me, in the middle of the night, in thin slippers in wet grass, in my nightie & in the drizzle, at the expense of my (absent) health.
Total cost: *Nix*. Signed L. K. J. witness HJ

Such is the last written evidence we have of Loë Kann Jones, Freud's 'treasure of a woman'. Sometime in early 1944, when Ernest Jones was recovering from a massive heart attack, Anna Freud informed him that Loë had recently died.

8

LOU ANDREAS-SALOMÉ: 'THE FORTUNATE ANIMAL'

Lou Andreas-Salomé arrived in Vienna to study psychoanalysis on 25 October 1912. She was fifty-one years old, a striking, splendidly female woman, with thick, wavy hair and clear, blue eyes. Pictures of the time show her swathed in vast furs: she looks bold, proud, confident, but also strangely innocent, confiding. Her notoriety as one of Central Europe's leading *femmes fatales* seems to sit on her lightly: there is nothing *soignée* about her. Nor is there anything to suggest the high seriousness of the unflinchingly independent bluestocking of rigorously philosophical formation. Lou is simply, grandly, Lou. Contemporary gossip and history may have placed her as many men's Woman — Nietzsche's, Rilke's, Freud's, sometimes even her husband's — but the only certainty about Lou is that she was first and foremost her own.

Frau Lou's reputation had, of course, preceded her in Freud's circle. She was known as the creator of numerous fictional heroines, many of them acclaimed as examples of the 'new woman': the dreaming ardent Ruth, who denies flesh and its attendant bonds of marriage to embrace the world of spirit; Fenitschka, who believes that sexual passion must be free, spontaneous, undemonic, 'like the good blessed bread eaten each day'; the painter, Adine, who rejects men when she recognizes that she can only be masochistically attracted to them; the widowed mother, Ma, who chooses a solitary loneliness over love's trap. The prolific, widely travelled and widely read Frau Lou was also known for her study of *Ibsen's Heroines* and for the first monograph on Friedrich Nietzsche, the philosopher 'who signified a nobility to which I could not attain' for the young Freud and whose thought was so rich — and one imagines so near to Freud's own — that he renounced the attempt to read too closely a thinker who 'had a more penetrating knowledge of himself than any other man who ever lived'.

But above all, in the hot house of gossip and ideas which was turn-of-the-century Vienna, the extraordinary Frau Lou was known as the particular friend of the great. Indeed, Lou's intimacies and acquaintanceships constituted a contemporary European hall of cultural fame. Nietzsche and Rainer Maria Rilke apart, there were, to name only a few, the dramatist, Gerhard Hauptmann; the socialist politician, Georg Ledebour; the director, Max Reinhardt; the feminist, Helene Stöcker, writer-explorer Frieda von Bülow and the influential popularizer of Darwin, Wilhelm Bölsche, in Berlin; the writers Frank Wedekind (whose 'earthspirit', Lulu, owes something to Lou), Max Halbe and Jakob Wasserman in Munich; and in Vienna, Breuer's close friend Marie von Ebner Eschenbach, Hugo von Hoffmanstahl and the man Freud liked to see as his literary double, Arthur Schnitzler.

Little wonder then that Freud, feeling somewhat embattled by the splits amongst his followers and by the continued resistance to psychoanalysis in the psychiatric establishment, welcomed the arrival of Frau Lou. Despite what he initially called her 'dangerous intelligence', he saw her interest in psychoanalysis as 'a favourable omen'. His obituary of her states it firmly: 'I am not saying too much if I acknowledge that we all felt it as an honour when she joined the ranks of our collaborators and comrades in arms, and at the same time as a fresh guarantee of the truth of the theories of analysis.'

This sense of Lou's usefulness to the analytic cause, of her acting as its guarantor, is one of the first notes sounded in her relationship with Freud. It is instantly joined by a second note, a scepticism, however courteous, surrounding her abilities as a theorist. In January 1912, Jung had written to Freud concerning an article on 'Sublimation' (the correct analytic, rather than chemical, term was 'Sublimierung', though Nietzsche had used 'Sublimation') which Frau Lou of Weimar fame had submitted to the Jahrbuch, which then only had a circulation among specialists. Jung noted the publication of the article, 'if it amounts to anything, would be a step towards the "secularization" of the Jahrbuch, a step to be taken with great caution but one which would widen the readership and mobilize the intellectual forces in Germany, where Frau Lou enjoys a considerable literary reputation because of her relations with Nietzsche.' Freud answered: 'We ought not in principle to decline, provided she contents herself with sublimation and leaves sublimates to the chemists. If it turns out to be idealistic chit-chat, we can reject it politely but firmly.'

This clatter of male intellectual superiority grows faint without ever altogether disappearing in the face of the third and omnipresent note in the Freud–Salomé relationship. Karl Abraham sounds it first in his letter of 28 April 1912, recommending Lou to Freud: 'I have never met anyone with so deep and subtle an understanding of psychoanalysis.'

Over the course of the next twenty-five years, Lou emerges as the great 'understander' of Freud and of Freudian metapsychology, as well as of her patients. The same age as Martha, and Freud's partner in the analysis of 'Daughter-Anna', it would be appropriate to see Lou as the mother of psychoanalysis: the good mother whose life-loving optimism imbues all her writings, which appropriately focus on female sexuality, on love and on questions of narcissism and sexual difference. The mother, too, whose roots (like Jung's) lie in turn-of-the-century romantic Lebensphilosophie, that peculiarly German hankering after that oceanic spirituality, that sense of wholeness, which Freud had rejected and which Lou never altogether leaves behind. Lou, in this optic, becomes the Aryan partner Jung had failed to be.

Decidedly her own 'sovereign' person at a time when that did not come easily, Lou was 'a remarkable woman', as Freud noted in his obituary, and one devoid of 'all feminine frailties and perhaps most human frailties'. She was glad to be female and, in the midst of all her pre-eminent men, she saw women as the superior and happier sex. Men and women both were drawn to her, admired her, saw their ideas reflected in the subtly responsive mirror of her mind, loved her and remained her friends. Though Lou never gave *herself* away, she had a gift for identifying with what her lovers and friends held dear and bolstering where support was needed. In that sense, she was a superb psychologist. Nietzsche called her 'shrewd as an eagle and brave as a lion, and yet still a very girlish child'. Anna Freud noted that 'the unusual thing about her was what ought actually to be quite usual in a human being – honesty, directness, absence of any weakness, self-assertion without selfishness.' The portrait Rilke draws is perhaps most evocative:

This woman has the ability to penetrate the most marvellous, the most splendid things; she turns all that books and people bring her at the right moment into the most blessed comprehension; she understands, loves, and moves fearlessly among the most burning mysteries. These do nothing to her, only beam at her with pure firelight. I know no one else – and since those far-off years when she first met me and brought such infinite significance into my life I've never known anyone else – who had life so much on their side. ...

Lou's life – a life which has all the inflections of high romance – began on 12 February 1861 in St Petersburg, capital of Imperial Russia, where her father, a Baltic German of Huguenot descent, was a general who moved in elevated aristocratic circles. Her mother, Louise, had previously given birth to five sons and little Louise von Salomé or Lyolya's arrival – just three weeks before the emancipation of the serfs – in the family's sumptuous apartment in the General Staff building across from the Winter Palace, was the occasion for numerous congratulations, including a message from the Tsar.

In her memoir, *Lebensrückblick*, Lou describes the warmth and affection which attended family life, her father's chivalrous, passionate nature, her mother 'Mouchka's' sincere piety and courageous rectitude. It was the atmosphere of love and fidelity which enveloped the family, she writes, that created in her a trusting confidence, a belief in gifts and an attendant sense of gratitude. To illustrate how deeply rooted this childhood aura of benevolence can become, she tells a story from her old age:

Walking in the woods one day, I happened upon some blue gentians which I would have liked to bring to a sick friend. But I was so buried in the thoughts that I wanted to pursue during this morning stroll, that I talked myself out of the wearisome act of picking them. A little while later, when I was on my way home, I was astounded to find the richly round bouquet in my hand. ... I could have sensed this as a miracle. But not at all. Nor did my 'distraction' make me laugh. My first reaction was a feeling of pure joy and I heard myself shout, 'Thank-you.'

Throughout her days, Lou never lost the feeling that life, with all its horrors, was bounteous and beneficent; that some benign power construed out of the paradise of early childhood was looking after her. And she was always grateful.

It is this constellation of intuitions and attitudes which shapes her later understanding of femininity and of feminine narcissism as a positive force. For Lou, the feminine in its essence partakes of a 'primordial fusion with the All in which we repose'.

With her father, who was fifty-seven when she was born, the young Lou had 'a secret bond of affection', a manifest tenderness which was hidden when her mother, who didn't believe in overt displays of sentiment, walked into the room. It was her father whose arm she held on their various walks through St Petersburg; her father, too, who taught her the important lesson of not giving *all* her allowance to one of the many street beggars, but of dividing it in appropriate parts. When the family dog had rabies, Lou's greatest fear was that she would catch it and bite her father. Towards her mother, there was more evident ambivalence. Lou recalls how when very young and watching her mother swim, she shouted, 'Dear mother, please drown.'

The St Petersburg childhood instilled in Lou a sense of her own specialness. She was distinct by wealth, rank and nationality. At home, German and French were spoken rather than Russian; the family religion was a pietist Protestantism and not the common Russian orthodoxy which her mother considered uncivilized. Unlike Kafka, say, whose feeling of difference resulted in a profound sense of alienation, Lou's encased her in the good fortune of specialness and made her value everything that distinguished itself by an intensity or excellence of feeling and thinking. 'Home' was so thoroughly grounded in her that even if it were not here, it was elsewhere and she belonged in it. It was this sense of at-homeness in the world which permitted her to flout convention and to embark on what was a singular trajectory for her, and indeed for any, time.

Lou's specialness extended to her very sex: a single girl amidst five brothers, though these soon dwindled to three. Her childhood idea of women's internal organs was that they were 'like the inside of the mountains filled with precious stones'. Her favourite fairy tale evoked a Russian princess 'from whose mouth jewels gushed with every word'. The mirror of brothers cast a favourable reflection, which never disappeared. It also gave her a sense of happy kinship with the male sex. 'The feeling of being tied to men by fraternal bonds was so evident for me in the family circle', she writes in her memoir, 'that it radiated out to all the men in the world.' Her 'openness and trustfulness' towards men, the confidence of 'belonging among older male persons', the sense, which Freud often teased Lou about, of the world – and the psycho-analytic circle – as inhabited by good brothers never left her, even in her moments of greatest self-doubt.

Despite her loving brothers and parents, Lou was a lonely, inward-looking child for whom fantasy and daydream acquired a very particular reality, one which often took precedence over shared events. She would weave elaborate stories around the passers-by in the St Petersburg streets. When, with the years, the burden of these intricate imaginings grew too great for her memory, she began to write down the detailed histories of the inhabitants of her invented world. At first this day dream sphere was suffused with the 'fine glow' of her unquestioning faith in God, a God who was her earliest memory and who existed secretly and solely for her. She told him everything and he listened so well that she assumed a dialogue, never questioning his inaudibility or invisibility. But one day she demanded an answer, which didn't come. God and her belief in him vanished simultaneously. So crucial was this loss of faith that Lou makes it the originary experience of her memoir.

One icy winter's day a servant from the family's country estate told Lou that he had seen a couple standing in front of her own little summer house and hoping to come in. Lou worried about them and feared that they would suffer cold and hunger. When the servant came to see her on his next visit to St Petersburg, she asked him where the couple had gone. He told her that they hadn't gone, but had simply grown thinner and thinner until they had disappeared and one morning, when he was sweeping the ground, he had found only their traces in buttons and hat and frozen tears.

Lou was devastated by what an adult would have termed a sense of the insubstantiality of things, of the transience of life. She demanded an explanation from God, a simple affirmation. 'Mr and Mrs Snow' would have done. But nothing came. Unbelief invaded her. Her sheltering God, who fused both mother and father and held in his pockets all the gifts in the world, melted away. And in the wake of his disappearance came a barren gloom, a desolating burden of responsibility for her own imaginings.

Lou later claimed that her loss of faith at so early an age – before rational doubt was possible – enabled her forever to maintain the childlike *feeling* of faith without any equivalent need for an object of belief. Certainly her life-long and strangely generous self-sufficiency, a state of being she came to give expression to in her ideas about narcissism, acts as proof of her own interpretation.

Her story of her first encounters with a mirror provides further insight into this aspect of her character. When as a child she looked into the mirror, she was astounded to discover that she was only what she saw: a being enclosed in narrow limits and constrained not to exist in other objects. Away from the mirror, she refused this lack of extension. Her sense that the physical was not an insurmountable boundary, that the visible and material did not define the limits of self or imagination, that there was no inviolable breach between self and other, persisted throughout her life. She had a 'solidarity in fate with everything' that exists, big or small. Lou later identified this feeling with the feminine in her, an emphasis that transcended the masculine impetus to reason which separated and divided.

Lou's father died when she was seventeen. The event coincided with her open breach with the parental religion and hence with the one community in Russia she knew – the German Protestants. She had for some time been preparing for her confirmation with the family minister, Pastor Dalton. His dogmatic narrow-mindedness and woolly arguments incensed her, and Lou delayed the date of her confirmation. Meanwhile, she went to hear Hendrik Gillot, the unorthodox pastor of Petersburg's most fashionable Protestant church and a known opponent of Dalton's. Gillot was by all accounts both a rigorous thinker and an impassioned orator and, as soon as she saw him, Lou had that sense of immanent recognition that characterized the beginning of all her important relationships. She describes it thus:

childish dreams and fantasies were integrated into reality. A flesh and blood being took their place: he didn't come to *join* them, but he united them, embodying in himself all reality. The revolution he caused in me can only be translated by the words, 'a human being'. It was the most surprising and unbelievable and at the same time the most familiar thing – the one I had always awaited.

Gillot filled the place that God had left, was at once embodiment and representative, the gift good faith awaited and instantly acknowledged. As Nietzsche and particularly Freud were to become, he was the teacher who chased away her phantoms and pointed her in the direction of truth.

Lou wrote to Gillot a polite but ardent letter, describing herself as a girl 'lonely in the midst of her family and surroundings, lonely in the sense that no one shares her views, let alone satisfies her longing for fuller knowledge.' She began secretly to see Gillot and to study with him. He took her through the history of philosophy and comparative religion. She read Kant with him and studied Spinoza, the thinker to whom she was most attracted, as well as Kierkegaard, Rousseau, Fichte and Schopenhauer. In her largely auto-biographical novel, *Ruth* (1895), she describes the course of what was a fervent relationship, the pain it cost her to yield her imaginary world to Gillot, the force of his intellectual clarity and the absolute trust she put in him. The lessons were intense, mentally and emotionally taxing, and once she fainted while sitting, as she often did, on his lap. Physical proximity was not uncommon between them, though only later did it develop an erotic overtone. When Lou realized that Gillot, who at thirty-seven was married with two grown children, had begun to make 'family arrangements for a union with me', she was horrified. 'With a single blow, what I had worshipped dropped out of my heart and senses and became alien.' The sudden revelation that Gillot, whom she had trusted as a guide on the demanding by-ways of spirit and intellect, should be a mere man with a man's needs, was a devastating parallel to her earlier disappointment in God. Lou, already weakened by the exertions of her studies, fell ill with a pulmonary haemorrhage.

The Gillot experience was the formative one of her adolescence. In retrospect, she realized her own failure as well as his. Slow to develop physically, she had been unable first consciously to recognize and then to respond to his needs. Her own desire was directed at something bigger than the man. Nor perhaps was the young Lou altogether unaware of the kind of subjection that a physical and permanent link with Gillot would entail. In her early fictions, though her heroines were often willing fervently to worship and to subjugate themselves to supposedly superior intellectual men, to yield sexually ran the risk of imprisonment, a masochistic trap of which Lou, though she toyed with it, was always mistrustful.

In February 1879, in the midst of Lou's relationship with Gillot, her father died. It was then that she told her mother that she had secretly been seeing the rival pastor. Distracted, her mother said to a relative that she had had to call on all her moral strength to get over this shock: she described Lou as a 'stubborn girl who always and in everything insists on her own way.' Lou got it. Her mother allowed the lessons with Gillot to continue and, when Lou broke with him, she took her ailing daughter to Zurich. Since a passport required church membership, Gillot arranged a special permit for Lou and a church ceremony, which included the text from *Isaiah 43*: 'Fear not, for I have redeemed you; I have called you by your name.' The name he gave her, since he found it difficult to pronounce Lyolya, was Lou.

During the year she spent in Zurich, Lou studied logic, metaphysics and history at the university. She also wrote poems. Though these, like so much of her writing, ring with an effusive and overblown romanticism, a diffuse sexuality somewhat embarrassing to contemporary ears, they were admired at the time. One of these early poems, '*Lebensgebet*' (Prayer to Life) was to be set to music by Nietzsche and come Freud's way. The erotic charge of the poem, the fact that though a love poem, it invokes 'life' in terms usually directed at either man or God, is pure Lou – here, an adolescent Lou hungering for an intensity of pleasure and if not that, as the final stanza of the poem states, an intensity of pain:

> If you have no more joy to give me –
> Millennia-long to live! To think!
> Clasp me in both your arms:
> Well, you still have your pain.

This summoning of all that life at its most extreme could bring struck a chord in Nietzsche, who called the poem heroic. Freud, on the other hand, who thought at first that the poem had been written by Nietzsche, told Lou that a good head cold would quickly cure him of the desire expressed in the poem's last stanza. The responses characterize the differences between the two men. It is telling that Lou, who never altogether lost her youthful heroic ardour and lived by the precept that intensity is all, could wholeheartedly admire both men.

Lou met Nietzsche in April 1882 in Rome, where she was staying with her mother. She was twenty-one, an exceptional young woman, with what contemporaries described as a cold, analytical and male intelligence, yet extremely amiable, sincere and friendly. The idealist feminist, Malwida von Meysenbug, had taken Lou under her wing and introduced her to the positivist philosopher, Paul Rée, a kind, reliable, melancholy man, who frequented her salon. Rée grew rapidly enamoured of Lou, who, on those midnight walks with him which threatened her reputation, fervently engaged *only* in philosophical debate. He proposed to her and was rejected, a rejection he seems to have accepted quietly since he thought himself a fundamentally unattractive and unloveable man. But Lou, with her hunger for ideas, won Rée over to her radically unconventional dream of living fraternally together in a small, sexless, intellectual community. Her notion brings to mind a monastic Oxford or Cambridge in which Lou, flirting with sexuality but keeping it at bay, chooses for herself only the most exceptional dons and Socratic exchange takes place from morn to midnight. It was Rée who suggested his admired friend Nietzsche as the third member of this community. Malwida von Meysenbug, though she worried about the way Lou flouted public opinion, interestingly approved of her as a 'companion' for Nietzsche and wrote to the philosopher, recommending her young protégée. Nietzsche was in Messina and was summoned to Rome to meet Lou.

Nietzsche, aged thirty-seven and 'seven-eighths blind', had just finished *The Gay Science*. Zarathustra was already in his mind, that figure who joyfully heralds a transformation of values and beckons in an era of higher beings. Personally, however, Nietzsche was lonely and somewhat isolated, and he was instantly taken with the young Russian woman who listened and argued so intensely and whose free spirit easily followed the flow of his thought. Lou's particular brand of ardent discipleship spoke to him and he considered marriage, a proposal deflected by the still adamantly virginal Lou, sometime during their subsequent meetings in Orta in Northern Italy, where she was travelling with her mother in May, and then in Lucerne. It was in Lucerne that the photograph which shows a kneeling Lou in a cart taking a whip to her two companions was taken.

Whatever the erotic connotations of this image, it is clear that Lou and Nietzsche remained only 'friends' during the eight months of their relationship, much of which evolved in letters. None the less, there is little doubt that Lou was his single mature passion. It is also not unlikely that her sexual refusal was a relief to him. Certainly, his early talk of marriage was quickly forgotten as relations progressed with this 'bold and rich soul', whom he initially saw as his 'heir'. They were kindred spirits, their intelligence and tastes 'related at the deepest level', sharing what he called a 'sibling brain', the 'urge to give oneself up to a great aim'. In their heroic ideal of voluntary suffering for the sake of truth and knowledge, in their particular religiousness without deity, in their outspoken embrace of a morality which went beyond any traditional understanding of good and evil, they were one.

Gillot, whom Lou had written to from Rome about her plans for living in a fraternal community, chastized her severely for again embarking on childish projects. Her eloquently defiant response to him is a clear indication of the motor forces of her character:

I can neither live according to models nor shall I ever be a model for anyone; on the contrary – what I shall certainly do is construct my own life according to myself, come whatever may of it. In this I have no principle to represent, but something far more wonderful – something that is inside oneself and is hot with sheer life, and rejoices and wants to get out. You also write that you had always considered this sort of wholehearted giving up of oneself to purely intellectual goals only as a 'transition' for me. What do you mean by 'transition'? If there are supposed to be other goals, goals which would make one give up the most magnificent and most hard-won thing on earth, namely freedom, then I want to stay forever in this transition, for I shall not give that up.

Defying all conventions, Lou lived out her 'project', convincing her recalcitrant mother that life with Rée was part of her study plan. Rée's mother would act as their chaperone on the Rée family estate in Stibbe in Germany, where she and Rée would live fraternally. Rée's sole aim, he told Lou in a letter in August 1882, was to be her '*Hüsung*': 'that you have a home in me. Someone on whom you can securely rely in the great world, who, except for his book, regards you as the sole task of his life.' Nietzsche, meanwhile, was the great heroic teacher. From her home with Rée, Lou travelled in August 1882 to spend three weeks with Nietzsche in the village of Tautenburg in Thuringen. On the way there, she stopped in Bayreuth, met Wagner and his circle and also Nietzsche's rigorously conventional sister, Elisabeth, who instantly took a jealous dislike of the uninhibited Lou. None the less, the two women continued their journey together and, despite a heated row about the saintliness or otherwise of Nietzsche's character, they stayed together in the same house in Tautenburg. Here between the perpetual and peaceful exchanges which filled Lou and Nietzsche's days, the women's rows continued, always and ever turning on the subject of what Elizabeth considered Lou's flagrant sexuality.

Nietzsche wrote to his friend Paul Overbeck about Lou: 'Our intelligence and tastes are related at the deepest point. ... I wonder if there has ever existed before such a philosophical openness as exists between us. ... I have never known anyone who could draw from their experiences so many *objective insights*, or anyone who knew how to derive so much from everything they'd learnt.' Lou, it seems, held her own with this kindred spirit, though it is hardly surprising that the twenty-one year old's thinking on religion, on love, on woman, should be profoundly marked by her understanding of the period's greatest philosopher. What is surprising, however, is that faced with Nietzsche's incisive intelligence, Lou was none the less capable of forming her own views and keeping a measure of independent criticality. Nor was she submerged by Nietzsche's overarching mysogyny. As her diary of that time shows, Nietzsche's nihilism, his scathing mockery, already separated them. It was this nihilism which formed one aspect of her critique of Nietzsche in the important book she was to write about him twelve years later. By then Nietzsche's last works had been published, and Lou condemned what she understood to be his praise of criminals, his attacks on democracy, his insistence on disorder and cruelty as necessary steps towards the creation of the Superman, that ideal who for her is ultimately an aesthetic image – a 'Supernietzsche'.

Lou's posture towards life was always one of reverence. Though she shared Nietzsche's disposition towards excess and his heroic suffering for truth, though she valued any emotion or thought which ruptured mundane stabilities, she couldn't follow him into the void where language and meaning itself stood to be reinvented. Lou was not an adept at Nietzsche's particular masquerade of irony. In herself, however, she incorporated so many of the elements that Nietzsche postulated it was necessary to strive for, that it was almost as if she had bypassed any tedious stage of 'overcoming' and was by nature the 'Overman' who was soon to emerge from his pen. Vigorous, unconventional, guiltless, intense in feeling and in her intellectual pursuits, Lou seemed the very embodiment of his philosophy. Little wonder that he saw her as 'a genius and of quite heroic character', 'prepared, as no other person is, for the hitherto unexpressed part of my philosophy'.

Whether in part because of this over-idealization, certainly in part because of his jealously protective sister's poisoning invective against Lou, Nietzsche had turned fiercely against her by the end of 1882. Rée, Nietzsche and Lou had spent three weeks together in Leipzig in the autumn of 1882 and then Lou had returned to Rée to nestle in the wing of his 'supraterrestrial kindness' and to take in the cooler air of his stringent analytic mind. It is telling that though she calmly measured their differences and valued Nietzsche's greater depth, Lou chose to live with Rée in a sheltered equality. Throughout her life this pattern of two men – one 'safe' or made safe, the other passionate and potentially dangerous – persisted.

Lou's link with Rée, together with Elisabeth Nietzsche's repeated slanders and her insistence that Lou was maligning him, resulted in Nietzsche excoriating Lou after the weeks in Leipzig as violently as he had previously praised her. Perhaps inevitably, he also jealously maligned Rée. Lou now became the caricature of Nietzsche's ideals, a beast of prey masquerading as a domestic animal, a brain with an appendage of soul, faithless and shameless with a cruel sensuality cunningly deployed against men.

By August 1883, with *Thus Spake Zarathustra* finished, Nietzsche stopped cursing Lou. He now saw that his sister had harmed him by severing his relationship with her and Rée, and he told Elisabeth: 'Of all acquaintances I have made the most valuable and full of consequence is the one with Fräulein Salomé. Only since knowing her was I ripe for my Zarathustra.' When Lou's first novel, *Struggling for God*, appeared in 1885, he wrote to a friend and fairly assessed its strengths and weaknesses, saying that though it was girlish and in some ways absurd, it was serious and lofty. The book, published under the pseudonym Henri Lou, combines Lou's two main formative experiences to date: a Nietzschean hero, who happily endures pain and for whom God is a mistake, enters into an intensely holy and Gillot-like love for a young girl. When this topples over into sexuality, disaster ensues. It was of this book that Nietzsche made the statement that has haunted Lou's reputation ever since: 'and if it is certainly not the Eternal-Feminine that draws this girl onward, perhaps it is the Eternal-Masculine.' In the male mirror through which she is most often reflected, Lou appears as either the *femme fatale*, who pursues men only destructively then to reject them, or a striving bluestocking, conventional sufferer of a masculinity complex. These negative designations refuse Lou's salient characteristic, her unquestioned, almost innocent, assumption of independence – as if nothing in life had made her aware of the fact that women were not meant to enter into relationships and leave them as they chose without displaying overt wounds; or live seemingly unencumbered lives of the mind and still remain attractive.

Elisabeth Nietzsche, despite her brother's change of heart, continued to spread slanderous and salacious falsehoods about Lou well after Nietzsche's death. She said of Lou's book on Nietzsche – written because Lou felt that current commentators had misunderstood him – that it was the 'revenge of a woman whose vanity has been wounded, who attacks a poor invalid'. Elisabeth evoked a scandalous Lou, hated by Nietzsche: an ugly, pleasure-seeking, Finnish-Jewish (since Elisabeth was notoriously anti-Semitic) adventuress who had had a notorious affair with a priest in St Petersburg, presumably Gillot. Lou never responded to Elisabeth's diatribes, nor to those of any of the loyal keepers of Nietzsche's flame who read history through Elisabeth's eyes. In May 1932, fifty years after the original meeting between Lou and Nietzsche, Freud wrote to her to say:

I am very pleased to hear that you are working at your memoirs. It has often annoyed me to find your relationship to Nietzsche mentioned in a way which was obviously hostile to you and which could not possibly correspond with the facts. You have put up with everything and have been far too decent; I hope that now at last you will defend yourself, even though in the most dignified way.

Lou characteristically chose not to sully her memoir with poison: Elisabeth's part in turning Nietzsche against her, her repeated slanders, never appear in the book. Lou makes no attempt to counteract the flow of rumours. Interestingly, too, her chapter on this part of her life gives Nietzsche no undue emphasis: what she evokes is the fraternal threesome – Rée, Nietzsche, Salomé – under the title, 'Experience of Friendship'. Whatever the salon gossip, Lou certainly never considered herself Nietzsche's woman.

Paul Rée was more important to her. Until the mid-1880s, they defied bourgeois morality, travelled together and shared a home in Berlin, if not a bed and a marriage. More importantly, they shared a life of intellectual equals, writing and studying, gathering around them a salon of historians, critics, natural scientists and philosophers. Gradually, however, they grew apart, perhaps because of the success of Lou's book and the failure of Rée's to gain him the academic post he hoped for. Rée determined to study medicine and moved to Munich, living with Lou only on weekends. Then with a suddenness which mystified all her friends, since she had previously refused all offers of marriage, Lou, in November 1886, became engaged to Friedrich Carl Andreas, an Orientalist, a passionate teacher who imbued his students with long-lasting devotion. Rée, disconsolate, despite Lou's promises of their friendship continuing unchanged, left her. She was never to see him again, except in her dreams where he appeared with uncanny frequency. The loss of this friendship was one she felt above all others and she spoke of it until late in life as 'the irreparable'. Rée dedicated his remaining and reclusive years to working as a doctor with the poor. In October 1901, he fell to his death from a steep cliff in the Engadine, where he and Lou had walked together in happier times.

The death shook and haunted her. She told a friend that she had reread all of Rée's letters and understood many things: 'I've had too much! Too many good things for a single life. That makes one humble.'

Lou's relationship to Andreas, like so much else about her, fits into no ready-made categories. Perhaps its very strangeness was partly responsible for making Lou so alert to questions about the nature of love and men and women, and eventually to the power of the unconscious. Lou 'recognized' Andreas as soon as he came through the door of the boarding-house where she then lived. What she recognized was the force of a pre-existing bond between them, the voice of an 'inner command', which made their union a necessity. This sense of recognition, which Lou never characterizes as the more traditional blinding of chemistry or sexual appeal, suggests the return of a childhood constellation: a powerful and inescapable paternal figure. The fact that the twenty-four-year-old Lou felt required by the inner command never to consummate her marriage with the forty-year-old Andreas points to another buried childhood prohibition: against incest.

Lou's continuing resistance to sex, however, seems to call for more than an explanation based on incestuous fears. In her fictions, sexual desire is an overpowering force, so strong that its fulfilment shatters the woman's individuality. The strength of the desire is only equalled by the strength of the resistance to it – a refusal to succumb to disintegration; and, more simply, to have freedom constrained. This fear in Lou has a shadow side. Desire is so intense, the man who elicits it is so awesome in his power, that there is a fear that in desire's fulfilment, both intensity and power may melt away. The man would then become merely man; Lou's charged and benevolent universe would be ruptured by the disappearance of its controlling force. Reading between the lines of Lou's considerable oeuvre, it would seem that Lou's greatest fear remained throughout her life a fear of loss, of a diminishment in plenitude, almost of a spiritual aridity. Once she had encountered sexual love, she saw it as a spiritual and physical aggrandizement. Never, even in her psychoanalytic days, did sex become a Freudian discharge of energies or simply pleasure, but rather a voluptuous fusion with the wonderful vitality and fullness of life.

To show how far from rational choice Lou's insistence on her virginity then was, she tells a story from the early days of her marriage to Andreas. In the midst of an afternoon nap, she was woken by a strange sound and by the sensation that her arms were not where they should be, but above her. When she opened her eyes, she found that her hands were around Andreas's throat, strangling him. The noise that had woken her was the rattle of his throat. He had tried to take her in her sleep.

The sexual prohibition was never broken, though the marriage remained intact until Andreas's death at the age of eighty-four. Despite her independent professional pursuits and the eventual list of her lovers, this was Lou's only marriage. She always returned to Andreas and from 1904 to *Loufried*, their home in Göttingen, where Andreas came to hold a university post.

Marriage, for Lou, it seems, could only be unconventional. Her diary of her Tautenburg days with Nietzsche had noted, in terms that lack the epigrammatic fineness of her teacher's, that marriage was a sphere of triviality which killed love and was thus less important than friendship. Lou, intent on intensity, married without entering into marriage. Appropriately – though only within the contours of Lou's altogether extraordinary psychic map – Lou prevailed upon her mentor and former suitor, Gillot, to preside over the religious ceremony which sanctioned her marriage. She remained in her own way as faithful to Gillot, whom for years she returned to see on her regular visits home to St Petersburg, as she did to Andreas.

Lou described her affinity with Andreas as a 'creaturely' kneeling before a power greater than them both. She was enthralled by his extraordinary intensity: a violence which expressed itself in an early suicide attempt in front of her just before their engagement; and a greater than usual sensitivity, a kinship with animals and plants which she learned to love through him. She was happy to follow him wherever his work might lead him, and she did. For the first ten years of their married life, it is probable that Lou, despite her ample and increasingly separate social and intellectual life, despite, too, the ardent pursuits of a number of admirers, maintained her magical virginity. Later in life, she recalled Joan of Arc and how in school she had been taught that there is nothing on earth so powerful that a pure virgin cannot achieve it. She noted, too, that it was a mistake to cease valuing virginity in girls, since it could lead them to intellectual productivity, even to heroism.

Certainly these early years of Lou's marriage were marked by productivity and a growing reputation as a writer. She became a well-known figure in the literary salons of Munich and Berlin. Her essays had a wide circulation and the theory of religious *Rückwirkung*, or back-effect, she developed at this time continued to be discussed well into this century. Lou's basic notion, influenced by Nietzsche, is that the divine has a history in two stages. First man made god(s) and worshipped him. Then this deity invented by humans made man into god-made man, that is, man with a need for a god to satisfy his aspirations and explain his idealisms and nature's mysteries. These needs, like Lou's childhood ones, survive the death of god, who continues to have an influence on man after his demise. Lou's essay, *Jesus the Jew*, marked the point of her first contact with Rilke, who recognized his own notions in Lou's thinking.

Lou's study of *Ibsen's Heroines* (1892) was the first monograph on Ibsen to be written by a woman. Using the central motif of the wild duck – whom she sees as a symbol of the positive striving towards a boundless freedom, towards everything that is nobler and grander than the arid prison of the bourgeois marriage – Lou interprets six of Ibsen's heroines and measures them against the ideal of the wild duck. Lou was also undoubtedly measuring herself. 'Marriage' with Andreas in the early days had inevitable constrictions, including depression verging on joint suicide during the socialist politician, Georg Ledebour's hot pursuit of Lou. And when Lou says of Nora that 'not for the sake of liberty does Nora wish to free herself, but only for the purpose of discovering her full resources ... as a fully conscious human being', it is only one of the many places where we hear Lou's autobiographical voice.

Lou's *Friedrich Nietzsche in his Works*, sadly dedicated to a 'stranger', namely the estranged Paul Rée, appeared in 1894. It is amongst the finest of her books, written with a firm, unadorned clarity, which in other works too often bows before a sweep of unspecific poetic images and intricate psychologizing. Perhaps Lou here remembered the lessons in writing Nietzsche had given her in Tautenburg, his councils against lengthiness, unfelt thoughts and the lure of the poetic – as well as Rée's precision. Though Elisabeth Nietzsche attacked the book vociferously, Nietzsche's friend, Peter Gast, applauded it as 'an extraordinary achievement' and, waxing lyrical, extolled Lou's 'mind, her spirit and understanding which is of a kind that only appears four or five times in a century amongst women'. Lou begins her study by quoting from *Human all too Human*: 'However far a person may reach with his knowledge, however objective he may seem to himself, he finally takes nothing away but his own biography.' Lou was concerned to show how for Nietzsche 'the outer work of the intellect and the inner image of the life' coincided completely. It is an appropriate starting-point for a woman whose own work was infused by her biography and who was to turn to psychoanalysis, the theory and practice built upon the assumption of reflexivity. Interestingly, Anna Freud, writing to Lou in 1923, after she had read the book, asks with girlish excitement: 'Was it not written very long before your analytic period? ... But so much in it has an altogether analytic tone. Did people then already think like this or was it all only your very own perception?'

By the time Lou met Rilke in May 1897, she was an established writer; he, thirteen years younger than her, was a youthful poet still only recognized by a few. Textual evidence suggests that he was her first lover: 'If for years I was your wife, it was because you were something *real* to me for the first time, at once and inseparably man and body....' Certain commentators, however, have suggested that there were other firsts, perhaps the Viennese doctor, Friedrich Pineles, known as Zemek, whom Lou called her 'good blessed bread', a phrase she repeats in her fiction, *Fenitschka* (1896), as a description of simple and healthy love. She was certainly pregnant by Pineles in 1902, only to lose the child, either by miscarriage or abortion because to divorce Andreas was impossible. It is this event Freud undoubtedly refers to in his obituary of her when he writes: 'It was in Vienna that long ago the most moving episode of her feminine fortunes had been played out.' However, it is perhaps more in the character of Lou's magical virginity and her fictionally expressed fears of subjugation to imagine Rilke, young, at once 'vulnerable and so male', as her first lover.

Whatever the case, her intimacy with Rilke lasted for four years and was then, after a rupture, transformed into a friendship which endured until his death. Indeed, on his death-bed in 1926, Rilke asked his doctors to call for Lou: 'Ask Lou what is wrong with me. She is the only one who knows.' Throughout his letters to her – which form one of the greatest of all literary correspondences of this century – the phrases 'You alone know who I am,' 'You alone are real' echo. His *Book of Hours* is dedicated to her, 'Laid in the hands of Lou'; the language he uses about her in his letters merges in his poems with the language he uses about God. He sees her and idolizes her as boundlessly generous, a good mother, who makes his terrors bearable and shields him from them – a mother who is also 'home', the home which for Lou was always happiness. Her presence is so directly and indirectly woven into his work that its manifestations are too numerous to chart here. It is worth noting, however, her kinship with that narcissistically perfected being, distant from all anguish, who is the Angel of the *Duino Elegies*. Lou, Rilke's earliest 'editor', also influenced his feeling for Russia, where they twice travelled together, once with Andreas, and his thinking about religion, the matter of their earliest discussions. Perhaps Lou's ultimate and benevolent importance for him can best be gleaned in the statement he made to Marie von Thurn und Taxis in 1924: 'without the influence of this extraordinary woman my whole development would not have been able to take the paths that have led to many things.' It was Lou who 'masculinized' Rilke, urging him to change his name from René to Rainer.

For Lou, Rilke acted as a release into love, a love which didn't require subjugation or a fracturing of herself since it was a meeting between 'whole' people, both conscious of the male and female in themselves, a union, she later writes, like that between brother and sister in a distant age before incest became sacrilegious. He made her grow into her youth 'for only now am I young, only now may I be what others are at eighteen: wholly myself'. Reversing the usual course of human, and particularly female, development, Lou began with intellectual dedication and only then proceeded to love and sexual awakening. At the age of thirty-five, she was launched into the world of love.

Sexual passion, love, now emerged as a primary concern in that prolific succession of novels, stories and essays which span the period of her affair with Rilke up until her encounter with psychoanalysis. Certain of Lou's preoccupations at this time run parallel to Rilke's: the purity of sexuality which has needlessly been sullied; the fusion (or the terrible rupture) between inner and outer, the self and the world, the spiritual and the physical. But the inflection is altogether Lou's own. As is the language: Lou has a propensity to rhapsodize, to evoke a superabundance of images, to throw a heavy curtain of rhetoric over her subject, to indulge in lofty philosophical flights. It is not a style which accommodates itself to English or to contemporary ears. The subject matter however retains its resonance and has in some instances a feminist ring. In *Fenitschka*, we see a young woman's intellectual passion replaced by physical passion, in a fiction which is a hymn to sexual spontaneity, a celebration of an open and noble sexuality which cannot exist in the constraints of marriage. In the collection *Children of Man* (1899), Lou explores the differing fates of women in love: several of the stories show women embracing an ample solitude, resisting the ties which men embody. It is almost as if, for Lou, men, passion, are only a step on the path to something at once more heroic and more abstract. Lou's romantically independent women resist ties, or are masochistically destroyed if they allow the bond with a man to be central to their lives. Bonding, for Lou, is bondage. *The Years Between*, her

1902 collection, reinforces this theme. Its adolescent heroines grow into the painful realization that the great men they worshipped are dangerously unworthy. Lou's most mature heroines, like *Ma* (1901) and Anneliese in *The House* (written in 1904), find their fulfilment, whether attached to a man or most often not, simply in *being*, being amply, generously, lovingly.

Given the emphatically independent, if none the less peculiar, nature of her heroines, it is perhaps surprising that Lou never directly took up the 'woman question'. Despite her friendships with the feminist writer Frieda von Bülow and the radical feminist Helene Stöcker, Lou identified with none of the numerous feminist campaigns of the day – for equality before the law, for legalizing abortion and contraception, or for fairer divorce laws. Social conditions were never a primary concern for the philosophical Lou. What did interest her during these early years of the century and for the remainder of her life were questions of sexual difference and the nature of sexuality, as well as sexual passion. Though her views, expressed in articles and reviews, shifted somewhat through the years, it is clear from the beginning that her measure of all things is not man, but woman – the woman who is herself. All beings are bisexual, but woman for her is superior by her very instinctual plenitude. She is whole, complete, like the original egg cell; she exists in a unity of spirit, intellect, body and feeling. Man, more differentiated than her, is forced by his dissatisfaction into ceaseless searching and Don Juanesque pursuits. This striving is a sign of male inadequacy. For woman – and Lou insisted on this for herself and always saw her own writing as secondary to her 'being' – ambition is unnecessary.

Woman in Lou's writings thus emerges as a romanticized life spirit, a noble eternal feminine, biologically harmonious, attuned to instinct and impulse, at home in the cosmos and a self-sufficient home in herself, whether she is a working woman or a wife. If these notions are like a composite of *fin-de-siècle*, aesthetic idealizations of Woman – and in certain respects hark forward to contemporary American eco-feminism – Lou none the less inflected such idealizations with the specificity of her own experience. Her heroines are never vacuous ideals, but intelligent, thinking beings, who make difficult choices about where their at-homeness lies. In these choices, in their generous plenitude, in their independent, unconventional passions, they are, of course, not unlike Lou. It is these writings which invest Lou's reflected image of *femme fatale* and philosophical bluestocking with an individual content that renders the separate terms inadequate.

Where *The Erotic* (1910) is concerned, Lou's flavour is again late-romantic, and again her lens is decidedly female. Sexual love is analogous to the passion of the artist or to the fervour of the mystic. It is an intoxication, a great regenerative force, in which the boundaries between two beings merge, as do the oppositions between egoism and altruism. For woman, the sexual and the spiritual are one, and in erotic passion Lou sees the psychical or spiritual arising out of the bodily and material. Since it is based on the principle of infidelity, the erotic in its highest forms cannot be contained by marriage. Happiness resides not in loving, but in being loved. The sexual moment may be one of self-surrender; but the loved person is an addition, 'the cause that gives rise' to our deepest entry into our self, who turns us back to our original links with all existence. In gratitude we idealize him. These were thoughts Lou was to develop more fully in her essay 'On Narcissism'.

During the time of her affair with Rilke, Lou also began to give special consideration to that particular being who is the artist and to the nature of creativity. Eventually, she came to see the artist – who struggles for the union between the bodily and the spiritual – as a somewhat less perfected form of woman, since he has to produce objects: but he is still far more admirable than mere man. In all this the influence of her experience of Rilke is palpable.

Crucially, too, Rilke marked the path which brought Lou to the study of psychoanalysis. With his bouts of anguished and uncontrollable depression, his existential dread of the physical, the separateness of body from soul, he led Lou into a terrain which psychoanalysis helped her to understand. Rilke's writing is permeated by a physical anguish – a profound fear of the very body he inhabits. As Angela Livingstone points out in her fine biography of Lou, Rilke, from his childhood, had been pursued by a terror of the 'Big Thing', 'like a second head', 'a dead animal which, when it was alive, had once been my hand or my arm'. The 'Big Thing' fed off his blood and threatened to destroy him. Lou later linked this dread to his adolescent experience of erection, which seemed to him at once a living thing and apart from him. The images of the too Big, the hard, the stony, the near, which possessed him, are also used in relation to Lou in the moments when he hates her: her size, her fearlessness come to represent for him the awesomeness of the bodily which is his other. But Lou is also his lover. In her love, his anguish is contained. And he is able to speak of it to her, knowing that she will listen, understand and sometimes advise.

Lou broke with Rilke in 1901, in part because his depressions wore her down. He began to write to her again in 1903. These letters cloak her in a therapeutic mantle. Long before Lou embarked on her systematic study of psychoanalysis, Rilke confesses to her in his letters as if she were already an analyst. He describes his intimate fears and his illnesses to her, as to no one else. And she accepts him, not only as friend, but also as patient, a poet-patient for whom she does not later recommend a formal analysis, but whose anguish preoccupies her analytically during the year of her *Freud Journal*.

It is likely that Lou was aware of Freud and his work as early as 1895. She was in Vienna in May of that year when the *Studies on Hysteria* appeared, and her circle of friends, which included Arthur Schnitzler and, in the first years of the century, her lover, Dr Friedrich Pineles, crossed over with Freud's. It was a city she frequented with some regularity. Indeed, Lou may have met Freud prior to the Congress of 1911. Certainly, as his obituary notice shows, he was aware of the part Vienna had played in 'the most moving episode of her feminine fortunes'. Perhaps, in his emphasis on Lou's treating psychoanalysis as a wonderful gift, there is a hint that Freud sees her turn to psychoanalysis, her return to Vienna, as a search for the child she had lost there. Psychoanalysis becomes Lou's baby.

Speculation aside, we know that Lou came to the Weimar Psychoanalytic Congress of September 1911 with Poul Bjerre, a Swedish psychotherapist who was then her lover. Freud laughed at her 'vehemently expressed desire to study psychoanalysis'. In her naïve enthusiasm she was acting like a child attracted by a wonderful new toy. Did she perhaps mistake him for Santa Claus, he asked her with a twinkle in his eye.

But Lou's sense of psychoanalysis as a particularly precious gift persisted, despite Freud's irony. Her joy in it and even more emphatically her joy in Freud – for she was certainly alert to the pun in his name – continued for the remainder of her life, as did her sense of gratitude. Her *Freud Journal*, the letters between her and Freud, are replete with festive imagery. For Lou, there is always a 'Sunday quality behind all the weekday work'. Freud calls her his Sunday child, the same name he gave his favourite daughter, Sophie. She quotes him laughing at her: 'I really think you look on analysis as a sort of Christmas present.'

For Lou, it was. Lou felt that the study and experience of psychoanalysis gave her a means of probing the obscure roots of life, those roots 'by which it is embedded in the totality'. Her philosophical pursuits had never permitted her to grapple directly with her own life; and though her *Journal* shows her grafting psychoanalysis on to the philosophical concepts which are part and parcel of her language, it is clear that she feels the tools of analysis are more valuable to her. For her, psychoanalysis put the body back into philosophy; one is almost tempted to say, the woman's body. It permitted her to contend rationally and scientifically with the material that had always fascinated her – the inner workings of the human mind, fantasy, sexuality, psychic extremes, childhood and its residue. Certain of its concepts merged happily with her own ideas and clarified them. She had already grappled with the notion of bisexuality as well as with the primacy of the sexual in her essay on *The Erotic* (1910); and with female masochism in her stories. The Freudian Unconscious, which showed the proximity of good and bad, love and hate, and revealed them to be spurious opposites, coincided with her own intuitions.

Psychoanalysis also allowed her to delve into and come to terms with her own life. Without feeling precisely guilty, Lou was haunted by the sense that she had sinned against the men in her life – Gillot, Nietzsche, Rée with his tragic end, Rilke, perhaps also Pineles and Bjerre and eventually Tausk – by letting them go. She had 'so swiftly and so forcefully penetrated the partner that he too soon and to one's own disappointment was left behind'. What she found in analysis, what made it a turning-point in her life, was a way of understanding a person 'that goes beyond all affect toward him: somewhere in the depths both aversion and love become only differences of degree.' Analysis permitted a relation 'beyond one's own fidelity and infidelity'. It allowed all the 'vanished persons of the past' to arise anew. To be 'close anew to all, and in it, to oneself'.

Indeed, from her various tributes to Freud and her memoir, it seems clear that Lou felt that everything in her life had conspired to bring her to the study and practice of analysis. Not only was she Russian, part of a people 'who had the ability to find words for complex things and could give expression to psychic difficulties', not only was there Rilke's plight, but the entire philosophical trajectory of the nineteenth century which she had studied and lived led her to Freud. The decline of the great Hegelian metaphysical systems in the face of Darwinism and positivism (incarnated for her by Rée, who she always felt looked backward where Nietzsche looked forward) meant taking a heroic attitude, a Nietzschean attitude to new godless truths. The only way to explore the lived and living reality of these rudderless truths, escape their evolutionary thrust into the 'superhuman', or the dead letter of moribund systematization, was Freud's way: 'to indicate what is repressed in the subterranean layers of the human being or what his resistance only allows to surface in the most ambiguous deformations'. Ironically, it was in this ultra-historical reading of Freud, this reading which saw psychoanalysis as tightly wedded to the task of restoring to man what he has forgotten, that Lou found the path away from the history of philosophy she had so acutely observed and lived. Psychoanalysis was in the vanguard of twentieth century thought, where she belonged, because it rubbed man's face in the mud of his own history.

With Freud's dispensation, Lou attended the Wednesday meetings of the Vienna Psycho-Analytical Society from 30 October 1912 until 2 April 1913. Although there were four women on the rolls, she was often the only one there amidst some fifteen to nineteen men, including Tausk, Rank and occasionally Ferenczi, who became a friend and in whom Lou, already then, presciently recognized the seeds of what would become his later divergence from Freud. Sometimes Lou's travelling companion, Ellen Delp, would accompany her to meetings. Once Lou brought her feminist friend, Helene Stöcker, along. A sign of the importance the Society attributed to Lou's presence can be seen in the fact that the week before her arrival, Hugo Heller presented a paper to the group on Lou Andreas-Salomé, the writer.

Freud, himself, was then working on *Totem and Taboo* and reflecting on narcissism, a subject close to Lou's nearest concerns. In her *Journal*, a documentary gold-mine for historians of analysis, Lou faithfully records the proceedings of the analytic meetings she attended in Vienna, as well as her responses to papers and her impressions of participants. She quickly grew close to Freud, often walking home with him after meetings or going to the Ronacher Café, where discussion extended into the night. On several occasions she was a guest at his home. Although their conversations probed her childhood and covered analytic terrain, Lou never underwent anything approaching a formal analysis with Freud or anyone else. Given the resolutely intellectual thrust of both Lou's *Journal* and her memoir, it is not always easy to glean what specific interpretations Freud might have made. None the less, her *Journal* entry of 2 February 1913 gives us a tantalizing glimpse into what may have been a key moment in her analysis. On that Sunday, Freud spoke to her about his life. What she notes as perhaps 'most personal of all' was his charming account of the 'narcissistic cat'.

The cat, so the story goes, had come in through an open window, arousing mixed feelings in Freud,

especially when it climbed down from the sofa on which it had made itself comfortable and began to inspect in passing the antique objects which he had placed for the time being on the floor. But when the cat proceeded to make known its archaeological satisfaction by purring and with its lithe grace did not cause the slightest damage, Freud's heart melted and he ordered milk for it. From then on the cat claimed its rights daily to take a place on the sofa, inspect the antiques, and get its bowl of milk. However, despite Freud's increasing affection and admiration, the cat paid him not a bit of attention and coldly turned its green eyes with their slanting pupils toward him as toward any other object. When for an instant he wanted more of the cat than its egoistic-narcissistic purring, he had to put his foot down from his comfortable chaise and court its attention with the ingenious enticement of his shoe-toe. Finally, after this unequal relationship had lasted a long time without change, one day he found the cat feverish and gasping on the sofa. And although it was most painstakingly treated ... it succumbed to pneumonia, leaving naught of itself behind but a symbolic picture of all the peaceful and playful charm of true egoism.

Lou makes no comment on this story, leaving it to hang enticingly in the text and moving on to what is certainly related material: Freud's query to her about why she had become so deeply involved in psychoanalysis. Her immediate answer to the question is hardly relevant. What is important is the intervention: it is almost as if Freud is asking her to reflect on her similarity to the cat and asking her what she, Lou, so like the cat in her narcissistic feline distance and self-containment, wants from him. Is psychoanalysis simply the gift of a sustaining bowl of milk and a purring exploratory stroll through the archaeological depths? Lou's answer lies in her later and most important psychoanalytic paper, 'Narcissism as Dual Orientation' (1921). Meanwhile, Freud penned what is certainly the best psychoanalytic portrait of Lou, in his own paper 'On Narcissism: An Introduction', where the cat duly features:

Women, especially if they grow up with good looks, develop a certain self-contentment which compensates them for the social restrictions that are imposed upon them in their choice of object. Strictly speaking, it is themselves that such women love with an intensity comparable to that of the man's love for them. Nor does their need lie in the direction of loving, but of being loved; and the man who fulfills this condition is the one who finds favour with them. The importance of this type of woman for the erotic life of mankind is to be rated very high. Such women have the greatest fascination for men, not only for aesthetic reasons, since as a rule they are the most beautiful, but also because of a combination of interesting psychological factors. For it seems very evident that another person's narcissism has a great attraction for those who have renounced part of their own narcissism and are in search of object-love. The charm of a child lies to a great extent in his narcissism, his self-contentment and inaccessibility, just as does the charm of certain animals which seem not to concern themselves about us, such as cats and the large beasts of prey. ... There are other women, again, who do not have to wait for a child in order to take the step in development from (secondary) narcissism to object-love. Before puberty they feel masculine and develop some way along masculine lines; after this trend has been cut short on their reaching female maturity, they still retain the capacity of longing for a masculine ideal – an ideal which is in fact a survival of the boyish nature they themselves once possessed.

However contested Freud's views on female narcissism may have been in recent years, it is hard to see anything but praise in this sketch of 1914 which has Lou as its original. And the narcissist, for Freud here, is the 'purest and truest' female type. There is nothing about her which signals Freud's later account of woman as in so many respects a failed man; a being with some 'inborn deficiency', who can only obtain 'undiluted satisfaction ... in her relation to her son' and whose every other relation in life – as Joan Riviere put it in her 1934 critique of Freud – will thus inevitably be 'accompanied by disappointment, a sense of loss and feelings of inferiority'.

For Lou – and one strand of psychoanalytic commentators on femininity have taken her lead – woman was the narcissist par excellence, 'the fortunate animal: really just as prone to regressive narcissism as the neurotic, not really undifferentiated like animals, but a regressive without a neurosis: For a neurotic, the wish to become a woman would really mean the wish to become healthy. And it is always a wish to be happy.' This novel view of woman as an independent, self-contented and enviable being underscores Freud's 'On Narcissism'. As Sarah Kofman has commented, 'What is attractive in woman', for the Freud of this period, 'is that she has managed to preserve what man has lost, the original narcissism for which he is eternally nostalgic. It may thus be said that man envies and seeks that narcissistic woman as the lost paradise of childhood ... and is condemned to unhappiness.' So, too, for the contemporaneous Lou of the *Freud Journal*: 'Only in womankind is sexuality no surrender of the ego boundary, no schism; it abides as the homeland of personality, which can still include all of the sublimations of the spirit without losing itself.' Under the aegis of Lou, the feminine enigma took on for Freud an altogether alluring, 'blissful' and 'self-sufficient' aspect.

Lou's charm and the attraction of her personality quickly earned her a special status in Freud's circle. Freud gave her extraordinary dispensation to attend meetings of Adler's rival group as well as his own: 'I only request of you that with due regard for the situation you make use of an artificial psychic split, so to speak, and make no mention there of your role here and vice versa.' A week later, he wrote to her to say:

I missed you yesterday at the lecture and am happy to hear that your absence was not occasioned by a visit to the camp of masculine protest. I have acquired the bad habit of directing my lecture to one particular person in the audience, and yesterday I stared as if spellbound at the vacant chair reserved for you.

Freud, like so many before him, was hardly immune to Lou's particular magic.

Much of the early part of Lou's *Journal* is devoted to discussing her disagreements with Adler and Jung and to detailing her growing admiration for Freud. She charges Adler and Jung with arriving at a 'premature and therefore quite sterile synthesis', an intriguing comment given Freud's veiled criticisms later of her own synthetic powers. Adler's 'masculine protest', Lou felt, led to a negative estimate of woman – something she interestingly never charged Freud with. Jung, whom one might have expected her to have great affinity with, she charges with diluting the concept of libido by including other than sexual drives in it.

This is not to say that she was always and ever in whole-hearted agreement with Freud. Her *Journal* shows frequent diversions and criticisms, for example on his use of the expression 'archaic' instead of 'infantile' with reference to the child's way of thinking – 'for surely primitive people, and animals too, distinguish sharply between the sexes, in contrast to the youngster for whom the genital sphere does not yet exist.' She quickly recognized the fundamental differences between herself and Freud. Late in life, she summed them up like this: 'His merit comes from having reestablished man, not by intuition but rationally, in his unity with all life. That which distinguished him from me from the very beginning is that he would have preferred to liberate man altogether from the Unique, while I feel the presence of the All-powerful even in the morbid and the pathological.' But for Lou – and the pupil and daughter who always inhabited her – Freud became the great teacher. She was surprised and impressed by how open and flexible he was: when she once commented on how his books stated something quite other than what he had just agreed with her about, he replied, 'My latest formulation.' Lou writes:

And that corresponds with my general impression: that the theory is by no means hidebound, but is adjusted to further findings, and, further, that this man is great simply in that he is the man of research advancing quietly and working tirelessly.

What she admired about him was that all his findings had been made against the grain, that his 'personal inclination ran counter to the dredging up of discoveries from such profound depths' and that once discovered he 'subjected them to a doubly exacting and sober scrutiny, so that their value might in no wise be overestimated.' In other words, what she revered in Freud was precisely what ran counter to her own inclinations. For Lou, Freud was the consummate rationalist who had no time for the mystical; and it was this very rationalist who indirectly unmasked the irrational. He was the painstaking researcher of independent mind, who did not baulk at shocking or repulsive discoveries. And here is where they met; for Lou, too, was unshockable. Her curiosity, her joy in plenitude, made her welcome 'the most horrible things' as Christmas presents.

The admiration between them was mutual. Very quickly, Freud learned to trust this famous outsider and set her up as a judge of the wrangles amidst the psychoanalytic brothers. In June 1914, he wrote to her: 'one cannot help feeling a covert desire to find out how the whole thing might appear to another person, to a judge male or female, and I confess that it is to you that I would most gladly have entrusted such an office.' Lou became the 'great understander', performing her office of judge with tact and skill. Freud allowed himself to criticize the 'brothers' to her with a personal zest he generally refrained from, eagerly awaiting her verdicts. His correspondence with Lou numbers over 200 letters. She is the only woman, outside the family circle, to participate in a sequence of letters which lasted over so many years. Through these letters an intimate portrait of Freud's intellectual procedures emerges.

Though Freud said that he never felt any sexual attraction for Lou, the fact that she was a woman was hardly irrelevant to their closeness and to the role of judge and understander he attributed to her. Lou was certainly aware of this. As she noted, perhaps with an uncharacteristic trace of irony, in the last line of her article in honour of Freud's seventieth birthday, 'Men argue and squabble. Women bestow grace.' Freud was always and ever aware of what he called her 'exquisitely feminine' qualities. Although these are occasionally chivalrous expressions, which cloak a put down or ambivalence about Lou's work, there is little doubt that it was her very *femaleness* which allowed him to negotiate with her over contentious matters and be led to explore avenues that he normally refused.

Her *femaleness* certainly played a role in one of the murkier stories in psychoanalytic history, in which Lou for a time acted as mediator. Viktor Tausk had been Freud's disciple since 1908, a man whom he supported at first both financially and emotionally. By the time Lou arrived in Vienna, Freud had grown distrustful of him, feeling that Tausk took over his ideas and over-ambitiously exploited them before Freud had painstakingly thought them through. Lou instantly judged Tausk, eighteen years younger than her, to be Freud's most brilliant disciple. Attracted to this volatile, introspective man, she started an affair with him which lasted until around August 1913. Lou was quick to understand the crux of Tausk's conflict with Freud:

There is no doubt about it that Freud acts with complete conviction when he proceeds so sharply against Tausk. But along with this 'psychoanalytic' fact (that is, bearing in mind Tausk's original neurotic disposition), it is also clear that any independence around Freud, especially when it is marked by aggression and display of temperament, worries him and wounds him quite automatically in his noble egoism as investigator, forcing him to premature discussion, and so forth.

Either because of or in spite of her affair, Freud allowed himself to discuss Tausk with Lou, and she stood up for her lover, as she had always done for the intense, troubled 'geniuses' in her life, and urged Freud to greater patience. So much so that Freud ironically read out to her the joke about the marriage broker and the young man which he had used in *Jokes and their Relation to the Unconscious* to illustrate sophistry or faulty reasoning. In the joke, the young man catalogues a succession of complaints to the matchmaker about the prospective bride: her stupid and spiteful mother, her own ugliness and lack of youth, her poverty. To each of these the matchmaker has a ready answer. 'But she's got a hunchback too,' the youth finally protests. To which the matchmaker replies, 'So what do you want? That she should be perfect!'

There was a sense in which Lou, here cast as the sophistical matchmaker, was being used as a conduit by both Freud and Tausk – a willing one, since she thought initially that she could be helpful to Tausk. By August 1913, in characteristic fashion, however, it was she who was breaking up the affair with the passionate Tausk and effectively giving herself over to the more reasonable and non-sexual relation with Freud. Her grasp of the Tausk-Freud battle shows all her usual psychological penetration:

Only now do I perceive the whole tragedy of Tausk's relation with Freud: that is, I realize now that he will always tackle the same problems, the same attempts at solution, that Freud is engaged in. This is no accident, but signifies his 'making himself a son' as violently as he 'hates the father for it'. As if by a thought transference he will always be busy with the same thing as Freud, never taking one step aside to make room for himself. That *seemed* to depend so much on the situation, but ultimately is his own doing.

Despite the fact that Lou seems here to be accepting Freud's verdict on Tausk, she remains clear not only about Tausk's character, and the inevitable end of their affair, but also about what she continues to value in him:

there still remain those irreconcilable contradictions between that which Freud calls the 'beast of prey' (which at least helps him in the practical management of life) and his over-sensitivity to the point of self-dissolution.

It is all so painful to behold that one would like to look the other way and run away. He is deceiving himself about me with his fantasies. In the long run no helpful relationship is possible; there can be none when reality is cluttered by the wraiths of unabreacted primal reminiscences. An impure tone resonates through everything, buzzing as it were with murmurings from within.

Yet from the very beginning I realized it was this very struggle in Tausk that most deeply moved me – the struggle of the human creature. Brother-animal. You.

By July 1919, Tausk was dead, in a double act of self-murder, having both shot and hung himself. Active war years had taken their toll, as had the difficulty of establishing himself from scratch for a fourth time, financial problems, and Freud's unremitting distance from a follower who sought closeness. Lou could not altogether exonerate herself: she had left unanswered Tausk's lonely and pleading letters through the war years and after. As others, not least among them Freud and she herself, had had occasion to notice, Lou could run hot and then, like the narcissistic cat, altogether cold.

Lou's 'exquisitely feminine' properties rendered Freud not only uncharacteristically tolerant towards her as mediator but also extended to a tolerance for her particular cast of mind. Through Lou, it could be said, Freud came to look a little less negatively on his *bête noire*: spiritual thinking, thinking which strives for synthesis or unity. There was a certain glimmer of admiration for what he called her visionary synthesizing ability, her leaps into philosophical generalization and speculation – characteristics he hotly rejected in his male followers. Without attributing too great an influence to Lou, it is interesting to note that it is during the years of their friendship that Freud allowed himself to indulge in his more speculative philosophical writings. Under the aegis of Lou, Freud occasionally fulfilled that very desire for philosophical speculation he had repressed in himself from his youth – almost as if it were a form of sexual promiscuity – in order to make psychoanalysis a sound empirical science. One could speculate that the experience of Lou was partly responsible for allowing him to acknowledge the 'exquisitely feminine' in himself: a feminine which for her always included an optimistic unity of disparate elements.

The letters make their differences clear and show the delicate negotiation that took place between them. Freud calls Lou the 'poet of psychoanalysis'. It is she who 'knits together the disjecta membra won through analysis and clothes them with living tissue.' In May 1916, in reply to a letter from her in which she worried that she had misunderstood something of Freud's, he wrote:

I cannot believe that there is any danger of your misunderstanding any of our arguments; if so it must be our, in this case my, fault. After all, you are an 'understander' par excellence; and in addition your commentary is an amplification and improvement on the original. I am always particularly impressed when I read what you have to say on one of my papers. I know that in writing I have to blind myself artificially in order to focus all the light on one dark spot, renouncing cohesion, harmony, rhetoric and everything which you call symbolic, frightened as I am by the experience that any such claim or expectation involves the danger of distorting the matter under investigation, even though it may embellish it. Then you come along and add what is missing, build upon it, putting what has been isolated back into its proper context. I cannot always follow you, for my eyes, adapted as they are to the dark, probably can't stand strong light or an extensive range of vision. But I haven't become so much of a mole as to be incapable of enjoying the idea of a brighter light and more spacious horizon, or even to deny their existence.

There is no more telling description of how Freud saw his own procedures and also their possible lack.

Lou often struck a female note and talked about the importance of the mother Freud was slow to acknowledge. At the start of 1919, she responded thus to Freud's 'The Taboo of Virginity':

It occurred to me that this taboo may have been intensified by the fact that at one time (in a matriarchal society) the woman may have been the dominant partner. In this way, like the defeated deities, she acquired demonic properties, and was feared as an agent of retribution. Also her defloration by deity, priests, etc. points back to a time when she was not the 'private property' of the male, and in order to achieve this she had to shake off the shackles of her impressive past – which may still play its part as the earliest positive basis for the precautionary measures of the male.

In January 1930, after she had read *Civilization and its Discontents*, Lou argued with Freud about his contempt for religious feeling. For her the oceanic feeling, 'alongside purely regressive or retarded elements', is 'closely allied to those powers of imagination which form part of all creative activity'. The link between religious feeling and the creative imagination lies, for Lou, in a pre-genital sphere, prior to the castration fears which introduce sexual difference. This is Lou's narcissistic home where there are no oppositions, in particular between fantasy and reality. There is a 'dim memory' of this 'quite vague and indistinct region of emotion' where one is lulled in 'a kind of maternal embrace'.

Lou, a philosophical idealist to the end, plunges in where Freud treads with intellectual caution. Throughout the correspondence there is the recurrence of his gentle reprimand: 'At some points I can only conjecture what you mean, where you venture to describe things which I have avoided as being not yet expressible in words.'

In March 1930, in response to her letter about religion, he writes to her using one of his rare musical analogies:

I am delighted to observe that nothing has altered in our respective ways of approaching a theme, whatever it may be. I strike up a – mostly very simple – melody; you supply the higher octaves for it; I separate the one from the other, and you blend what has been separated into a higher unity; I silently accept the limits imposed by our subjectivity, whereas you draw express attention to them. Generally speaking we have understood each other and are at one in our opinions. Only, I tend to exclude all opinions except one, whereas you tend to include all opinions together.

Throughout their friendship, Lou played the optimist to Freud's pessimist. In *My Thanks to Freud*, her gift to him on his seventy-fifth birthday and also her summary of the benefits of psychoanalysis, she even managed to cast Freud's theory of the death drive in a positive light, by interpreting him to mean that life is worth living despite any lack of illusions about it. Freud as ever was grateful, even if alert to the idealizing tendencies of his life-loving model narcissist:

It has certainly not often happened that I have admired a psycho-analytical work instead of criticising it, but this time I can't help doing so. It is the finest thing of yours I have read, an involuntary proof of your superiority over all of us – in accord with the heights from which you descended to us. It is a true synthesis, not the nonsensical therapeutic synthesis of our opponents, but a true scientific one, in which one can have confidence that it can transform back again into a living organism the collection of nerves, muscles, tendons and blood vessels, into which the analytical knife has turned the body. If only it were possible to coarsen and make tangible all that you sketch with your fine brush, we should perhaps be able to grasp the final truths.

The trust Freud put in Lou, the aura, if never the fact, of a love affair between them, found one particularly significant expression. Freud asked Lou to partner him in the analysis of 'Daughter-Anna', as they both came to refer to Anna Freud in their letters.

Lou's six-week stay at the Freud home in 1921 was in part occasioned by Freud's desire that, as he wrote to his colleague Max Eitingon, she develop a friendship with Anna. Whether he already had it in mind that Lou serve as Anna's analyst is not certain. What is certain, despite Anna's later denials, is that Lou took on the role, and that Freud was clear that he needed to be replaced by a woman as his daughter's analyst. A female analyst would be better placed to probe any resistances arising from Anna's hostility towards her father, and her flight from the feminine and sexual side of her life. When Freud renewed his analysis of his daughter after a lapse of two years, Lou received the equivalent of progress reports from them both. The analytic parenting of Anna brought the two of them so close that, in later years, Freud said that Lou stood next in line of intimacy to his daughter.

Lou's analysis of Anna was hardly conventional. It unfolded during long discussions (both in Vienna and in Lou's home in Göttingen and in letters) of their shared interests − beating fantasies, anal sexuality and masochism − in which Anna tried to keep up with Lou's astonishing 'thought tempo'. Anna said that Lou helped her to overcome her fear of speaking and theorizing in public − so much so, indeed, that it was Anna who delivered Lou's membership lecture to the Vienna Society in 1922. (The rule of personal attendance was specially waived in Lou's case.) She also stated that she could not have written her paper on beating fantasies without Lou, and that Lou had helped her in a 'strange and occult way'.

What Lou did not do was to fulfil Freud's increasingly ambivalent wish that his daughter be prised away from him. Indeed, Lou, who had always seen a self-surrendering dedication as the height of feminine love, was well-placed to understand Anna's desire to stay at home and dedicate herself to Freud and psychoanalysis. The wry intimacy of the Lou−Freud correspondence on this count is worth noting. On 6 May 1922, after one of Anna's visits to Göttingen, Lou wrote: 'Altogether Anna has stirred up quite a storm of passion here, as she will tell you, but nevertheless returns home totally unseared by these flames. Nor should I be at all surprised if this sequence of events were to be constantly repeated, so much does she enjoy every homecoming.'

Good mother to Anna, Lou was also herself above all a fellow daughter to Freud, whose work she valued, honoured and explicated in a variety of writings including her *Thanks to Freud*. At the age of seventy-three, a year before her death, Lou sent the second photo of their correspondence to Freud and wrote: 'If only instead of that I could look for just ten minutes into your face − into the father-face which has presided over my life.' Freud, for Lou, came to stand for all her teachers, and in certain respects, in his absent-presence, for that aura of godliness which had accompanied her from her youth.

It is always difficult to assess analytic practice. After her initial study period in Vienna, Lou began to see patients, some referred to her by Freud. By 1923, she was seeing ten a day, a strenuous schedule which received a stern, if humorous, rebuke from Freud:

I regard it as a badly concealed attempt at suicide, which very much surprises me, since as far as I know you have very little neurotic feeling of guilt. I conjure you to put a stop to this by raising your patients' fees by a half or a quarter to correspond with the cascading collapse of the mark. The fairy godmother who stood at your cradle apparently omitted to bestow on you the gift of reckoning. Please do not wave aside my warning.

During the post-war period when soaring inflation made the mark worthless, Freud offered to send Lou money and delivered on his promise. His kindness affected her deeply, but she continued to see as many patients as she could. Analysing, which she felt allowed her to bring into play both the masculine and feminine sides of herself, her intellect and her intuition, gave her immense pleasure: 'psychoanalytical work makes me so happy that even if I were a millionaire I would not give it up.' It is the special relationship between the analyst and analysand which is the starting-point of *My Thanks to Freud*; she sees it as a relationship which makes vivid the significance and dignity of every human being. For Lou, the person who is psychically ill is someone who has tried to go to his 'uttermost extreme', whereas the healthy simply put up with what they've got. She saw patients not only at home in Göttingen, but also, after the war, in Königsberg, where she helped Otto Bruns organize his Polyclinic along psychoanalytic lines. She also worked with Eitingon at the Berlin Polyclinic. In her letters to Freud, she discusses her patients and problems, as well as her insights; his responses comment and guide.

In the practice of analysis, Lou found a point of fruition for her considerable talents. Her famous ability to identify with a person, to listen to anything no matter how shocking and to make those she listened to feel better and wiser here had a professional use. Anna Freud and Rilke, whose correspondence with her after 1912 has the undeniable flavour of an analysis, both in their different ways provide testimonials to Lou's analytic flair. So does the following account from a doctor in Königsberg, – one of the five who underwent 'teaching analyses with her':

I confess that the way Lou analysed me left a deep impression on me and has been a great help to me all my life. Since then I have been much less inclined to be shocked by the actions of others. For if you have once faced your own 'inner scoundrel' – and we all have him – you are far less ready to be morally outraged by the behaviour of your fellow men. ... She had a very quiet way of speaking, a great gift of inspiring confidence. I am still a little surprised today how much I told her then. But I had always the feeling that she not only understood everything but forgave everything. I have never again experienced such a feeling of conciliatory kindness, or if you like, compassion, as I did with her. ... She was a great listener.

There is a sense in which the formal and contained structure of the analytic session released Lou. The sexuality which she seemed to exude, often despite herself – something which in life often had problematic ends – could here be accommodated, analysed and turned to constructive use. Alternately, what she experienced as her lack of interest in ordinary people – that coldness which Freud had apparently attributed to her and she seemed unquestioningly to have acknowledged – a coldness which was perhaps in part a learned defence against her attractiveness, was transformed within the analytic chamber into warmth. 'In myself,' she wrote to Freud in discussing a difficult and inarticulate patient he had sent her, 'I am a cold fish who is fond of only a few people; for that very reason I am so grateful that within the sphere of psychoanalysis my feelings are able to flow so warmly and freely.' Lou never had any doubts about the value of psychoanalytic work. She sadly reflected that had psychoanalysis been discovered in time, Paul Rée might have been saved.

Lou's publications on psychoanalytic theory are relatively few. On the whole these recast her own prior concerns in the language of psychoanalysis and refine them with her new understanding. Thus her article, '*Zum Typus Weib*' ('On the Feminine') published in *Imago* in 1914, shows her once again pondering woman's nature and the difference between the sexes. Responding to Freud's *Three Essays* and using his terminology, Lou inflects the whole question of the girl's development with her own particular preoccupations. For instance, taking Freud's insight that at puberty the young girl suffers a new wave of repression, particularly of her clitoral sexuality, Lou reinterprets puberty as the moment when the girl, in the process of her own maturation, is sent back to herself – a self which, for Lou, is a primal fusion with everything. This passivity may well be the ultimate mark of woman's difference, but for Lou it is a passivity which is the basis of all virtue. It is what gives woman her superior talent for happiness. In her passive return to her self, her self-abnegation, woman's sexual instincts and ego (self-preservative) instincts come together, are unified, just where the male's are in conflict, separated. Thus, in woman the passive sexual drive can abandon itself to what seems supremely desirable to the ego instincts: the father, man in the father, god. For woman, the spiritual and the erotic come together. She is at one, a blessed undivided being.

Man is less fortunate. His 'activity', his aggressivity, turns towards the passive woman and even if he idealizes her from the sexual point of view, his ego ideal can never be realized in his sexual partner. That has to be found in the same sex: it is the father, the male principle, that man – searching for himself, seeking to replace and surpass the father – has to adore. Thus, for the male, sexual and spiritual impulses are inextricably divided.

Lou finds a biological metaphor here to back up her case. 'In looking for himself as active producer, man loses himself as possessor of himself – just as in the function of reproduction, he loses what he possesses and becomes, in Freud's term, an altruist.' Woman, on the other hand, turned passively inwards, has a happy egoism, a sovereign indolence, like the egg, which has no need to be needlessly active. It is the woman's passive inwardness, her link with a primordial unity, which makes of the male for her a mere individual representative of the 'whole'; through this individual male, it is the generalized spiritual whole she loves. For Lou, this linking in woman of the sexual and the spiritual, this grounding in a primordial unity, means that woman, in herself, has an independent cultural value: artists strive to express and attain that unity which is already hers.

As in so much of her writing, Lou casts her theories here in her own image. The cheerful egoism, the gift for happiness she attributes to the feminine, the intuition of a primal unity, is all hers; as is the spiritualization of the sexual, the ability to identify wholly and merge with man – the representative of a god – while still maintaining the sovereign integrity of her own person.

Lou's essay '"Anal" and "Sexual"' of 1916 received Freud's unmitigated praise and the greater accolade of being twice referred to in his works. It forms a long footnote to the *Three Essays* and is worth quoting both for Freud's assessment and the different emphases of his language and Lou's:

Lou Andreas-Salomé, in a paper which has given us a very much deeper understanding of the significance of anal erotism, has shown how the history of the first prohibition which a child comes across – the prohibition against getting pleasure from anal activity and its products – has a decisive effect on his whole development. This must be the first occasion on which a child has a glimpse of an environment hostile to his own instinctual impulses, on which he learns to separate his own entity from this alien one and on which he carries out the first 'repression' of his possibilities for pleasure. From that time on, what is 'anal' remains excluded from life. This clear-cut distinction between anal and genital processes which is later insisted upon is contradicted by the close anatomical and functional analogies and relations which hold between them. The genital apparatus remains the neighbour of the cloaca and actually (to quote Lou Andreas-Salomé) 'in the case of women is only taken from it on lease'.

Excellent though this precis is, it misses out some of Lou's emphases. The child, for Lou, is catapulted out of the bliss of primal unity with mother and world by the force of the first exclamation of parental repugnance, the first 'Pfui!' or 'ugh', as Lou so graphically puts it. This first prohibition is a lesson in disgust which lasts a lifetime. Not only does it become identified with pleasure, but excrement comes to represent all that is alien, deathly, not-us. Through the first 'ugh' the child becomes, however dimly, aware of a conscious self, one born through prohibition and in division. The anal experience, first the repression of anal pleasure and then its eventual control, thus become linked to all human creative production. The most transcendent art, the greatest human actions, are often linked to the dim memory of that first unity and the first powerful repression of anal pleasure, which is the Cinderella amongst the step-sisters.

For Lou, anal erotism is a rehearsal for genital erotism, which is its double and repeats the struggle between desire for pleasure and its increase through prohibition, this time with another person to whom the self is given up in an ultimate intimacy. The material excretions parallel each other, but whereas excrement comes to stand for dead matter, sexual fluid is associated with life. Moving fluently within her poetic register, Lou then asserts that the physical proximity of anus and genitalia means that in the sexual act death, the realm of excrement, is transcended by the forces of life and generation.

It is worth remembering that the significance Lou gives to anal erotism is part of the special importance she attributes to the earliest phases of life, an importance which has a metaphysical inflection over and above its usual psychoanalytic one. Her long text, 'Narcissism as Dual Orientation' (1921), makes this clear. For Lou, narcissism is not only the primary stage of the infant's life, but is also the libidinal complement of egoism: that is, a primary self-love which extends through life and is much more generalized and omnipresent than Freud's. The reading she gives to the Narcissus myth underpins all her ideas and links back to her childhood memory of seeing herself as so bleakly limited in a mirror. Narcissus, Lou emphasizes, saw himself in a natural mirror, not a man-made one. Perhaps, when he gazed into the pool, he saw not only himself, but himself as everything, his body not as boundary of the self, but as an undivided part of the whole.

The self-love Lou focuses on is good, a *Lebensrauch* or life-intoxication. It is not only an assertion of the ego, but also a force which propels identification with the world, fusion with the other. Narcissism is like a bridge of love towards other beings, objects, value systems. Sexual love is a coupling with the other person and with the 'everything' that the person represents; this fusion is a replay of the original unity, the bliss of the child in the womb. The image of ourselves that we narcissistically project on to an ideal works back upon us, like God's *Rückwirkung*, and improves us. Indeed, all cultural activity finds its origin in this narcissism: just as the infant sets up her toys as symbols of the 'one and all' that was recently hers, so the lover idealizes the beloved and the artist makes works of art. The objects we make, the relations we enter into, are all propelled by an attempt to recreate the lost paradise of original unity.

Unlike Freud's, Lou's account of the individual in the world is a non-conflictual one. There is no sense in her work of displaced libido at odds with the real, of creative activity as a futile search for self-satisfaction. Lou's world begins with a good – a primal unity – which is always and ever remade in our actions. It is a world of plenitude, ever awake to ugliness, strangeness or fundamental antagonisms, but ever optimistic about their harmonious possibilities. In her psychoanalytically informed expressionistic drama, *The Devil and his Grandmother*, published in 1922, Lou found an uncharacteristically humorous and ironic metaphor for her world-view. She created a mischievous excremental devil who lives in his own grandmother's bottom, that stinking hell we prefer to hide. Grandmother is vast, her head poised in the clouds, from where the angels look longingly down at the steamy playful world of shit. Lou's dark devil, at the end inevitably excreted, commits suicide and merges into the bright sphere of love – Lou's world.

Lou spent her last decades at one remove from the sophisticated salon circles of her pre-war years. Dedicated to her work as an analyst, she travelled little. She found a new sense of communion with animals and plants, with the 'presentness' of the natural world. She lived quietly with Andreas: old age had brought them closer together than they had ever been. In the final ten years of her life, she produced three of her best books: *Rainer Maria Rilke* (1928), *My Thanks to Freud* (1931) and her memoir, *A Look Back at Life*, published posthumously. The superabundance of her life provided her with ample material for reflection. And meditation rather than narrative was the mode she chose for her memoir. Looking back on her trajectory, she pondered over the fact that she had never experienced the three forms of love which generally characterize women's lives. She had never taken the risk of having a child and had thus been excluded from 'what is most precious in a woman'. Nor had she ever had a real marriage, or experienced the 'pure erotic bond'. In all this, Lou judged herself as not having scaled the heights that other women had. But regret was not Lou's register. No sooner does she note lacks, than she wipes them away with her far more customary tone of gratitude. What she has lived, she has lived fully. To use her own image, she has plunged her hand into the rosebush of life and grasped a handful of flowers. Not all, since that is impossible: the bush is too abundant. But the flowers she holds in her hand are enough to allow her to experience the whole of the rose bush.

Lou seized life, uncomplainingly, with both hands. Despite the repeated illnesses which plagued her towards the end – diabetes, breast cancer, loss of sight – she worked stoically until the last. Her letters to Freud in her final years have an aura of quietude, ruptured only by Lou's anger and grief over Freud's, though never her own, suffering. Their last meeting took place in 1928, after Freud had undergone one of his numerous operations. They walked together in the Tegel park, where the pansies bloomed. Freud, hardly able to speak, presented her with a bouquet. Lou, distressed at the suffering of her friend and teacher, asked him if he remembered the poem, 'Prayer to Life', which he thought Nietzsche had written. He smiled and said he did. 'And then something happened I did not understand myself, but no power in the world could have stopped me: my trembling lips in revolt against his fate and martyrdom, burst out: "The very thing I once babbled about in my heated enthusiasm, you have done it."' Startled by her own words, Lou burst into tears. Freud did not answer. He simply put his arm around her.

Lou's youthful ardour for Nietzschean heroism had been replaced by the more down-to-earth model of Freud's stoic endurance.

A good pupil, she remained grateful to both teachers, tempering the excess of one with the realism of the other. But however great and important her teachers, Lou had throughout remained primarily herself: a woman, instilled with a sense of life's bounteous plenitude, navigating her own radically unconventional course. 'It does not matter what fate one has if one only really lives it,' she had once said to Anna Freud, who often returned to the thought. Lou lived that fate fully until the moment of her death on 5 February 1937. 'There will be arms outstretched to receive me,' she is reported to have said at the end. Characteristically, this most grateful of women, who had seen life as boundless, held out hope even of death. In this as in so much else, Freud's most intimate female friend was certainly the least Freudian of Freud's women.

9

ANNA FREUD:
THE DUTIFUL
DAUGHTER

The early edifice of psychoanalysis was an extended family home. Its originary members were linked to the patriarch at its centre by ties of friendship and blood, as well as by the highly charged transferential bond. Freud sought for sons to whom to pass on the succession. He found them, then found them wanting, and also found that he was never quite ready to be the murdered father of the 'horde'. Instead, the line of succession passed through his youngest daughter, vestal virgin Anna, who guarded the shrine of psycho-analysis and the word of the father.

'St Anna'. Anna, the holy spinster who, in what she herself named 'altruistic surrender', gives herself up to the care of Freud and his legacy. Anna-Cordelia, youngest of three daughters, who in adolescence feels herself *'dumm'* and leaden, yet loves most and remains ever loyal to her father. 'Anna-Antigone', the indomitable daughter, not eyes and sight, but mouth and speech to the increasingly silent inventor of the talking cure. Anna, who is *'stärker wie ich'*, stronger than me as Freud says, and leads her ailing Oedipus out of the dangers of Nazi Vienna to the safety of Britain.

In the Freudian arcana, Anna Freud holds the card of the mythical daughter. The Freud Museum in London has a video which shows her introducing and commenting on the family 'home movies': a tiny old woman with a girlish modesty and a ready girlish laugh, which erupts into a giggle as she introduces her favourite image of Freud, a secret picture, because he does not know he is being filmed. In charting the passage of faces across the screen, she repeatedly omits to name her own, except once, when she says dismissively, 'and that is me in the background'.

But myths are idealizations. And around the common rooms and dinner tables of psychoanalytic culture, where gossip rumbles as copiously and dangerously as free associations do on couch or armchair, Anna Freud takes on a different aura. Here her spinsterhood and loyalty are laid as failings at her father's door. How could the daughter of the man who put sex on the public agenda never have done it! Enter Anna, the spinster fearful of being a woman, who, maimed by paternal power, lived in her father's shadow because she had nothing of her own. Enter too, the sacred monster: Anna, the closet lesbian, the fierce censor, guarding the sacred portals of the Freud Archive so that no insalubrious whiff may emerge to taint the family name. Perhaps more damaging than all this in the psychoanalytic gossip mill is the suggestion that Anna Freud was improperly analysed: a daughter analysed by her own father, even if that father was Freud, must inevitably – by the laws which govern transference – be improperly or 'insufficiently' analysed.

Somewhere between these poles of myth and gossip, Anna Freud led a full, exacting and productive life. It should be noted that Freud, whatever the popular version of analytic lore, never stated that repetition of the sexual act constituted the royal road either to maturity or redemption. Nor did he lay down a code for 'normal existence' to which individuals could aspire and which provided a goal at the end of analysis. If there was a member of the Freud family who invoked norms for others to follow, then it was Anna.

But then she invoked them for herself first of all. As the youngest of the six Freud children, the one whose conception provoked a good deal of ambivalence, and as the least favoured girl, she had, after all, a great deal of striving to do simply to be noticed. This assiduous and dutiful striving marks one of the principal strains in her character. It is not surprising that Lou Andreas-Salomé, lifelong friend and Anna's 'second' analyst, dedicated her 1923 novel *Rodinka* 'To Anna Freud, to tell her of that which I have loved most deeply.' One of the key themes of the novel is that a quiet receptivity to everything that life brings is a more fruitful way of being than any frantic, desirous striving, however purposeful.

Anna was born on 3 December 1895. It seems that by this time Martha, who had borne five children in eight years, had had enough of infants. She took a long time to recover her strength fully after the birth. Little Anna or Annerl was formula fed and she always remembered her early childhood as unhappy: 'the experience of being left out by the big ones, of being only a bore to them, and of feeling bored and left alone.' It was certainly the memory of bitter childhood hurt and her intense jealousy of Martha's favourite, Sophie, which later fuelled her particular empathy with children. A lecture she delivered at the age of fifty-eight speaks for her sense of her own childhood: 'It is only when parental feelings are ineffective or too ambivalent, or when aggression is more effective than their love, or when the mother's emotions are temporarily engaged elsewhere that children not only feel lost but, in fact, get lost.'

On Freud's side, however, and in terms of the history of psychoanalysis, Anna's arrival had a somewhat different aura. He dreamt the founding dream of psychoanalysis just five months before her birth and days after it wrote to Fliess: 'We like to think that the baby has brought a doubling of my practice.' Though pretty sister Sophie was certainly the parental favourite, Anna pleased her father through her '*Unartigkeit*', a cheeky naughtiness which earned her the affectionate title of Black Devil. Something of his relish for his mischievous youngest daughter is evident in his account of her in *The Interpretation of Dreams*, where nineteen-month-old Anna, deprived of food for a day after an attack of vomiting, is heard to call out excitedly in her sleep: 'Anna Fweud, stwawbewwies, wild stwawbewwies, omblet, pudden.' Freud comments:

The menu included pretty well everything that must have seemed to her to make up a desirable meal. The fact that strawberries appeared in it in two varieties was a demonstration against the domestic health regulations. It was based upon the circumstance, which she had no doubt observed, that her nurse had attributed·her indisposition to a surfeit of strawberries. She was thus retaliating in her dream against this unwelcome verdict.

Interestingly, Freud links toddler Anna's dream to an analogous one dreamt by his mother. If it is to stretch a point too finely to suggest that there is something of a self-fulfilling prophecy in this early linking of the youngest and eldest Freud female – just as in 'The Theme of the Three Caskets', the first and last of the fates are linked – it is none the less the case that Anna cared for the aging Freud much as Amalie had cared for little Siggy and with the same attention to his greatness. 'I am, of course, more and more dependent on Anna's care,' he wrote to Lou in May 1935, 'just as Mephistopheles once remarked:

> In the end we all depend
> On creatures we ourselves have made.

In any case it was very wise to have made her.'

The young Anna's demonstrations and retaliations against the minimal role family life offered her took the form of daydream, storytelling and reading – all of which provided ways of identifying imaginatively (and sometimes masochistically) with characters whose place in the sun was greater than her own. They also provided ways of 'getting lost'. Often, the characters Anna identified with were heroic men, who unflaggingly and self-sacrificially served their 'Emperor' – an emperor in whom it is difficult not to see Daddy. It is this Daddy whose approval and love Anna jealously seeks and worries over, against a host of rivals who number not only her mother, her sisters – the pretty Sophie, the rational Mathilde – but also her second mother, Minna, and eventually any number of women analysands who are also friends and future analysts. A letter of September 1913 captures the tone of her anxious longing:

Dear Daddy!
I received your pretty card today and am afraid that if you now have daily access to such views, you will never get used to our Berggasse again, although it is also very nice here. ... I am already very curious about everything Tante Minna will recount. There are already a great many people asking after you. ...

Her letters are filled with eager demands for more from him, as well as with hugs and kisses, all the more ardent in their appearance, since the family was on the whole physically reserved.

However radical his professional views, Freud did not consider sending his daughters to the Gymnasium, the secondary education which would have permitted them an entry to university. Anna, like her sisters, attended the Lyceum. Schooling meant once again striving diligently to be what parents and teachers wanted her to be, which was, by this stage, a good girl. The anxiety school filled her with, the attendant flight into daydream, lies at the root of her later pedagogical experiments and her exploration of school phobias. But if Freud was conservative about his daughters' formal schooling, he seems to have had no reservations about Anna listening in on the Wednesday evening meetings of the Vienna Psycho-Analytical Society, which she did from the age of fourteen. Her passionate desire to accompany him to America that year was, however, not fulfilled.

By the summer of 1912, her *matura* complete and the decision as to what to do next weighing on her, Anna's health suffered. An extended tour of Italy in the company of Tante Minna was called off: Sophie was getting married and Minna was needed at home. Instead, Anna was sent to Merano for a rest-cure that stretched for five months and, through parental orders, beyond the date of Sophie's wedding. It was a troubled time, as the surviving correspondence between Freud and Anna indicates. An end-of-the-year response to one of Anna's daily letters seems to walk a tightrope between judicious parental discipline and a cruelty of convenience: it was simpler to keep the jealous sisters apart.

My dear little Anna,
I hear you are again worrying about your near future. A gain of $1\frac{1}{2}$ kilos has not yet changed you so very much. I want to calm you about all this and remind you that the plan was to send you to Italy for eight months, so that you could come back all round and at the same time altogether down to earth and reasonable. We didn't really dare hope that a few weeks in Merano would accomplish this transformation and had thus already decided when you left that we would not see you in Vienna for the wedding or immediately thereafter. I think that you will now slowly accustom yourself to this horrid prospect. The ceremony can very well proceed without you. In fact also without guests, company and so on, in which you really have no interest. As for your school plans, these can very well wait until you have learnt to take things in less heated a fashion. Nothing will run away from you. To idle away your time a little and take pleasure in the fact that you can have such lovely sunshine in winter, will also do you good.

Freud goes on to reassure Anna that they enjoy her letters, but would also not mind if she felt too lazy to write daily. She is as yet too young for drudgery.

Anna accommodated herself to the paternal dictate – if not altogether easily. The new year brought a wry letter from Freud expressing his happiness at the fact that she was making herself strong and healthy in order earnestly to take up her duties as 'only daughter', while her predecessor played out her last part. But a few days later, Anna suffered a relapse. Freud offered an 'interpretation' – something it is worth noting he refrained from doing with his other children. Anna's condition, he emphasized, had no physical basis:

You know that you are a little silly. I've persecuted you for a long time already with this and always hope that your insight will overcome it. It was hardly a mystery to me, that you should come down with backache as soon as you were knitting – trying with ambivalent feelings to finish Sophie's wedding present. Now you are suddenly unwell again and as far as I can make out, it has to do with Max's [Sophie's fiancé] presence in Vienna and the promised (or repudiated) visit they were both to make to you on their honeymoon.

Your age-old jealousy of Sophie, for which you, as I know, are not alone responsible, – far more she – seems to have passed over to Max and to disturb you. You are hiding something from us, perhaps also something from yourself.

Anna's instant response was to deny any jealousy of Max, though the way in which she linked her own rejected love of Sophie and stranger Max's ability to win it so quickly suggests Freud's greater insight. Anna acknowledged, however, that she could not make head or tail of her sudden changes of mood, 'how it can sometimes be so stupid'; and she ardently stressed that she wanted to become a reasonable person and would become one 'if you will help me'. Meanwhile, she began to read her father's books.

On the first Sunday after Sophie's wedding, Freud wrote again, addressing her as 'My dear only daughter' and making it clear what was expected of a 'reasonable' young woman:

You will have understood from the books you have read that you were so over-ardent, restless and unhappy, because, like a child, you ran away from many things of which a grown girl does not need to be afraid. We will see the change in you when you no longer ascetically withdraw from the pleasures of your age, but willingly do what makes other girls happy. There is hardly enough left over for real interests when one is too ambitious, too sensitive; and when a piece of life and one's own nature remain strange to one, then one finds oneself disturbed in those very areas one wants to throw oneself into.

This advice to follow the course of other girls, to cease being over-zealous and ambitious, rings a little oddly when we remember that many of the daughters in Freud's near circle of friends were entering university. But perhaps the feminine model Freud and certainly Martha had in mind was that of his own two elder daughters, who were now both married. Freud's aspirations for his daughters were always conservatively conventional.

If the plunge away from maidenly asceticism was stated as a clear wish for Anna here, it soon took on an ambivalence which, though recognized, coloured Freud's relations to Anna for the remainder of his life. On the one hand, he was all too happy to have his only daughter, indeed his only remaining child, at home, at his side – not an unconventional wish, since the lot of youngest daughters was often that of caring for aging parents. On the other hand, Freud wished her a man, the pleasures appropriate to her age, something of her own.

Anna soon became 'reasonable' enough to engage on an elementary school-teaching apprenticeship and, having sat her entry exam, to travel to England in the summer of 1914. No sooner did Freud hear from Loë Kann Jones of Anna's warm reception by Ernest Jones than he was warning her firmly against any leap into marriage. There is a note of almost comic paternal panic here:

I know from the best sources that Dr Jones has serious intentions of wooing you. It is the first time in your young life and I have no thought of robbing you of the freedom your two sisters have enjoyed. But it has been the case that you have lived more intimately with us than they and I comfort myself with the hope that it will be more difficult for you than for them to make a decision about your life without assuring yourself first of all of our (in this case, my) consent.

He then reminded Anna of Jones's age – he was an experienced thirty-five to her innocent eighteen; hinted that Jones's interest might be as much in Professor Freud as in Anna herself; and recommended that she talk to Loë Kann, who could warn her about more intimate and evidently sexual matters. All sound and reasonable advice, of course, but at the same time saturated not only with the tone of jealous, possessive fatherhood but with Freud's self-acknowledged homosexual tendency to identify himself with the maidenly and passive feminine vis-à-vis the aggressor male. In a letter a week later, he further counselled Anna to remain on a friendly and equal footing with Jones, but never to let herself be alone with him so that he can do something decisive: 'You'll find the means: you are, after all, also a female [*Frauenzimmer*].'

Anna's response to these warning letters was at once dutiful and teasing. She was grateful for her father's advice – and one imagines for the attention shown in such long and impassioned letters – and would do what he recommended; but she also tantalizingly outlined for Freud the glorious excitement of a double-date trip to the countryside with Jones, an occasion she remembered fondly up to the time she wrote a memoir about Jones in 1979. Her dreams, however, were not about Jones, but continuously about Loë Kann, one of a number of Freud's remarkable friends – beautiful, childless, older women – whom Anna admired, grew close to and perhaps dreamt of growing into so that she too could be the object of her father's regard.

Freud's ambivalence about his youngest daughter being possessed by another man was perhaps no greater than that of most patriarchal fathers. What was rare was his acknowledgment of it. In March 1922, after his first analysis of Anna, he wrote to Lou Andreas-Salomé,

I too very much miss Daughter Anna. She set off for Berlin and Hamburg on March the second. I have long felt sorry for her for still being at home with us old folks [...], but on the other hand, if she really were to go away, I should feel myself as deprived as I do now, and as I should do if I had to give up smoking! As long as we are all together, one doesn't realize it clearly, or at least we do not. And therefore in view of all these insoluble conflicts it is good that life comes to an end sometime or other.

Freud was as addicted to his youngest daughter as he was to his cigars: his self-analysis had already led him to see the links between the pleasures of smoking and the pleasures of women. And if it was in vain that 'an old man yearns for the love of woman as he had it first from his mother', as he had said in his daughter-Anna-inspired meditation on King Lear in 'The Theme of the Three Caskets', he could none the less not let Anna-Cordelia go. Only death would release him from the conflict. And Anna, as his essay signalled, was ironically also his champion against death. So Freud continued to worry. After his analysis of Anna was renewed in 1924, he wrote again to Lou: 'The child gives me enough worries: how she will bear the lonely life [after his death] and whether I can drive her libido from the hiding place into which it has crawled.' And again on 10 May 1925: 'I am afraid that her suppressed genitality may some day play her a mean trick. I cannot free her from me, and nobody is helping me with it.'

Yet some had tried and Freud had not been over-eager to welcome their help. Amongst Anna's suitors, there was Hans Lampl, a long-time friend of her brother, Martin's, and of the family's. Freud had financed school and skiing trips for the young Hans, who could not afford them, and had given him presents, including a dressing-gown Lampl long cherished. Lampl had attended Freud's lectures since 1912 and reported on them to Anna, then in Merano. In a letter home from England in July 1914, Anna expressed her sorrow at Lampl's unhappiness in Reichenau and reminded Freud to keep on sending him the *Wiener Klinische Zeitung*. In 1920, all three attended the Hague Congress together. But, for whatever constellation of reasons, Lampl did not live up to Freud's hopes for his daughter and by the summer of 1921 she was writing to her father: 'I am often together with Lampl in a friendly relationship, but I also have daily opportunities to confirm our judgment of him from last year and to rejoice that we judged correctly.' Nor did anything come of Anna's rumoured love for the rather more brilliant Siegfried Bernfeld, a Zionist and socialist educator and organizer of youth projects, who later wrote the first well-researched biographical studies of Freud. Anna's attraction to Bernfeld in the early 1920s may in part account for the hostility towards him Freud expresses some ten years later in his letters to Jeanne Lampl de Groot, the woman Hans Lampl eventually married.

If Freud was worried about his daughter's celibacy and suppressed sexuality, and was simultaneously reluctant to let his 'little only daughter' grow up, Anna's ambivalence to remaining his 'dear only daughter' was somewhat less, particularly after she had thoroughly established herself as the Professor's chief nurse and closest colleague, and effectively all but displaced Martha and Minna. If Freud had been single-minded in his desire to see Anna married, it is likely that she would have done so – if only in order to please him. As it was, there was a role waiting for her which was altogether more impressive than that of 'wife'. Abram Kardiner, one of Freud's analysands in the early 1920s, makes the point well: asked why 'quite an attractive girl' like Anna Freud did not marry, he responded, 'Well, look at her father. This is an ideal that very few men could live up to, and it would surely be a comedown for her to attach herself to a lesser man.'

Anna's 1914 stay in England was cut short by the outbreak of war. Her return to Austria from what was now an enemy nation was managed by Loë

Kann Jones and her husband, Davy, who arranged for Anna to travel in the entourage of the departing Austrian ambassador. Back in Vienna, she launched eagerly into a teacher-training course. Freud's letters to his friends reflected his growing admiration for her: 'She is developing into a charmer, by the way, more delightful than any other of the children,' he wrote to Ferenczi on 8 April 1915. He had already had occasion to note that Anna was the 'most gifted and accomplished of my children, and a valuable character besides, full of interest for learning.'

Successful in her teacher's examination, Anna began her work as an apprentice teacher in 1915 at the Cottage Lyceum. She charmed her young pupils and earned the approval of her superiors, who spoke of her 'gift for teaching' and offered her a four-year contract to start in the autumn of 1918. She combined her apprenticeship with studies in psychoanalysis, translating in 1915 an article by James Putnam into German and Hug-Hellmuth's writing on play therapy into English, asking her father to elucidate technical terms. In 1916, she attended Freud's course of introductory lectures on dreams at the university and, in 1917, the series on neuroses. Psychoanalysis was evidently a more abiding interest than teaching, and though Freud put paid to her wish to study medicine, like Helene Deutsch – the sight of whom in a white doctor's coat at Freud's lectures had inspired Anna – he did not discourage her from becoming a lay analyst. Indeed, the fact that he took her into analysis sometime in 1918 is certain indication that he supported her professional aspirations: Freud had long thought it necessary that a personal analysis should be part of every analyst's training.

Analysing family members or friends in those early days of psychoanalysis was hardly the irregular occurrence it is today, and Anna's analysis with Freud was not then the quite so closely guarded secret it later became. They were both, none the less, acutely aware of the particular problems transference – and counter-transference – might pose between daughter and father. And Freud's dissatisfaction with the progress of the analysis after three years is evidenced by his calling on Lou Andreas-Salomé to partner him in it; and then in 1924 engaging upon a second analysis of Anna. It was, for the time, an unusually long analysis, and Anna's flight from sexuality and her unshakeable focus on Daddy was, as we know, never resolved to his unambivalent satisfaction.

Anna's analysis was thus not simply or only a training analysis. In her exemplary biography of Anna Freud, Elisabeth Young-Bruehl details the symptoms which made Anna a suitable case for treatment. Her low self-esteem had long led her to a flight into fantasy. Anna told herself 'nice stories', extended complicated daydreams that first accompanied and then substituted for masturbatory pleasure. These nice stories in which she often played a heroic and self-sacrificial male role left her feeling depleted and '*dumm*', unable to work or make decisions. What she called her 'night life', which she recorded for her father from 1915 on, was on the other hand distressingly turbulent. There are repeated and violent dreams of going blind, 'of shooting, killing or dying' she writes to him in 1919; of defending her father from enemies and finding her sabre broken; of Tausk's bride attempting to shoot Freud. Striving to defend or serve the father figure and failing to do so is a recurrent theme. The underlying wish of both night life and nice stories is manifest in a dream of 1915: 'Recently I dreamt that you are a king and I a princess, that people want to separate us by means of political intrigues. It was not pleasant and very agitating.'

Out of Anna's analysis came not only her paper on 'Beating Fantasies and Daydreams' of 1922, in which her own experience serves as the prime case, but also her confidence, her ability to write it and deliver it to the Vienna Society and thereby be granted membership.

With a systematic lucidity which is the mark of all her analytic writings, Anna uncovers the Oedipal core of the girl child's masturbatory fantasy of being beaten and its relation to 'nice stories'. Masochistic pleasure and guilt attend a fantasy constructed to prove that 'Father loves only me'. In Anna's paper, the 'patient' meets with a happy end. She transforms her personal daydreams into stories: 'By renouncing her private pleasure in favour of making an impression on others, the author has accomplished an important developmental step: the transformation of an autistic into a social activity. We could say: she has found the road that leads from her fantasy life back to reality.'

In Freud's 'A Child Is Being Beaten' of 1919, which incorporates Anna's case amongst other similar material, the prognosis is not quite so optimistic. He sees in the three stages of the beating fantasy the girl's escape 'from the demands of the erotic side of her life altogether. She turns herself in phantasy into a man, without herself becoming active in a masculine way, and is no longer anything but a spectator of the event which takes the place of the sexual act.' Daddy Freud continued to worry over his youngest daughter. But in the event, they were both right, and he had equal reason to be proud of her.

At the International Psychoanalytic Congress of 1918 in Budapest, the first since the outbreak of war, Freud evoked a psychoanalysis which stretched beyond its present limits to include 'the wider social strata' and through institutions and out-patient clinics would treat 'a considerable mass of the population', so that 'men who would otherwise give way to drink, women who have nearly succumbed under their burden of privations, children for whom there is no choice but between running wild or neurosis, may be made capable, by analysis, of resistance and of efficient work.' Anna took his words to heart, particularly in their application to children.

Despite the ill-health which plagued many during the wartime shortages of fuel and food – and which in Anna's case resulted in tuberculosis – Anna during the time of her teaching apprenticeship had worked in a day-care centre for working-class children and for Bernfeld's American Joint Distribution Committee, which found homes for orphaned children. She grew close not only to Bernfeld, but also after the war to August Aichhorn, who became an acknowledged authority on juvenile delinquency. She shared with them an interest in the education of troubled and socially deprived youngsters, in welfare work, and in the application of psychoanalytic insight to pedagogy – all concerns that she would later bring to fruition. In the early 1920s, she began to analyse children: first, her sister Sophie's orphaned boys, particularly Ernst, whose mothering she shared with Mathilde, her childless elder sister; then two girls she housed with the Rosenfelds in 1924; and, the following year, the Burlingham children and their friend, Adelaide Sweetzer.

After Freud's first cancer surgery in 1923, Freud and Anna grew increasingly close. She became not only his chief nurse, changing his prosthesis when he had trouble with it, but also his secretary, spokesperson and colleague. So intimate were they that although Anna did not take over the organization of domestic life in Berggasse, she did in other respects displace Martha. It was certainly the realization of this which allowed Freud, then recuperating from his heart condition at a sanatorium with Anna in 1926, to comment wryly to Max Eitingon – to whom Anna also wrote familiarly – that his 'sick nurse ... in the course of the day separates out into wife and daughter, but through the night will doubtless regularly remain the latter.'

With Otto Rank's resignation late in 1924, Anna became the sixth member of Freud's inner circle, the committee governing the affairs of psychoanalysis. She worked energetically at the *Verlag*, amongst other tasks putting together the German edition of Freud's *Gesammelte Schriften*, and acting as a consultant to the English edition of his *Collected Papers*. With the establishment of the Vienna Institute and its training programme under Helene Deutsch, Anna became one of the Institute's teachers in child analysis and a training analyst. By the end of the 1920s, two-thirds of her work was with children, one-third with trainee child analysts.

If Anna was aware that many of the honours and responsibilities conferred on her came to her as her father's daughter, her growing self-confidence, coupled with her father's evident admiration for her, as well as their acknow-ledged inter-dependence, greatly eased her inner sense of strain. It did not, however, do so altogether. The intimacy with her father, so long sought in fantasy, could, after all, only be partially realized in reality. Anna's childhood jealousies resurfaced in relation to Freud's female colleagues and analysands; Freud continued to express concern to friends. Anna masochistically drove herself too hard, strove too hard: 'like all women, she is always fanatical and makes herself very tired.' Anna needed an existence which was not subsumed in an identification with Freud: the ego ideal he provided could only be punishing since Anna inevitably could not live up to it. Anna needed something, someone of her own. She found it in Dorothy Burlingham, daughter of the legendary creator of Tiffany glass, who had come to Vienna in the autumn of 1925 in search of psychoanalysis.

Freud was not altogether appeased. He wrote to Lou: 'Since the poor heart must absolutely have something, it clings to women friends, one taking the place of another.' Dorothy had taken the place of Eva Rosenfeld, a mother of two, Maedi and Victor. But Eva had a husband in situ, and Dorothy did not. (When Eva grew jealous of Dorothy, Anna assuaged her by offering her an analysis with Freud; there were advantages to being the Professor's daughter.) And though Freud continued to worry about Anna's lack of a sexual life, there is no question but that with Dorothy, Anna had the equivalent of a marriage, complete with four ready-made children who could be mothered both analytically and familially. Indeed, with the entry of Dorothy into her life, Anna gained an independence which increasingly put Freud into the emotional background of her life. The two women holidayed together, and instead of lengthy detailed letters home to Daddy, there are mostly only clipped telegrams. The Burlinghams, after only nine months in Vienna, moved into an apartment in Berggasse 19. The two families began to spend their summers together in Semmering. Freud wrote to Ludwig Binswanger: 'Our symbiosis with an American family (husbandless), whose children my daughter is bringing up analytically with a firm hand, is growing continually stronger so that we share with them our needs for the summer.'

Dorothy Burlingham

Dorothy Tiffany Burlingham, born on 11 October 1891, was the youngest of the glass millionaire Louis Comfort Tiffany's eight daughters and the fourth by his wife, Louise, a feminist and intellectual who died when Dorothy was twelve. Although in certain respects, Dorothy's lavish American childhood lived under the erratic tyranny of an eccentric father was poles apart from Anna's *gemütlich* and *bürgerlich* Viennese rearing, in other respects they shared enough to make them feel they were somehow twinned. Like Anna, little Dorothy felt left out by her siblings: she was nicknamed, 'me too', her constant cry. Her parents had wanted a boy and the feeling of being the unwanted, odd-child-out was exacerbated by the death of a sister three years older than herself, a prettier and favoured sibling much mourned by mother and nurse. Next in line by age were the beautiful twins, talented scene-stealers and wrapped up only in each other.

One of Dorothy's childhood memories was of her mother's closest friend, Julia de Forest, reading and translating *The Interpretation of Dreams* for her mother, while young Dorothy sat at their feet. Louise Tiffany was a trustee of the New York Infirmary for Women and Children, a pioneering teaching hospital staffed by women. She was also a delver into texts on mental disorder. The brilliant Julia lived in a 'Boston marriage' with a doctor who had been the resident physician at the Infirmary. Despite or perhaps because of her mother's early death – before Dorothy had had a substantial opportunity to engage with a woman who visibly preferred older children – Dorothy always identified with the maternal side of the family rather than with her highly talented but autocratic and alcoholic father. It was Julia de Forest who arranged, against Louis Tiffany's wishes, that Dorothy attend a good boarding-school. Dorothy's relationship to her excessively temperamental father, though diametrically opposed to Anna's with Freud, had the same effect of making her relationships with men problematic.

In September 1914, Dorothy married Dr Robert Burlingham, a Harvard graduate whose pedigree stretched back to the *Mayflower*. Their first child, Bob, was born within ten months. It is not clear whether Robert Burlingham's sequence of nervous breakdowns – he was later diagnosed as manic depressive – started before or after the birth. Whatever the case, the violent eruptions of his illness coloured the remainder of Dorothy's life with her husband. Three more children, Mabbie, Tinky and Mikey, were born in quick succession in a union which was visibly crumbling and punctuated by separations. Finally in 1925, Dorothy and the children fled America without Robert's knowledge. They stopped first in Switzerland and then moved to Vienna. Under the strain of Robert's violent breakdowns, a disintegrating marriage, a fearsomely interventionist mother-in-law, and troubled children about whom she was obsessively anxious – Bob was particularly sensitive to family moods and had become hyper-allergic and asthmatic in his first months – Dorothy turned to psychoanalysis for help. She had heard of Anna Freud's work with children.

After Anna's preliminary interview with Dorothy in the spring of 1925, she agreed to take Bob into analysis and arranged for Dorothy to have an analysis with Theodor Reik. In September, the Burlinghams settled into the suburban mansion of a Hungarian prince just outside Vienna, the first of several opulent residences. Bob began his 'lessons' with Anna. Mabbie followed shortly after and then Adelaide Sweetzer, the daughter of Dorothy's Switzerland-based friends.

The relationship between Dorothy and Anna blossomed quickly. The women met frequently to discuss the children and, by spring, they were making trips to the Vienna Woods in Dorothy's Model T, often with Freud – 'the Professor' to Dorothy – in tow. To Lou, Freud wrote that Anna had made friends with 'a quite congenial American woman, an unhappy virgin'. But he was obviously fond of both Dorothy, whose distant reserve made many wary of her, and the 'naughty American children' Anna was treating. He gave the darkly dramatic Dorothy with her luminous suffering eyes an opal brooch: she lost it almost immediately and he replaced it with another. (When the first was found by Eva Rosenfeld, Anna's now somewhat displaced friend, Freud told her to keep it.) Dorothy, in turn, gave Freud his first dog, a chow – the Chinese Emperor's breed – called Lun Yu, who, together with his replacements from then on, feature regularly in Freud's reflections.

The circle of Anna's friends was now also Freud's own: in the close identification between father and daughter, it becomes increasingly difficult to disentangle whether friends are there for Anna's sake or because she serves as a conduit to, or a more socially active embodiment of, Freud. When Dorothy broke off what she felt was an ineffective analysis with Reik in 1927 and went into analysis with Freud – an analysis which, with the inevitable ruptures of operations and emigration, lasted the twelve years until Freud's death – the circle was, in any event, complete. So complete that Freud, Dorothy, Anna and the children were drawn into making telepathic observations via analysis on each other's unconscious. Family life and analysis were one.

Anna, for whom Dorothy in part took on the aspect of the good older sister who the now dead Sophie had never been, increasingly became the second parent to Dorothy's children. Though Robert Burlingham travelled to Vienna on several occasions in an attempt to convince Dorothy to return to America, she feared life with him and his influence on the children too much to do so. Robert, between the bouts of his illness, was a devoted father, distressed by the absence of his family. The children's loyalties were torn. But both Anna and Dorothy felt the children's place was with their mother(s) in Vienna. In 1929, Freud was drawn into a series of interviews with Robert and his formidable jurist father – interviews with the aim of bringing all or part of the family back to America; and failing that, obtaining custody of the children. Robert met with no success then, though the business of meeting him to reject him took a serious toll on Dorothy's health. Gradually – perhaps with the help of an analysis which it seems was geared towards giving Dorothy greater independence and self-mastery – she arrived at a point where she could permit the children to visit their father for holidays, though never all at the same time for fear of abduction.

In May 1938, Robert found a radical solution to his side of the family tug of war: he jumped to his death from the fourteenth floor of his New York apartment. Freud was quick to write to Dorothy and exonerate her from any guilt:

I am beset with worry that you may cause yourself pain, unjustifiably so, by an understandable effort on your part to grant your love (which never died) one last expression. Therefore, someone outside the family should be allowed to remind you of how little guilt, in the ordinary sense, there was in your relationship with your husband, but instead how overpowering was the influence of his illness, which made it impossible to have a satisfactory relationship, and which has to be accepted as yet another of those acts of fate that fall upon us human beings and cannot be changed by any brooding or self analysis.

Dorothy could take Freud's words only partly to heart. She wrote to her friend Edith Jackson: 'My one sorrow is, & has been, that I could not help him or do anything to give him happiness. I would have given a very great deal to have been able to do so.'

The 'tragedy' of her husband's illness had certainly been one of the factors to stimulate Dorothy's entry into the world of psychoanalysis. In 1926–7, she audited Anna Freud's lectures on child analysis at the Vienna Institute and participated in her seminar. Urged on in her studies by Anna, in 1932 she became an Associate Member of the Vienna Society. The paper she presented, 'Child Analysis and the Mother', drew on her own mothering experiences and gave a succinct and deeply felt portrait of the mother's reaction to the analysis of her own child. One can only wonder at the strength of her relation with Anna if it could survive the emotions Dorothy, the mother, here describes:

She feels herself being dragged into the analysis. Her relationship toward her child, her actions and behaviour toward him, what she says to him, and how she says it, her moods and her tempers, everything is studied from the analytic angle. That is bad enough, but when she realises that her whole private life is also being brought in, she naturally feels abused. She can understand why all that concerns the child is necessary material for the analyst, but when it comes to her private life – that seems to her to be going one step too far. She will not stand for it and struggles against it. Naturally, she feels injured, criticised, misunderstood. Furthermore, she feels jealous even of the attention which is now being given to her child. It was she who suffered from her child's behaviour, and now it is her child who gets all the sympathy and help. She, who was most affected by his difficulties, now not only is not being considered, but an even more difficult situation is being made for her. Moreover, she feels her child loving someone else more than herself, turning to someone else with all his troubles as he previously did to her. It does not make it easier for her to realise that this person really does understand her child better than she does. She feels humiliated. And then, added to all of this, the child begins to look at her, the mother, with newly opened eyes, even criticising her, her actions, her very thoughts; and she knows that the child finds sympathy in all of this with his newfound friend, the analyst. Is it astonishing that the mother resents the analyst's efforts? Is it strange that analysts often lose cases just because parents cannot stand the analysis and suddenly break off the treatment?

Given this sense of analysis as an invasion, it is a measure of Dorothy's bond with Anna that she did not break off the particularly all-encompassing brand of child analysis – one which included analytic sessions, pedagogical monitoring and surrogate mothering – the early Anna advocated. Then, too, one might speculate that it was the strength of Dorothy's parental feelings that led Anna's technique of child analysis to be so staunchly protective of parental primacy in the child's affections, as compared to Melanie Klein's. Klein, perhaps on the basis of her very different experience of analysing her own, rather than her best-friend's children, advocated the analyst taking over *all* parental functions in the transference. Anna, sensitive to Dorothy's parental fears, left a space for the parent and Dorothy remained staunchly 'Anna Freudian'.

Until her death in 1979, Dorothy was Anna's resolute supporter and partner in her various clinical ventures. They lived and worked together in Austria and in England. If Dorothy's habitual reserve and self-effacement made her sometimes appear to be a mere shadow of the emphatic and energetic Anna's, this was to belie the truth of Dorothy's character. Dorothy had considerable talents of her own as her war nursery work and work with the Hampstead Clinic and blind children make clear. This last was primary and wholly original work and remains so. It is the model for Oliver Sacks's study of the deaf, *Seeing Voices* (1990). Dorothy also had a particular kind of prescience, an intuitive skill which heightened her effectiveness as a child analyst. Her first paper had dealt with what Freud in his *New Introductory Lectures*, mentioning Dorothy, called 'thought transference' between mother and child: an unconscious force 'so subtle and uncanny that it seems at times to approach the supernatural'. This was not a talent the insistently rational Anna shared.

The two women, joined in what after Freud's death could effectively be called a Boston marriage, complemented each other. It is not certain that

Anna, with her somewhat austere asceticism, and Dorothy, with her fear and reserve, shared a sexual relationship. Rather they had what Anna in a 1927 letter to her father called 'the most agreeable and unalloyed comradeship'; and a way of life within the embracing challenges of psychoanalysis. All, of course, for the first formative years, under the wing of Freud.

If Dorothy was to write after Freud's death, 'The years in which I knew him were the most important of my life,' then for Anna they were the years in which she finally acquired something of her own. That something was not only Dorothy, but also the children who were to form the bedrock of her first substantive work.

From the moment the Burlinghams moved to Vienna, Anna's story is not recountable apart from them.

Analysing Children

Before Anna started to practise, the history of child analysis is very brief. Freud, on the whole, focused on childhood only as a residue, and a constructed, if determining one at that, in the shadowy layers of adult memory. The exceptions were the case of Little Hans, the 'Analysis of a Phobia in a Five-Year-Old Boy', published in 1909, whose treatment, alongside other material, had also been used in two earlier short papers on the sexual theories of children and their sexual enlightenment. Little Hans was not, however, analysed by Freud; Max Graf, Hans's father, a musicologist who for some years had been a member of Freud's Wednesday-night group, was in the position of the analyst. Freud, effectively, acted as the control analyst receiving reports from the father and advising. Little Hans's mother had already been in analysis with Freud. Only once during the period of the analysis did he see Little Hans formally and then it was *with* his father. This is worth stressing when we come to assess Anna's early work with children and her heated disagreements with Berlin-based Melanie Klein – by then, since Hug-Hellmuth had died, the only other major worker in the field – over the place of the parent in the process of child analysis. Anna, in stressing the importance of regular contact with the child's parents, with so to speak the child's actual environment, was in fact taking her cue from her father.

It is possible too that her argument with Klein for going too 'deep' too soon with her interpretations similarly stems from the case of Little Hans. Freud had rebuked Hans's father for pressing the little boy too hard: 'Hans's father was asking too many questions, and was pressing the inquiry along his own lines instead of allowing the little boy to express his thoughts. For this reason the analysis began to be obscure and uncertain.' Anna, who knew her father's work by heart, who had so internalized it that it had become second nature, might well have been fuelled by this rebuke in criticizing what she saw as Klein's over-hasty interpretations. Klein, Anna felt, saw in every instance of a child's play an aggressive impulse or a sexual connotation, to the exclusion of all other factors. Pushing the child too hard in this way often resulted in a sudden end to the child's analysis. Dorothy Burlingham's influence is perhaps at play in all this.

If Anna was following in her father's footsteps and was instinctively cautious, she was none the less a pioneer who diligently broke new ground in her chosen byway of psychoanalysis. Only one analyst had been there before her : Hermine Hug-Hellmuth, whose many observations of children, and whose key 1920 paper 'On the Technique of Child Analysis', bears a remarkably close parallel to Anna's first book (1927) on the subject. Anna must have known the article by this early member of Freud's circle – she had been at the Hague Congress in 1920, where the paper was first delivered – but she showed a marked recalcitrance, perhaps because of the scandal attending Hug-Hellmuth's death, in acknowledging any direct debt to her forerunner, who, like herself, had been a teacher.

There were other influences. The brilliant Sándor Ferenczi had as early as 1908 lectured on psychoanalysis and education, and his thinking on how education could be structured so as to help rather than to thwart children's instinctual lives had certainly had an impact on Anna – as it had on Klein, who worked with children in Ferenczi's Budapest Clinic towards the end of the war. So too had the work of her Viennese colleagues Bernfeld and Aichhorn : Anna's psychoanalytic bent, rooted as it partly was in her own experience as a teacher, always had a pedagogical cast. Her early Utopian hope was that through a conjuncture of education and psychoanalysis one could somehow create happier children and a happier world. The first generation of child analysts were trained in Vienna under her aegis. It could be said that in the 1920s and early 1930s, Anna's Vienna became the capital of child analysis for continental Europe and America : the adult centre had shifted to Berlin. London, where Melanie Klein emigrated at Ernest Jones's invitation in autumn 1926, was to have its heyday a little later.

Anna's bent was pragmatic. In this she differed from her father, whose interests in 'cure' always came second best to the more challenging scientific task of discovering the laws of the unconscious. In 1928, comparing herself a little mournfully to her colleagues at the Institute, she wrote to Lou :

You know, when I am analyzing or when I imagine something in my own mind, then it appears to me as totally clear and, if not 'simple,' then at least transparent. But if I listen to others in the Society, then things look more complicated and difficult, as if I myself wanted to see a simplicity where there is none. This probably comes from the fact that the others understand things better when they distance themselves from the human beings and put things in coldly theoretical terms. And with me understanding just disappears very easily when it is detached from the human being. ... My way is totally practical, but I would like to learn the other way too. Papa thinks it will come with more experience.

Papa was undeniably pleased with his youngest, at least where her work was concerned. While Anna was preparing her lectures for the Training Institute, the lectures which were to become her first book,

Introduction to the Technique of Child Analysis, Freud wrote to Eitingon:

The most enjoyable event right now is Anna's course on child analytic technique ...
it is really the general opinion that she knows how to hold the attention of her
audience. She tells me the content of each lesson on the evening before, and I am
especially gratified that she does not, like a student, simply apply what she has learned
elsewhere; she is unconstrained as she deals with the subject, she judges for herself
and knows how to assert the particularities of this kind of analysis. Compared to the
opinions of Klein, hers are conservative, one might even say reactionary, but it looks
as if she is right.

When Anna's book appeared in 1927, Freud wrote to Lou: 'You will
not believe how little I contributed to her book, nothing but curtailing her
polemic against Melanie Klein. Apart from that it is completely independent
work.'

If Freud had curtailed Anna's polemic against Klein, it was still amply in
evidence. Anna had heard Klein's pioneering lecture on the compelling case
of Erna; her eventual objections to her method were succinctly put in a style
which is a model of pedagogic clarity. Anna was writing a training manual
and effectively laying down the basis for a school.

Anna's argument with Klein focused on one cardinal difference. Klein
believed, unlike Freud, that the super-ego develops in tandem with, rather
than as an effect of, the Oedipus complex and both emerge very early from
'the deprivation experience of weaning, that is, at the end of the first or the
beginning of the second year of life' – far earlier than Freud had set out.
This Kleinian super-ego is not formed from any identification with parents,
but has its source in the child's own anxiety experience of weaning and its
attendant aggressive and sadistic impulses.

For the more 'conservative' Anna, the young child's super-ego is in a state
of formation which is not resolved until the Oedipal conflict has played itself
out. The developing child is thus still dependent on parental influence and
his environment.

For Klein, the child in analysis is no different from an adult. If language
cannot be depended on as the medium of communication, then play takes its
place and is the medium for interpretations which are as 'deep' or as sexual
in their content as they would be for an adult. Transference is as full as with
adults and is present from the start, always available for interpretation.

For Anna, as for her predecessor Hug-Hellmuth, the child is not a
minuscule adult. He or she is *sent* to analysis, does not come of her own
accord and must thus be won over. Parents must be kept in touch with;
there must be some preparatory knowledge of the child's environment so that
such external factors can be correctly interpreted within the analysis. Ideally,
too, for the analysis to be successful, there should be some co-operative
linkage with schools, so that education and 'reality factors' do not undo
analytic progress. As for transference, Anna's experience had, she felt, shown
her that 'a child is not ready to produce a new edition of his love relationships
because, as one might say, the old edition is not yet exhausted. His original

objects, the parents, are still real and present as love objects, not only in fantasy as with the adult neurotic.'

Ten analyses featured in Anna's book, the two elder Burlingham children and their friend, Adelaide Sweetzer, among them. Through dreams, daydreams, drawings and play, their cases emerge. Ten-year-old Bob Burlingham is 'the boy who could never tell the truth and wanted to give up this habit'; Mabbie, the eight year old who 'cried so often and was angry with herself for doing so' and wanted to come back into the world 'as a doll who belonged to a little girl – with whom my nurse was before – who is specially nice and good'; and Adelaide, the girl who had a devil in her and wanted it taken out.

Bob Burlingham was intensely hostile to Anna at the start of analysis; she uses his case to show how a child needs to be won over – effectively seduced by the analyst – for analysis to have any effect. Anna protected Bob from punishment, returned money he had stolen, did him favours and eventually won his 'most extensive co-operation'. It was only then that she felt the real work of analysis could begin:

We have to free a part of this boy's masculine aggressiveness and his object love for his mother from repression and from the overlay by the present passive-feminine character and mother identification. The conflict involved is an inner one. While the fear of his real father in the external world originally drove him into carrying out the repression, the success of this achievement depends for its maintenance upon inner forces. The father has been internalized, the superego has become the representative of his powers, and the fear of him is felt by the boy as castration anxiety. At every step which the analysis takes on the path toward making conscious the repressed oedipal tendencies, it encounters outbreaks of this castration anxiety as an obstacle. Only the laborious historico-analytic dissolution of this superego permits the work of liberation to progress.

Anna's tone about Bob is didactic: there is a clear normative impulse. Bob's 'passive feminine character', his super-ego, need to be worked on, the study makes clear, so that he can free himself from the feminine attitude and progress to normal heterosexual development. Anna's role, part analyst, part surrogate parent, is to help shape him, and in some measure to act as an ego ideal. If this method is fraught with the dangers of creating dependency in the patient, this was, certainly in the case of the Burlingham children, something Anna did not fear but rather desired.

Anna was not unaware of her normative impulses. She wrote to Lou after Lou had praised the book: 'I was not at all sure that you would be satisfied, especially because they are children, whom I always want to change, while you prefer to leave as they are.'

Anna's tone of knowing what was right and best for a patient is one that is rarely heard in Freud's case histories, which read rather more like artful enquiries into the labyrinth of the human psyche, more dominated by scientific curiosity than the desire to change. It is perhaps this which in part led him to designate his daughter as 'reactionary' when compared to Melanie Klein. He certainly had long had misgivings about combining pedagogy and psychoanalysis; before the war, he had warned Maggie Heller, the daughter of the publisher and analyst Hugo Heller, to keep psychoanalysis distinct from the inevitable normative demands of pedagogy. And, for all her heat and occasional theoretical fuzziness, Klein is never normative. As Joan Riviere said in her inimitably clear and decisive way at the London Symposium Ernest Jones organized in 1927 to allow Klein and her English supporters to respond to Anna Freud's work:

Psychoanalysis is Freud's discovery of what goes on in the imagination of a child [...] But analysis has no concern with anything else: it is not concerned with the real world, nor with the child's nor the adult's adaptation to the real world, nor with sickness nor health, nor virtue nor vice. It is concerned simply and solely with the imaginings of the childish mind, the fantasied pleasures and the dreaded retributions.

It is interesting to note that Freud never publicly disclaimed or argued against Melanie Klein's work, as he did with so many other supposedly renegade followers. Privately, however, his feelings were inevitably with his daughter. Small wonder: Ernest Jones had entered the child analysis fray on Klein's side and hit below the analytic belt. 'It is a pain to me that I cannot agree with some of the tendencies in Anna's book, and I cannot help thinking that they must be due in part to some imperfectly analyzed resistances; in fact I think it is possible to prove this in detail.'

Freud hit back. The imputation that his daughter's Oedipus complex was still unresolved, that she had been imperfectly analysed, and that this kept her from delving into her own analysands' muddied Oedipal waters, could not go unanswered. At first his rebuke to Jones was gentle enough:

When two analysts are of different opinions on one point, the assumption that the erroneous view of one may originate in the fact that he is not completely analysed, so that he allows himself to be influenced by his complexes at a cost of science, may in some cases be completely justified. But in practical polemics I consider such an argument is not admissible, because each party can make use of this argument and it does not help to come to a judgment as to which party is in error.

Freud is even willing to concede in agreement with Klein 'that children are much more mature than we previously thought', though he holds out on the question of the formation of the super-ego: 'I would like to challenge Frau Klein's statement that the superego of the child is as independent as that of the adult. It seems rather to me that Anna is right in emphasizing the point that the superego of the child is still the direct parental influence.'

But after the Innsbruck International Congress and the publication of the London Symposium material in the *International Journal* edited by Jones, Freud's anger peaked. Amongst the various attacks on Anna, the charge of her insufficient analysis had been repeated. Ella Freeman Sharpe, for example, had noted:

The problem of child analysis seems more subtly implicated with the analyst's own deepest unexplored repressions than adult analysis.... Rationalisations that the child is too young, that the weakness of the superego makes an admixture of pedagogy with analysis indispensable, and so on, are built upon the alarms of that very same infantile superego in the analyst that he has to deal with in the child before him.

Freud wrote his sharpest letter yet to Jones:

You are organizing a veritable campaign in London against Anna's child analysis. In this you make the accusation that she has not been deeply enough analysed, and you repeat this accusation in a letter to me. I must point out to you that such a criticism is as dangerous as it is impermissible. Who, then, has been sufficiently well analysed? I can assure you that Anna has been more deeply and thoroughly analysed than, for instance, yourself. The whole criticism is based on a slipshod assumption which with a little good will could have been avoided. Frau Klein concluded from a remark of Anna's to a child, which was intended to spur the child on to find the material by itself, that Anna avoids the Oedipus complex in her analyses. She draws this conclusion without any knowledge of the rest of the analysis. The whole attack is based on this belief. At the Congress Frau Klein taxes Anna with this, and in response to Anna's reply: 'What else but the Oedipus complex would I be analysing in the child?' admits that she has misunderstood. But it is just this attack to which you are wanting to give the greatest publicity – a complete translation in the periodical, and publication as a separate brochure. In this symposium even such an otherwise intelligent person as Riviere permits herself theoretical assertions which are in conflict with all our knowledge and beliefs and which open the way to the removal of analysis from the sphere of reality. What is the meaning of all this? I believe I have a right to an explanation. The differences of opinion between two analysts about the development of the superego in children and about techniques of analysis are not so important that they cannot be left to history to decide, nor should they provoke such a hasty, violent and unjust reaction. Is this aimed at me, since Anna is my daughter? A fine motive amongst analysts who demand from others that they control their primitive urges!

The Anna Freud–Melanie Klein controversy was to run and run. It reached its height in wartime with the British Society's Controversial Discussions and achieved a very English compromise thereafter: an umbrella of consensus which permitted differences to live side by side despite continuing rumbles from opposing troops.

In truth, it is not hard to imagine that there was almost a visceral antipathy between the two women, so different were they in style and personality and hence, also, in their analytic undertakings: Anna with her hard-working rectitude, her vestal's hopes that people be good and the world the nice place of her nice stories; Melanie, with her vociferous blousiness, her forceful appetites, her passionate imprecisions. Alix Strachey, that wickedly shrewd, if somewhat anti-Semitic, observer of the social life of early analysis, in her letters home to her husband, characterizes Anna as 'that open or secret sentimentalist'; and Klein as a vulgar Cleopatra, 'a sort of ultra heterosexual Semiramis in slap-up fancy dress waiting to be pounced on.' And, she parenthesizes, 'I now think Anna Freud simply hates her on personal grounds because she thinks she's a "low" woman. Someone ought to speak to her about her general sniffiness, don't you think?'

If Anna was 'sniffy', it was because she did not like mess. Nor could she have felt a kinship with the uncontrolled cannibalistic and sadistic impulses, the rampant aggression, with which Klein inflected the child's imaginings.

The two women's relations to mother and mothering also mark their difference. By using her own children as her analytic subjects, Melanie Klein compounded the functions of analyst and parent, but named these as the function of analyst. In her work, the real mother disappears only to be apotheosized in theory in her iconographic function as breast.

Anna, never a mother herself, worked alongside real mothers as a kind of family aide and kept the maternal function intact, perhaps even isolated and idealized. Analysis, for her, remained separate from mothering, though it operated in alliance (or sometimes in conflict) with parental functions. These functions were idealized in their power and goodness. Anna, after all, was the dutiful daughter, her superego formed by Sigmund and Martha. If her link with her own mother was the less easily acknowledged one, it shaped her view of the maternal without allowing her to assimilate it openly within herself. The formative influence of Anna's tie with her sister Sophie should also not be minimized. When Sophie died, Anna took her son, Ernst, on as her first 'patient'. She did not attempt to supplant and was perhaps scared of supplanting her dead rival, Sophie, whose image, idealized by her family, she continued to maintain. Analytic mothering and real mothering remained distinct in Anna's life and work, each acting upon the other without ever being transcended into a theoretical construct or linked wholly in the figure of the analyst.

Anna's view that children and adults were different in the crucial matter of the fluidity of the child's super-ego made schooling and environmental factors particularly important to the child's development. In this latter emphasis Anna's was at one with the socialist hopes of Vienna's therapeutically inclined radicals, her friends Bernfeld and Aichhorn. She was part of the entire tradition of liberal political reformism to which so many early feminists, including Bertha Pappenheim, belonged. In a 1927 lecture, she claimed that the most important future application of psychoanalysis must be 'to pedagogics or the sciences of upbringing and education'. Normal development and preventive therapy were her primary interests and these took on physical form in her first educational experiment.

The Hietzing or 'Matchbox' school was built in Eva Rosenfeld's backyard with Dorothy Burlingham's money in 1927. The impetus for the school came from Anna's and Dorothy's sense that the Burlingham children, 'being both American, and worse still, analysed', were not fitted for conventional Viennese schooling. This was compounded with Anna's belief that children in analysis would benefit from schools which co-operated with analytic values.

The school stayed open for five years and had some twenty pupils, about half of whom were in analysis. Anna's nephew, Ernst, whom she had virtually adopted, was one of these. He later became an analyst and changed his name to Freud. The teachers, who implemented a broad project-based curriculum designed to engage the children's imagination, were Peter Blos and Erik Erikson, then an artist and later a leading analyst in America.

Reflecting on the Hietzing experiment in 1937 and taking into account the difficulties her own children had faced in adapting to ordinary forms of schooling, Dorothy Burlingham was muted about its success. In her paper, 'Problems Confronting the Psychoanalytic Educator', she notes that such 'protected' children are 'especially oversensitive', 'not readily inclined to accept restrictions', 'can scarcely tolerate any criticism or admonition', and need particular help in adapting to the demands of external reality. Hietzing shared the problems of many other idealistic educational ventures. Since it is impossible to gauge what alternate lives people might have led if conditions had been different, it is difficult to judge whether the Burlingham children were hindered or helped by the experience of analysis combined with special schooling and Anna's analytic mothering. Certainly the children, especially the two eldest, though they loved Anna, felt trapped by her double role and by the constant glare of analysis on their feelings and actions – much as Anna, as she had confessed to Lou, had felt 'pulled apart ... mishandled and mistreated' in her analysis by her own father. This, compounded by their fractured loyalties to warring parents, did not help to make their emotional trajectory through life particularly smooth. Mabbie committed suicide at the age of fifty-seven while staying at Maresfield Gardens. Bob repeated his father's manic-depressive cycles, and, despite continuing analysis with Anna, who never recommended the use of drugs, declined and died at the age of fifty-four.

Anna and Dorothy were not unaware of the burden of being analysed and its hazards. Its antidote was the idyll of simplicity and naturalness the countryside provided. Hiking weekends and holidays in the open air were the order of family life, complete with *dirndls* for the women. Eventually, in 1930, there was the farmhouse Dorothy and Anna bought forty-five minutes from Vienna. *Hochroterd*, complete with cow, flock of chickens, vegetable and flower gardens and extravagant views, became their refuge. As Anna said, 'I like it about farm life that it brings down to a simple formula, even psychic things.'

With the extension of her analytic practice in the late 1920s, Anna's interests began to focus on very young or pre-latency children, which brought her a fraction closer to Klein, and on adolescents or post-latency children like the elder Burlinghams. Here was the groundwork for her second and perhaps most important book, *The Ego and the Mechanisms of Defence*, which appeared in 1936 as an eightieth birthday present for Freud, though portions of it had been delivered as lectures from 1929 on. The book had a decisive impact on what was to become a particularly American brand of psychoanalysis, with its emphasis on ego development.

Anna was concerned to deny, perhaps once again so as to counter Melanie Klein, that psychoanalysis must deal only with depth psychology – with unconscious psychic life, the repressed instinctual impulses, affects and fantasies. Clinical practice, psychoanalytic therapy, she claims, makes nonsense of this. 'From the beginning analysis, as a therapeutic method, was concerned with the ego and its aberrations: the investigation of the id and of its mode of operation was always only a means to an end. And the end was invariably the same: the correction of these abnormalities and the restoration of the ego to its integrity.'

However contentious some found and continue to find this, it is part and parcel of Anna's chosen emphasis on psychoanalysis as primarily a therapy rather than a theory, and as a psychology of the normal.

The book is particularly acute in its insights into teenagers, the way in which this phase of life, with its pendulum swing between asceticism and self-gratification, re-enacts earlier infantile sexual configurations. Anna gives a lucid account of the ten means by which the ego defends itself against incursions from the unruly impulses of the id: repression, reaction-formation, projection, introjection, regression, sublimation, isolation, undoing, reversal, and turning against the self. She shows how these can help the ego to adapt to reality and also how in excess they fail. To these ten, Anna adds two original defence mechanisms, both of which are linked to her own self-analysis, and both of which have become classics of ego psychology.

The first is 'identification with the aggressor', which, Anna points out, is a common 'stage in the normal development of the superego'. The child internalizes the criticism of his elders, making their characteristics and opinions his own. But if the child introjects both rebuke and punishment and then regularly projects this same punishment on another, 'then he is arrested at an intermediate stage in the development of the superego', never having quite completed the internalization of the critical process. Alternately this aggression may be directed too severely inwards and the child becomes melancholic or depressed. Of the many variations on the theme of identification with the aggressor, Anna herself was prone to the depressive one, directing what she perceived as others' hostility inwards on herself and gauging her own lack of value by their estimation.

The second syndrome which Anna newly identifies as a defence is 'altruistic surrender'. Here she examines the case of a governess who gives up her own instinctual impulses in favour of other people, displacing her ambitious fantasies on to her men friends and her libidinal wishes on to her women friends. The governess lives wholly in the lives of other people, instead of having any experience of her own. Anna traces the governess's problem back to her early family life and finds there 'a narcissistic mortification', a disappointment with herself, which prevented her from living her own life and caused her to displace her wishes on those better qualified to fulfil them. This altruistic surrender, as Anna makes clear by quoting the example of Cyrano, can extend to the point where the subject's own life is less valuable than another's and one's own death is attended with no fear:

In conclusion, we may for a moment study the notion of altruistic surrender from another angle, namely in its relation to the fear of death. Anyone who has very largely projected his instinctual impulses onto other people knows nothing of this fear. In the moment of danger his ego is not really concerned for his own life. He experiences instead excessive concern and anxiety for the lives of his love objects.

Like Cyrano and the altruistic governess, Anna may indeed have given up some of her own instinctual impulses and lived in part vicariously in an identification with her father. She was an adept at the very defences she chose to study. Some of the older members of the Society were a little resentful to find her spare, austere figure increasingly in his chair. As Eduard Hitschmann acidly put it: 'There Freud sat and taught us the *drives*, and now Anna sits there and teaches us the *defences*.'

But Anna's self-surrender served the Freud family well, when the Nazis invaded Austria in 1938 and made their iron presence increasingly felt. Freud, unlike so many of his colleagues and despite urgent advice from all sides, still refused to leave Vienna. Only after two visits from the Gestapo and Anna's round-up did he concede. Anna, armed with the veronal she then always carried, had been taken in for questioning in March 1938. In the Gestapo headquarters, she had the wit to get herself transferred from an endless wait in a corridor to an interrogation room, and then to give so cool a description of the scientific work of the International Association that she was released. When she returned home, seemingly unperturbed, it was Freud who lost his composure. He was seen to weep for the first time. He also at last announced that the family would leave Vienna.

Together with Princess Marie Bonaparte, Anna worked tirelessly to arrange the necessary passes, sift the Vienna Society archives and Freud's papers, and crate up their belongings. On 4 June 1938, the Freuds left the birthplace of psychoanalysis and made their way via Paris to London.

Ends and Beginnings

Freud died on 23 September 1939. Stoical to the end, he had finally asked his doctor, Max Schur, to administer morphine: 'Now it's nothing but torture and makes no sense any more.' He had asked Schur to communicate his wish to Anna, who only acceded to it on Freud's insistence.

Dorothy was in America, trapped by the war into extending what had been intended as a brief visit. In what was now characteristic fashion, Anna relieved her acute mourning with hard work. Five days after the funeral she was seeing patients. Work, even if only for a few minutes at a time, made her forget; afterwards, she would always recommend it for mourners. But forgetting is only one half of mourning; remembering is the other. And there is a sense in which Anna's vast archival enterprise is a memorial to her father: when she was reading his handwriting, she felt him near. The vigilance she exercised in the future over these writings – tantamount to censorship in the historian's eye – was no less than the jealous protectiveness with which she had surrounded her father.

By the time Dorothy returned to England in April 1940, Anna seemed at least superficially her old energetic self again:

I can only admire Anna, how very wonderful she is. She goes on with life more intensely than she ever has, has many ideas & plans. She is building up her life without her father & yet somehow it is still his personality & his life which you feel in everything she does. Everything is simple, natural, and real that she does....

In certain respects, London, a bastion of the Kleinians, was the worst place to which Anna could have come. America would have been far more welcoming, but for a technical hitch: the American Society did not permit lay analysts. Then, too, for Freud and Anna, there were sentimental reasons. Freud's admiration for England dated from his youth, from the heady years in the 1870s of English positivism and of liberal democratic ideals, the land of Cromwell and Mill; so he had his boyhood ideals to draw on when he reflected, on arriving in England in 1938, that now he could 'die in freedom'. It would have been unthinkable for Freud to emigrate to America, the land he had once called a 'gigantic mistake'. And it would have been equally unthinkable for Anna to leave behind her the land in which her father's remains rested. Nor should one underestimate how congenial the British psychological temper, with its J. M. Barries and Lewis Carrolls, was to prove to a psychoanalysis centred on children, as both Anna Freud and Melanie Klein were to discover. It was in Britain that Anna and Dorothy were to consolidate the work for which they became deservedly famous.

The two women had already run an experimental nursery in Vienna, the Edith Jackson project – a nursery which catered for the children of families under financial duress. The wartime Blitz produced an even more pressing need: a home for young children who ought to be evacuated from the most heavily bombed areas and who in certain instances had already posed billeting (or fostering) problems. In January 1941, the Children's Rest Centre in Wedderburn Road, Hampstead, was opened and by the summer two further addresses were acquired, one in Netherhall Gardens, Hampstead, the other, New Barn in Essex, a residence for older children. With a staff which included psychologists like Ilse Hellman, also a Viennese refugee, and care professionals, an assortment of refugees and the occasional mother of a billeted child, the homes catered for some 120 children, amongst them a proportion of tiny babies. Apart from the immediate and vital war work the Hampstead Nurseries provided, the insights garnered from the experience significantly shaped fostering and welfare policy, social work and paediatrics after the war in Britain and America.

Anna's and Dorothy's work with the War Nurseries is systematically documented in *Infants Without Families and Reports on the Hampstead Nurseries 1939–1945*, a short version of which was published in 1944, as well as the shorter *Young Children in War-Time* of 1942. Both books show an underlying concern with determining the advantages and hazards of institutional life. They also make manifest the psychoanalytical backdrop of the nurseries: the advantages and disadvantages of institutional rearing vary according to the child's phase of psychic development.

What comes clearly to the fore here is the singular importance of the mother in the child's emotional life. It is almost as if Anna Freud has taken on Melanie Klein's seminal insights, rid them of their revolutionary excess, their aura of an original and hence unmoveable sin, and translated them into the register of 'normal' development.

For the small child, the air raids are 'simply a new symbol for old fears'. The four year old's bad conscience – usually externalized in fear of thunder and lightning, devils and lions and tigers and bogeymen – now names fear as Hitler and German planes. 'We shall know that peace has returned when nothing is left for the children to be afraid of except their own former ghosts and bogeymen.'

But air raids, the real effects of the Blitz, provoke anxiety insofar as the mother is anxious.

A child in the infant stage of 1, 2, 3, 4 years of age will shake and tremble with the anxiety of his mother, and this anxiety will impart itself the more thoroughly to the child the younger he is. The primitive emotional tie between mother and baby, which in some respects still makes one being out of the two, is the basis for the development of this type of air raid anxiety in children. The quiet manner in which the London population on the whole met the air raids is therefore responsible in one way for the extremely rare occurrence of 'shocked' children.

What does have a crucially formative impact on the child is separation from the mother. In case after case, the War Nurseries Records document the adverse effects of the child's separation anxiety, from the babe in arms to the five year old. This is so even if institutional conditions are materially healthier and happier than the child's home life. The tiniest child, whose difficulties may be compounded by weaning, may find seeming solace in the nursery's maternal substitute after only a few days since 'his needs are overwhelming, his helplessness is extreme, and his distinction between one person and another is still in the beginning stage.'

But for the 3–5 year olds, separation acts as an intolerable confirmation of all their negative feelings. All the inevitable hate and attendant guilt, which are part and parcel of child–parent relations, are held in check and neutralized in ordinary family life by affection. 'It does not seem so very dangerous to kill a parent in fantasy if at the same time outward evidence shows that this same parent is alive and well.' But with the absence of the parents, 'the child is frightened ... and suspects that their desertion may be another punishment or even the consequence of his own bad wishes. To overcome this guilt he overstresses all the love which he has ever felt for his parents. This turns the natural pain of separation into an intense longing which is hard to bear,' and into a rage against himself. All the effects of this are exacerbated when it is the mother who is absent. Acquiring language, toilet training, eating, play – all are affected by the ruptured emotional bond with the mother.

As the result of such observations, after a year the Nurseries introduced a new organizational practice: children were grouped into family-like modules, four or five children to a staff 'mother' according to mutual choice. Real mothers were encouraged to visit. Recommendations were also made that children be gradually prepared for separation, since their later difficulties often depended on the manner and suddenness with which this had taken place. This preparation was equally important in moving them from the institution (or foster family) back to their own parents. After the war, Anna and her nursery social worker, James Robertson, campaigned for similar preparation to be made for sick children going into hospital and for mothers to stay close to them during the period of hospital care. She also kept in touch with the Nurseries' children, sending them birthday and Christmas presents well into the 1950s.

In November 1941, Anna and Dorothy set up an informal training programme for the younger members of the Nurseries' staff. Linking theoretical lectures, practice with all age-groups and aspects of the Nurseries' work, and supervision by more experienced staff, the programme served as a foundation for the post-war Hampstead Child Therapy Clinic and Course.

While the sirens blared across London and world war raged, the British Psycho-Analytical Society mirrored its aggressions within its more contained theatre. Melanie Klein had reacted with anger and anxiety to the arrival of a large group of Viennese analysts, Anna Freud at their head. She was angry at Jones, her staunch supporter, for aiding their immigration and anxious that the British Society would be swamped by their anti-Kleinian views. Rumours and accusations flew between the opposed camps, increasing distrust. The culmination was a series of public 'scientific' debates, which came to be known as the Controversial Discussions. It is impossible here to detail what is now published as a thousand-page document covering these discussions. The opponents were formidable. Ranged behind Klein were amongst others, the brilliant Susan Isaacs, Joan Riviere and Paula Heimann; and with Anna, Edward Glover, President of the Society since Jones had retired to the country, and Melitta Schmideberg (Klein's estranged daughter) – both, for Anna, somewhat uncomfortable bedfellows.

At the core of this psychoanalytic war lay the body of the father: the daughters and sisters were fighting over Freud and perhaps, as Antigone had done for her brothers, the right to bury him in their own way. At issue was the question of what was psychoanalysis and who was the purer Freudian – Anna or Melanie. The crusading Melanie certainly thought she was, and she was effectively more like Freud, the adventurous conquistador, than the conservative Anna, though he, himself, had always sought to keep this characteristic in himself under tight rein. In a letter to Ernest Jones, Klein claimed that Freud had not drawn the full conclusions from his work and that 'It is tragic that his daughter, who thinks that she must defend him against me, does not realise that I am serving him better than she.' Anna, of course, begged to disagree: where her father's sacred ashes were concerned, she was intransigent. James Strachey characterized the battle between the two women in his own wryly sensible way:

My own view is that Mrs K. has made some highly important contributions to Ψa [psychoanalysis], but that it's absurd to make out (a) that they cover the whole subject or (b) that their validity is axiomatic. On the other hand, I think it is equally ludicrous for Miss F. to maintain that Ψa is a Game Reserve belonging to the F. family and that Mrs K.'s ideas are fatally subversive.

These attitudes on both sides are of course purely religious and the very antithesis of science. They are also (on both sides) infused by, I believe, a desire to dominate the situation & in particular the future....

As the salvoes sounded, the substantial differences between the Anna Freudians and the Kleinians did emerge clearly. At their centre were disparities in their understanding of the infant's earliest life. Where for Klein there was the encompassing influence of innate unconscious fantasies on development, for Anna there was a mix of innate and environmental factors. Klein argued that 'as a result of his own uncontrollable greedy and destructive fantasies and impulses against his mother's breasts' the infant in his second six months was thrust into 'the depressive position', thereby stressing the primacy of aggressive instincts, or what for Freud came under the aegis of the death instinct. Anna argued that the earliest instinct was for self-gratification and that the infant went through a narcissistic phase first.

In the discussion of 7 April 1943, Anna, in response to a paper by Susan Isaacs, put her case with her usual terse lucidity:

The following seems to me an outstanding difference between Mrs Klein's theories and psychoanalytical theory as I understand it. For Mrs Klein object relationship begins with, or soon after, birth, whereas I consider that there is a narcissistic and auto-erotic phase of several months' duration, which precedes what we call object relationship in its proper sense, even though the beginnings of object relation are slowly built up during this initial stage. According to Mrs Isaacs' descriptions, the new-born infant, already in the first six months, loves, hates, desires, attacks, wishes to destroy and to dismember his mother, etc. He has feelings of guilt towards her, commits acts of aggression, of reparation, and does things on her behalf or against her wishes. This means that his attitude towards her is that of a fully developed object relationship.

According to my own conception of this same period, the infant is at this time exclusively concerned with his own well-being. The mother is important, so far as she serves or disturbs this well-being. She is an instrument of satisfaction or denial, and as such of extreme importance in the child's narcissistic scheme of things.

Anna then asked whether Mrs Isaacs would agree with the two following formulations:

One of the outstanding differences between Freudian and Kleinian theory is that Mrs Klein sees in the first months of life evidence of a wide range of differentiated object relations, partly libidinal and partly aggressive. Freudian theory on the other hand allows at this period only for the crudest rudiments of object relationship and sees life governed by the desire for instinct gratification, in which perception of the object is only achieved slowly. ...

The assumption of early object phantasies in Mrs Klein's theories is bound up with the theoretical substitution of a very early stage of rich and varied object relationship, for the early phase of narcissism and auto-erotism as described by Freud.

The second area of disagreement, Anna went on to point out, lay in the dating of the synthetic function of the ego, which 'consists in correlation between an inner urge and an inner prohibition'. Here too, her own observations made her more Freudian than Klein:

This achievement which, in Kleinian theory, is ascribed to the very beginning of life, belongs, in Freudian view, to the development of the Oedipus complex and its consequences for the formation of the superego. The affect which accompanies this unification is guilt. I cannot see evidence of this reaction before the third year.

As for early fantasy, that hoary disagreement which had made the Kleinians label her as a hater of the 'deep' and unpsychoanalytical, Anna is quick to defend herself:

Mrs Isaacs believes that we object to the concept of early phantasy because of a prejudice against psychic reality as such; if it were so, this would disqualify us as psychoanalysts ... the term 'phantasy', in its new use in Kleinian theory, covers modes of mental functioning for which we use other terms: thinking, reality-thinking, remembering, wishing, longing, in short all mental activities of the infant.

Moreover, Anna argues:

The early phantasies most frequently described in Kleinian theory are violently aggressive phantasies. This seems logical to the analysts who are convinced of the preponderance of the death instinct at the beginning of life. The existence of these same phantasies is widely questioned by those to whom the libidinal impulses seem of overwhelming importance for this time of life. Again, the underlying difference of opinion does not refer directly to phantasy activity but partly to dating as before, and partly to a divergence of views about instinct theory.

It is evident that under the influence of Klein and with the growth of her clinical work, Anna had come some way towards Klein in the years since her first book. However, the differences between the two women remained substantial. Anna may have moved towards an understanding of the importance of the mother in the child's early development, but this was a real 'environmental' mother, not a fantasy object whose name was breast. Nor was the child, for Anna, a traumatized bundle of innate sadistic phantasms, but a developing creature whose ego had to be nurtured in order to achieve mature strength and robustness. These differences played themselves out in *The Psychoanalytic Study of the Child*, the first volume of which appeared in 1945. Edited by Anna Freud, Heinz Hartmann and Ernst Kris – the latter two had both settled in America – its first number was devoted to a critique and history of Kleinian analysis, and included Ernest Glover's attack on the Kleinian project as 'a bio-religious system which depends on faith rather than science ... [and] is a variant of the doctrine of Original Sin.' Anna and Klein may both desex the Oedipal triangle and reduce it to a mother–child dyad, but whereas Klein's version leads to an interest in psychoses, Anna's tends to a shoring up of the normal ego.

The Freud–Klein controversy affected the whole tangled question of how training should proceed in the British Society, given that it contained these warring forces. Anna resigned from the Training Committee when a 1944 draft report on training suggested that her views represented one of the 'extremes' of opinion in the divided Society. And she simply ceased to attend meetings of the Society for almost two years. Only in November 1946 was the matter finally resolved following lengthy discussions between Anna and the President, Sylvia Payne. John Bowlby, the new Secretary of the Training Committee, adapted a training proposal from Anna based on the principle of separate but equal. The training reflected what effectively became the constitution of the British Society: an A Group of Kleinians; a B Group of Anna Freudians; and a middle Group of Independents. The compromise training scheme set up two parallel programmes, a Course A taught by teachers from all groups; and a Course B taught by 'Miss Freud and her colleagues'. Both courses would function under one Training Committee and students would come together for lectures and seminars other than those on technique.

The battle over Freud's legacy, together with the work at the Hampstead Nursery and the continuing strain of war, took their toll on Anna. The war's end brought a roll call of the dead, including that of her aunts, one at the Theresienstadt concentration camp – the very camp from which in August 1945 came the pack of six 'wild' children whose case she charted later in her 'Experiment in Group Upbringing' of 1951 – the others at Auschwitz and Treblinka. There had been other deaths too, following that of her father's on the eve of war. Aunt Minna had outlived Freud by less than two years. Her death allowed Dorothy to move into Maresfield Gardens, but increased Martha's loneliness. Then early in 1946, two more friends from Vienna died.

Anna fell ill, her flu quickly aggravating itself into a severe pneumonia, which almost resulted in her own death. As Elisabeth Young-Bruehl evocatively demonstrates, in her illness Anna identified with her father, relived her past and, for the first time since Freud's death, allowed her grief to overcome her. The helplessness of being ill thrust her back into the helplessness of childhood. Many of her dreams of the time centred on her father; their recurrent theme was losing and being lost:

I dream, as I have often done, that he is here again. All of these recent dreams have the same character: the main role is played not by my longing for him but rather by his longing for me. The main scenes in the dreams are always of his tenderness to me, which always takes the form of my own, earlier tenderness. ... In the first dream of this kind he openly said: I have always longed for you so.

The main feeling in yesterday's dream is that he is wandering about (on top of mountains, hills) while I am doing other things. At the same time, I have an inner restlessness, a feeling that I should stop whatever I am doing and go walking with him. Eventually he calls me to him and demands this himself. I am very relieved and lean myself against him, crying in a way that is very familiar to both of us. Tenderness. My thoughts are troubled: he should not have called me, it is as if a renunciation or a form of progress had been undone because he called. I am puzzled. In the dream the feeling is very strong that he is wandering around alone and 'lost'.

Anna interpreted this and other dreams in an extended process of self-analysis. The dreams formed the core of her insights in 'About Losing and Being Lost', which was first drafted in 1948. In this paper, she shows how losers in a process of identification project on to the object they have lost their own emotions. So too the person in mourning. Freud, in the above dream, expresses the longing that Anna feels. The subject's own feeling of being lost, rejected, alone – a childhood constellation – is displaced on to the lost object, whether person or thing. But the mourning 'dreamer feels in the grip of conflicting emotions and alternates between pure joy about the reunion and remorse and guilt for having stayed away from the dead one, neglected him.' Such dreams are the means of overcoming mourning. They show 'simultaneous urges to remain loyal to the dead and to turn toward new ties with the living.'

Anna did both. She remained more loyal and protective of her father than he would certainly ever have been of himself – assiduously monitoring editions of his letters or stories of his life, fighting battle after battle in his name. But she also intrepidly set out into territory he never entered, organizing clinics and schools, engaging with the 'real world' of welfare, battling for children who were not hers, but perhaps lost, like her. Dorothy Burlingham, on the third anniversary of Freud's death, strikes the note:

We are lucky in Anna Freud. It's amazing that there should be two such personalities in one family. It had to be a woman, only a woman could have been able to enjoy & grow from such a father & yet to be able to keep independent of thought & to continue as she does now growing & giving out. I have often seen a person who has lived for another person, sort of shrink & lose whatever they had gotten when that person is gone – but there is none of that with Anna Freud. Her meetings are brilliant. ... I often look around at those young faces and enjoy their enthusiasm, their earnestness and appreciation of what has come their way.

The death of her mother at the age of ninety in November 1951 did not evoke the same extensive mourning in Anna as had her father's. Martha had never been a point of identification or longing, only a rival to be displaced, a figure who up until the very end criticized Anna's clothes or demeanour, was sceptical about child analysis (as indeed about analysis generally), and was particularly scathing about its cost in biscuits and knitting wool. Yet they had lived together the whole of Anna's life and, despite her usual restraint, Anna wept openly at her death. If Anna's work with children had gradually allowed her to see the importance of the maternal role, she could with Martha's death begin to acknowledge some of her own mother's virtues: her unflappable bravery when faced with the Nazis; her skilful management of their large household; her high standards.

The Hampstead Clinic

A few months after Martha's death, the Hampstead Clinic, funded with money from the United States, opened its doors. Anna was fifty-six years old and the Clinic was to provide the main forum for her prodigious activities until her death thirty years later. The Clinic combined all Anna's youthful aims. It linked treatment of disturbed children from any variety of backgrounds with their education, child therapy with family life. From the base of a training programme, the Clinic gradually acquired a number of other dimensions: a nursery catering mainly for children from poor and immigrant backgrounds; a well-baby clinic providing medical and psychological counselling for mothers; child analysis, sometimes combined with analysis of mothers; a unit, run by Dorothy, for blind children and their mothers; and a research section, which developed the Hampstead Diagnostic Profile, a unique system for assessing the multifarious aspects of a child's development. This was based on the detailed Index instituted by Dorothy, a veritable mine of child observation data to be shared with all workers in the field. As the work of the Clinic progressed, so too did its publishing programme.

The Clinic was the 'something of her own' Anna had always wanted. Sometimes she talked of it as her child. Certainly, it fulfilled the child in her: 'It looks so gay and charming that one regrets not being a problem child oneself,' she wrote to an American contact in 1952.

Freud had worried about Anna working too hard. In the second part of her life, this work continued unabated. The clinic and analysis aside, Anna taught, wrote, lectured, edited and organized symposia. Freud's centenary celebrations in 1956 bore her stamp and were marked by the start of the *Standard Edition* and the completion of Ernest Jones's biography, on both of which she had been consulted closely. But perhaps the most influential of her undertakings was the Child Developmental Profile, formulated, reformulated and tested in the decade after the centenary. Designed to assess both a child's normality or abnormality, and chart development along a series of different lines, this diagnostic tool marked the culmination of Anna's difference from her father. The profile, culled from numerous observations, is based on the understanding that the child's condition is in flux and, unlike the adult's, cannot be gauged by a fixed symptomatology or simply charted on an instinct-based unilinear sequence which runs through oral, anal and phallic stages. There is a libidinal base, but a further series of composite lines mark the way a child matures, moving 'from dependency to emotional self-reliance and adult object relationships'. These include a line which moves from primary narcissism through to relations with others; another that moves from a child's play with its own and its mother's body through transitional objects to work. The Profile as a diagnostic method and Anna's concept of a developmental psychopathology continue to be of considerable importance, particularly in the United States.

Anna's interests in the 1960s moved more decisively than they had before from psychopathology to normal development, the first informing the second. Various research groups at the Clinic investigated learning disturbances and eating disorders, delinquency and promiscuity, as well as what was becoming increasingly Anna's concern, child and family law. One of the comments which made the round of the Clinic's students evokes an understanding which had informed her work from its earliest Vienna days, but which now was clearly on the surface. About a child, whose troubled mother was seeking the Clinic's help, Anna was heard to say: 'It is not quite clear yet whether the child needs analysis or the mother needs a housekeeper.' This was a very far cry from the Freudian or Kleinian focus on the deep unconscious. But then, Freud has been noted as saying about a woman who during her divorce was seeking analysis, 'She doesn't need psychoanalysis, she needs resignation.' If not in her wit, then perhaps in her practice, Anna had moved a considerable distance from Freud.

At the turn of the decade, following a period both as lecturer and informal student at the Yale University Law School, Anna extended psychoanalysis into family law in a project which was to have far-reaching consequences. With Albert Solnit and Joseph Goldstein, and with the collaboration of Dorothy Burlingham, she co-wrote *Beyond the Best Interests of the Child* (1973), which was followed by *Before the Best Interests of the Child* (1979) and *In the Best Interests of the Child*. Together these books helped to shape child custody legislation in the United States and provoked a debate whose repercussions continue – including Jon Elster's recent attacks on the arrogant irrationality of assuming that the act of calculating the best interests of the child can be accomplished without exacerbating the conflict in which the child is already caught up.

Based on the lessons garnered from the work of the wartime nurseries, the shaping emphasis of these books lies in the understanding that a child's perspective of the world is different from an adult's. A child's experience of time, of the length of a parent's absence or presence, is not the same as an adult's. For 'sound development' to take place, stable bonds need to be formed. A child's fundamental need is for 'unbroken continuity of affectionate and stimulating relationships'. A 'psychological parent', who genuinely cares for a child, can provide this as well as a biological parent. It follows then that protracted custody decisions, temporary foster placements, the shuttlecock business of joint custody, are not in the child's best interests. What the courts and welfare agencies need to take into account in disputed cases, the authors argue, is what is 'the least detrimental available alternative for safeguarding the child's growth and development.' As for state intervention, the authors take a minimalist line: it should occur 'if and only if it provides the child in jeopardy with a less detrimental alternative'. What may seem to state officials as questionable parental behaviour may be less detrimental to a child than being severed from parents. This is re-emphasized in the third book in the series, which examines the problems care professionals encounter, and probes their normalizing points of view and personal psychology. Too often, a social worker's 'rescue fantasies' may lead them to overstep bounds and confuse their own role with that of a saving parent.

If the note these volumes strike is a cautionary one, so too is that of many of Anna's last psychoanalytic writings. Whatever her idolization of her father, she did not see psychoanalysis as a universal panacea. When Marilyn Monroe's California analyst grieved her suicide and his failure to help the actress, Anna consoled her old friend and long-standing colleague, emphasizing that 'In these cases we are really defeated by something which is stronger than we are and for which analysis, with all its powers, is too weak a weapon.' Marilyn Monroe seemed to disagree with this pessimistic vision of the efficiency of psychoanalysis: she left a substantial legacy to her New York analyst, Marianne Kris, who in her turn made it over to the Hampstead Clinic.

The limits of analysis were clear to Anna. She may have moved beyond her father and accepted the importance of the mother-child relationship and the pre-Oedipal phase, but she did not believe that the analyst could stand in for the mother and make good primary lacks. After, and perhaps because of, the working through of her own 'nice stories', Anna was always firmly grounded in the real. Life was no more about restoring the bliss of a primal unity than it was about the easy enacting of any fantasies. It was always and ever, as Freud had insisted, the site of conflict. Psychoanalysis focused on the 'conflict within the individual person, the aims, ideas and ideals battling with the drives to keep the individual within a civilized community.' 'It has become modern', she wrote to a friend in 1974, 'to water this down to every individual's longing for a perfect unity with his mother, i.e., to be loved only as an infant can be loved. There is an enormous amount that gets lost this way....'

For Anna, the work of psychoanalysis was to enable an individual to live productively with – to use her own recurrent phrase – the inevitable vicissitudes of life. Psychoanalytic understanding, her own analysis had shown her, did not eradicate conflicts, the complex pain of living. Desires and life were reconciled in an uneasy truce, which had from time to time to be renegotiated. She did so herself, with an increasing stoicism which mirrored her father's. With old age, the circle of friends and family grew steadily smaller. When Dorothy died on 19 November 1979, after repeated bouts of illness, Anna mourned, wrapped herself in Dorothy's hand-knitted sweaters and carried on, battling against her severe anaemia, against a new host of her father's detractors, including Jeffrey Masson and Peter Swales, and organizing the second and third of the Hampstead Symposia. In March 1982, she suffered a stroke, which left her speech and motor abilities impaired, but not her humour. When her hands refused to knit as they had always done, she laughed at their unwillingness to comply in those feats of sublimation which she had required of them throughout her life: 'Look at what that hand did, it is angry because I controlled it for so long.'* The body Anna had sought to control finally gave out on 9 October 1982.

---

*One could write a whole alternate biography of Anna through the metaphor of knitting, an activity engaged in by Martha and all the Freud girls. Knitting, this most feminine of activities, with its auto-erotic subtext, was something Anna excelled in, first in competition with Sophie, perhaps in an attempt to win her mother's love, then throughout her life as a kind of meditative recreation, raised to the level of a craft, an idealized function in the dream of the 'natural life' she and Dorothy established in their country retreat. Knitting is also Anna's single visible point of identification with her mother and the feminine domain. Anna often knitted through analytic sessions; she and Dorothy knitted together and, after Dorothy's death, Anna wore one of her partner's knitted cardigans. Her sweaters were auctioned to raise money for the Hampstead Clinic. Freud once jokingly said to her: if all else failed, she could earn her keep by knitting. Appropriately, in the Freud Museum, Freud's presence is memorialized by his desk, couch and collection of antiques. Upstairs, in Anna's space, the dominant object is Dorothy Burlingham's loom.

At the end, a tiny Anna would have herself wrapped in Freud's capacious Lodenmantel – the green Austrian coat which now hangs in the Freud Museum – and wheeled to nearby Hampstead Heath. Her father's mantle had indeed always covered her, and she had kept the coat, like his memory, clean and intact through all the vicissitudes of her own and psychoanalysis's shared life. But Anna was more than the keeper of her father's shrine. The annals of analysis and child welfare, as well as the seven volumes of her writings, are testimonial to that. If she lived and thrived under the maidenly sign of the daughter and within the folds of what she conservatively understood as his psychoanalysis, she was also a remarkable woman who translated her appetites, her call for a double portion of 'wild stwawbewwies', into prodigious achievement.

10

HELENE DEUTSCH: AS IF A MODERN WOMAN

Helene Deutsch, the first of Freud's women to make a substantial and influential contribution to the analysis of the feminine, begins her autobiography, *Confrontations with Myself,* like this:

Only after completing this autobiography did I realize that it forms a supplement to the autobiography hidden in my general work *The Psychology of Women.* That is why I have decided to call this book an epilogue. I feel that the phrase 'one for all and all for one' could serve as a motto for my collected works, including this autobiography – a collection I would entitle simply *The Woman.*

Deutsch's insights into women are generalizations from herself: her life and her analytic writings are one. If she herself sees her condition and experience as emblematic – those of *The Woman* – then she is not far from wrong. This is particularly the case if we put the adjective 'modern' in front of 'woman'. The contradictions which bedevilled Deutsch, the trajectory of her own life, have a far more contemporary ring than is the case with any of the other early women analysts. Indeed, considered in the abstract, the ruling concerns of her life bear a striking resemblance to those of women who participated in the second great wave of feminism in the 1970s: early rebellion against mother and the confines of conventional feminine and family life, struggle for independence and education, self-identification as a socialist feminist, marginal disillusion with socialism, pursuit of a professional life, conflict between the demands of career and family, ambivalence over motherhood, split between sexual and maternal feminine identities.

   To cap the parallel, Deutsch's psychoanalytic preoccupations were with the key moments of female sexuality: menstruation, defloration, intercourse, pregnancy, infertility, childbirth, lactation, the mother–child relation, menopause. Translated into another idiom, this is the underlying agenda of any contemporary women's magazine – an agenda which her writings helped in some measure to create.

   That said, it comes as something of a surprise to find that in feminist circles Deutsch is the most reviled of all Freud's women, her name tarnished with the brush of a 'misogynist' Freud whose servile disciple she is purported to be. Glimpsed from under Freud's bruising patriarchal wing, Deutsch emerges as the reactionary apologist of female masochism, echoing a catechism which would make of woman a failed man, a devalued and penis-envying servant of the species. Yet reading Deutsch's life and not inconsiderable work afresh, a somewhat different image comes into focus. True, she took shelter in and inspiration from Freud's presence. Never primarily a theoretical thinker, she often reduced his insights by not distinguishing 'more clearly and cleanly between what is psychic and what is biological'. She took penis envy as a simple given rather than as a sign of that castration, which, either as fear or acceptance of loss, instigates the psychic construction of sexual difference. She also recast the imaginary eternal feminine into the mould of a real 'feminine erotic' mother and prescribed it as a norm.

None the less, when we unpack her multiple understandings of masochism, motherhood and motherliness, it is hard to see in these any devaluation of women. Nor, in her own masterly work as a clinician and teacher, is there any sense of her being less than equal to the male. If anything, the opposite is closer to the truth.

She was born Helene Rosenbach on 9 October 1884 in Przemyśl, a garrison town in Polish Galicia, then an outpost of the sprawling Austro-Hungarian Empire. Like Anna Freud, she was the third and youngest daughter, a late arrival in a family which already comprised the saintly and self-sacrificing eleven-year-old Malvina, the docile and artistic seven-year-old Gizela, and ten-year-old Emil, the only boy, whose poor academic performance, later gambling and wastrel tendencies gravely disappointed his parents. Helene's father, Wilhelm, was a prominent and respected lawyer, a liberal and a specialist in international law. His Jewishness, at a time when Jews were invariably second-class citizens, did not prevent him from becoming Galicia's representative at the Federal Court in Vienna: he was the first Jew in the region to be allowed to represent clients in court. Her mother, Regina, shared none of her husband's intellectual interests. As Helene described her, her own family was largely comprised of business people and her own aspirations were social and materialistic.

In the autobiography which she wrote in her late eighties, Deutsch evokes her Polish years with a textured and romantic intensity which is present nowhere else in this memoir. Przemyśl remained throughout her life 'the centre of the earth'. She also, and perhaps predictably after so many years spent as a practising analyst, casts her childhood in the terms of an Oedipal family romance and all but writes her life as an affirmation of the theories she has generated through its length. Her mother is a hated, malevolent figure, an irascible narrow-minded despot, prone to eruptions of temper during which she beats her children; she is particularly vengeful towards the young Helene, who disappointed her hopes by not being a boy. All Regina Rosenbach's motherly ambitions are 'centered around the good reputation of her daughters in the eyes of the world'. In contrast, Helene's father is idolized, a point of love and identification, a figure whom her shallow mother, only concerned with social forms, cannot understand or appreciate in the way that the young Helene can.

Wilhelm Rosenbach's office was in the family apartment. The young Helene – not unlike Anna and a similarly father-oriented Simone de Beauvoir – often occupied a chair under his desk from where she would watch and listen to clients and other lawyers arguing. Helene travelled with him to see clients and went to court with him. She thought at first of becoming a lawyer, but women were excluded from the law faculty. In Przemyśl, she became known as 'the old Rosenbach' and was lauded as the family's most beautiful daughter – and brilliant enough to be a son.

In *The Psychology of Women*, Deutsch links one kind of feminine masochism to an active identification with the father. She seems here to be speaking both for Anna Freud and herself, in evoking the third and youngest daughter whom the father chooses as the receptacle for his spiritual values:

It is as though the father's relation to the daughter has got rid of its dangers and freed itself from the fear of incest with the two older daughters. The third one – Cinderella – seems to be particularly suitable for the father's love choice because of her helplessness and apparent innocuousness. The need to save the little daughter from the aggressions of the mother and the older sisters certainly plays a great part here.

The 'powerful sensual current' that puberty brings may result in such father-identified girls splitting the father in two, finding a father figure who is also a lover – which was Helene's case – or in sublimating the erotic capacity altogether, which was Anna's. Deutsch notes:

The girl's renunciation of erotic fulfilment must not be judged by stereotyped standards. Observation teaches us that a strongly sublimated father–daughter tie does not necessarily involve neurosis or feelings of frustration and privation, even if it impairs the girl's erotic life. Fulfilment of the positive goal of life is not necessarily connected with normal sexuality.

She also remarks that:

the danger of such a relation to the father arises from the fact that sometimes he grants his daughter's request for an alliance and later abruptly breaks the bond. The father suddenly realizes, often under the prompting of the mother, that his daughter is approaching sexual maturity and should have more feminine interests; he refuses to have 'active' communion with her. Very often his own subsequent anxiety drives him to repudiate this relation.

This was how Deutsch understood Wilhelm Rosenbach's unwillingness to support her own desires for education beyond the age of fourteen. She had exhausted the academic possibilities that Przemyśl afforded women, and she was now 'expected to live the idle life of a debutante under my mother's tutelage until I married.' She had to run away from home twice before her parents gave in to her greater will, her fierce desire for independence and for some kind of professional status. On the second occasion, the condition of her return was that her father sign a contract binding him to help her obtain her *Abitur*, the diploma necessary for any entry into tertiary or professional education. Even then, Wilhelm Rosenbach, trapped in a cultural conservatism where women were concerned, did so only reluctantly. Helene was sent away briefly to a private girl's school in the larger town of Lwow and then to Zurich to study sociology. But in the event, it took her five years of erratic tuition to obtain her *Abitur*.

Helene's active rebellion against her mother's restrictive proprieties, and her father's compliance, was fuelled by the fate of her sisters, both of whom were propelled into early and socially appropriate marriages. Her beloved sister Malvina, whom Helene in later years said had saved her for femininity since she was the only benevolent maternal presence she had experienced, was prevented from marrying the man of her choice. When she finally did marry and left home, the ten-year-old Helene went into lonely mourning. Her sister Gizela's marriage followed four years later; Helene had acted as voyeuristic chaperone, her erotic fantasies activated by the courting couple.

These fantasies had already had fertile stimulus. Helene was sexually seduced by her brother at a young age, an experience which was uncovered in her analysis. In her autobiography, and more fully in an article on the pathological lie where it appears as a veiled case history, she sees this illicit seduction as the root cause of her tendency not only secretly to fantasize, but to relay these fantasies to friends as truth. Helene revived the pleasurable masochistic side of the childhood seduction by inventing make-believe secret love affairs, which gave her the reputation of being a fallen woman amongst her friends. In later life, she linked her own imaginative powers – in adolescence she had dreamt of being a writer – to her attempt to escape from a real seduction whose memory she wished to avoid. But it is noteworthy that in her exploration of the various types of female masochism, this kind of childhood abuse plays no decisive role. The parental figures, particularly the father, are seen to be the psychic determinants here, alongside anatomical development and an overlay of cultural factors. But we might speculate that, just as her overt hatred for her mother and the inevitable (covert) ambivalence which attended it were instrumental in channelling her professional interest into a study of motherhood, so too her secret experience of childhood seduction as well as her fixation on her father spurred her crucial interest in feminine masochism. Her first (or we might say her third, after her brother and father) love affair, this time with a married man fourteen years older than her, Herman Lieberman, provided the final impetus.

The affair with Lieberman played a decisive part in Helene's political formation and coincided with her phase of political activism. Affair and activism, sex and politics, were openly hostile challenges to her mother's dream of a thoroughly bourgeois respectability. Helene had always spoken Polish, in opposition to her mother's German – ironically her later professional and authorial language – and now she identified herself wholeheartedly with the cause of Polish nationhood. Against her mother's upward social aspirations, Helene channelled her youthful zeal into the workers' movement and social revolution. She demonstrated, threw herself under police horses, courted arrest and wrote for the Przemyśl newspaper. She was passionate about the condition of women, organized the first group of working women in the town, and led an abortive women's strike in a shirt collar factory. All this she did in part under the aegis of Lieberman, who, if he was not her father, was, as she says in her memoir, suitably 'endowed with qualities that would make a transition from my father identification possible'.

Lieberman was a significant figure in Polish socialist history. Born in 1870, he was by the age of fourteen committed to the labour movement, national independence and the socialist cause. He studied law in Vienna, travelled on behalf of the cause, spent a period in a French jail, joined the Polish social democrats and became a leading criminal lawyer. An eloquent public speaker, an idealist as well as a fine politician, he was eventually elected as a Polish member of the Vienna Parliament. On his death in 1941, he was the Minister of Justice in the London-based Polish government in exile.

At the time that he met the fourteen-year-old Helene, Lieberman was already a prominent figure in Przemyśl, a colleague of her father's and a frequent guest at her sister Gizela's house, where they first met. One can imagine that his idealism fired her, as much as his reputation as something of a seducer. His wife seemed to share little of his interests, but he was none the less tied to her, in part because of their child, in part because of the respectability demanded of even radical politicians. Helene had chosen an apt figure to whom to transfer her feelings for her father: apt because he incarnated ideals and romantic aspirations, but also because Lieberman permitted a repetition of the original Oedipal scene of a weak, enslaved father bound to an ignorant conventional mother.

In *The Psychology of Women*, Deutsch wrote:

The woman who is harmoniously erotic, who is most 'feminine' and represents the best achievement of her Creator, often declares in the evening of her rich and happy love life: 'I have not always been faithful, but actually I have been in love only once.' Some crumpled picture in her album or an image in her memory represents for her a figure to which in her early youth she attached her great yearning and readiness to love, and through which she unconsciously preserves her faith to her first love object, her father.

There are two very trivial and fully conscious fantasies of the normal young girl that relate to the father. In one he is a great man who deserves a better fate, a victim of the prosaic mother who has tied him to the grey business of earning a living. She, the little daughter, would be a more suitable object for him, though he must painfully renounce it. In a large number of instances, a psychologically sound woman may have as her first love object − an object to which she often remains attached for life − an unfree man, often a married man, who fans her love and responds to it, but cannot break his old tie. Such a man reproduces the situation described above. The fantasy of his painful love yearning and the woman's own suffering, shared with him, often prove stronger motives for faithfulness than the fulfilment of love.

What started as a schoolgirl infatuation slowly blossomed into a full-scale grand passion. Lieberman helped and encouraged Helene in her prolonged attempt to get her *Abitur*, nurtured her ambitions to further study and spurred her social commitment. But it was probably not until 1904, when she was twenty, that their love was mutually acknowledged. It is clear from his letters to her, which she kept until her death, that she meant as much to him as he to her. Though they talked of a life together, a life committed to socialist struggle and women's emancipation, she never urged him to a divorce, which she may have sensed he would not and could not obtain – particularly after the death of his second child, a son born during his affair with Helene, a son whom in imaginative terms both of them seemed to think of as theirs.

Helene was one of seven women to gain entry to the University of Vienna Medical School in 1907, and one of three to complete the course. Though it was technically illegal, her examiner in internal medicine refused women permission to enter his ward or his lectures. Helene nevertheless sat his exam, something he could not disallow. He addressed her throughout, without looking at her, as Mr Rosenbach and was astonished when, in part out of spite, she performed brilliantly. She was a good student, though as she later confessed her medical studies meant little to her: 'I needed my status as a medical student primarily as something that could lend me an identity in this otherwise insecure period of my life. And I needed it for my father's sake, to give him the reassurance that I would soon be entering a respectable profession.'

Helene's move to Vienna coincided with Lieberman's election to Parliament. The city became the stage for their increasingly troubled and still illicit love. Its secrecy both shamed Helene and nourished her passion. She felt galled by her inability to break the affair, passively trapped in heroic resignation and a self-sacrifice which spilled over into social idealism. Two events precipitated the end of the relationship. In the summer of 1910, Lieberman and she travelled together to an International Socialist Congress in Stockholm. Here, amidst such legendary socialist figures as August Babel, Karl Kautsky and Jean Jaurès, were the equally legendary women, Angelica Balabanoff and Rosa Luxemburg, the latter, like Helene, a Polish Jewess. Their unflappable composure amidst these great men, their independence, their fiery intelligence and commitment to the cause, led Helene to examine her own position and find it sadly wanting. In a mood of sober evaluation, she realized that her socialist zeal was

fatally amalgamated with my love for the socialist leader. This realization cast a shadow on both my love and my social idealism. In my early adolescence I had longed for great experiences transcending the helpless dependence of love for *one* man. Meanwhile as I ripened into womanhood, ideology and passionate love had become closely interwoven, with love dominating and swallowing up most of my creative endeavours. Thus, as I came to see after the 1910 Congress, my love was in conflict with my own ego-ideal....

The rupture with Lieberman found its final act in pregnancy and abortion: 'I was ripe for motherhood, and the nature of our relationship made it out of the question.' Helene's will at last reasserted itself: she had an abortion and moved to Munich to complete the final year of her degree. She finally broke with Lieberman and entered into a relationship with Felix Deutsch, the man who became her husband and lifelong companion.

If in Lieberman Helene had found her paternal ego-ideal and replayed her identification with her father, in Deutsch, she found the good mother she might have wished for and had experienced in her older sister. Small, elegant, something of a dandy with at least one long-standing homosexual affair in his past, a talented musician, a Zionist rather than a socialist, Felix Deutsch freed Helene from what had become Lieberman's oppressively male and demanding presence. Felix was the same age as her, but further advanced in his studies. A Viennese, he had a Fellowship in internal medicine at the Munich University medical school, where he and Helene met. Helene calls this first encounter a '*coup de foudre*'. As she writes in her memoir, Felix lifted the burden of an obsessive relationship from her shoulders, gave her 'a grandiose feeling of liberation' and cleared the air for her. What some people interpreted as Felix's naïveté, a kind of simple optimism, was for Helene, a wise innocence, a goodness, a 'psychic "clear air"'. It was what drew her to him. They shared a devotion to work, and Felix, particularly, fuelled and abetted Helene's sense of vocation, taking on a role highly unusual in a man of his time. Helene later sometimes felt he was not quite ambitious enough for himself. Indeed, as she grew increasingly successful, the Vienna gossip mill had it that it was she who wore the trousers in the family. From the very beginning, the familiar names they used for each other in their letters evoke children playing at mums and dads: he was known as Papuschkerl, she as Mamuschkerl. Or alternately, he is her own dear boy. The high drama of the relationship with Lieberman is replaced by the cosy *Gemütlichkeit* of sentimental Vienna. It was an atmosphere which served Helene's professional ambitions well, though the sexual problems it eventually posed may have been instrumental in sending her first to Freud, then to Karl Abraham.

Felix and Helene married on 14 April 1912. The following March, Helene completed the qualifications for her medical degree. She had already determined to specialize in psychiatry and after her exams she began to make a systematic study of the work of Kraepelin and Pierre Janet. She had also read Freud's *The Interpretation of Dreams* in Munich and, some years earlier, his interpretation of Jensen's *Gradiva* – as we have seen, a most appropriate introduction to psychoanalysis for a woman who would eventually become an analyst. She had a vivid interest in psychoanalysis, shared by Felix. But though she accepted psychoanalysis's basic tenets and was excited by Freud's work, psychoanalysis then provided no formal training. In part because she had no independent means, in part, too, perhaps because she was a woman in a world of male professionals, Helene had a need for conventional structures, which could ensure professional status. It was this need, shared by others, which made her instrumental in bringing formal training structures into psychoanalysis in the 1920s.

In 1913, as part of her psychiatric training, Helene Deutsch went to work in a hospital for mentally retarded children headed by Erwin Lazar. She thought at the time that her future psychiatric work might focus on children. The experience was useful, but intellectually dissatisfying. Helene felt that she was groping in the dark and needed theoretical supervision as well as exposure to a far wider range of material. This perpetual need to see more cases and learn through direct clinical work is a recurring theme in her early years. Deutsch was always first and foremost a clinician; and by all accounts a formidable one. In their emphasis on case history, her writings bear witness to this.

After some six months with Lazar, Deutsch joined the staff of Wagner-Jauregg's famous Clinic for Psychiatry and Nervous Diseases, the largest in Austria. As a woman, she was effectively barred from work anywhere but in women's and children's wards. Dissatisfied, Helene realized that she could only get more useful training in Munich or Switzerland. In what she calls a 'great heart-sacrifice to my brain', sacrifices that were to be recurrent in her relationship with Felix, in February 1914 Helene set off for Kraepelin's famous Munich hospital without her husband.

In her memoir, she characterizes her restlessness, both with her satisfactory though somewhat sedate marriage, and with any fixed position thus:

We were happy – but my old friend and enemy, the restless desire for excitement and, above all, for learning and achievement, did not let me fully enjoy what we possessed. 'The air was clear,' but somehow I longed for storms. This longing was not silent and from time to time forced me to get away. It was my own inner battle for liberation, no longer raging, but now and then making ghostlike noises. I always wanted to learn something that could only be learned somewhere else – I wanted to repeat my adolescent flight from home. Or to say it even more simply, I longed for new longings.

Helene's repeated longing for new longings, her inability to accept a sedately contented *modus vivendi*, was a characteristic which later informed her understanding of female masochism. In the meantime, the solution to her longings involved a simple reversal of roles: Felix, the good wife, her good mother, stayed at home.

Kraepelin may have been a great theoretician and brilliant diagnostician, but the work Deutsch did under his auspices was, she felt, both tedious and fruitless. Her research consisted in determining through word tests what influence feelings had on the ability to remember. Helene wrote to Felix: 'I am supposed to do something which is against my good conscience and my bad knowledge. I am supposed to talk about memories, search out complexes, and, completely neglecting my psychoanalytic convictions, I am supposed to act as though I did not know that there is a subconscious, and finally bring evidence against Freud!!!' She envied Felix, who, while she was in Munich, was attending Freud's Saturday evening presentations and reading case histories; and she dreamt of establishing an institution near Vienna for neurotic and psychotic girls, a dream that was not to come to fruition, though she encouraged Felix to approach possible backers. In April, she returned to

Vienna and joined Wagner-Jauregg's Clinic again. She also attended Tausk's seminars. She had an active desire to move into psychoanalysis. But Tausk's difficulty in finding patients was a clear disincentive, particularly for a woman who was part of a struggling young couple.

The war, which provided so many women with work experience they would otherwise not have got, made it possible for Deutsch to become one of Wagner-Jauregg's assistants, an elevated position to which in peacetime she would not have been officially entitled. She was put in charge of the Women's Division. Though he respected Freud and increasingly Deutsch, Wagner–Jauregg was well known for his antipathy to psychoanalysis. The fundamental task of a psychiatrist, then, was to diagnose quickly and accurately according to an existing typology of diseases or syndromes. With her affinity to psychoanalysis and her interest in patients and the possibility of slow cure, Helene often found herself teased by Wagner–Jauregg if she spent too long with a patient. 'He could even go so far as to ask that patient, "Well, did Dr Deutsch manage to convince you that you want to have a child by your father?"'

Cases from the Clinic provided Deutsch with material for her first psycho-analytic papers on induced insanity and on the mechanism of regression in schizophrenia, a subject in which she and Tausk had a shared interest. Her position at the Clinic also provided her with access to Freud's lectures. It was here, in her white coat, that Helene, unbeknownst to her, stirred Anna Freud's ambitions to become a doctor.

In 1916, Deutsch moved one step closer to psychoanalysis and Freud by seeking admission to the Wednesday evening meetings of the Vienna Psycho-Analytical Society. As a condition of her acceptance, she had to comment on Lou Andreas-Salomé's paper, '"Anal" and "Sexual"'. Lou's dense theorizing was not for Helene and she found the task difficult. This is perhaps at the root of Helene's later dislike of Lou, though one can imagine that the ambitious Helene also felt a certain rivalry for the older woman with her easy glamour and by then notorious record of sexual conquests. Yet Helene was structurally to replicate Lou's role as a conduit between Tausk and Freud when, for three months in 1919, she acted as Tausk's analyst.

Before Helene was to enter into a personal rather than a merely formal relationship with Freud, an event intervened which fundamentally shaped both her personal and professional preoccupations: the birth of her son.

Helene had been several months pregnant when war broke out and had lost the baby. This was the first of several deeply troubling miscarriages. In *The Psychology of Women*, she devotes a large section to spontaneous abortion and miscarriage and is at pains to show the frequency with which it is influenced by psychogenic factors. Amongst these, a crucial one is the pregnant woman's unconscious rejection of an identification with her own mother. Under the pseudonym of a patient called Mrs Smith, Deutsch tells a story which is undoubtedly her interpretation of her own:

The patient ... was the youngest in a family with many other children, one boy and several girls. After this boy had disappointed the ambitious hopes of the parents, they wanted to have another son, but instead my patient was born. Her mother never concealed her disappoinment over this fact, and her attitude toward the girl was unmistakeably: 'It would have been better if you had not been born.' The patient was saved from traumatic reactions to this attitude by two compensations – her father's deep and tender love for her, and the maternal affection of one of her sisters, twelve years older than herself. Her father's love aroused in her the wish to become a substitute for his son and she successfully turned her interests and ambitions toward this goal. She was saved from the dangers of the masculinity complex because her father's love for her emphasized and encouraged her femininity. The two tendencies frequently conflicted but did not lead to a neurotic result.

Only after she had married and conceived an ardent desire for a baby did her childhood difficulty come to the fore. As a little girl she had reacted to her mother's rejection with conscious hatred and devaluation. The idea of identification with her aggressive mother had filled her with almost conscious horror. Up to her pregnancy she had been able to be feminine by disregarding her mother problem; but this method no longer worked when she herself was about to become a mother. ... Her tragic feeling that she would never achieve motherhood was intensified when she gave birth one month before term to a stillborn child.

Mrs Smith's inability to bring a pregnancy to full term is happily resolved. In her memoir, Deutsch takes up the story and explains how her next pregnancy was brought to full term by the intercession of a friend, a 'goddess of serenity', also pregnant, with whom Helene could identify:

through identification with her my motherhood changed its character. Through a psychological impact on biological forces, my desire for a child was fulfilled: my friend gave birth to her son one month later than she had expected – just when my pregnancy reached its term. My son was born six hours after hers.

In *The Psychology of Women*, the story is given a slightly different and fuller gloss. It is not identification with the calm friend which makes Mrs Smith's pregnancy successful:

Only later, during her analysis, did she realize that the success of her identification with her friend was not due to the latter's inner harmony but to another motive. The friend had a mother who was the opposite of her own. While her own mother was tall, domineering, cold, and aggressive, her friend's mother was very small and full to the brim with maternal warmth. She spread her motherly wings both over her own loving daughter and Mrs Smith, who was thus able to achieve motherhood by sharing in this benign mother–daughter harmony.

The identification with a good mother may be important, but equally important for Helene was the possibility of leaning on a female friend, a surrogate sister. Indeed, the story of Mrs Smith goes on to reveal that the two women conceived again at the same time. This time Mrs Smith had no fears about the pregnancy, but when the friend suddenly had to move to another town, Mrs Smith started to miscarry the following day. The clinical diagnosis was 'over-excitability of the uterus'.

Psychoanalytic treatment did not remove her difficulties. She ironically called herself an 'appendix mother' who could bring her pregnancy to a successful conclusion only by leaning on another woman. Beyond this she was not neurotic, and could solve all the other problems of her life. It was only to the heavy task of pregnancy that she was unequal, for reasons of which she herself became aware. After her friend had failed her she could no longer chase away the shadow of the mother she had rejected.

Nor could Helene, who amongst all the early analysts apart from Freud and Lou was one of the few to have no moral revulsion at the fact of homosexuality, do without her female friend.

Martin Deutsch was born on 29 January 1917. It is in her problematic relationship to mothering him that Helene most poignantly evokes a contemporary woman. The emotional and what she calls the 'libidinous' demands of motherhood conflicted with the demands of her professional life. She was tormented by guilt, which expressed itself not in a slackening of her professional abilities or productivity, but rather in an over-anxious worrying about her little boy. It would not be stretching a point to suggest that the pride of place Deutsch gives to mothering in *The Psychology of Women*, her insistence on motherhood as woman's culminating task, is an attempt to compensate for and repair what she saw as her own deficiencies in this area:

While trying to cope with the heavy professional workload caused by the war, I always had the painful suspicion that I was depriving both my son Martin and myself of a rich source of happiness, the mother–child closeness that is most significant to a baby during the first two years. I loved my child deeply, but the two of us could only occasionally experience the blessing of the mother–child bond with all its tenderness and care. My motherly feelings, moreover, were disturbed by anxieties of a deeply neurotic character concerning my little son.

Nursing was an 'excruciating' business that drained her physically and psychically. Felix, increasingly the good mother, eventually came up with a wartime solution: his piano was exchanged for two goats tethered in the Clinic yard near the room little Martin and his nanny inhabited during the day close to Helene's office; the goats provided the necessary milk. But soon Helene also developed a competitive relationship with Martin's nurse, who seemed to be taking over all the maternal space. She was fired and a new nurse sought – a pattern which was repeated time and again. Meanwhile, Felix seemed to have no trouble in 'naturally' displaying all the motherly ease which Helene lacked. 'Even in situations in which a child usually calls for his mother, he turned more often to Felix than to me,' Deutsch writes, underlining not only the strong bond between father and son, but also intimating that to her competitive eyes, it was effectively a bond in which Felix displaced her as mother.

The story now sounds all too familiar. We can imagine that it left Helene with a deep 'maternal' wound, which is also of course a narcissistic one. Its pain was exacerbated by the fact that Martin's relations to her, though not to his father, were always tinged with resentment and hostility. The 'torments', the repetition of unrequited longing that she suffered, echo through the pages of *The Psychology of Women*, that paean to motherhood where amongst so much else she also notes the cases of women who 'put too much of their whole rich emotional world' at the disposal of a single child and identify with it to such an extent that it is unbearable for them to think of having another 'who would compete with him for her motherly love'.

It was these 'torments' – professional interests notwithstanding – which also finally brought Helene to analysis with Freud in August 1918. Personal needs coincided with professional aspirations in what she called a 'didactic analysis'.

She had been attending Freud's Wednesday evenings regularly from early in 1918 and was formally elected to membership of the Psycho-Analytical Society in February of that year. Her first paper as a member to the group on 13 March drew on the memory association experiments she had carried out in Munich. When Deutsch learned that another woman psychiatrist, Dr Elisabeth Revesz, Sándor Rado's wife, was in analysis with Freud, she thought that he might have her as well. In the event, when her sessions with Freud began in the autumn, she took over Revesz's hour; just as a few years later in Berlin, she was for a brief time to take over Revesz's husband in a short-lived affair.

The relations between the Freuds and the Deutschs were friendly. Through his connections Freud got Felix a post as doctor to the English legation, a job which in impoverished post-war Vienna assured the Deutschs access to food. In return, Helene would always arrive at her analytic session bringing goat's milk for an ailing Martha and ring the bell to the private side of the Freud apartment, before continuing on to Freud's analytic chamber.

We know little of the content of Helene's analysis, and even less of Freud's assessment of her. What is evident is that her standing as a psychiatrist – and one who carried a glowing testimonial from Freud's friend and rival Wagner–Jauregg – made her a valuable acquisition for the Freud circle. It is also clear that Helene felt she could not combine working in a clinic where the atmosphere was hostile to psychoanalysis and carry on an analysis with Freud. Despite the practical and initially material disadvantages, she chose Freud:

Psychoanalysis was my last and most deeply experienced revolution; and Freud, who was rightly considered as conservative on social and political issues, became for me the greatest revolutionary of the century. Looking back I see three distinct upheavals in my life: liberation from the tyranny of my mother; the revelation of socialism; and my release from the chains of the unconscious through psychoanalysis. In each of these revolutions I was inspired and aided by a man – my father, Herman Lieberman, and lastly Freud.

Helene's analysis began on the day her own father left Vienna. Freud took over the role. Though she knew that she could never displace Anna, she actively felt herself to be Freud's daughter. She identified with him, was inspired by him and wrote first for his eyes. Freud, she felt, had released her talents and it is true that after her analysis with him, at the age of thirty-five,

Helene Deutsch entered the most productive phase of her life. Under the aegis of the Father, she begins an analysis of the Mother.

The aspects of her analysis which she features in her memoir all point to the predominance of the 'Oedipus complex and the feminine castration complex' in her transference. She evokes a scene of 'primitive oedipal fantasy', in which she is standing in front of a men's clothing store near Freud's apartment and weeping bitterly as she thinks, 'What will the Professor's poor wife do now?' She is convinced that Freud is in love with her and about to leave Martha.

Another memory from the period of analysis consists of a dream in which Helene has both masculine and feminine organs. 'Freud told me only that it indicated my desire to be both a boy and a girl. It was only after my analysis that it became clear to me how much my whole personality was determined by the childhood wish to be simultaneously my father's prettiest daughter and cleverest son.'

The pretty and clever daughter/son, who Helene was, was distraught when Freud abruptly terminated her analysis after a year, in order to give her hour to the Wolf Man. His reported statement – 'You do not need any more; you are not neurotic' – did nothing to mollify the depression the severance of analysis thrust her into. It is clear that Freud found the Wolf Man a far more interesting case. Perhaps, too, he felt that Helene had wallowed long enough in the Oedipal quagmire. He matter-of-factly told her that continuing her pursuit of professional and scientific goals, 'thus sustaining my old identification with my father', would not conflict with her womanhood. It is important to note that Helene's case makes it clear that for Freud there was no problem in a woman having a masculine identification once this was combined with motherhood. Nor, given these two factors, did there seem to be any problem with the non-resolution of the relationship to the mother. Since for Freud the psychic bisexuality of every being was a given, and the signal for the lack of neurosis was the patient's ability to love and to work, there seemed no particular need for Helene's analysis to go on interminably. Helene, none the less, suffered from the termination and felt in retrospect that Freud had not gone far enough in analysing her 'feminine castration complex'. Perhaps she responded to the termination very directly in the language of that castration complex: feeling she had been cut off, in favour of the male.

Is this an instance of the hoary misogynist Freud of feminist criticism who was insensitive to his women patients' real problems? It is true that Freud fell asleep during Helene's analysis when she talked about her nursing problems, and since he was suffering from prostate difficulties, often went to the toilet in the middle of sessions. True, too, that the sexual side of Helene's marriage with Felix did not improve, and mothering side by side with work was stressful. And Helene *still* longed for the grand and secret passions Lieberman had given her, with their painful pleasures. But was this neurotic misery demanding treatment or simply an ordinary case of everyday unhappiness? Freud thought the latter, trusted Deutsch enough to name her unofficially his 'assistant' and proceeded to send her cases. And though he only mentions her work five times in the *Standard Edition* – and then in the same breath as several others – it is clear that he respected her clinical abilities and continued to act, when she called upon him, in the role of a 'control' analyst, discussing cases with her and then often emphasizing the trust she should have in her knowledge of her own patients.

The tangled case of Tausk is perhaps the exception. Freud sent Tausk to Deutsch after she had only been in analysis herself for some three months. It was an odd referral, since Tausk was older and, as Deutsch also recognized, far more versed in analysis than she. One can only conjecture as to why Freud – given that he felt unable to take Tausk on himself – chose Deutsch to be Tausk's new analyst. Did he infer that because Helene was in analysis with him, he could thus keep an eye on Tausk, whose war experiences had left him even more deeply troubled and still dependent on Freud? Was there a further motive in sending Deutsch an attractive man with whom he suspected she could repeat, within the confines of counter-transference, her basic and obsessively Oedipal love pattern and thereby free herself from it? We can only speculate about such motives. What is evident is that a triangle – not unlike the earlier Tausk–Lou–Freud triangle – developed in which Tausk talked of Freud to Deutsch, elaborating on his fears that Freud was stealing his ideas and would never acknowledge his unique worth; and Deutsch, hardly immune to Tausk's charm, talked of Tausk to Freud and developed similar fears about the Professor, so that her own analytic hours were effectively usurped by Tausk. Freud called a stop to the untenable situation after three months: either Deutsch had to give up Tausk or give up her analysis with Freud. Deutsch inevitably gave up Tausk, feeling in doing so that she had betrayed her patient. When Tausk committed suicide, an event which utterly surprised Deutsch, she judged the responsibility to be in no way hers. She had been a mere go-between.

Whatever Deutsch's personal unhappiness at this time, her work flourished. At The Hague Congress of September 1920, where Abraham delivered his important paper on femininity, penis envy and the castration complex, Deutsch gave her own first paper on 'The Psychology of Mistrust'. This was followed by her work on the pathological lie, where, thanks in part to the insights her own analysis had given her about her childhood seduction, she characterizes lying as at once a defence against real events and an act of creativity. It is worth noting that Deutsch's continued interest in imposters, 'as if' and multiple personalities all have at their root a preoccupation with disturbed identifications – something which she saw in herself. At the same time, this line of her work attempts to grapple with pre-existing psychiatric categories in a psychoanalytic fashion.

It was not, however, till after her analysis with Abraham that Deutsch began actively to consider the question of woman. Indeed, it was his paper on femininity and the feminine castration complex delivered at The Hague Congress in 1920 which prompted her to seek a second analysis with him. The paper 'impressed me all the more because Freud had not perceived this

complex in me in spite of the dream in which I had a double set of genitals.'
It was on hearing Abraham that she realized that Freud had missed something
out. Then, too, Helene's intimate relations with Felix were at a low ebb. There
was friction between them, the old problem of what Helene called some
months later 'our libidinous deficiencies toward each other'. Felix had been
accepted into the Vienna Society at the beginning of 1922 and by the summer
had become the Freud family doctor. But Helene wanted him to have analysis,
and thus far Felix had resisted.

Driven by her old restlessness, her continuing depression over the severance
of her first analysis, and her sense that Freud had not come to grips with the
feminine in her, Helene moved to Berlin to enter analysis with Abraham at
the beginning of 1923. Her son Martin went with her, but the separation
from his father tormented the boy and, after the summer break, he remained
with Felix in Vienna.

Deutsch was full of admiration for Abraham's cool analytic style and his
objective insight 'without any reeling experience of transference'. She felt he
was probing deeper than Freud, that the analysis was 'an all-absorbing nuclear
point' which 'devours all my psychic energy'. She was plunged into an
oppressive melancholy, a repetition of some early infantile period. Work
seemed impossible: 'I was in a stupor-like condition for days on end, standing
beside the stove, in fantasies that could not be grasped, confused and
tormented.'

Despite all this, she had a sense that the analysis could not be successful.
In his biography of Helene Deutsch, Paul Roazen states that early on in
Helene's analysis with Abraham, he had shown her a letter from Freud which
told him in no uncertain terms that Helene's marriage with Felix was one
that ought not to be disrupted by analysis. The Freud–Abraham correspondence, shortly to be published in a complete edition, contains no such letter. It
is highly unlikely that the letter was destroyed. But it is not impossible that
Helene, remembering her past for Roazen's ears, wanted to believe in and produce a sign of Freud's attentive intervention, a mark of his care for her and for
the Deutsch marriage, whatever her residual anger at supposed interference
from above in her analysis.

Whether a letter ever existed or not, it is plausible that behind her coming
to Berlin lay the desire, perhaps unconscious, to rupture her marriage: a new
analysis was in part the excuse. In fact, as Roazen reports, early in her stay in
Berlin Helene lived out her wish in a brief affair with Sándor Rado. Amongst
her papers, Roazen found her own analysis of a dream she had at the time. On
top of the sheet is the equation Felix = Mother; and then a series of further
equations which show that just as her sense of being betrayed, 'not loved
enough', by her father had led her to Lieberman, so Felix's betrayal had now
led her to Rado. A further equation which she does not chart is how Freud's
lack of love had thrust her into Abraham's arms. Indeed, Abraham's apparent
confession to her that he had written to both Freud (though again no trace of
this remains in the correspondence) and Felix to say that he had not really
been able to analyse her, since he had too much feeling for her, suggests that

it was the seductive closeness of their analysis which made him fear failure. Freud perhaps in abruptly terminating Helene's analysis was trying to break her repetitive cycle. He was refusing Helene's tendency to love by identifying herself with the object, then experiencing that love as betrayed and running to the next object. It was a tendency she herself explored in her various studies on the 'as if' personality. Indeed, her memoir sometimes fills one with the sense that she experienced her own existence to be an 'as if' – living her life first 'as if' a socialist in her identification with Lieberman; 'as if' a conventional wife with Felix; 'as if' a mother in her identification with her saintly friend; then 'as if' a psychoanalyst in the identification with Freud.

Whatever the exact status of a letter from Freud to Abraham stating that Helene had to return to Felix, it was clear to all that Helene's compulsion to repeat had to be side-stepped. She had come to Abraham to explore her femininity, her first and ravaging failed mother identification and the whole murky pre-Oedipal scene, from whence she had run into Daddy's arms. Her ability to recognize Felix not only as betraying Father, but also as Mother, both good and bad, and, most importantly to return to him despite the inevitable rage, denotes a certain success in her two analyses. Perhaps it was also in this return that Helene was able to live out – by conscious identification – the anger, mingled with love, in her own mothering of Martin. To go *back* was to return not to Father, but to Felix = Mother, and in part to accept the mother in herself. Only after her return to Vienna does Deutsch's writing about the psychology of women really come into its own.

It is worth noting here that in describing the feminine woman, Deutsch, whose first subject is so often herself, marks out the tendency to identification as a salient and positive feature. Only when the protective mechanisms that narcissism affords go wrong does this tendency work masochistically against the individual. At this extreme, we have an 'as if' personality, a person with only fleeting identities acquired from others, a person with no narcissistic core. It was this danger which Helene so nearly and neatly skirted. And she did so in order to become what she hoped was the 'feminine woman', whose tendency to identify, as she explains, is part and parcel of 'intuition', that very constellation of qualities which made her a good analyst. In a 1926 paper on the 'Occult Processes Occurring during Psychoanalysis' – a paper which Freud later cited – she emphasizes that intuition, the analyst's ability to identify with the patient's transference fantasies, is a potent therapeutic tool.

After her return to Vienna, Helene stayed loyal, if not perhaps altogether faithful, to both Felix and Freud. Felix had entered analysis with Bernfeld. Whatever Helene's irritation with him over the years – with his lack of 'masculine' self-assertion, the cooling of his relationship with Freud in 1923 after Felix had hidden from the Professor the serious nature of his cancer, his hesitation about moving to America – their marriage lasted until Felix's death in 1964. Indeed, in her memoir, she paints Felix as the ideal loving husband and father, and a great pioneer of psychosomatic medicine. In memory, identification is free from the possibility of betrayal.

With Freud, too, there were continuing irritations. Their relationship remained friendly but centred on work. Freud never let her forget what he saw as Felix's treachery in lying to him. Helene was irked when Freud in his paper 'On the Psychical Consequences of the Anatomical Distinction between the Sexes' (1925) only devoted one line to her by then substantial contribution to the field of female sexuality. And even that, a line she had to share with Abraham and Horney. She was even less pleased when in his essay on 'Female Sexuality' he linked her contribution to that of Jeanne Lampl de Groot and Ruth Mack Brunswick, both younger and, as far as she was concerned, lesser analysts; though he did acknowledge the 'full justice' she had done to the question of feminine masochism. What Deutsch felt as Freud's insufficient acknowledgment of her original work was certainly exacerbated by what she remembered as Tausk's obsessive concentration on this theme. It must have been in part the niggling competitiveness of the Viennese Circle, the vying for rank in the Professor's eyes, which made her see America as a joyful liberation from 'that stupid, stuffy atmosphere'.

Yet Helene remained loyal. After Freud's death, the identification did not diminish and she referred to herself as his ghost. She was thrilled when, on her first trip to America, the newspapers hailed her as 'A woman envoy from Freud' and 'the master's foremost feminine disciple'. By 1930, Helene Deutsch was at least that.

After her return from Berlin in 1924, Deutsch set to work with a new energy, which flowed undiminished well into her old age. Her monograph on *The Psychoanalysis of Women's Sexual Functions* came out in 1925 and already held in germ many of the ideas more fully presented in her wartime *The Psychology of Women*. A range of clinical papers followed, as well as in 1928 a psychohistory of George Sand, and in 1930 a second book, *Psychoanalysis of the Neurosis*, which became a standard teaching text.

Clinical practice aside, teaching was Deutsch's forte. In 1924, the Vienna Psycho-Analytical Society still had no training institute. Deutsch became its midwife as well as its first President in 1925 at the formal inauguration. Bernfeld was Vice-President and Anna Freud Secretary. Over the next years, until her departure for America in 1935, Deutsch was the first port of call for any candidate who sought psychoanalytic training in Vienna. Like Anna Freud, therefore, she taught many of the next generation of analysts. She became known as a brilliant teacher. Her remarkable seminars – which introduced the study by case histories – often ran until the early hours of the morning. She was also much sought after as a training analyst and supervisor. Analysis filled nearly every hour of her life and the circle of her friendships. On Saturday evenings, the Black Cat Card Club met in her apartment – a group of young psychoanalytic couples called together by Deutsch, in contrast to the even younger 'singles' who gathered round Anna Freud. Amongst those who played cards and informally discussed psychoanalytic problems in the Deutschs' flat were the names who would come to prominence in America – the Hartmanns, the Hoffers, the Krises, the Waelders and the Bibrings.

At the Bad Homburg Congress of 1925, Deutsch set out the lines of the Vienna Training Institute, which was modelled on its Berlin predecessor. The two-year course would include a period of analysis for the purposes of instruction; a theoretical training by means of lectures, seminars, demonstrations and the use of the Institute's library; and practical training by conducting analyses under the supervision of the Institute. Wary of any rigidities in training or breakdown into warring schools, Deutsch believed that technique could not be formally handed down without the kind of ossification she was later critical of in American training institutes. Analytic technique was not 'a complete, learnable entity which can be taught by thorough and regular drilling.' Free association aside, 'every individual has his own methods and variants which correspond to his personality'.

It is in fact in her understanding of psychoanalysis as a clinical practice that Helene Deutsch is closest in spirit to Freud. By 1926, she was without illusions about the existence of any magical method leading to a certain cure. A letter to Felix makes the point:

I don't want to practice my profession ... with this rigid adherence to the phantom of 'Freudian Method,' which, as I now realize, I must regard as an *area of research* and not as a therapeutic method. The 'swindle' is based on the fact that certain people (Professor himself!) in full awareness, for the purpose of scientific and material exploitation, do not openly disavow the therapeutic – whereas others, on the one hand out of identification, and on the other hand out of the narcissistic need to have some special ability, unconsciously elevate psychoanalysis to be their battle cry, to be the one and only path to blessedness. ... To give psychic treatment, yes – but with full awareness that success is only minimally connected with the uncovering of infantile libido fixations and with transference agencies.

It was out of her understanding of psychoanalysis as a site of research as much as a method for cure, that Deutsch's culminating work on the psychology of women takes on the form of a typology of the 'normal', based on an assortment of cases, including her own. The impetus to typology of course harks back to her psychiatric training, and was very much a dominant trend in psychiatric and psychological thinking of the time in, for instance, the work of Jung and Ernst Kretschmer.

In 1934, like so many of her Austrian and German counterparts, Deutsch left what was becoming an increasingly intolerable political climate. Felix joined her the following year. They settled in Boston, where Helene already had important contacts, including the admiration of the influential neurologist, Stanley Cobb. The move was made, much to Helene's distress, against Freud's will. But the Deutschs had pressing reasons. Their son, Martin, had been involved in the general strike against Dollfuss's repressive regime and, as a result, could no longer go to school in Vienna. He was sent to Switzerland, from where he continued actively to participate in what was now the underground socialist movement. America would provide a refuge for the entire family in more respects than one.

Indeed, Helene experienced Boston as a breath of fresh air, compared to Vienna. She wrote to Felix who was less eager to leave Vienna than she: 'Here is life, and there is dull, narcissistic brooding round about people's own intellectual fog. What is good for Freud's genius and his age, and for Anna's yielding herself up to the paternal idea, is becoming for others a mass neurosis.'

The Deutschs' departure left Freud 'loving but unreconciled', as he pointed out in a card sent in response to their birthday greeting in 1936. But by 1938, he wrote to Helene to say that she must not feel too guilty about having left Vienna against his will. He believed and trusted she would remain faithful to psychoanalysis. Helene did, but in her own way.

Attacked, as she has been by feminist critics, in the same breath as the 'patriarchal' Freud, it is useful to ask ourselves just how Freudian Helene Deutsch, that supposed arch disciple, effectively *is* in her thinking about women. True, in her most influential book, *The Psychology of Women* (1944, 1945), she situates herself in the Freudian tradition and acknowledges the Professor at relevant intervals. True, too, she takes up the terms 'passivity' and 'activity' to characterize feminine and masculine dispositions. But there are substantive differences.

Freud posited a single libido which was at the service of both male and female sexual functions. He emphasized the psychic bisexuality of all individuals. Most importantly, he stressed that 'psychoanalysis does not try to describe what a woman is – that would be a task it could scarcely perform – but sets about enquiring how she comes into being, how a woman develops out of a child with a bisexual disposition.' The Freudian project is thus clearly one which seeks to uncover how children *become* psychically man or woman, and not, quite emphatically, to determine the properties *essential* to *being* man or woman.

In her 1925 *The Psychoanalysis of Women's Sexual Functions*, Deutsch's most theoretical attempt to amplify Freud's ideas on how the child becomes a woman, she seems superficially to follow the lines laid down by Freud. Oral and anal stages of development are followed by a genital or phallic stage. It is in her interpretation of this last that she diverges from Freud and introduces the particular emphasis which will be amplified in her *The Psychology of Women*. In the phallic stage, the little girl's primary erogenous zone is the 'masculine' clitoris: a diminutive and insufficient organ which compares unfavourably to the penis in energy and size. How much easier things would be for the girl, Deutsch intones, if the vagina could be mobilized at this early stage, rather than having to wait to a later stage of maturity to be brought into sensation – and then only by the intervention of a penis. But no, the little girl is only aware of her insufficient clitoris. Shamed by its smallness, envious of the male's larger organ, aware of her lack, narcissistically mortified, having made these unhappy comparisons, the little girl turns away from her active sexuality and grows passive, inward-looking. It is here that Deutsch finds the genesis of that passivity which for her differentiates women from men.

Freud did not give a pre-eminence to the anatomical as such. For him, it was the anatomical as transformed by imaginative experience which had a shaping power. Unlike Freud in this, Deutsch generally remains on the level of the anatomical. The penis emerges as a *real* penis, not a psychic determinant.

This tendency to a biological determinism is even more pronounced in *The Psychology of Women*. Despite her claim there that she is steering a psychic course between biological and sociological factors, Deutsch constantly turns to the 'natural' world to find back-up for her arguments about female passivity and male activity, and calls on innate characteristics to bolster her arguments.

This primary and substantial difference between her and Freud is followed by a second. For Deutsch the child's relation to the mother is crucial:

Freud raised the problem regarding the manner in which the girl's love object changes from mother, hitherto the only object of her attachment, to father. Numerous attempts to explain this, on the part of Freud and other authors, have been based on the assumption that this change is accomplished during childhood, but according to my views, it is never completely achieved. In all the phases of woman's development and experience, the great part played in her psychologic life by her attachment to her mother can be clearly observed. Many events in that life are manifestations of attempts to detach herself, attempts made in thrusts, and the woman's psychologic equilibrium and eventual fate often depend on the success or failure of these attempts.

The little girl's sexuality takes her from the breast, through the sucking inherent in the movement of vagina around penis in intercourse, to the masochistic identification with mother in sex, in pregnancy and in childbirth. Giving suck to her own child, woman has at once moved forward and back. The feminine cycle is complete. Many of women's difficulties arise from their unconscious unwillingness (or overwillingness) to identify with their mothers both in their sexual and childbearing functions.

The Psychology of Women, written after Freud's death and in the atmosphere of American ego psychology, takes Deutsch even further away from Freud. With its emphasis on the normal, it is effectively an encyclopaedia of essential feminine types. Bringing together case histories of her own as well as hospital and welfare cases, examples from literature such as *Anna Karenina* and Balzac's *Two Women*, and the life of George Sand, Deutsch gives us a typology of woman, her development and behaviour through all the key, biologically activated moments of a woman's life, from menstruation to menopause. In its psychosomatic emphasis, the book is not a little influenced by Felix Deutsch. Hidden in its essentialism is a prescriptive agenda: Deutsch has an ideal woman in mind – 'the feminine erotic type' – against whom all other types are to some extent measured, their cases subsumed to her pre-existing and normative typology.

What makes woman woman, for Deutsch, is that passivity – now redefined with her critics in mind as 'activity directed inward' – which is the result of the girl's experience of the phallic phase. It is this activity directed inward which accounts for woman's rich fantasy life, her intuitive sensitivity and her ability to identify with others, in particular men and children. Side by side with this passivity is a kind of generic masochism: in order to turn towards the male sex, the woman has to seek an object which is in the first instance harmful to her. Defloration, menstruation, childbirth are all painful: 'The origins of masochism and passivity', Deutsch writes, 'are intimately connected

They are both the outcome of the feminine constitution and of a mechanism of instinctual reversion related to it that turns energies directed toward the outer world inward.' This specifically feminine masochism, she hastens to point out, is governed and held in check by an equally feminine narcissism: 'Since the sexual tendencies of woman are directed toward goals that are dangerous for her ego, the latter defends itself and strengthens its inner security by intensifying its self-love, which then manifests itself as "narcissism".' In its 'harmonious' interplay with masochism, this healthy narcissism marks the erotic feminine type, which is Deutsch's ideal.

In describing this ideal, Deutsch seems almost to replicate the magazine romance notion of the man's perfect woman. Here is the woman who experiences herself in identification with the man, adapts herself to him, is an unaggressive helpmate whose narcissistic method of making the man happy can be expressed in the formula, 'He is wonderful and I am a part of him.' All such women ask for in return is love and ardent desire, 'finding in these a satisfying compensation for the renunciation of their own tendencies'.

In contrast, the activity of the masculine woman is, in Deutsch's description, directed outwards towards the world; in so doing, she unhappily betrays her own femininity.

If these descriptions negate everything that the last decades of feminism have taught us, then Deutsch superficially emerges as even more of a conservative in the second volume of *The Psychology of Women*. It is wartime. All around her women are at work, taking on what she defines as masculine roles. Seeing their psychic difficulties, she locates the apotheosis of woman in her species role as mother. Both her feminine and even her masculine types find the culmination of their achievement in childbirth and breastfeeding.

It was Deutsch's eulogy of motherhood which made her so popular as an authority, so eminently quotable in the 'back-to-the-home' 1950s and unleashed the feminist backlash against her in the next decades.

Yet on closer reading, her conception of women emerges as anything but limiting. Her descriptions of motherhood and motherliness convey a supreme sexual plenitude, indeed a phallic power. Through mothering, it is as if Deutsch's mutilated feminine takes the phallic force back into herself. She is a complete feminine being, free from envy and reminiscent of that resplendent ideal evoked by Lou Andreas-Salomé – a being to which the male is wholly secondary or unnecessary. Indeed for both Deutsch and Lou, this phallic motherhood need not entail the possession of *real* children: 'woman can also make enormous contributions in the social, artistic, and scientific fields by drawing indirectly upon the active aspirations of motherhood and the emotional warmth of motherliness.' The cumulative impact of Deutsch's subtext is thus hardly one which confines woman to the roles of helpmate and traditional mother, a secondary appendage to the bold male. Rather, it is men here who emerge as incidental and almost irrelevant appendages to the triumphal Mother.

Deutsch has created for herself the mother she never had, a complete woman modelled on her own image. *The Psychology of Women* has at its main thrust a wish-fulfilment as much as it has any normative impulse. This central core aside, the book is replete with sensitive insight into the problems women confront at all stages of their lives. Case histories illuminate the various kinds of splits between sex and mothering that women suffer, and detail the distortions in the crucial identification with the mother. Deutsch is hardly altogether 'conservative' here. Nor is she indifferent to the cultural pressures which misshape women's lives. She can see in lesbianism a successful psychic resolution of an early disturbed attachment to the mother. Rebellion against authority – like the feminist rebellion – may in part be 'psychologically infantile', but it may also be 'more adapted to reality and more rational than so-called "adult" behaviour that conforms to the demands of society'.

Deutsch was in her early sixties when *The Psychology of Women* was published, a prospective grandmother, a successful Boston analyst and Associate Psychiatrist at the Massachusetts General Hospital. America had been kind to her: she had leapt the hurdles of immigration and become part of an American psychoanalytic establishment of which she did not always approve, though she did head the Boston Institute for several years. The new land also brought the fulfilment of a long-held dream. She and Felix purchased a farm in New Hampshire, an echo of Anna Freud's *Hochroterd*. Helene called the farm, *Babayaga*, after the good witch of Polish folklore. When her grandchildren came here, Helene fulfilled that second long-held wish – to be a good mother.

In 1963, Deutsch retired as a training analyst. Felix's declining health and memory loss had forced his removal from the Boston Society and Helene retired too in a gesture of solidarity. After his death in January 1964, she continued to work and to write – essays on narcissism, on the ego ideal and mother–son identification – well into her eighties. Her autobiography appeared in 1973, just before her ninetieth birthday. Near the end of that book she rues the fact that 'nowadays there are so few women in psychoanalytic training, because I believe that psychoanalysis is *par excellence* a profession for women'.

Intuition, a facility for identifying – the very characteristics Helene Deutsch looked for in an analyst – were also those she attributed to her ideal feminine. For Deutsch, to be a good woman and to be a good analyst were one.

By the time of her death on 29 March 1982, two years before her hundredth birthday, there had been many witnesses to the fact that she had been both.

11

MARIE BONAPARTE AND FREUD'S FRENCH COURT

'Facteur de la Vérité'

Great-grand-niece to the Emperor Napoleon I, wife to Prince George of Greece, aunt to the present Duke of Edinburgh and heiress to the vast Blanc fortunes which built Monte Carlo, Marie Bonaparte was an unlikely figure to find herself, at the age of forty-three, on Freud's couch. Yet Marie Bonaparte was central to the establishment of psychoanalysis in France. Nicknamed 'Freud-a-dit' by the French analysts of her day, she was also a key player in the first of French psychoanalysis's many institutional battles and in the expulsion of that native son of French analysis, Jacques Lacan, who saw himself as a truer bearer of the Freudian word than she. Marie was Freud's postman to France – his *'facteur de la vérité*, as the philosopher Jacques Derrida punningly entitles his long text on Lacan and the destiny of the purloined letter of psychoanalysis.

As such, Marie Bonaparte was a thoroughly loyal if not always reliable postman. In her capacious sack, Freudian 'truth' was transformed into a biological message, anatomy into a castrated destiny, rather than into a dynamic symbolic structure. But for all that, the Freudian letter, supported by that other potent means of exchange, Marie's millions, reached its destination. Psychoanalysis proliferated in France. If its contents were purloined to produce truths other than those she saw, there is none the less an irony in the way in which the phallus she so obsessively felt she lacked was returned to a determining place by her supposed enemies.

'Letters' were singularly important in Marie's life. From the age of seven, she was filling her copy-books with them – grotesque, cruel, magical tales and poems in those secret languages, English and German; stories overflowing with the recurring characters of her fantasies. These copy-books, presented to Freud in 1926, marked a turning-point in her analysis and served as the basis of her own self-analysis. They were only the beginnings of an activity of writing which filled Marie's years: countless letters, diaries, journals – one for each of her principal lovers, her children, her grandchildren, her analysis.

At one juncture in her analysis, Freud asked her to stop writing everything down. Writing was a refuge, an armed frontier post against the problematic country beyond. Marie stopped keeping an analytic diary, but she never stopped writing: articles, books, stories, thousand-page memoirs. Writing, she herself said, was her phallic activity in the world, an act libidinized through its identification with her father, an act at once intimate and public.

But intimacy made public could also pose a threat. Marie's adolescence was made miserable by the menacing possibility of her own letters reaching an improper destination. Her father's married secretary, the Corsican Antoine Leandri, had encouraged the sixteen-year-old Marie to engage in a flirtation, during which she wrote him the love letters which he was soon to use for the purpose of blackmail. If Marie did not pay, pay too for his unfair dismissal, Leandri would expose behaviour unsuited to a young princess. Marie paid secretly and then after her twenty-first birthday paid so to speak 'through the nose' for her indiscretion: in the tense weeks before a trial set for July 1904, she inadvertently banged her face against her piano and suffered a deep cut at the base of her nose. So disfiguring did she feel this trace of the Leandri affair to be that in subsequent years she had several operations to remove it. These surgical interventions seemed no more successful than those other, nether ones, which Marie underwent in an obsessive quest to cure what she understood as her frigidity by re-siting her clitoris closer to that most recalcitrant of feminine organs, the vagina.

If this story of black-*mail* reads like the libretto of a romantic opera, like so many of the broad strokes of Marie's life and the rhetorical flourish of much of her own writing, another set of letters, a second post, brings her firmly back into the history of psychoanalysis. In January 1937, Marie purchased Freud's letters to Fliess – that correspondence seminal to his creation of psychoanalysis – from a German bookseller. Heedless of Freud's exhortations, Marie refused to hand the letters over to him and watch him burn them. 'You belong to the history of human thought like Plato, let us say, or Goethe …', she told him. 'What a loss it would have been, for us, for posterity, if the conversations with Eckermann had been destroyed, or the dialogues of Plato, these latter out of pity for Socrates, in order to keep posterity from learning that Socrates practised pederasty with Phaedrus and Alcibiades?' Without the letters, Marie stresses, 'Something would be lost to the history of psychoanalysis, this unique new science, your creation which is more important than even Plato's ideas.'

Marie sternly defied her revered 'dear father'. It is probable that had she not, in her last embattled years, listened to the injunctions of the more cautious Anna Freud, the Freud–Fliess correspondence would have been available in an uncensored form well before Jeffrey Masson's 1985 edition. Marie had after all been an inveterate defender of the 'warts and all' school of biography. And she was certainly not afraid of any homosexual undercurrents. In a 1939 article published in the *International Journal of Psychoanalysis*, she had emphatically stated that 'a biography that is as real and human as possible will not detract from the reputation of the dead.' She added, [it was] essential that the subject's most loveable characteristics, although they may be considered by some as the least desirable, should not be removed for what is supposed to be respect but is in reality sacrilege. And these are the very characteristics that are usually preserved in intimate papers such as letters or diaries, which are so often threatened by the devoted persons who inherit them.

Certainly Marie, a compulsive scribbler, was also unashamed when it came to exhibiting her own secrets – in the light of the greater truth which her psychoanalytic mission bestowed on her. If in her last years she grew rather more conservative under the sway in part of her loyalty to Anna Freud, in part of the factions within the Paris Society, it was none the less remarkable, given her status, that her early intellectual radicalism had existed at all.

Marie's was not only a hunger of the mind, a perpetual search for clarity and understanding – however one judges the fruits of that search. This 'energy devil', as Freud called her, also had a thirst for experience, which translated itself into radically unconventional behaviour. The ease with which she moved from dinner at Buckingham Palace to lectures on female sexuality at the British Society, from court to couch, is only one of the many signs of this.

Freud remarked that Marie had 'no prudishness whatsoever'. In this, he noted, 'Nobody understands you better than I. But in my private life I am a petit bourgeois. ... I would not like one of my sons to get a divorce or one of my daughters to have a liaison.' The 'but' speaks volumes about the split in Freud himself between the good Victorian, faithful to wife and home, conventional in his opinions about women, and the revolutionary explorer, charting the rank and fetid jungle of the psyche. Marie, on the other hand, did more than talk dirty. She became one of those 'excessive Bonaparte women' whose legends peopled her childhood. And she took steps to live out not only her ideas, but also that *wilde Phantasie*, which Freud said existed in her as an admixture to her realism. Marie even went so far as seriously to consider committing incest with her twenty-four-year-old son. Perhaps it was only Freud's measured reflection that the trespass could well be 'followed by feelings of guilt against which one is quite helpless' that stopped her.

This redoubtable Bonaparte was born on 2 July 1882. Marie's father, Roland Bonaparte, an officer and dedicated naturalist, was an impoverished grandson of Napoleon I's renegade and profligate brother, Lucien. Her mother, Marie Blanc, the dreamy, sheltered daughter of a wealthy entrepreneur, was tubercular and died a few weeks after Marie's birth. She bequeathed the Bonapartes a vast fortune and baby Marie more than the usual share of a poor little rich girl's lacks. Marie, or Mimi as she was called, was left in the care of a string of nannies and governesses, whose speed of departure seemed to quicken in proportion to Mimi's attachment to them. Her father was absent even when present and all of little Mimi's energies were focused on winning the unattainable love of this cold man, lacking in affection. Bestriding the household in St Cloud like a one-eyed colossus was Princesse Pierre, Marie's paternal grandmother, 'a truly phallic woman', ambitious in her struggle to overcome her peasant origins, devious, a legendary huntress and horsewoman, who could 'piss standing up like a man, in the very midst of a crowd, merely by spreading her legs and skirts'. Her Amazonian displeasure often covered Mimi, who was terrified of her and jealous of her closeness to Prince Roland. Yet from a young age, Mimi knew that she would rather be like her censorious grandmother than like any other of her entourage of women who weakly bemoaned their sad fates.

Gossip about 'upstairs' bubbled in the Bonapartes' 'downstairs', where young Mimi spent most of her days. It was spiked with the proverbial envy and malice, in this instance with some cause. Rumour had it that the fierce Princesse Pierre had collaborated with her son in murdering *'petite-maman'*, Marie's mother, having first forced her to sign a will in Roland's favour. The insinuations coming fast on the heels of tales of other murderous Bonaparte exploits, not least those of Napoleon himself, made an indelible impression on little Mimi's imagination. She was haunted by the notion that she was implicated in a crime, responsible by her birth for her mother's death. But she also identified with *petite-maman*, who loved music and poetry and, like herself, was a victim of the malevolent Bonaparte couple, her Oedipally bound father and grandmother. To complicate matters further, Mimi adored her father, was dazzled by the horror of the rumoured ill-doings and felt guilty in her adoration.

As if in revenge, or as if she were bound to repeat the downstairs gossip eternally, Marie remained fascinated by murderers for the rest of her life. Madame Lefebvre, who in 1925 murdered her pregnant daughter-in-law – an incestuous murder which echoed the rumours in Marie's own family – served as the subject of one of Marie's finest and earliest papers (1927), the first to bear the imprint of analysis. On Madame Lefebvre's behalf, Marie became the first expert psychoanalytic witness in France. In her last years, at the age of seventy-seven, Marie struggled to have Caryl Chessman's death sentence repealed. Freud, it is worth noting, considered the final section of her lengthy study of Edgar Allan Poe, where she deals with sexual murderers, as the best thing she had written. In Poe himself, she found her mirror image. He, too, was inhabited by a dead mother who was persecuting and idealized by turn, but always incapable of being fully revitalized. Marie's search for cures for her frigidity is in certain respects an attempt to bring to life the dead woman in herself, a quest which was doomed to failure. Reborn, the murdered mother might seek retribution. For all its dangers, the father's line was safer. Where her mother should have been, there was, instead, the huge legacy: mother love had been replaced by the comforts of wealth and the secret excitement of murderous and covetous fantasies. Indeed, Marie often thought wealth was her major 'feminine' attraction, the cause which brought men to her.

Isolated from other children by her status, the parental preference for a sheltered austere existence which it was thought would appropriately prepare her for an aristocratic destiny, Marie's life was further constrained by what was wrongly suspected to be a tubercular condition. Raised as an invalid, she was allowed neither to run nor to play with potentially germ-ridden friends.

The anxiety about her health had, she later discovered, money at its core: if Marie were to die, the family fortunes would shrivel. Its immediate effect was to turn her into a lonely, fearful child, whose one solace was her heated imagination, and to fill her with phobias. Marie was frightened of buttons and red wine; of illness and possibly poisonous medicines; of contagion, constipation and ghosts. She had terrifying nightmares. In one series of dreams, a panting, steaming, iron monster, which she named the *Serquintué*, recurred, bursting into her room and threatening her with death. In another, a creature with a red finger growing out of its white neck tried to penetrate her fragile flesh.

Marie took refuge in daydreams about her glorious ancestors, whose feats she would one day equal. She read and wrote stories. By the age of seven, she could speak and write in three languages. She had a great hunger for learning in which her studious father served as a model. Her happiest childhood moments were spent with him gazing at the stars through his telescope, learning to draw or experimenting with magnets and electricity. But Prince Roland did little to encourage his daughter's scientific curiosity and the governesses the parental couple hired were not chosen for their intellectual accomplishments. Marie's skills were to be only those suitable to a royal heiress. Her education, until she was old enough to insist on better, was minimal; even then, examinations were prohibited to her. But education could at least be demanded; the affection she so ardently desired could not.

The melancholy Marie's first love – her father and her devoted, but jealously simple and superstitious nanny, Mimau, aside – was the theatre. At the age of fourteen, she was taken to see *Oedipus Rex* and *Hamlet*, both enacted by the great tragedian Mounet-Sully. She was as fascinated by the actor as she was shaken by the plays which seemed to resonate so closely with her life.

In the summer of 1898, Hamlet gave way to Leandri, who secretly wooed the impressionable Marie during a family expedition to Switzerland. A stroke here, a kiss there, and a great many verbal declarations set Marie on fire. Leandri made her aware of her femininity. He told Marie that her grandmother was making her ugly by dressing her badly and cutting her hair. He enjoined her to defend herself and her interests against the old virago. Primed by his insistence, Marie began to rebel, to make demands, to show her 'will power'. In some things she held sway: she was given fashionable clothes and allowed to visit her mother's grave. She also began to write Leandri the letters he seemed so ardently to desire from her.

Prince Roland, who had one of his few close friendships with his secretary, gradually woke to the fact that not only were rumours circulating about Marie and Leandri, damaging her reputation, but also that his secretary's meddling in his daughter's life was culminating in social treachery. Leandri had first had Marie attend mass in the church which the Radziwills, her maternal aunt's family with whom Roland had long since broken, frequented. He had then arranged a meeting between Marie and the Radziwills.

Prince Roland put Leandri on indefinite leave. Marie battled to have her father change his mind and began to write passionate letters to Leandri in earnest. Then, when Leandri committed a second treachery by accepting a large sum from a potential suitor of Marie's with the promise that he would further his suit, Prince Roland fired him outright. It was after this that the blackmail of Marie began: the Leandris, husband and wife, threatened that if Marie did not pay them – a regular stipend now, a larger sum later – they would sue Prince Roland and allege that he had fired Leandri in order to cover up Marie's sexual indiscretions. Her letters were their evidence.

Marie at last recognized how Leandri and his wife had used her. She sank into a depression, and produced a series of physical symptoms, to the point where Princesse Pierre called in an assistant of Charcot's to advise on this 'hysteric'. Marie swung between the conviction that she would die before the age of twenty-one – the time at which she came into her inheritance and her final blackmail date with Leandri – and dreaming of becoming a doctor, something her father would certainly not allow.

In certain respects, Marie, like Anna von Lieben, had the classic symptomatology of an aristocratic hysteric. Too intelligent and wilful to subside passively into the restrictive feminine mould demanded of her by her time and her social status, she found expression for her rebellion in a rush of illnesses and phobias. In later life, the discourse of bisexuality – the masculine mind trapped in a feminine body – provided her with a ready formula for a condition which others took as the starting-point of a feminist account. The medical studies her father prevented her from pursuing became the emblem of the liberation she had failed to attain.

Marie's obsessive respect for medicine lasted all her life and retained its importance for her throughout her engagement with psychoanalysis – founded, after all, by a doctor. Indeed, in her theoretical writings, Marie often gives greater weight to anatomical facts than psychic ones, and there is an overriding biologism in her last work. She might not have trained as a doctor, but her knowledge of medicine grew formidable; and although she was an avid champion of lay analysis, she was, as Heinz Hartmann said, 'more of a doctor than most doctors are ... among all of us she was the only one who really understood medicine. ... She took medicine more seriously than most analysts do.' So seriously, one might add, that the greatest and longest-lasting love of her life was for a doctor. So seriously too, that she regularly had recourse to the scalpel – a form of penetration that did not threaten the arousal of the dead woman in her and which progressed, happily, under anaesthesia.

Marie was fourteen when she learned from her new German governess that sexual intercourse did not involve the man making 'pee pee' on the woman but penetrating her. The notion petrified her. No wonder, she thought, *petite-maman* had died. Although she gradually 'accepted the law of nature to which I would have to submit', Marie did not take to submission unambivalently. She never, it seems, found any particular satisfaction in penetrative sex: the sadistic conception of intercourse, formed in childhood, left its residue. It combined with her sense that had she been a boy, the parental couple would never have curbed her activities and treated her as unjustly as she felt they did. Woman's lot was a poor one on all fronts. Even at the end of her long and full life, she was able to write: 'In the culture created by men, women do not have the position, the freedom, the happiness that they ought to; I feel myself to be one of the oppressed.' Her marriage was, despite its pomp and circumstance, one of the aspects of her oppression.

Marie was twenty-three before she had sufficiently recovered from the trauma of Leandri's blackmail and its effects to take up social life fully again. Prince Roland, having paid off Leandri just before his suit was to be taken to court, had renewed his efforts to find a noble husband for Marie. At first, there was only a string of doddering old men. Then enter, Prince George of the Royal House of Denmark, the son of King George I of Greece. Prince George, though he was not in direct line to the throne, was an altogether suitable candidate, indeed, something of a catch. In comparison to Marie's other suitors, George had all the attributes of a fairy-tale prince. He was a tall, blond Viking, kind, gentle and disinterested. But he was disinterested too in the literature which Marie loved and, as it transpired, in the woman she was. During the courtship meetings in which he slowly narrated his life to her, Marie found herself fending off sleep rather than any anticipated advances. She resigned herself to the marriage, still hoping for love; but it was the wedding preparations which really excited her. She was lavishly extravagant in purchasing her trousseau. The Paris newspapers carried headlines about it and about the civil wedding which preceded the grander religious ceremony in Athens. So did Proust.

Prince George's great passion was his Uncle Waldemar, ten years older than him and his lifelong friend. In one of her notebooks, entitled *The Old Companion*, Marie describes her wedding night. George came to her having seen Waldemar first: 'You needed the warmth of his voice, of his hand, and his permission, to get up your courage to approach the virgin. ... You took me that night in a short, brutal gesture, as if forcing yourself, and apologized, "I hate it as much as you do. But we must do it if we want children." '

This introduction to the act of love was hardly calculated to make Marie any more comfortable with her femininity than her father's earlier somewhat brutal disparagement of her had been. He had said to her a few years before her marriage: 'If I saw you in a brothel, you are certainly not the one I would pick.' Certainly, the homosexual orientation – if not provenly the practice – of these two men in her life, did nothing to assuage Marie's fear of childbirth. Haunted by her mother's fate, she awaited the birth of her two children in terror of her life. As it was, Peter and Eugénie (the first born on 3 December 1908, the second on 10 February 1910), once born safely, gave her great pleasure. None the less, Marie was at loose ends. The husband who kept her in what she experienced as the chains of boredom and royal propriety left her with time and too much energy on her hands. She was not one passively to accept what she called 'the oppression of marriage', this 'universal, if necessary malady'. In Paris, she began to frequent intellectual salons, and then run her own. She had made a close friend of the doctor and sociologist, Gustave Le Bon, who had written on the psychology of the crowd and, through him, she entertained *le tout Paris*, intellectuals, writers and politicians.

It was also Le Bon who first introduced her to Freud's writings.

Athens did not provide the same intellectual stimulation as Paris and it was probably here that Marie began to take lovers. Also here, that she became something of a heroine to the people through her war work, organizing and financing hospital ships and nursing on naval ambulances. Her sexual excursions only served to heighten what she had begun to see as the problem of her sexuality. Even the two great loves of her life did nothing to resolve it. In her *Notes diverses*, she writes:

After a few vain and unhappy attempts at love, I experienced two great passions. Between the ages of thirty and fifty, two men were my companions. The first, by his age and authority, could have been my father, and no one has loved me so much. The second was an older brother, and it was he whom I loved the most and the longest.

Aristide Briand, who became Marie's lover in 1916 after an ardent courtship which had lasted over two years, had been Prime Minister of France four times before he met her, became Prime Minister again during the height of their affair and was to fill the post six more times before his death in 1932. A formidable orator, a man of the people, he had started life as a socialist and, during his long political career, introduced a variety of liberal measures. His politics became Marie's own in many respects, and the book she wrote immediately after the 1914–18 war, *Guerres militaires, guerres sociales*, shows how she had imbibed French socialism as well as Lenin and Trotsky. The love affair with Briand was one of intellectual passion, at its height before any physical consummation. It ended when Marie discovered in May 1919 that Briand had been in love with another woman throughout that year. The two remained friends, though Marie, despite her new-found confidence in her desirability, retained her sense of sexual failure. In the journal she kept during her analysis with Freud, she noted having remarked to Freud about the affair: 'His ardour found me too frigid, from every standpoint'; to which Freud apparently answered: 'And he wasn't wrong!'

Her frigidity continued to haunt Marie. The second great love of her life, a physician, who remains unnamed and whom she simply calls 'the friend' in her journals, was similarly unable to dispel it, though she maintained relations with him until his death in 1945. The fact that 'the friend' callously told her early in their affair that he carried on making love to his wife since she gave him the pleasure the frigid Marie didn't, did nothing to lessen Marie's passion for him. In fact, his little cruelties probably increased it. The affair was at its turbulent peak while Marie's father lay dying in 1923–4. Prince Roland, now dependent and childlike in his needs, at last gave Marie all the attention she had once craved. She would escape her father to meet her lover in the garden, where they would make love under the stars. The new love was a retribution for the lacks of the old. Its little punishing sadisms only assuaged Marie's guilt at leaving the dying man.

It was at her father's bedside that Marie read Freud's *Introductory Lectures on Psychoanalysis*. And it was here, at the age of forty-two, that she began to feel the stirrings of what she calls '*l'appel du père*', the call of that second father who is, for her, Freud. Marie's life in psychoanalysis began with Prince Roland's death.

Marie had already met Dr René Laforgue, one of the three key figures in early French analysis, who was a psychoanalytic consultant at the psychiatric clinic of Sainte-Anne. They saw each other regularly, not so much for an analysis as for conversation. Marie's obsession with her own frigidity had led her in 1923, during the time of her father's illness, to do research on female sexuality. This had consisted of talking to some 200 women about their sex lives and measuring the distance between their clitoris and vagina – an eccentric notion and one which has since caused a measure of hilarity. But Marie undertook her task with scientific precision and with the indomitable flair of a veritable Bonaparte: in pursuing her preoccupations, Marie was never anything less than courageous and altogether immune to public opinion. None the less, when the results of her research appeared in a Brussels medical journal in April 1924, the month of her father's death, the name at the top of the article, entitled 'Considerations on the Anatomical Causes of Frigidity in Women', was A. E. Narjani. The article comes complete with statistical tables and anatomical drawings. Amongst her sources, Marie quotes not only Freud, whom she hotly disputes, but also Adler, Wilhelm Stekel and Krafft-Ebing. Her readings in psychoanalysis and sexology were already voracious.

The article begins by making an important distinction between two kinds of female frigidity, that catch-all term which covers a multitude of conditions. There are women who have an overall absence or a very low level of sexual *desire* and thus experience libidinal frigidity. Then there are women who experience 'violent desire' but are frigid with regard to vaginal *pleasure*. It is these latter who interest Marie. Amongst them, she distinguishes two further types. Those whose frigidity has a psychic determinant – women who are frigid as a result of disgust at their partner and, more gravely, those who suffer from a general sexual anaesthesia – may benefit from psychotherapeutic intervention. Then there are those whose vaginal frigidity has an anatomic cause – too great a distance between clitoris and vagina. This latter group, her researches had shown her, were often very tall women, like herself, and the only possible cure for their condition would lie in surgical intervention, still in its infancy. In describing these women, one senses that Marie is describing herself:

There are numerous women whom we haven't the right to qualify as sexually anaesthesic and who, though they are very passionate, desire men's love and are susceptible by various caresses to the greatest pleasures, remain implacably insensitive during coitus and only coitus, and this whatever the love which draws them toward their husband or lover. At the beginning of their sexual life they often blame this deficiency on their partner, accusing him of being too hasty and of not knowing how to go about it. But these women may change lovers time and again, even meet some with whom the act lasts over an hour, and still their insensitivity in the ultimate embrace persists. Such women usually end up by understanding that the deficiency is in themselves, and they console themselves with the idea that all women must be like them and that only in novels does shared pleasure between man and woman exist. These women do not reject men and are glad to give pleasure, contenting themselves with their lover's caresses before and after. But when they happen to love an egotist, who has no thought for the woman, their situation becomes dramatic. They are reduced either to chronic voluptuous disappointment which leads to a variety of nervous problems, or to masturbation which is always psychically unsatisfactory, or to the search for a more attentive new lover.

Even if this attentive lover is found and his caresses 'before, after or even during' lead to orgasm, these women will never be fully satisfied. Because it isn't these 'ersatz' of *voluptas* that Nature demands of love. And though these women may well sometimes want to convince themselves of their perfect happiness, perfect it isn't: they remain, despite all caresses, all the tendernesses of love, eternally unsated in their bodies.

In making her case, Marie takes a side-swipe at Freud for having imputed that there is something wrong in the clitoris maintaining what she insists is a 'normal sensitivity' beyond its due date: that is, beyond the time when the little girl supposedly becomes a woman by displacing clitoral sensitivity for vaginal sensitivity; and for attributing this retention of clitoral sensitivity to excessive infantile masturbation. Marie will have none of it:

The clitoris remains the central organ of sexual pleasure for all women, and this whatever the diffuse sensitivity of the vagina which never manages to supplant it. Because the clitoris is homologous to the penis ... the normal woman can no more do without it to experience voluptuous contact, than the normal man can do without his penis.

Neither the psychotherapeutic interventions of Freud, whom, whatever her criticisms, she insisted on seeing, nor the surgical interventions of another Viennese, Professor Halban, whose clitoral operations she championed, were ever to relieve Marie of her fixation with her frigidity.

Her father's death threw Marie into despair. As was her way, she expressed it in part somatically and submitted repeatedly to the knife. In the year before she turned to Freud, she had an ovarian cyst removed, had the scar on her nose retouched for the third time and had plastic surgery on her breasts. She also wrote a suicidal story, *Les glauques aventures de Flyda des mers*, in which her thinly disguised heroine drowns herself in desperation at her life.

It was after a dinner with Otto Rank at her house that René Laforgue wrote to Freud on her behalf:

I do not know if Rank has told you that we spent an evening at the house of Princess George of Greece. The lady in question suffers from a rather pronounced obsessional neurosis, which, though it has not impaired her intelligence, has nevertheless somewhat disturbed the general equilibrium of her psyche....

This lady intends to go to see you in Vienna, and she asks me to inquire if you could possibly undertake a psychoanalytic treatment of her.

Freud responded with no apparent enthusiasm. He would only take on even a princess if Laforgue could 'guarantee the seriousness of her intentions and her personal worth', if she had German or English, and 'accepted precisely the same obligations as all the other patients'. Laforgue vouched for Marie's seriousness, said that she was so set on a two-month analysis that she wanted two hours a day and that she would certainly submit to the general conditions, and if necessary come back for another two-month season. Any resistances did not lie there, but in the intellectual domain, where the Princess, because of her superior mind, challenged everyone. Laforgue further explained that it was not so much a 'cure' the Princess was seeking as a didactic analysis. 'In my view she has a pronounced virility complex, as well as numerous difficulties in her life, so that analysis would in any event be indicated.'

Freud was even less impressed than after Laforgue's first letter. On 16 June 1925, he replied to say that he could do nothing for the Princess. Given the limited number of his working hours, he was not prepared to squander anything on an analysis without a serious goal. 'Since I take only very few cases, an analysis of six to eight weeks, forcing me to give up another one and extending over a season, cannot tempt me.' Nor, for the same reasons, could he devote two hours a day to the same case.

But no sooner did Marie appeal to Freud directly than he changed his mind. He would expect her in Vienna on the afternoon of 30 September. The stage was set for a meeting which would procure for psychoanalysis a potent champion in France. Marie brought with her not only the force of her own personality, soon to be doubly fuelled by a new loving father and the sense of a genuine cause, but also the superior confidence of one who belonged to an aristocratic and intellectual old-established elite. In her, the 'Jewish science' found a formidable French defender against those who, like Edouard Pichon, might want to hijack its insights and give them a chauvinistic slant. For the rest of her life, Marie was to put her Napoleonic talents to the task of building a French psychoanalytic empire. To do so, she had initially to defy the vigorous protests of her husband, her lover and her children and to suffer the blandishments of the conservative circles which were her own.

Where Marie's commitment went, there went her wealth. On repeated occasions, she succoured Freud's ailing publishing enterprise; she undertook translations and financed the French psychoanalytic journal, as well as premises for the Paris Society. She was also a loyal and supremely generous personal friend, showering Freud and the family who became hers with gifts, presenting him with his favourite chows and with antique statuary – including the urn in which his ashes were ultimately placed; and paying the fee to the Nazi authorities which enabled the Freuds' departure from Vienna.

Freud was obviously as enchanted with the woman he loved to call 'Princess' – the endearment he had used for Martha during their engagement – as Marie was with him. After less than a month of meetings, he was writing to Eitingon about his 'dear princess' who was 'a quite outstanding, a more than just half masculine female'. Laforgue, who had recommended her, was told. 'The Princess is doing a very fine analysis and is, I think, very satisfied with her stay. I rejoice now that I submitted to your wish and to the impression her letter made on me.' The analysis, conducted in German or

English, continued over six somewhat interrupted months in the first year, then for one or two months a year until Freud's death. It quickly merged into friendship: both Marie and her daughter were recipients of Freud's rings. How successful the analysis may or may not have been is as tangled a question as ever. Certainly, the encounter with Freud and with psychoanalysis gave Marie what she called a 'new life' – a cause – and released powers which had been dormant or turned in on herself. She had come to analysis, she noted in her unpublished *Journal d'analyse* on 28 October 1925, in search of 'the penis and orgastic normality'. Whereas the second, it seems, was not to be found, it could undoubtedly be said that analysis freed the first, the phallic woman in her, allowing her to give full rein to an intellectual Marie who played an important part on the professional psychoanalytic stage. Freud became the loving father who supported her activities, thus displacing a real father who had been cold and disapproving.

The impression Freud made on her, she wrote to Laforgue after her first session, 'surpasses everything I expected. First his great kindness, combined with so much power. One feels him in "sympathy" with all humanity, which he has been able to understand and of which one is only an imperceptible fragment.' A few weeks later, she told Laforgue that analysis was the most 'gripping' thing she had ever done. Freud both analysed and chatted, answering her eager curiosity about him with unusual confidences – or perhaps only unusual in that Marie, inveterate scribbler, recorded them. The confidences only went up to a certain point. On the hoary question of his own sexual life, Freud drew a modest curtain. To Marie's teasing comment that 'he must have had a supernormal sexual development', he only replied, *'Davon werden Sie nichts erfahren* [You'll discover nothing about that].' And added, with an old man's irony, *'Vielleicht nicht so sehr!* [Perhaps not so very!]' According to Peter Swales, he also told Marie that he had not been a virgin at marriage, but when she pressed him on whether he had had other relations with women since marriage, he declined to answer. It was to Marie too that Freud wryly remarked on his golden wedding anniversary that though his old passion for Martha was now the faintest of memories, for all that, 'It was really not a bad solution of the marriage problem.'

The analysis itself provided Marie with startling revelations. In its first month she recounted a dream to Freud, which, like a kingpin, began to topple all the fixed points of her childhood universe. She was sitting in a little bed in the Bois de Boulogne and watching a couple making love on a large bed. Freud instantly offered the interpretation that she had, as a small child, actually *seen* a couple making love in broad daylight. Marie resisted the interpretation, pointing out that she had not had a mother. Freud insisted, suggesting a nanny in the mother's place in this primal scene. Still resisting, Marie came up with a screen memory: her nanny's room. Seated on a little chair, Mimi is watching her nanny. The nanny, her face unusually yellowish and horse-like, is pommading her hair in front of the chimney-piece where a fire burns. 'I feel disgusted,' Marie declares.

With that puzzle-solver's clinical intuition which was superbly his, Freud picked apart the elements in the dream – the nanny's uncharacteristic horse-like face, indicating a displacement from a man who dealt with horses; the fire, sexual relations; the sooty fireplace, the cloacal inside of the woman's body and so on – to imply that Marie must indeed have seen her nanny in coitus with the family groom and that this scene provided her with her first perception of sexual difference. Still resisting Freud's interpretation, Marie, on her Christmas return to France, sought out the Corsican family groom to determine the truth of dreams, memory and the linkage with childishly perceived family gossip. Now an old man of eighty-two, the groom, Pascal, refused to confess to any sexual misdemeanours. But the more he talked, the more the details of his refusal only coincided with what Freud had suggested. This time, on her return to Vienna, Marie brought her childhood copy-books to Freud. She had unearthed these dusty notebooks shortly after her father's death and her total inability to recall having written them – this incomprehensible hiatus in her memory – together with the startling nature of her childhood fabulations, had been one of the factors which had led her to seek out Freud. Freud's comments on these grotesque childhood tales, notably his assertion that she had witnessed fellatio amongst other repeated variations of the sexual act, made Marie seek out the aged Pascal once more. This time, he confessed to his relations with her nanny, often carried out in front of little Mimi, from the time she was six months old to when she was three and a half; he also confessed to the administration of Syrop de Flon, the potion which put Mimi to sleep while the nanny was busy with him.

Marie, the practical realist, had her proof of the scientific validity of analysis.

The copy-books, not published until after Freud's death, but with his agreement, provide a remarkable document of the history of an analysis. Buried in Marie's tales are early memories later transmuted into fables. Her commentary on them, which integrates Freud's interpretations with her own, vividly represents the circuitous path by which repressed memory is unearthed and translated. Marie's infantile voyeuristic experience of variations of the sexual act; her double Oedipal load of groom and nanny, father and grandmother; her dead mother; her half-heard narratives of household intrigue – all these had been transformed by Marie into fears and desires, masturbation and guilt, and into the girlhood grotesques she had penned in secret foreign languages. Analysis illuminated childhood terrors and wishes, the lonely frightened child she had been, and the unfolding of her later destiny.

The Serquintué, the steaming monster engine with its one eye, who threatened the little girl, once analysed, was seen to be the male in coitus who would kill the 'little voyeuse' to punish her for her sin of seeing. Dismantled, Serquintué yielded the composite word, *cercueil* (coffin) and *tué* (killed).

The railway train, in the guise of which the Serquintué appeared, puffed and panted much as a man in the act of intercourse, which I had so often watched. ... Also, a train rushes on one like an angry bull; woe to him who falls beneath it, it passes over his body, and it crushes him – as man crushes woman in normal coitus; that was why my mother had died – from having lain beneath a man; for me the infantile sadistic conception of coitus had been carried out to the letter.

That is why the train, bull and voyeur at the same time, was a slayer; if at the same time it represented a hearse, my mother's hearse with her body inside it, that is because there was condensed in it my picture of the 'combined parents'; on the one hand the murdering male, who rushes upon the female in the sadistic act of intercourse, on the other the woman attacked and slaughtered, actually laid in her coffin, from which she returned to slay me in my turn – me, the child who had been the man's accomplice in her death, since she had died from giving birth to me. Thus the coffin holding the slain woman in turn slew the wicked little girl, who had seen, with feelings of satisfaction, the accomplishing of the fatal sex act.

Mimi, that 'poor body ink' who always had black fingers, was like her mother Blanc, 'quite black' in death and predestined to be a victim of men, as well as a writer and man's intellectual rival.

At the conclusion of the analysis of one tale, Marie writes:

The real fact of my mother's death and my father's survival made a strange impression on me, which still survives in my unconscious; namely, that all women are more or less dead, or at least candidates for death, while men, the bearers of the phallus, are immortal. Sometimes, in certain semi-conscious hypnogogic states, I still find myself astonished that there are innumerable women on the face of the earth, and not men only. Doubtless this odd idea of the 'annihilation of the female universe' is a belated trace of some grandiose Oedipal wish-fantasy, in which I imagined myself left alone on earth with my father, or with 'men', all duplicates of him.

If Freud, the father, analysed Marie's paternal identification and allowed her to make use of her 'masculine' talents, there were still problems, she felt, with her femininity. Marie became productive in her male role. The good fairy of her copy-books – in her analysis both nanny and mother – has bequeathed her the 'mouth-pencil' – Pascal's penis and her father's essential paternal attribute, at once penis and writing tool. But her feminine side was still free to roam destructively, present recurrent symptoms and determine her *idée fixe* about the anatomical basis of frigidity. Perhaps it was the fear Marie and Freud shared of the dark and savage female side that meant he would not touch on it too deeply; when Marie once remarked to Freud, 'Man is afraid of woman,' he exclaimed, 'He's right.'

Marie, too, was still afraid. The dead woman, the annihilated female universe, haunted her lengthy study of Edgar Allan Poe. Sometimes turgid in its mechanical application of psychology to literature, sometimes brilliant, this psycho-biography interprets Poe's oeuvre as his attempt to come to terms with the dead mother who obsessed him and rendered him impotent.

Marie's femininity similarly remained frozen, impervious to analytical penetration. 'Every living thing', she wrote in her commentary on the copy-books, 'fears being broken into, for this threatens it with destruction.' The fear of penetration was for her a 'vital', biological fear, and not one which could be shifted or dispersed by psychological means. Her frigidity continued to obsess her and she still saw it as an anatomical problem. During her time in Vienna, she and Ruth Mack Brunswick, whom she at first perceived as a rival, became intimate friends and sexual confidantes. Ruth gave her advice on masturbation techniques and told her she was 'prouder of her masturbation than of 10 doctoral degrees'. Marie still believed that her 'masculine' clitoris, for which all her erotic sensations seemed to be reserved, was at the root of her sexual unhappiness.

In 1927, she decided to undergo the operation with Professor Halban she had once written about and have her clitoris moved closer to her vagina. Freud admonished her, telling her that being an analyst requires restraint and reminding her that analysis frees the instincts, but it should also allow one to master them. Marie resisted him: her *idée fixe* was still in place. In 1929, after four years of analysis with Freud and a top-up with Rudolf Loewenstein, who also became her lover, and after she had already started seeing her own patients, she wrote in one of her many notebooks: 'Psychoanalysis can at the most bring resignation. ... The analysis has brought me peace of mind, of heart, and the possibility of working, but from the physiological point of view nothing. I am thinking of a second operation. Must I give up sex? Work, write, analyse? But absolute chastity frightens me.' Marie underwent a second clitoral operation, no more successful than the first, despite her continuing championing of the technique. But then, she also continued to champion analysis.

Marie's tenacity had some impact on Freud. In his 1932 lecture on 'Femininity', he conceded that the all-too-frequent sexual frigidity of women could perhaps in certain cases be determined by 'a contributory anatomical factor' – surely a vague phrase for the misplaced clitoris that Narjani–Bonaparte had so assiduously investigated. It was also perhaps in part because of the obstinacy of his dear friend Marie's symptoms that Freud in his 1931 essay on 'Female Sexuality' emphasized the difficulty of grasping everything 'in the sphere of this first attachment to the mother', 'so grey with age and shadowy and almost impossible to revivify', so impenetrable, that he had not 'succeeded in seeing my way through any case completely'. Marie had been able to cling with Freud to 'the very attachment to the father in which [she] had taken refuge from the early phase that was in question'.

Marie's particular inability to come to terms with her own femininity – that realm for her of the dead woman, the murdered and thus potentially murderous mother – inflects all her writings on female sexuality. These contain a significant admixture of *'wilde Phantasie'* along with her more 'realist' insights. Where Freud dips into the biological only in order finally to construct sexuality along a psychical plane, for Marie anatomy adamantly determines destiny.

Fascinated by the female body, she examined women's corpses and investigated sexual parts. Female circumcision preoccupied her and she avidly read and frequented anthropologists who could inform her about tribal practices. At one point she asked Jomo Kenyatta, the future President of Kenya, then a graduate student, to write up what he had told her about female initiation rites and excision in his country. She went so far as to give credence to the evolutionary theses of Gregorio Maranon, who held that at birth every human being is endowed with the potentialities of both sexes, the progressive male and the regressive female. The general development of woman comes to a stop at puberty, Maranon claims, when the specialized organs designed for maternal function take over. Femininity, for Maranon, thus becomes 'a stage of evolution which has stopped midway between adolescence and the adult man, this last being the true terminal form of organic evolution'.

Obsessed by her female body, in which the one vital part seems to her male; convinced that a masculine mind and will are trapped in her female form – a form responsible for the parental couple's restrictive and contemptuous treatment of her, treatment which her own husband in certain respects repeated with their daughter Eugénie – Marie translated her fixations into a theory which takes bisexuality as its basis. Her organic inflection here is the characteristic feature of her theorizations. The first paper she gave to an international psychoanalytic congress, 'The Erotic Function in Woman' (1932), focuses on women who have not renounced their masculinity and who therefore preserve the 'phallic organization with regard to the erogenous zones'. They become heterosexuals, Marie declares, 'in whom the clitoral zone nevertheless stubbornly remains the dominant one'. Her 1933 article, '*Les deux frigidités de la femme*', takes up Narjani's old theme and now states that frigidity caused by clitoridal fixation can only be cured by a mixture of surgery and psychoanalysis – until, that is, hormonal medicine will be able to '*viriliser l'homme*' and '*féminiser la femme qui le désireraient*'– masculinize men and feminize the woman who wishes it. *Female Sexuality* (1951) amplifies on all these themes, with an insistent emphasis on the psycho-biological. And her final collection of papers bears the revealing title, *Psychoanalysis and Biology*. By the end of her life, Marie was postulating a determinative organic unconscious, deeper than Freud's.

In *Female Sexuality*, Marie's most widely read book, she uses Freud's paper on the subject in order to encompass her own particular emphases on genitality. Her *idée fixe* about her frigidity, the too great distance between her dormant vagina and her sensitive 'masculine' clitoris, permits her to quote approvingly Freud's 'in human beings pure masculinity or femininity is not to be found either in a psychological or a biological sense', and twist this to conclude that 'we are justified in thinking that libidinal fixation on the clitoris, in woman, when tenaciously maintained, corresponds to a basically biological masculine character incorporated in the feminine organism.' Like Helene Deutsch – although Marie partially disputes her essential feminine masochism – Marie proposes a relatively static typology of woman, basing herself on Freud's descriptions of the possible orientations to sexual difference in reaction to the castration complex. Marie's feminine trinity includes the *revendicatrices* – the women who claim back the absent penis by investing their sexuality in their clitoris and assuming male attitudes; the *acceptatrices* – the ideally and biologically well-adapted women who replace the desire for a penis by a desire for the child; and the *renonciatrices* – the renouncers, who, 'biologically outclassed by the male', abandon all sexual rivalry and make up the ranks of saintly spinsters.

Absorbed by the problem of her own sexual frigidity, Marie effectively gives up the psychoanalytical for a determinative biology. It is not surprising that in her last years, in a moment of despair in part caused by the battles within the Paris Society, she should note in her diary, alongside a list of mistakes, this last:

A bigger error, it is Freud who was wrong. He overestimated his power, the power of therapy. The power of childhood events. ... It was in the depths of the maternal flesh ... that nature made me, by sex, a female misfit – but otherwise, in the brain, almost a man.

Whatever the failures of psychoanalysis, Marie remained a close and lavishly generous friend of Freud's and Anna's until the end. When Anna was arrested by the Gestapo, Marie tried to have herself arrested as well, but the Nazis were too cowardly or clever, it seemed, to implicate royalty. She worked tirelessly to facilitate the family's flight to England, using the many diplomatic connections she had access to and the strength of her title.

On the Austrian front, she was helped by Margaret Stonborough-Wittgenstein, one of Freud's few female friends who was neither analyst nor analysand. The elder sister of Ludwig Wittgenstein, a highly cultivated and independent woman, as well as a respected patron of the arts, Margaret's friendship was one Freud had greatly valued since near the beginning of the century. From her philosopher brother's musings over a comment about dreams Freud had made to his sister, we can infer that Margaret valued Freud's friendship to an equal degree. Though Jewish by origin, the Wittgenstein family had converted generations back. This, together with their wealth and status, rendered them non-Jews in the Nazi categorizations – though even they had to fight and pay enormous amounts of money to secure their special status. Margaret used what influence she had to help Freud and others, but would herself never accept the official designation of 'honourable Aryan'.

Marie welcomed the Freuds and their contingent in her home in Paris on their migration to England. One of Freud's first letters from London was to her, thanking her, with a warmth characteristic of their correspondence, for a day which 'restored our good mood and sense of dignity; after being surrounded by love for twelve hours we left proud and rich under the protection of Athene' (the statuette Marie had smuggled out of Austria and returned to him in Paris). Marie battled tirelessly to obtain exit visas for Freud's sisters and was desolate when she could not, but she managed to bring Oliver Freud to France, as well as Heinz and Dora Hartmann (the latter a grand-niece of Josef Breuer and former paediatrician, who was also another trainee of Freud's), not to mention some 200 other persecuted Jews.

Marie herself, together with George, her daughter Eugénie, who had also grown close to Freud, and Eugénie's husband and daughter, survived the war years in South Africa. Depressed by world events, feeling deeply uprooted, Marie none the less kept herself busy. She saw a few patients, lectured, wrote and collected material for her *Myths of War*. This fascinating monograph of 1946 shows the structural similarity between narratives which circulated orally during the war on Axis and Allied sides and their link to traditional myths and fables. Late in 1944, Marie and George sailed for England, returning at last to France in the new year. She was sixty-three years old and, for her remaining years, she continued to champion what she understood as the Freudian cause in the tangled politics of French psychoanalysis.

As early as March 1926, Marie had attended a meeting of a small group of Freud's followers in Paris and been recognized as his personal emissary. Worried about the vagaries of analysis in France, the International Psychoanalytic Association had settled four Berlin- and Vienna-trained analysts in Paris, who, together with Marie, effectively established the Freudian line over and above the home-grown one. When, in November 1926, the Paris Society was established, Marie played a considerable part in ensuring that its rules were ones Freud approved of. From 1934 she was the Society's Vice-President. The year before she had been instrumental in establishing and financing the first Paris Society Headquarters and Training Institute and had become a member of the Training Committee. That same year, Freud proposed her for the Vice-Presidency of the International Psychoanalytic Association – a post left vacant by Ferenczi's death.

His letter to Jones of 23 August 1933 is revealing. He was making the nomination not only because Marie was a person who could be shown off to the outside world, but because

she is a person of high intelligence, has the working capacity of a man, has done nice work, is fully devoted to the cause, and as you know, is also in a position to give material help. She is now 50 years old, will presumably turn increasingly away from her private interests and devote herself to analytic work. I need not mention that she alone holds the French group together and pays for the *Revue Française*. Her good practical sense and charming, sociable manner will make her a delightful colleague on the executive.

Moreover, Freud added, Marie was not a physician and to invite a layperson to fill so exalted a post would be a definite strike 'against the undesirable arrogance of the physicians who like to forget that psychoanalysis is after all something other than a part of psychiatry'. Marie, with her avid respect and recourse to medicine, was destined to champion lay analysis and, in the 1950 French test case of the American child analyst Margaret Williams, to hire her lawyer and take her cause to the highest courts.

The post-war analytic situation distressed Marie. The Paris and British Societies were riven by conflict, as much the psychic and political residue of war as of theoretical differences. In Britain, where she went frequently, Marie noted that there were in fact two societies which did not mingle. 'When one visits London, one goes to the two of them, as formerly in Rome to visit the Pope and the King.' In France, things were, if anything, worse. Loewenstein, her closest colleague and friend, had left for the United States in 1940. It was to him she communicated her distaste for the Paris Society's internal wranglings and her disapproval of, amongst others, Lacan, its rising luminary: 'As for Lacan, he is rather too tinged with paranoia and questionable narcissism, allowing himself too much personal interference.' Worse, Lacan 'the paranoid' played havoc with rules of time and the increasingly ritualized aspects of technique.

Loewenstein had analysed Lacan, Marie for a short while and her son, Peter. During the bitter wrangles which eventually resulted in the Paris Society's split in 1953, both Lacan and Marie, fully aware of the other's links with him, communicated their complaints about each other to him. Lacan informed Loewenstein that Marie's actions had always had disastrous consequences for their group:

The social prestige she represents can only falsify relations. What she derives from her role with Freud makes everyone listen to her with a patience which takes on the semblance of approval. The respect due to an old lady brings with it a tolerance for her opinions which demoralises the young, in whose eyes we appear in a state of ridiculous subjection.

There were no saints in the psychoanalytic squabbles. With her weight on the Training Committee, Marie refused to have three of Lacan's pupils considered. She used her influence with the International, her friendship with Anna Freud, her position as Honorary President of the Training Committee and of the Executive Council, to make certain that Lacan and Daniel Lagache's new Société Française de Psychanalyse was not recognized by the International, going so far as to orchestrate their exclusion from the administrative debate about their personal futures at the London Congress of 1953 – a move that Loewenstein thought 'abnormal and unjust'. Marie, on her side, did not understand why Loewenstein could not be as tough as she was: in her anger at Loewenstein there was not a little residue of her sense that he had not successfully analysed her son.

The personal asperity between Marie and Lacan has something in it of mutual envy. Marie's 'social prestige', her wealth, the aristocratic standing which allowed her flagrantly to transgress all rules, was something Lacan always aspired to. As for Marie, Lacan had that coveted medical degree. He also had, as Marie was perhaps the first to spot, a particular talent, she noted in a letter to Loewenstein, sensing in Lacan the theoretical architect and sect builder who would draw disciples to him, something Marie perhaps had the ambition but not the talent to realize. Interestingly, the two shared a fascination with extreme criminal acts and both looked to anthropology as a seed bed for psychoanalytical insight.

Certainly, for all Lacan's ostensible contempt for Marie, he was all too aware of her study of Poe. In his brilliant analysis of Poe's *The Purloined Letter*, he dismisses her textual attention to whether the exact hiding-place of the letter is above or below the mantelpiece (was he deliberately alluding to Marie's preoccupation with the exact location of the clitoris?) as the 'inferences of those whose profession is grilling'. As Jacques Derrida has wryly suggested, Lacan in fact arrives at the same truth as the redoubtable Bonaparte, finding as the ultimate meaning of the purloined letter, the castration of the woman, and the truth, *la réadéquation*, or the reappropriation, as the desire to fill the hole.

Marie was long dead by the time of this later post-structuralist twist in the affairs of French psychoanalysis, over which she had so ardently presided. She had remained active in its affairs until the end, though squeezed into mere honorary positions. As ever, depression increasingly led her to find solace in writing. Her lengthy memoirs and her book on the miscarriages of justice, inspired by the Caryl Chessman affair and which championed the abolition of the death sentence, were all produced in her seventies. As she had noted in the second volume of her commentary on her copy-books: 'This reflex of taking refuge in writing whenever I have been hurt by life has remained with me. Disappointment or grief, far from preventing me from working, always drives me irresistibly to seek solace in literary or scientific creation.'

Medical science remained a passion. In her will she left generous bequests to the Institut Pasteur amongst others. Her final thoughts on psychoanalysis are perhaps best expressed in her address to the executive committee of the Twentieth International Congress held in her house at St Cloud. Amongst its accomplishments, she noted the liberation of the irrepressible sexual instincts, greater frankness with our children and greater sexual freedom for women. 'Mankind has ... become a little less hypocritical, and, perhaps a little happier.'

The woman whom Freud had numbered amongst his closest friends, who thought of herself as the last Bonaparte, died on 21 September 1962.

Eugénie Sokolnicka, 1884–1934

Freud had sent a previous emissary to France, one whom he had not been so close to as to Marie Bonaparte, and one who had sadly proved less successful in the organizational affairs of French psychoanalysis, though she had the reputation of being a brilliant clinician.

Eugénie (Kutner) Sokolnicka was born in 1884 into a family of Polish Jewish professionals and battlers for the cause of national liberation. She had studied science and biology at the Sorbonne and taken Pierre Janet's courses there, before returning to Poland to marry a man she had met in France. In 1911, Eugénie went to Zurich to become Jung's student. Then in 1913, at the moment of his falling out with Freud, she turned to the Professor and became Freud's analysand. In 1916, she was made a member of the Zurich Society and started taking patients; she began attending meetings of the Vienna Society early in 1916 and became a member on 8 November. At the war's end, she made her way to Budapest and worked with Ferenczi for two years. Ferenczi reported to Freud in detail about his analysis of Sokolnicka, also using it in the paper he presented at the Sixth International Congress in 1920: 'Further Developments of an Active Therapy in Psycho-Analysis'. The Hungarian experience stayed with her: she was known for her short-term therapies, one of which was the subject of her first psychoanalytic paper in

1920: a striking exposé of her method of dealing with the obsessional neurosis of a ten-year-old boy, who had suffered traumatic separation from his parents during the Bolshevik occupation of the town of Minsk. In a 1929 lecture to the conference of French psychoanalysts, Eugénie lucidly presented her views. The aim of the cure is to allow the patient to reunite his sexual desire and his tenderness in one object. In order to reach that point, masturbation and work inhibitions must be analysed. There are two possible kinds of analysis: the minimal, which sees as its end the disappearance of symptoms; and the maximal, which includes the freeing of the ability to love and the avoidance of repetition. A more succinct description of the tasks of analysis would be hard to find.

Having failed to integrate herself in the Warsaw psychiatric milieu and found a psychoanalytic society there, on Freud's advice Sokolnicka returned to Paris in 1921. Here, her Polish difficulties were repeated on a grander scale. The French psychiatric establishment had little confidence in lay analysts, let alone women whose principal expertise was with children. No sooner did Sokolnicka acquire a position at the famous Sainte-Anne hospital, than Henri Claude, friendly to Freud but hostile to lay practitioners, became its new head and fired her.

Sokolnicka's fame was to lie elsewhere. Contacts brought her close to the illustrious group around the Nouvelle Revue Française, who had an enthusiastic literary interest in psychoanalysis. During 1921–2, the writers André Gide, Jacques Rivière, Roger Martin du Gard, Gaston Gallimard and Jean Schlumberger met for weekly sessions at Sokolnicka's home and discussed clinical and theoretical aspects of analysis with her. They called her the 'Doctoresse' and named their group the *Club des Refoulés* (Club of the Repressed). Gide went so far as to attempt analysis, but, when the going got tough after some six weeks, abandoned it. Instead, he turned the experience into the matter of his most accomplished novel, *The Counterfeiters*, in which Sokolnicka is transformed into Doctoresse Sophroniska, and her famous cure of a childhood obsessional neurosis is turned by Gide, who knew the material, into an abject failure: Boris, her fictional patient, kills himself in a game of Russian roulette.

Sokolnicka's literary influence moved hand in hand with her clinical successes. In 1923, she became training analyst to two figures key to the development of analysis in France: René Laforgue and Edouard Pichon; and in 1926 she was named Vice-President of the fledgling Paris Society, a post she held for two years. But, by the 1930s despite the continuing loyalties of Laforgue and Pichon who sent her patients, Sokolnicka's practice dwindled: the weight of the French predilection for medically trained practioners counted against her. Poverty, growing depression, the rise of Nazism and her own sense of rootlessness weighed on her and, in 1934, at the age of fifty, this brave and talented woman took her own life.

It is one of the ironies of French psychoanalysis that Eugénie Sokolnicka's obituary – a glowing one – was written by the nationalist and anti-Semitic Edouard Pichon. Her former analysand had remained her friend to the end, having even provided her with a flat throughout her last lean years.

Maryse Choisy, 1903–79

One other French woman who became an analyst had a brief encounter with Freud. In 1924, Maryse Choisy, an adventurous and impetuous twenty-two-year-old journalist, who both flew planes and tamed lions, had three analytic sessions with Freud. After the third, in a response which is in some ways reminiscent both of Dora's to Freud's emphatic interpretations and of Marie's triumphant confirmation of Freud's uncovering of dramatic childhood sexual scenes, Maryse fled.

She had related an obscure dream of being a cat in her parents' castle and offered some brief associations:

Freud pondered for a few minutes over my dream, then uttered without warning: 'Such and such an event happened in your family when you were still in the cradle.'

[...] I did not believe Freud. I even became indignant.

'What you say is quite impossible. I would have known it. Such things are simply not done in *my* family. It's against their principles.'

Though I could not see him behind me, I knew he was smiling. He just gave me the following advice: 'Well, you'd better ask them.'

I jumped on the first plane back to Paris. I ran to my aunt's house. I spoke to her the moment I got there. Believe it or not, Freud's extravagant story of an event which I had never even suspected (at least consciously), turned out to be true.

The 'truth' that Freud revealed was that Maryse was an '*enfant naturel*', an illegitimate child.

There was something uncanny about this dream interpretation. I did not return to Vienna. Freud now symbolized for me the magical father, the medicine-man. He saw through me. I felt as transparent as glass. I was scared. I was so scared that I would go to great lengths to avoid analysis. It took me eight years to overcome my panic. Freud had overestimated me. He believed he could tell me anything. In spite of my independent airs there was still a truth I could not face at twenty-two.

Maryse Choisy, this evoker of medicine-men, converted to Catholicism in 1936 through the offices of Teilhard de Chardin; she also went through two training analyses, one with René Laforgue, another with Charles Odier. Seeing herself as a rival to the legitimate daughter, Princess Marie Bonaparte, in 1946 she founded the Centre d'Étude des Sciences de l'Homme, with its own royal sponsor, Prince Louis de Broglie, and numerous luminaries (Janet, Laforgue, Chardin). Its monthly organ *Psyche*, an international review of psychoanalysis and the human sciences, she hoped would rival the existing *Revue Française de Psychanalyse*. The Centre and the journal addressed the great spiritual problems of the age and attempted to find for psychoanalysis the larger public which would recognize in it a new spiritual solution. She was attempting to counter Bonaparte's brand of Freudian atheism with a synthesis of Rome – she had asked for the papal blessing for psychoanalysis – and oriental religions. But she was also the first in post-war France to direct attention to the larger public arena that Jacques Lacan's followers would, a few years later, make their own – and some of her protégés were later to become his. In the same vein, she also later collaborated with Father Leycester King of Oxford, in founding the International Association of Psychotherapy and Clinical Psychology. She carried on writing, producing a spirited study of Freud and a book on the prostitute.

Choisy was part of the post-war movement in France to develop what could be called a Christian psychoanalysis. Her search for a benediction for psychoanalysis from the Church runs parallel to Jacques Lacan's, who similarly sought the papal blessing for himself and his new school. Whereas Lacan's was distinctly a move within the power politics of psychoanalysis – the Pope's blessing would establish the pre-eminence of his new school and allow priests, attracted by his logocentric theories, to swell its ranks – Choisy's search for the Pope's approval had a religious base. In the event, she and like-minded colleagues did manage to obtain a papal view on psychoanalysis. It was hardly one which would have sat well with Freud, that radical critic of the illusory nature of religion. Pius XII spoke out in two addresses, one to an international congress on the histopathology of the nervous system, another to Maryse Choisy's Association in 1953. He distinguished psychotherapy from Freudian psychoanalysis, declaring that, 'It is not proven, it is even untrue that the pansexual method of a certain school of psychoanalysis is an integral and indispensable part of any serious psychotherapy worthy of the name.' 'Serious psychotherapy' could proceed so long as it did not look for sexual causes, violate the confession and accepted the existence of sin and error beyond guilt, absolvable only through contrition and sacramental pardon.

Freud, that adamantly atheistic Jew who had laid the basis of psychoanalysis on the very insight that the motor force of the psyche was sexual, and that guilt was a perverse attack on repressed sexual impulses, was discounted in one papal blow. Maryse Choisy's flight from Freud had taken her a long way.

JOAN RIVIERE AND ALIX STRACHEY: TRANSLATING PSYCHOANALYSIS

Though Freud himself was shaped by that laboratory of the modern which was turn-of-the-century Vienna, English-language Freud came as part and parcel of a very different hothouse of the avant-garde: Bloomsbury. The rapid dissemination of Freud's ideas in the English-speaking world after the First World War, the depth with which they took hold, owed much to the manner in which Freud was reimagined in English. And this manner – in its seductiveness, its liveliness, erudition, refinement, lucidity and wit – is as thoroughly Bloomsbury as Virginia Woolf herself, whose works, after all, bear the imprint of the same publisher as the *Collected Papers* – the first attempt systematically to order Freud's writings in English. Two women played a central role in this major task.

The Freudian trajectory in England had another simultaneous line of transmission in which women were predominant. In 1913, the same year as Ernest Jones's 'official' London Psycho-Analytical Society was founded, two women, Dr Jessie Margaret Murray and Julia Turner, with financial backing from the 'psychoanalytic' novelist May Sinclair, had founded the Medico-Psychological Clinic in Brunswick Square. The women were feminist in orientation and eclectic in drawing upon various psychiatric and psychotherapeutic, including psychoanalytic, ideas; the Clinic initially treated mainly women patients. During the war, the demand for treatment of shell-shocked soldiers led to its expansion under a new partner, Dr James Glover.

Murray died in 1919 and, following Glover's analysis with Abraham in 1920, he enthusiastically set about making the Brunswick Square Clinic the London version of the psychoanalytic Polyclinics he had seen growing up on the Continent. Turner resisted his pure Freudianism, and Glover left the Clinic, taking most of the women students and staff with him, amongst them Ella Freeman Sharpe, who had come to the Clinic as a patient, trained there from 1917 on and, like Glover, gone to Berlin for analysis in 1920. Turner was forced to close the Clinic in 1922. Most of the workers at the Brunswick Square Clinic emigrated to the British Psycho-Analytical Society founded by Ernest Jones in 1919, where Glover's and Jones's versions of orthodox

Freudianism were to be promoted and defended. The immigration into the Society of these already experienced practitioners, imbued with the high ideals of philanthropy, feminism and socialism, in part explains why the British Society had so many lay women members from so early on – the list Jones mentioned to Freud in 1927 included 'Miss Low, Miss Searl, Miss Chadwick, Miss Sharpe, Mrs Isaacs, Miss Lewis, Miss Terry'. It was also again in part from these women members that the interest in child analysis, which was to become such a characteristic feature of psychoanalysis in Britain, originated.

But the work of translating Freud and of giving literary life and substance to Freudian orthodoxy fell not to the offspring of the Brunswick Square Clinic but to the Bloomsbury set. Two women analysed by Freud, Joan Riviere and Alix Strachey, put their highly original stamp on this task.

Joan Riviere, 1883–1962

Freud was fortunate to find in one of his first English translators, the elegant and acerbic Joan Riviere, a writer of psychoanalysis to rival him for both vigour and subtlety. That Joan Riviere also 'rendered' the work of Melanie Klein into English, and communicated her ideas with 'a vividness that ... neither Mrs Klein nor any of her other collaborators achieved', is perhaps an irony, but one altogether emblematic of the destiny of Freudianism in Britain. The international transmission of Freud's work and that of his followers, together with the establishment of institutional structures, were crucial to the status and impetus of early psychoanalysis. Joan Riviere's role in that history, though largely unsung, was hardly a negligible one.

She was born Joan Hodgson Verrall in Brighton, Sussex, on 9 July 1882, the eldest surviving child of a publicly spirited solicitor, Hugh John Verrall, and his wife Anna Hodgson, daughter of a Devonshire parson. The Verralls were an old county family of considerable intellectual standing and literary connections. Joan's uncle was the classicist, A. W. Verrall, whose lectures James Strachey, Freud's other major English translator and editor, singled out as the only ones worth attending in Cambridge. Joan was sent for schooling to Wycombe Abbey and then to Germany to learn the language that was to prove so valuable to her. Despite the family's academic connections, she did not go to university. Instead, her design and drawing talents – that aesthetic bent her later colleagues so remarked on – were put to use and she served for a period as a court dressmaker with the firm of Nettleship. On the intellectual side in this golden Edwardian age of her youth, there was her uncle's glittering Cambridge circle. Her presence at social gatherings stayed with Strachey for over half a century: 'I still have a vivid visual picture of her', he wrote in 1962, 'standing by the fireplace at an evening party, tall, strikingly handsome, distinguished-looking, and somehow impressive.' There were also meetings of the Society for Psychical Research in which Verrall – whose ability to 'cut through conventional attitudes and superficial shams' so reminded both Strachey and Joan of Freud – played a considerable part. At the turn of the century, it was this Society which was instrumental in fostering interest in Freud amongst intellectuals in England: in 1912, Freud even contributed 'A Note on the Unconscious in Psycho-Analysis' to its *Proceedings*.

Joan's county origins and her links with the Cambridge and then Bloomsbury elites were undoubtedly in part responsible for what Ernest Jones, a Welsh mining clerk's son, later described to Freud as her 'strong complex about being a well-born lady', who 'despises all the rest of us, especially the women', and her 'disdainful way of treating other people like dirt beneath her feet'. Unsurprisingly, the notorious British sense of class found its way into analytic chamber and analytic society as dangerously as any unconscious sprite, colouring all relations. But Joan's arrogance had more than a class base: it grew equally out of her trenchant intellect and acid wit, characteristics Freud was swift to admire, calling her 'clever and clear-headed', 'a powerful helpmate', 'a real power and ... a concentrated acid'. Quick to make enemies because of her haughty manner and her willingness to voice judgments and sometimes unpopular convictions, the redoubtable Joan was also quick to enlist admirers.

At the age of twenty-three, Joan married Evelyn Riviere, a Chancery barrister who was the son of an established Royal Academician. Two years later, their only child, Diana, was born. Not long after, in 1909, Joan's father, to whom she had been close, died and she suffered a breakdown, retreating to a sanatorium. It was perhaps this breakdown, followed by further 'nervous' as well as physical illness, which led her to seek analysis with Ernest Jones sometime in 1916. With a break of about a year during which she suffered from tuberculosis, she was still seeing him in June 1921. Recognizing how 'unusually intelligent' she was, Jones had won her to the cause of psycho-analysis. By the end of the war Riviere was amongst Britain's first lay analysts, a practising member of the newly formed British Psycho-Analytical Society and had translated Freud, in particular the *Introductory Lectures*, setting up a 'new standard' which made it 'possible for the first time for readers of English to realize that Freud was not only a man of science but a master of prose writing'. Despite all these achievements, Jones confessed that her case was 'the worst failure I have ever had' when he referred Riviere to Freud for analysis.

What we know of Riviere's troubled analysis with Jones comes from her fraught letters to him now lodged in the archive of the British Society and from the rather different but equally charged correspondence between Jones and Freud just prior to and during Riviere's year of analysis with Freud in 1922. It is clear that Riviere fell in love with the mercurial Jones, declared her love and bitterly suffered what she experienced as his refusal, a '"hardness" quite brutal in *my* then "quivering" and "wounded" state.' During the period of her analysis, Jones, it should be remembered, had broken up with Lina, Loë Kann's maid who had replaced her in his affections, and had rapidly married Morfydd Owen, who died tragically just over a year later in the summer of 1918. As he wrote in his memoir, undoubtedly thinking of Joan Riviere, this was a time when 'patients naturally expressed their resentment' – at the three-week interruption in analysis that Jones, in acute pain at his wife's sudden death, found necessary – 'by finding opportunities to flick my still unbearably raw wound; psychoanalytic treatment does not bring out the most charming aspects of human nature.' Then, in October 1919, Jones married Katherine Jokl, a marriage which endured until his death in 1958. All this coupling inevitably provided a stimulus to 'transference love'.

What is less clear, and was indeed not altogether transparent at first to Freud, is how much Jones had initially encouraged Riviere's love, and how much reality it had taken on for him outside the transference. On balance, the evidence of the letters would suggest that Jones – aside from having badly mishandled the transference and perhaps having innocently led Riviere on by behaving like a friend, that is, seeing her outside analytic sessions – was not a particularly guilty party. None the less, their extra-analytic relationship, together with the inevitable complexities of transference, had sufficiently fuelled Joan's imagination to occasion a crisis. By November 1918, Riviere was desperate and considering suicide.

Jones almost came clean to Freud in his first detailed letter about Riviere. With only a little special pleading about her possessing the 'most colossal narcissism imaginable' and a 'strong complex about being a well-born lady', he confessed that he had been mistaken to try to enlist her for the cause while analysing her:

I underestimated the uncontrollability of her emotional reactions and in the first year made the serious error of lending her my country cottage for a week when I was not there, she having nowhere to go for a holiday. This led to a declaration of love and to the broken-hearted cry that she had never been rejected before (she has been the mistress of a number of men). From that time on she devoted herself to torturing me without any intermission and with considerable success and ingenuity, being a fiendish sadist. ... The treatment finally broke down over my inability to master this negative transference, though I tried all means in my power.

Freud reprimanded Jones sternly. This was, after all, the second analytic triangle Jones had entangled him in.

You may imagine how little charmed I was by the prospects opened in your letter. I will spare myself any further remarks on the subject as you seem to have suffered sufficiently for your mistake. But let us hope that all these adventures belong to the past.

Mrs Riviere appeared to him not 'half as black as you had painted her. ... In my experience you have not to scratch too deeply the skin of a so-called masculine woman to bring her femininity to the light. I am very glad you had no sexual relations with her. ... To be sure it was a technical error to befriend her before her analysis was brought to a close.' As always, Freud stood by his patients, praising Riviere's valuable qualities.

His criticism, both overt and implicit, piqued the younger Jones, who protested at Freud's being able even to suspect that he would have sexual relations with a patient. Freud must have misunderstood his use of the expression

'declaration of love', which was of course on her side only. To satisfy her vanity she has always maintained the theory that I also was in love with her but was not honest enough to confess it, but I have never been able to confirm this in my self-analysis. She is not the type that attracts me erotically, though I certainly have the admiration for her intelligence that I would have with a man. But speaking more generally, you need never have any fear about me in such respects. It is over twelve years since I experienced any temptation in such ways, and then in special circumstances. . . .

Then, too, as Jones was perhaps pleased to stress, Freud was not yet aware of the savagery Riviere, undoubtedly as intelligent and valuable as Freud said, was capable of: Freud had not yet reached the critical ninth month of analysis, 'when the expected child did not arrive' and when 'she regressed to identification with her father and treated me ... like her younger brother, whose sole function in life was to admit that he was nothing by the side of her greatness'.

Enmeshed in this correspondence – which for all the passion of its attack, counter-attack and self-exoneration, shows both Freud and Jones at their diplomatic and manipulative best – is the story of how Freud, recognizing Riviere's intellectual and literary skills, persuaded Jones to establish her as the translation editor of the *International Journal*. The post was a supremely important one, since in those early days many of the articles printed in the *Journal* were by Freud or were translations from *Zeitschrift* and *Imago*. Riviere thus became the person responsible for the way in which much of psycho-analysis was disseminated in English. She remained translation editor until 1937, when she resigned in order to devote herself to clinical work and her own writing.

Jones, hardly blind to Riviere's skills since he had been the first to see and enlist them, none the less resisted Freud's initial proposal. He sensed that Freud, seduced by Riviere's evident charms, was also trying to ensconce her as editor of his *Collected Papers*, the pre-Second World War version of the *Standard Edition*. This, Jones intimated, ran not only counter to his own personal aspirations for that post, but would also be impossible should Riviere continue to be 'intolerably dictatorial', one of those domineering and 'hectoring women'. Then Jones launched his challenge: 'The saying here is that her visit to Vienna will be the final and most severe test of Ψa and people are most curious to see if her disdainful way of treating other people like dirt beneath her feet will undergo any modification.'

Freud, his clarity of analytic vision defied, rose to the bait and wrote his severest letter to date:

Somehow I imagine I guess your opinion of me in this matter. You think Mrs Riviere has put on her sweetest face and moods, has taken me in completely and seduced me to defend her against you in a chivalrous manner, so that now I am a puppet in her hands, show her the letters I get from you and give you away to her. I am sure you are wrong and I feel rather sorry there should be a need to point it out to you. But if I have misconstrued your opinion I beg you will pardon me.

A secondary analysis like this is no easy or pleasant task. Special duties were imposed on me which I am to discharge with the least possible damage to the parties concerned. You are not consistent on the matter of her coming over to me, but finally you took the stand that you had sent her for finishing and correcting the analysis she had with you. You confessed to some technical errors in analysis which you regretted in so serious a tone that I was led into a misconception about the nature of your wrong. Now this situation given you must be prepared to my taking her side, defending her interest and even turning against you in favour of her analysis. It means simply doing my duty as an analyst. It would not have worked, had I announced from the very beginning your dissension with Dr Jones must not be mentioned in our analysis or: Be sure, whenever you were at variance with him you must have been wrong and he right, for he is an old friend of mine, foremost among my pupils and the actual leader of the Ψa movement. Better not to have started her analysis at all! So I had to go through the matter, to listen to the details and to give you away, before I could get you back. There was no chance of making her see the abnormality of her reactions unless she had got the acknowledgment of your errors where you had committed them.

And in fact I cannot praise the way you handled her. You seem to have soon lost the analytic superiority especially required in such a case. I may not dwell on criticising your ways, if you will not miss it, it may be the subject of oral conversation between us and in German.

Freud then succinctly outlined his diagnosis of Joan Riviere:

Let us turn to Mrs Riviere. If she were a sheer *intriguante* she would have insisted on her sweetness with me until she had got out of me all she needed. Now she did not. She soon became harsh, unpleasant, critical even with me, tried to provoke me as she had done with you. I made it a rule never to get angry at her. Now I cannot give you the result of our analysis, it is not yet definite nor complete. But one important point soon emerged. She cannot tolerate praise, triumph or success, not any better than failure, blame and repudiation. She gets unhappy in both cases, in the second directly, in the first by reaction. So she has arranged for herself what we call *'eine Zwickmühle'* [a dilemma], ask your wife for the explanation of the term. Whenever she has got a recognition, a favour or a present, she is sure to become unpleasant and aggressive and to lose respect for the analyst. You know what that means, it is an infallible sign of a deep sense of guilt, of a conflict between Ego and Ideal. So the interest in her case is turned to the narcissistic problem, it is a case of a character-analysis superadded to that of the neurosis. To be sure this conflict, which is the cause of her continuous dissatisfaction, is not known to her consciousness; whenever it is revived she projects her self-criticism to other people, turns her pangs of conscience into sadistic behaviour, tries to render other people unhappy because she feels so herself. Our theory has not yet mastered the mechanism of these cases. It seems likely that the formation of a high and severe ideal took place with her at a very early age, but this ideal became superseded, 'repressed' with the onset of sexual maturity and ever since worked in the dark. Her sexual freedom may be an appearance, the keeping up of which required those conspicuous compensatory attitudes as haughtiness, majestic behaviour etc.

Now I don't know if I will succeed with her better or how far success may go, but for the time being we are getting on quite satisfactorily and analysis is full of interest. I confess to a kind feeling towards her, partly based on her intellectual capacity and practical efficiency. I would not give her a bit of chance if she was not possessed of these highly valuable qualities. But so she is and 'active therapeutics' could make use of this fact to initiate the reconciliation of her Ideal to her Ego. A due recognition of her ability, while the treatment conquers her incapacity for her enjoying success, is to her advantage as well as to ours.

At the time he wrote this, Freud was developing his notions of the super-ego and the unconscious sense of guilt. From the similarities between his description of Joan Riviere and the 'clinical facts' on which he based his account of the relations between ego, ideal and super-ego, it would seem clear that she served as a prime model for his second topography of the mind: the id, ego and super-ego.

Interesting as Riviere may have been as a spur to Freud's developing ideas, how successful was she as a test of Freud's psychoanalysis? Did Freud, despite his prognosis that Riviere 'will require special care and regards indefinitely' meet the challenge that Jones had set him? Certainly, from the remainder of the Freud/Jones correspondence over her case, it would seem that Riviere's relations both with Jones and other colleagues had suffered a remarkable sea change after her analysis with Freud. By December 1922, Jones was writing that Mrs Riviere 'made an excellent impression on her return and I think we shall work well together'. And early in 1924, he emphasized that 'she has proved a most valuable and loyal cooperator, has given not the slightest trouble to anyone, and is on the best of terms with myself.' None the less, Joan Riviere's 'ego ideal' continued to be a rigorous one and over the years students and colleagues continued to fear her sharp tongue and the severity of her judgments. And the perfectionist demands she made on herself continued to prove no less than those she made on others.

If in 1922 Freud was defending Joan Riviere to Jones, by 1927 the tables had turned and it was Jones's turn to defend her to Freud. The 'severe test' their friendship had withstood over Riviere, that invaluable acquisition to the movement, was now once again at risk and Riviere again played her part in it. This time, it was Freud's turn to be the stricken party, the man who felt betrayed by her savage tongue and unflinching strength of mind. But what was at issue now was not the fate of a single mishandled analysis, but the very direction of psychoanalysis itself in Britain.

Joan Riviere probably first met Melanie Klein at The Hague Congress of 1920. But it was at the Salzburg Congress of 1924, where Klein read her controversial paper on child analysis, that they struck up the friendship that was to become so important to both. The haughty, genteel Riviere and the plump, unconstrained Klein may have made an odd couple, but between them there was a meeting of minds. In Riviere, Klein found an English champion who could not only vividly render her work into English, but also communicate her ideas and inflect them with her own inimitable trenchancy. In Klein's work, Riviere evidently found a strain of Freudian thinking which struck a particularly rich chord in her: a violent, infantile world where sadistic and aggressive impulses were rampant, whatever the external frame family life provided. Undoubtedly, too – though little had been made of this before Athol Hughes's excellent recent work on Riviere – once impelled by the Kleinian vision, Riviere proceeded to chart highly original ground, linking morbid jealousy to envy of the primal scene some twenty-five years before Klein did so. Klein's failure adequately to acknowledge that Riviere had been there – and brilliantly – first was perhaps one of the factors that led to the ultimate cooling in the two women's relations in the 1950s.

But in 1927, when the British launched their counter-attack on Anna Freud and her view of child analysis, Riviere was in the forefront of the British Kleinians. In her paper in the Symposium on Child Analysis, she incisively criticized Anna Freud for the logical inconsistencies in her position: for saying that 'analysis cannot be done in the customary way with children because they are not like adults' and then saying that 'they are not like adults because analysis is not done in the customary way with them'. More substantially, Riviere attacked Anna for making nonsense of 'the true nature of the Oedipus complex, i.e. its unconscious character':

It is surely clear enough from adult analyses that it is not the *reality* of the patient's relations with his parents at any age that is reflected in his neurosis. The Oedipus complex and the pregenital phantasies woven into it originate and have their existence in the mind – or in the 'imagination', as we might express it in ordinary everyday speech – and are quite independent of any correspondence with reality, as every transference-neurosis shows us. These phantasies are played out in the *Unconscious*, and the objects of them are not the real father and mother at all, but the unconscious imagos of them. The unconscious relations with these imagos are then *transferred* to the *real* parents and worked off on them (just as they are worked off on the analyst in the transference-neurosis), and this gives rise to the morbid behaviour of which so often a child's neurosis largely consists.

Imagine reminding Freud's daughter, with italics, of the importance of the unconscious and transference! Analysis, for Riviere, is not concerned with education, or with the 'real' world – so pre-eminent in Anna Freud's thinking – but with the child's unconscious, her fantasy life. Nor is the super-ego, for her a much earlier formation than for Anna, the product of 'real' parental prohibitions:

the child's ideal of goodness – its superego – is derived from the bitterness of its experience in frustration and is simply an item in its phantasy-life. It is not so much the 'nursery conscience', the lessons in cleanliness and so on, that begins to instil morality into children. When we think of their rich phantasy-life, which analysis reveals to us, we see that it consists of things unimaginable to our conscious civilized minds, things that *never could* be realized in any environment; even in regard to pregenital pre-Oedipus phantasies, therefore, the factor of frustration operates. It is not actual threats or prohibitions, or moral or ethical injunctions, which instil a sense of guilt into the child; it is the fact of its own inferiority and the unattainability of its sexual desires....

Interestingly, in his correspondence with Ernest Jones over the British Kleinians' attack on Anna, Freud is relatively sanguine about Klein herself. His only real sense of outrage – apart from his condemnation of Jones for ever having let matters go so far – is over Joan Riviere: his former analysand, the woman whose mind he so respects, and whose characteristic of rewarding praise with aggression he had personally experienced – and tried to analyse away – five years earlier.

More disconcerting to me than these tempests in a teacup are the theoretical statements of Riviere, especially because I have always had such a high opinion of her understanding. Here I must reproach you with having carried tolerance too far. If a member of any of our groups expresses such mistaken and misleading basic views, that is good reason for the group's leader to give that person a private lecture, but not a case for which one seeks to ensure the widest publicity, without critical comment.

It was Jones's turn to defend Riviere and he did so in his usual negotiating fashion, attempting to exonerate himself in Freud's eyes, while simultaneously backing Riviere's views:

To begin with, I did not find her views untrue in themselves, though they are presented in a one-sided and therefore misleading way. This I certainly endeavoured to influence to the best of my ability, but you know that she is a person of considerable determination and in any case there was no question of refusing to publish them.... She insists that the child's unconscious picture of the parents to which it reacts in such manifold ways is far from being a photograph of them, but is throughout coloured by entirely individual contributions from the child's own component instincts, e.g. the idea of the parent may be much more sadistic than the reality, etc. etc. This I should have thought was common ground in psycho-analysis; if not, it is in my opinion easily demonstrable. It also seems to me worth insisting on because of the tendency at times to identify the growing super-ego with the *actual* parents rather than with the child's particular picture of them. Naturally Mrs Riviere would not deny the influence of real attributes to the parents in this compound, and I told her she was making a mistake in dwelling only on what might be called the phantastic half of the picture.

Freud's response, though now devoid of outrage, likens Riviere to that arch-betrayer Jung in her recourse to a 'phylogenetic imago'. None the less, even while invoking the original apostate, Freud is prepared to acknowledge her perspicacity. His admiration of her overrides any sense of a need to defend his daughter.

I learn that your assessment of Mrs R. is exactly the same as mine. Naturally I criticize her for denying half the facts, while the other – what you call the phantastic half – is alone proclaimed; incidentally, in an excellent way. This makes her viewpoint 'heretical', contains an unfortunate similarity to Jung's and, like his, is an important step towards making analysis unreal and impersonal. The clarity of her style precludes any misreading of her meaning. Just read the last paragraph of her article again. If she has experienced a case which proved to her the importance of the phylogenetic imago, then only a greater number of cases can be useful to me to put the influence of real, personal factors beyond any doubt. It is remarkable that people find it most difficult to recognize overdetermination and the multiplicity of aetiological factors. All our apostates always grasped part of the truth and wanted to declare it as the whole truth.... Incidentally, Mrs R.'s logic and perspicacity are revealed even in her error; she has quite rightly discovered the theory which alone fits Mrs Klein's technique. Is it not time to end this not altogether agreeable episode? I should be sorry if Mrs R. continued to be discouraged or estranged.

No wonder that Anna much later confessed to Jones that she had once been very jealous of Riviere.

Riviere's advocacy of Melanie Klein continued. In one of the exchange lectures organized in the 1930s to keep the Viennese and British Societies better informed about each other's thinking, Riviere addressed the Vienna Society 'On the Genesis of Psychical Conflict in Earliest Infancy'. The date was 5 May 1936, the eve of Freud's eightieth birthday. There is no better introduction to Kleinian thinking than Riviere's brilliant paper. The verbal felicity she had brought to her finely honed translation of *Civilization and its Discontents* six years earlier is everywhere in evidence here in service to the bleak Kleinian world-view. Riviere is as adept at making complex theoretical insights persuasively straightforward as she is at invoking the aggressive expression of the infant's sadistic inner life:

Limbs shall trample, kick and hit; lips, fingers and hands shall suck, twist, pinch; teeth shall bite, gnaw, mangle and cut; mouth shall devour, swallow and 'kill' (annihilate); eyes kill by a look, pierce and penetrate; breath and mouth hurt by noise, as the child's own sensitive ears have experienced. One may suppose that before an infant is many months old it will not only *feel* itself performing these actions, but will have some kind of *ideas* of doing so. All these sadistic activities in phantasy are felt not only to expel the danger from the self but to transfer it onto the object (projection).

By the time the war time Controversial Discussions were in full swing, Riviere could leave the arguments to others who quoted her. Her task was mainly to organize and forcefully to intercede when the clash between warring groups had left all 'scientific' differences behind and descended to the humiliating level of mere personal hostilities.

Despite her advocacy of Klein, Riviere never turned against Freud. Her admiration for the Professor persisted and was openly spoken. Always a woman of trenchant judgment, she had never been prone to idealize; as a result, nor did she demonize. Astute criticism was a constant in her repertoire, even when it came to the founder of psychoanalysis. Thus, when her pen etches out praise, one is tempted to trust it. In the same year as she wrote her wholly Kleinian Lecture for Freud's eightieth birthday, she reviewed his *Autobiographical Study*. Her closing comments give us an insight not only into Freud, but also into what it was that stirred her always recalcitrant approval:

Between the lines of his life's story the features of the man himself appear. On the one hand there stand out his innate gifts – the power of imagination, of vision, of perception; on the other the strength of his character traits that balance and complement these gifts – the fearlessness, patience and indomitable persistence, the candour and inflexible honesty. These two sides of his nature were welded into a whole for the pursuit of truth by the absorbing aim that dominated his life: to discover a unity and reconciliation of the subjective experiences of men's minds and the tangible, demonstrable reality of their lives, and so for the first time reconciling them.

A few years later, on 23 September 1939, a week after Freud's death, Riviere made a more personal tribute, moving, yet precise, and, as always, with a sting in its tail. It was difficult for the Bloomsbury Freudians to have to acknowledge that the founder of psychoanalysis was a mere Jew and Riviere's anti-Semitism was true to the group. She is eager to exonerate Freud from too great a taint: 'His appearance was not … particularly Jewish,' she writes, combining this with a graphic physical description which ends with the comment, 'this rather awe-inspiring appearance was lightened by the glow of an enchanting humour, always latent and constantly irradiating his whole person as he spoke, which reassured one that the Olympian was indeed mortal, too.'

Recalling the start of her own analysis in which Freud, contrary to his own rules, began by saying, 'Well, I know something about you already: you had a father and a mother!', Riviere humorously notes his impatience with 'preambles and polite nothings'. She then evokes Freud's curious impersonality, 'reserve behind the eagerness, as though it were not for himself that he so peremptorily demanded to understand things, but for some purpose outside himself'. She comments on the 'inimitable dry humour of his writings [which] became in ordinary intercourse a charming gaiety and capacity for finding amusement in most situations'; but she is quick to add that though he could be 'tolerant and philosophical, he was apt to be both impatient and intolerant' – not someone who suffered fools gladly. What she admires most in him is 'the conjunction of a hunter on an endless trail and the persistent, immovable watcher who checks and revises. … Indomitable courage and tenacity, coupled with an unswerving honesty, were the characteristics supporting his gifts of observation, his "intrepid imagination" and insight, which led to his great achievements.' But – and with Riviere there is always that necessary 'but'– Freud's 'power to see new facts and to check his observations diminished considerably in him after his operation in 1924', which, of course, made him incapable of perceiving the importance of Kleinian insights.

Riviere's intellectual rigour, her ability to see – clearly and unimpeded by prior schema – what her patients presented to her, resulted in several seminal papers. In 'Jealousy as a Mechanism of Defence' (1932), she probed beneath that very defence to unearth a deeper primal envy in which the child's desire to despoil and ravage the mother – container of milk, breast, penis and children – results in a guilt, which later projects that aggressive desire on to the 'loved' other, who then emerges as the subject of suspected infidelities and cause of the patient's persecutory jealousy. In 'Womanliness as a Masquerade' (1929) – a subject which concerns us more closely here – Riviere drew on Ernest Jones's paper on female sexuality (1927) to introduce into the clinical typology of psychoanalysis a feminine character far more resonant with contemporary experience than any Freud or even Helene Deutsch had explored. Her subject is the intellectual woman – a subject, given herself and the high proportion of women in the British Society, which she knew well. And for Riviere's generation, more modern than Freud's, the absence of a Victorian scheme of moral reference allows this type to emerge in an altogether new configuration:

Not long ago intellectual pursuits for women were associated almost exclusively with an overtly masculine type of woman, who in pronounced cases made no secret of her wish or claim to be a man. This has now changed. Of all the women engaged in professional work to-day, it would be hard to say whether the greater number are more feminine than masculine in their mode of life and character. In University life, in scientific professions and in business, one constantly meets women who seem to fulfil every criterion of complete feminine development. They are excellent wives and mothers, capable housewives; they maintain social life and assist culture; they have no lack of feminine interests, e.g. in their personal appearance, and when called upon they can still find time to play the part of devoted and disinterested mother-substitutes among a wide circle of relatives and friends. At the same time they fulfil the duties of their profession at least as well as the average man. It is really a puzzle to know how to classify this type psychologically.

Riviere then proceeds to do so. She draws on the analysis of a woman of this kind who, despite her success and ability as a writer and speaker, had a need for reassurance from men, which led her compulsively to seek from them sexual and professional compliments after any public engagement. This need was shown to have its source in identification, then in a castrating rivalry, with her father: by eliciting approval from men who had watched her perform, she was warding off any possible retribution for being in possession of the father's penis. But Riviere takes matters further. The patient's obsessive need to flirt with and seek a response from the men was not merely

to secure reassurance by evolving friendly feelings towards her in the man; it was chiefly to make sure of safety by masquerading as guiltless and innocent. It was a compulsive reversal of her intellectual performance; and the two together formed the 'double-action' of an obsessive act, just as her life as a whole consisted alternately of masculine and feminine activities.

She then concludes that for this patient, womanliness could be assumed and worn as a mask, 'both to hide the possession of masculinity and to avert the reprisals expected if she was found to possess it.'

Beyond her observations, what is radical in Riviere's position is that for her mask and essence are one where womanliness is concerned. 'The reader may now ask how I define womanliness or where I draw the line between genuine womanliness and the "masquerade". My suggestion is not, however, that there is any such difference; whether radical or superficial, they are the same thing.'

It is interesting that Riviere described this woman as 'homosexual' – that is, not having fully achieved heterosexual womanhood – though what full achievement might mean where one is postulating the masquerade as a constant is not altogether self-evident. Her clinical picture is the following: as a result of inevitable disappointment or frustration during sucking or weaning, the child desires to bite off the nipple; or, if there is an extreme intensification of oral-sadistic desires, to 'destroy, penetrate and disembowel the mother and devour her and the contents of her body', which includes the father's penis. The oral-sadism extends to the father in the desire to castrate him by biting off his penis. Thus both parents are feared rivals, but it is the mother who is most hated and most feared: in retribution for the child's sadistic act she could destroy the girl's body, her beauty, her children. The girl's only safety then lies in identifying with the father, using the masculinity she thus obtains and 'putting it in service of the mother': that is, she becomes the father so that she can restore him to the mother. But the restitution can only take place if the mother recognizes the girl's 'supremacy in having the penis to give back'. If maternal gratitude is withheld, the girl is subject to paroxysms of oral-sadistic fury. Later the girl averts her anxiety at having robbed her mother by denying her mother existence. The guilt of having triumphed over her can then only be absolved by the father, who, by giving her recognition, is giving her the penis instead of the mother. But this supremacy entails an exclusion from enjoying much that the mother had. Full heterosexual femininity becomes an impossible attainment.

What then, Riviere asks, is the 'essential nature of fully developed femininity', *das ewig Weibliche*? She responds by pointing to the conception of womanliness as a mask, behind which man suspects some hidden danger. Fully developed heterosexual womanhood may be founded on the oral-sucking stage – receiving the '(nipple, milk) penis, semen, child from the father'. The acceptance of 'castration' – humility, the admiration of men – may come partly from the over-estimation of the object on the oral-sucking plane. But chiefly it derives from the renunciation of sadistic castration-wishes on the later oral-biting level: 'I must not take, I must not even ask; it must be *given* me.'

Both the 'normal' woman and the homosexual desire the father's penis and rebel against frustration (or castration); but one of the differences between them lies in the difference in the degree of sadism and of the power of dealing both with it and with the anxiety it gives rise to....

In this analysis, where the mask rules over the constellation of the feminine, the difference between homosexuality and heterosexuality is only a question of a fractional degree.

During her long years of psychoanalytic practice, Joan Riviere numbered among her analysands and trainees some of the most notable of British analysts: D. W. Winnicott, Susan Isaacs, Hanna Segal and Herbert Rosenfeld. By all accounts, she was a formidable lecturer and an inspired teacher. In a psychoanalytic Society where women's influence was strong, hers was particularly so. Yet within all this institutional and public life, it is tempting to see in Joan Riviere what she so subtly – and perhaps with a degree of projection – saw in Freud. The insight comes in her last published paper, a contribution to Freud's centenary celebrations. Written after her explorations of the 'inner world' in literature and Ibsen's *Master Builder*, Riviere here chooses to see Freud as a writer: a thinker whose ideas need to be embodied in creative form outside himself before they take on life. It was Freud the writer who drew her to analysis and made of her the person who wrote him into English. And it is Joan Riviere, the writer, who speaks to us most directly; her words which breathe reality into theoretical constructs. Her description of the depressive position evokes a state of being in terms which would rival that of any writer of her time:

The content of the depressive position ... is the situation in which all one's loved ones *within* are dead and destroyed, all goodness is dispersed, lost, in fragments, wasted and scattered to the winds; nothing is left *within* but utter desolation. Love brings sorrow, and sorrow brings guilt; the intolerable tension mounts, there is no escape, one is utterly alone, there is no one to share or help. Love must die because love is dead. Besides, there would be no one to feed one, and no one whom one could feed, and no food in the world. And more, there would still be magic power in the undying persecutors who can never be exterminated – the ghosts. Death would instantaneously ensue – and one would choose to die by one's own hand before such a position could be realized.

British psychoanalysis was lucky to have her.

Alix Strachey, 1892–1973

The energetic Ernest Jones, with his imperialist ambitions, had dreamt of a complete and standardized English edition of Freud's works as early as 1913. In the event, he served as godfather to a project which fell into the talented hands of Joan Riviere and, gradually, James Strachey and his wife, Alix – both mainstays of the Bloomsbury group. It was to these latter two that the task of transforming Freud fully into 'an English man of science of wide education born in the middle of the nineteenth century' finally fell, as the *Collected Papers* gave way to the twenty-four-volume *Standard Edition* in the post-Second World War years. If Alix Strachey's name appears under the words 'Assisted by' on the title page of this *Edition*, we know that she shared amply in the work of translation and had been James Strachey's constant critic and collaborator for nearly half a century – ever since Freud, after only a few weeks of the Stracheys' analysis, had suddenly instructed them to translate a paper he had recently written: '*Ein Kind wird geschlagen*'.

Alix Sargant-Florence and her elder brother Philip were born in New Jersey, where her American father and British mother had settled in the lively artists' colony of Nutley. Six weeks after Alix's birth, her father was drowned and Mary Sargant returned with her children to the Britain she far preferred. A feminist and dedicated painter, Mary Sargant lived a bohemian life, travelling frequently with her children to the Continent from her home base in Chelsea and, by 1900, from their newly built house in Buckinghamshire, Lord's Wood: a name she wanted but failed to have changed to Lady's Wood. The children's schooling was irregular. It was only at the age of ten that the headstrong Alix was enrolled in a preparatory school, eventually going from there to Bedales. However, Mary Sargant's artistic aspirations for the children were great: music and art were always a part of the informal curriculum. Though Alix had no talent for the first, she was adept at the second and in 1910, recalcitrantly following her mother's wishes, she attended the Slade School of Art for a year. Then she rebelled: she was far more interested in philosophy and anthropology than in becoming a practising artist. In 1911, she went to Newnham College, Cambridge, and though she chose to read modern languages, she continued to pursue other interests, even purportedly reading Freud. She also grew close again to her brother, Philip, a scholarship student at Caius College, and joined him on the editorial committee of the *Cambridge Magazine* and in the interminable late-night philosophical discussions of the rationalist Heretics Society. Here the cutting wit and finely tuned ironic intelligence so evident in her later letters made her reputation amongst the largely male membership.

Early in her Cambridge years, Alix suffered from what was diagnosed as 'degeneration of the heart', but was probably a nervous breakdown involving some kind of anorexic condition. She was transformed from a 'beefy' young woman into that tall, gaunt, mannish and troubled figure, who appears in photographs and is evoked in Virginia Woolf's impressions. We know little of the details of Alix's state, which persisted beyond Cambridge into the war years, and was perhaps exacerbated by her hatred of war: one of the two books she published under her own name – and then not until 1957 – was *The Unconscious Motives of War*. But it seems clear that she had a melancholic disposition and suffered from *ennui*, a lack of direction, both intellectual and sexual. As Virginia Woolf put it in her inimitably catty way, Alix was possessed of 'a good brain, but not enough vitality to keep it working' and 'an air of level-headed desperation, solid, capacious, but as low in tone as a coal cellar'. She was perpetually mired in a 'sort of morbid scrutiny of values & motives', a profound blackness which undermined desire. Social gatherings apart, Woolf had had experience of Alix when she came to work very briefly for the Hogarth Press: after two hours training as a printer, Alix had 'solemnly & slowly explained that she was bored'. None the less, she became for a while Leonard Woolf's 'dame secretaire', helping him research a report which grew into *Empire and Commerce in Africa*. Virginia Woolf's most telling description of Alix, reminiscent of Alix's own pointed caricatures, evokes her on an afternoon when Woolf had bumped into her in the West End:

As we walked up & down Dover Street she seemed on the verge of rolling up the usual veil of laughter & gossip & revealing her sepulchral despair – poor woman.
Where are you going now Alix?

I really don't know.
Well that sounds dismal! Don't you look forward to say eleven tomorrow morning?
I merely wish it didn't exist that's all!
So, I left her, hatless, aimless, unattached, wandering in Piccadilly.

Having initially been caught out by the war in St Petersburg, Alix returned to London in January 1915 to settle in Bloomsbury in her brother's flat. Here she became a Bloomsbury regular, attending the weekly salons which James Strachey also frequented, joining the pacifist movement and participating in meetings of the socialist 1917 Club, where Woolf imagines her sitting eternally like 'a kind of Fate, surveying the passage of moral generations'. Though Alix was a 'crophead' and the sexual ambivalence of so many of the group was also hers – James Strachey in his first mention of her in a 1910 letter to his brother Lytton had singled her out as 'a delightful Bedalian ... an absolute boy' – her love affairs at this time, though not later, were it seems all with men. The writer David Garnett featured amongst these. In his memoir, published in 1955, he vividly describes an Alix who, 'by her intelligence, her coldness and her apparent detachment', excited 'a high degree of physical love', a 'longing to commit murder and rape'. Whatever temporary excesses Alix may have inspired, lifelong friendships with lovers were maintained – as was the Bloomsbury norm.

Despite the various love affairs, heated or cold, it was James Strachey whom Alix desired: James, who had been a member of that elite, quasi-secret Cambridge Society, the Apostles, and whose modernist artistic tastes, intelligence, irony and lassitude so directly reflected hers. But initially James's attentions were elsewhere – first with the poet Rupert Brooke, then with the Rubenesque Noel Olivier, a passion that continued late into his life. And so Alix, according to Virginia Woolf, set out to woo a James as uncertain about the goals of his life as she. She wooed him intellectually, with her knowledge of Freud; and practically, with an invitation to share her new flat in Gordon Square rent-free. And she won. On 4 June 1920, Alix and James, to the surprise of many of their friends, were suddenly married. That very day a letter arrived from Freud – to whom James had written five days earlier – stating that he was prepared to take James into analysis in the autumn, for a fee below the usual rate since his was 'the case of a man who wants to be a pupil and become an analyst'.

In the last week of September, James and Alix arrived in Vienna. Initially, only James was to be analysed, but then – after an attack of agoraphobia, or what James called her palpitations, during a performance of *Götterdämmerung* in the Staatsoper – Alix asked James to approach Freud on her behalf. Though Freud had begun by thinking that the concurrent analysis of husband and wife would be a 'technical impossibility', he soon became 'fascinated, partly by her case, & partly by the effect of the actions & re-actions caused by his taking both of us at once.'

We know little of the interstices of this double analysis, except that for James it provided 'a complete undercurrent for life', whereas for Alix it was an unsatisfactory affair. She later compared Freud unfavourably with Abraham – with whom Freud had recommended she continue her analysis – and called Abraham 'far and away the best analyst'. Part of the problem with Alix's analysis by Freud may have been the fact that it was never properly terminated. In February 1922, Alix contracted influenza, which led to bronchial pneumonia. She was confined to the Sanatorium Loew, where Felix Deutsch attended her until June of that year, by which time Freud pronouced both James and herself as 'fit to practise'. He wrote to Jones about them:

As regards [John] Rickman and the Stracheys I send them back to you within a week. Both will prove of great help to you if you treat them generously. I propose the Stracheys should become members (full) of the Society as they have gone through 1½ years of serious analysis, are theoretically well informed and people of a high order. To be sure their conflicts have not been decided, but we need not wait so long, we can only instigate the processus which has to be fed by the factors of life. Becoming full members ... would bind them to the interests of the Society. [...] Do not put back her for him, she is very valuable.

Even if analysis with Freud had not 'decided' the Stracheys' conflicts, it did provide both Alix and James with a lifetime dedication to psychoanalysis. Psychoanalytic culture and the work of translation became from then on the centre of their lives. And after their first year with Freud, even the sceptical Virginia Woolf was able to pronounce: 'Freud has certainly brought out the lines in Alix. Even physically, her bones are more prominent. Only her eyes are curiously vague. She has purpose and security.' And then, she adds, as Freud himself – often equally doubtful of the comparative benefits of analysis vis-à-vis marriage – might have: 'but this may well be marriage'.

In 1921, before their double analysis was terminated, Alix and James began their collaborative translation of what became known as the *Case Histories*, or Volume 3 of the *Collected Papers*, which emerged as a tome of over 600 pages in 1925. Freud had been called on to settle 'doubtful points': he had also, as he acknowledged in his 'Additional Note' to the Dora case, 'corrected a few oversights and inaccuracies to which my excellent English translators, Mr and Mrs James Strachey, have directed my attention'. The careful attention the Stracheys gave to their work, the constant decisions and revisions they engaged in, reflected the importance the British Society had given to the enterprise of translating and publishing the collected Freud. There was even a Glossary Committee – made up of Ernest Jones, Anna Freud and Joan Riviere, whose translation of the *Introductory Lectures* had appeared in 1922, and the Stracheys – which met regularly to determine how technical terms should be translated.

In September 1924, when the substantial work on the *Case Histories* was complete, Alix travelled to Berlin to be analysed by Abraham, as Freud had recommended – perhaps because of the important work Abraham had done on melancholia. She remained there for a year until Abraham's unexpected and fatal illness terminated this second analysis. During her time in Berlin, Alix was initiated into the hectic world of German psychoanalysis. Apart from her analysis with Abraham, she went to lectures and seminars at the Polyclinic, heard amongst others, Otto Fenichel, Franz Alexander, Siegfried Bernfeld and Sándor Rado. She dined regularly with the Abrahams, met Lou Andreas-Salomé, Helene Deutsch and Hanns Sachs. She also met Melanie Klein, then, like her, in analysis with Abraham, and became her champion, first at the meetings of the Berlin Group, where Klein was regularly attacked by the men – 'I can't make out whether they hate her because they have frightful affective resistances against Frühanalyse; or whether they have those f.a.r.'s because they hate her' – and later in London. All these frenetic comings and goings, Alix described in vivid letters home to James – letters packed not only with flurried shorthand reports of psychoanalytic meetings and forays into Berlin dance halls with 'die Klein', but also with cameo portraits of the psychoanalytic tribe. Never quite part of the tribe, yet deeply engaged with its intellectual adventure, Alix's account bears her own indelible imprint: her letters sparkle with mockery of herself and others, astutely observed surface detail and racy irony battling with a genuine excitement in newly discovered ideas.

Central to that excitement as the year progressed was the work of 'die Klein'. The unlikely friendship between these two women, so different in all respects, blossomed. And Klein's warm reception in England was certainly in some part due to Alix's efforts: she tutored Klein in English and in English psychoanalytic terms, helped Klein arrange her visit to London in the summer of 1925 and translated the six lectures Klein delivered there. James's suggestion that 'You'll not only have to *translate* but also to *write* Melanie's lectures' may bear more than a grain of throwaway truth if the evidence of Klein's own later writing in English compared to her work in Alix's translations is anything to go by. Certainly, Alix's gift for rigour and clarity played its part. As Alix graphically comments in one of her letters: 'Melanie swam up & was *most* gracious, & all over the place – *how* had I kept it all so clear, etc. etc.; and she swooped off with the paper.' Several letters reiterate the groan: 'I wish to God she had the art of expressing her views with some degree of coherence.' In May, a few months before Klein's English debut, Alix suggested to James: 'one of the things I'll try & do ... is to write to you to explain what exactly each lecture is supposed to say – for in conversation she can be perfectly clear, if forced – so that you can ask intelligent questions afterwards & make the discussion "*préciser*" what the actual paper may fail to do.' Whatever the division of labour between translator and conceiver, Alix remained impressed with Klein's brilliance. Her translation of Klein's work continued hand in hand with that of Freud's for some years and included the important *The Psychoanalysis of Children* (1932), the book which grew out of and included the six lectures translated for Klein's first British visit.

On her return from Berlin, Alix played her part, alongside James, in the requisite committee and organizational meetings; she also took patients. Her own analysis continued, first with Edward Glover and later with Sylvia Payne. Her devotion to the psychoanalytic cause went hand in hand with the never-ending work of editing and translating the growing psychoanalytic canon. Amongst other projects, Alix translated Karl Abraham's *Selected Papers*, in collaboration with Douglas Bryan, and prepared a complete index of psycho-analytic terms – a mammoth undertaking which was not finished until 1943. But for all her immersion in psychoanalytic work, Alix maintained a certain measure of her Bloomsbury scepticism. She appreciated Virginia Woolf's unwillingness to engage in analysis, noting, as Lou Andreas-Salomé had of Rilke, that her artistic imagination was so enmeshed with her madness that stopping the latter could well endanger the former. It is also interesting to note that, for all her work on behalf of and friendship with Klein, Alix never became a 'Kleinian'. In this respect she was akin to another literary analyst who trod her own path between Freud and Klein – Ella Freeman Sharpe, who was, during the inter-war years, a far more influential training analyst than Klein, training twelve candidates to the latter's four.

With the outbreak of the Second World War, Alix and James retreated from Bloomsbury to the relative safety of Lord's Wood, her mother's one-time home. They remained there after the war; it was the base from which they carried on their translation work and the vast labour of the *Standard Edition*.

But the phenomenon of Nazism, of war and its attendant threat of atomic proliferation continued to preoccupy Alix. When she came to write a book of her own, it was to these subjects that she turned her extensive knowledge of psychoanalysis. *The Unconscious Motives of War* brings to the fore the radical political consciousness which had been hers since the 1917 Club days and marries it with the depth of her psychoanalytic culture. While the first part of the book gives a lucid exposé of the main tenets of psychoanalysis, the second uses psychoanalysis to explore the behaviour of people in groups. In the action of the crowd, Alix sees a regressive force at work: not only does the person in a group 'lose his super-ego', but he also feels the need once more 'for an external authority to take its place ... who shall dominate and guide'. Linked by libidinal (and often homosexual) ties, as well as by ties of identification and mental dependence, the group induces an unrealistic state of mind, and indifference as well as outright hostility to those outside the group. Herein lies its destructive potential.

Amongst Alix's examples of the regressive group mentality are not only the classical Freudian instances of public school, church and army, but – and this is the radical core of her study – the national sovereign state. Give the sovereign state weapons of mass destruction and the world as a whole is in acute danger. 'The dangers of State-mentality in these days are so great that one is almost tempted to recommend that States should be altogether abolished and that people should co-operate freely as private individuals in attending to all matters that are necessary for their survival and well-being.' Never a Utopian though, Alix acknowledges that this is impossible, since people also need groups. All that can be done is that the mental attitudes of the individual be tackled in order to mitigate the regressive influence the group can have on him. There are two ways in which such mitigation might be effected: one is feminist, the other is psychoanalytic. Blithely aware of her own fancifulness, Alix postulates that 'the growing independence of the female sex and their

increasing entrance into public affairs' may moderate such destructive tendencies, since women, 'besides being relatively immune to State-mentality, as
a whole possess much less destructive energy'. But the benign public influence
of women is only one answer; the other, to her more practical suggestion, is
to enlist psychoanalysis.

What *The Unconscious Motives of War* and Alix's second book *The Psychology
of Nationhood* (1960) reveal are one set of motives which underpin her lifelong
devotion to psychoanalysis: its prophylactic potential. Even if not everyone
can undergo therapy, a knowledge of the theory of psychoanalysis may help
us live and bring up our children in such a way that our destructive potential
is allayed. It was to this end that Alix's lifelong task of translating and
disseminating psychoanalytic ideas had been devoted.

The twenty-four volumes of the *Standard Edition* were published over a
span of twenty-one years, the first ones appearing in 1953, the last in 1974.
In 1966, James Strachey was awarded the Schlegel-Tieck Prize for translation.
He and his 'assistant' celebrated with a winter cruise to the Caribbean. In
April 1967, a month before the official award ceremony, James died. Alix
lived on alone at Lord's Wood until her own death almost six years to the
day later: 28 April 1973. The final volume of the *Standard Edition*, completed
by Angela Richards, is fittingly dedicated to the memory of both Stracheys.

13

THE FRIENDSHIP OF WOMEN

Freud's friendships in the last decades of his life were notably with women. Lou Andreas-Salomé, the first in a long line, had been the recipient of confidences attesting to his disappointments with male colleagues – from Jung to Adler to Rank. There had always been women, on his couch and in his intimate circle. But after the war and the loss of his favourite daughter, Sophie, and the grandchild she bore, Freud's daughters multiplied: it is as if Freud, growing older and increasingly ill, were seeking Sophie's diffused essence in a number of younger women. The daughters, Anna legitimately though jealously at their forefront, hovered around him like the good sisters of his childhood, providing him with admiration, love, gifts and emissaries. They were at once friends and rivals for his attention. In his relations to them, Freud was analyst, teacher and father; he was also courteous and courtly, with that wry seductiveness of a bygone age, which chided, flattered and advised, erasing the boundaries between analytic chamber and daily life.

Amongst the Freud demonologists, as plentiful these days as their next of kin the idolizors, it has been suggested that Freud encouraged these daughters to be dependent on him; that he never fully analysed their father transference; and that he seductively trapped them into disciplehood. This would be to cast Freud into the role of a vain, doting, senescent Lear, whose days were so sadly impoverished that only the adulation of a feminine court gave him a *raison d'être* – something the productivity of his last two decades instantly gives the lie to. Another charge levelled at Freud is that he preferred his women rich and made use of their wealth. If Freud accepted high fees from Marie Bonaparte at her insistence, if he permitted Marie and others to put money into the *Verlag* and other psychoanalytic projects, it is equally true that he redistributed wealth, sending money to Lou and to other friends, colleagues and patients in need, whom he often treated free of charge.

Such accusations, such interpretations of Freud's female friendships, also severely denigrate the women who chose, in one way or another, to be his daughters. If they learned from Freud and loved him each in her own way, their lives were hardly impoverished by the fact. Nor, judging by their individual achievements, were they insubstantial figures, mere shadows of the great man, passive victims of potently magical and charismatic authority.

Not all these women may have been quite as formidable as Marie Bonaparte or as wide-ranging in their clinical practice and writings as Helene Deutsch. None the less, the analysts Ruth Mack Brunswick, Jeanne Lampl de Groot, Kata Levy; Anna's friends, who also to a greater or lesser degree clustered round Freud – Eva Rosenfeld, Marianne Kris, Anny Rosenberg Katan, Dorothy Burlingham, Edith Jackson, Muriel Gardiner – and the American poet Hilda Doolittle, were all characterized by an independent spirit and a professional zest which were rare for the time. For all Freud's conventional utterances about women, he showed a marked preference in his *friendships* for women who bore little relation to the model. Little wonder that under the impetus of these women, Freud in his last decades, when not exploring the general condition of humankind, ventured increasingly into a terrain which had previously only been of peripheral interest: the specificities of female sexuality.

The American Connection: Ruth Mack Brunswick, 1897–1946; Muriel Gardiner, 1901–85

Two years younger than Anna, Ruth Mack arrived in Vienna in 1922 at the age of twenty-five. A Radcliffe graduate with a medical degree from Tufts and a completed psychiatric residency behind her, she wanted to train with Freud. Her father, Judge Julian Mack, was a noted jurist and Jewish philanthropist; her husband, whom she was in part fleeing, a heart specialist. Ruth herself was a vigorous, independent spirit, a daring woman with a fine mind, cultured, vivacious and elegant; with her, Freud had none of his customary reservations about Americans. She quickly grew to be not only a friend of the Professor's, receiving one of his rings, but also a family friend, a member of that close circle who accompanied Freud on his summer vacations. Ruth also became the conduit for Freud's American patients, often looking after them while they were in Vienna. In time, too, she took on the emissary's role, reporting to Freud from America on the doings of American psychoanalysis. Their closeness was such that Ruth was present at his April 1931 operation, alongside Dr Max Schur.

Of her analysis with Freud we know little, except that, as with so many of his trainees at this time, a first sequence was followed up by later ones. 'Every analyst should periodically', Freud wrote in 1937, 'submit himself to analysis once more, without feeling ashamed of taking this step.' By that time, Ruth would have had several follow-up analyses. In a letter to Jeanne Lampl de Groot of 22 August 1928, Freud notes: 'Ruth ... is taking on a portion of follow-up analysis, which will probably do her a lot of good.' We can almost hear the sigh, as he adds, 'How incomplete were all my early analyses.'

Paul Roazen has suggested that Ruth's was an addictive personality and that she had both a drug and a Freud habit. Certainly, Ruth suffered from stomach and gall bladder problems and as a doctor could prescribe drugs for herself – morphine, painkillers, sleeping tablets – which she did to the point that addiction developed. Freud, writing to Lampl de Groot in 1932, hinted at the problem: 'Ruth is a very erratic patient and because of organic complications, highly elusive.' So elusive, that her analysis seemed interminable and her dependency on Freud was marked. She arranged for her future husband, Mark Brunswick, who had followed her to Vienna, to be analysed by Freud. And Freud in that now criticized blurring of the boundaries between analysis and daily life with which we have become so familiar, effectively sanctioned their marriage. Indeed, Freud acted as a witness for Ruth at her wedding to Mark in 1928; his lawyer son Martin had drawn up the marriage contract.

Apart from a year in the United States in 1928–9, when her daughter was born, and the summer trips to visit family, Ruth stayed in Vienna until 1938. Advice from Freud, both analytic and non-analytic, became something of a way of life for both the Brunswicks. Freud, it seems, was not averse to Mark's having an affair with a young girl he was later in love with, nor was he against the couple's divorce in 1937; but the repetition of the marriage vows some six months later did not meet with his approval. In this intermingling of analytic and what were effectively extended family relations, dependency could certainly be said to have existed on both sides. Or to translate this into another and non-analytic register, Freud and the younger, though hardly from all accounts passive, Ruth were intimate friends. It seems illogical to presume that because both Ruth and Mark were at various intervals in analysis with Freud that this gave him, as is sometimes suggested, a near magical power over their relations, a power so incomparably greater than another equally close, trusted and respected friend might have had.

Gossip aside, it is clear that Freud valued Ruth's analytic abilities greatly, as much as he was frustrated by her continuing addictions and his inability to help her emerge from them. He urged her to write. In 1928, he personally forwarded a paper of hers, 'A Note on the Childish Theory of Coitus a Tergo', to Ernest Jones for the *Journal* – a paper which Jones, according to Anna Freud, disdained because Ruth did not seem to be familiar with the work of Melanie Klein. The paper was, however, published. It seems that throughout their friendship, Freud encouraged her to write, providing her with topics she might pursue: one cited by Roazen focused on the argument that the relation of the infant to the mother's breast plays an exceptional role in the development of the aesthetic sense. Ruth was slow to produce; and how much of Freud's encouragement was based on his sense that publication would shore up Ruth's insecurities, how much on his recognition of her considerable ability to put arguments forcefully and succinctly on paper, is not clear. Certainly, her published work is proof of a remarkable skill greatly under-used.

Freud also respected Ruth's clinical talent: he felt that she had a natural bent for 'smelling' the unconscious. From very early on in her training, he sent her patients and the list of Ruth's analysands grew long. Amongst Freud's referrals to her was the Wolf Man, perhaps the century's most famous patient.

It was a referral which made Helene Deutsch extremely jealous.

From October 1926 to February 1927, the man who had served as the subject for Freud's 'From the History of an Infantile Neurosis' came to Ruth. In her 1928 paper, Ruth detailed this new phase in the Wolf Man's analysis, modestly calling her own work 'a supplement' to Freud's. The paper gives evidence of the terse brilliance with which Ruth handled clinical concepts and the incisive acuity she brought to summarizing the progress of a case. She modestly saw her own part in the Wolf Man's treatment as negligible: 'I acted purely as mediator between the patient and Freud,' she later wrote. Not altogether negligibly, however, since she stresses that the fact that she was a woman was crucial to the process:

it seems improbable to me that analysis with a male analyst would have been possible. It is one thing to play the persecutor's role towards a female paranoiac – already castrated! – and quite another to play it toward a man for whom castration is still a possibility. It must be remembered that in the psychoses the things feared are actually believed in: the psychotic patient is afraid of the actual cutting off of his penis, and not of some symbolic act on the part of the analyst. Fantasy has become reality. Thus the situation is too dangerous for the patient. This is perhaps the one situation where the sex of the analyst is of importance.

Apart from her work with the Wolf Man, Ruth is best remembered for her article, 'The Preoedipal Phase of the Libido Development', published in the 1940 issue of the *Psychoanalytic Quarterly* commemorating Freud's death. According to her, the ideas contained in the piece grew out of close discussions with Freud from 1930 onwards, two years before his own article on 'Female Sexuality' appeared. Ruth is at pains to underline that she is here acting as Freud's mouthpiece, thus undercutting our ability to recognize her independence or originality, even if it existed.

As early as 1929, Ruth had emphasized the importance of the pre-Oedipal phase; and Freud acknowledged that she had been the first 'to describe a case of neurosis which went back to a fixation to the pre-Oedipus stage and had never reached the Oedipus situation at all'. So the legacy of the theory of the pre-Oedipal, although it has always since been associated with Freud, is also Ruth Mack Brunswick's. And, ironically reproducing the developmental sequence Freud and she were to give it, her contributions came to be seen as either precursors or as valedictions. Like the pre-Oedipal mother herself, it is almost impossible to unearth what belongs to her from beneath the overwhelming mass of material associated with the father.

Her major contribution to psychoanalytic theory, in her 1940 article, was the rewriting of the early history of the girl and the boy in terms of the active and passive Oedipus complexes – terms used with Freud's approval to replace the positive and negative Oedipus complex. The pre-Oedipal period is characterized by a seamless shift from an exclusive attachment to the mother in both sexes into the active Oedipus complex, again in both sexes, where the child actively takes the mother as the object, the father appearing only as rival: 'the preoedipal sexuality of the girl becomes her active oedipus complex with the mother as its object.' In girls, the shift into the passive Oedipus complex, with the father as preferred object, takes place late, with reluctance and with difficulty; but it is already grounded in the earlier system of 'Oedipal' relations centred on her mother. The seemingly stark contrast between Oedipal relations with the father and pre-Oedipal relations with the mother has been entirely reduced. Depending on one's perspective, Ruth's theory can either be seen as recognizing but then quickly assimilating the pre-Oedipal mother into the (passive) Oedipus complex, superficially so dominant in those women who in later life cannot detach themselves from the admired paternal figure; or it can be seen as a subtle reform in which the mother finally occupies her rightful place centre stage, the father being granted his part only as an epilogue, an attempt at a happy ending, to the central tragedy.

On some issues, Ruth went out of her way to correct Freud; she was quite firm on the reinterpretation of penis envy the early relation to the pre-Oedipal mother requires:

The little girl's desire for a child precedes penis envy and is linked to the desire to possess the attributes of the omnipotent mother. Therefore penis envy is not motivated solely by the narcissistic urge to have that which one does not have, but also by the object-oriented cause of possessing the mother.

And, if this point were not sufficient to win the case, the little girl in her account is sufficiently realistic to give up the impossible desire for a penis in favour of a wish in the realm of possibility, that for a baby. Not all children are penis-substitutes, she is saying.

In her last years in Vienna, Ruth Mack Brunswick, like her fellow Americans, worked tirelessly to provide affidavits to permit her friends to emigrate to the United States. She returned there herself, just before war broke out, and settled in New York. Though she carried on working through the war years, her health deteriorated. Increasingly she turned to morphine and other opiates for relief both from physical ills and the emotional upheavals caused by the death of her parents and Mark's second divorce suit. When Marie Bonaparte visited Ruth in New York in the winter of 1945–6, she was dismayed by her friend's condition and the toll morphine addiction, ill-health and depression had taken. On 23 January 1946, Ruth, confined to bed, none the less arranged a supper party for Marie. The following morning, probably heavily drugged, she slipped in the bathroom and fell, fracturing her skull. The sudden tragedy of her death at what amongst the women analysts was the startlingly early age of fifty marked Ruth out as a case for private mourning and almost unbroken public silence. No obituary of Ruth Mack Brunswick appeared in the *International Journal of Psychoanalysis*. Yet amongst her many patients and trainees, she was respectfully remembered.

One of these was a young American heiress who had come to Vienna in 1926. Muriel Gardiner was a radical young literature graduate of Wellesley College, who had also studied at Oxford. Divorced, mother to a small daughter, she had arrived in Vienna hoping to have an analysis with Freud, who promptly referred her to Ruth Mack Brunswick. The personal analysis, together with the study of psychoanalysis, was initially intended to act as a prelude to a career in teaching. In the event, she graduated from the University of Vienna medical faculty after the Nazis had already come to power.

Muriel Gardiner's studies, serious in themselves, also served as a cover for her 'real' work – her covert and by all accounts heroic activities in support of the Austrian socialist underground and eventually of Austrian left-wing and Jewish refugees. It was in fact the ruthless 1934 fascist suppression of the socialist opposition which made Muriel decide to stay in Vienna rather than return, as she had planned, to the United States to study medicine. Her apartment became a 'safe house' for resisters and there she eventually sheltered the head of the central committee of the Austrian Revolutionary Socialists, Joseph Buttinger, who was to become her husband.

In her resistance work, Muriel was joined by another young American friend, who had been briefly analysed by Freud and supervised in her child analysis training by Anna Freud: Dr Edith Jackson. Edith, who, like Muriel, came from a wealthy family, also put up money and negotiated with the Viennese authorities for the establishment of Anna Freud's first group project, the Jackson Nursery.

Unbeknownst to her, Muriel served as the model for Lilian Hellman's novel *Pentimento*, later made into the film, *Julia*. The notoriety which attended the publication of this book, couched as an autobiography, led the modest Muriel Gardiner to break her own silence: *Code Name 'Mary'* was her attempt to tell her own story of the difficult and dangerous resistance years in Austria. This self-effacing and understated memoir also gives us an insight into Muriel's analysis and her relations with Dr Mack. Referred by Freud to Ruth Mack Brunswick, Muriel set off in great trepidation to her first meeting, but 'everything she said made such good sense and seemed so down-to-earth that I decided to be analysed.' The analytic bond became a close one: in order not to interrupt her analysis during the summer holidays, Muriel followed Ruth to the United States in the summers of 1926 and 1927. The analysis went on for several years and was then renewed again as a training analysis. It overflowed into social relations, and when Muriel wanted Russian lessons, Ruth sent her to the Wolf Man, who needed any income he could lay his hands on. Just after the Nazis annexed Austria, Muriel bumped into a distressed Wolf Man on the street. His wife had committed suicide, and he was in despair. Muriel pulled strings, prepared affidavits and finally, in August 1938, the Wolf Man made his way to Ruth in London. The respect Muriel bore her analyst found its way into her book, *The Wolf Man by the Wolf Man*, which puts Freud's and Ruth's case histories side by side with the Wolf Man's own memoirs and Muriel's narrative of his later life. The royalties from the book, with Muriel's characteristic generosity, went to the Wolf Man himself and provided him with a much needed income, to supplant the one Freud could no longer supply.

Though Ruth introduced Muriel to Freud, it was principally with Anna that a friendship was struck up, one that was to grow stronger in the post-war

years when Muriel returned to the United States. Anna's words are the last
in *Code Name 'Mary'* and they are touching both in what they reveal about
Anna and the tribute they pay to Muriel Gardiner: 'I had not known of the
intensity of your political activities in Vienna, only the vaguest rumours, and
I was quite fascinated, even a bit envious. I like my own life very much, but
if that had not been available and if I had to choose another one, I think it
would have been yours.'

Muriel's activities in the Austrian socialist resistance were in line with Ruth's
and her husband's political sympathies – ones shared by many of the younger
analysts, including Anny Rosenberg Katan, who, like Muriel, served as courier
to the underground. They were not, however, shared by Freud. In 1934, when
Dollfuss's fascist government brutally put down the general strike, Freud
wrote to Hilda Doolittle:

We passed through a week of civil war. Not much personal suffering, just one day
without electric light, but the '*stimmung*' was awful and the feeling as of an earthquake.
No doubt, the rebels belonged to the best portion of the population, but their success
would have been very shortlived and brought about military invasion of the country.
Besides they were Bolshevists and I expect no salvation from Communism. So we
could not give our sympathy to either side of the combatants.

Freud's old man's pessimism, his lack of sympathy for the socialists, caused
consternation amongst his younger analysands and friends, and some of them
say it went so far as to hamper the transference. None the less, political
differences aside, they remained largely loyal to the Professor and the cause
of analysis. This was emphatically the case with Muriel Gardiner, who belongs
in this story of Freud's women not so much for her links with the living
Freud, as for the fact that, with Anna, she became the guardian of Freud's
shrine.

When she returned to the United States with the outbreak of war, Muriel
practised as a psychiatrist and analyst, also undertaking work in prisons with
those whom she calls *The Deadly Innocents; Portraits of Children Who Kill*, a book
prefaced by her long-time friend, the poet Stephen Spender. It was under her
auspices and with her family wealth that the New-Land Foundation was set
up – the Foundation which helped finance Anna Freud's Hampstead Nurseries
and one of whose projects was the establishment of the London Freud
Museum. Muriel Gardiner died on 6 February 1985, just over a year before
the dream she had shared with Anna Freud took on visible reality and the
Freud Museum opened its doors.

Anna's Circle

If Anna had a sense of rivalry with Freud's young female acolytes, she was
equally adept at bringing them to his attention and then maintaining the
friendships formed in the family circle for the whole of her long life.

Two of her childhood friends, daughters of the Freud family circle, became
analysts like her and, like her, had analyses with Freud. Sent for training to

other analysts, they maintained close bonds with the Freuds. Marianne Kris
was the daughter of Freud's friend, family doctor and card-partner, Oscar
Rie. Unlike Anna, her family encouraged her to train as a doctor. Just after
the war, she had an analysis with Freud, who then recommended her to Franz
Alexander in Berlin for her analytic formation. In 1927, she married the art
historian/analyst Ernst Kris, who trained with Anna Freud; together the
couple took part in the weekly meetings of Helene Deutsch's Black Cat Club.
One of their children was named after Anna, the other after Kata Levy's
brother, Anton von Freund; both became first psychiatrists then analysis. The
Rie line was, it turned out, more prolific of analysts than the Freud line:
Marianne's sister, Margarete, much admired by Anna Freud, had an analysis
with Freud, became an actress and married Herman Nunberg, one of Freud's
earliest followers, who had come to psychoanalysis from Cracow via the
Burghölzli of Jung and Bleuler. In later life, she helped her husband edit and
translate the Minutes of the Vienna Psycho-Analytical Society.

During the war, Dorothy Burlingham helped the Krises to move to the
United States, where, amongst other activities, they worked on projects for
the Yale Child Center. After Ernst's death in 1957, Marianne grew ever closer
to Anna, coming to see her often in what she thought of as her second
home; and turning over her bequest from Marilyn Monroe to her Hampstead
Clinic. She died in Anna's and Freud's house in Maresfield Gardens in 1980,
just after the second Hampstead Symposium had run its course.

Anny Rosenberg Katan was the daughter of another of Freud's card-playing
friends, the paediatrician, Ludwig Rosenberg. Three years older than Anny,
the prim Anna Freud took on a special significance for the younger, more
rambunctious girl. The two children were playing by a creek into which Anny
dropped a rock, thereby muddying and drenching the bigger girl. As Anna
made to run home, Anny challenged her: 'You could just let it dry.' When
years later, Anny, now like Marianne Kris a young doctor, was seeking analytic
training with Anna and the latter hesitated, she again defiantly teased her:
'You aren't going to let a splash stand in the way, are you?'

Analysed by Anna Freud for free, Anny was referred to Theodor Reik for
a training analysis. She coupled her work as an analyst with resistance work
for the socialist underground; and after she emigrated to Holland with her
ten-year-old son, she and her second husband, Morits Katan, were active in
the Dutch resistance. After the war, the couple moved to Cleveland, Ohio,
from whence they travelled often to see Anna in London and Walberswick.
Here they bought a house. The childhood friends stayed together, both socially
and analytically: in 1962, Anny and Marianne Kris with several other analysts
formed a special interest group for child analysts within the American
Association. Together with those other Viennese friends, Jeanne Lampl de
Groot and Muriel Gardiner, they attended Anna's Hampstead Symposia in
1979 and 1980.

Kata Levy, an analysand of Freud's – again free of charge – in the years
just after the war, was another friend of Anna's, but this time in the model
of those admired elder sister surrogates, like Loë Kann. A Hungarian social

worker, then painter and finally analyst, Kata was the beautiful wife of Ferenczi's analysand, Lajos Levy, the director of the reputed Jewish Hospital in Budapest and one of the founders of the Hungarian Psychoanalytic Society. Her brother, Anton von Freund, was the wealthy businessman whose wife had been analysed by Ferenczi while he sought an analysis with Freud.

Kata grew close to Freud. After her analysis was over, Freud wrote to her saying how pleased he was that he could now communicate with her simply and warmly, 'without the didactic rudeness of analysis, without having to conceal my cordial friendship for you.' Their correspondence continued over the years, intimate and friendly; Freud even confided to her about finances. 'One can no longer make a living from the Viennese, the Hungarians, the Germans,' he told her. 'It is really no activity for a dignified old man. *C'est la guerre.*' He would now have to take English and American patients, who could pay in hard currency. Freud also persuaded one of his daughters-in-law to name her son after Kata's brother, Anton.

Anna became friends with Kata in 1917, when she travelled to Budapest and served informally as the resident tutor for the von Freunds' daughter. In a telling letter describing the course of what was to be a lifelong friendship with Anna, Kata wrote in 1952 that, whereas she had begun as 'dear old Kata', she had quickly turned into the sister who aroused jealousy: 'you seem to have felt at that time like the rich girl who, on account of her money, fears to be loved or, more precisely, to get married. You seem to have felt, for example, that my interest in you was really an interest in your father.... But then you started to march forward in seven-mile-a-step magical boots ... you became the *older* sister.'

Kata and her husband managed to survive the war years in Budapest, but after it Stalinism threatened the small analytic community. In 1956, Anna and Eva Rosenfeld, together with a group of Hungarian-born émigrés in London banded together to raise funds to permit Hungarian analysts to emigrate. The Levys arrived in England and lived in a small house adjoining Anna's garden. Kata took up work at the Hampstead Clinic, focusing particularly on the simultaneous analysis of mothers and children. She died in London in 1971.

Eva Rosenfeld, 1892–1977

Amongst the Vienna-based women who moved in Freud's and Anna's orbit, Eva Rosenfeld was, next to Ruth Mack Brunswick, Freud's undoubted favourite. Given that she was not only a lively cultivated woman with a gift for friendship, but also the niece of the famous French singer Yvette Guilbert, whom Freud had idolized ever since Madame Charcot had recommended that he go and hear her sing, this was perhaps not altogether surprising. It was Eva who brought Freud the photograph of her aunt he so cherished, inscribed '*A un grand savant, d'une artiste*'; and who reported Freud's apologetic quip to Yvette Guilbert and her husband during one of their regular meetings at the Hotel Bristol – '*Meine Prothese spricht nicht französisch*', 'My prosthesis doesn't speak French.'

Eva's father was a Berlin-based theatrical impresario, who, having grown rich on music hall, redirected his wealth into attempting to introduce the German Expressionist dramatist, Gerhardt Hauptmann, and contemporaneously Yvette Guilbert, his new sister-in-law, to the United States. Though the Hauptmann venture proved a resounding failure, it resulted in Eva being born on Manhattan's Fifth Avenue. Over the years, all the women in Eva's family grew friendly with Freud, not only Yvette Guilbert, but also Eva's mother, universally known as Omi, to whom in 1937 he wrote acknowledging that he would enlist Marie Bonaparte's help with the British royal family should Yvette Guilbert decide to emigrate to Britain.

Freud's connection to the Rosenfeld family predated Eva's friendship with Anna. Her husband, Valentin (or Valti) Rosenfeld, had attended Freud's lectures in 1905–6, probably at the time that Freud was formulating his conception of the family romance. In 1910, Valti, who was contemplating marriage, wrote to Freud seeking advice. Would it be advisable to marry his first cousin? Freud is said to have replied that such marriages always brought out the characteristics in common, but if they didn't mind that, the young couple should go ahead and enjoy themselves. And so, Valti Rosenfeld married his cousin, Eva.

Eva, herself, came to Freud through Anna, whom she had met in 1924. She quickly became a family friend, helping Martha out with the preparations for summer holidays and generally, with her marked talent for organization, making herself useful. Her adolescent daughter, Maedi, went into analysis with Anna and, in turn, Anna housed some of her young patients, including her nephew, Ernst Halberstadt, in the bustling and friendly, though far from affluent, Rosenfeld house. Valti practised criminal law and in 1927 defended the members of the radical socialist group who had set fire to the Palace of Justice in July, as an act of reprisal for the authorities' acquittal of nationalist perpetrators of political murder. As a consequence of this defence, Valti Rosenfeld's practice in bourgeois Vienna suffered and the family's financial circumstances were strained – not enough, however, to prevent him from pursuing his passion for Goethiana and putting together a remarkable library of first editions. When Eva and Anna met, the Rosenfelds had two children, two having previously died in a diphtheria epidemic. Their home, ruled over by the cultured, energetic Eva, always buzzed with talk and activity and hummed with the music they all loved.

Before the Burlinghams arrived in Vienna, it was the Rosenfeld family which provided Anna with something of her own. On Anna's thirtieth birthday, Eva presented her with a long cord to which she had attached thirty presents. And Anna's letters to Eva in the 1920s have the tone of love letters where a kiss takes the place of everything as yet unspoken: the bond between the two women was a particularly deep and intimate one. The arrival of the Burlinghams strained it. Eva felt that she was being displaced in Anna's affections; but the Burlingham children fell in love with the *Gemütlichkeit* of the Rosenfelds' home and soon, despite Eva's continuing sense of injury, the three families were always together. The death of Eva's fifteen-year-old daughter Maedi, in a mountaineering accident in the summer of 1927, was a singular blow which Anna tried desperately to help her overcome, writing: 'I so much wish I could become a small piece of Maedi for you. I wish I had a small daughter, whom I could share with you.' In the same letter, obviously in response to a request from Eva about what books of Freud's to read, Anna suggests among others '*Trauer und Melancholie*' and *Totem and Taboo*. Eva's sense of tragedy was certainly compounded by the fact that she had replicated her mother's fate, both having lost three out of four children, leaving only the youngest alive: Eva herself, and in her case, her son, Victor. Eva tried to overcome her grief in her work for the Matchbox school, built that autumn in the Rosenfelds' backyard. In her unpublished memoir, she records that it was Maedi who was 'the real spiritual founder of the school', of which Eva, Anna and Dorothy were the guiding forces. Peter Blos, the school's first teacher, describes Eva at the time as 'a resourceful, intelligent, gifted woman who created around her an atmosphere of humanity, culture and music'.

It was Eva who was indirectly responsible for the death of Freud's first chow, Lun, in the summer of 1929. She was taking Lun home to Vienna when he broke free at the Salzburg station and was run over by a train. Freud wrote to her telling her that she must not reproach herself or feel responsible for the small tragedy: 'But it is very distressing, and I am tempted not to repeat for myself this attachment to an animal.'

The incident could not have eased Eva's already ambivalent relations with Dorothy, who had given Freud the dog. None the less, Anna's letters to Eva at the time offer constant reassurance about a friendship Eva may have doubted: 'You are me and I am you and everything of mine that you could use you should take, because it is rightfully yours.' In September of that year, Anna wrote to her more irritably on the same matter: 'Why do you believe that I have only thoughts about Dorothy and want to be reassured only about her condition?' It is this same letter which offers Eva a free analysis with Freud. For two months, Eva saw Freud six times a week; and after that on Sunday afternoons and daily throughout the holidays. Analysis gave her a way of working through her mourning. It also gave her, what she called in her memoir, 'a viable universe'. It was the beginning of Eva's path towards becoming an analyst. Only much later, when she was herself an analyst, did she recognize the crucial significance of one of Freud's interventions, which she had resisted at the time. Freud had told her that if her idealized father had lived longer, that is beyond her fifteenth year, she would have hated him. In retrospect, Eva realized that Freud was telling her that she was repressing her hatred for father Freud: a hatred based on her sense that, throughout her analysis, 'I must have repressed the wish to be analysed by Anna, my dear friend, whom I loved so much'. With this buried hatred – and the sense that she had been displaced in Anna's affections – it is perhaps not surprising that Eva, for a time at least, turned to Melanie Klein.

In 1931, Eva moved with her son to Berlin, where she worked as matron at Ernst Simmel's psychoanalytic sanatorium, the *Schloss* Tegel, until it closed in July of that year. But Berlin, with the rising Nazi threat, was not a place to settle and, sometime in 1932, Eva set out for Moscow idealistically thinking that a future might be found there. She came back, as her son, Victor Ross, graphically puts it, with 'her tail between her legs'. Eva began to see patients and continued her psychoanalytic training, taking courses at the Berlin Institute of Psychoanalysis, then headed by the gentiles acceptable to the Nazis, Felix Boehm and Carl Müller-Braunschweig. In 1936, the family moved to London and Ernest Jones, undoubtedly spotting Eva's considerable organizational talents, appointed her secretary of the Rehabilitation Fund. It was Eva who did the lion's share of the endless bureaucratic work required to bring analysts out of Austria.

The political situation and the disorientation involved in uprooting her life deeply distressed Eva. Klein's paper on depression, which she read during her first months in Britain, impressed and affected her. She considered a second analysis, a brief four-week one with Freud or one with Klein. Although certain commentators have implied that Freud resentfully cut her off when she decided on Klein, his letter to her reads rather more like an attempt to allow her to think the matter through clearly for herself and points her in the direction of Klein, a direction, he suggests, she has already decided on. It is a telling reminder of Freud's impartiality, at least towards some of his friends and former patients:

There are other aspects of the matter to consider, one that could prove disagreeable for you, another that could prove disagreeable for me. You know what my attitude to Melanie Klein's work is. I too think that she has found something new, but I don't know if it means quite so much as she believes, and I am certain that she has no right to use it to place theory and technique on a new basis. Our four weeks would naturally attempt critically to unravel what you have found in yourself to confirm the Kleinian theories. It is possible that I might bring you to another judgment of these things. Then you would go back to London and find yourself in opposition to the circle and direction of work when you would manifestly prefer to stay in tune with both. On the other hand, it wouldn't be possible for you to hide from the English group the influence that you have experienced through me, and that would kindle an antagonism I have gone out of my way up until now to avoid.

The other possibility, that in four weeks you would convince me of the fundamental significance and correctness of Kleinian findings, I do not really think is a probable outcome. I think then that the piece of inner work that is now thrust upon you, the resolution of your intellectual allegiance [*Parteinahme*] as well as of your father or mother influence, is something that you will have to sort out without help, at least without mine. Because as always I take a lively interest in your destiny, I am naturally unhappy that such a problem should have posed itself, particularly for you.

If Freud seems altogether sanguine here, and more concerned about Eva than about psychoanalytic politics, then it is more than possible that Anna, on the other hand, took her decision to begin a Kleinian analysis as a sign of betrayal. Clearly Eva herself, once the Freuds had arrived in London, felt torn between the Kleinian and Freudian camps. It was she who suggested that a small group of Kleinians be formed who could work out how best to present their ideas to the Viennese. Susan Isaacs wrote of the matter to Clifford Scott: 'She feels that we don't make it easy for the Viennese to understand our views, and that one ought to give much more attention to the educational side of our work – to find ways of putting things which will get rid of *intellectual* obstacles at least.' The Internal Object or I.O. group was duly launched with the task of defining a communicable theoretical framework. Eva valiantly tried to be a peacemaker. She remained near-invisible during the Controversial Discussions in the British Society during the war, and on Anna's invitation attended some of her weekly seminars at Maresfield Gardens with the specific purpose of explaining Klein's theories to Anna's group.

Willi Hoffer got such an attack of fury with what I was saying that I said to him, 'Willi, next time we must come in arm-in-arm or people will think we are really cross with each other and they mustn't think that, that isn't our way of being friends. You were cross with me, but never mind,' and we came in together arm-in-arm. Yes, that was our Viennese tradition; nothing could disturb a personal friendship.

Old friendships died hard, in Eva's case at least. In 1955–6, Eva and Anna Freud worked together to raise money to resettle the endangered Hungarian analytic community. As late as 1967, though the relationship between the two women no longer had the intimacy of their Vienna days, Anna was writing to Eva, still in German, asking why Eva didn't visit Walberswick. The friendship had become increasingly a family affair. In the 1970s, the two women would visit Mathilde Freud together, and in the last year of Anna Freud's life, it was Eva's daughter-in-law who drove her home from the Royal Free Hospital.

Perhaps not surprisingly, Melanie Klein felt that Eva had sacrificed her analysis to Anna Freud. Meeting her on the bus one day just after the war when the controversy over training had been resolved, Klein emphatically told Eva that she would now have to belong to the Middle Group. Eva, it seems, was relieved, 'because I thought I could not become a Kleinian. How could she think I wanted to be?' Klein, Eva is said to have remarked, had no friends, only disciples or opponents. The contrast with Freud is implicit. For Eva, herself, psychoanalysis was a matter of drawing the best from all positions and using this to inform her practice. A much-loved and humane clinician who lives in the memories of patients and friends far more than through any publications – writing was a task which continually defeated her – Eva Rosenfeld continued to work as a Middle Group analyst until her death in 1977.

Jeanne Lampl de Groot, 1895–1987

In the summer of 1921, Jeanne de Groot, a newly graduated twenty-six-year-old doctor from a wealthy and cultured Dutch family, approached Freud for a training analysis. In responding to her, Freud for the first time set down in written form what he now required of students. Apart from the preparatory self-analysis, there was literature to be read, lectures to be attended and meetings to be participated in. After the '*Autoanalyse*', it would be necessary for Jeanne to work in the Berlin Polyclinic in order to familiarize herself with the treatment of patients. It was the beginning of one of Freud's most extended and cordial correspondences of the 1920s and 1930s, and eventually, after Jeanne's time in Vienna, one replete with exchange of family news and gossip.

Jeanne arrived in Vienna for her analysis in April 1922. Fresh-faced, petite, she must have charmed Freud as much as he charmed her, for apprenticeship quickly merged into long-lasting familial friendship. She found Freud to be a 'charming and considerate, old-fashioned gentleman, humane and generous'. He asked her whether he or his daughters could help in getting her settled. Jeanne mentioned that she was looking for a piano. Freud confessed to her that he, himself, was unmusical, fearing perhaps that the later discovery of this lack might hinder the analytic process. He also told her that his daughter, like Jeanne's sister, had died of influenza while pregnant. Such was the way in which Freud ensured a positive transference at the beginning of analysis.

Freud's friendship with Jeanne, formed in the same year as those with Ruth Mack Brunswick and Joan Riviere, aroused Anna's jealousy, like these others. It could not have been weakened by the fact that Jeanne broke off her engagement with one of the members of Wagner-Jauregg's staff to marry, in 1925, Dr Hans Lampl, Anna's recurrent suitor. A Viennese gossip column noted that 'Lampl got his Jeanne and Anna got her Wolf' – Wolf being the large male dog Freud had given Anna at that time. Yet Anna maintained her humour, and the women became friends, if not intimates, Jeanne attending Anna's child analysis seminar when this was established. Later, after the war, the two women did battle together to convince the International Association that child analysts should be International members. And after Hans Lampl's death in a motor accident in 1957, Jeanne drew even closer to Anna, travelling frequently to London from Holland, where she and her husband had settled just before the war.

Freud's correspondence with Jeanne is avuncular and gossipy. He gives her advice about family problems and her relationship with Hans; he also counsels her not to worry about feeling she needs a follow-up analysis. He reports in detail on his health, expresses his anxiety about Anna's and once tells her to keep Hans away while Anna is so exhausted. Jeanne, now working in Berlin, is also the keeper of his cigar ration and the letters are full of thanks for these and settling of financial accounts. In 1933, he signs himself '*der alte Taube* [old pigeon]'.

Lampl de Groot's early work was largely concerned with female sexuality. Her paper on 'The Oedipus Complex in Women' (1927) was one Freud referred to approvingly in his own 1932 paper on 'Female Sexuality', criticizing only Lampl de Groot's lack of emphasis on the hostility which accompanies the girl's turning away from her mother in the move from the negative to the positive Oedipus complex.

Known as a Freudian loyalist, Lampl de Groot, however, did have her own emphases. She notes in this paper, somewhat diffidently, that though Freud attributed the difficulty of getting at early or pre-Oedipal material in women to the profound repression to which this was subjected, she in part thinks otherwise: 'The greater difficulty of understanding these particular mental processes in little girls may arise on the one hand from the fact that they are in themselves more complicated than the analogous processes in boys and, on the other, from the greater intensity with which the libido is repressed in women.' She then adds, attributing the thought to Karen Horney but seemingly approving it: 'Horney thinks that another reason is that, so far, analytical observations have been made principally by men.' Though kept on a low note, in her conclusion Lampl de Groot again reiterates the point about the importance of the woman analyst: 'with a male analyst it may be very hard to bring this period to light at all. For it is difficult for a female patient to enter into rivalry with the father-analyst, so that possibly treatment under these conditions cannot get beyond the analysis of the positive oedipus attitude.' Undoubtedly in part under the pressure of his young female disciples, Freud made the same point himself in 1931.

Lampl de Groot's second paper, 'Problems of Femininity', written in 1932 and published in 1933, is one Freud at first firmly criticized in his correspondence with her. So sharply did she feel the criticism that in a subsequent letter, he felt the need to apologize and did so humbly and humanely, saying that there was too much subjectivity in his criticism, something Jeanne could not have been aware of:

I am suspended, quite literally, on the question of the *passiven Triebziele* [passive instinctual aims], a problem I sometimes almost grasp and which then again veils itself. When I read your work, I grasped it again for a moment and then when your elaborations didn't meet the point, I was deflected from my appreciation and wrote down what I now recognize as incorrect. Now I'm once again groping in the dark.

Freud then re-emphasizes how rich her paper is in content. This epistolary instance of Freud criticizing and then apologizing to Jeanne gives us some insight into how Freud negotiated discussions with his female disciples.

For all his apology, when Lampl de Groot came in 1985 to reprint her 1933 paper on 'Problems of Femininity', one senses that Freud's criticisms of a half-century earlier still carry their sting for her. She introduces the paper by calling it 'partly a youthful sin: perhaps I should have changed more than a few of the formulations.' Then, in defiance of the Professor, she adds: 'Be that as it may, I have decided to publish it with only slight differences in wording because I myself cannot reject it altogether, though I am quite aware of its speculative side.'

In the long span of her life, Jeanne Lampl de Groot went on to become an important figure in Dutch psychoanalysis. She was a co-founder of psychoanalytic training in the Netherlands and of the Psychoanalytic Institute connected with it. Her articles ranged over a wide variety of psychoanalytic fields. She herself always felt it a privilege to have been close to Freud and to have played a part in the Vienna Society when it was at its height.

H. D. – Hilda Doolittle, 1886–1961

Amongst the women who peopled Freud's later years, the American poet and writer Hilda Doolittle was the recipient of a particular, almost an amorous, tenderness. Only perhaps with Lou Andreas-Salomé, his other literary patient-pupil, did Freud display a similar tone – a loving care, compounded with respect and imaginative interest.

Hilda Doolittle returned Freud's tenderness many times over. Freud had said to her abruptly, in the midst of a session: 'The trouble is – I am an old man – *you do not think it worth your while to love me.*' Her *Tribute to Freud*, written in 1944, ten years after her analysis, was proof of the love which formed her part in what she called the 'most luscious sort of vers libre relationship'. Here H. D. evokes Freud as the 'blameless physician', an incarnation of the Asklepios of the Greeks, half-man, half-god. In its fine literary allusiveness, in its sensitive immediacy, this brief memoir – together with *Advent*, the journal H. D. kept during her first months in Vienna – captures the tone and movement of an analysis, that free unconventional play of associations and memory not so different in certain respect from *vers libre*, as it has rarely been caught. Freud would have had reason to be grateful for H. D.'s gratitude.

Hilda Doolittle, co-founder with Ezra Pound and her then husband, Richard Aldington, of the Imagist movement, was well-known as a literary figure, at once poet, editor, classicist and experimental novelist. A shy, somewhat withdrawn woman, she had been through a number of breakdowns, experienced hallucinations, and at the time she came to Freud in March 1933 was suffering from a loss of artistic direction, as well as from the fear that personal breakdown, like war, which had in part occasioned a prior breakdown, would come again. She wanted to be strong enough to meet that second war, 'to help in some subsidiary way, if my training were sufficient and my aptitudes suitable, with war-shocked and war-shattered people'. 'There was something that was beating in my brain: I do not say my heart – my brain. I wanted to free myself of repetitive thoughts and experiences – my own and those of many of my contemporaries.' She saw Freud five times a week for some four months in 1933 and then returned again in October 1934 for about six weeks. The analysis took place in English. The two corresponded and then met again briefly in London.

H. D. was already familiar with psychoanalysis. As an avant-garde writer in Europe in the 1920s, it was difficult not to see modernism and analysis as in some ways foraging the same terrain. Then too, H. D.'s lifelong friend and sometime partner, the writer Bryher (Winifred Ellerman), had been friendly with the Freuds since 1927 and had been analysed by Hanns Sachs. A powerful advocate of psychoanalysis, Bryher also over the years donated substantial sums to various psychoanalytic ventures including the training of lay analysts. From 1933 on, she was instrumental in helping refugee analysts flee Germany and settle in safer lands. It was Bryher who convinced H. D. to have analysis, first with Mary Chadwick in London in 1931, a relationship which did not work, and then briefly with Hanns Sachs in Berlin. It was Sachs who recommended H. D. to Freud and wrote a letter of introduction. Bryher made the final arrangements.

It is likely that Freud read some of H. D.'s work before her arrival. An American friend had given him *Palimpsest*, three overlayered stories tracing woman's development as artist, using antiquity as a psychological trope. The burrowing in the past, the writing over of one personality with new ones which are yet determined by the old, signalled a set of interests not so dissimilar from Freud's own – though not in an idiom with which Freud, thoroughly un-modernist in his tastes, was familiar. H. D. on her side prepared for analysis by immersing herself in a reading of Freud.

No sooner had the analysis begun than Freud, according to Bryher, was writing to her to say that 'he has no exciting patients' apart from H. D. and the Dutchman, who had the hour prior to hers and who features largely in her *Tribute*; and 'that seldom if ever had he come into contact with a mind so fine, a spirit so pure, as that of our esteemed Kat [H. D.] and he hoped that after a summer rest, she would return to resume an analysis of months of weeks or even years as she so desires, and she would have preference over all others.'

As early as May 1933, H. D. conveyed equal enthusiasm:

I wish he had a thousand lives and arms and brains ... the world is literally his 'child'. He is so impersonal and tender ... Freud is simply Jesus-Christ after the resurrection, he has that wistful ghost look of someone who has been right past the door of the tomb, and such tenderness with such humour, he just IS all that. I am sure he IS the absolute inheritor of all that eastern mystery and majic [*sic*], just IS, in spite of all his monumental work and all that, he is the real, the final healer.... He is very sharp like a little adder when he wants to be, but has not been with me, except to show he CAN be.

The analytic love affair between Freud and H. D. – which extended to embrace her daughter, Perdita, and her friend Bryher – continued until Freud's death and beyond. It continued despite Freud and H. D.'s very marked differences. Where H. D. insisted on the reality of her hallucinatory experiences as poetic and prophetic vision, Freud understood these as dangerous symptoms. Her manifestations of the occult were his signals for the return of the repressed. Where H. D. believed in a transcendent world, Freud insisted on a material universe, bounded by death. Yet there is a sense in which these differences added to the excitement of the analytic adventure they were engaged upon: an archaeological foray into the strata of the psyche, where the 'gods', the antique denizens of Freud's collection, may be unearthed in their fearful glory or revealed as household familiars in the light of analytic scrutiny, 'goods' rather than 'gods' – to take up one of their own punning refrains.

H. D. was as much student as she was patient, one of those remarkable and, in the terminology of the time, 'masculine' women, whom Freud, whatever his pronouncements about the feminine, seemed to cherish. She was born in Bethlehem, Pennsylvania. Her father, whom she idolized, was a well-known

Professor of Astronomy, but a cold, distant man whose only passion was the science H. D. never felt she could successfully aspire to. Her mother, Helen, Doolittle's second wife, belonged to the strict Moravian Church, which, as H. D. later discovered, had a hidden mystical and hermetic tradition she claimed as her own maternal legacy. An artistic woman, she denigrated her own talents better to serve her husband and her five sons, particularly, it seemed to little Hilda, her favourite, Gilbert. Hilda, 'wispy and mousey' amongst the 'glowing and gold' boys, felt unloved and torn in her adolescence between the maternal and paternal models. She was an early rebel against familial expectations, leaving Bryn Mawr before completing her degree. A long friendship with Ezra Pound ended in a ruptured engagement, in part because she felt suffocated by the muse-like perfection Pound demanded of her, in part, too, perhaps because of a sexual fear. Instead of marriage, H. D. left America for England at the age of twenty-five, in the company of Frances Gregg, an early homosexual love. In 1913, her first poems as H. D. were published: it was Pound, still a friend, who signed her 'H. D. – Imagiste', the tag which brought a modernist movement into being and which H. D. was to wear with increasing frustration in years to come, as she struggled with new voices and new forms.

The year 1913 also brought marriage to the writer Richard Aldington. Two years later, their child died, stillborn: H. D. always felt that the premature labour had been brought on by the shock of hearing about the *Lusitania* disaster, as well as by a war-changed Aldington's increasing hostility. In 1919, towards the end of her second pregnancy, this time by the critic and composer Cecil Gray, a series of further shocks combined with influenza and double pneumonia to threaten her own and her unborn child's life. There was news of her brother Gilbert's death in France, closely followed by the report of her father's death from shock; Aldington suing for divorce, and the rupture of her close friendship with D. H. Lawrence, whose presence in *Advent*, as her absent, yet betraying, twin, continued to be strong. H. D.'s daughter, Perdita, survived, but H. D. herself suffered a breakdown. Her new friend Bryher saw her through it: together they travelled to Greece, where H. D. experienced the visionary hallucinations she brought as 'symptoms' to Freud.

H. D.'s career and her writings have served as something of an exemplum in feminist literary history. What H. D.'s personal trajectory and her work make clear is that in order to forge an identity which would encompass her both as woman and writer, battle had to be waged on several fronts simultaneously. There was the struggle against the constraints of a male literary tradition to find her own unique and authoritative poetic voice, a voice that could contain her sexual ambivalence, her femaleness and her visionary premonitions. There was the struggle against social expectations, a series of conventional assumptions about woman's place which put obstacles in the way of her being poet but not muse, lover but not wife. Finally there was the struggle with her own femininity, an attempt to come to terms with the woman she was. It is on this last front that her analysis with Freud is particularly interesting not only for what it reveals about H. D., but also for the insight it gives us into Freud and his ideas about femininity.

Through the brilliantly allusive lines of H. D.'s *Tribute*, one can begin to reconstruct some of the landmarks of her analysis. Freud understood H. D.'s coming to him in Vienna as her unconscious attempt to find her mother whose place he was made to assume: Vienna was the city where her mother, Helen, had spent her honeymoon. He felt that H. D.'s difficulties lay in her longing to be re-united with her lost pre-Oedipal and phallic mother, the mother who presided over those early years before sexual difference had positioned Hilda as a girl. To this mother she could still in fantasy be the infant boy-god of her crucial analytic dream of Moses in the Bullrushes, rather than the little girl, Miriam, who looks on wistfully as the Princess/Mother makes her way towards the cradled boy child, the 'founder of a new religion', whom H. D., before Freud's intervention, had interpreted as representing Freud himself. For Freud, cast in the role of the analytic Mother, H. D. can assume the role of Moses and take on the place of the male disciple she imagines he values highly: she can become the favoured brother with whom she had associated the Flying Dutchman, whose analytic hour preceded hers – the eminent scholar and occultist J. J. van der Leeuw, killed after H. D.'s first analytic sequence and in part responsible for her return to Freud.

This search for union with the mother, we see Freud implying, is also at the root of H. D.'s homosexual loves; and the motive force of her hallucinated 'writings on the wall' is 'a sort of display or entertainment for my mother'. It was H. D.'s mother-fixation which needed to be brought analytically to light if her 'dangerous symptoms', the encroachment of unconscious hallucinations on daily life, were to be put to rest. As H. D. put it in her idiomatic slang in a letter to Bryher, her 'mother-fix' was special: 'F. says mine is absolutely FIRST layer, I got stuck at the earliest pre-OE stage, and "back to the womb" seems to be my only solution. Hence islands, sea, Greek primitives and so on. It's all too wonder-making.'

As Susan Stanford Friedman has so convincingly shown, it would seem that Freud interpreted H. D.'s predicament along the lines he had laid down in 'The Psychogenesis of a Case of Homosexuality in a Woman'. She had never, in her passage through the Oedipus complex and its partial repetition in puberty, altogether transferred her feelings from her mother to her father; and the loved woman for her was still the whole woman imagined in infancy, the phallic, uncastrated or masculine woman, the ideal woman with whom, in her homosexual loves, she recreated the mother–child relationship.

Freud's interpretations, as H. D.'s brief reports of them in her *Tribute* suggest, were mainly geared towards making her aware of her mother-fixation and thus dispelling the hallucinations propelled by it. There was also, by implication, a second step: an attempt to move H. D. beyond the mother to an acceptance of the father. Freud insists to H. D., despite her protests, that in the transference she has cast him in the role of mother. Many years had passed since the case of Dora, and Freud was now able consciously to see and say, both honestly and presumably too for therapeutic effect, that it was not a role he enjoyed: 'I do *not* like being the mother in transference – it always surprises and shocks me a little. I feel so very masculine.' Interestingly, this is one of the few recorded instances we have of Freud analysing the mother transference and delving into pre-Oedipal material. We should perhaps remember that we are dealing here with the late Freud, the Freud who is possibly released by his own mother's death, the Freud who has, through the impact of analytic experience and the pressure of his female colleagues and analysands, altered and deepened his views on the development of the feminine.

Recognizing the 'mother-fix' went in hand in hand with recognizing the potentially benevolent role of the father. The force of Freud's exclamation, 'I am an old man – *you do not think it worth your while to love me*,' can be read in this light. The intervention, of course, emphasizes Freud's age and the proximity of death which H. D. feared for him, but also feared all around her: the deaths of her child, her brother, father, mother, friends had crystallized into the debilitating war phobia, which was one of the prime catalysts in her coming to Freud. But Freud's exclamation has further force. At once an abrupt analytic intervention to jar H. D. from ideas to feeling – to force her to see *him* and not him-through-the-objects in his collection she seemed to prefer – and an overtly seductive call to transferential arms, it is also a statement emphasizing that Freud is worth loving in his maleness. H. D. needed to recognize and love him as a man, to replay the movement from mother to father. We might even go so far as to suggest that the whole seductive tenor of their relationship, as H. D. recreates it, was part of Freud's analytic intent, transforming the 'cold man', the rejecting man who had been H. D.'s father, into a loving man, a fallible man capable of maternal tenderness, a man moved by affection. 'I had imagined', Freud writes to her on 24 May 1936, 'I had become insensitive to praise and blame. Reading your kind lines and getting aware of how I enjoyed them I first thought I had been mistaken about my firmness. Yet on second thoughts I concluded I was not. What you gave me was not praise [but] affection and I need not be ashamed of my satisfaction. Life at my age is not easy, but spring is beautiful, and so is love.'

There is no evidence to suggest, however, that Freud, apart from bringing into conscious play H. D.'s mother-fixation in order to dispel her 'dangerous symptoms', her hallucinations, attempted directly to steer H. D. away from homosexuality. At only one point in the *Tribute* does she mention him commenting on this. Freud tells her that she would not have been 'biologically' happy with Gregg, her first homosexual love – words that hurt her. But, on the other hand, Freud remained affectionate towards Bryher, accepting and never judging the relationship between the two women: his friendship and respect for both of them was wholehearted.

Be that as it may, H. D., who was nothing if not independent and who had managed to maintain her independence of spirit in the face of the hardly inconsequential powers that Ezra Pound, Richard Aldington and D. H. Lawrence were, was quite capable of judging that 'the Professor was not always right'. Against Freud's instructions – since writing about analysis during its course functioned, he believed, as a form of resistance – she took notes on her analytic sessions and then, having stopped doing so at his urging, replaced these by discussing her analysis in almost daily letters to Bryher. Then, too, H. D. was neither prepared to accept Freud's materialist world-view, which equated 'gods' with 'goods', nor wholly to abandon the realm of the mothers. Her 'dangerous symptoms' were to her a mystical vision, an occult message. Despite Freud's disapproval, she persisted in her beliefs, continuing to find significance in occult teachings. During the period of her analysis with Freud, she was able, for instance, to recognize her belief in astrology as her way of being 'in love' with her astronomer father, but she none the less understood astrology as a hermetic parallel to astonomy. To Bryher, she wrote on 28 May 1933 about Freud: 'he has to stick to his scientific guns, but I have to stick to mine too. These Jews, I think, hold that any dealings with "lore" and that sort of craft is wrong. I think so too, when it is WRONG !!!!! But it isn't always.' Spiritualism – a set of mysteries to place alongside psychoanalysis, a further set of correspondences from which to wrest meaning – was to inform H. D.'s poetic work and her life until its end. And able to argue Socratically with the rationalist Freud, she maintained her emphasis on intuition over reason throughout her analysis. 'The Master', as her poem of that title reveals, sometimes made her rage at his certainties.

> I was angry with the old man
> with his talk of the man-strength,
> I was angry with his mystery, his mysteries,
> I argued till day-break.

But from the tone of her letter to him on his final birthday, 6 May 1939, it would seem that they finally agreed respectfully and playfully to disagree. With the spectre of war drawing ever closer, H. D. writes: 'I can only hope that you feel secure and protected by the eternal verities and their symbolic, stabilized presences. Your Egyptians and Greeks (the gods or "goods") watch over you.'

There remains the question of how effective H. D.'s analysis was. Her *Tribute to Freud* leaves little doubt as to the value the experience held for her. The richness and new voice of her many post-analytic writings are further evidence of the beneficial quality of the experience: they show her in control of that visionary realm which fuels her work. Interestingly too, in her Freud memoir, we see her identifying Freud as a good father, one of the few patriarchal figures in her late work who do not act as victimizers or betrayers. Freud as the sensitive scientist, the intuitive rationalist, could encompass both sexual poles and thus, as blameless physician, as fatherly and motherly friend, heal.

It is perhaps not surprising that in this H. D.'s views tally with Bryher's, who wrote:

Freud in himself was not what his admirers wanted him to be, a silent sage or hermit sitting on a rock and staring at the horizon. He reminded me rather of a doctor of the nineties, full of advice and kindness, who would have gone out in all weathers to help his patients and turned no one away from his door. He had his wish, nobody this last century has helped humanity so much.

However blameless H. D.'s physician, there was nothing so simple as a 'cure' at the end of an analysis with Freud or even after continuing analysis with Walter Schmideberg in 1936 and 1937. During the long London years of the war she had so feared, H. D. kept her grip on life by writing – it was in 1944 that she began her *Tribute to Freud* – and by immersing herself in occult teachings: meaning, a semblance of order, could be found here to be pitted against the nightmare realities of daily life. But in 1946, the concatenation of circumstances which she had come to recognize as the triggers to her repeated breakdowns occurred again. Wartime bombings and the trauma of so many deaths fused with a personal betrayal. The friend in question was Lord Dowding, retired Air Chief Marshal of the Royal Air Force, who had become an advocate of spiritualism and lectured widely on his communications with his dead pilots. H. D. had heard him lecture, read his work and struck up what was to her an important friendship with him. But when she herself began to receive messages from Dowding's dead pilots warning of the terrors of atomic war and tried to tell Dowding of this, he refused to acknowledge her communications and recommended that she give up her spiritualist work. Dowding's rejection, experienced as a deep betrayal, was the catalyst for breakdown: H. D. entered a state where she could no longer differentiate between external reality and the hallucinated vision of a new war, an atom bomb exploding St Paul's Cathedral, a repetition of her old war phobia. She took refuge at the Swiss Küsnacht Klinik, a residential sanatorium, for six months. By her own account, she got better there, using what she had learned from the blameless physician.

In 1953, at the age of sixty-seven, H. D. returned to Küsnacht for an operation. During her stay, she met Erich Heydt, a doctor and existential analyst, who became a close friend and colleague and who recurs as a prominent figure, both compassionate and erotic, in her late work. It was the continuing analytic self-exploration that she engaged in with Heydt during what she called 'tea sessions' which undoubtedly brought H. D. back to Küsnacht for several long recuperative periods following physical illness during the 1950s. Indeed, the work of self-analysis marked the remainder of H. D.'s life, work that she transformed into the poetry and prose of her last years. This substantial post-war oeuvre, with its exploration of sexuality and of what it means to be woman, stands as a tribute to H. D.'s formidable poetic and recuperative powers and, in a small way, to the value of psychoanalysis and Dr Freud, for one woman at least.

Part IV

THE
QUESTION
OF
FEMININITY

14

FREUD'S FEMININITY: THEORETICAL INVESTIGATIONS

If you reject this idea as fantastic and regard my belief in the influence of lack of a penis on the configuration of femininity as an *idée fixe*, I am of course defenceless.

Whatever Freud's hedging of the bets, history has indeed interpreted his belief in the influence of the lack of a penis on the configuration of femininity as an *idée fixe*. And attackers of it have not been in short supply, while its defenders have not been vocal. Yet the idea has not perished, or faded away, and still lives on as the most notorious and popular version of the Freudian view of men, women and sex. How did this little idea of his, this *idée fixe* that girls become women impelled by a deeply and passionately felt envy for the penis, come to have such a grand, infamous and frankly unlikely destiny? After all, the theory of penis envy was seemingly only an afterthought, an appendage to a theory of sexuality whose fundamental tenets allowed little room and assigned little importance to the differences between the sexes.

With great theoretical astuteness and cunning, Freud had for thirty years managed to make the differences between men and women irrelevant to the psychoanalytical theory of sexuality. However, as he followed his path from the theory of hysteria of the 1890s – when he discovered sexual trauma as the hidden causes of his female patients' neurotic miseries – via the bold theory of infantile sexuality of 1905, the cornerstone of all later psychoanalytic theory, through the revisions of 1914 and 1915 made necessary by the introduction of narcissism and libido theory, he was accumulating a series of hypotheses and insights, findings and prejudices, which would make it imperative for him to confront the question of sexual difference.

It was not only the inner logic of Freud's own theoretical development that was to make it urgent to address the question. His followers, prominent amongst them the younger women analysts, were also in the late 1910s and early 1920s pressing the theory towards this problem of sexual difference. And when Freud published his three seminal papers in 1923–5, those other younger analysts would also publish papers on the topic, sometimes in counterpoint to his, sometimes in disagreement. The first psychoanalytic

debate on female sexuality had already begun; it was to be the first psychoanalytic debate in which Freud's own theories were to be seen as only one
wing, and an extreme wing at that, of admissible psychoanalytic views. That
debate in part tailed off into unresolved silence; in part it was mothballed by
the more pressing exigencies of emigration and war. Then came a second
debate opened by a series of scathing critiques of Freud and psychoanalysis
mounted by the new feminists of the late 1960s and early 1970s; it was
joined by Freud's defenders – of varying degrees of orthodoxy. From them,
psychoanalytic feminism emerged. In the course of the twenty years from the
late 1960s to the late 1980s, Freud was transformed from being the chief
ideological opponent of feminism into its patron saint.

The Making of a Theory

When Freud returned to Vienna from Paris in 1886, he was the embodiment
of the enlightened and progressive medical views of Charcot: 'I regarded the
linking of hysteria with the topic of sexuality as a sort of insult – just as the
women patients themselves do.' Freud combated the view that hysteria was
causally linked with anatomical changes in the female genitals. But within two
years, he had come to recognize that 'conditions related *functionally* to sexual
life play a great part in the aetiology of hysteria (as of all neuroses), and they
do so on account of the high psychical significance of this function especially
in the female sex.' As his researches unfolded in the 1890s, Freud discovered
the pathogenic significance of factors of sexual life, both in the actual neuroses
(neurasthenia and anxiety neuroses) and in the psychoneuroses (obsessional
neurosis and hysteria). In the former, he drew the portrait of the cloistered
virginal bride whose sexuality is brutally awakened by her husband, who then,
either for reasons of his own impotence, or because of the contraceptive
measures the couple are forced to adopt, fails to satisfy her and instead lays
the foundation for her anxiety neurosis and her permanent frigidity. The
neuroses these women brought to Freud very much conformed to Breuer's
dictum that 'the great majority of severe neuroses in women have their origin
in the marriage bed.'

These women were the symptoms of their husbands' neuroses; they were
the most visible, yet silenced and most easily discountable victims of the
sexual gloom of the period. Freud's descriptions of their lives constitute a
tableau vivant of the figures of sexual doom harrying everyone: of rampant
venereal diseases, producing the same symptomatology as hysteria; of coitus
interruptus, threatening every marriage; of masturbation, reducing potency and
causing neurasthenia; of fathers and brothers seducing the maids within households and the women workers without. Marriage, for these women, is the focus
of all economic and idealistic desires. And for Freud marriage is also the
prism which reveals all the desires that are refracted through it to be illusory.

In the psychoneuroses, scenes of seduction functioned as the sexual core
of his patients' secret lives. The neurotic woman now is the principal witness
to the social arrangements of hypocrisy, secrecy and sacrifice in which these

scenes flourish. And she is exemplary of the failings of all: 'In matters of sexuality we are, all of us, the healthy as much as the sick, hypocrites nowadays.' Two figures of the hysteric emerge: the sacrificed young woman who cares for others (Bertha Pappenheim, Fräulein Elisabeth von R.) and the rebellious young woman, simultaneously scapegoat and embodiment of the prevailing moral turpitudes (Fanny Moser, Fräulein Elisabeth von R., Ida Bauer). Freud's theory of neurosis arising from a conflict brings these two types of women together as two sides of the same coin. The hysteric suffers from those rebellious, sexual desires that she repudiates: they are incompatible with her higher moral ideals.

This is the portrait of the hysteric which emerges from the *Studies on Hysteria*: the woman who is gifted, ambitious, of high moral seriousness, caring and humble, often highly educated and a sincere lover of truth, yet is also independent in spirit beyond the feminine ideal, obstinate, pugnacious, and harbouring unacknowledged and forceful sexual desires. To account for both major psychoneuroses with the one specific causal factor, sexual seduction in childhood, Freud distinguished between unpleasurable pre-pubertal sexual experiences – 'that is, of a passive nature'– leading to hysteria, and those accompanied by pleasure (either an active experience in boys or a passive one in girls), which lead to obsessional neurosis. 'The natural sexual passivity of women explains their being more inclined to hysteria.' The scene is already set for a sexual division of labour amongst the neuroses: men are more prone to the symptoms of guilt, of self-reproach, of scrupulous conscientiousness and compulsively frightening thoughts; women are more prone to fright, to flight in repugnance at the emergence of a desire-laden memory, to reacting with shame and disgust at their own mental products. Despite these early attempts, Freud did not pursue very vigorously the link between, on the one hand, the 'natural sexual passivity of women' and the presumed 'activity' of men, and, on the other, the causal sequences by which different neurotic symptoms are to be explained when traced back into the prehistoric past. His attention turned more, as we saw in Chapter 3, to the details of the perverse scenes his patients remembered for him. He began to draw distinctions within the sexual material these scenes presented, concluding that 'hysteria is not repudiated sexuality but rather *repudiated perversion*'. And he began to define what constituted perversion: the use of the sexual zones abandoned since childhood – the anus, the mouth, the throat – whose later stimulation in memory leads to the unpleasure from which consciousness turns away in disgust. These abandoned, *non-genital* sexual zones were to become the foundations of Freud's theory of sexuality, the sources of the component drives of infantile sexuality. By focusing on how what was once pleasurable in childhood becomes the source of disgust and the occasion for repression, Freud finally decided to give up 'the idea of explaining libido as the masculine factor and repression as the feminine one' (an idea which, despite himself, continued to intrigue him, so that he repeatedly rehearsed arguments for rejecting it).

Freud had transformed his view in gradual stages. First, he had considered that a pre-pubertal sexual experience was sufficient to generate neurosis. Next, he considered that only perverse sexuality was noxious. Now he explained that perversity meant sexuality attached to erogenous zones active in childhood but abandoned by adults. This account allowed little difference between the sexes, and Freud recognized this fact without being disconcerted by it. In a November 1897 letter to Fliess, he stated for the first time a thesis which was to remain canonical for all his later psychoanalytic theories:

the main distinction between the sexes emerges at the time of puberty, when girls are seized by a *nonneurotic sexual* repugnance and males by libido. For at that period a further sexual zone is (wholly or in part) extinguished in females which persists in males. I am thinking of the male genital zone, the region of the clitoris, in which during childhood sexual sensitivity is shown to be concentrated in girls as well. Hence the flood of shame which the female shows at that period – until the new, vaginal zone is awakened, spontaneously or by reflex action.

The model was now established for later psychoanalytic explanations. Neuroses stemmed from regressions to fixations of abandoned erogenous zones, whose primary characteristic was that they were non-genital: the anus and the mouth were non-gender specific, and yet were the chief source for repellent sexual ideas defended against later. If what counted for later development took place in childhood, before puberty, then one would not expect the sexual lives of adult males and females to differ in any significant respect. There is one 'but' here: in girls, there is one more zone whose excitability will, like the anus and the mouth, be extinguished later (the male clitoris); and there will later be added one more zone which has no precedent in childhood and has no precedent in the male, who persists in his childhood genital activities: the vagina. Yet, given his views on the infantile determination of neurosis, this shift from the traditional clitoris to the novel vagina in puberty is of secondary significance for the future sexual life and pathology of the girl; the shift takes place at puberty or after, whereas the dice have already been thrown long before, in childhood; they were thrown amidst the abandoned prehistoric erotics of non-genital sexual play.

The sexual theory Freud developed in these fertile years at the end of the 1890s was very much addressed to his friend Wilhelm Fliess; there was one essential component of it which was borrowed from him – the notion of bisexuality. Originally, Freud followed Fliess in conceiving of bisexuality as being due to two different chemical substances, somewhat like hormones, or perhaps to being due to the effects of the two fundamental biological rhythms Fliess had discovered: the twenty-three-day male and the twenty-eight-day female cycles. Freud was immensely attracted by the grand idea linked to this, namely that conflict between the masculine and the feminine principles in each individual was the primary cause of repression, both in Fliess's version and in Alfred Adler's later concept of masculine protest (neurosis is a protest of the feminine against the masculine; it is a striving on the part of the feminine to become masculine). Yet Freud's theory of infantile sexuality was in part an *alternative* to this vision which sees an eternal struggle between the masculine and the feminine principles in every individual as being the primary cause of repression. Infantile sexuality was a theory of the essential *poly-* or *plurisexuality* of human beings. The conflict Freud called repression did not necessarily have to be organized along the lines drawn by a biochemical or mathematico-biological conception of bisexuality; it could take place between the various components of that plurisexuality.

Bisexuality was, from 1896 on, a permanent member of Freud's fundamental concepts; but it led a kind of shadow existence for many years, being introduced into his *Three Essays on the Theory of Sexuality* only to be repudiated because its biological connotations made it less than helpful in understanding the love felt for a person of the same sex. By then, Freud's more fundamental concepts of the sexual object and the sexual aim, and the looseness of the bond that unites them in the sexual act, had far greater power for the understanding of sexuality. The most intriguing long-term effect of Freud's continued espousal of the concept of bisexuality was that it allowed him perpetually to *postpone* answering the question: what do the terms masculine and feminine really mean? In this sense, it functioned like the principle of wave/particle duality of matter, allowing the theorist to tack between a variety of analytic methods without any sense of bad faith at this refusal to answer either/or questions. Recognizing 'every sexual act as a process in which four individuals are involved', and that both men and women are mixtures of the masculine and feminine principles is a liberation from the necessity of deciding what a man is, what a woman is. So the ever available recourse to bisexuality explains much about Freud's long-held indifference to the question: what is femininity? Freud's theory became a faithful replica of the bisexual fantasies and gestures of the hysteric he described in 1908, embodying both a masculine sexual fantasy and a feminine sexual fantasy, 'simultaneously playing both parts', constantly switching his associations, as though to an adjoining track, into the field of the contrary meaning.

It is the child who is the leading actor in the *Three Essays* of 1905. The first of the three essays discusses the sexual aberrations, involving deviations of either sexual object ('the person from whom sexual attraction proceeds') or sexual aim ('the act towards which the instinct tends'). Freud's survey of deviations with regard to the object slowly and surely produces a topography of sexual behaviour which loosens the link between the sexual drive and its object, showing how the instinct and the object 'are merely soldered together': 'the sexual instinct is in the first instance independent of its object; nor is its origin likely to be due to its object's attractions.' His account of the deviations with respect to aim reveals how sexual satisfaction is always a precarious achievement, which 'has to struggle against certain mental forces which act as resistances, of which shame and disgust are the most prominent.' The very terms which Freud employs in his dissection of sexual perversity oblige the reader to recognize the proximity of sexual activities to those which produce disgust and loathing:

the kiss ... between the mucous membrane of the lips of the two people concerned, is held in high sexual esteem among many nations ..., in spite of the fact that the parts of the body involved do not form part of the sexual apparatus but constitute the entrance to the digestive tract.

In this description of the culturally favoured kiss, Freud evokes the sensations more usually associated with vomiting, all so that he can convince the reader to confront as if for the first time the true enormity, the utter perversity, of the act. At such times, Freud is himself identified with the sexual instinct, which 'in its strength enjoys overriding this disgust'. The deviations of aim – use of the lips and mouth, of the anus, of touching, of looking, of hair, skin and clothing, of domination by aggressive or passive impulses – demonstrate the ubiquity of variety of perversity: 'the sexual instinct itself may be no simple thing, but put together from components which have come apart again in the perversions.' Whilst still using the language of normality and perversity, Freud has entirely undermined the concept of the sexual instinct and its activity as being one unified act; he has undermined the notion that there is one 'natural' or authorized version of sexuality, which forms the standard against which all other versions can be measured: 'the exclusive sexual interest felt by men for women is also a problem that needs elucidating and is not a self-evident fact based upon an attraction that is ultimately of a chemical nature.'

The first essay concludes with demonstrating the closeness of fit between perverse sexuality and the forms of sexuality found to be active, under repression, in neurotic symptoms. Here, Freud advances his argument that neurosis arises from the repudiation of perverse sexuality in a more complete form: 'symptoms are formed in part at the cost of *abnormal* sexuality; *neuroses are, so to say, the negative of perversions.*' The seat of this abnormal sexuality is the collection of component instincts, each of which is linked to an erotogenic zone, an organ capable of excitation. The exemplars of these zones and instincts would always be the oral and anal orifices, and the skin.

The second essay is called 'Infantile Sexuality'. The way has been well prepared by the survey of the sexual aberrations; Freud will demonstrate that the neuroses and perversions of adult sexual life will map exactly on to the infantile sexual activities of childhood. Thumb-sucking, auto-erotic activity, the activities associated with the variety of erogenous zones: all these polymorphous perverse activities are universal in childhood, the peak of the activity of what Freud called component drives being around the age of four. Within a few years, these activities will be given up, will succumb to the rigours of toilet-training and education in manners and propriety; a period of latency sets in, to be disrupted by the second wave of sexual activity that commences with puberty.

The third essay, 'The Transformations of Puberty', depicts the emergence of the form of sexuality to which much adult life is restricted: the dominance of the newly enlarged genital zone. And now, for virtually the first time in his *Three Essays*, Freud recognizes the difference between the sexes: 'As we all know, it is not until puberty that the sharp distinction is established between the masculine and feminine characters. From that time on, this contrast has a more decisive influence than any other upon the shaping of human life.' Freud goes on to acknowledge a series of differences: the greater precocity of inhibitions (shame, disgust, pity) in girls; the more marked tendency to repression, the predominance of passive rather than active sexual aims in girls. Yet Freud is eager to belittle the significance of these differences, both in his final word on the topic, in 1932, and here in 1905:

The auto-erotic activity of the erotogenic zones is, however, the same in both sexes. ... So far as the auto-erotic and masturbatory manifestations of sexuality are concerned, we might lay it down that the sexuality of little girls is of a wholly masculine character. Indeed, if we were able to give a more definite connotation to the concepts of 'masculine' and 'feminine', it would even be possible to maintain that libido is invariably and necessarily of a masculine nature, whether it occurs in men or in women and irrespectively of whether its object is a man or a woman.

A significant part of the manifestation of the masculine libido in girls is her attachment to the clitoris:

The leading erotogenic zone in female children is located at the clitoris, and is thus homologous to the masculine genital zone of the glans penis. All my experience concerning masturbation in little girls has related to the clitoris and not to the regions of the external genitalia that are important in later sexual functioning. I am even doubtful whether a female child can be led by the influence of seduction to anything other than clitoridal masturbation. If such a thing occurs, it is quite exceptional. The spontaneous discharges of sexual excitement which occur so often precisely in little girls are expressed in spasms of the clitoris. Frequent erections of that organ make it possible for girls to form a correct judgement, even without any instruction, of the sexual manifestations of the opposite sex; they merely transfer on to boys the sensations derived from their own sexual processes.

As in 1897, Freud is in no doubt that the clitoris, like the penis in the boy, becomes very early on the centre of the sexual world. And yet he recognizes that the clitoris does not play the dominant role in the sexuality of adult women and men; a change comes about. The 'vaginal orifice' becomes the 'new leading zone'; this change of zone, specific to women, together with the wave of repression at puberty in which women 'put aside their childish masculinity, are the chief determinants of the greater proneness of woman to neurosis and especially to hysteria. These determinants, therefore, are intimately related to the essence of femininity.'

In this, Freud's first public account of the difference between the sexes, we see the weight of the underlying assumption that boys and girls have, to all important intents and ultimate purposes, the same course of development of their erogenous zones. It is only very late in the day, well into puberty, that a fundamental difference emerges. And even then, Freud recognizes that a woman whom a respectable marriage or medical science may determine to be lacking in sexual sensation may not be so at all: 'They are anaesthetic at the vaginal orifice but are by no means incapable of excitement originating in the clitoris or even in other zones.' The unease that will plague Freud's account on this point is already implicit: is the vagina a legitimate, let alone feasible, focus for sexual pleasure for the adult woman? What underpinnings can psychoanalytic theory find for the undoubtedly common inclination of adult women to engage in vaginal intercourse?

The *Three Essays* was not restricted to an account of how genital sexuality came to dominate adult life, and how the manifold failure of genital sexuality in so many people, men and women, perverts and neurotics, revealed the richer and more varied substructure of infantile sexuality. At puberty, an object for the new sexual aim has to be found; finding that object, it turns out, is always a refinding, a rediscovery of the objects that had given satisfaction in infancy and childhood. 'There are thus good reasons why a child sucking at his mother's breast has become the prototype of every relation of love.' Yet Freud, atheistic citizen of Catholic Austria, knew full well that the picture of the child satisfying itself at the mother's breast was not always taken to be, as he asserted, 'a prototype of the expression of sexual satisfaction in later life'. So he was quick to assert and underline the identity between the child's affection for its caretaker and later sexual love, clinching the argument with what he knew would be regarded as the 'sacrilegious' reflection that the mother 'herself regards [her child] with feelings that are derived from her own sexual life: she strokes him, kisses him, rocks him and quite clearly treats him as a substitute for a complete sexual object.'

To prove, then, that affectionate relations in childhood are sexual, that they are exactly the same in character as later adult sexual relations, Freud paints motherly love as a sexual perversion – the primary sexual perversion in women, he might have added. The pincer move becomes complete when he observes that 'children themselves behave from an early age as though their dependence on the people looking after them were in the nature of sexual love', since their libido is so often transformed into anxiety, just as Freud had earlier postulated occurs with sexually unsatisfied women. The sexuality flows both ways, from parent to child, and from child to parent. When the requirement of choosing an object again reawakens in puberty, the choice is first made in ideas, or fantasies, using as its model the memory of forgotten infantile tendencies, in particular the child's desires for its parents, 'which are as a rule already differentiated owing to the attraction of the opposite sex – the son being drawn towards his mother and the daughter towards her father.' Puberty requires the overcoming of these plainly incestuous fantasies, and psychoanalysis demonstrates how girls especially may retreat into an infantile, asexual version of these incestuous love relations. Here, in 1905, is Freud's version of the Oedipus complex.

The main drift of these arguments is to affirm the continuity between sexual and nonsexual love: between maternal solicitude and perverse sexual relations between mother and child; between the anxiety of unfulfilled sexual longing and the child's fear of the dark; between the affectionate fondness of girls for their aged parents and the intensely passionate sexual desires of daughters for their fathers and mothers. In the 1905 version of the Oedipus

Sigmund Freud and Anna at The Hague Congress, 1920

Sigmund Freud and Anna in Maresfield Gardens, spring 1939

Dorothy Burlingham (left) and Anna Freud in Maresfield Gardens, 1979

Eva Rosenfeld (sitting) with her daughter
Maedi and friend, c.1922

Ruth Mack Brunswick with her daughter
Mathilda, named after Freud's daughter, c.1930

Marie Bonaparte with her children, Eugénie and Peter, c.1913

Joan Riviere with her daughter Diana, c.1913

Helene Deutsch in 1936

The murder of Dr Hug-Hellmuth as imagined by the Illustrierte Kronen Zeitung, *11 September 1924*

WIENER STADT UND LANDES ARCHIVS

Caricatures from the Eighth International Psychoanalytical Congress, 1924: (clockwise from top left) Dr Hermine Hug Hellmuth, Melanie Klein, Dr Karen Horney and Alix Strachey

Hilda Doolittle – H. D. – by Man Ray

complex, there is no hostility paired with and restraining the incestuous attachment of children and adolescents, yet Freud made quite explicit that the process of desexualising the incestuous choices, of desexualising the erogenous zones of childhood, was a complex, fragile and by no means natural process. The overriding tone of the *Three Essays* is the establishing of the *continuity* between adult and childhood sexuality, to the enrichment of both. Adult sexuality can only be understood in its full diversity if seemingly non-sexual or perverse activities are given back, via their universal occurrence in childhood, their rightful place in the natural history of sexuality. And infantile sexuality can only be understood rightly if its passions and jealousies are seen to be as wholeheartedly carnal as those of adulthood.

As we have seen, the figure of the sexual mother is crucial here. The child's sexual desires for her are met at least half-way by her desire for it. The most explicit description comes from Freud's study of Leonardo da Vinci, written in 1910:

A mother's love for the infant she suckles and cares for is something far more profound than her later affection for the growing child. It is in the nature of a completely satisfying love-relation, which not only fulfils every mental wish but also every physical need; and if it represents one of the forms of attainable human happiness, that is in no little measure due to the possibility it offers of satisfying, without reproach, wishful impulses which have long been repressed and which must be called perverse. In the happiest young marriage the father is aware that the baby, especially if he is a baby son, has become his rival, and this is the starting-point of an antagonism towards the favourite which is deeply rooted in the unconscious.

The portrait of the mother in writings of this period is not fundamentally different when we turn from the boy's to the girl's relationship to her. Whereas the infant boy can take full possession of the plenitude offered by the mother's sexual openness to him, the girl must also confront the sexually active mother – but now in the negative form, of rival and hindrance:

Occasions for conflict between a daughter and her mother arise when the daughter begins to grow up and long for sexual liberty, but finds herself under her mother's tutelage; while the mother, on the other hand, is warned by her daughter's growth that the time has come when she herself must abandon her claims to sexual satisfaction.

The figure of the sexually active mother – either subject, object or rival – is the dominating image. Freud does not even feel it necessary to complement this image with that of the sexually active father, which he takes as a given; the rapacious sexual tyranny of the father was to become the cornerstone of his speculative anthropological essay, *Totem and Taboo*: 'a violent and jealous father who keeps all the females for himself', not unlike the sexually megalomaniacal Freud, who, in 1895, dreamed of having all the women, daughters and patients alike.

So the sexual theory Freud was proposing in the first decade of the twentieth century did not distinguish between the development of boys and girls. Both were akin to adults in the depth and sexuality of their passions; both had richer and more diverse non-genital sexual lives than adults; both were, in reality in infancy, and later in revived fantasies of puberty, deeply involved with the sexual mothers and fathers of childhood. Even when sexual difference began to assert itself, in puberty, there was a seemingly natural symmetry in their incestuous fantasies, the boy taking his mother as sexual object, the girl her father.

Yet Freud had already proposed that the fact of heterosexual attraction was a *problem* to be *explained* – as much of a problem as any other stable fixation in erotic life, such as homosexuality. The *Three Essays* undermined the very notion of a unified model of human sexuality, in the process detaching sexuality from reproduction. Freud now showed how the mystery of reproduction was the first human mystery, the first problem small children confronted: the riddle of the Sphinx. There is no instinctual knowledge of the mystery of sexual reproduction – and this was continually to prove a stumbling-block in the later psychoanalytic debates, as theorist after theorist seemed to forget this fundamental datum of psychoanalysis, incredulous that children might not know something as fundamental as the facts of life. The answers children find in childhood pave the way to further diversity, in line with their own sexual activities, and children are not preordained to discover the biology of human reproduction as the norm to which their sexualities will eventually be subjected. To start with, they do not organize the world into two sexes; the implication of Freud's writing here, as later, is that to understand sexuality we are obliged to follow their lead – we should recognize our seemingly spontaneous belief in the all-importance of the division between the sexes as a prejudice, not unlike the sexual theories of children, perhaps just the adult version of one of those theories:

If we could divest ourselves of our corporeal existence, and could view the things of this earth with a fresh eye as purely thinking beings, from another planet for instance, nothing perhaps would strike our attention more forcibly than the fact of the existence of two sexes among human beings, who, though so much alike in other respects, yet mark the difference between them with such obvious external signs. But it does not seem that children choose this fundamental fact in the same way as the starting-point of their researches into sexual problems.

Children – and by implication the unconscious – neglect the difference between the sexes; their first sexual theory 'consists in *attributing to everyone, including females, the possession of a penis*'. The boy in particular cannot imagine a person like himself without this essential constituent and little girls 'fully share their brother's opinion of it. They develop a great interest in that part of the boy's body. But this interest promptly falls under the sway of envy. They feel themselves unfairly treated.' So Freud's investigations of the childish imagination led him to what would become crucial theoretical terms in his later accounts: the fear of loss for the boy and the envy of difference for the girl. They come together as one package, in the period in childhood before the vagina is discovered, when children cannot imagine more than one genital: the castration complex.

Alongside the repudiation of the absence of the penis are other theories: babies are born through the anus, like a piece of excrement. Asserting the universal significance of the penis, children also 'refuse to grant women the painful prerogative of giving birth to children'; anyone can give birth, just as anyone can excrete. And when children catch wind of parental sexual intercourse, they invariably interpret it as being a sadistic act and, precisely because of this interpretation, fail to perceive it as the missing link solving the problem of the origin of babies. Frequently other candidates for what parents do together are put forward: urinating together, showing their behinds, inserting something into the navel.

In an important sense, in the unconscious, no one ever solves the mystery of the origin of babies – it remains the riddle of the Sphinx. The diversity of component drives, of infantile sexual aims and objects, are matched by the diversity of imagination expressed in the sexual theories of children. When children grow up, they often restrict their sexual activities, centring them on the genitals; when they grow up, they give up their sexual theories and centre their sexual imaginings around a new sexual theory, a starkly dualistic one they subsequently construct: that concerning the essential natures of men and women. They imagine a uniquely privileged version of the sexual act, modelling it on what Freud was to call the primal scene – the scene of parental sexual intercourse – and they imagine themselves in the scene, destined to play one or other of the parts. They imagine for themselves the sexual division of labour as their new adult version of the sexual theory of childhood – the only one that, in its impoverished simplicity, remains to them.

The concept that developed most directly out of the work on the sexual theories of children was the Oedipus complex. In childhood, sexual theories express the diversity of erotic life and the diversity of individual expressions of it; somewhat later, as the child struggles to achieve independence of the parents, it constructs family romances, stories of replacement parents, of its mother's secret affairs and lofty family connections, more in conformity with the child's erotic wishes – and also a way of settling accounts with the mother who betrayed the son with the father; in adulthood, these theories and romances are the scripts for the dramas played out in real life – or that part of life studied in the psychology of love. In three essays – devoted in turn to the woman who must be saved from her promiscuity, to the universal requirement to solve the conflict between the idealization of the loved object and its essential debasement in sensual satisfactions, and finally to the cultural significance of virginity – Freud continued his exploration of the fantasies surrounding the sexual mother. The fragile and puzzling restrictions that adults place on their erotic lives are the continuations of the failures and disappointments of infantile sexual life, of the 'fixation of tender feelings on the mother'. The influence of the mother in the mental life of boys and men is expressed, on the one hand, in the overvaluation of the loved object masculine love is prone to, and on the other, in the condition that the loved women be debased, attached to another man and rescuable. In rescuing her from another man – in raising her from being the debased, fascinating whore to being once again the idealized, untouchable mother – the male lover reverses the bitter defeat he once suffered when his mother was repeatedly unfaithful to him with his father. He also proves himself not forever indebted to his parents for his life, but instead asserts that he alone is the all-powerful giver of life. The two women in the story – the mother and whore, the idealized and the debased – demonstrate the fragile potency of men, who fail to unify in later life the sensual and affectionate currents that once belonged to the love for the mother, before her treachery, before the boy's bitter disappointment. In the second of the papers, Freud reflected:

It sounds not only disagreeable but also paradoxical, yet it must nevertheless be said that anyone who is to be really free and happy in love must have surmounted his respect for women and have come to terms with the idea of incest with his mother or sister. Anyone who subjects himself to a serious self-examination on the subject of this requirement will be sure to find that he regards the sexual act basically as something degrading, which defiles and pollutes not only the body. The origin of this low opinion, which he will certainly not willingly acknowledge, must be looked for in the period of his youth in which the sensual current in him was already strongly developed but its satisfaction with an object outside the family was almost as completely prohibited as it was with an incestuous one.

The debasement of the object is necessary, in the sense that one must commit incest in one's heart if one is to be able to love another woman freely. The restrictions from which women suffer in 'our civilized world' have no less significant effects:

In the case of women there is little sign of a need to debase their sexual object. This is no doubt connected with the absence in them as a rule of anything similar to the sexual overvaluation found in men. But their long holding back from sexuality and the lingering of their sensuality in phantasy has another important consequence for them. They are subsequently often unable to undo the connection between sensual activity and the prohibition, and prove to be psychically impotent, that is, frigid, when such activity is at last allowed them. This is the origin of the endeavour made by many women to keep even legitimate relations secret for a while; and of the capacity of other women for normal sensation as soon as the condition of prohibition is re-established by a secret love affair; unfaithful to their husband, they are able to keep a second order of faith with their lover. The condition of forbiddenness in the erotic life of women is, I think, comparable to the need on the part of men to debase their sexual object.

Freud sketches the portraits of the man who can only be potent with a debased woman and of the woman who can only free herself from frigidity in the forbiddenness of secrecy – a characteristic that could be linked to women's 'age-old foible of orgasmic pretence', since what better demonstration of secrecy could there be than the deceiving of one's own sexual partner? Such impoverished and restricted sexualities are the consequences of the unresolved component parts of the Oedipus complex. It was precisely at this time, in the period 1909–12, that Freud began to assert that the Oedipus complex was the core complex of the neuroses, to which all other pathological formations would eventually be traced. The various figures Freud had depicted – the sexual mother, the phallic mother and the menace of castration, the anal theory of birth, the family romance – were all to be articulated into one central drama: the passionate love of the child for the parent of the opposite sex, a love which is doomed to disappointment because of hostile rivalry with the parent of the same sex. The growing centrality of the Oedipus complex represented the development of the account of the child's sexual relations to its objects, rather than to its aims. Whereas Freud had previously emphasized the arbitrariness of the subject's relations to its objects, the Oedipus complex began to represent a normative account of the necessary sequence of the child's objects if it is to enter adulthood relatively free of pathological residues from its polymorphous prehistory. As Juliet Mitchell argues, its original formulation as the desire for the parent of opposite sex 'acted as a conservative "stopper" when it came to understanding the difference between the sexes'; it became 'a notion of a natural and normative heterosexual attraction', whereas everything else in the theory of infantile sexuality ran counter to the normative sexual symmetry and complementarity of the early conception of the Oedipus complex. However, just as the Oedipus complex began to prescribe the restricted range of objects to be expected in the infancy of all subjects, Freud conducted a revolution in the very concept of the object itself.

The revolution went under the name of narcissism. The impetus to this revolution came initially from two directions, around 1910. Firstly, from the study of homosexuals, who 'take *themselves* as their sexual object. That is to say, they proceed from a narcissistic basis and look for a young man who resembles themselves and whom *they* may love as their mother loved *them*.' Secondly, partly under the stimulus of Jung's study of the psychoses and of Schreber's *Memoirs*, Freud posited a stage in development short of object-love, in which the subject takes himself as his love-object; the noisy symptoms of psychosis often represent the catastrophic consequences of a regression to this stage – in returning to the safety of love of the self, the psychotic has given up the world, often despairing of ever recovering it.

In 1914, Freud finally wrote his paper on narcissism. There he distinguished two types of love: anaclitic, or 'leaning upon', where the subject loves the person who tends to him, or protects him; and narcissistic, in which the person loves an object on the model of his love of himself. He may love, narcissistically, either what he himself is, what he himself was, what he himself would like to be, or someone who was once part of himself. With this new model of love as primarily the love of oneself, new figures of love relationship emerge. Not only the homosexual, who attempts to save the perfect love of the sexually overwhelming mother by loving young males the way she once loved him. But also, a new and more womanly model of love to set alongside the romantic one of self-sacrificing, overvaluing love to which men were so prone, and which guaranteed their eventual marriages to the temporarily overvalued woman, despite her only being a pale reflection of the mother. Before he described this model in print, he had met her in person, in Lou Andreas-Salomé – the figure of the narcissistic woman:

Women, especially if they grow up with good looks, develop a certain self-contentment which compensates them for the social restrictions that are imposed upon them in their choice of object. Strictly speaking, it is themselves that such women love with an intensity comparable to that of the man's love for them. Nor does their need lie in the direction of loving, but of being loved; and the man who fulfils this condition is the one who finds favour with them. The importance of this type of woman for the erotic life of mankind is to be rated very high. Such women have the greatest fascination for men, not only for aesthetic reasons, since as a rule they are the most beautiful, but also because of a combination of interesting psychological factors. For it seems very evident that another person's narcissism has a great attraction for those who have renounced part of their own narcissism and are in search of object-love. The charm of a child lies to a great extent in his narcissism, his self-contentment and inaccessibility, just as does the charm of certain animals which seem not to concern themselves about us, such as cats and the large beasts of prey. ... It is as if we envied them for maintaining a blissful state of mind – an unassailable libidinal position which we ourselves have since abandoned. The great charm of narcissistic women has, however, its reverse side; a large part of the lover's dissatisfaction, of his doubts of the woman's love, of his complaints of her enigmatic nature, has its root in this incongruity between the types of object-choice.

The contrast between men and women is no longer between the overvaluing – and therefore debasing – man and the transgressive, secretive woman. Now it is the woman who makes no secret of her love – for herself. And it is the man whose fascinated love amounts to an envy for a state he has given up. The man now loves this sort of woman in the way a parent loves its child: 'Parental love, which is so moving and at bottom so childish, is nothing but the parents' narcissism born again, which, transformed into object-love, unmistakably reveals its former nature.' The portrait of human love is transformed. Everyone now searches for the ideal and perfect being they once were, or wished to be, finding echoes of it in others; everyone seeks once again the haven of narcissism, the garden from which they were expelled. Instead of the sexual mother providing the prototype for all later object relations, it is the love of the self that takes over from the sexual mother the image of plenitude. And the narcissistic woman becomes the inheritor, in Freud's writings, of the sexual mother's fullness of being in the world.

Yet with the concept of narcissism as a new origin for human love relations – an origin that, throughout Freud's paper on narcissism, threatens to take over and subordinate the other, anaclitic way of loving – the problem of entry into the world of objects is posed in a new and pressing way. Why should the human subject ever leave the blissful state of narcissistic love? How is he or she driven out of this Eden? How does one ever come to love an object beyond one's own self? The masculine model Freud had previously used can still be usefully invoked. The man loves not only himself, but also 'the woman who nurses him', and simply transfers his narcissism to that object; hence the 'sexual overvaluation' that the now impoverished ego accords to the privileged love-object. Here, however, the argument is shaky; why should the male give up his narcissism in favour of the object, especially since Freud quite rightly regards this male model of love as akin to a neurotic compulsion, and had already demonstrated its genealogy more satisfactorily in the lack of resolution of the Oedipus complex than through this gratuitous ceding of narcissistic plenitude to the object? There is something altogether more plausible in the account of the narcissistic woman's path to object-love:

Even for narcissistic women, whose attitude toward men remains cool, there is a road which leads to complete object-love. In the child which they bear, a part of their own body confronts them like an extraneous object, to which, starting out from their narcissism, they can then give complete object-love. There are other women, again, who do not have to wait for a child in order to take the step in development from (secondary) narcissism to object-love. Before puberty they feel masculine and develop some way along masculine lines; after this trend has been cut short on their reaching female maturity, they still retain the capacity of longing for a masculine ideal – an ideal which is in fact a survival of the boyish nature they themselves once possessed.

This self-sufficient woman is poised, as narcissism allows one to be, half-way between the passivity of being loved and the activity of loving (after all, she is active in her own love of herself and her body) – in the reflexive, middle voice of object choice. But she is wrenched out of this state of equilibrium by a ruse of nature, which 'consists in leading the woman toward object love in spite of her narcissism, even by means of this very narcissism': she ends up loving the baby as she once loved herself, just as the man loves the woman as he once loved himself. Yet the explanation works better for the woman precisely because the precious 'part of the body' makes the sacrifice of narcissism for the object more plausible. The love of man for woman is more easily modelled on the narcissistic love of a woman for her child, or of what she once wished to be, than vice versa.

This is, in fact, the model that Freud will follow for both sexes in his later work. The bridge from narcissism to the object will for boys and girls be found in a 'part of their own body' which 'confronts them like an extraneous object'. For the male, this object is the penis. For the female, this object will be the penis she comes to recognize she does not have; it will be supplemented with a series of symbolic equivalences that Freud elaborated on in papers following 'On Narcissism': penis = faeces = gift = baby. The name Freud will give to this route that both sexes take out of the narcissistic world will be one he knew already: the castration complex. The castration complex will come to mean that the subject is expelled from the narcissistic world precisely in order to preserve or acquire what comes to symbolize narcissism: the penis.

Yet alongside the revolution of narcissism, Freud's growing conviction of the centrality of the Oedipus complex resulted in an investigation of childhood sexual fantasies which had important consequences for his theories of femininity. In 'A Child Is Being Beaten' (1919), he showed that even sexual aberrations, previously associated with autonomous component drives, were also precipitates of the Oedipus complex. Patients with such beating fantasies regressively reworked pleasurable but guilt-inducing incestuous love of the father into a masochistic but guilt-free form. The enquiry into masochism continued in 'The Economic Problem of Masochism' (1924), in which Freud for the first time postulated a primary masochism: a portion of the destructive instinct, or instinct for mastery, fails to be diverted outside the organism as object-libido, but is retained within, in a pure sexual form. On top of this primary masochism is built feminine masochism, whose fantasies 'place the subject in a characteristically female situation; they signify, that is, being castrated, or copulated with, or giving birth to a baby.'

This phrase demonstrates how developments in Freud's theories were intersecting more and more with the view of femininity he was working his way towards, which he set out in three papers in 1923–5: 'The Infantile Genital Organization', 'The Dissolution of the Oedipus Complex' and 'Some Psychical Consequences of the Anatomical Distinction between the Sexes'. He maintained these ideas, with one fundamental change, in his expositions of 1931 ('Female Sexuality') and 1932 ('Femininity'). Indeed, his starting-point had remained remarkably stable since 1897: the view that in childhood female genital activity centres on the clitoris, and is fundamentally the same as the boy's penile masturbatory activities. The distinctiveness of females emerged in puberty, with a specific and severe wave of repression, in part required by social mores and the restrictive education of young women, in part inherited from his early neo-Fliessian views that repression is aimed more at 'feminine' wishes than masculine ones. Freud now transposed this specific wave of repression from puberty to childhood. This earlier dating was to have momentous consequences for his theory of femininity. It was occasioned by his changing account of the development of boys' sexuality. He now saw the Oedipus complex in boys not only as the model for all later object-love, but also as the crisis of narcissism. What brings about the destruction of the phallic-genital organization in which the Oedipus complex is now embedded is the threat of castration: the boy gives up his libidinal wishes to save his narcissism – his penis. This account of libido being sacrificed to save narcissism was soon to be reapplied to the girl: she gives up her masculine sexual drives and retreats, when possible, to the haven of passive narcissism. The Oedipus complex is then shattered, dissolved, by being transformed into the parental agency within the psyche that regulates the subject's sexual and aggressive wishes: the super-ego. This takes place just when the pre-genital sexual impulses are being organized under the primacy of the genital organs: the phallic phase. It is the active phallic masturbatory sexuality directed towards the mother that is destroyed and transformed into the super-ego; the boy's realization that the alternative trend – the passive libidinal wishes directed towards the father – would also involve the loss of the penis, reinforces his decision to turn away from the Oedipus complex.

In 1923 Freud postulated that this additional phase of pre-genital sexuality, the phallic phase, occurs in boys and girls, and that it is to all intents and purposes a complete version of later adult sexuality. He had for a long time – since 1908 at least – been convinced that neither boys nor girls know of the existence of the vagina; for both sexes, genital masturbation means active phallic (clitoridal) sexuality and both sexes do not recognize the existence of women. The mother is phallic, and the opposition that corresponds to masculine and feminine is that between phallic and castrated, just as the preceding anal-sadistic phase, with its characteristic object, the stool, only recognizes the opposition active-passive.

Yet Freud found himself increasingly perplexed by the little girl's development. Since the fear of castration could not be the motive for the destruction of her phallic phase activity – she recognized that she was already castrated, whereas the little boy feared its occurrence – he fell back on those external, social factors, which, in truth, he had always accepted as bearing down on the girl so hard: 'these changes seem to be the result of upbringing and of intimidation from outside which threatens her with a loss of love.' The vulnerability of the little girl to the loss of love is, as we have seen, the feminine version of narcissism, in counterpoint to the masculine version (fear of the loss of the penis). He concluded:

The girl's Oedipus complex is much simpler than that of the small bearer of the penis; in my experience, it seldom goes beyond the taking of her mother's place and the adopting of a feminine attitude towards her father. Her Oedipus complex culminates in a desire, which is long retained, to receive a baby from her father as a gift – to bear him a child. One has an impression that the Oedipus complex is then gradually given up because this wish [for a baby from her father] is never fulfilled.

With these papers describing the phallic phase and the dissolution of the Oedipus complex, Freud was centring the drama of the child's development in the *final* period of infantile sexuality, before the latency period set in following the catastrophic downfall of the Oedipus complex. He was acutely aware that other analysts proposed different accounts of the castration complex, and rebutted them in notes and references as he went along. Lou Andreas-Salomé had proposed the loss of the stool as the model for the loss of the penis; earlier, in 1910, A. Stärcke had proposed that the original exemplum of castration is weaning, in the loss of the nipple from the baby's mouth; now in 1924, Otto Rank was proposing that the original castration, the original expulsion from Eden, was the act of birth itself. So Freud's assertion of the centrality of the phallic stage, the Oedipus complex and the castration complex for the organization of the child's later internal psychic economy was a way of asserting that, despite the determining role of infantile sexuality, the almost exclusively genital sexuality which dominates the impoverished imaginations of adults would still remain the battleground on which an account of the neuroses, and of masculinity and femininity, would be given.

Freud's difficulties were considerable, as his uneasy discussion of castration anxiety in *Inhibitions, Symptoms and Anxiety* of 1926 was to show:

there is no danger of our regarding castration anxiety as the sole motive force of the defensive processes which lead to neurosis. I have shown elsewhere how little girls, in the course of their development, are led into making a tender object-cathexis by their castration complex. It is precisely in women that the danger-situation of loss of object seems to have remained the most effective. All we need to do is to make a slight modification in our description of their determinant of anxiety, in the sense that *it is no longer a matter of feeling the want of, or actually losing the object itself, but of losing the object's love* [emphasis added].

Is it the loss of the object itself – the penis, for example, though it might also be the nipple – or is what is feared the loss of what the object symbolizes? Freud's account of the centrality of the castration complex seemed to make it clear that the penis was more than just another element in the series of separable objects, beginning with birth (baby separating from mother), passing via nipple separating from mouth and the stool separating from the anus – the partial objects, as Abraham had christened them. Yet what precisely specified the privileged character of the penis, if the more fundamental fear was that of 'losing the object's love'? His theory lacked a decisive means for answering that question. But he was clear that if one interpreted castration as a concept not restricted to the loss of the penis, then the theory would no longer explain the differences between the sexes – it might explain something else, but certainly not that.

It was at this point that Freud struck an entirely new note in his consideration of the psychology of women, thus allowing him to recognize how evasive he had been on this issue: 'we have been in the habit of taking as the subject of our investigations the male child, the little boy. With little girls, we have supposed, things must be similar, though in some way or other they must nevertheless be different.' Quite: similar ... but different. Here was Freud's old problem, now reformulated and newly confessed to. Freud thought that he now had a new approach to the question:

In little girls the Oedipus complex raises one problem more than in boys. In both cases the mother is the original object; and there is no cause for surprise that boys retain that object in the Oedipus complex. But how does it happen that girls abandon it and instead take their father as an object?

This is certainly a new starting-point, but what Freud went on to say in this 1925 paper was not in its essentials new. He immediately invokes 'certain women who cling with especial intensity and tenacity to the bond with their father and to the wish in which it culminates of having a child by him.' But this seemingly snug and conventional version of the normal Oedipus complex has a long prehistory: a prehistory of the momentous discovery by the girl of the boy's larger organ, her castration and her consequent penis envy: 'she has seen it and knows that she is without it and wants to have it.' There follows a list of the various possible consequences of this desire to have a penis. The desire to become a man may persist and dominate her later life; she may even deny that she is lacking in the penis, 'and may subsequently be compelled to behave as though she were a man.' When she realizes that she is not alone in lacking a penis, she may decide to throw in her lot with the sex that is contemptuous of penis-less creatures. Or, the penis envy may be transformed into the character-trait of jealousy, which, in Freud's opinion, 'plays a far larger part in the mental life of women than of men'. And penis envy may finally turn her against her mother, who is 'almost always held responsible for her lack of a penis'. Freud was still preoccupied with the masochistic beating fantasies he had described a few years previously, perhaps still reaping this surprising fruit of his analysis of his own daughter: the jealousy expressed in the beating fantasy is an expression both of masturbation – a clitoris is being beaten – and of jealousy of the sibling more favoured than the subject, whose mother deprived her of a penis.

This turning away from the mother is mentioned, but passed over quickly. What strikes Freud more forcibly is that he might now be able to explain his conviction, the fruit of long experience, that 'masturbation is further removed from the nature of women than of men'. Recognizing that 'masturbation, at all events of the clitoris,' – and Freud never discusses any other method of masturbation – 'is a masculine activity and that the elimination of clitoridal sexuality is a necessary precondition for the development of femininity', it seems probable that what turns the girl violently against that pleasurable activity is 'her narcissistic sense of humiliation which is bound up with her penis-envy'. In this sphere, she retires in favour of boys, forced away from masculinity by her inability to compete.

For some little girls, the culminating consequence is now open: she can take up the distinctively feminine position of wishing for a child instead of the penis – 'and *with that purpose in view* she takes her father as a love-object. Her mother becomes the object of her jealousy. The girl has turned into a little woman.' That is, she has arrived at the haven of the Oedipus complex, from which, as so many analyses show, it is so difficult to prise her.

What is new in this familiar story is the picture of the girl entering the Oedipus complex *reluctantly*, turning to the father only because of her penis envy, because of her narcissistic wound. She turns to him as if to a new object, in hope and, perhaps, in hope of revenge. But there is something else that is fundamentally novel, if only implicit here: the father is the *epilogue* to the story, not its main protagonist. If he enters into it so late in the day, who is the main protagonist for all those years before the little girl in final resignation turns to him? The mother.

When Freud, in 1925, had asked how it was that little girls abandon their relations to their mothers and turn to the father, he had not answered the question so much in terms of the relation to the mother, or the details of that early relationship, but in terms of the crisis of the castration complex. The concept of penis envy still dominated the account. By 1931, Freud was ready, perhaps under the influence of the psychoanalytic debate that his papers of the mid-1920s had been a part of, to explore the importance of the figure of the pre-Oedipal mother. Indeed, he now granted her some of his most opulent rhetoric:

Our insight into this early, pre-Oedipus, phase in girls comes to us as a surprise, like the discovery, in another field, of the Minoan-Mycenean civilization behind the civilization of Greece. Everything in the sphere of this first attachment to the mother seemed to me so difficult to grasp in analysis – so grey with age and shadowy and almost impossible to revivify – that it was as if it had succumbed to an especially inexorable repression. But perhaps I had gained this impression because the women who were in analysis with me were able to cling to the very attachment to the father in which they had taken refuge from the early phase that was in question. It does indeed appear that women analysts – as, for instance, Jeanne Lampl-de Groot and Helene Deutsch – have been able to perceive these facts more easily and clearly because they were helped in dealing with those under their treatment by the transference to a suitable mother-substitute.

The 1925 paper had opened with the observation that certain women 'cling with especial intensity and tenacity to the bond with their father', and Freud eventually explained this intense bond as their haven from their bitter disappointment at not being given a penis. Now, in 'Female Sexuality' of 1931, this intense bond was evidence of an earlier relationship with the mother of equal, if not greater, intensity. The relationship to the father is not a reaction-formation, but a less malignant repetition; the love of the father is not the culmination of female development, but a pale shadow of an altogether more powerful relationship.

Freud now explores relations with men not for their own internal dynamic, but as a guide, sometimes the only guide, to the earlier relations with the mother. Relations with men simply replay the fateful twists and turns of the protracted early relationship with the mother. 'With many women we have the impression that their years of maturity are occupied by a struggle with their husband, just as their youth was spent in a struggle with their mother.' Women may spend their later lives repeating the fated relationship with the pre-Oedipal mother, but these are just so many ways of commemorating the *loss* which is at its core.

This authentically Freudian model of the destiny of later relationships arising from their being repetitions of earlier, now hidden, ones is applied with full force to the development of women. More emphatically than with the boy, the little girl's destiny is recounted in terms of primordial loss: a double loss, now, of the penis and of the mother. While Freud had maintained in the *Three Essays* that the finding of an object was always a refinding, thus installing the idea of implicit loss at the heart of all later sexual discoveries, it was only with 'Mourning and Melancholia' (1917) and *The Ego and the Id* (1923) that the accent fell primarily on the losing rather than the finding: the process of losing and giving up the object became the fundamental process by which the super-ego and the ego were built up. Objects are abandoned and the ego and its narcissism are constructed at their expense, through the incorporation or the mirroring of the object. The little girl will, throughout her life, adopt towards her id the mimicking posture of the ego Freud describes: 'Look, you can love me too – I am so like the lost object (the mother).' The woman is clearly the product of her mourning.

Just as women had presented Freud's theory of narcissism with a new question – what calamity would require a narcissistic being to turn outside to objects? – so the discovery of the pre-Oedipal mother requires Freud to ask why the little girl turns away from the mother. It is not so much the fact that she turns to the father that is now the focus of enquiry; it is the fact that she turns away at all. Behind every significant relation – to men, to her own children – Freud can now detect the mourning of the relationship to the mother. His explanations for why she gives up her mother become less and less satisfactory the more complex they become. Both in 'Female Sexuality' and the lecture on 'Femininity', Freud gives a list of reasons for this turn, some of which contradict one another, some of which are in no sense specific to the little girl: 'she failed to provide the little girl with the only proper genital, that she did not feed her sufficiently, that she compelled her to share her mother's love with others, that she never fulfilled all the girl's expectations of love, and, finally, that she first aroused her sexual activity and then forbade it.' He finds himself dissatisfied with this list; 'the real fact is that the attachment to the mother is bound to perish, precisely because it was the first and was so intense'. The little girl is condemned to this unmournable loss, one which colours all future love relations. The analogy Freud immediately invokes is a significant one, when we bear in mind how the young Freud, forty years earlier, just starting out on his own medical practice and his own marriage, painted marriage as the breeding ground of frigid and frustrated young wives – their sexual lives and their nervous systems destined to be crucified on the cross of their husbands' impotence, their repressive education and rampant social hypocrisy:

just as one can often see happen in the first marriages of young women which they have entered into when they were most passionately in love. In both situations the attitude of love comes to grief from the disappointments that are unavoidable and from the accumulation of occasions for aggression.

And yet such a reason applies to the little boy as well. Freud is forced to confess that 'unless we can find something that is specific for girls and is not present or not in the same way present in boys, we shall not have explained the termination of the attachment of girls to their mother.' Recognizing that here was a major problem for his account – which was, after all, directed primarily to the question of what distinguishes the development of girls from boys, rather than to a general psychology of differences – Freud none the less wavered on this point, seemed to forget it and then recalled it only to forget it once again. Perhaps he did not wish to countenance seriously the negative conclusion of so many years' work, that maybe there are no significant fundamental differences in the development of boys and girls. So, a year later, when he wrote 'Femininity', Freud was back on his old track again, less impressed by the doom that befalls all great loves and less suspicious of his own plethora of reasons for why the girl turns away from the mother: 'girls hold their mothers responsible for their lack of a penis and do not forgive her for their being thus put at a disadvantage.' Hence their flight to their father, from whom some girls hope for the penis in the form of a baby. 'The turning away from the mother is accompanied by hostility'; it ends in a hatred which 'may become very striking and last all through life'. She takes revenge on the mother, pledging herself to the phallic father instead.

Identification with her mother can take the place of attachment to her mother. The little daughter puts herself in her mother's place, as she had always done in her games; she tries to take her mother's place with her father, and begins to hate the mother she used to love, and from two motives: from jealousy as well as from mortification over the penis she has been denied.

Having established that the castration complex is now not only the answer to why she turns *to* the father, but is also why she turns *away* from the mother, Freud is quite ready to describe the girl's earlier relations to her mother as being as rich and varied as any other infantile relation; indeed, the description of the relations between girl and mother apply equally and without need for qualification to those between boy and mother. *There is no lack in the girl's relations with her mother.* The girl's sexual aims are active as well as passive; they occur in all registers of the libidinal phases she passes through, including both passive and active clitoral aims – being passively seduced and, on the occasion of the birth of a sibling, being the active progenitor of the new baby.

Yet when she repudiates her mother, she still inhabits the phallic world of castrated and phallic beings; she is still the little man. The question becomes: does she ever leave this world? The boy, of course, destroys the Oedipus complex precisely so as not to face the full consequences of his realization of the fact of castration. And Freud's later papers on male sexuality revolve around the seeming impossibility of the boy ever recognizing a beyond of the phallic phase. In describing the mechanism of disavowal, Freud showed how the boy may establish a permanently psychotic relation to the fact of castration: by erecting a fetish, the substitute for the mother's penis, he splits his ego. The fetish both affirms and acknowledges the absence of the penis, commemorates it, and also fills in the absence, disavowing it. The twin possibilities that Freud envisaged for the little boy's reaction to his sight of the mother's genitals – horror at the possibility of castration and contempt for the castrated sex – haunt the male ever after, infusing the idealizing and denigrating cycles by which he attempts to gain access to woman while denying her castration. It is only through denial that a man can attain a woman.

And what of the girl?

During the First World War, Freud had explored the interconnections between anal erotism and the castration complex:

We can say that the ultimate outcome of this infantile wish for a penis is in women in whom the determinants of a neurosis in later life are absent: it changes into the wish for a *man*, and thus puts up with the man as an appendage to the penis. This transformation, therefore, turns an impulse which is hostile to the female sexual function into one which is favourable to it. Such women are in this way made capable of an erotic life based on the masculine type of object-love, which can exist alongside the feminine one proper, derived from narcissism. We already know that in other cases it is only a baby that makes the transition from narcissistic self-love to object-love possible. So that in this respect too a baby can be represented by the penis. ... The importance of the process described lies in the fact that a part of the young woman's narcissistic masculinity is thus changed into femininity, and so can no longer operate in a way harmful to the female sexual function.

Here is an explicit account of how narcissism can be transformed into 'femininity', accepting the man, desiring him even, but only as an appendage to the penis. Yet renaming this end-result 'femininity' simply because the woman in question now desires a man, rather than a penis or the more primordial first gift of faeces, does not alter the underlying structure of things. This woman does not desire a man *qua* man ; she desires something else. Her sexual aim is masculine not because of the accident of wanting a man, but because it is an active aim, rather than the more passive, more equilibrated, aims of narcissism.

Similarly, in 1932, Freud shows how the woman may come to love a man because she hopes to receive a penis-baby from him, yet may focus her love on the baby when it arrives. So the marriage is not secured 'until the wife has succeeded in making her husband her child as well and in acting as a mother to him.' Yet again, the woman's first love is for her mother, and only the thin and fragile bridge of penis envy connects her to the male sex. There is very little the male sex can offer a woman. Within the phallic world that both men and women inhabit, women are neither the first nor the second sex ; they are not even the separate sex.

From the standpoint of the phallic phase, there is only one sex. The question is : is there an intelligible alternative standpoint, is there a stage beyond the phallic phase? The difficulties of later psychoanalytic theory confronted with the problem of masculinity and femininity open up here, because exploring the earlier oral or anal stages, or the complexities of the relation to the pre-Oedipal mother, cannot provide an answer. To see these problems clearly, we must retrace our steps and investigate from another starting-point why Freud arrived at this account of the differences between the sexes. We must consider what are the meanings of the terms masculinity and femininity.

One answer to the question, 'is there a beyond to the phallic phase ?', would be : Yes, it is given in the forms of knowledge made available by science. In the same way as children can eventually learn the facts of life, become enlightened and reject the anal, cloacal or sadistic sexual theories of their earlier years, so can women and men recognize in biology the essence of the difference between the sexes. It is precisely this answer that Freud refuses. Just as his study of the sexual theories of children undercuts the efficacy of sexually enlightening education – after all, the unconscious of normal and neurotic subjects alike are untouched by such enlightenment – so the truths of biology, whether the narratives of spermatozoa and ova or of penis and vagina, are not only less than enlightening but prove entirely ambiguous. On this point, common sense views of the differences between the sexes are ultimately not only more tenacious and consequential, but also more relevant.

'When you meet a human being, the first distinction you make is "male or female?" and you are accustomed to make the distinction with unhesitating certainty.' Echoing very clearly the opening of his paper on 'The Sexual Theories of Children' quoted above on page 406, Freud surprises us by pointing to the un-self-critical expectations we bring to our social world. We unhesitatingly expect the social world to be organized into clear-cut types, into males and females, as if we were convinced that the spaces devoted to excretion in public, our 'Ladies' and 'Gentlemen', those words the courteous and seductive writer Freud was so adept at employing, reflected the human essence. Psychoanalytic science, however, immediately undercuts this habitual certainty of ours, because it shows that each individual is neither wholly a man nor wholly a woman, but rather both at once. Not only that: anatomy and embryology conspire to unsettle our clear-cut distinctions, revealing the variability of secondary sexual characteristics; 'in human beings pure masculinity or femininity is not to be found either in a psychological or a biological sense.' When one turns to the sociological meaning of masculine and feminine, one is simply reduced to observing actually existing behaviour, that is, observing that those human beings who go into doors marked 'Gentlemen' must be men.

Freud had little interest in these 'conventional' or 'sociological' distinctions. More generally, he regarded studies of the differences between the sexes as both untrustworthy and inconclusive, just as in 1905 he had belittled the differences between the sexual life of the two sexes. In his lecture on 'Femininity' in 1932, Freud ran through a series of differences between little girls and boys – girls are less aggressive, defiant and self-sufficient, they have a greater need to be shown affection, are more dependent and pliant and thus more easily toilet-trained; girls are more intelligent and lively, 'they go out to meet the external world and at the same time form stronger object-cathexes.' But to Freud these differences are of no great significance: 'For our immediate purposes they can be disregarded.' That is, these differences do not have the consequences for the sexual destinies of girls and boys that the castration complex has; only something that touches the child to the core, in its sexual life, in its narcissism, can have serious consequences.

This consistent disregard for the psychology of gender difference makes all the more striking Freud's subsequently notorious conjecture about the weakness of the super-ego in women:

I cannot evade the notion (though I hesitate to give it expression) that for women the level of what is ethically normal is different from what it is in men. Their super-ego is never so inexorable, so impersonal, so independent of its emotional origins as we require it to be in men.

Freud was well aware of the storm of protest this view would elicit. In his lecture on 'Femininity', he described how the girl lacks the boy's motive (the fear of castration) for surmounting the Oedipus complex; hence 'the formation of the super-ego must suffer; it cannot attain the strength and independence which give it its cultural significance, and feminists are not pleased when we point out to them the effects of this factor upon the average feminine character.'

Freud had never been reluctant to contradict the claims of feminists. As early as November 1883, in a famous letter to Martha about J. S. Mill's *The Emancipation of Women*, which Freud had himself translated into German a few years earlier, he had vigorously critized Mill's programme for the equal rights of women, all as part of his courtship of his fiancée. In this letter, each of his general criticisms of Mill's political arguments is followed by a personal conclusion, addressed to Martha, addressed, therefore, to the woman he loved and the woman who would become the embodiment of the female virtues he was criticizing Mill for ignoring:

a main argument in the pamphlet I translated was that the married woman can earn as much as the husband. I dare say we agree that housekeeping and the care and education of children claim the whole person and practically rule out any profession; even if simplified conditions relieve the woman of housekeeping, dusting, cleaning, cooking etc. All this he simply forgot, just as he omitted all relations connected with sex. This is altogether a topic on which one does not find Mill quite human. His autobiography is so prudish or so unearthly that one would never learn from it that humanity is divided between men and women, and that this difference is the most important one. ... In all his writings it never appears that the woman is different from the man, which is not to say that she is something less, if anything the opposite. For example he finds an analogy for the oppression of women in that of the Negro. Any girl, even without a vote and legal rights, whose hand is kissed by a man willing to risk his all for her love, could have put him right on this.

It seems a completely unrealistic notion to send women into the struggle for existence in the same way as men. Am I to think of my delicate sweet girl as a competitor? After all, the encounter could only end by my telling her, as I did 17 months ago, that I love her, and that I will make every effort to get her out of the competitive role into the quiet undisturbed activity of my home. It is possible that a different education could suppress all women's delicate qualities — which are so much in need of protection and yet so powerful — with the result that they could earn their living like men. It is also possible that in this case it would not be justifiable to deplore the disappearance of the most lovely thing the world has to offer us: our ideal of womanhood. But I believe that all reforming activity, legislation and education, will founder on the fact that long before the age at which a profession can be established in our society, Nature will have appointed woman by her beauty, charm and goodness, to do something else.

No, in this respect I adhere to the old ways, to my longing for my Martha as she is, and she herself will not want it different; legislation and custom have to grant to women many rights kept from them, but the position of woman cannot be other than what it is: to be an adored sweetheart in youth, and a beloved wife in maturity.

The young Freud was intent on persuading his wife-to-be of the higher virtues of the economics and morality of the doctrine of separate spheres. The arguments are strung together somewhat uneasily: the economic arguments concerning the division of labour sit alongside a peroration about the higher moral and aesthetic virtues of the beloved woman; the morality of the family should be entirely different from that of the market. What is more, Nature will resist social reform: woman's destiny is a higher one than is possible in the hurly-burly of public life. Each of Freud's arguments rings many bells, mostly alarm bells, over a century later, when many of Mill's arguments have been endorsed in law. Freud even managed to contest Mill's use of the word 'emancipation', so resonant with the nineteenth-century political struggles in Europe and with the Civil War in the US fought over the emancipation of the slaves. Can the positions of the black and of the woman really be compared, Freud asks, when the black is despised and feared, and the woman is admired and revered?

His own later writings on the psychology of love would show that contempt and fear can be more easily combined with idealization and deference than this superficial psychology of consciousness allows. Yet there are themes in this sermon on the necessity of the doctrine of separate spheres which reappear later in psychoanalytic theory, in both more subtle and less domineering forms. The key to Freud's objection to Mill is his perception that Mill overlooks the places of both sexual pleasure and of sexual difference in human life. In his letter to Martha, Freud does not dwell at length on the importance of sexual pleasure, except by implication, when he dismisses the inhuman prudishness of Mill's account of a human life. What if, Freud implies, sexual pleasure is the highest good in life – or if human beings behave as if it were? What consequences will there be for the organization of human society? Mill refuses to address this question, he implies. And yet – as he would put it later, echoing his own reply to Mill – human beings do treat the distinction between the sexes as the most basic one, despite this distinction not being a psychologically valid one before the changes of puberty reduce sexuality down to the two socially acceptable forms of masculinity and femininity. In Freud's work there is a tension between people's beliefs about the gendered division of sexuality and the reality of infantile sexuality and its consequences in later adult neurosis and perversion. In his later work, he would himself put in question his own assumption that the distinction between men and women is the fundamental one, but only to reinforce his sense that the distinction is still regarded as fundamental in ordinary human social life.

The closest to a Mill-like liberal reformist position Freud came was over the question of the pernicious effects on the capacity for sexual fulfilment of civilized sexual morality. On the campaigning sexual issues of his day, such as divorce law reform, the legalization of homosexuality and abortion, Freud was an unambiguous liberal. In early 1907, he invited Fritz Wittels to join the Vienna Psycho-Analytical Society because of his complete agreement with Wittels's controversial pamphlet calling for the freedom of women to have abortions. He might even, during this, his most liberal period, on occasion defend, if in distinctly patronizing prose, a policy of positive discrimination: 'Woman, whom society has charged with a heavier burden (in particular in relation to reproduction), must be judged with indulgence and tolerance in those domains where they lag behind men.' Yet the underlying principles of Freud's liberalism were the opposite of the egalitarianism of Mill. Freud saw sexuality and morality, sexuality and civilization as fundamentally at odds; no law could efface the frustrations of sexual life, since the law would always be at odds with its enemy, the demand for sexual gratification. Thus Freud might attack the hypocrisy of the double standard from which women suffered far more than men, but in so doing he was subtly identifying women with the demand for sexual gratification – and endorsing this demand; and he would persist in this identification in his later work.

In his speculative reconstruction of human history in *Civilization and its Discontents*, it is woman's demands for love that lay the foundation of civilization. However, 'women soon come into opposition to civilization and display their retarding and restraining influence. ... Women represent the interests of the family and of sexual life.' The claims of civilization call men away from the home and the family towards public life and activity. Men also organize social groups in such a way as to exclude libidinal relations to both women and men: 'In the great artificial groups, the Church and the army, there is no room for woman as a sexual object. The love relation between men and women remains outside these organizations.' The groups organized around the leader, from whom that bulwark of higher civilization, the super-ego, is later derived, depend on the capacity for sublimation, in particular of the sublimation of homosexuality: 'it is precisely manifest homosexuals, and among them again precisely those who set themselves against an indulgence in sensual acts, who are distinguished by taking a particularly active share in the general interests of humanity.'

It is here that Freud's ambiguous attitude to the importance of the personal life over and against the claims of civilization, which underlies his response to Mill, becomes more explicit. In Freud's eyes there are two fundamental social institutions, in tension with one another: the group constituted around a leader, uniting men around one man, in which libidinal relations are aim-inhibited and desexualised; and the family, constituted around man's relationship to woman and the culture founded on this erotic bond. As the group gains in power and complexity, 'the woman finds herself forced into the background by the claims of civilization and she adopts a hostile attitude towards it.' The sexual life of the family and the public life of civilization emerge as fundamentally at odds, and women always represent the claims of the sexual and the family. As he had put it in 1908, women are 'the actual vehicle of the sexual interests of mankind'.

However, these ascetic male groupings of public life are not ones that Freud, with his virulent distrust of religion and all its institutions, and living in the age of fascism and the politics of the masses, would endorse. These groups will, in the end, always tend to revert to their original model, the murderous brother band, docile in its admiration of its leader one moment, triumphant in his murder the next. So the other great institution of civilization, the family, and woman as its lynch-pin, begins to seem more like the true defender of the rights of Eros against the pressures of Thanatos. After all, hadn't he argued in *The Ego and the Id* that the super-ego was 'a pure culture of the death instinct'? Women's weaker super-egos and their lesser capacity for sublimation are at one not only with their hostility to civilization, but their greater fidelity to the claims of Eros. So the pessimistic culture-critic Freud held no enthusiastic brief for the masculine rigours of the triumphalist super-ego. His deep conviction of the superiority of the patriarchal principles of intellectuality and impersonal justice was always tempered by a nagging doubt that it might be women who could best counteract the repressions of civilization, because they are more firmly held by Eros.

Freud never went so far as to equate Eros with femininity and Thanatos with masculinity. Such a stretching of his categories would have revealed their fundamental fragility. Even in his more down-to-earth accounts of the development of boys and girls, he was acutely aware of the unsatisfactory character of the distinction between masculinity and femininity with which his late theories on female sexuality were so concerned. How then, was he to characterize the psychoanalytic distinction between masculinity and femininity? Throughout Freud's writings, this issue elicited a characteristic double gesture. In the first moment of this gesture, Freud identifies the pair masculinity/femininity with another pair of concepts, 'active'/'passive'. Having done so, in the second moment, he immediately warns against doing exactly this:

For psychology the contrast between the sexes fades away into one between activity and passivity, in which we far too readily identify activity with maleness and passivity with femaleness, a view which is by no means universally confirmed in the animal kingdom.

Freud never resolved the indecision that this double gesture reveals. He was never happy with the equation 'maleness/femaleness = activity/passivity', but he could see no more plausible equation, and often resorted to it, usually, although not always, surrounding it with provisos and self-criticisms. Before we consider the distinction between masculinity and femininity in greater detail, one remark would be useful. What is striking and conspicuous in all of Freud's discussions of the conceptual content of the contrast of masculinity and femininity is that he nowhere considers the external genitalia. The internal genitalia – the presence of spermatozoa and ova – are the core of the biological criteria, and these are, for human beings rather than scientists, unavailable as evidence. On the other hand, possessing a penis or a vagina does not figure as a possible candidate for distinguishing the masculine and the feminine. A moment's consideration reveals why. 'Possessing a penis' is precisely the child's phallic theory of the distinction and, therefore, must be differentiated from this other, non-fantasied way of drawing the distinction, the way which presents Freud with such perplexities. Possessing a penis or vagina is an anatomical rather than a biological criterion and, therefore, it is one which spills over into and is suffused with fantasy, with mental, even hysterical, representations of the body. The idea of 'the anatomical sex-distinction' and the famous phrase 'anatomy is destiny' with which Freud's theory of the stunted, castrated female is associated could not count as possible *scientific* means of distinguishing masculine from feminine, precisely because these are the spontaneous theories of the phallic boy and his accomplice, the penis-envying girl.

It is undoubtedly for this reason that Freud prefers the 'grammatical' definitions of masculinity and femininity to the 'anatomical' ones; he prefers to call active sexual aims 'masculine', and passive ones 'feminine'. Freud's grammatical sense of the passivity is clarified if we compare his view briefly with that of Helene Deutsch, for whom passivity is activity directed inward, and activity means acting on the external world. Freud pays exclusive attention to the verb, rather than to the subject's stance: for him, the opposition is 'acting upon'/'being acted upon', not the *direction* of the subject's acting, outwards or inwards.

So Freud follows the masochist, who, as we have seen, picks out the following characteristic female situations, grammatically passive ones: 'being castrated, or copulated with, or giving birth to a baby'. And it was in following his equation of activity and masculinity that he asserted in 1905 that 'the sexuality of little girls is of a wholly masculine character'. He had always assumed that adult female sexuality was more passive than male sexuality, and he reworked this equation to try and align it with the later, more sophisticated sense of femininity and masculinity. One important reason why Freud persisted in aligning femininity with passivity had to do with the question of the vagina.

It is almost inconceivable that Freud was not aware of the orthodox views of contemporary anatomists and physiologists, who had, from well before the early nineteenth century, demonstrated that the clitoris was the specific site of female sexual pleasure, and who, in the medical writing of his time, had asserted that the vagina had virtually no erotic functions at all. Nineteenth-century medical encyclopaedia writers closed the file on the vagina in the same way as Alfred Kinsey in the mid-twentieth century, with a flourish of definitively and chillingly rank-pulling medical rhetoric: virtually the entire vagina could be operated on without need of an anaesthetic. Freud's view of the vagina, therefore, is not intended as the story of its developmental physiology; it is intended as the story of its destiny in the sexual lives of women. However, lurking within the account was the teleology – the ultimate biological aim of reproduction – that Freud himself very rarely made explicit.

There was a theoretical need to arrive at an account of childbirth, of passive sexual intercourse and so forth, which Freud struggled against, but allowed and sometimes encouraged in his less fastidious followers, such as Sándor Ferenczi and Helene Deutsch, who equated all biologically female attributes with sexual femininity, which thus becomes entirely subject to the teleology of childbirth and motherhood. In Freud's theory, the suppression of clitoridal sexuality was not only part of the implicit teleological account that led to the vaginal genital sexuality; it had become an essential part of the story of how the little girl finally stopped being a little man.

One of the paradigmatic forms of adult female sexual activity is submitting to sexual intercourse. The additional erogenous zone the girl acquires in puberty, the 'truly feminine vagina', has, it appeared to Freud, a passive sexual aim, no matter how actively the woman pursued that aim. But the vagina does not figure in the unconscious; therefore, the deeper motivations for vagina-oriented sexual behaviour must come from elsewhere: on lease from the passive sexual aims of anal sexuality, as Lou Andreas-Salomé so aptly put it, or from the rhythms of suckling at the breast, and displacement of oral libido to the genital, supplemented by identification with the penis, as Helene Deutsch in 1924, Ernest Jones in 1927 and Melanie Klein in 1928 were to emphasize. The only way the vagina can come to function as a sexual organ, then, is in the imaginary: 'the switch from clitoris to vagina ... is hysterical, a recathexis that works against the organic structures of the body. Like the missing-limb phenomenon, it involves feeling what is not there. Becoming a sexually mature woman is therefore living an oxymoron, becoming a lifelong "normal hysteric".'

There were two entirely different questions here, which have often been confused. Freud needed to find a way of explaining how the new erogenous zone of the vagina acquires its connections with infantile sexual activities and, therefore, its sexual interest for the adult woman. But he also maintained that clitoridal sexuality *disappears* and must cede its rights in favour of the vagina at and after puberty. 'With the change to femininity the clitoris should wholly or in part hand over its sensitivity, and at the same time its importance, to the vagina.'

Freud persisted in seeing the vagina as a privileged organ in women's sexual lives, something more than a biologically useful appendage to the clitoris. It was as if this organ, the only non-infantile sexual organ either sex possesses, was the last and only refuge for the elusive femininity that his monistic phallic theory proved time and time again had roots in penis envy and the masculinity complex. In addition, by the 1920s, Freud had linked the turning away from the mother, so crucial to the girl's development, to the giving up of clitoridal sexuality. It was giving up the clitoris that was crucial to the theory, not the consequent handing over of its rights to the vagina. Freud never used the phrase 'vaginal orgasm' – in any case, he used the word 'orgasm' itself in its general sense very infrequently, preferring the less physiological phrase 'sexual satisfaction'. 'The myth of the vaginal orgasm' cannot be attributed to Freud. None the less, throughout his work he insisted that there was a destiny of the sexual lives of women, normal femininity, in which the leading erogenous zone was the vagina.

If the vagina has no original erotic function, then that function has to be acquired. But it has to be acquired both as an erotogenic zone or organ and as part of a more general relation to the object. Here Freud argues that the passive aims of vaginal intercourse go hand in hand with the passive relation to the object, maybe even that they follow on from that passive relation. Therefore, the turn away from the active relation to the mother to a passive relation to the father is doubly significant. Not only does the girl change her object from mother to father, opening up her access to the Oedipus complex in its normal configuration, but the passive relation to the father paves the way for the later passive function of the vagina. The turn to the father is 'accomplished principally with the help of passive instinctual impulses', which 'clears the phallic activity out of the way, smooths the ground for femininity'.

Freud recognizes the dangers to the undisturbed construction of 'femininity' in his account. He paints a picture of three lines of development for the little girl who has discovered that she is castrated. Firstly, she may, through her penis envy, turn away from sexuality altogether, and certainly from her phallic mother; passivity gains the upper hand, and through the set of symbolic equivalences her wish for a penis becomes a wish for a doll-baby, then the wish for a baby. Here is one of the most surprising and constant features of Freud's account: the masculine wish for a penis is the direct antecedent of the most feminine of all wishes, for a baby; 'perhaps we ought rather to recognize this wish for a penis as being *par excellence* a feminine one.' Pure masculinity is transformed, under its own inner logic, into pure femininity.

The second alternative is the defiant and obstinate refusal to believe that she does not possess a penis. This 'masculinity complex' may later be the seed-bed of an active homosexual relation to the object. Freud's case of female homosexuality was the clearest expression of this posture. The case describes a young woman whose mother had had a child just when the young girl was herself coming to maturity. 'Furiously resentful and embittered, she turned away from her father and from men altogether. After this first great reverse she forswore her womanhood and sought another goal for her libido. ... She changed into a man and took her mother in place of her father as the object of her love.' Most significantly for Freud, the most interesting determinant of her homosexuality was not the nature of her object so much as the relation she had to it:

in her behaviour towards her love-object she had throughout assumed the masculine part: that is to say, she displayed the humility and the sublime overvaluation of the sexual object so characteristic of the male lover, the renunciation of all narcissistic satisfaction, and the preference for being the lover rather than the beloved. She had thus not only chosen a feminine love-object, but had also developed a masculine attitude towards that object.

What of the third alternative, 'normal femininity'? Freud has nothing to say of it! Why? Because normal femininity is, in fact, covered by the first alternative: the most masculine of all the little girl's wishes, her wish for a penis so that she can continue, undisturbed by reality as it were, her phallic pleasures, is also the most feminine of her wishes, since it leads eventually to the baby that is the unique mark of mature femininity: motherhood. 'Normally, large portions of the [masculinity] complex are transformed and contribute to the construction of her femininity: the appeased wish for a penis is destined to be converted into a wish for a baby and for a husband, who possesses a penis.' As Sarah Kofman puts it, 'what is most specifically feminine in woman is in fact her masculine desire to possess the penis, her penis envy. This desire thus becomes at once the vestige of woman's "masculine" sexuality that *must* disappear in order to leave room for femininity and also what allows woman to bring her femininity to the best possible fruition.'

It is such arguments that suggest to one that there is no theory of femininity *as such* in Freud's work. There are, at most, accounts of how such distinctively 'feminine' wishes as the wish for a baby, or how such distinctively 'feminine' attitudes as a passive attitude towards men, in particular the father, arise. Even these accounts are continually hedged in with provisos. In his last extended account of the destiny of femininity, 'Analysis Terminable and Interminable', Freud concluded:

We often have the impression that with the wish for a penis and the masculine protest we have penetrated through all the psychological strata and have reached bedrock, and that thus our activities are at an end. This is probably true, since, for the psychical field, the biological field does in fact play the part of the underlying bedrock. The repudiation of femininity can be nothing else than a biological fact, a part of the great riddle of sex.

There is no further analysis possible. We must accept the repudiation of femininity by both men and women as a biological fact. Indeed, repudiation seems at times to be the very essence of what femininity is; on this point, there is the constancy, over more than thirty years, of Freud's conviction that there exists a wave of repression at puberty that is a fundamental feature of the changes that bring femininity into existence, and his parallel conviction that masturbation provokes a greater struggle, and is always more at odds with the ego, in girls and women when compared with boys and men. Yet the question, 'what exactly *is* this femininity that is repudiated?' nags away at Freud as he writes this swansong on his life's work. He adds a footnote:

We must not be misled by the term 'masculine protest' into supposing that what the man is repudiating is his passive attitude [as such] – what might be called the social aspect of femininity. ... What they reject is not passivity in general, but passivity towards a male. In other words, the 'masculine protest' is in fact nothing else than castration anxiety.

Is passivity as such simply conventional femininity, what society expects of women? No, Freud is musing, there is more to femininity than simply what society expects or requires of women. Femininity in a deeper sense than the social necessarily includes a reference to the phallus. Yet exactly how this clarifies the essence of femininity, the essence of what each and every human being repudiates, still escapes him.

Perhaps Freud was having second thoughts about his decisive and somewhat ill-tempered refutation of Adler's theory of the masculine protest in 1914. Then, he had closed off the question with the following argument:

It is impossible, and is disproved by observation, that a child, whether male or female, should found the plan of its life on an original depreciation of the female sex and take the wish to be a real man as its 'guiding line'. Children have, to begin with, no idea of the significance of the distinction between the sexes; on the contrary, they start with the assumption that the same genital organ (the male one) is possessed by both sexes; they do not begin their sexual researches with the problem of the distinction between the sexes, while the *social* underestimation of women is completely foreign to them. There are women in whose neurosis the wish to be a man has played no part. Whatever in the nature of a masculine protest can be shown to exist is easily traceable to a disturbance in primary narcissism due to threats of castration or to the earliest interferences with sexual activities.

By the end of his life, however, Freud was committed both to the views which he had used to criticize Adler's thesis and to the thesis they were meant to criticize. Borrowing the terms he employed in 1914, we can put it as follows. Life as a sexed being is a disturbance of primary narcissism. Boys only ever become men, and girls only ever become women, by being expelled by the castration complex from primary narcissism into masculinity and femininity.

15

THE DISPUTE OVER WOMAN

Freud was adept at constructing psychoanalytic debates as he went about the business of building his theory. His texts abound with imaginary objectors, pertinent disinterested questions and invectives against heretic disciples. The topic of femininity is no exception to this combative or dialectical feature of his writing. Indeed, one of the two first-generation psychoanalytic heretics, Alfred Adler, had, as we have seen, with his concept of masculine protest raised a question concerning the nature of repression and femininity which Freud repeatedly returned to consider, from 1911 to 1937. On two occasions, Adler's name was linked to that of Fliess, a longer-standing influence on Freud, as Freud debated the relationship between repression, femininity and bisexuality.

Yet the challenge to Freud's theories, which gave rise to what has since become known as the first psychoanalytic debate on femininity, came from another quarter – from the pupils of Karl Abraham: Karen Horney and Melanie Klein. Horney and Klein found a somewhat unlikely but deft spokesman in Ernest Jones, whose three papers on female sexuality of 1927, 1932 and 1935 summed up a view that was fundamentally at odds with Freud's. On Freud's side, there were his (more or less) faithful Viennese: Helene Deutsch, Jeanne Lampl de Groot and Ruth Mack Brunswick, backed up by the later arrival, Marie Bonaparte. The debate was not acrimonious, although it was deep and never resolved; all participants in it presented themselves as engaged in fine-tuning Freud's overall theory of sexuality. And so they appeared to be. But at issue in the debate were questions which reappeared in some of the larger subsequent splits within the psychoanalytic world (the Kleinians versus the Freudians in London; the Lacanians versus the Bonapartists in Paris). And the issue of femininity came to be seen as having much larger consequences outside the technical papers of psycho-analytic journals; the issues in the debate exercised the feminist critique of psychoanalysis and the question of psychoanalysis's relation to a science of sexuality in general.

Nor did the debate lack in historical ironies and paradoxes. If ever there were, in the psychoanalytic terms chosen by Jones and his group, an enthusiast for the importance of the clitoris, then Freud was that enthusiast. Yet thirty years later, it was Freud who was regarded as the major theorist of the 'oppressive' myth of the vaginal orgasm. Through an irony of history, Freud came to be seen as a champion of the vagina, whose importance in childhood he had repeatedly denied.

'The ultimate question is whether a woman is born or made.' So Jones put the central issue. Freud was reluctant to assume an innate femininity or masculinity, although he did posit an innate, virtually contentless bisexuality. Until proven otherwise, he wished to pursue enquiries on the assumption that there was no fundamental difference between the sexes until the period of hegemony of the Oedipus complex: the little boy and girl alike constituted their first genital organization around the phallic organ – the penis or the clitoris. He had weighty reasons for *ignoring* certain sorts of argument and evidence; it was his followers' eagerness to make use of these that often placed him in an uncomfortable position. His refusals of certain patently evident truths gave a structure, as if in chiaroscuro, to the debate. Firstly, Freud was not interested in a psychology of sexual differences. He might at times catalogue such differences, only to dismiss them as of little interest for the questions psychoanalysis addressed. Most prominently, he described the activity of little girls, which was quite the equal of their male peers, but refused to see anything of significance for the question of femininity in such an observation. Freud also eschewed a path which he had opened up, particularly in *The Ego and the Id*, and which was to come to dominate later psychoanalytic theories of sexual difference: the path of identification. One does not in his view arrive at a primary 'gender identity', as it came to be called in the 1970s, through identification with the parent of the same sex; as with so many other theories that look to inter-subjective or social relations for the origin of sexual difference, the concept of identification leads to an infinite regress: the father's masculinity is as much a question as the son's.

Thirdly, and most importantly for the debate of the 1920s and 1930s, Freud eschewed innate biological dispositions or propensities. A letter whose significance Juliet Mitchell has done much to highlight puts Freud's positions clearly. In 1935, a Berlin analyst, Carl Müller-Braunschweig, sent a paper to Freud for his comments. Freud replied in a gruff and acerbic tone:

I object to all of you [Horney, Jones, Rado, etc.] to the extent that you do not distinguish more clearly and cleanly between what is psychic and what is biological, that you try to establish a neat parallelism between the two and that you, motivated by such intent, unthinkingly construe psychic facts which are unprovable and that you, in the process of doing so, must declare as reactive and regressive much that without doubt is primary. Of course, these reproaches must remain obscure. In addition, I would only like to emphasize that we must keep psychoanalysis separate from biology just as we have kept it separate from anatomy and physiology.

The separation of psychoanalysis from biology was clear to Freud even when he respected the contribution that Fliess's biology could make to his work. It was reiterated often in the decades when Freud was developing his theory, and is conceptually determined by the concept of instinct, 'lying on the frontier between the mental and the physical'. What is more, having separated psychoanalysis from biology, Freud then went on to indicate that biology can actually be ignored in constructing psychoanalysis – that biology can be actively misleading as a guide for psychoanalytic theory. Didn't his own mental and cultural Lamarckianism, constant over the years when it increasingly fell out of favour in biological circles, indicate a cavalier attitude to biology? In the letter to Müller-Braunschweig he rubbed the point home in the following way: 'Sexual-biology seems, at the time being, to lead to two substances which attract one another. There is only one libido, a male one.' The implication is clear: whatever biology tells us of the biochemistry of sexuality, psychoanalysis deals with one, male libido. *Ergo* libido is not a biological concept.

A more specialized but connected issue in the debate concerned the relation between the weight to be attached to traumatic ('environmental') or to constitutional and dispositional ('heredity') factors. Freud's critics thought it *biologically* implausible that anything as important and universal as femininity could be decided by the influence of an external trauma, such as perceiving the anatomical difference between the sexes. As Helene Deutsch put the argument: 'Even a priori it seems unlikely that a trauma of external and accidental origin should play a fundamental part in the formation of feminine personality.' Hence Freud's critics leaned, almost by scientific temperament, towards the view that there are predetermining biological dispositions, a constitutional femininity, and it is the task of the psychoanalyst to analyse until these are ascertained as the basic elements of the psyche.

Freud's view was the opposite. Psychoanalysis, for him, is *restricted* to the field of the accidental, the traumatic. He had expounded this view in a letter written in 1911, in reply to a question from a philosopher, Else Voigt-länder:

You suggest that I overestimate the importance of accidental influences on character formation and in contrast you stress the importance of constitutional factors, of disposition, which selects from among the experiences and allows them to become significant. ... The question as to which is of greater significance, constitution or experience, which of the two elements decides character, can in my opinion, only be answered by saying that δαίμων καί τύχη [daimon kai tuché] (fate and chance) and not one *or* the other are decisive. ... If in our analytical work we concentrate more on the accidental influences than on the constitutional factors, we do so ... because on the basis of our experience we know something about the former, while about the latter we know as little as – non-analysts. ... We are also of the opinion that by appreciating the importance of the accidental we have taken the right road towards the understanding of constitution. ... What remains inexplicable after a study of the accidental may be put down to constitution.

So the field of operation of psychoanalysis is, according to Freud, the accidental, the traumatic. Not just adult traumas, as in Charcot's sense, but infantile traumas, such as the Oedipus complex and all the fixation points (the after-effects of traumas) that are unearthed in the course of analysis. What is left over, what is still inexplicable, what is provisionally attributed to constitution, is not therefore the most important, the most fundamental, but rather the point at which explanations fail, the point at which science falls silent. To try and bolster with biology the necessarily fragmentary explanations of psychoanalysis – which is, after all, not a religion, automatically offering total explanations in the face of the unknown, or a paranoid system, which requires an explanation for everything – is to lack trust in the work of the analyst. On this point, Freud's biologically inclined followers betrayed an eagerness for the final and complete explanation that positing a fundamental underlying biological disposition, such as an inherent 'biological principle of heterosexual attraction' or an 'essential femininity', superficially offers.

In point of fact, such explanations do nothing of the sort, unless they are backed up with biological theories (such as the biochemistry of hormones) with substantive content: they simply name a problem. None of those ready to contest Freud's account offered such substantive biological theories; hence their references to biology were simply promissory notes, respectful attitudes towards the authority of a science other than psychoanalysis. Freud's dicta to Müller-Braunschweig made it clear that biology was irrelevant to psychoanalysis, whether it supported psychoanalytic findings or contradicted them (as in the case he cited). But the implication was also that if one is going to invoke biology, then one must supply some content for this invocation, otherwise it is too transparently an argument from authority. And, as with all such respectful attitudes to authority, they close off enquiry – in the name of a conventionally acceptable explanation – rather than open it. So his followers filled in the perceived holes in Freud's theories with hypothetical biological entities. Where Freud's blithe dismissal of biological theories was, for him, a sign of scientific independent-mindedness, many of his followers regarded it as something of an obstinate shortsightedness, if not a scandal, on Freud's part, that he refused to recognize the fundamental and original reality of sexual difference from the start.

All participants in the debate agreed that at its centre was Freud's interpretation of femininity as constructed out of the disappointment of the little girl at not having a penis; the primary evidence for the supremacy of the phallus throughout the early phases came from this later vestige of the little girl's earlier phallic activity. It might be assumed that other analysts would contest the *very existence* of the fact of the little girl being disappointed at not having a penis. But not one of the participants disputed Freud's facts: not one contested the clinical reality of penis envy. In 1926, Karen Horney, the most outspoken of Freud's critics, put it more strongly than anyone else:

Every little girl who has not been intimidated displays penis envy frankly and without embarrassment. We see that the presence of this envy is typical and understand quite well why this is so; we understand how the narcissistic mortification of possessing less than the boy is reinforced by a series of disadvantages arising out of the different pregenital cathexes: the manifest privileges of the boy in connection with urethral erotism, the scoptophilic instinct [the visual drive], and onanism.

And Jones, following Horney closely on this, wrote: 'no woman escapes the early penis-envy stage'. So the debate was never about the existence and ubiquity of penis envy, which all agreed upon; rather it was about the interpretation to be put on it. Horney was quite forthright on this question. Freud's and Abraham's theory of the castration complex amounted to saying that in reality 'one half of the human race is discontented with the sex assigned to it and can overcome this discontent only in favorable circumstances'. This, she contended, 'is decidedly unsatisfying, not only to feminine narcissism, but also to biological science.' The allusion to 'biological science' is immediately striking; she interpreted Freud's conception of the castration complex as being a theory about the essentially biological nature of women: they were biologically castrated men. Throughout her work on femininity, there was to be an insistence on the biological reality of these questions – an insistence that Freud always regarded as fundamentally misplaced in psychoanalysis.

Her critique of Freud was spelled out in a series of papers, beginning in 1922 (published in 1924) and ending in the early 1930s, shortly before her emigration to the United States. In her first paper she outlined the three reasons for the ubiquity of penis envy in little girls: her inadequate pleasure in urinating, owing to the narcissistic overestimation of excretory processes in children; the advantage the boy has in the visual pleasures associated with his visible genitals, which, Horney adds, has the enormous consequences of obliging women to display their whole bodies, décolleté if possible, instead of the visible penis; and the manual advantages the boy has in masturbation, which the girl perceives as his having been permitted to masturbate. These three reasons mean that

as an actual fact, from the point of view of a child at this stage of development, little girls *are* at a disadvantage compared with boys in respect of certain possibilities of gratification. For unless we are quite clear about the *reality* of this disadvantage we shall not understand that penis-envy is an almost inevitable phenomenon in the life of female children, and one that cannot but complicate female development.

Yet this realistic envy of the penis is not the fundamental problem for the girl's development, Horney suggests. This realistic penis envy becomes of long-term significance because the intrinsic femininity of the girl is wounded. Her fundamental feminine wish is to be given a baby by her father. The 'primal feminine phantasy' is of being raped by the father; the 'penis had become the object of envy in place of the child'. It is the frustration and guilt that stem from this disappointed fantasy that constitute the primary wound to femininity: it is 'wounded womanhood that gives rise to the castration complex'. Horney postulates a 'wholly womanly relation to the father', which is then abandoned in disappointment; instead, the girl turns her object-relation to the father into an identification, identifies with the masculine position and revives the urethral, scoptophilic and onanistic penis envy. But the much deeper feminine fantasy, whose repression starts off this chain of events, is the fantasy of having been raped and thus castrated by the father's enormous penis.

Penis envy for Horney thus becomes crucial in women's development because of the regressive identification with the father. Implicit here was the view that normal sexual identity is constructed by a natural identification with the parent of the same sex. This fresh start to the problem of sexual difference was to have an influential future: it forms the basis of object-relations theory of sexual differences. Instead of forming the identification with the parent as a result of the catastrophe of the castration complex, the identification precedes it, is in some sense given (biologically, usually) and is certainly normative in a sociological sense. In her 1924 paper, Horney implicitly opposes Freud's conception of the girl as a little man, by invoking the heterosexual attraction the little girl already feels for her father; in normal women, this heterosexual attraction would be permanently supported and secured by a normative identification with the parent of the same sex. Horney's 1926 paper, 'The Flight from Womanhood', made these assumptions explicit. There is a 'biological principle of heterosexual attraction', which gives rise to the primal rape fantasy of the little girl; the masculine phase the girl passes through is a defence against the primary anxiety arising from the father's violation of her. But if the primal fantasies invoke the gigantic paternal penis, this implies foreknowledge of the vagina. Here is the basis of the major thesis of a paper Horney wrote in the early 1930s: that 'the undiscovered vagina is a vagina denied', that 'behind the "failure to discover" the vagina is a denial of its existence', that the (Freudian) observation – the theorist repeating the vigorous defences of little boys and girls – that a girl knows nothing of her vagina is a secondary defensive stunting of the original knowledge of her own biological capacities and destinies.

Horney observes that the very universality of the wish to be a man that nearly all women analysands confess to should alert us to the fact that it is defensive in character. This wish is immoveable, is clung to in order to conceal the deeper relation to the violating father, the girl's deeper 'feminine wishes'. Her defensive wish to be a man results in her abiding sense of inferiority; but this feeling is easier to bear than the guilt she would otherwise have to face:

The fiction of maleness enabled the girl to escape from the female role now burdened with guilt and anxiety. It is true that this attempt to deviate from her own line to that of the male inevitably brings about a sense of inferiority, for the girl begins to measure herself by pretensions and values that are foreign to her specific biological nature and confronted with which she cannot but feel herself inadequate.

It is our foreknowledge, our deep common-sensical perception of this specific biological nature, that should warn us that 'we must resist the temptation to interpret in the light of penis envy the manifestations of so elementary a principle of nature as that of the mutual attraction of the sexes.' This mutual attraction between the sexes is so fundamental that even if we discovered penis envy at this level, we should have to reinterpret it. However,

Horney still wants to hedge her bets. What if penis envy were still discovered at this deep level of primal feminine wishes for the potent primal father? Horney suggests that if this were the case, we should instead view it as the primordial desire of the female for the opposite sex:

it is just the attraction to the opposite sex, operating from a very early period, which draws the libidinal interest of the little girl to the penis ... if penis envy were the first expression of that mysterious attraction of the sexes, there would be nothing to wonder at when analysis discloses its existence in a yet deeper layer than that in which the desire for a child and the tender attachment to the father occur.

Thus Horney wins whichever which way. Penis envy stems either from the urethral, scoptophilic or onanistic impulses of infantile sexuality. Or it stems from defence against deeper feminine fantasies of penile rape by the father. Or it is itself the expression of the femininity of the girl, the primordial tender attachment to the father. The one thing penis envy is not is the last and most salient outcrop of the little girl's masculinity, from which her later femininity develops.

One senses that Horney's importance in the debate did not stem primarily from these striking but hardly rigorous arguments. In part this is due to the curious fact that on certain points she was being more faithful to Freud's earlier views than Freud was about to become. The central and primal fantasy of early femininity is, for Horney, the primordial paternal rape fantasy; it is the defence against this that leads to neurotic identification with the father. So the primal scene she evokes is one we are very familiar with from the beginnings of psychoanalysis: the father–daughter rape/seduction scene, the primal father who possesses all the females. In 1925, Freud was to start the turn away from this primal scene towards the murkier and older relations of little girl to her mother. Eventually, he was to bring the history of the seduction theory to a close with the observation that, because mothers unavoidably, through their cleansing of the genitals, excite their daughters genitally, it is the father who so regularly appears in later fantasies as the sexual seducer. 'When the girl turns away from her mother, she also makes over to her father her introduction into sexual life.' In contrast to Freud's changing views, in which the father increasingly figured as a cover for the mother, Horney's papers of the 1920s give very little hint that the relationship to the mother is of great significance. She asserts the independence of feminine development on the basis of the primal relationship to the father and the innate femininity of the girl.

There is another reason for coming to the conclusion that Horney's detailed theories were not what made her contribution of fundamental significance. It was not so much her declaration that the castration theory entailed that women were 'biologically' handicapped, which appeared totally implausible to Horney's biological intuitions – 'what biological value could there be in such an adaptation?' was her implied rhetorical question. It was not so much her declaration that feminine narcissism was wounded by this theory – not in itself a strong argument, no matter how true. Nor even was it her observation, never followed up until Erikson developed his theory of inner space and womb envy, of the intensity of the male envy of women's capacity for pregnancy, childbirth and motherhood, as well as of the breasts and suckling. Rather she set the agenda for the later feminist critique of Freud, by pointing out that Freud's theory of femininity 'differs in no case by a hair's breadth from the typical ideas that the boy has of the girl.' Horney was suggesting that Freud's own realization that 'the sexual theories of a child are a mirror of its particular sexual constitution' should now be applied to the theories of analysts about masculinity and femininity: Freud and other male analysts were unable to see the distinctive features of the girl's development because they themselves were 'stuck' in the little boy's phallic phase, dominated by the division of the world into beings possessing a penis and beings who are castrated. It is this suggestion that later appealed to a generation of feminists infused with the doctrine that the 'personal is the political', and that the political argument was often best, as well as most effectively, conducted by unpacking the personal underpinnings of political positions, or the political underpinnings of personal desires and prejudices – Mandy Rice-Davies's famous principle, 'Well, he would, wouldn't he?' Horney was claiming that the closeness of fit between the boy's horrified view of girls and the analyst's theory of femininity should, at the very least, give us pause for thought.

In 1931 Freud responded to this claim, and to the table of striking similarities between the boy's ideas concerning girls and the psychoanalytic view of their development that Horney drew up in her 1926 paper:

It is to be anticipated that men analysts with feminist views, as well as our women analysts, will disagree with what I have said here. They will hardly fail to object that such notions spring from the 'masculinity complex' of the male and are designed to justify on theoretical grounds his innate inclination to disparage and suppress women. But this sort of psycho-analytic argumentation reminds us here, as it so often does, of Dostoevsky's famous 'knife that cuts both ways.' The opponents of those who argue in this way will on their side think it quite natural that the female sex should refuse to accept a view which appears to contradict their eagerly coveted equality with men. The use of analysis as a weapon of controversy can clearly lead to no decision.

Freud was attempting to neutralize this new manoeuvre of Horney's before it would lead to a polarization of views along sexual-political lines. In that, he certainly failed.

Horney was an established figure before she had opened the debate on femininity with her clear challenge to the Freud–Abraham position. She was a Berlin analyst, an analysand of Abraham's and a mainstay of the Society by the end of the war – the equivalent of Vienna's Helene Deutsch. Now it was Deutsch, also under Abraham's influence, who took up the topic of female sexuality. Her impulse to undertake a second analysis with Abraham had, as we have seen, stemmed from hearing Abraham's 1920 paper on the castration complex in women – the paper to which Horney's 1922 paper had originally been a reply. Deutsch's paper is also a reply to Abraham, and, despite the fact that Horney and Deutsch profoundly disagree on the fundamental question of the significance to be attached to penis envy and the castration complex, there is one very important assumption, common to them both and entirely at odds with the approach of Freud and Abraham:

The first thing that strikes us is that it is always, or principally, the genital difference between the sexes which has been made the cardinal point in the analytical conception and that we have left out of consideration the other great biological difference, namely, the different parts played by men and by women in the function of reproduction.

Whereas Horney, the author of this declaration of conceptual intent, characteristically shifts away to consider another question altogether, Deutsch doggedly pursued exactly this question in her first paper, and in her definitive account of the psychology of women published twenty years later. Her 1924 paper, 'The Psychology of Women in Relation to the Functions of Reproduction', written after she had completed her analysis with Abraham, begins with the discovery of the vagina, which is the signature of woman's entry into true womanhood, and of the boy's entry into manhood:

man attains his final stage of development when he discovers the vagina in the world outside himself and takes possession of it sadistically. ... The woman has to discover the new sexual organ *in her own person*, a discovery she makes through a masochistic submission to the penis, thus becoming also a guide to this new source of knowledge.

The un-Freudian note of requisite and normative symmetry between the sexes – the sadistic man triumphing, the masochistic woman submitting – is characteristic of the ever-present teleological pressure of Deutsch's writing on women. Yet in other respects, she is more orthodoxly Freudian: when she is excavating the more ancient roots of these final libidinal positions, exposing the oral antecedents, the equation of the breast and the penis, the primary fantasy of fellatio and fertilization through the mouth, and pinpointing the anus as the natural antecedent of the vagina on account of its passivity and common cloacal origin. But, following Freud, she is obliged to emphasize the tenacity of clitoridal sexuality, adding, almost with regret, that 'one would suppose it an easy task for feminine libido in its further development to pass on and take possession of the third opening of the female body – the vagina', if it were not for the intervention of the clitoris in the developmental sequence. But it is not until the penis actively stimulates the vagina into taking on the passive-oral function of sucking and the vagina is identified with the penetrating penis that the vagina comes fully into its own. And now Deutsch adds another characteristic note, fateful for its future consequences: 'the orgastic activity of the vagina is wholly analogous to the activity of the penis. I refer to the process of secretion and contraction.' Deutsch is amplifying Freud's remarks about the shift in leading zone from clitoris to puberty, recounting a dramatic struggle between clitoris and vagina: which organ is to be identified as the rightful heir of the phallus? She portrays this struggle as a biologically preordained one, one the clitoris should lose, since it is an inadequate version of the penis. Implicit, therefore, in her account is the view that the phallus is the exemplary pleasure-organ for both sexes, even after the phallic phase has ended, whether it is the clitoris or the vagina that takes over the phallic function for the girl.

Deutsch is not content in showing how the vagina becomes the equivalent of the phallus; she also is eager to demonstrate its successful fate as final fully maternal receptacle for what had once been phallic narcissism:

In its role of organ of sucking and incorporation the vagina becomes the receptacle not of the penis but of the child. ... The vagina now represents the child, and so receives the cathexis of narcissistic libido which flows on to the child in the 'extension' of the sexual act. It becomes the 'second ego', the ego in miniature, as does the penis for the man. A woman who succeeds in establishing this maternal function of the vagina by giving up the claim of the clitoris to represent the penis, has reached the goal of feminine development, she *has become a woman*.

But once the vagina has attained its womanly supremacy, a new function emerges, which will later be closely allied to masochism, tying the woman even more intimately to her reproductive function:

Orgasm in the woman appears not only to imply identification with the man but to have yet another motive; it is the expression of the attempt to impart to coitus itself in the interest of the race the character of parturition (we might call it a 'missed labour') ... the act of parturition contains the acme of sexual pleasure ... coitus acquires the character of a pleasure act mainly through the fact that it constitutes an attempt at and beginning of parturition.

Parturition, Deutsch adds, is 'an orgy of masochistic pleasure'. But she does not assert this primarily because the phenomenology of the sensations of parturition shows similarities to those of orgasm, as Masters and Johnson were later to do, but because she wished to bring male and female reproductive roles into exact parallelism. Where in his orgasm the male ejaculates semen, in hers the female ejaculates a baby:

parturition constitutes for women the termination of the sexual act, which was only inaugurated by coitus, and ... the ultimate gratification of the erotic instinct is analogous to that in men and takes place at the moment when soma and germ-plasm are separated.

Where Freud had assumed that the pleasures of little boys and girls were similar, centred on the active phallic organ, the penis–clitoris, Deutsch had now demonstrated that the entire sexual destiny of men and women is ruled by the same sexual rhythm. But note that where the basis of Freud's argument was the pleasure principle, which regulates how boys and girls cling to and then renounce their phallic activities, Deutsch's argument posited the reproductive teleology of the separation of the old generation and the new.

Deutsch was postulating a far-reaching parallelism between mother and child, a parallelism that culminated in the return of the original oral satisfactions when the baby sucks at the breast: the uterus convulses as the child is put to the breast, in one movement handing the dominant sexual organization back to the penis. The circle is now closed: 'in coitus the penis takes on the role of the breast, while in lactation the breast becomes the penis.'

However, this cyclical pattern, in which the 'act of reproduction, begun in oral incorporation, completes the circle by representing the same situation at the end as at the beginning', is interrupted by two elements. And the fact that Deutsch sees these as interruptions shows how far she is from Freud's conception of an original plural sexuality that is only shoe-horned with difficulty into the socially acceptable forms of masculinity and femininity. The two interruptions stem from the woman's inherent bisexuality, and its principal expression, the masculine strivings of the clitoris.

With this cyclical closure, this perfect repetition and completion that the mother–child – in reality, the mother–daughter – relation embodies, Deutsch has given a decidedly new element to Freud's theory, something Horney, with her vision of the primal rape as the central fact of femininity, was never able to do. Deutsch has written the father out of the theory, except insofar as he is represented by the awkward clitoris, the stumbling-block that women must surmount if they are to achieve true femininity. If we pause for a moment, though, we notice that the mother of Deutsch's cycle is the phallic mother – the equation of breast and penis certifies that. This strand of Deutsch's work can be seen extending well into her later writings, where the account of female homosexuality she gives centres on the regression – on account of penis envy, fear of the pains associated with masochistic femininity and disappointment at not receiving a child from the father – to the fullness of the mother–daughter relation. And Volume II of *The Psychology of Women* is one long paeon of praise to the mother, both as privileged first object and as ultimate feminine destiny. It is also the point where Klein and Deutsch are at one, although, as our discussion of Jones's use of Klein's work will show, Klein and Jones are careful to include the father within their conception of the phallic mother.

In a paper of 1930, 'The Significance of Masochism in the Mental Life of Women', Deutsch added a crucial new element to the story: the essential feminine traits of passivity and masochism. She asks what becomes of the active clitoral aims when they are given up in disappointment; she answers that they are transformed, by being turned inwards, into passive aims, ones that will be conducive to the passive feminine destiny that awaits the girl. The protest against castration, giving expression to the masculine narcissistic desire to have a penis and associated with the active libidinal strivings, is now transformed into the wish to be castrated by the father (here Deutsch echoes the primal rape scene of Horney). Here is the generation of the key elements of Deutsch's reinterpretation of Freud, which became widely perceived as the Freudian orthodoxy after the Second World War: femininity is now synonymous with passivity and masochism. The sexual life of the woman is dominated by the masochistic triad of castration, rape (coitus) and parturition, each linked in the mother–daughter cycle Deutsch had already outlined in her paper on femininity and reproduction. And it is this characteristic emphasis on the subordination of femininity to the rigours of reproduction, with their inevitable link to the essential passivity and masochism of femininity, that is the distinctive feature of Deutsch's work.

Deutsch's later work shows some departure from what she had conceived of as her rigorous defence and development of Freud's theories. But the style she had set for the publicly orthodox Freudian – the biologistic interpretation of a fundamental penis envy expressing a constitutional lack, which inhibited the expression or development of a true femininity, whose 'three essential traits' were 'narcissism, passivity and masochism' – was to be very influential. Despite Marie Bonaparte's disagreement with Deutsch over the importance of masochism for women's capacity for orgasm, the biological reading of Freud that Bonaparte gave in her papers of the 1930s, through to her book, *Female Sexuality*, of 1951, was very much in the vein that Deutsch had opened up. Because they start life with a biologically inferior organ, the clitoris, that is destined to lose its function, women will always have difficulty in adapting to the necessary passivity imposed upon them by their cloacal vagina. In the face of these biological facts, women's attitude to their sexual life should be one of resignation.

There were, however, different ways of responding to Freud. If Deutsch and Bonaparte cast themselves as defenders in the debate, whilst offering interpretations of Freud's writings which were quite alien to the sceptical distance Freud attempted to put between psychoanalysis and biology, then the most outspoken critic of Freud, Ernest Jones, presented an entirely different biological subversion of Freud's theory of femininity.

Jones's doctrine of the unconscious knowledge of sexual intercourse was part of a larger set of doctrines with which he countered Freud's theory of femininity. From 1925 on, Melanie Klein began to have a profound influence not only on Jones, previously as orthodox as any Freudian, but on the bulk of analysts in England, where she eventually settled in 1926. From 1927 on, the debate between Anna Freud and Klein and her new and enthusiastic followers over the theory and practice of child analysis erupted. Not for the first time, Freud's relationship with Jones was caught up in political, professional and personal tensions; not for the last time, it survived intact. Jones was, when all was said and done, the indefatigable organizer ready to jump on a plane in 1938 to save the Freuds from the Nazis and, following Freud's death, to complete his life's work with a magisterial biography of his master. However, by 1926, Jones was the only one of Freud's early living major disciples who had not had a public disagreement with the master.

In 1927, Jones and Freud had three major and institutionally significant disagreements: one over the question of lay analysis; one over Klein's and Anna Freud's differing views of child analysis; and one over female sexuality. In each of the debates, one catches an almost clipped military style in Jones's conduct of the battle, as he draws up plan A against plan B in the debate over lay analysis, draws as sharply as possible the two opposed views of the super-ego in the debate over child analysis, and sets out, to strategy B's advantage, the two distinct views A and B of female sexuality (i.e. the 'essentially male' view of Freud on the one hand vs. the 'essential female' view of Jones, Horney and Klein). These differences of opinion, particularly over Klein's theory and the linked topic of female sexuality, appeared to lead to a gradual curtailing of Freud's and Jones's theoretical exchanges of view. And, in a more mysterious way, it dried up the flow of Jones's previously seemingly inexhaustible analytic pen; his paper of 1935, 'Early Female Sexuality', delivered as part of the scientific exchanges intended to heal the growing rifts between London and Vienna, was Jones's last major psycho-analytic publication.

Freud's own concerns were, as we have seen, dictated by his starting-points: the fact that adult sexuality is a delicate construction, welded out of parts that are not functionally preordained to work well together, and that adult sexuality, with its emphasis on two – at most, and certainly not one – sexes is neither the only nor the 'natural' way to look at human sexuality. We could, Freud's *Three Essays* implied, have ended up divided into oral, anal, urethral and voyeuristic types, rather than into 'simply' men and women: 'it does not seem that children choose this fundamental fact [of the existence of two sexes among human beings] in the same way as the starting-point of their researches into sexual problems.' It is this basic Freudian datum that Ernest Jones does his utmost to undercut. The fact of the existence of the two sexes, each with full knowledge and interest in both sets of erogenous and reproductive organs, he takes as the absolutely fundamental starting-point for discussion of the phallic phase: 'the boy may be supposed to have had from very early times an unconscious knowledge that the mother has an opening – and not only the mouth and anus – into which he could penetrate.'

Our source of knowledge of the boy's very early unconscious knowledge is Melanie Klein. Her theories pervade Jones's rebuttal of Freud's model of the 'essentially male' little girl. Jones's starting-point, however, is more sensitively directed at Freud; he picks up on the weakness we have already seen exhibited in Freud's complex and ambiguous 1926 refutation of Rank's birth trauma theory. 'What precisely in women', Jones asks, 'corresponds with the fear of castration in men?' Freud's somewhat clumsy formulation had been: losing the object's love. Jones proposed a more radical conception, one that covers both sexes: 'in both sexes castration is only a *partial* threat, however important a one, against sexual capacity and enjoyment as a whole. For the main blow of total extinction we might do well to use a separate term ... *aphanisis* ... both sexes ultimately dread exactly the same thing, aphanisis.' Jones goes on to argue that what Freud had called the phallic phase in girls is not a normal part of her development, but a neurotic regression, under the threat of aphanisis. Most importantly, what the girl is protecting through this defensive identification with the male is her femininity. Whereas Freud had posited one original sex – a phallic sex – which divides into two, masculine and feminine, through their different responses to the castration complex, Jones posits two original sexes – 'male and female created He them', as the final words of his 1932 paper put it – which respond distinctively to the different forms in which they perceive the threat of aphanisis. To protect her femininity, the girl masquerades as a boy.

What does Jones mean by an original femininity, which each female is born with? He denies the significance of both of Freud's problems: the first concerning the late but all-important shift from clitoris to previously undiscovered vagina, and the shift of object from the mother to the father. The structure of his argument is thus close to that of Horney, as he himself recognizes, whilst its detail, and the greater force of its psychoanalytic argument, derives from the work of Klein. Firstly, the question of the vagina. Through exploring the early partial objects of the little girl, Jones depicts the complex links between the oral, anal and vaginal trends, emphasizing that the late onset of the sadistic wave allows the vagina to emerge as a passive, receptive organ. 'The two alimentary orifices thus constitute the receptive female organ.' 'Normal' penis envy emerges, as Horney had pointed out, through autoerotic – urethral and exhibitionistic – sources; but the second important form is an erotic, Oedipal form, for which Jones prefers the term penis desire to that of envy. It results from the frustration of the girl's relations with her father; it is the bitter disappointment 'at never being allowed to share the penis in coitus with the father, or thereby to obtain a baby, that reactivates the girl's early wish to possess a penis of her own.' However, the primary motivation for this defence is the autonomous attack on the girl's sexual desires mounted by the super-ego, itself created by the unbearable frustration of the Oedipal desires.

Here we see the importance of Klein's claims that the Oedipal drama is played out extremely early. Where Freud saw the attachment to the mother as pre-Oedipal, the Kleinians, askance at such a departure from Freudian orthodoxy, declared themselves *plus royaliste que le roi*, as Jones put it. There is no such thing as a pre-Oedipal phase. So Jones could agree with Freud that the turning away from the mother, which Freud linked to penis envy, is the crucial moment in the girl's development. But for Jones this 'hate' is very early on 'essentially a rivalry over the father's penis': there is 'at a very early age hetero-erotic incest, with Oedipus hate of the mother'. Thus, like Horney, Jones commits himself to both the girl and the boy having established a relation to the father extremely early, and having established the existence of the vagina. The primal scene is the fantasy of the combined parent figure inside the mother's body. Jones admonishes Freud on this:

In the boy's imagination the mother's genital is for so long inseparable from the idea of the father's penis dwelling there that one would get a very false perspective if one confined one's attention to his relationship to his actual 'external' father; this is perhaps the real difference between Freud's pre-Oedipal stage and the Oedipus complex proper.

The *plus royaliste* Jones wishes to establish the Oedipus complex as the model of all relations; he does so by portraying the early relations to the mother as including relations to this internal father: the father's penis perpetually in coitus, the combined parent, inside the mother's vagina. There is no phallic mother: the woman with a penis is always the mother with the father's penis.

From very early on, children *already know* that the penis is the father's attribute; they know that women don't have penises, and they know that they haven't been castrated.

In his 1927 paper, Jones placed great emphasis on the combined parent and on the fundamental aim of early sexual fantasy: the union of the penis and the vagina. In defence against the dangers associated with the desire for this union, the girl can either give up her object, the father, or give up her sexual organ, the vagina. Whichever she gives up, the eventual outcome is liable to be either an identification with the father, Freud's masculinity complex, or straightforward denial of the vagina and penis envy; the two solutions lead to interconnecting, non-feminine positions. 'Freud's "phallic phase" in girls is probably a secondary, defensive construction rather than a true developmental stage.' In Jones's account, the subject is already sexed: she gives up her sex to enter into penis envy; whereas in Freud, the girl only becomes sexed when penis envy is transformed into something else.

Jones was hurt by being treated by Freud as, in effect, an appendage of Horney's arguments concerning the defensive and secondary character of penis envy. In a letter to Freud, he managed to combine both a hurt and a lofty tone, awarding Freud good marks for discovering for himself things that 'we in London' – and from the mid-1920s on, Jones's royal 'we' always signified the Kleinian 'we' – had already discovered:

It was, however, gratifying to find you laying stress on the prolonged early mother attachment in women with a strong father-fixation (in my experience the same is true in cases, which perhaps you do not see so often, of strong father-aversion) and on the early aggressivity towards the mother, for in London we have for some time been emphasizing these two points. But we do not find that this stage is entirely a matter between the girl and the mother *alone*, the phantasy of the father (especially of his penis in her womb) playing also a part of some importance.

Switching from patronizing Freud to implying that he was about to make the same mistakes as Jung had made – 'Previously he forgot the mother, and now he has forgotten the father' – Jones insistently urged Freud to join the Kleinians in seeing Oedipal conflicts as present virtually from the beginning of psychic life:

Hitherto you have laid such stress on the father and male side (owing to the obscurity of the female) that I hope some passages in your essay discounting the father and the triple Oedipus situation in the young girl will not influence some analysts to proceed to a similarly one-sided view as you then indicated.

Freud's reply was dignified but unmoved:

That I am supposed to have forgotten the father is generally not like me. I state that the father does not yet play a role, or only a negligible one, in a certain developmental phase. It seems to me that in your circles this chronological order is neglected, and that too many disparate elements are thrown on to the same plane, probably under the influence of Kleinian interpretations, whose justification I dispute in accordance with my latest experiences.

While Freud was intransigent on his clear disagreement with Klein's interpret-ations, there were issues that might be misunderstandings rather than dis-agreements:

However, I also sense a misunderstanding between us. Can it be that what you denote as the phallic phase in the girl means something different to us; that you make a distinction between phallic and clitoral, which mean the same to us? It seems to me to be so.

Jones's second paper on female sexuality, 'The Phallic Phase' of 1932, set out to show that he understood Freud quite well, but was determined to carry through an even more thorough downgrading of the concept of the phallic phase, which had been introduced in Freud's 1923 paper, and upon which his entire conception of the development of female sexuality rested. Not only is the phallic phase not a true developmental phase in girls – and here already is Jones's unambiguously biologistic reading of the concept of development stages, which, unlike in Freud, are to be sharply distinguished from neurotic deviations, which are 'secondary and *komplexbedingt* [conditioned by com-plexes]'; it is not a true developmental phase in boys. Neither sex displays ignorance of the vagina; so neither sex can ever, except through neurotic denial, inhabit a world in which there is only one sort of sexual being, the phallic being.

At every stage, both the boy and the girl have intuitive knowledge of the difference between the sexes: 'the proposition that the boy has no intuition of the sex difference is on logical grounds alone hard to hold ... intuition of a penetrable cavity is an early underlying assumption in the whole complex reaction.' And if logic were not sufficient, Jones points to the 'boy's own libidinal sensations in his penis with their inevitable accompaniment of penetrative impulses.' Thus from early on the boy has libidinal strivings towards penetration and infers that there is a cavity that the mother has that will match these strivings. The dread of the vagina derives not from the fear of ridicule that Horney had imputed to the boy as he compares the smallness of his organ with the vastness of the space it is required to fill; rather, the boy knows that he will encounter in that space the hostile and rivalrous paternal penis. The boy's phallic phase is inaugurated in the face of this danger, with its denial of the vagina and its giving up of penetrative desires: 'the typical phallic stage in the boy is a neurotic compromise rather than a natural evolution in sexual development.' It is a deviation from his natural propensity for sadistic penetration into the vagina: 'later to retrace his steps in order to evolve, he has to claim again what he had renounced – his masculine impulses to reach the vagina'.

In girls, the assertion of primary femininity again follows Klein: the work of the English child analysts 'shows that girls had from very early times definite impulses towards an imaginary penis, one incorporated into the mother but derived from the father, together with elaborate phantasies on the subject of parental coitus.' The hostility towards the mother may be manifest at one level of analytic interpretation in penis envy and the charge that the mother failed her by not giving her a penis. But deeper (i.e. Kleinian) analysis shows that the charge against the mother is a more feminine one, unconnected to the girl's own lack of a penis: 'she has thwarted the true, feminine needs of her receptive and acquisitive nature and has threatened to destroy her body if she persists in them.' The mother is a threat because her aim is 'to destroy the real feminine penis-receiving and child-bearing organs'. Jones had come a long way from Freud's firm conviction that the vagina is unknown in childhood: 'The vagina is the seat of the deepest anxieties, so an extensive displacement outwards takes place.' Both sexes, therefore, react to incestuous Oedipal wishes with guilt; the super-ego instils in both a fear of mutilation for their own genitals: 'the central dread of the guilty girl – even in consciousness – is that she will never be able to bear children – i.e. that her internal organs have been damaged.' As is appropriate for the little girl, with her knowledge of her vagina and her preponderant preoccupation with the internal organs, she may locate the fear in the destructive penis of the father; but this destructive penis is always already the penis derived from the fundamental fantasy, highlighted by Klein's work: 'the father's penis incorporated in the mother'.

Jones's paper of 1935, his sortie in the prolonged struggle for theoretical supremacy between Vienna and London, a struggle replayed during the war in the Controversial Discussions, added little of substance to his two earlier papers. However, it increased the distance between Freud's views of the late and contingent acquisition of the fateful penis envy and its desire for a penis-child and the Kleinian reversion to a primordial feminine desire for sexual intercourse:

There is, in our opinion, such a thing as a primary natural wish for a penis on the girl's part, but this we regard not as a masculine striving in clitoris terms, but the normal feminine desire to incorporate a man's penis inside her body – first of all by an oral route, later by a vaginal one. This wish seems to us to lead on directly to the wish for a baby, the normal wish to take in a penis and convert it into a child.

The only feature that distinguishes this account of femininity as a psycho-analytic account, rather than as the pre-Freudian wisdom of the ages about woman's desire for man, and man's desire for woman, is the assertion that the original form of this feminine desire is oral. Interestingly enough, this was one of the fundamental tenets of Klein's account of early fantasy that Freud wholeheartedly accepted. In a letter to Jones sceptical of the value of Klein's very early interpretations concerning the development of the super-ego and early femininity, Freud ventured the following view:

Everything we know about early female development seems to me unsatisfactory and uncertain. I see only two points clearly: that the first representation of sexual intercourse is an oral one – sucking on the penis, as earlier, at the mother's breast; and giving up clitoral masturbation on account of the painful realization of the inferiority of this organ. On everything else I must reserve my judgement.

Freud never developed the view expressed in this letter; it is not clear from whence he derived the idea. Klein had claimed it as her own, noting in a paper published in 1926 how in a paper delivered in 1924 she had previously given examples 'to show that children at first conceive of, and desire, coitus as an oral act.' And it certainly has the hallmark of Klein's work at this time, when she was attempting to show how the Oedipus complex was active much earlier than Freud had envisaged, and, in a sense, made this a necessary conceptual consequence of one of the basic principles of the Freudian psychoanalytic method as she interpreted it: 'we should discover the primal scene'. Jones made use of Freud's confession in his letter, drawing out its latent Kleinian implications and adding some more for good measure. Firstly, he interpreted Freud as holding that 'the girl seeks for a penis in her mother' – a view to which Freud would probably have assented. But Jones then asserts that the girl links the idea with the mother having received the father's penis in an act of fellatio. Here is the combined parent, here is the discovery of the primal scene that Klein requires. An internal process transforms this penis into excrement and eventually into the anal-child. This, Jones affirms, 'is, though still on an alimentary level, nevertheless akin to the allo-erotism of the adult woman.' By subtle progression of argument, Jones used Freud's slim certainty about the oral conception of coitus, when combined with the Kleinian view of the innate unconscious knowledge of parental intercourse (purportedly Freud's primal scene), to arrive at a goal which was diametrically opposed to Freud's: the original feminine desire to take the penis into her body and turn it into a child:

Freud holds that when the girl's wish to own a penis is disappointed it is replaced by a substitute – the wish to have a child. I would, however, agree with Melanie Klein's view that the penis-child equation is more innate, and that the girl's wish to have a child – like the normal woman's wish – is a direct continuance of her allo-erotic desire for a penis; she wants to enjoy taking the penis into the body and to make a child from it, rather than to have a child because she cannot have a penis of her own.

Jones, relying on the work of the women analysts Horney and Klein, had, in order to criticize Freud, developed a view that posited an innate femininity, consisting in the innate desire to have children, which was intimately tied to the wish to incorporate the penis into the leading erogenous zone. Whereas Freud and Klein expressed the view that this zone was the mouth, Jones, in part following Horney, had put forward arguments – based on the opposition between the knowledge children have of the external male genitalia and the internal female genitalia – to the effect that the vagina was innately primordial in this respect, that the vagina was the innate seat of feminine desire and, therefore, the innate seat of the deepest feminine anxiety.

What final judgment should we pass on this theory, which was intended to remove what Jones called – introducing into the English language a word that was to have a long and important career in feminism – Freud's unduly 'phallocentric' bias? As we have seen, we could with justice call his theory a vaginocentric theory, though it would be more accurate to call it coitocentric.

And therein lies the historical irony. Freud's phallocentric theory of femininity made the attachment of women to men, their interest in sexual intercourse, a fragile and contingent event – the product of a series of difficult transitions. Jones had made coitus the supreme and inflexible destiny of woman, an instinctual aim to which she is born. So the anti-phallocentric Jones is by no means a feminist, no more than Horney's theories of paternal rape and vaginal predestination made her one. One can see as much in a curious, quite definitely Freudian, slip with which he closed his third and final paper on female sexuality:

[the girl's] femininity develops progressively from the promptings of an instinctual constitution. In short, I do not see a woman – in the way feminists do – as *un homme manqué*, as a permanently disappointed creature struggling to console herself with secondary substitutes alien to her true nature. The ultimate question is whether a woman is born or made.

Where Jones had written 'feminist' in this passage, many other people would see the passage making more sense if he had written 'Freudian'. Of course, in Jones's eyes they would be right. For the Freudian view of the woman as a man who has been castrated (by nature?) and the feminist view of woman as a human being who has been deprived and frustrated (by culture?) both deny the deeper truth: of woman becoming woman in fulfilling her innate feminine destiny.

If Jones's papers were the most explicit challenge to the Freudian model, the work of Jeanne Lampl de Groot and Ruth Mack Brunswick self-consciously developed Freud's contrasting of the development of the little girl and boy into a less counter-intuitively contentious model. The main theme of their revisions to Freud's model were direct developments of his ideas concerning the complete Oedipus complex, due to the inherent bisexuality of children, as set out in Chapter 3 of *The Ego and the Id*. In his 1925 paper on 'Psychical Consequences', Freud had spelled out the problem: how does it happen that girls abandon their first object, the mother, and turn to the father? His answer had concentrated on the castration complex and the subsequent penis envy. Lampl de Groot interpreted both the boy's and the girl's relation to the first object as already an Oedipal relation. Instead of the contrast Freud implicitly drew between the early attachment to the mother, what he would call in 1931 'a phase of exclusive attachment to her mother', and the later Oedipus complex, Lampl de Groot portrayed both boy and girl as already lodged in an incipient Oedipus situation. Except that, for the girl, this early phase represents her 'negative oedipus attitude'. It is Lampl de Groot who underlines that the reason why a girl is so overwhelmed by the sight of the boy's penis is precisely because the sight threatens, competitively as it were, her relation to the mother: 'When she has discovered and fully accepted the fact that castration has taken place, the little girl is forced once and for all to renounce her mother as love-object and therewith to give up the active, conquering tendency of her love-aim as well as the practice of clitoral onanism.' Freud had emphasized as a new and momentous discovery the fact that there is an elaborate development in girls before the Oedipus complex is entered into: 'So far there has been no question of the Oedipus complex. ... In girls the Oedipus complex is a secondary formation.' Lampl de Groot shifts the emphasis, in part to lessen the importance of the castration complex:

in contradistinction to Freud, we are assuming that the castration complex in female children is a secondary formation and that its precursor is the negative oedipus situation. Further, that it is only from the latter that the castration complex derives its greater psychic significance, and it is probably this negative attitude which enables us to explain in greater detail many peculiarities subsequently met with in the mental life of women.

In her second paper on problems of femininity, published in 1933, Lampl de Groot followed Helene Deutsch's recent emphasis on the passive and masochistic trends essential to the development of femininity: the dominant sexual events of a woman's life are painful. In her first paper, she had argued that the fact that girls have to give up their first love-object, never to regain it, is the source of women's lack of capacity for full object-love, which has here, in a subtle twist of Freud's account, become a normative goal of adult maturity: 'she can only "let herself be loved"'. The passivity of this position – which Lampl de Groot seems to link closely with narcissism – is the distinctive characteristic of femininity. Her argument now pursues the development of femininity as being synonymous with passivity: women who love men, rather than let themselves be loved, are masculine; maternal love is also masculine, because it is active; the passive and purely feminine woman has no super-ego because the creation of the super-ego requires active and aggressive instinctual components. But the full implications of Lampl de Groot's first paper were only to become clear with the final 'Freudian' statement in the debate, Ruth Mack Brunswick's paper of 1940.

Bearing the indeterminate but none the less considerable authority of being the product of conversations with Freud over a period of some ten years, her paper set out the definitive view of the pre-Oedipal phase and its influence on the development of both boys and girls. Yet there were two theses developed in her work, one of them explicitly at Freud's suggestion, which came into considerable tension with each other. The paper opened with the statement of one of them, that 'an exclusive relation exists between mother and child' before the advent of the father. This exclusive relation is dyadic, as later theorists would put it, in contrast with the Oedipus complex, whose fundamental character is that of a triangle. 'At the beginning of her life the little girl is to all intents and purposes a little boy.' However, in boys the pre-Oedipal mother attachment is short, merging very early into the Oedipus complex; whereas, in girls 'something surprisingly like the oedipus complex of the boy' develops. Like the boy, she is attached to the mother and the father enters the scene as a rival.

Brunswick sets out to explore the three antithetic pairs of concepts that are fundamental to understanding infantile life: active–passive; phallic–

castrated; masculine–feminine. It is in exploring the first of these that she introduces a new conception, the second of her novel theses:

I should like to offer a suggestion made by Freud in our early discussions of these problems. The terms 'active' and 'passive' oedipus complex are more comprehensive and accurate in their application to both sexes than the usual positive and negative oedipus complex. According to this new terminology, the preoedipal sexuality of the girl becomes her active oedipus complex with the mother as its object.

With this suggestion, Lampl de Groot's focus on the negative Oedipus complex as characteristic of the little girl becomes assimilated back into a new symmetric account of boys and girls: both take up the position of the active Oedipus complex following the period of exclusive attachment to the mother. What then follows is the destruction of the boy's Oedipus complex and the girl's move, following the discovery of castration, into the passive Oedipus complex, in which she (passively) takes the father as her object. Freud's suggestion thus allows the Oedipus complex to regain its supremacy as the central organizing event of infantile sexual life. Where Freud had, in 1925, recognized the asymmetry of the boy's and the girl's developments, particularly with respect to the Oedipus complex, his disciples Lampl de Groot and Brunswick restabilized an account common to both girls and boys around a redefined Oedipus complex.

Not only that: both boys and girls now have a period of exclusive attachment to the mother, which precedes the active Oedipus complex. The earliest period of infancy is one of an exclusively passive relation, derived from the infant's 'nuclear passivity', to the active mother: 'not only active, phallic but *omnipotent*'. All later activity, in both sexes, depends upon an identification with the primordially active mother. Girls now differ from boys only in that they have a supplementary period of rejection of the active Oedipus complex, in which they passively love their fathers and, somewhat late in the day, construct the wish to have his baby. This supplementary period, once known as the girl's Oedipal relation to the father, becomes of less and less significance in Brunswick's account. Only 'partial success [in transferring libido to the father] is the rule rather than the exception, so great is the proportion of women whose libido has remained fixed to the mother.'

On the question of the origin of the wish for a baby, Brunswick breaks with one of the oldest of the Freudian findings, that the wish for a child is the outcome of a complex set of equations between stool, penis and child. The wish for a child is very much older than penis envy; it is primarily an asexual wish, 'based wholly on the primitive identification of the child of either sex with the active mother'. Penis envy itself is no longer only conceived of as a narcissistic wound: it becomes part of a seductive calculation within the active Oedipus complex, within the girl's amorous relation to her mother. 'An object root [of the active wish for a penis] is formed when the little girl realizes that without the penis she is unable to win the mother' – an argument that Jacques Lacan would take up and extend considerably. Nor is penis envy translated into the wish for a child, as Freud had argued; Brunswick implies, rather, that it dies a slow death, as the child acquires the sense of the impossibility of such a desire for a penis and puts away such childish things:

Contrary to our earlier ideas, the penis wish is not exchanged for the baby wish which, as we have seen, has indeed long preceded it. In the course of normal development the impossible is given up and the possible retained. The little girl concentrates her energy on the permissible and legitimate wish for a baby. The active penis wish, the wish for a full and permanent possession of a penis, makes way for the passive penis wish, the wish to receive the penis from the man in coitus.

As a result of her collaboration with Freud, Brunswick had transformed many of the theses Freud had advanced in the 1920s and early 1930s. Prior to any castration complex, the active Oedipus complex dominates the infantile genital organization. The focus now inevitably shifts to the primary passivity of both sexes in their initial dyadic relation to the active mother and its relation to the activity of this active Oedipus complex. Thus Brunswick's argument subtly reinforces one underlying and very long-standing tendency of Freud's reflections on femininity: the similarity between the development of boys and girls. However, Freud's stark accent on the sudden divergence of their development is almost entirely lost in Brunswick's account; for her, the most salient influence of the pre-Oedipal phase – by which she means the active Oedipus complex – on later femininity is the complete absence, in many women, of the normal (passive) Oedipus complex. Freud, she implied, never saw such a woman:

The undeveloped, primitive woman with scant heterosexuality and a childish, unquestioning attachment to the mother, presents herself almost regularly to the woman analyst. This type of individual does not consult the male analyst because of a total lack of contact with the man.

Without positing an essential femininity, without invoking a primordial rape fantasy, without assuming the primacy of the early vagina or the combined parent, Brunswick had centred the 'Freudian' theory of femininity entirely on the relationship to the mother. And had underlined, as if it were not already clear, that the woman analyst was in a privileged position to discover this.

By the time Brunswick published this paper in 1940, most of the European analysts were émigrés in the USA, like her, or in Britain. Some precariously, others with trumpeted success, they were preoccupied in constructing new lives. And in the process they constructed a different, non-European version of psychoanalysis. The debate over female sexuality, conducted between the three centres of psychoanalysis, Vienna, Berlin and London, had slid into silence as the Berlin, and later the Viennese analysts, were forced to emigrate. When the theoretical debates along the Vienna–London axis were renewed in the much more urgent form of an institutional crisis within the British Psycho-Analytical Society during the war, the Viennese were scandalized at the radical interpretations of Freud that Klein and her followers now took as the essential basis of psychoanalysis. But the issue of female sexuality was secondary and superfluous to the vitriolic disagreements in these debates:

over fantasy, over the early life of the infant, over the pre-eminence of the libido as opposed to the destructive instincts, over the relations of psycho-analysis and biology, over Klein's fidelity to Freud. Although, as we have seen, the best organized criticism of Freud's views of female sexuality had come from Ernest Jones, in the first full flush of his enthusiasm for Klein's theories, little of Kleinian theory bore directly on the topics Freud was addressing. However, as Jones's papers indicate, Klein's work had the pro-foundest repercussions for a theory of femininity.

Melanie Klein had recognized this on one occasion in the late 1920s, at the time when the debate over female sexuality was at its height. In one paper she wrote then, and only in that paper, she delivered a direct challenge to Freud's views on female sexuality, by positing a primary femininity phase for *both* sexes, characterized by the incorporative, receptive and passive aims of the oral and anal phases. Klein's intentions in this paper were wider: she wished to reaffirm her finding that the Oedipus complex comes into operation very early, much earlier than Freud envisaged, and that the super-ego is also in operation long before the child has been threatened with castration. There is no doubt that the argument of the paper is somewhat confused, in part because of the complexity of the factors Klein is bringing together; it is probable that the confusion and complexity led her to refrain from using the concept of the femininity phase again. But this does not entail that the concept was not a natural development of her thought; quite clearly it was.

Klein argues that the frustrations suffered in weaning and interference with anal pleasures lead to an intensification of sadism, which is concentrated on gaining access to and taking possession of the mother's body and its contents. The crucial shift is when these contents come to include the babies inside the mother; when the super-ego forbids these sadistic attacks on the mother's body, an identification with the mother ensues. This 'very early identification' constitutes the femininity phase. It is feminine because in fantasy the mother's body now contains children: it is the womb that is being attacked and coveted.

As in the castration complex of girls, so in the femininity complex of the male, there is at bottom the frustrated desire for a special organ. The tendencies to steal and destroy are concerned with the organs of conception, pregnancy and parturition, which the boy assumes to exist in the mother.

What is feminine about the femininity phase is the desire for children. Yet what the child would meet if it were to enter the womb to steal the children is the hostile penis of the father. 'Thus the femininity phase is characterized by anxiety relating to the womb and the father's penis, and this anxiety subjects the boy to the tyranny of a super-ego which devours, dismembers and castrates and is formed upon the image of father and mother alike.'

The girl's early maternal identification is also governed by the sadistic desires to rob and destroy the mother. Thus Klein establishes a feminine identification in both sexes prior to the phallic phase, prior to the onset of the castration complex and penis envy. And this identification is fully Oedipal in its implications and its genesis. Freud singled out this trend in Klein's argument for rebuttal in 'Female Sexuality': Klein's early dating of the Oedipus complex 'is especially incompatible with my findings as to the long duration of the girl's pre-Oedipus attachment to her mother.' Freud was starkly contrasting the pre-Oedipal attachment to the mother with the Oedipal love of or rivalry with the mother, and affirming that Oedipal conflicts do not interfere with the lengthy honeymoon period of the girl's attachment to her mother. Yet, in an ironic twist, it was Ruth Mack Brunswick's paper which was to bring the 'Freudian' position much closer to Klein's some twelve years later, with the similarities between the early Oedipus complex of Klein and the new concept of the active Oedipus complex. Both organize the child's later genital impulses around the mother as primary object, with whom an identification is crucial to later development. Both portray the father as embodying a hostile element – the hostile penis in Klein, the Oedipal rival in Brunswick. Both assert the wish for children as primordial and prior to the later transformation of penis envy into the desire for a child from the father. The only difference is that Brunswick posited a very early phase, almost a pre-pre-Oedipal phase, accentuating 'exclusive attachment to the mother' – one in which the father does not figure at all. In contrast, Klein had long before discovered the father – in the form of the phallus of the combined parent figure – active in fantasies from the very earliest months of the infant's life.

The overall drift of Klein's paper of 1928 was to support those arguing against Freud. She supported Horney's contention that penis envy was a secondary and superficial formation; penis envy is a cover for the more profound 'dread of injury to her womanhood', to her own capacity for motherhood and her internal organs. From very early on, Klein sees the little girl as already committed to the problem of her own reproductive organs and her deep fears bound up with babies. She endorsed Deutsch's 'Kleinian' – or should one say Abrahamian – argument that 'the genital development of the woman finds its completion in the successful displacement of oral libido on to the genital'; she added that vaginal sensations play a part as soon as Oedipal impulses arise. All in all, Klein was endorsing each of the separate arguments that the psychoanalytic debate over female sexuality levelled against Freud's construction. And, as we have seen, her theories unquestioningly and assertively embodied precisely those assumptions of innate femininity and masculinity that Freud's own theories had been designed to avoid.

However, Klein's significance was not so much in the steadfast manner in which she politely picked apart Freud's arguments concerning female sexuality as in the overall long-term influence of her theories. With other British theorists such as Brierley, W. R. D. Fairbairn and Winnicott, each profoundly influenced by her whilst not necessarily being her followers, Klein established a psychoanalytic school, that of object-relations. This tradition would eventually, in the 1970s and 1980s, provide the conceptual tools to challenge Freud's theories, whether these were confronted in the orthodox form of his own papers, or in the revised ego-psychology of his daughter and her American co-workers that dominated American psychoanalysis from the Second World

War to the 1970s. Most importantly, Klein's work pioneered a slow and subtle shift, one, perhaps, that transformed psychoanalysis more than any other single factor: the reorientation of the understanding of the child's inner world around its relation to its mother. Mothers became models for the profession of psychoanalysis, mothering provided descriptions of what psychoanalysts were supposed to be doing; via the mother, the normative life-story was introduced. 'In the work of the British School, psychoanalysis was not being used as a new way to understand mothering, but mothering was being used to understand psychoanalysis.' By promoting the view that the most salient, and certainly the most important, transferences are to the analyst *qua* mother, the Kleinians – now joined by their bitter opponents the Anna Freudians, as well as Winnicott and Wilfred Bion – eventually proposed norms for psychoanalytic treatment (and theory) which focused entirely on the mother: the internalization of the good breast, the achievement of the depressive position. Freud's sexual mother had been ushered blushing from the analytic scene. And, with the eclipse of the sexual mother, the British school's psychoanalytic child was itself to be desexualised, in that very British tradition which had also created *Alice in Wonderland* and *Peter Pan*.

Although the early debates on femininity and sexual difference in the 1920s and 1930s seem to have been internal to psychoanalysis, when we look at their return in the 1970s and 1980s we can be in no doubt of the influence of feminism on psychoanalytic theories of female sexuality. The occasion for the second debate was a wholesale onslaught on Freud's views by the new feminists of the 1960s and 1970s. The criticism initially came most powerfully from well outside the established profession of psychoanalysis. And that fact, that it was feminism which ignited a new debate over Freud's views of female sexuality, should encourage us to enquire whether the same was not true of the first debate. Horney was alone amongst psychoanalysts (at least amongst those who contributed to the debate in the journals) to address the anti-feminist tenor of Freud's original argument. However, the allusions, by Jones, by Freud himself, by others, to the wider stakes at issue remind us that this first debate was not conducted in a vacuum either. Far from it. Noisy intruders, the return of the repressed, were already making themselves heard in the lecture-halls, seminar-rooms and consulting-rooms. It is also too much of a coincidence that the period of most intense debate in the inter-war years, and its falling away, coincided with the rhythms of expansion and contraction, the post-war rise and fading away towards the end of the 1930s, of the political and social feminist movements of Europe and America. The destinies of psychoanalysis and feminism were for much of this century closely intertwined.

16

FEMINISM AND PSYCHOANALYSIS

'A new prophet arrived upon the scene to clothe the old doctrine of the separate spheres in the fashionable language of science.... Sigmund Freud, beyond question the strongest individual counterrevolutionary force in the ideology of sexual politics.' So wrote Kate Millett, the first in a line of contemporary feminists for whom Freud loomed large in its demonology. Freud becomes the principal ideologue in the modern oppression of women, the patriarchal apologist for male chauvinism. The new feminism's relation to Freud was initially one of, quite literally, visceral hostility.

However, the new feminism's relation to Freud and psychoanalysis became more complex than this, the dominant critical note. To the extent that feminists perceived the twentieth-century 'sexual revolution' as a positive and liberating force, Freud's association with that movement accorded him a respected place amongst the antecedents of progressive contemporary movements. Feminists might approve of his general critique of social and sexual repression, yet regard his views on women as execrable instances of traditional patriarchal contempt. In this attitude to Freud, a deeper tension was being expressed. The women's liberation movement had emerged in part as a result of the 1960s sexual revolution, with its emphasis on free love, on the self-determination of one's sexual life, and on the explosive and Utopian potential of freedom of sexual expression. To that extent, it could regard the metaphysics of Eros that the more radical readings of psychoanalysis offered (Wilhelm Reich, Herbert Marcuse) as an endorsement of the new lives the radical movements of the 1960s were attempting to live. Insofar as the women's liberation movement arose out of the discovery that the oppressive character of relations between men and women are starkly revealed, rather than transcended, in the sexual revolution, a distrust of these prophets of sexual liberation, and of their paternal antecedent, was formative. Free love, it turned out, was free only for men; the woman paid, in many small and indeterminate ways. The recounting of the many small ways in which each woman paid was intimately bound up with the sense of taking control of their lives that was so much a part of the growing movement. At the same time, it created a universal consciousness that the endemic historical experience of women was one of sexual and social oppression.

The new practicality of the ideal of each individual woman taking control of her life was also a development of the transformations in legal and medical sexual technology of the 1960s. The Pill symbolized both the possibility of sexual pleasure without painful consequences and women taking control of their sexual and reproductive lives; it promised freedom and control. The struggles for abortion law reform were a further element in the movement for self-determination and individual control, superficially less permeated by the ideal of redemption through sexual pleasure. In as much as these movements were a continuation of the struggle against social structures that were tightly restrictive of sexual life in general, and of women's sexuality in particular, they were a continuation of the struggles to which Freud's critique of modern sexual morality had also contributed. However, insofar as they were also struggles against the confining of women to their tightly defined social and biological roles, Freudian psychoanalysis was seen as the legitimator of the doctrine that woman's social place was in the home caring for her penis-substitutes, that her fulfilment lay in marriage and in passive submission to the sexual and social will of the male.

Much however had changed between the 1930s and the 1960s. Feminist texts bear witness to this: they often speak of that historical epoch as if it were alien and utterly prehistoric. For Kate Millett, the period 1930–60 was that of the sexual counter-revolution, whose political arm was Nazi Germany and the Soviet Union and whose ideological arm was Sigmund Freud and sociological functionalism. The ubiquitous self-consciousness of the 1960s as being a new era in the history of the world went hand in hand with a sometimes involuntary, sometimes deliberate quasi-Brechtian effect of alienation from this recent history, well described by Betty Friedan's *The Feminine Mystique*. Freud figured prominently herein as the spirit of the time:

Freud was accepted so quickly and completely at the end of the forties that for over a decade no one even questioned the race of the educated American woman back to the home. ... After the depression, after the war, Freudian psychology became much more than a science of human behavior, a therapy for the suffering. It became an all-embracing American ideology, a new religion. ... Freudian and pseudo-Freudian theories settled everywhere, like fine volcanic ash.

The ingredients of the Freudian Zeitgeist that oppressed women varied. Sometimes it was the Victorian model embodied in Freud's own relations with his beloved sweetheart, mistress of hearth and home. Always it was the vision of the girl as a castrated, stunted man. Freud's opinions that the super-ego of women was weak, dependent, never so inexorable as in men, so that 'for women the level of what is ethically normal is different from what it is in men', together with his emphasis on the role of jealousy and envy in women's lives, were repeatedly held up as the clinching evidence both of Freud's personal contempt for women, and of the necessary conservatism of psychoanalytic theories. Sometimes it was the phallocentricity of his theory that doomed it in the eyes of feminists. Often it was the 'Freudian' dictum, usually as read in the extremely influential and many times reprinted *The Psychology of Women* by Helene Deutsch, that the mature woman's sexuality was naturally passive and masochistic. Or the fact that sexuality was so central to Freud's version of psychoanalysis made it complicit with visions of women as beings closer to nature, ruled by their biological animal urges, condemned by their bodies to the natural function of serving their cultural masters. Time and again, psychoanalysis was seen, even by those more sympathetic to the idea of such a theory, to be not a theory of sexual differences, but a rationalization and legitimation of already existent social roles.

Two specific theses aroused the greatest anger and opposition to Freud's work: 'penis envy' and the 'vaginal orgasm'. The attacks on Freud over the second of these best capture the new mood of 1960s' feminism. Freud's early notion that women change their leading sexual zone in puberty from the clitoris to the vagina was seen as the foundation for the widely disseminated requirement that, to be sexually normal, a woman could only have vaginal orgasms: 'clitoral women were deemed immature, neurotic, bitchy, and masculine; women who had vaginal orgasms were maternal, feminine, mature, and normal.' The physiological findings of Masters and Johnson's *Human Sexual Response* of 1966 were seen to be the definitive refutation of the Freudian thesis concerning vaginal orgasm: there is only one sort of female orgasm – the 'clitoral body' is, to use Masters and Johnson's own words, 'the primary focus for sensory response in the human female's pelvis'. The symbolic power of Masters and Johnson's work, while in part stemming from the predominantly physiological vocabulary which replaced the suspect Freudian vocabulary of subjective meanings and imaginary bodies, arose from their fundamentally masturbation-centred account of both female and male sexuality. The assertion of the rights of the clitoris and the myth of the vaginal orgasm went hand in hand with women's assertion of their own control over their bodies, even their sexual pleasures, and their fundamental independence of male sexuality, in particular the penis. Masters and Johnson's emphasis on the capacity of women for indefinitely many orgasms encouraged the view of women's pleasure as inevitably restricted if they are dependent in any way on men. 'A woman needs a man like a fish needs a bicycle' was a famous feminist slogan; the implicit message was that a woman needs a man no more than her rampant clitoral sexuality, previously symbolized by the vagina's humble receptivity to the phallic god, needs a penis.

The critique of penis envy was from the beginning the shibboleth of feminist criticism of Freud. There were two very common responses. The first was to express disbelief that such a phenomenon exists; it became the myth erected by a systematically diseased man who could not face woman's otherness, a myth in the service of, and giving a pseudo-scientific basis for, traditional misogynistic views of women's supposed enviousness and jealousy. Following this view, the theory of penis envy could be analysed and interpreted as a scientific myth, perhaps even a projection of men's far greater envy of women's capacity for child-bearing. As common as this interpretation, was its almost exact opposite: the view that Freud's observations on penis envy were correct, but had been entirely misinterpreted. Instead of envying the male's sexual 'privileges', penis envy was a veiled expression of envy of the male's social privileges: his power, his status, his capacity to dominate others. The penis of penis envy is not a real, bodily penis; it is simply a phallic symbol, but not a Freudian phallic symbol. The young girl immediately perceives it as a symbol of power and prestige. In this interpretation, penis envy is a real and justified index of female oppression in a patriarchal society. Interpreting penis envy like this links closely with arguments found in the feminist historiography of hysteria discussed in Chapter 3, the 'male oppression model'. The sick or neurotic woman of the nineteenth century is in reality a victim of the social order she inhabits; Freudian theories of hysteria and later of penis envy were just one of many attempts to maintain the status quo, the existing hierarchy of gender roles. Repossessing history, giving women back their silenced voices, would reveal a quite other order of female desire than the cold phallic stone of patriarchy, than the insistent voices of the male totems of Freud and Lawrence. The genealogy of patriarchy's silencing of the voice of female desire showed how Freud's theories translated directly into the psychoanalytic therapies and marriage manuals of the mid-twentieth century, with their aim of restoring distressed women to their proper places as mothers, helpmates and housewives. In these popularizing works, any attempt to compete with men, to disrupt the hierarchy, is attributed to her envy of the penis. The prescribed treatment is to transform her penis envy into the authorized passive feminine virtues; the index of success will be her capacity for vaginal orgasm.

One of the favourite catch-phrases of the early 1970s was 'consciousness-raising'. This programmatic phrase, redolent of the primary givens of the psychoanalytic theory of the unconscious and of the psychoanalytic practice of bringing the repressed into consciousness, named one of the major political practices in the first years of the modern women's movement. Groups were constituted for the purpose of consciousness-raising. In the sharing with other women of personal, autobiographical and quotidian details, the wider social and historical sweep of patriarchal oppression was revealed. Women who had previously felt that they lived isolated, impoverished lives now shared their individual experience with others, their sisters, and were euphoric in gaining recognition from others, in the simple naming out loud of bitterly humiliating experiences in common – the political economy of sexual bartering, the furtive pleasures of childish masturbation, the shame of possessing a woman's body in a man's world. Simultaneously, a new group consciousness was created, that of the universal category of women, often conceived of in Marxist terms as a class whose coming to consciousness is the necessary basis for any political action.

The practice of consciousness-raising fed off a political axiom of the era: 'the personal is political'. However, rendering the political personal and the personal political did not suffice for long. Notwithstanding its creative originality and genuine political novelty, the women's movement had firm, historical links with already existing political movements and theories, whether Marxist, socialist or liberal democratic and rights oriented. Part of the new movement's significance lay in its challenges to the categories of those political theories – for instance, to the economic definition of class, to the male property-owning norm of the human right. Yet the development of its distinctive political practice and theory could only occur if the personal were equally made the object of theoretical reflection. If the political innovation of consciousness-raising had a family affinity to the talking cures invented in the twentieth century under the pressure of the therapeutic imperative, then a turn by members of the women's movement to consider the utility of revising, for their own purposes, an already existing theory of the personal and of the talking cure became, by the early to mid-1970s, attractive.

There were other, perhaps more pressing reasons for the shift from consciousness-raising to a more personal, more theoretically reflective mode of analysis. The relief and catharsis flowing from self-revelations of the social injuries and injustices common to all women – for instance, the demeaning sexual strategies required to gain and hold on to jobs, marriages and economic security in general – did not prevent questions of the correct or progressive individual and communal courses of action, of life style, from being raised. Consciousness-raising could often be confused with or degenerate into organized self-criticism, whose moral claim was vouchsafed for some by the respect given, at the time, to Maoist political models. And a new moralism, perhaps not unrelated to the higher ethical norms thought by some early twentieth-century feminists to be the special gift of women, could grow out of the slogan 'the personal is political'. Personal sexuality was sometimes required to prefigure the liberated sexuality of a transformed society. 'Heterosexist assumptions' had to be expunged without mercy. Thus, for example, in the early 1980s a major controversy broke out between feminist groups who wished to restrict discussion of questions of power and domination within lesbian relationships, on the grounds that any hint of such inequalities of power were simply examples of complicity with male heterosexual oppressive practices. What had started off as a liberatory movement seemed to some to have become a new and deeply prescriptive moralism. Feminism now confronted the question that had given psychoanalysis in its early days such power to shock: does the understanding of human sexuality require dispensing with ethical norms, whether conventional or radical?

There were other reasons for a turn to psychoanalysis. The sexual libertarian aspects of Freud's theories were not the only ones to attract the positive interest of feminist thinkers. Understanding the family, an institution so bound up with the recent historical destinies of women, was an urgent need, especially since the youth movement and the anti-psychiatry movement, both historical antecedents and coeval with the emergence of modern feminism, had viewed the family as one of the core reactionary institutions of modern society. If penis envy were itself an accurate clinical observation, if psychoanalysis were a reliable means for uncovering hidden structures of everyday life, then it might have other things to say about the sexual position of women, both historically and in the present. Shulamith Firestone had outlined this view as part of her critique of psychoanalysis:

Both Freudianism and Feminism came as reactions to one of the smuggest periods in Western civilization, the Victorian Era, characterized by its family-centeredness, and thus its exaggerated sexual oppression and repression. Both movements signified awakening: but Freud was merely a diagnostician for what Feminism purports to cure.

Freud proposes, feminism disposes. The historical link between psychoanalysis and feminism asserted here is one that has emerged repeatedly in our study. The notion that there is an intimate, perhaps even fated, historical link between the two has haunted one substantial section of feminist thought in the last twenty years, even when the specific content not only of Freud's theories of femininity but of many other aspects of psychoanalytic theory have been censured. '"We were made for each other", says one partner in the first flush of rapture; only to be followed at a later, more bitter stage by a transformed insistence that "the relationship was doomed from the start" ... neither side ever lets go ... psychoanalysis and feminism seem to be locked into combat or copulation unto the death.'

The union was first proposed in the early 1970s, when a more reflective, more theoretically aware development in feminism found in Freudian psychoanalysis the elements of a theory of sexual difference – anthropological, sociological and psychical – which feminism required. As Gayle Rubin shrewdly, wittily and absolutely seriously wrote: 'Psychoanalysis is a feminist theory *manqué*.' Rubin's 'The Traffic in Women' and Juliet Mitchell's *Psychoanalysis and Feminism* proposed that feminism needed psychoanalysis for its own purposes: to develop a theory of sexual difference in patriarchal society, in order to answer 'the question of the nature and genesis of women's oppression and social subordination', and of 'how society transforms biological sexuality into products of human activity'.

Mitchell's ground-breaking work put the thesis of the psychoanalytic feminists boldly: 'a rejection of psychoanalysis and of Freud's works is fatal for feminism. ... If we are interested in understanding and challenging the oppression of women, we cannot afford to neglect it.' Her sustained attack on her contemporary non-feminist and feminist critics of Freud – on the Reichians, on the anti-psychiatry movement associated with R. D. Laing, on the feminists Simone de Beauvoir, Eva Figes, Betty Friedan, Shulamith Firestone, Germaine Greer and Kate Millett – uncovered the extent to which the Utopian revolutionary movements of the 1960s were antipathetic to the core ideas of Freudian psychoanalysis: to the unconscious and sexuality, and to the very idea of an autonomous psychic reality. The venomous sting of the indictments and the muscular certainties of the solutions of the radical feminists so often assumed direct translation from social reality, whether it be one of oppression or of liberation, to the condition of the individual agent or subject. Psychoanalysis as a theory interposed psychic reality between the subject and the social order, thus making possible the pursuit of the feminist project of revealing the construction of the subject, without necessitating a mirroring relation, in which the constructed subject matches perfectly the roles and categories of the social world.

Mitchell drew a map of the misreadings of Freud. She also specified what an adequate feminist theory of the family, sexuality and the feminine might look like. Crucial to this specification was the division between nature and culture, and the requirement that a theory place both women and men, in their different subjective positions, on the side of culture; there was to be no place for a theory which had women playing nature to man's culture. Simone de Beauvoir, in the most important work on women published this century, had opened her chapter on psychoanalysis with the following assertion of the importance of Freud's legacy for the study of women:

> The tremendous advance accomplished by psychoanalysis over psychophysiology lies in the view that no factor becomes involved in the psychic life without having taken on human significance; it is not the body-object described by biologists that actually exists, but the body as lived in by the subject. Woman is a female to the extent that she feels herself as such. There are biologically essential features that are not a part of her real, experienced situation: thus the structure of the egg is not reflected in it, but on the contrary an organ of no great biological importance, like the clitoris, plays in it a part of the first rank. It is not nature that defines woman; it is she who defines herself by dealing with nature on her own account in her emotional life.

The advantage of psychoanalysis is that it operates entirely in the human, in the cultural field. Mitchell followed Beauvoir in this respect, despite her disagreements over the existentialist-phenomenological critique of psychoanalysis which Beauvoir appended to her account of Freud's significance. And this vision of psychoanalysis as an account of the cultural generation of human sexed subjectivity was allied with another axiomatic position arrived at by Mitchell and many other psychoanalytic feminists following her: psychoanalysis is the best guarantee against a lapse back into the essentialist doctrine of original femininity. As long as psychoanalysis is an account of the becoming of a woman, not of her being – her essence, her substance – it offers feminism what it needs. And its theories of the unconscious and infantile sexuality will allow feminism to avoid the traps or blind alleys into which other theories have led it. Thus the common view of American feminists, that it is the social conditions of patriarchal society, not penis envy, which are solely responsible for women regarding themselves as inferior, postulates the little girl as a passive transmitter of social and cultural values, obliterating her individual subjectivity, making her far more passive – but now in relation to social values and forces – even than the little boy *manqué* of Freudian theory. It turns the little girl into a victim, just as the first feminist histories of hysteria of the early 1970s had painted the hysteric as a victim. Such deterministic arguments only make it both more difficult and more imperative to discover a feminine subject who is untouched by the social beyond the roles and rules of patriarchal society. Thus the social determinism of feminist critiques of Freud – deterministic because they posit a direct, unmediated *and uncontested* translation and transference of patriarchal values and roles from family and social ambience to potential feminine subjects – requires, in a second stage of the analysis, recourse to a feminine subjectivity which lies untouched and recoverable, beyond the social. And here essentialism makes a comeback: the feminine that is recovered from this beyond becomes for such theorists the 'essence' of femininity. However, the various essentialisms associated with earlier versions of Freudianism – primordial rape, innate heterosexual principles, the biological underwriting of femininity by the capacity to give birth – complicated the question of where psychoanalysis stood in relation to Freud's original project, which had repudiated both biological and social varieties of essentialism.

What complicates the history of the relation between psychoanalysis and feminism is the appearance of a third element in the debate: French psychoanalytic theory as developed by Jacques Lacan in the context of structuralist linguistics and anthropology. Mitchell's work bears the influence of Lacan's return to Freud, from which emerged a radically distinct, resolutely symbolic (as opposed to naturalist) Freud, full of significance to the future development of feminism's relations to psychoanalysis. Yet the curious irony of employing Lacanian psychoanalysis as the fertilizing agent in the union of psychoanalysis and feminism was that he highlighted the essential function of the *father* in the constitution of the human subject. Lacan systematically questioned those psychoanalytic developments from the 1930s to the 1970s, which were increasingly and almost exclusively focused on the child's early relations with the mother. He reiterated the centrality of the Oedipus complex to any psychoanalytic theory or effective clinical interpretation, making common ground with the Kleinians' suspicion of the very idea of the pre-Oedipal. And it is the father who introduces the Oedipus complex. The Lacanian father is the representative of the law, of the existence of human culture (as opposed to nature); he supplies the third term or mediating function that allows the child to find a place in the symbolic order (language) and escape from the blind alley of fascination with the image (other) of the mirror stage, experienced in fantasy as fascination with the mother. However, the father's function is strictly metaphorical – he functions neither as real father (flesh and blood), nor as imaginary father (though the latter figures in fantasy as an ideal and punitive agency), but as the Name of the Father, with his family name assigning the child a place in the social world. It is this metaphor that allows the child to become a sexed being through the phallic function to which the Name of the Father refers.

Lacan's suspicion of the pre-Oedipal or Kleinian mother was shared, although for different reasons, by Mitchell and others, who knew the conservative impact of popularizations such as *The nursing couple* in the post-war effort to rebuild the family. The necessity of the father and the phallus in the Lacanian scheme guaranteed that psychoanalysis was removed from the ambiguously *ewige mutterliche*, or eternally maternal, tendencies that British Kleinian and object-relations theories were encouraging. The father is always symbolic, even in the most basic empirical sense that Freud had often alluded to: 'turning from the mother to the father', Freud wrote, 'points in addition to a victory of intellectuality over sensuality – paternity is a hypothesis, based on an inference and a premise.' More significantly, an anthropology can be constructed around a psychoanalysis centred on the father; Lacan's enthusiastic use of Claude Lévi-Strauss's theories of kinship and the exchange of women could become the model for Mitchell's and Rubin's feminist psychoanalytic anthropology, answering one of feminism's most basic questions: why is patriarchy the universal template of society?

The Lacanian answer to the feminists' ever-present stumbling-block of penis envy is the concept of the phallus. Where the penis refers to the anatomical part, and even the imaginary organ of fantasy, the phallus is the name of a function, and specifically a signifying function. No one *has* the phallus, though distinct sexual positions are marked out by desires to have it and to be it. Lacan's account of sexual difference posits the mother as desiring; the recognition of her desire, the desire of the other, is the starting-point of the desire of the child. The subject desires what the mother desires: the object, the signifier, of that desire is the phallic function of the father. In this account, desire is born in the child in the double recognition of lack: the mother desires, is thus lacking, yet simultaneously the child realizes that it lacks what the mother desires. The third term of this triangle enters in, the father; he necessarily enters in as rival since the child posits the father's very existence as the object of the mother's desire following the recognition that he or she does not have what the mother desires.

The phallus is thus a symbol founded on absence, a symbol of lack. It manifests itself not in its immobile presence, but in the exchange, the exchange between the father and the mother. In this sense, Lacan's theory picks up on one of Jones's Kleinian deviations from Freud: the fact of sexual intercourse is primary in the organization of sexual difference. But Lacan's version is structuralist: sexual intercourse is defined by an exchange, a transaction, of symbols (or signifiers). No one has the phallus; it is only manifest in the act of exchange; it is the letter of credit in the domestic sexual economy. This 'socialization' of the penis in the form of the economy of the phallus resonated well with the project of a feminist psychoanalytic anthropology. Yet, as sceptics sometimes doubted, it was by no means clear that it solved the problem of power and patriarchy. Even Lacan was equivocal on this point, seemingly attributing the privilege of the phallus to its being doubled up in the symbols of political power:

the law would not apply any the less if women were placed at the centre of this system, receiving the phallus in exchange for which they would give a child. If one must however describe this exchange as androcentric, it is, Lévi-Strauss tells us, on account of effects which make themselves felt, of political power that it is incumbent on men to exercise. The phallus prevails, then, because it is also the sceptre, in other words because it belongs to the symbolic order.

But the symbolic logic of the phallus has other creative resonances, besides its potential for building a political economy of sex. When the subject gives what he does not have, according to Lacan, he loves. And love is thus always Oedipal, positing an imaginary rival who has the something the loved one desires. It is Julia Kristeva who has most recently picked up on this Lacanian account and developed it into a far-ranging theory of the father of personal prehistory, whose very early intervention in the relation to the pre-Oedipal mother brings about a split in primary narcissism.

Lacan's account of the introduction of the Freudian signifier of sexual difference, the phallus, into the economy of the child's relations to the mother does not specify the gender of the child. The difference between boy and girl emerges out of the differing positions that they take up as the schema unfolds. It is this aspect that makes it attractive to a feminism that requires an account of the generation of sexual difference in the imaginary and symbolic relations between the child and its entourage. It renders Freud's account of the generation of the phallic phase less dependent on the equation of the clitoris and penis. And it robs the crucial moment when the girl perceives her own anatomical lack of its gender-determining function. What replaces the moment when 'she has seen it and knows that she is without it and wants to have it' is the recognition that the mother desires something that is beyond the child – the name given to this beyond is the phallus. So the person who is castrated in the Lacanian model is the mother – any being who desires is castrated – and then the child. *Both* boy and girl are castrated. Implicit in the account is that both boy and girl come to perceive lack itself as a sign of prohibition: a being that lacks (desires) was once a being that did not, was self-sufficient. An event took place that deprived it of its original state of non-desiring plenitude. Castration has always already happened. It is the father who is introduced into the psychic economy with lack; and it is the father who is, therefore, perceived as being the efficient cause of that lack. He is the castrator. Mitchell reads this account back into Freud: 'For Freud the absence of the penis in women is significant only in that it makes meaningful the father's prohibition on incestuous desires.'

Thus the problem becomes for Lacan to explain how boys can ever come to equate their little penis with the phallic function concealed in the mystery of the father's relation to the mother. 'What the boy has, as an appurtenance, he must take it as from another; this is what we have called the *symbolic debt*.' On this point, another rapprochement between psychoanalysis and feminism opens up, through the Lacanian perception of the instability of gender roles – for example, the castrated little boy who later becomes in someone's imaginary the man with a penis, or the little girl who awaits the unique gift and must make do solely with counterfeit substitutes. These ways of being sexed are difficult to achieve under the best of circumstances, always place the subject permanently in debt to another, and are thus invariably precarious – the debt must perpetually be serviced. The child continues to resist castration, continues to resist becoming a human being. 'Feminism's affinity with psychoanalysis rests above all, I would argue, with this recognition that there is a resistance to identity at the very heart of psychic life.'

However, the Lacanian reading of Freud's account of femininity, centring on the phallus as a signifying function rather than an anatomical part, does not satisfy everyone. Hence vociferous debates, often uncannily reminiscent of the debates of the 1920s and 1930s, have been conducted over the last fifteen years. Critics of the phallocentric Lacanian system often link it to Freudian phallocentrism and, just as Ernest Jones, the coiner of the word phallocentric, had done, posit an autonomous feminine sexuality – for example, Luce Irigaray's echo of Horney's vision of the primordial rape, in the interruption of the autoeroticism the woman needs to experience sexual pleasure: 'the brutal spreading of these two lips by a violating penis', an interruption that denies the multiplicity of feminine pleasure and the specificity of the feminine in relation to language. For Irigaray, then, the Freudo-Lacanian theory of the phallus is simply the 'contemporary figure of a god jealous of his prerogatives'. And the figure of the little boy who sees the woman with no penis reappears on stage again, now as the little boy who sees that the Emperor has no clothes. Jacques Derrida's critique of the transcendental phallogocentric Lacanian system opens with this story as the allegory of psychoanalytic interpretation itself. Stephen Heath and David Macey have mounted violent attacks on the Freudo-Lacanian phallic orthodoxy, tearing aside veils that do not exist, since, as they lay out the texts, the question is always: 'How could any reader not see that these texts are sexist and trivializing of women?'

Lacanian psychoanalytic feminists had followed Lacan in viewing his reformulations of Freudian theory as being clarifications of Freud's ambiguities, rendering consistent or more usable the complex tensions of psychoanalytic theory as Freud developed it over forty years. As a result, Lacanian theory sometimes adopts the posture – Jones's posture in defending Klein's theory of the early Oedipus complex – of being *plus royaliste que le roi, plus phallique que le phallus*. Yet the interminable ambiguities of the relation between the penis and the phallus render the correct reading of the Lacanian theory an unceasing hermeneutic labour in defence of a thesis that is never secure. 'If the phallus is distinct from the penis, then feminism's battle against phallocentrism is not a battle against men. But if it is nearly impossible to keep the distinction phallus/penis clear, that may account for the constant return of the assumption that men are the enemies of feminism.'

Despite the infusion of the radically novel Lacanian interpretations of Freud from the mid-1970s on, the suspicion remained for many that psychoanalysis did not quite meet the need that feminism had of it. Was the relation between feminism and psychoanalysis a contingent one? Could there have been another theory of the construction of sexual identity which would have been more satisfactory for feminism's needs? Did psychoanalytic feminists espouse the psychoanalytic theory of sexual difference *faute de mieux*? These questions have persisted, even amongst those who are enthusiastically and professionally committed to psychoanalytic theory and practice. Nancy Chodorow writes: 'Until we have another theory which can tell us about unconscious mental processes, conflict, and relations of gender, sexuality, and self, we had best take psychoanalysis for what it does include and can tell us rather than dismissing it out of hand.' But the questions, the haverings about the virtues of psychoanalysis, have contributed to the currents of feminism which are less enamoured of the union of feminism with a theory whose language and popularizations can still evoke the visceral hostility that it aroused in the first wave of the new feminism.

These currents were dominant in American psychoanalytic feminism of the 1970s, which regarded the hostile critiques of Freud's phallocentricism as valid and rejected Freud's theories of female sexuality. Psychoanalytic feminists in the United States, taking the prominent examples of Dorothy Dinnerstein, Nancy Chodorow, Carol Gilligan and Jessica Benjamin, have followed different post-Freudian psychoanalytic traditions. These are ones which do not parade themselves as ultra-orthodox, and which are convinced that they have made discoveries that contradict and render obsolete Freud's theories: theories of the pre-Oedipal mother and the object-relations theories of the British school, and theories of the core gender-identity. As Dinnerstein put it with her typical generosity in opening her remarkable book: 'I am disinclined to let the presence of [Freud's sexual] bigotry deflect my attention from the key to a way out of our gender predicament that Freud, in a sense absent-mindedly, provides.'

Chodorow indicates quite clearly her conceptual allegiances. She is in sympathy with Horney and other critics of Freud insofar as they declare the implausibility of Freud's account, for instance his denial that the vagina is of significance in the early years, and of its phallocentric one-sidedness and bigotry: 'Horney asserts a model of women with positive primary feminine qualities and self-valuation, against Freud's model of woman as defective and forever limited.' Chodorow argues that Freud's account is the product of 'patriarchal assumptions about passivity and activity' and of a biological determinism concerning the function of the genital organs. In her eyes, his critics had successfully challenged his assumption that sexual difference is defined for both sexes in relation to the absence or presence of the male genital, rather than to 'two different presences' – although she remains non-committal about the biological essentialism upon which this refutation was founded. But Chodorow's main aim is not to revise Freud's theory of sexual difference, in part because she regards it as irremediably distorted and incorrect, but also in part because she regards much of the general Freudian psychoanalytic project as flawed and misguided. Indeed, Chodorow's central feminist question in *The Reproduction of Mothering* arises from perceiving that 'women's mothering is one of the few universal and enduring elements of the sexual division of labor.' She asks: 'How do women today come to mother?' By the end of the book, she has supplied answers to these and other questions as well:

women's mothering ... creates heterosexual asymmetries which reproduce the family and marriage, but leave women with needs that lead them to care for children, and men with capacities for participation in the alienated work world. It creates a psychology of male dominance and fear of women in men.

The heart of the psychoanalytic argument that leads to this conclusion depends firstly on rejecting the instinctual theory which Freud and his opponents in the psychoanalytic debate over femininity had shared: these theories see people (in this case women) as appendages of their drives and genitalia. On this point, Chodorow was very much in sympathy with the earlier wholesale rejection by feminism of the psychoanalytic vocabulary of 'objects', of the assumption that the 'self', the person, can be described as an assemblage of autonomous sub-systems or processes. The feminist demand that women not be treated as (sex) 'objects', appeared to intertwine with the 'humanistic' plea that persons not be treated as (psychoanalytic) 'objects', but as 'subjects'. With this criticism, Chodorow indicated a fundamental break with classical analysis, and more particularly with its French Lacanian version. In turn, Freudo-Lacanians regarded such conceptions of a self which was ontologically prior to and more fundamental than its bodily desires and activities as a revival of the pre-Freudian masterful ego that Freud's discovery of the unconscious had undermined forever.

Beyond the instinctual theory, Chodorow endorses an object-relations theory and Margaret Mahler's account of child development as a continual process of separation-individuation. Object-relations theory, in Chodorow's interpretation, allows her to flesh out the criticism of Freud's Oedipus complex, on the grounds that it takes account only of the child's desires and fears in relation to the parents, omitting the relationship established by the parents' wishes and behaviour towards the child. Object relations for Chodorow means patterns of family relationships; this is the advance that feminism requires. The gendered specificity of the mother-child relationship can now be described: girls have greater difficulty separating from their mothers, precisely because *their mothers* regard them as being 'the same' as themselves; boys separate more easily from their mothers because, from very early on in life, the mother regards the boy as 'different', as belonging to the other gender.

It was Robert Stoller who provided one crucial aspect of this argument for Chodorow, in a series of explicit criticisms in the 1960s of Freud's account of the generation of masculinity and femininity. Just as Masters and Johnsons' work of the 1960s had been read by feminists as a definitive refutation of the Freudian claim about the change of the girl's leading zone from the clitoris to the vagina, so Stoller's underpinned many later refutations of Freud's account of the difficult construction of maleness and femaleness. Stoller's studies of the development of 'core gender identity' demonstrated that children have a certainty of their gender – 'the simple acceptance of the body ego, "I am a female"' – from an early age, perhaps as young as twelve months. Stoller's explanation did not attribute this acceptance to knowledge of the vagina or other genital signs: the single causal element is the fact that 'their parents have no doubt that they are females.' Freud's assumption that the theory the child holds about itself and its sexual identity is bound up with *its* desires, rather than its parents or general entourage, is certainly ignored, and implicitly denied. The sociological account, so rhetorically powerful in the 1960s and 1970s, wins the day and dissolves all the debates about the complex process through which masculinity and femininity are acquired.

Chodorow adds a further twist to Stoller's basic thesis. Core gender identity, 'the fundamental sense of being female', is acquired very early; but the development of the girl and boy towards their *sexual*, as opposed to gender, identity is a more complex affair, in which the process of individuation and separation is crucial. Here the model of the child receiving messages directly from the parent, including the parent's desires and internal mental states, is retained but made more elaborate. For Chodorow, 'the establishment of an unambiguous and unquestioned gender identity and realistically sexed body-ego is a preoedipal phenomenon.' It is entirely bound up with the messages, or imprinting, received from the primary care-taker, who contingently happens, because of the near universal division of labour, to be the mother. And there the tragic part, for feminists, of the story begins. It is girls who have difficulty establishing their separate identities and acquire, in consequence, certain emotional characteristics and aptitudes, such as privileging the self-in-relation, the self that defines itself through its relations with others. It is these aptitudes that then lead to many of the distinctive traits of adult women, in particular that they wish to be mothers, and to mother. In boys, a different process occurs, including the construction of a core gender identity by a repudiation, by being not-mother; as one of its distinctive characteristics the male self denies relatedness. Thus, 'the maternal identification represents and is experienced as generically human for children of both genders'; it is the Oedipal phase which reverses the earlier mother-centred definition of the human, making maleness the new standard of the human.

One of the conclusions Chodorow came to was that the fear and loathing of mothers in western culture, together with all the fateful consequences of the doctrine of separate spheres, will only be dissipated if men become mothers. Non-gender-specific parenting became the key item on the political agenda; 'women's mothering was *the* cause or prime mover of male dominance.'

Chodorow's thesis was very influential, not least because it showed many feminists how the earlier criticisms of Freud's bigotry and phallocentric theories could still stand without their being obliged to discard psychoanalytic theory in its entirety. Theorists such as Carol Gilligan could follow the path that Chodorow had trod, from social theory and psychology towards psychoanalysis, bringing with them the evidence and argument of more academically based disciplines, thus sidestepping rather than readdressing the fatally flawed Freudian account of sexual difference. Gilligan emphasized the different modes of social being in the world of girls and boys, which could be interpreted in the light of their different early experiences of mothering. Yet her project picked up, curiously enough, on one of Freud's most heavily censured reflections: 'for women the level of what is ethically normal is different from what it is in men. Their super-ego is never so inexorable, so impersonal, so independent of its emotional origins as we require it to be in men.' Gilligan's experiments on moral reasoning in children and adolescents revealed that girls' morality is distinctly, though not of course universally, different from that of boys: it is a morality of responsibility (to others), rather than the often mechanical morality of rights and abstract justice of boys. Her work converged with Chodorow's in the emphasis on connection, on relatedness, harking back to the girl's experience with her pre-Oedipal mother. At the back of both was the empirical and analytic work elaborating on the primordial rhythms of attachment and separation of Margaret Mahler's studies of mothers and children.

The psychoanalytic feminism of Chodorow and many American feminists and analysts is thus very different from European psychoanalytic feminism. The psychoanalytic traditions which are used to consummate the union are different, as are the personal, political and metaphysical requirements and expectations of the products of the union. The American analytic traditions have, ever since the 1930s, regarded Freud's 'biologism' with distrust and disbelief, preferring instead to emphasize both the immediate impact of the social world and the autonomy of the self, even if that autonomy is an ever-receding personal and theoretical ideal. The culturally specific tradition of individualism and self-help, of therapeutic optimism and the cult of self-esteem which had become such an integral part of psychoanalytic culture in the United States finds a reflection in psychoanalytic theory in the liturgy of the self that psychoanalytic feminists have willingly participated in. Curiously and yet so persistently, the optimism of this rhetoric of selfhood is always accompanied by the rhetoric of the victim.

In addition, American psychoanalytic feminists centre their account on the mother, pre-eminently the pre-Oedipal mother, whereas many of the European psychoanalytic feminists follow both Lacan and Klein in clinical and theoretical scepticism about the possibility of talking plausibly about a mother, no matter how early and how omnipotent, devoid of a relation to a father, as if a theory of the pre-Oedipal mother were just a theoretical version of an infantile sexual theory of maternal and social parthenogenesis. We can adapt the famous and often interpreted phrase of Winnicott's 'There is no such thing as an infant' – 'meaning of course that whenever one finds an infant one finds maternal care'. In the unconscious, there is no such thing as a two-person relationship – meaning of course that whenever one finds a mother, one finds the (symbolic or imaginary) paternal principle that transforms a woman into a mother. As Jessica Benjamin, in an interview, astutely described the European psycho-analytic feminists: 'all these people ... claim that the father is going to spring the child from the dyadic trap'.

Benjamin herself introduced new themes into the analysis of feminine subjectivity with her focus on the question of power and domination in sexual relationships, suggesting, in a Hegelian spirit, that the desire for recognition is the principle which opens up the dyadic relationship, but also allows the closure, through fear and defence, of the relationship which leads to the ubiquity, if not universality, of masochism in women's sexual relationships. Yet many of the materials with which she fashions her theory are those we have seen employed in Chodorow's theory: the accent on the differentiation of self and other, on loss and separation, on the all-important pre-Oedipal relation to the mother, hence on primary maternal identification, and the postulate of a core gender identity. All these theoretical arguments, while focusing sharply on recognizably Freudian and feminist problems, at the same time shunt to the sidelines Freud's original questions concerning the construction of sexual personae in the resolution of the principal struggles between desire and anxiety, libido and defence, in early childhood.

By no means every European feminist writer conceded the supremacy of the Oedipal schema. Just as American feminists often turned to post-Freudian theories of the pre-Oedipal mother, asserting the primacy of the mother in the construction of feminine identity, so did European feminists look 'beneath' the Oedipal, patriarchal order for a different, feminine ordering of the unconscious. Whilst the claims on behalf of the nomadic, schizophrenic, desiring body without organs of Gilles Deleuze and Félix Guattari's influential book *Anti-Oedipus* were not often taken up by feminists, the argument expressed a mood that was pervasive. 'Beneath the paving stone, the beach' was a slogan from May 1968. 'Beneath the Oedipal law, feminine *jouissance*' was a formula that, although promoted by Lacan in his ironic, offensive and oracular 1973 seminar on female sexuality, his reply to the feminist movement, was echoed in radical feminist views. Hélène Cixous's work on the alternative feminine spaces of writing, of maternal presence, outside the masculine order, the 'universal battlefield' of binary oppositions, shares in this search for a radical alternative to the patriarchal and Oedipal order. Julia Kristeva's early work on the semiotic as the locus of a specifically feminine counterpoint to the masculine order of signifier and Symbolic (linked as it then was in a startling if unlikely juxtaposition to the importance of the phonic in Chinese and the repression of the phonic in many western language-systems) has since developed a more recognizably psychoanalytic concern with the 'pre-Oedipal', informed by Winnicott's conceptions of transitional space and Kleinian investigations of early fantasy. In the different language of French writing, here are approaches to the centrality of the mother, not only in psychoanalysis but also in a radical theory of femininity.

The development of psychoanalytic feminism and its critics became even more complex in the 1970s and 1980s with the rise of textual psychoanalysis. Mitchell's defence of Freud had been mounted to demonstrate that psycho-analysis was not only a possible additional tool in the armoury of feminism's analysis of patriarchal culture, but also one that was necessary and acceptable to feminism. The positive theories she had advocated owed much not only to Lacan, but also to Lévi-Strauss and the conceptual scaffolding offered by French structuralism. However, it was not only feminists such as Mitchell and Rubin who were making use of 'French theory', as it was sometimes later called. Structural anthropology; Althusserian Marxism; Foucaultian history; Derridean deconstruction; structuralist poetics; narratology; post-struc-turalism: all these intellectual projects came into existence in the Anglo-American academic world in the 1970s and 1980s; all of them traced their lineage and point of departure to varieties of French theory; all of them married different ideas from France to create novel academic cults, some ephemeral, some less so. If there was one thing that Lévi-Strauss and Lacan,

Foucault and Derrida, Barthes and Althusser, Kofman and Kristeva, Irigaray and Deleuze, Ricoeur and Todorov had in common, it was their saturation, nearly always with admiration and indebtedness, however critical might be the final response, in Freud's writings. French theory transmitted to Britain, America and many other countries a new unquestionable status for Freud's writings as an essential prerequisite for the self-understanding and self-representation of literary criticism, social theory and philosophy. No longer did one have to be a clinician or accredited psychoanalytic theoretician. '*Freud studies*' became a discipline in its own right, practised in seemingly bold, although not always risky, world-wide interdisciplinary ventures, across the whole intersecting network of the humanities.

The example Lacan set, with his 'Seminar on *The Purloined Letter*' of 1954, of showing how a literary text exemplifies certain psychoanalytic concepts, such as repetition, the theory of the lost object and the relation of transference, was very important for textual psychoanalysis. So too was the work of Derrida, with his virtuoso demonstration of how texts undermine themselves, how texts perform their very own self-analysis. His persistent fascination with the complexity and reflexive character of Freud's texts set an example to many others. The tradition can be seen as a long one; it was Karen Horney who first criticized Freud's theories by drawing up a two-column table, in which the first column represents psychoanalytic theory, and the second the little boy's theories that are the object of psychoanalytic theory, thus revealing, without need for further commentary, the closeness of fit between theory and object. In that respect, she was following Freud, and many theorists and critics since have discovered Freud's texts as veritable cornucopias of blindnesses revealed in the very act of illumination, of counter-transference revealed in the very act of theoretical analysis. The collection *In Dora's Case* is the most concentrated example of this approach to Freud's writings, doing to Freud what Freud did to Dora, putting his text on the couch just by letting it free associate within itself, hoisting Freud with his own petard of proto-deconstructionist analysis of the patient. In this way, the very techniques of analysis have become indispensable to textual criticism, whether philosophical, literary or cultural; the *tu quoque*, so prominent a part of Freud's own dream analyses, from his very first analysis of the dream of Irma's injection, becomes the hallmark of the textual critic, prominent amongst them feminist literary critics.

It was Shoshana Felman who highlighted a fundamental methodological problem in this kind of interdisciplinary, intertextual study. In her 'Introduction' to a collection on 'Psychoanalysis and Literature', she queried the meaning to be attributed to the innocuous word 'and' in the very project she and her co-authors were engaged in. Is a study of psychoanalysis and literature one in which psychoanalysis will be in a position of mastery over the literary text, on the model of an analyst who knows, who achieves mastery over his patient's pathology, her hysteria, her access to femininity? Or will it be a study in which psychoanalysis finds itself subject to the same laws of textual analysis and deciphering as any other text, laws and methods which are the esoteric techniques proper to literature, to fictional structures? This ambiguity, already to be found in Freud's analysis of fictional writing, in Lacan's and Derrida's readings of philosophy and literature, is one which can be generalized to all those projects which attempt to link psychoanalysis *and* ... another disciplinary project. Is psychoanalysis the master discourse, or are its claims to hegemony being cut down to size as it is reclaimed as just one part of western intellectual and literary traditions? The question is now addressed to the uncomfortable shotgun marriages and separations of psychoanalysis and feminism. Whether the question can be resolved is as yet unclear, and its answering promises to be a busily interminable vocation.

Of course, one could describe the recent pre-eminence of Freud as an inevitable part of the process whereby each new generation rediscovers, in its own way, according to its own dominant modes of communication and intellectual reappropriation, the work of this century's most influential writer. The somewhat disconcerting feature of Freud's public face is that he often appears at his most influential when he is the object of most opprobrium, when his theories are subjected to the greatest opposition. This chapter began with the near universal clamour of feminists against the damage done by the principal ideologue of male supremacy; they too, we now perceive, were Freud's women. And the ever-present dialectic within feminism, between virulent hostility towards and fascinated admiration of Freud's work, has taken new forms since the late 1960s. In the late 1970s and early 1980s, two seemingly independent but related feminist arguments again took Freud as the target within much broader social campaigns. In an influential work on rape, Susan Brownmiller found in the theories of the Freudians a pernicious male ideology claiming that 'all women want to be raped'. The principal witness for the prosecution was, naturally, Helene Deutsch. Brownmiller's powerful book focused attention on male violence against women. Brownmiller also raised the question for many, feminists and non-feminists alike, of what an account of human sexuality should be like – an account which addresses both male and female human sexuality or sexualities and one which can address rape with the seriousness, urgency and subtlety the question deserves. Once again, Freud came on the agenda for feminists, nearly always as bogeyman, very sporadically as potential mentor.

Freud was, curiously, brought further into an urgent contemporary sexual-political debate in the early 1980s, with the uncovering of the extent of the sexual abuse of children. In 1977 Florence Rush argued that Freud had both discovered and covered up the extent of such abuse. In 1984, J. M. Masson, historian and at the time a practitioner of psychoanalysis, mounted the same case against Freud. He argued in detail that key psychoanalytical concepts, amongst them infantile sexuality and the Oedipus complex, were founded on Freud's moral and intellectual cowardice: his refusal to believe his patients' stories of sexual seduction in childhood. At the same time, Alice Miller's work on the long-term effects of 'real' infantile trauma also challenged the orthodox Freudian account of Oedipal fantasy, in a sustained indictment of the moral and pedagogical underpinnings of the therapy industry. Masson's and Miller's attacks linked up with the feminist therapies which had always included a reference to the real conditions of women's oppression as a necessary part of the therapeutic process.

The long-standing feminist groundswell of feeling against Freud now found new voice and expression. Many were indignant that Freud, and the complacently complicit psychoanalytical profession in his wake, had refused to believe the evidence of childhood sexual abuse, and had tried instead to convince their patients that their memories were fantasies disguised as reality. Once again, defenders of Freud argued the case for psychic reality against the overwhelmingly immediate rhetorical force of the call on the socially real. Somewhat at a loss, they were obliged to recognize that the political demands made on psychoanalysis require it to be a voice of condemnation, whereas the ethos of its clinical practice requires it to abstain from moral condemnation, from being either for or against. The stark differences of view are captured in the semantics of description; where Freud had consistently used the term 'seduction' to describe children's sexual relationships to adults, the keyword of the 1980s was invariably 'abuse'.

Freud's views on sexual ethics were permissive. As he put it to Marie Bonaparte when she asked him for his views on mother–son incest, at a time when she was considering sleeping with her adult son, the question bears comparison with cannibalism: there are

no grounds whatever against eating human flesh instead of animal flesh. Still most of us would find it quite impossible.... Incest is not so remote, and indeed happens often enough.... In individual exceptional cases incest would even to-day be harmless, although, it is true, it could still be unsocial as abrogating one of those sexual restrictions necessary to the maintenance of civilization.

On other occasions he could be less Olympian, at least if we trust Joseph Wortis's account of his analysis with Freud:

Relations with children ought not to be encouraged or tolerated, said Freud; in fact they ought to be prevented with the severest measures. Nobody ought to be permitted to have sexual relations with people who did not enjoy freedom of choice and judgement: an employer, for example, had no right to make advances to an employee, because free choice was not possible there.

Here, there is almost an anxious modern tone in the pressure Freud allows ethical imperatives to exert on sexual life, which may be a reason for doubting the accuracy of Wortis's account. Perhaps the following story captures the classical analyst's sense of the marginality of questions concerning sexual ethics within professional analytic practice. In the early 1980s, when Miller's and Masson's criticisms of Freud were being widely discussed, a classically trained Freudian analyst was asked for her views on the question of the reality of childhood sexual trauma, or what is now popularly called sexual abuse, as it emerges in analysis. 'An important question', she mused, 'and one that has preoccupied me for much of my professional life. My view is that if the patient is acting out by having sexual relationships with children, then one can assume that the infantile trauma were real.' For the practising analyst, the ethical questions about sexual life that preoccupy so many other workers in the sphere of the sexual abuse of children do not acquire urgency. She does not interrupt the analysis, or call the police; her only action is to integrate the new material into the work of the therapy. After all, it is her adult patient's pressing present-day problems that require her attention; it is not the analyst's task to settle scores with the past. Nor, most importantly, is it her task to intervene with either the past or the present of the patient, in the name of a higher good.

The Freud that has emerged in this seesaw of attacks and revisions is a figure who is assumed to be an active participant in the politico-sexual issues of this end of the twentieth century, implicated, if only negatively, in the responses of modernity to the deepest fantasies of both men and women. He is also a Freud whose privileges are now threatened by the redundancy notice that those who have inherited his profession wish to serve on the patriarchal father. The man who, in his youth, told his fiancée that 'the position of woman cannot be other than what it is: to be an adored sweetheart in youth, and a beloved wife in maturity' invented a profession in which women figure prominently neither as sweethearts nor wives, and in whose iconography the father is in danger of being pensioned off, rather than murdered, in favour of a mother who asserts her rights to be regarded as the origin of all things.

An eminent British Kleinian analyst, Hanna Segal, has an incisive view on Freud's entire relations to women:

I think Freud's theory that little girls think they have got a penis and then discover they don't is bunko. On the other hand, Freud was the first to treat women as human beings in the sense that he gave a proper place to female sexuality. He didn't consider them asexual beings. And even more important, I think, psychoanalysis is the first organized profession in which from the beginning women were treated exactly the same as men. ... People sometimes ask if women are more talented as psychoanalysts than men because they are more turned inwards. I don't think so.

It would be eccentric to come to the conclusion that Freud's significance for the history of women in this century lies in his having been the first equal opportunities employer. As this book has shown, there is more at stake in the prominence of women analysts – and patients – in the history of psychoanalysis than a somewhat out-of-character even-handed liberalism which gives access to the new profession. The development of psychoanalytic theory was inseparable from the distinct and important part women patients and then analysts took in its creation. Contemporary thinking about what woman is is so permeated with the discourse that Freud and his women invented that it is impossible to conceive of a future language of sexuality that does not call on the name of Freud. The twentieth-century love affair with Freud may have followed the patterns of idealization and debasement he himself described so well, but it remains, none the less, a love affair.

THE SUMMING UP

As the Freudian century drew to its close, the disparate figures of 'Freud' that presided over it refused to fade into cultural memory. Repeatedly proclaimed dead by scholars or pundits, Freud declined to rest in peace. He popped up here, there and everywhere: to act as a foil to Darwin, where once he had been used to confront Marx; to perform a comic turn in any number of Hollywood films; to engage in the science and the memory wars of the 1990s. Meanwhile, the purportedly 'real' Freud was exhumed in any number of guises – from fraud to literary genius. It now seems abundantly clear that a single image of so pervasive a presence is unlikely to emerge. Different facets of 'Freud' matter to different subcultures and interest groups – whether they seek to disparage, dismantle, honour or simply use his work.

A careful sifting of historical materials does, of course, bring a fuller picture of Freud into view. *Freud's Women* engaged us in precisely this kind of intricate inquiry. It is one which speaks to immediate intellectual and cultural concerns. In the opening section of the book, we noted that in the cultural imagination of our time, Freud stands accused on several damning counts. He was a conservative Victorian patriarch who saw woman's primary place as being that of reproductive servant of the species. He transformed his subtle misogyny into a model of the world in which women could only be failed men. He is also charged with having falsified his patients' evidence, metamorphosing their own accounts of real childhood abuse into the register of fantasy, and throwing over his early seduction theory for a more palatable – to us at least – version of events in which Oedipal desire shapes memory.

Our book set out to explore the history which had given rise to these accusations. The process of research and writing made clear that such excessive concentration on and condemnation of Freud's failings was itself a way of denying the women who figured in the history of psychoanalysis – specifically Freud's patients and colleagues – their rightful place. Once one gave them this, not only Freud but psychoanalysis itself began to look subtly different. When we spoke of Freud's women we were also, of course, speaking of Freud in so far as he and his ideas were shaped by women. The portrait that emerged of this figure crucial to the thinking of the twentieth century was rather more nuanced than the court-room sketch of the man in the dock.

Freud's Women examined four aspects of Freud's relation to women. In Part I, our focus was on women as experienced by Freud the man – his mother, his fiancée and wife, his daughters. The Freud in question here is son, lover, father – and dreamer. In Part II, we traced the development of Freud's practice and his theories through his collaboration with and 'laying bare' of his women patients. These, the famous hysterics of the late nineteenth century, were his natural and historically fated partners in the creation of psychoanalysis. The Freud who fig-ured here was doctor, conquistador, discoverer and, above all, listener and story-teller. His women patients elude us more than he does. The exact place that Freud occupied in their lives remains shadowy; they left few narratives of their own to chart their relations with him.

In Part III, we looked at Freud in another guise: that of patron, father-figure, friend, analyst, colleague. With the distinguished and idiosyncratically individual women who became some of the first analysts in his circle, Freud was not first and foremost their personal analyst. He was primarily a friend and companion – a mentor channelling their enthusiasm for that energetically disputed discipline which was the psychoanalytic process. Yet with each of these women, his func-tion as 'The Analyst' might emerge unexpectedly. Indeed, one of the most intriguing questions in all of Freud's friendships, both with men and with women, is where the fine line between analytic intervention and the ordinary toing and froing of amicable intimacy can be drawn. Whether it was the complex quadrille of Freud, Ferenczi, Ferenczi's lover Gizella Pálos and her daughter Elma, with whom Ferenczi fell in love and who was analysed by both Ferenczi and Freud, or the even more curious ménage of Sigmund, Anna Freud, his daughter and ex-analysand, and Dorothy Burlingham, his long-term analysand throughout the 1930s, Freud was breaking most of the rules in the analytic book. He did so again with the remarkable Lou Andreas-Salomé, who was his partner in the analysis of daughter, Anna; and with Princess Marie Bonaparte, who amply documented both analysis and friendship. Who is to say whether the analyses conducted under such conditions were the better or the worse for it? Certainly Freud seems to have been able to remain a colleague, father and friend in the process. In fact as Freud grew older, his aspect as a benign paterfamilias towers above all others. It persists well beyond the time that his own theories of the murder of the father would have fixed as its sell-by date.

The theoretically inclined may be rather sceptical of the historical inquiry con-cerning these real women, from Anna von Lieben, Freud's patient and teacher, via Ida Bauer (Dora) to Lou Andreas-Salomé and Marie Bonaparte. What is the interest of these real women, when it is the figure of Woman as she appears in psychoanalytic theory and practice that is important for psychoanalysis itself? There are two immediate replies to this question. First, psychoanalysis is a his-torical phenomenon, as a theory in the history of science and as a cultural move-ment. As such, when writing the history of psychoanalysis, there will always be occasion to concern oneself with the quasi-biographical and historical relations of its founders and chief figures. Second, psychoanalysis has a kinship to biographical investigation and, in Freud's own book on dreams, to an auto-biographical one. Given that its fundamental rule, 'say everything that comes into your head', superficially appears to be an injunction to reveal every last personal detail in the name of scientific inquiry, a critical examination of psychoanalysis, as a movement, a science and a method, may feel obliged to follow in its path.

Many of the present wave of Freud critics believe that everything wrong in psychoanalysis can be traced back to the fraudulent deception of Freud himself. Frederick Crews, for example, characterizes Freud as 'a saturnine self-dramatizer' who remorselessly destroyed countless lives. If one takes such criticisms seriously, then biographical facts really do count in this debate. So, writers on psychoanalysis inevitably ask a series of biographically inflected questions. How significant is it for the foundations of psychoanalytic theory that Freud – not to mention so many analysts then and now – was a Jew? What consequences, if any, can be deduced from the fact that this theory was created by a rather correct bourgeois professional with conventional tastes and habits? And how significant is it that Freud's collaborators in developing this theory – his patients rather than Josef Breuer or Wilhelm Fliess – were women? Finally, is there any significance in the fact that this theory was proposed by a man rather than by a woman?

In Part IV, we examined Freud the theoretician of the feminine – the thinker who played the role of contested founder and sometime figure of fun in the evolving annals of psychoanalysis and feminism. Many millions of pages, countless column inches and magazine headlines around the world, have been devoted to the theory of femininity he propounded. This Freud of penis envy and the 'mythical' vaginal orgasm, this theorizer of woman as failed man, feminism's very own Cassandra, would perhaps have had to be invented as a sounding board against which feminist thought could shape itself if he didn't, at least in part, exist. This aspect of his work has provided the late twentieth century with one of its many embattled Freuds. Despite his own perpetual shunning of politics, Freud here becomes distinctly political – the shuttlecock of feminist debate. On one side of the court, he is the patronizing patriarch condemning women to the single satisfaction of motherhood. On the other, he is the potential liberator, denying any determining essence of femininity.

It has become a commonplace that Freud didn't understand women, that he failed to recognize the importance of the mother for psychic life because of his refusal to recognize the significance of his own mother. Didn't he say, 'The great question that has never been answered and which I have not yet been able to answer, despite my thirty years of research into the feminine soul, is "*Was will das Weib?* What does woman want?"' Surely this question is a confession of Freud's fundamental lack of understanding?

The provisional reply that his theory gave to the question of woman's desire – that woman wants a penis – has rankled feminists since the 1920s. Such a view of Freud's limitations allows contemporaries to feel secure in the progress their own psychoanalytic groupings have made. In a recent conversation, an eminent French woman psychoanalyst noted that it was quite obvious that the Freudian theory of penis envy, of *Penisneid*, was quite unsatisfactory; but everything had been sorted out since Jacques Lacan replaced the penis with the phallus, signifier of signifiers. In other words, Freud's partly personal, partly theoretical problem in understanding women's desire has since been corrected without too much difficulty.

There is a contradiction at the heart of the classical account of the history of psychoanalysis which has Freud founding the field through his unprecedently original work with his female patients, the famous hysterics, while simultaneously being devoid of a capacity for understanding women. While he is much derided for his question, 'What does woman want?', as if the rest of the world can plainly see the simple answer to this question and his very asking of it were a confession of an irremediable failure of his humanity, the more obvious inference is not drawn: that Freud established his project for understanding women on the basis of a prior not-understanding. Without that prior not-understanding, there would have been no psychoanalysis. 'The not-understanding of women cannot be placed "outside" analysis, as if it were something one could add on to analysis, or say of analysis, without finding it already at the heart of analysis.' What is more, the context of his oft-quoted remark '*Was will das Weib?*' – addressed to Marie Bonaparte, friend and sometime analysand, a woman of particularly extreme wants and desires – brackets it in irony. Whether Freud was addressing her as analyst, friend or mentor, or as an amalgam of all three, remains unclear.

Is it important that psychoanalysis was invented by a man rather than by a woman? We can readily point out 'masculine' characteristics that find expression in the discovery of psychoanalysis. There is Freud's identification with great explorers, with conquistadors, with men of science who penetrate the deep secrets of mother nature. Freud himself speaks in terms of penetration, of revealing the naked truth. It is easy to see in his fantasy of the defloration of a young girl or woman the foundation of his interpretative practice: snatching away a young girl's flowers, penetrating to the heart of her soul, stealing a woman's most precious possession. His sexual megalomania, as he himself called it, was – and is – in no sense exceptional or out of the ordinary. His Don Juanism is usefully transformed into his refusal to hear the word 'no' as meaning 'no'. It is no coincidence that he called his first theory of the neuroses the seduction theory. And he saw *l'amour médecin*, the love of doctors, following Molière, as one of reason's ruses; for him, as for a Hegel crossed with Casanova, transference love was always a question of technique – a technique elaborated against the grain. Lou Andreas-Salomé, Freud's disciple and friend, writer and psychoanalyst, lover of Nietzsche, Rilke and many others, said that she admired Freud more than Nietzsche and Rilke because his work was accomplished despite himself, against his own inclinations. What she meant was that, at heart, Freud was not a technician of eros or of thanatos, but a grand romantic, a sentimentalist, an idealizer of women.

Freud's response to declarations of love in the consulting room brings into relief the crucial moment of transference. It is easy to forget how difficult, how perverse even, it might be to respond to the words 'I love you' by saying, 'I think you are deceiving yourself, you are really thinking of someone else.' This gesture of Freud's is entirely characteristic: it is the postman's gesture, the gesture of passing the message on to another – the gesture of 'tele-'. Thus, at the beginning of psychoanalysis, one can postulate a libidinal economy of placing-at-one-remove: on Freud's side, as a founding practice; on the side of the patient, as the inaugural concept of repression. When Freud writes about this transference-love, the analyst is a man, the subject of the positive transference is a woman and the subject of the negative transference is a man. Closely linked to this conception of the transference is his conception of the classical Oedipus complex, that of the boy who loves his mother and fears his father. The masculine bias of psychoanalysis is plainly there.

But there are arguments on the other side. Post-Freudian psychoanalysis suggests that the basic transference within analysis is always to the mother. Here the argument goes that, from the beginning, Freud, in creating the analytic situation, which he recognized was very much a personal working environment, positioned himself as the mother in the transference. Winnicott thought that Freud's fundamental and unconscious presupposition was the experience of mothering. Thus he constructed the analytic setting so that it was a prolongation or evocation of mothering: the analyst who is always there, on time, alive, breathing, awake, preoccupied with the patient, free from fits of anger, free from the compulsion to fall in love with the patient. So the analyst, Freud, is, from the start, a mother.

We sometimes forget that Freud clearly often found himself to be the mother in the transference and no doubt carried on analysing this maternal transference just as he would any other. To Hilda Doolittle, his most eloquent patient, he said:

'I do *not* like being the mother in transference – it always surprises and shocks me a little. I feel so very *masculine*.' I asked him if others had what he called this mother-transference on him. He said ironically and I thought a little wistfully, 'Oh, *very* many.'

It is the response to her question that is telling in favour of the Winnicottian sense. Freud certainly did not say to H.D., 'I refuse to play the role of the mother.' He was pretty good at it, even if he didn't enjoy it. In fact, if we look closely at the case of Dora, we find him playing the role of the experienced, worldly-wise woman who knows the secrets of sexual life, who is well aware that in sexual matters it is the little stories, the little details, which sustain an erotic relationship. But in the case of Dora, Freud did not ask himself quickly enough how the analytic situation could become, for this young girl, the site of an eroticization of speech shared between intimates. Nor did he interrogate sharply enough any pleasure he found in it. Only later, when Dora had left, did he oblige himself to transform this pleasure into analytic knowledge.

In discovering psychoanalysis, Freud, we suggest, had to play the part of a woman at least as much as that of a man. But what of the patients, both his and those who have come to psychoanalysis and psychiatry since his death?

Freud's initial gesture on his return to Vienna from Charcot's Paris in 1886 was to claim hysteria for men as well as for women. Leaving aside the disputed originality of this move, we have emphasized how Freud resolutely attempted to ignore the gender specificity of the nervous diseases, despite the fact that so many of his patients were hysterical women. As he developed psychoanalytic theory, he steadily retreated from any close correlation of hysteria with women and obsessional neurosis with men. Hysteria could be diagnosed in both sexes. The First World War corrobated this stance. The thousands of soldiers suffering from 'shell shock' displayed bodily, yet non-organic symptoms similar to those of hysteria. This produced a fundamental psychiatric re-evaluation of the notion of hysteria as a women's condition, as well as of the traditionally valued masculine character traits. In brief, psychiatry and psychoanalysis drew further and further back both from linking hysteria closely to the feminine, and, in the middle years of the century, when psychiatric classification was regarded as a poor substitute for causal therapies and theories of the origins of symptoms, from hysteria itself as a category.

With the reforms of the 1970s in psychiatric classification and the successful attempts at global uniformity of psychiatric categories under the domination of the anti-psychoanalytic and supposedly theory-free DSM-III, hysteria disappeared as a term of psychiatric classification. It fragmented into a variety of diagnoses: borderline personality disorder, multiple personality disorder, anorexia, psychosomatic illness. Among these, the DSM's classification of a 'histrionic personality disorder' seemed almost to pathologize old-fashioned notions of femininity (as well as play on two entirely different Greek words – that for 'uterus' and that for 'theatrical' – as if the doctors now thought that 'hysteria' and 'histrionic' had the same etymology). The histrionic personality disorder is characterized by excessive emotionality and attention seeking. The patient is always performing, choosing parts to suit the environment; placating and demanding in quick succession.

Yet the spectre of gender-specific conditions would not go away, not least because certain feminist theorists and activists wished to claim these as a visible mark of the injustices and noxious effects of a social, medical and familial system which produced illnesses in and then discriminated against women. On the one hand, the categories of hysteria retain a currency in the humanities and in gender studies courses, whatever the medical schools and insurance companies have decided. 'Self-diagnosis', like self-pleasuring, is no longer entirely in the hands of the medical establishment. Feminists and others have sometimes disowned, sometimes embraced the gender-specificity of so many of the chronic and non-specific illnesses of the late twentieth century, from ME via MPD to anorexia. 'Anorexia is the most common modern dress of hysteria,' writes Elisabeth Young-Bruehl; it is a means of avoiding sexuality or transposing sexuality into other modes. And these non-specific and disturbing conditions tell us a story of our times, not just of a body in pain: 'Anorexia is – culturally speaking – an antiliberation mode, a type of conservatism, a personal puritanism.'

If hysteria and hysterical patients are largely no longer recognized as such by the medical establishment, while 'hysteria' still retains a complex life outside of medicine, the 'talking cure' they gave birth to is everywhere – though in forms its co-founder would perhaps have given short shrift. Talking therapies, from re-covered memory therapy to bereavement counselling, abound in our time. Psy workers of varying designations appear in the wake of wars and natural disasters; they are omnipresent whenever marriages are in trouble and children are in distress. And, despite the much-vaunted scientific superiority and cost-effective-ness of the new psychopharmacologies, the talking cures are an essential part of the overall treatment of depressives and others who are the target of the new pharmacopoeia.

Beyond any designation of illness or disorder, speaking the emotions is acknowledged as a cultural good. Openness, an ability to negotiate personal rela-tions and feelings, is valued. Corporations hire relations counsellors and that bastion of the stiff upper lip, the British royal family, has yielded to moments of public confessional. (In the movement from court to couch, Princess Marie Bonaparte proves a fitting ancestor to Princess Di, though not one who made the front pages.) All this could be read as a feminization of culture. And Freud's practical and theoretical innovations are among its principal sources.

There is an irony in the fact that this feminization of culture – what some might even call its hystericization, given the post-modern emphasis on femin-inity as masquerade or as performance of gender – has come hand in hand with an attack on Freud as a scientific impostor. The most famous of these assaults is by Frederick Crews. Underpinning Crews's critique of psychoanalysis is his sense that the analyst, by developing a relationship with the patient, allows feel-ings or suggestions to contaminate the empirical data. Psychoanalysis can thus never provide the hard facts by which a science can be tested and proved to work. In its epistemological stance, it would seem, it is feminine. Never, given the permeability of both players in the talking cure, can it attain to the objectiv-ity, the indifference to the needs of a particular case, which hard, one might say masculine, science demands.

Crews, like the best of rhetoricians, would, of course, like to have it all ways. He uses the classic, feminist critiques of Freud's case of Dora to draw attention to the sexual aggressiveness of Freud's own behaviour, his withholding of sympathy, his assailing of Dora's self-esteem at every turn, his exploiting of the power-imbalance already inherent in the clinical setting. The case of Dora, for Crews, is 'one of the worst instances on record of sexist hectoring by a reputed healer'. Nowhere does Crews allow for the possibility that Freud's de-liberate and knowing self-exposure in publishing his errors as a clinician may be geared to pedagogical ends, that he may be underlining his own mistakes in order to point out the workings of transference to fellow and future clinicians. Not to mention to temper the therapeutic enthusiam which accompanies all medical innovations.

Crews purports to ally himself with feminism, but does not go so far as to embrace what became perhaps the dominant form of feminist therapeutic prac-tice in the US in the last decades of the century – the recovered memory and trauma therapies. Quite the reverse; his assault on Freud is also an assault on the recovered memory movement. He assimilates one into the other. They make strange bedfellows.

Since the first edition of *Freud's Women* appeared, questions of abuse, trauma and the nature of repression have moved centre stage in the relations between psychoanalysis, women and feminism. With the publication in 1992 of Judith Herman's *Trauma and Recovery*, a purportedly psychoanalytic and feminist project opened the gates to the anti-Freud battalions. On the first page of this influential study, Herman states: 'This book owes its existence to the women's liberation movement. Its intellectual mainspring is a collective feminist project of reinventing the basic concepts of normal development and abnormal psychology, in both men and women.' Her reinvention, in fact, draws on the virulently anti-Freudian wing of the American feminist movement which emphasized the social oppression of women and patriarchy's violent crimes – rape, physical and sexual abuse. For her, 'hysteria is the combat neurosis of the sex war'. This archaic phrase – most feminists would think of it now as a 'gender war' if war it ever was and still is – gives a hint that the categories Herman is employing are very much pre-Freudian, when sex was a tightly guarded and policed domain, a domain of pain as much as of pleasure. And a domain that was heavily gendered.

One aspect of Freud's sexual theory still has the power to shock: his discovery of infantile, polymorphous, ungendered sexuality, with its far-reaching consequences for adult sexuality. We would still prefer to think of childhood as a sphere of untainted innocence, as if the movement from child to adult had to replicate the story of origins and Edenic paradises lost. Our horror at child abuse is reinforced by this wish. A rising tide of seemingly random violence has combined with this to create in the figure of the paedophile a veritable monster of satanic proportions, a bogeyman with which we adults, huddled together round our children, frighten each other as we tell story after warped story.

The loss of the innocence of childhood can be placed alongside the death of God as the great adventure of critical thought at the end of the nineteenth century; but it seems that the former is as tenacious in our cultural imaginations as the latter. The lasciviousness of children still disturbs. What is scandalous about Freud's account of infantile sexuality is twofold: first, there is the iconoclastic gesture of destroying the idol of the innocent child; and second, even this arena of sexual life does not elicit the law-maker and rule-invoker in Freud. Much of the new writing about sexuality at the end of the nineteenth century was informed by legal and forensic preoccupations, from medical judgements in which sexual perversions were the sign of insanity to sexological polemics against the unnaturalness of laws restricting homosexual acts. Yet Freud held himself back entirely from any involvement with this legal framework. Why?

The analytic position is negatively defined as a withholding – withholding of personal views, personal details, prohibitions, common sense about what is normal. This withholding thus becomes a mirror held up to the patient's own desires and the laws that contain them. Freud's theories, as they developed, became increasingly a theorizing of the process by which the analyst incarnated the inhibitions and prohibitions that the patient's own desires brought with them to the surface of consciousness – the resistances which, as they were dissolved, were in the same movement progressively incarnated in the analyst. That is, the analyst became the patient's super-ego – that system of compulsions and prohibitions which suppressed and distorted his or her desires. In order to be able to 'see' this super-ego system more clearly, the analyst's neutrality was essential. For the analyst to offer any moral or quasi-legal judgements concerning the patient's desire would be to become inextricably – and irreversibly – entwined with the patient's own super-ego.

Yet *Freud's Women* documents numerous occasions when Freud's friendships and intimate relationships were intertwined with analysis and, according to modern professional rules of conduct, were somewhat irregular. The real lesson, here, is not the loose morals of the founder or the licence he allowed himself that he (or more often others in his name) forbade others. Freud had little difficulty in manoeuvring and acting under conditions of such complexity because his pragmatic and non-moral conceptions of both private and professional relationships were of a piece with his developing theories of the super-ego. Giving advice to a mother about the erotic relationship between her lover and her daughter emerges as a technical problem; there is no moral problem, beyond the pain that any conceivable action in such circumstances entails. For Freud there appears to be a seamless continuum between the professional action of the analyst and the action that stems from friendship, even from courtesy. The only analytic virtue that Freud asked of his patients was freedom. He offered them freedom of speech. In turn, for the purposes of analysis, he expected the patient to be in the position of a free agent. It is hardly surprising then that an analysis with Freud often transformed and sometimes destroyed the affective and marital ties of women.

Freud's great discovery of the 1920s was the ubiquity of unconscious guilt and its far-ranging effects in the world. The concept of the super-ego is equivalent to the quasi-Nietzschean affirmation of the complete separation of ethics from the experience of guilt. Not only is this conception a-moral; it is also anti-legal. This is the conjunction – between guilt, responsibility and the relation of psychoanalysis to the real – which has proved to be so crucial to contemporary debates between psychoanalysis and women.

Our contemporary history in this area has many surprising twists and turns. Part of the critique of psychoanalysis in the 1970s was grounded in the feminist movement's general repudiation of psychological categories. Rape was an ordinary sordid crime committed by ordinary men against anonymous women. Psychology in all forms should be excluded from the courtroom where rape cases were heard. In this spirit, in the 1970s, the pioneer feminist investigators of the sexual abuse of children indicted adult men in general, not specific pathological men who were part of dysfunctional families, as the jargon puts it. These activist campaigns joined forces with the critics of psychoanalysis when Jeffrey Masson maintained that Freud had, in his seduction theory, been an early discoverer of the extent of the sexual abuse of children, but had lacked the moral courage to face the facts. In place of his dangerous discovery, he had erected the theory that universalizes the relations of Oedipus, Laius and Jocasta.

The first thing to note about this turn of events is that, in contrast with the early twentieth century, psychoanalysis becomes, here, the mortal enemy of a sexual reform movement. When Freud declared hysteria to be derived from women's repressed sexuality, often bisexual or perverted impulses, he could be seen as in concert with sexual reformers who campaigned for the recognition of both women's sexual natures and their rights – if not with those who promoted one more effort for the moral reformation of the male of the species. The thrust of the psychoanalytic theory of sexuality, with its emphasis less on sexual differ-ence than on sexual pleasure, was seen to be an implicit critique of moralism, hypocrisy and restrictions on women's freedom. In the 1980s, among feminist reformers concerned with sexual violence against women and children there was far less talk – indeed, a great deal of silence – about women's sexual pleasure (though other wings of the feminist movement became intensely preoccupied with the question of what might count as 'liberatory' pleasure). The politics of sexual crimes against women certainly overshadowed the investigation of women's pleasure, particularly in the courtroom and the legislature. There was much talk of rights – but this quasi-legal language is not of a right to pleasure or sexual satisfaction, but of the right to freedom and autonomy, perhaps even con-tinuous with a woman's right to choose.

The rights talk dovetails neatly with the legal imperative of the new political therapies. The new therapies constructed to speak to the plight of rape victims and the adult consequences of childhood sexual abuse are continuous with a forensic investigation, preparatory to a trial in court. As well as being helped by the therapist, that selfsame therapist is always grooming the patient or client for her appearance in court as witness for the prosecution. For Freud, there was no question of assisting a patient in his or her prosecution; he neither sued parents nor won claims for his patients. When patients went to court, Freud was more likely to offer the diagnosis of paranoia than bear witness to their pain. In 1906, when asked to indicate the relevance of psychoanalysis to the law, Freud argued that, in its very nature, psychoanalysis would not offer much aid to the law in the task of ascertaining whether a person was lying or telling the truth, guilty or innocent, since psychoanalysis is not interested in establishing guilt or inno-cence, reality or fantasy:

you [future judges and defending counsel] may be led astray by a neurotic who, although he is innocent, reacts as if he were guilty, because a lurking sense of guilt that already exists in him seizes upon the accusation made in the particular instance. You must not regard this possibility as an idle fiction; you have only to think of life in the nursery, where such events are often enough to be observed. It sometimes happens that a child who has been accused of a misdeed strongly denies the charge but at the same time weeps like a detected sinner. You may perhaps think that the child is lying when he asserts his innocence; but this is not necessarily so ... Many people are like this, and it is still open to question whether your technique will succeed in distinguishing self-accusing individuals of this kind from those who are really guilty.

Freud was indicating to the lawyers that psychoanalysis pursued its truths down different paths from those of the law and had very good reasons for so doing. What matters in psychoanalysis is the fact that a patient has *said* something, not whether that something is true or not. Law always requires an answer; psycho-analysis in its nature will produce only more questions.

This was, and remains, the fundamental parting of the ways between a psychoanalytic inquiry and a forensic inquiry, however sophisticated its psychotherapeutic style. It is also this issue which lies at the heart of the new feminist therapeutic critiques of Freud.

Like Masson, Judith Herman, foremost in a line of trauma and recovered memory therapists, states that 'Freud stopped listening to his female patients' – the evidence is clear in the Dora case, where he refused to 'validate Dora's feelings of outrage and humiliation'. As a result:

for close to a century, these patients would again be scorned and silenced ... Out of the ruins of the traumatic theory of hysteria, Freud created psychoanalysis. The dominant psychological theory of the next century was founded in the denial of women's reality.

What Herman posits is that the validation of women's reality, which is fundamentally one of sexual oppression, is the crucial starting point for and necessary element in the recovery movement. Like so many movements that began in the 1960s and early 1970s as political activism, this therapeutic version of feminism has been transformed into the individualism of juridical inquiry, shakily allied with the individualism of the therapeutic imperative.

The uneasiness of the alliance between a clamorous call for justice and the therapist's technique of disinterested inquiry is clearly visible in Herman's account of how the recovered memory therapist must work: 'the therapist promises to respect the patient's autonomy by remaining disinterested and neutral ... "Neutral" means that the therapist does not take sides in the patient's inner conflicts or try to direct the patient's life decisions.' But such quasi-psychoanalytic neutrality will not deliver the ideological goods, or promote the bond between therapist and patient required of a therapy that is also a political indictment of oppression, so Herman quickly insists, as if catching herself:

The technical neutrality of the therapist is not the same as moral neutrality. Working with victimized people requires a committed moral stance. The therapist is called upon to bear witness to a crime. She must affirm a position of solidarity with the victim. This does not mean a simplistic notion that the victim can do no wrong; rather, it involves an understanding of the fundamental injustice of the traumatic experience and the need for a resolution that restores some sense of justice.

The key terms here are 'committed', 'bear witness', 'solidarity', 'victim', 'fundamental injustice' and 'justice'. In them we can see that peculiarly modern fusion of the language of criminal and civil law, in which one wishes both to condemn a criminal, to secure revenge and to seek due financial compensation. It, of course, also insists on its status as a language of morality. Paradoxically, however, it reduces women who are the complainants to the infantalized status of victims, the very condition from which the first feminist movement tried to escape.

If we compare Herman's dicta with Freud's technique, we see how moralizing and ideologically primed such a conception of neutrality is. As Freud's analysis of civilization indicates, it may be necessary to have our own personal versions of the thought police, but the function of psychoanalysis is to give an exact accounting of what we lose in welcoming them into our inner lives.

That this mention of the thought-police is not an extravagant and rhetorical gesture can be seen from the development of case law in the United States concerning the duties of professional health workers. From the 1960s on, culminating in the Tarasoff case, a series of precedents has greatly curtailed the freedom of the mental space that a therapist can offer her patient. It is now obligatory in many states for a professional to report to the police – and this means the police, not a professional body or an advisory committee attached to an employing institution – any mention of a crime past, present or future. If, in the example chosen by Christopher Bollas and David Sundelson in their book *The New Informants*, a patient reports on a story he heard from a friend about her being sexually harassed at work, the therapist is now obliged to report this incident to the police. The true work of therapy, which would explore the patient's identification with the harasser and the harassed, the fox and the rabbit, is cut short by the imperative of introducing legal surveillance.

The deep belief in the patient that the ideas are in themselves evil and should be punished is now echoed in a cultural mentality that agrees that people must be held accountable for thoughts even if they are expressed in a space designed to be free of dire consequences.

Freud himself was adamant that any restrictions to the fundamental rule of free association would entail the death of analysis: 'I once treated a high official who was bound by his oath of office not to communicate certain things because they were state secrets, and the analysis came to grief as a consequence of this restriction.' In Freud's view, the resistance to the analysis retrenched in safety behind the wall offered by the law of the state. The absolutism of the analyst is the only adequate response and therefore itself must not admit of any restriction: 'Psycho-analytic treatment must have no regard for any consideration, because the neurosis and its resistances are themselves without any such regard.' There is a place for the violent implacability of the law in psychoanalysis, but it is set against the external laws of the state and of morality. This is the higher law of no law, of complete freedom of speech. Imagine how many rules and regulations the neurosis, in Freud's word, can find to hide behind in a Californian analysis. The sites of resistance to analysis do not have to be violent or sexual fantasies; the details of confidential state papers will function just as well. So how much more anti-analytic will rules concerning the required reporting of rape fantasies be!

This development in the therapeutic culture of the United States intersects with the topic of *Freud's Women* in two ways which then become linked. First, psychoanalysis is an anti-moral intervention in the moral culture of the twentieth century. How women and the feminist movement are situated, or locate themselves, in relation to the critique of this moral culture has been a fundamental feature of the history of psychoanalysis. Second, the profession of psychotherapist has become largely a woman's profession. In *Freud's Women*, we charted the rise of those women colleagues and disciples of Freud to positions of institutional and theoretical authority. In the last thirty years, this development has become even more marked. In 1976, women constituted just over

31 per cent of all recipients of US doctorates in clinical psychology; by 1990, the figure had risen to 58 per cent. By 1986 women constituted 34.9 per cent of all psychiatrists in the US under thirty-five and in 1988, showing the shape of things to come, 47 per cent of medical students who chose psychiatry were women. It is already rare to find a male counsellor.

So, at the start of a new century, we face a paradoxical historical scene. The unconventional and courageous characters we described as Freud's women were the cultural grandmothers of a generation of women who have become dominant in the quintessentially modernist therapeutic project; yet their metaphorical granddaughters are now practising a method marked by sexual fastidiousness and fundamentalist moralism. In the first half of the twentieth century, it was characteristic of psychoanalysis to enter into a system of alliances with social reform movements. These alliances had both institutional and ideological aspects. In the first half of the century, feminism and psychoanalysis made natural allies. In the second half, the second wave of feminism was divided in its appraisal of the value of an alliance with psychoanalysis. As liberatory feminism lost its impetus at the end of the 1970s, the sexually puritanical and morally evangelical developments of regulatory feminism quite understandably came to recognize in psychoanalysis a principal ideological enemy.

These movements within psychoanalysis and in the feminist appropriation of Freud's practical legacy have paradoxically occurred at a time when the collective sexual compulsions have become more and more visible and acceptable. Freud's texts on sexuality seem increasingly prehistoric to younger readers. Their language of 'perversion', of 'objects', of the 'phallic' is tame beside the sexual saturation of our media which will educate a teenager far more widely than any reading of sexological tracts of the early or mid-twentieth century. Set beside *Cosmopolitan*, late-night TV sex programmes or a stint at surfing the Net, Freud's *Three Essays on the Theory of Sexuality* can seem rather restricted. Certainly, by comparison, he is singularly lacking in graphic detail. Who needs Freud, then, to teach us about the once forbidden sphere of sexuality when we have porn websites, Viagra and tailor-made vibrators?

Indeed, an aside on the history of the vibrator might make us altogether revise our sense of Freud's place in our past. Sold to the medical profession for the treatment of neurasthenic or troubled women around the time Freud was inventing psychoanalysis, the electrical vibrator became an abandoned medical technology in the 1930s, just when Freud's talking cure for sexual problems was becoming widely disseminated and advocated as a universal panacea. The resurgence and retooling of the vibrator in the 1960s, now as a self-help sexual aid principally for women, in parallel with the laboratory-based sexual dicta and 'how-to' books of Masters and Johnson, was a boon for the generation of women determined to take, quite literally, their sexuality into their own hands. It would be going too far to map too precisely the rise and fall of Freudian theories of female sexuality on to the rise, fall and rise again of the political technology of the orgasm blackboxed in the vibrator. But it highlights the fact that our century has invented many sexual technologies, of which the talking cure is only one; and that the futures of the talking cure may be bound up with the fortunes and side effects of these other technologies.

While vibrators and masturbatory aids, mechanical and bookish alike, became everyday household appliances, as necessary to modern living as the remote control and the microwave, psychoanalysis shied away from its historical kinship with modern sexual technologies, preferring to settle for being what Michel Foucault called a 'technology of the self': a new communications technology to be placed alongside radio, the telephone and e-mail, those other principally oral or at least non-iconic modes. In the domain of the economies of pleasure, any observer of late-twentieth-century culture cannot help but notice that, alongside the alliance between the new moralism and 'post-Freudian' therapies, there are new forms of libertinage and new regimes of pleasure and its control. Furthermore, new competing ideological forms have arisen to challenge the 'market niche' occupied by psychoanalysis: for example, evolutionary-biology-speak and system-, cybernetics- and AI-talk. These ideologies have also established their own up-to-date technologies for delivering the message and corralling new enthusiasts: during the 1980s, anyone could obtain a free copy of software whereby they could turn their computer into a connectionist device and thus become part of the vanguard of AI investigators.

The new prosthetic communications technologies should be placed alongside the old, namely psychoanalysis. Psychoanalysis is not just a communications technology because it is a new form of speech, which it is, but because it creates a new kind of object in the world: a virtual addressee. To see this one need only ask the question which confronts the analyst every working day: is the transference a real relationship? As real as any other, Freud replied: 'We have no right to dispute that the state of being in love which makes its appearance in the course of analytic treatment has the character of a "genuine" love.' But how can it be, when it is entirely artificial and conducted under circumstances that make it more like an experiment, a simulation, than a piece of reality? The obvious word to use about the transference is now ready to hand: it is a virtual relationship, in very much the sense that we now refer to virtual reality.

If we look backwards in time from Freud's invention of the psychoanalytic relationship, we find earlier versions in the magnetists and hypnotists of the nineteenth century. And if we interpret the psychoanalytic relationship, along the lines of Lacan, as a relationship of pure demand, then we begin to see it as a purification and critique of the professional relationship in general, whether that be between patient and doctor, client and lawyer, or client and prostitute. Even Freud could see it in this light at times. When asked in 1909 about the new practice of psychotherapy, he replied, 'Psychotherapy is as old as illness, and we doctors could not give it up if we wanted to, because the other party to our methods of healing – namely the patient – has not the slightest intention of doing without it.' The analyst, in this quasi-Lacanian view, is the analyst of all promises, of all relations of exchange, transaction and generosity between humans. And by engaging in this analysis of the fundamental social bond, she has some hope of discovering or at least drawing upon the sources of the faith which transforms, at special sites such as Lourdes or even in the more mundane environment of the local health clinic, pure demand into cure.

But if we look forward in time from this invention of the psychoanalytic situation, we find ourselves in unexpected territory. On the fact that the figure of the psychotherapist is one of the great socio-technological inventions of the last century there is considerable agreement. Alasdair MacIntyre places the therapist alongside the manager and the hedonist-aesthete as the moral characters of our age, embodiments of ethical principles and practical modes of being in the world. Yet the therapist is Janus-faced – both a figure of knowledge and science, and a figure of care, in Lacan's words. Both the neutral mirror, the pure spirit of objectivity, and the pure embodiment of empathy, understanding, intimacy and at-one-ness.

That this invention – not Freud's but the invention he gave the clearest account of, especially in his *Papers on Technique* – is of fundamental importance to contemporary cultural developments is confirmed by the curious story of ELIZA, the first computer program to simulate conversation. Named after Eliza Doolittle in Shaw's *Pygmalion*, her Henry Higgins was a computer systems expert called Joseph Weizenbaum. Working in the mid-1960s in collaboration with psychoanalyst Kenneth Colby, Weizenbaum chose to make the first conversational computer simulate a therapist. Why did he choose to simulate a psychotherapist? First, because there already existed a theory of psychotherapy that reduced the task of writing a program considerably. This theory was that of Carl Rogers, whose linguistic technique consisted of reflecting back to the patient what he or she had just said – as captured by the catchphrase 'I'm OK, you're OK.' But more generally, we can observe that the basic rule of psychotherapy is that, just like a computer, the therapist knows nothing about the world. This is one of the consequences of Freud's decision to withhold judgement as to the truth or reference of what patients say to him, in favour of its meaning.

Weizenbaum quickly found out that people treated the program as if it were a person. This shocked and perturbed him. He discovered that people were enormously prone to overestimate, in his view, the capacities of computers. It was experiences such as the following that turned him against the project of artificial intelligence:

Once my secretary, who had watched me work on the program for many months and therefore surely knew it to be merely a computer program, started conversing with it. After only a few interchanges with it, she asked me to leave the room. Another time, I suggested I might rig the system so that I could examine all conversations anyone had with it, say, overnight. I was promptly bombarded with accusations that what I proposed amounted to spying on people's most intimate thoughts; clear evidence that people were conversing with the computer as if it were a person who could be appropriately and usefully addressed in intimate terms ... What I had not realized is that extremely short exposures to a relatively simple computer program could induce powerful delusional thinking in quite normal people.

Weizenbaum's consternation stemmed from his judgement that ELIZA's interlocutors deluded themselves into thinking that the computer understood something. He was also astounded when psychiatrists became excited at the prospect of a workable expert system providing automatic psychotherapy. Weizenbaum, innocently, presupposed that psychotherapy required sympathetic identification and recognition. Unlike Pygmalion, unlike Henry Higgins, Weizenbaum never bet that he could fool his colleagues – which, in his view, they now had been; rather, he was shocked when they were 'taken in', just like the secretary and the patients, by ELIZA. And, in keeping with his hostility to the computer, Weizenbaum resolutely refused to fall in love with ELIZA, as the story of Pygmalion and Henry Higgins required him to do.

The world of the computer has changed since 1966. There was only one place in the world you could talk to ELIZA then – in Weizenbaum's office. There are now in use, in many private homes throughout America, thousands of copies of a software program, DEPRESSION 2.0, developed by Weizenbaum's psychiatrist colleague Colby. This software is more sophisticated than ELIZA, but not that much more sophisticated. There is, perhaps, a more profound change afoot though. From the 1970s to the early 1990s, Sherry Turkle followed the change of attitude of her MIT students to the idea of having a computer, rather than a human psychotherapist. In the 1980s, most students thought the idea of a computer therapist silly if not insulting. No computer could understand human emotions, because they don't have bodies or participate in complex family relationships. This was their attitude even if they behaved differently when on-line with a computer therapist, when they would behave much more like Weizenbaum's secretary: intent, secretive and absorbed by the conversation. But by the 1990s, students more saturated in behavioural and cognitive approaches which concentrated on reprogramming bad habits were more open to the virtues of having a computer rather than a human therapist. Perhaps it was easy for them to model psychotherapy on the daily workout on the running machine at the gym. Most interestingly, many of Turkle's students saw nothing to debate. As one of them said:

Well, the computer therapist might not be involved with you the way a human would be, but that has a good side, too. These doctors who have sex with their patients are involved but in a bad way ... The computer couldn't even begin to give you these problems.

In the age of AIDS, it is not only imperative to have safe sex, one needs to have safe therapy. And there is nothing safer for the purposes of human relationships than a computer.

We already have a number of fictional texts by Nicholson Baker which analyse sex in the age of the gadget – and inversely, gadgets in the age of sex. Baker's *Vox* and *The Fermata* are meditations on sexual fulfilment in a world where nobody ever meets the other, mediated entirely by gadgets – SF ploys, like the ability to stop time, or more everyday items like vibrators, shower heads and telephones. These essays on postmodern sex are simultaneously a celebration of human inventiveness and the will to pleasure and intimacy, and also a poignant depiction of the essential solitariness of our attempts to stop 'Time's thievish progress to Eternity'.

People don't buy computers simply for their psychotherapist programs. One of their rapidly expanding functions is as a viable alternative to real life (or RL, as computer aficionados call it). Out there – is the electronic world out there, or is it more accurate to say in here? – out there, they go on-line as different personae, participating in MUDs (Multi User Domains) and creating alternative lives and electronic friends, crossing genders and countries with ease. Yet even in the world of the Internet, there is a founding cyberspace legend which involves a psychiatrist and a group of women.

In all versions of the myth, a male psychiatrist called Alex joins a chat line in the persona of Joan, a severely handicapped married woman – lusty, funny, a woman of appetites. Joan finds it easy to enter into strong and intimate relations with the other 'women' on-line, so strong that the other women wish to enter into Joan's real life to help her, to become true friends. Finding his electronic persona under extreme pressure to become real, Alex informs the group that Joan has had to go to hospital – the hospital where he works as a psychiatrist. By contacting this hospital by phone, the on-line friends of Joan discover that Joan is not Joan, but Alex the psychiatrist in drag. Shock and outrage are the result. In some versions of the story, Joan has had electronic sex with her women friends, and the shock and outrage is in part a response to this sexual betrayal. In other versions, Joan has introduced some of her on-line friends to Alex, a psychiatrist, who has had real-life sexual affairs with several of them.

These are myths for our time, stories connecting sex, psychiatry and identity. In the 1960s, it was the fact that humans treated the computer as an intelligent being, capable of understanding, that so shocked Weizenbaum. But, it now turns out, humans are very quick to get on friendly terms with electronic personae, whether there are computer programs or other human beings running them. As Turkle notes, in the 1980s the gender-shifting was the transgressive focus of the story; in the 1990s, it was the shifting back and forth between reality and virtuality that disturbed. If we wanted to, we could say that psychoanalysis both should not be surprised and also has much to learn from this capacity for massive projective identification. The issues now, as was so often the case in the 1990s, are not so much about whether machines can be like humans as what are the ethics that should be observed in human–electronic relations. The questions raised are as much about deception and being deceived, and then about confusing virtual reality and real life, as they are about being understood.

Without the psychoanalysts having done anything, prosthetic communications technologies alter the cultural conditions for a psychoanalytic culture. Alongside those changes are ones in the domain of sexual life. It is not clear whether the basic technology of sex has ever changed, but it is clear that the fantasy culture of sex has. The technology of identity and the technology of relationship have been, are being and will continue to be transformed. The importance of the figure of the 'shrink' in these transformations is clear. He or she is the exemplar of the intelligent computer, the stand-in for the fantasy of talk, the concentration of the threat to a safe intimate life – as well as the legal dispenser of identity-transforming drugs. The old-fashioned analyst presages these transformations; her technology of the transference was the first virtual relationship. The question is, can analysts survive in this new culture their techniques foresaw? Or will their moralizing antipathies to these technologies – to drugs, to computers, to virtual sex – do the job that the Freud-bashers have not yet succeeded in doing?

The signs are not good. In the arena of sex, where Freud's work was originally so subversive and so much aligned with other reform movements, the public faces of analysts have become reactive, resistant, maybe even reactionary, but, most tellingly, incurious. From their reactions to the Kinsey Report and to Masters and Johnson's sexual experiments, to their sniffy moralism in the 1960s and 1970s, they betrayed considerable disinclination to continue the revolutionary inquiries that the concept of infantile sexuality promised. There were exceptions of course, such as Masud Khan and Robert Stoller. Meanwhile, the British analysts used the theoretical advances of Klein and Winnicott as their alibi, replacing sex with the mother and passion with play. The French analysts transformed sexual experience into a mathematico-mystical contemplation of the relation of the Ø, *jouissance* and the 'objet petit *a*'. American and other analysts, subject to the relentless pressures of cultural globalization, now talk most heatedly about sex when it is a question of the ethics of the therapeutic relationship. Increasingly, they take their cue from the sympathetic non-analytic therapists, such as Peter Kramer, whose *Listening to Prozac* gives numerous case histories without mentioning sexuality, and notes, with some perplexity, how indifferent patients are to the dysfunctional sexual side effects of the social-identity-transforming wonder drug. If psychoanalysts succumb to the prevailing moralism concerning sexual practices – from the sexual abuse of children to sexual relationships between doctors and patients or between computers and humans – one can say that psychoanalysis may still go on in private, as a perpetually endangered species, but the psychoanalytic culture that formerly sustained it will no longer exist.

What kind of future will there be for psychoanalysis in an era of hypermoralism, when the constructing, securing and protecting of identities have become projects which are both political and technological and when sexuality has gone virtual? Will women still look to psychoanalysis as a privileged theoretical and practical resource in an era when not only gender but sexuality itself is incited for all by masquerade and performativity? These are questions which the project of *Freud's Women* can only raise. Their answers lie in the unknown terrain of the new millennium.

March 2000

ABBREVIATIONS

Bertin   Bertin, Celia, *Marie Bonaparte: A Life* (London, Melbourne, New York: Quartet, 1983)

Bloomsbury/Freud   *Bloomsbury/Freud: The Letters of James and Alix Strachey 1924–1925*, eds Perry Meisel and Walter Kendrick (London: Chatto & Windus, 1986)

CW   *The Collected Works of C.G. Jung*, eds Sir Herbert Read, Michael Fordham and Gerhard Adler, trans. R.F.C. Hull (London: Routledge & Kegan Paul, 1944–78)

FA   *A Psycho-analytic Dialogue: The Letters of Sigmund Freud and Karl Abraham, 1907–1926*, eds Hilda C. Abraham and Ernst L. Freud (London: The Hogarth Press and the Institute of Psycho-analysis, 1965)

FF   *The Complete Letters of Sigmund Freud to Wilhelm Fliess, 1887–1904*, ed. J.M. Masson (Cambridge, Mass.: Harvard University Press, 1984)

FJ   *The Complete Correspondence of Sigmund Freud and Ernest Jones, 1908–1939*, ed. R. Andrew Paskauskas (Cambridge, Mass., and London: Harvard University Press, 1993)

FJung   *The Freud/Jung Letters*, ed. William McGuire, trans. R. Manheim and R.F.C. Hull (Princeton: Princeton University Press, 1974)

FLou   *Sigmund Freud and Lou Andreas-Salomé: Letters*, ed. Ernst Pfeiffer, trans. William and Elaine Robson-Scott (London: The Hogarth Press and the Institute of Psycho-analysis, 1972 [a partial and edited selection])

FM   Freud Museum Collection

Freud Journal   Lou Andreas-Salomé, *The Freud Journal*, trans. from the German by Stanley A. Leavy, with an introduction by Mary-Kay Wilmers (London: Quartet, 1987)

FPf   *Psycho-analysis and Faith: The Letters of Sigmund Freud and Oskar Pfister*, eds Heinrich Meng and Ernst L. Freud, trans. Eric Mosbacher (London: The Hogarth Press and the Institute of Psycho-analysis, 1963)

FS	*The Letters of Sigmund Freud to Eduard Silberstein, 1871–1881*, ed. Walter Boehlich, trans. Arnold J. Pomerans (Cambridge, Mass.: Harvard University Press, 1990)
Freud–Klein Controversies	*The Freud–Klein Controversies 1941–45*, eds Pearl King and Riccardo Steiner (London and New York: Tavistock/Routledge, 1990)
Gay	Gay, Peter, *Freud: A Life for our Time* (London: Dent, 1988)
GW	Freud, Sigmund, *Gesammelte Werke*, 18 vols (London: The Hogarth Press, and Frankfurt a.M.: S. Fischer Verlag, 1940–68)
Int J Psa	*International Journal of Psycho-analysis*
J	Jones, Ernest, *Sigmund Freud: Life and Work*, vols I–III (London: The Hogarth Press, 1953–7); where vol. I is cited, the second edition (1954) is being referred to.
LC	Sigmund Freud Archives, Library of Congress, Washington DC
Letters	*Letters of Sigmund Freud, 1873–1939*, ed. Ernst L. Freud, trans. Tania and James Stern (London: The Hogarth Press, 1970)
Minutes	*Minutes of the Vienna Psychoanalytical Society*, eds Herman Nunberg and Ernst Federn, trans. M. Nunberg, 4 vols (New York: International Universities Press, 1962–76)
Reader	Fliess, Robert (ed.), *The Psycho-Analytic Reader* (London: The Hogarth Press, 1950)
SE	*The Standard Edition of the Complete Psychological Works of Sigmund Freud*, 24 vols, ed. by James Strachey in collaboration with Anna Freud, assisted by Alix Strachey and Alan Tyson (London: The Hogarth Press and the Institute of Psycho-analysis, 1953–74)
Secret Symmetry	Carotenuto, Aldo, *A Secret Symmetry: Sabina Spielrein between Jung and Freud*, (1980; trans. Arno Pomerans, John Shepley and Krishna Winston, 1982; 2nd edn with additional material, London: Routledge & Kegan Paul, 1984)
SFC	Sigmund Freud Copyrights, Wivenhoe, Essex
Stud	Freud, Sigmund, *Studienausgabe*, 10 vols with an unnumbered *Ergänzungsband* (abbreviated as *Erg*) (Frankfurt a.M.: Fischer Verlag, 1969–75)

NOTES

Preface pp. ix–x
p. ix *the science of psychoanalysis* *The Interpretation of Dreams*, *SE* V, pp. 452–5

Freud on Trial pp. 1–7
p. 1 *wife in maturity* *Letters*, letter to Martha Bernays, 15 November 1883, pp. 89–91
p. 2 *equality with men* 'Female Sexuality', *SE* XXI, p. 230
p. 2 *Marie Bonaparte* *J* II, pp. 468–9
p. 3 *women outdistance men* *Letters*, letter to Martha Bernays, 6 October 1883, p. 82
p. 3 *goes shopping* Reik, T., 'Freud in conversation', mimeo, p. 6, *LC*, Box B46
p. 3 *the most capable* *FJ*, Freud to Jones, 28 April 1938
p. 3 *better than men* Gay, Freud to Ernest Freud, 9 May 1938, p. 628
p. 3 *few individuals profit* *Minutes I*, p. 351
p. 3 *process of reproduction* Boyer, 'Freud, Marriage and Late Viennese Liberalism', p. 92
p. 3 *sexual freedom* Boyer, 'Freud, Marriage and Late Viennese Liberalism', p. 100
p. 3 *women on principle* *Minutes II*, 13 April 1910, cited in Gay, p. 503
p. 3 *future experiments* *Letters*, Freud to Jeanne and Hans Lampl de Groot, 11 November 1926, pp. 365–6
p. 4 *darken their lives* '"Civilized" Sexual Morality and Modern Nervous Illness', *SE* IX, p. 195. For an early, positive feminist response to Freud's theses about sexuality and morality, see Meisel-Hess, *Die Sexuelle Krise* (1909), excerpted in Brinker-Gabler, *Zur Psychologie der Frau*, pp. 229–35
p. 4 *as an illness* '"Civilized" Sexual Morality and Modern Nervous Illness', *SE* IX, p. 195
p. 4 *fifteen years earlier* *The Interpretation of Dreams*, *SE* IV, p. 154
p. 4 *excitation and satisfaction* *Three Essays*, *SE* VII, p. 223
p. 4 *complete sexual object* *Three Essays*, *SE* VII, p. 223
p. 4 *later sexual satisfactions* *Three Essays*, *SE* VII, p. 182
p. 5 *mother or sister* 'On the Universal Tendency to Debasement in the Sphere of Love', *SE* XI, p. 186
p. 6 *male or female patients* Glover, 'Psychoanalysis in England', pp. 543–4
p. 6 *the same period* Chodorow, 'Psychoanalyse und Psychoanalytikerinnen'; 'Seventies Questions for Thirties Women'
p. 7 *traditionally been women's* For a discussion of these questions, see Coleman, 'From "Dear Lou" to "Code Name Mary"'

1: The Young Freud pp. 11–41

p. 11 (*or of several*) Freud and Ferenczi, *Correspondence, 1908–1914*, Freud to Ferenczi, 9 July 1913, p. 528; see also Assoun, *Freud et la femme*, p. 39

p. 11 *of human life* 'The Theme of the Three Caskets', *SE* XII, p. 298

p. 12 *into her arms* 'The Theme of the Three Caskets', *SE* XII, p. 301

p. 12 *all their force* *J* III, pp. 487–8, Freud to James S.H. Bransom, 25 March 1934

p. 12 *impossible to revivify* 'Female Sexuality', *SE* XXI, pp. 226–7

p. 12 *note of inhumanity* *J* III, pp. 487–8, Freud to James S.H. Bransom, 25 March 1934

p. 12 *now I am* *Letters*, Freud to Ferenczi, 16 September 1930, p. 399

p. 12 *mother's death* See Anzieu, *Freud's Self-Analysis*, p. 297, and Assoun, *Freud et la femme*, pp. 26ff.

p. 13 *parents' sleep* *The Interpretation of Dreams*, *SE* V, p. 583

p. 13 *come to nothing* *The Interpretation of Dreams*, *SE* IV, p. 216

p. 13 *of his mother* See Anzieu, *Freud's Self-Analysis*, pp. 294 ff.; Rosenfeld, 'Dreams and Vision'; Assoun, *Freud et la femme*, pp. 28–9

p. 13 *at that time* 'Screen Memories', *SE* III, p. 322

p. 14 *scene breaks off* 'Screen Memories', *SE* III, p. 311

p. 14 *from this soil* 'Letter to the burgomaster of Pribor', *SE* XXI, p. 259

p. 14 *Ashkenasi origin* Martin Freud, 'Who Was Freud?', p. 203

p. 14 *highly intelligent* Martin Freud, 'Who Was Freud?', p. 202

p. 14 *and egotistical* Heller, 'Freud's Mother and Father', pp. 334–40

p. 15 *committed suicide* Balmary, *Psychoanalyzing psychoanalysis*, p. 73

p. 15 *was his mother* 'Notes upon a Case of Obsessional Neurosis', *SE* X, p. 233n

p. 15 *paternity in doubt* Schur, *Freud: Living and Dying*, pp. 190–1

p. 15 *indisputable favourite* *J* I, p. 6, citing Freud, 'A Childhood Recollection from *Dichtung und Wahrheit*', *SE* XVII, p. 156; see also *The Interpretation of Dreams*, *SE* V, p. 398n (added 1911)

p. 15 *all human relationships* 'Femininity', *SE* XXII, p. 133

p. 15 *her masculinity complex* 'Femininity', *SE* XXII, p. 133; see also Abraham, 'Freud's Mother Conflict'

p. 15 *before the term* *SFC*, Freud to Sam Freud, Manchester, 21 August 1925; see also Whyte, *Focus and Diversions*, pp. 110–11, for a report of Amalie's dream of Freud's funeral

p. 16 *long a life* *LC*, quoted in Gay, p. 573, Freud to Jones, 15 September 1930

p. 16 *end of it* Schur, *Freud: Living and Dying*, p. 529; supplemented by Gay, p. 651 & p. 740

p. 16 *entrusted himself* Sprengnether, *The Spectral Mother*, p. 178

p. 16 *and Sigmund* Sajner, 'Sigmund Freuds Beziehungen', p. 172

p. 16 *in June 1857* Krull, *Freud and his Father*, p. 111

p. 16 *my own capacities* *FF*, 3 October 1897, p. 268

p. 16 *washed herself* *FF*, 4 October 1897, p. 269

p. 16 *capacity for knowledge* Assoun, *Freud et la femme*, p. 41; see also Grigg, '"All Roads Lead to Rome"', and Hardin, 'On the Vicissitudes of Freud's Early Mothering'

p. 16 *to do anything* *FF*, 4 October 1897, p. 269

p. 16 *vocation and knowledge* Assoun, *Freud et la femme*, p. 43

p. 16 *very shrewd indeed* *FF*, 15 October 1897, p. 271

p. 16 *sharp and efficient* *SE* IV, p. 247; 'her treatment of me was not always excessive in its amiability and her words could be harsh if I failed to reach the required standards of cleanliness. ... It is reasonable to suppose that the child loved the old woman who taught him these lessons, in spite of her rough treatment of him.'

p. 17 *of the nurse* *FF*, 15 October 1897, pp. 271–2

p. 17 *of two mothers* Gay, p. 7

p. 17 *one mentioned above* 'In his father's house he found not only his kind stepmother, Donna Albiera, but also his grandmother, his father's mother, Monna Lucia, who – so we will assume – was no less tender to him than grandmothers usually are.' 'Leonardo da Vinci', *SE* XI, p. 113

p. 17 *father as well* 'Leonardo da Vinci', *SE* XI, pp. 113–14

p. 17 *by this wish*   *Group psychology*, *SE* XVIII, p. 121

p. 17 *living and surviving*   *FF*, 3 October 1897, p. 269

p. 18 *his early years*   Gallop, 'In Dora's Case', in *Feminism and psychoanalysis*, p. 213; Swan, '*Mater* and Nannie', *passim*

p. 18 *the child's rival*   *The Psychopathology of Everyday Life*, *SE* VI, p. 51 n.2

p. 18 *what is happening*   'Femininity', *SE* XXII, p. 123

p. 18 *a real basis*   'Femininity', *SE* XXII, p. 123

p. 18 *eight months later*   *J* I, p. 8

p. 18 *childhood jealousy*   *FF*, 3 October 1897, p. 268

p. 18 *in my memory*   'Screen Memories', *SE* III, p. 310

p. 19 *slender and beautiful*   *FF*, 15 October 1897, p. 271

p. 19 *his pet*   Heller, 'Freud's Mother and Father', p. 336

p. 19 *original catastrophe*   'Screen Memories', *SE* III, p. 314

p. 19 *too risqué*   Gay, p. 14

p. 19 *and 'Alexander'*   Book with dedication in personal collection of Victor Ross

p. 19 *give to them*   *Letters*, Freud to Martha, 19 June 1884, p. 129

p. 19 *mother and sisters*   *J* II, p. 429

p. 19 *of their lives*   *J* III, p. 246. After the war, Anna Freud was tormented by guilt over the old ladies being left in Vienna: 'It is, after all, our fault that we left them to be killed.' (Young-Bruehl, *Anna Freud*, p. 288)

p. 20 *treat in 1885*   *Letters*, Freud to Martha, 23 July 1885, p. 174

p. 20 *Eduard Silberstein*   *Letters*, Freud to Martha, 7 February 1884, p. 113

p. 20 *he gave money*   Young-Bruehl, *Anna Freud*, p. 31

p. 20 *congratulate her*   *J* I, p. 132

p. 20 *committee member*   *FPf*, Freud to Pfister, 9 May 1920, pp. 76–7

p. 20 *name came up*   See particularly Freud's unpublished correspondence with Samuel Freud, who lived in Manchester (courtesy of *SFC*)

p. 20 *distance from them*   *FF*, 23 March 1900, p. 406

p. 20 *double incest*   Freeman and Strean, *Freud and Women*, pp. 77–8

p. 20 *years his junior*   *FF*, 23 March 1900, p. 406

p. 20 *her education*   *FS*, 22–23 October 1874, p. 67

p. 20 *towards neurasthenia*   *Letters*, Freud to Martha, 10 February 1886, p. 223

p. 21 *least discreet*   Martin Freud, *Glory Reflected*, p. 15

p. 21 *shirts and boots*   *Letters*, Freud to Martha, 12 December 1885, p. 201

p. 21 *of Freud's*   *J* I, p. 180

p. 21 *long-standing affection*   *FF*, 17 May 1896, pp. 186–7

p. 21 *alone at Vienna*   *FJ*, Freud to Jones, 24 August 1922

p. 21 *in the 1950s*   See *J* III, p. 91, and Young-Bruehl, *Anna Freud*, pp. 96–8

p. 21 *grieved intensely*   *Letters*, Freud to Martha Freud, 29 April 1908, p. 282 n.5

p. 21 *killed himself*   Young-Bruehl, *Anna Freud*, pp. 96–7

p. 21 *petitioning*   *FF*, 26 November 1899, p. 389

p. 21 *family headquarters*   *FF*, 12 June 1900, p. 417

p. 21 *Freud family*   Clark, *Freud*, p. 195

p. 21 *like my own*   *FF*, 14 September 1900, p. 423

p. 22 *sensitiveness*   *Letters*, Freud to Martha, 9 September 1883, p. 72

p. 22 *of the mother*   'The Theme of the Three Caskets', *SE* XII, p. 301

p. 22 *first calf-love*   'Screen Memories', *SE* III, p. 313; Gay, p. 22, renders the phrase as 'first rapture'

p. 22 *twelve-year-old*   Swales, 'Freud, Martha Bernays and the Language of Flowers', p. 8n, gives her age as thirteen; Boehlich (*FS*, p. xvii) gives it as nearly twelve when Freud first met her in the summer of 1871, the year before his falling in love.

p. 22 *young lady*   *FS*, 4 September 1872, p. 16

p. 22 *my diffidence*   *FS*, 4 September 1872, p. 16

p. 22 *improve the past*   'Screen Memories', *SE* III, p. 313

p. 23 *near our home*   'Screen Memories', *SE* III, pp. 312–13

p. 23 *primeval past*   FS, 1 & 2 October 1875, p. 138; see Eissler, 'Creativity and Adolescence',
   p. 475
p. 23 *no more of these*   FS, 23 April 1876, p. 153; see also McGrath, *Freud's Discovery of
   Psychoanalysis*, p. 134
p. 23 *encountered since*   FS, 5 April 1876, p. 144
p. 23 *tenderer sex*   FS, 5 April 1876, p. 149
p. 24 *her own child*   FS, 4 September 1872, p. 18
p. 24 *can fully match*   FS, 4 September 1872, p. 17; see also Gedo and Wolf, 'The "Ich"
   Letters'
p. 24 *like himself*   'A Special Type of Object-Choice Made by Men', SE XI, p. 173
p. 24 *of my shell*   FS, 4 September 1872, p. 18
p. 24 *into passion*   'Femininity', SE XXII, p. 134
p. 24 *character-trait*   J II, pp. 482–3
p. 25 *desire and defense*   McGrath, *The Politics of Psychoanalysis*, p. 131
p. 25 *marrying Pauline*   J I, p. 29
p. 25 *did not belong*   The Interpretation of Dreams, SE V, p. 520
p. 25 *no empty flirtation*   McGrath, *The Politics of Psychoanalysis*, p. 89, quoting from Freud to
   Emil Fluss, 17 March 1873
p. 25 *sexual aggression*   'Screen Memories', SE III, pp. 316–17
p. 25 *sexual fantasy*   On this point, we agree with the general trend of Swales, 'Freud, Martha
   Bernays and the Language of Flowers', although there is much in Swales's work for
   which the Scottish judgment 'non proven' is necessary.
p. 25 *childish pranks*   'Screen Memories', SE III, p. 317
p. 26 *of my life*   The Interpretation of Dreams, SE IV, p. 172
p. 26 *probably Rosanes*   Swales, 'Freud, Martha Bernays and the Language of Flowers',
   p. 24
p. 26 *to do this*   The Interpretation of Dreams, SE IV, p. 173
p. 26 *coloured plates*   See also Grinstein, *Dreams*, p. 57, on the connection between the screen
   memory and the dream of the botanical monograph.
p. 26 *flower specimens*   Bernays, 'My Brother, Sigmund Freud', p. 141
p. 26 *its mycelium*   The Interpretation of Dreams, SE V, p. 525
p. 26 *into the unknown*   The Interpretation of Dreams, SE V, p. 525
p. 26 *of flowers*   See The Interpretation of Dreams, SE V, pp. 347–8, for the flowery dream and
   its symbolism
p. 27 *chopped in pieces*   Studies, SE II, p. 70 n. 1
p. 27 *peculiar idioticon*   J II, p. 498, Freud to Pfister, 6 November 1910
p. 27 *one who cuts*   See Swales, 'Freud, Martha Bernays and the Language of Flowers', p. 37
p. 27 *do with them*   FS, 5 April 1876, p. 146
p. 27 *him in 1885*   Letters, Freud to Martha, 24 November 1885, p. 198
p. 27 *Karl Bettelheim*   A colleague and friend of both Breuer's and Freud's, with whom Freud
   worked on a study of electricity.
p. 27 *Sigmund Freud*   Gedo, 'On the Origins of the Theban Plague', p. 252
p. 27 *answered 'No'*   Personal communication, Peter Swales, 1990
p. 27 *far between*   J I, p. 110
p. 27 *but elsewhere*   Letters, Freud to Martha, 7 February 1884, p. 113
p. 28 *worthy funeral*   Letters, Freud to Martha, 28 April 1884, p. 153
p. 28 *elimination of affects*   Hirschmüller, *Breuer*, p. 155
p. 28 *according to Peter Swales*   Swales, 'Freud, Martha Bernays and the Language of Flowers',
   p. 12n
p. 28 *choice of a wife*   Letters, Freud to Mathilde Freud, 19 March 1908, p. 281
p. 28 *Sephardic origin*   Martin Freud, 'Who Was Freud?', p. 203
p. 28 *two daughters*   Swales, 'Freud, Breuer and the Blessed Virgin', p. 26
p. 29 *I might marry!*   The Interpretation of Dreams, SE V, p. 476
p. 29 *you unsuspecting worm?*   Letters, Freud to Martha, 26 June 1885, p. 170
p. 29 *generous and reasonable*   J I, p. 113, Freud to Martha, 2 August 1882

p. 29 *with incredible fortitude* Martin Freud, 'Who Was Freud?', p. 211; see also Gay, 'Six Names in Search of an Interpretation'

p. 29 *stop at once* Martin Freud, *Glory Reflected*, p. 212

p. 29 *blessing of summer* FPf, Pfister to Martha Freud, 12 December 1939, p. 145

p. 30 *wish you weren't* J I, p. 186, Freud to Martha, 17 August 1884

p. 30 *to subordinate myself* Letters, Freud to Martha, 29 August 1883, p. 66

p. 30 *symbolic ones* Letters, Freud to Martha, 23 July 1882, pp. 35–6

p. 30 *Marty and me* Letters, Freud to Martha, 23 July 1882, p. 36

p. 30 *her wicked uncle* Letters, Freud to Martha, 14 July 1882, p. 33

p. 30 *everyone loved her* Letters, Freud to Martha, 23 July 1882, p. 35

p. 30 *compares with mine* Letters, Freud to Martha, 14 August 1882, p. 41

p. 30 *Understand?* Letters, Freud to Martha, 26 May 1885, pp. 159–60

p. 30 *household and nursery* J I, p. 154, 1884 letter

p. 31 *control of reason* J I, p. 124, Freud to Martha, 8 July 1882

p. 31 *Her reply was 'Nonsense'* J I, p. 126

p. 31 *seventy years later* J I, p. 131

p. 31 *of your family* J I, pp. 143–4, Freud to Martha, July 1884

p. 31 *heartlessness and caprice* Letters, Freud to Martha, 17 August 1884, pp. 138–9

p. 32 *in every family* Letters, Freud to Minna, 21 February 1883, p. 53

p. 32 *anything but egotistical* Letters, Freud to Martha, 17 August 1882, p. 42

p. 32 *ever will have* Letters, Freud to Martha, 17 May 1885, p. 157

p. 32 *nothing but you* Gay, Freud to Martha, 5 December 1885, unpublished, p. 50

p. 32 *head over it?* Letters, Freud to Martha, 29 March 1884, p. 117

p. 32 *the 'conquistador'* FF, 1 February 1900, p. 398

p. 32 *after all* Letters, Freud to Martha, 20 January 1886, p. 209

p. 32 *gigantic striving* J I, p. 187, Freud to Martha, 4 September 1883, also Letters, Freud to Martha, pp. 68–9

p. 33 *like a racehorse* Letters, Freud to Martha, 24 November 1885, pp. 196–7

p. 33 *still remain* J I, p. 191, Freud to Martha, August 1883

p. 33 *rattling noise* Letters, Freud to Martha, 18 August 1882, p. 45, also Gay, p. 41

p. 33 *so often despised* Letters, Freud to Martha, 23 October 1883, pp. 85–6

p. 34 *all later siblings* Stolorow and Atwood, 'A Defensive-Restitutive Function', p. 226

p. 34 *as you are* Letters, Freud to Martha, 2 February 1886, p. 214

p. 34 *urge for truth* See J I, p. 136

p. 34 *be mistaken* J I, p. 113, Freud to Martha, 2 August 1882

p. 34 *in short, the truth* Letters, Freud to Martha, 25 September 1882, p. 47

p. 34 *sure of mine* J I, pp. 122–3, quoting letter from end of June 1882

p. 34 *anything by it* Letters, Freud to Martha, 6 October 1883, p. 82

p. 34 *ashamed of it* Letters, Freud to Martha, 16 January 1884, p. 104

p. 35 *was very unhappy* Letters, Freud to Martha, 30 June 1884, pp. 132–3

p. 35 *of any love* J I, p. 151, Martha to Freud, 6 July 1886

p. 35 *atone for it* Letters, Freud to Martha, 2 February 1886, p. 215; see also J I, pp. 214–15

p. 35 *compact majority* An Autobiographical Study, SE XX, p. 9, and 'Address to the Society of B'nai B'rith', SE XX, p. 274

p. 35 *bedside manner* J I, p. 157

p. 35 *vowing to return* FF, 19 September 1901, p. 449

p. 35 *matter of principle* J II, p. 495, Freud to Ferenczi, 19 January 1910

p. 36 *for the insane* Hirschmüller, *Freuds Begegnung*; see also Stone, *The Passions of the Mind*, pp. 116 ff.; Vranich, 'Sigmund Freud and the "Case History of Berganza"'

p. 36 *a new era!* Letters, Freud to Martha, 7 January 1884, p. 99

p. 36 *electrical treatment* Letters, Freud to Martha, 29 May 1884, p. 127

p. 36 *on his door* J I, p. 174

p. 36 *in no time* Letters, Freud to Martha, 10 March 1886, p. 224

p. 36 *hospital for children* Kris, 'Introduction', *The Origins of Psycho-analysis*, p. 16, quoting the title of Kassowitz's 1890 account of the hospital's work.

p. 36 *interference by seniors*   See Gicklhorn, Joseph, 'Das Kinder-Kranken-Institut', *LC*, B 39, mimeo

p. 36 *children's paralyses*   'Zur Kenntniss der cerebralen Diplegien des Kindesalters (im Anschluss an die Little'sche Krankheit)' (1893); *Die infantile Cerebrallähmung* (1897); *J* I, pp. 237–8

p. 36 *another to distraction*   *Letters*, Freud to Martha, 18 August 1882, pp. 44–5

p. 37 *he needed it*   *J* I, p. 170

p. 37 *account ledger*   *Letters*, Freud to Martha, 30 March 1886, p. 228

p. 37 *150,000,000 Marks*   *Letters*, Freud to Martha, 10 March 1885, pp. 149–50

p. 37 *a rich wife*   See *Letters*, Freud to Martha, 7 February 1884, p. 113. The 'stupid rich girl' to whom Freud refers in this letter was probably Pauline Theiler, whom Silberstein married in 1881, and whom Freud treated for depression in 1891. She committed suicide by throwing herself from the third or fourth floor of Freud's building, while visiting Freud for her treatment in May 1891. (See *FS*, 'Introduction', pp. xiv-xv, and Appendix, p. 192)

p. 37 *I am rich*   *Letters*, Freud to Martha, 14 August 1882, p. 41

p. 37 *marriage in 1886*   *J* I, pp. 161–2, Emmeline Bernays to Freud, 27 June 1886

p. 37 *comfortably below*   *J* I, p. 148, Freud to Martha, 6 January 1886

p. 38 *lost long ago*   *Letters*, Freud to Martha, 19 June 1884, p. 128

p. 38 *never the rich*   *Letters*, Freud to Martha, 10 March 1885, pp. 149–50

p. 38 *unrestrained love*   *J* I, p. 143, re sciatica in 1883

p. 38 *to this rule*   See *J* I, p. 137

p. 38 *to the marriage*   *FF*, 21 December 1899, p. 392. See also Freud's interesting comments on the importance of Nathan Weiss's wife's dowry in his suicide shortly after his marriage, *Letters*, Freud to Martha, 16 September 1883, p. 80.

p. 38 *on this theme*   It has probably disappeared for good; when Marie Bonaparte allowed Freud to look through the Fliess letters, he singled that letter out as one of the few that was missing (*FF*, p. 10). The fact that Fliess married a rich woman might well have led to his censoring this dream, especially if thoughts of comparison between the two men entered into Freud's associations. But see *FF*, 9 June 1898, p. 315.

p. 38 *for each other*   *Letters*, Freud to Martha, 18 August 1882, pp. 44–5

p. 38 *deep significance*   For further discussion of the dowry question, see Anzieu, *Freud's Self-Analysis*, p. 546

p. 38 *of my patients*   *FF*, 4 October 1897, p. 269

p. 38 *equals my mother*   *FF*, 15 October 1897, p. 271

p. 39 *dismissed from service*   Rousseau, *Les confessions*, pp. 85–7; see de Man, 'Excuses (*Confessions*)'

p. 39 *going on living*   *FF*, 3 October 1897, p. 269

p. 39 *in sexual matters*   *FF*, 4 October 1897, p. 269

p. 39 *to do anything*   *FF*, 4 October 1897, p. 269

p. 39 *for later experiences*   *The Psychopathology of Everyday Life*, *SE* VI, p. 50

p. 39 *no grudge*   *An Autobiographical Study*, *SE* XX, pp. 14–15

p. 40 *100,000 gulden*   *J* I, p. 157

p. 40 *costs nothing*   *On Dreams*, *SE* V, pp. 638–9, 655; emphasis in the original; see Anzieu, *Freud's Self-Analysis*, pp. 531 ff.

p. 40 *a great detour*   'Afterword' to *The Question of Lay Analysis*, *SE* XX, pp. 253–4

p. 40 *a long time*   Reik, T., 'Freud in conversation', mimeo, *LC*, B46, p. 6

p. 40 *as my dowry*   Freud, Esti D., 'Mrs Sigmund Freud', p. 29

p. 40 *semi-unselfish capitalists*   *Letters*, Freud to Martha, 19 March 1886, p. 227

p. 41 *irreparable rupture*   *J* I, p. 151

2: 'Not a Bad Solution of the Marriage Problem' pp. 42–61

p. 42 *very often ill*   *Letters*, Freud to Max Halberstadt, 27 July 1912, p. 300

p. 42 *healthy, and active*   Gay, p. 613, citing *J* III, p. 209, Freud to Marie Bonaparte, 27 September 1936

p. 42 *my own wife*   *The Interpretation of Dreams*, *SE* IV, p. 110

p. 42 *wife in maturity*   *Letters*, Freud to Martha, 15 November 1883, pp. 90–1

p. 43 *as henpecked*   Gay, 'Sigmund and Minna? The Biographer as Voyeur', p. 44

p. 43 *of punctuality*   Gay, p. 59

p. 43 *in the house*   Freud to Anna, 12 October 1920, *LC*, in Gay, p. 428n

p. 43 *never abated*   Personal communication, Victor Ross, 13 October 1991

p. 43 *least is said*   Freud, Esti D., 'Mrs Sigmund Freud', p. 31

p. 43 *children's children*   Young-Bruehl, *Anna Freud*, Martha Freud to August Aichhorn, 27 July 1948, p. 308

p. 43 *word between us*   Freud, Esti D., 'Mrs Sigmund Freud', p. 31

p. 43 *content and meaning*   Martha Freud to Ludwig Binswanger, 7 November 1939, quoted in Grotjahn, 'Sigmund Freud and the Art of Letter Writing', p. 446

p. 43 *of the Seder*   Rosenfeld, 'Dream and Vision', p. 97; see *J* III, p. 375

p. 44 *from our home*   *Letters*, Freud to Martha, 23 July 1882, pp. 39–40

p. 44 *of her life*   Quoted in Freeman and Strean, *Freud and Women*, p. 46; quoted also in Clark, *Freud*, p. 89

p. 44 *brothers or sisters*   Gay, p. 600n; Martin Freud, 'Who Was Freud?', p. 203

p. 44 *on many tablets*   *Letters*, Freud to Martha, 21 September 1907, p. 270

p. 44 *foolish and superstitious*   Roazen, *Freud and his Followers*, p. 71, giving Isaiah Berlin as the direct source of the story

p. 44 *deferred to her*   *J* I, p. 154

p. 44 *practice fluctuated*   *FF*, 20 August 1893, p. 54: 'there are two factors of which she knows nothing: the necessity not to spend much more during these months in which I have no income....'

p. 44 *mushrooms as well*   *FF*, 4 July 1901, p. 443

p. 45 *quite ambitious*   *Letters*, Freud to Marie Bonaparte, 10 May 1926, p. 370

p. 45 *to his hotel*   *FF*, 23 March 1900, p. 407

p. 45 *in October 1883*   Book with dedication in personal collection of Victor Ross

p. 45 *form of pornography*   Laforgue, 'Personal Memories of Freud', p. 342

p. 45 *child analyst*   'A Disturbance of Memory on the Acropolis', *SE* XXII, p. 245

p. 45 *use her will*   Quoted in Freeman and Strean, *Freud and Women*, p. 47

p. 45 *like a swindle*   Stekel, *Autobiography*, p. 122

p. 45 *to keep silence*   Wittels, 'Wrestling with the Man: The Story of a Freudian', unpublished memoirs, quoted in Timms, 'The "Child-Woman"', p. 99

p. 45 *to the public*   Freud to Wittels, 8 January 1929, quoted in Timms, 'The "Child-Woman"', p. 104

p. 45 *traffic among mankind*   *FPf*, Freud to Pfister, 24 February 1928, p. 123

p. 46 *extremely unhappy Zweig*   Gay, p. 60

p. 46 *before her wedding*   *J* I, p. 142

p. 46 *lack of principle*   *Letters*, Freud to Martha, 5 July 1885, pp. 171–2

p. 46 *in the pregnancy*   Mathilde Breuer sent baby clothes to Martha, see letter dated 19 June 1887 (also letter c. February 1887), *LC*, Anna Freud Bequest E3

p. 46 *permit any pretences*   *Letters*, Freud to Emmeline and Minna Bernays, 16/17 October 1887, p. 234

p. 46 *to the midwife*   *Letters*, Freud to Emmeline and Minna Bernays, 21 October 1887, p. 235

p. 46 *Freud's patients, lived*   Bruno Bettelheim, 'Freud's Vienna', in *Recollections and Reflections*, pp. 20–1

p. 47 *her dowerlessness*   Unpublished letter to Minna Bernays, 15 April 1893, quoted in Ernst Freud *et al.*, *Sigmund Freud: His Life in Words and Pictures*, p. 148

p. 47 *this as well*   *FF*, 20 August 1893, pp. 53–4

p. 47 *seldom sharp-tongued*   Young-Bruehl, *Anna Freud*, p. 30

p. 47 *interest in us*   *J* I, p. 115

p. 47 *nice to you*   *Letters*, Freud to Minna, 28 August 1884, p. 140

p. 48 *bit of weaning*   Young-Bruehl, *Anna Freud*, pp. 33–4, based on Jones's letters to Anna Freud, 23 April, 18 and 26 November 1952

p. 48 *doesn't spare her*   *J* I, p. 129

p. 48 *attract each other*   *J* I, p. 180

p. 48 *I am alive* Letters, Freud to Martha, 23 June 1885, p. 167

p. 48 *he remains alive* Letters, Freud to Martha, 23 June 1885, p. 167

p. 48 *to stay alive* Letters, Freud to Martha, 14 August 1885, p. 182

p. 48 *laid for her* Letters, Freud to Martha, 18 December 1885, p. 202

p. 48 *our little circle* Letters, Freud to Minna, 7 February 1886, pp. 217–18

p. 49 *in Frankfurt* FF, 7 March 1896, p. 177

p. 49 *since their honeymoon* FF, 18 August 1897, p. 262

p. 49 *witty tongue* FPf, Pfister to Freud, 30 December 1923, p. 91

p. 49 *closest confidante* FF, 21 May 1894, p. 73

p. 49 *during the 1890s* Gay, p. 76, citing letter from Marie Bonaparte to Jones, 16 December 1953; J II, p. 432 gives Lucie Freud (personal communication) as source for this

p. 49 *further ostracism* FF, 7 November 1899, p. 383

p. 49 *a real woman* FJung, 212F, 24 September 1910, p. 353

p. 49 *Frau Professor Freud* Paula Fichtl, Interviews, FM; see also Berthelsen, Detlef, *Alltag bei Familie Freud*

p. 49 *recover in Sicily* FF, 24 September 1900, pp. 423–4; Freud calls the ailment a 'pulmonary apicitis (inflammation)'

p. 50 *has pointed out* Gay, pp. 752–3; see also Gay, 'Sigmund and Minna? The Biographer as Voyeur', and Gay, 'The Dog that Did not Bark in the Night'

p. 50 *Mathilde or Sophie* Secret Symmetry, Spielrein to Freud, 20 June 1909, p. 104

p. 50 *is convincing* Swales, 'Freud, Minna Bernays and the Conquest of Rome' is infuriatingly convincing and speculatively tenuous in almost equal measure.

p. 50 *founder of psychoanalysis* Gay, p. 163; Malcolm, *In the Freud Archives*, p. 24

p. 51 *vegetate harmlessly* FF, 11 March 1900, p. 404

p. 51 *of growing old* FJung, 177F, 2 February 1910, p. 292

p. 51 *than – die* FJung, Emma Jung to Freud, 6 November 1911, p. 456

p. 51 *life of Mankind* FJung, 45F, 19 September 1907, p. 89

p. 51 *entitled to* Letters, Freud to J.J. Putnam, 8 July 1915, p. 314

p. 51 *very indistinct* Gay, p. 163

p. 51 *psychoanalytic papers?* FJ, Jones to Freud, 22 August 1913. The paper was Putnam, 'Bemerkungen über einer Krankheitsfall mit Griselda-Phantasien'

p. 52 *of her father* Young-Bruehl, *Anna Freud*, p. 73

p. 52 *abnormal and scandalous!* Choisy, *Sigmund Freud*, p. 47: 'Freud ne trompe pas sa femme. C'est scandaleux! C'est anormal'

p. 52 *cholera would have* J I, p. 187, Freud to Martha, 2 March 1885

p. 52 *writing table* Letters, Freud to Martha, 13 May 1886, p. 230

p. 52 *wife in maturity* Letters, Freud to Martha, 15 November 1883, pp. 90–1

p. 53 *take care of* J I, pp. 180–1; no date for quote but probably in Freud-Martha correspondence

p. 54 *know so well* FA, Freud to Abraham, 18 December 1916, p. 244, cited Gay, p. 361

p. 54 *the spending itself* Letters, Freud to Martha, 18 August 1882, p. 45

p. 54 *died of diphtheria* J I, p. 167

p. 54 *lost my Mathilde* FF, 7 March 1897, p. 232

p. 54 *signs of puberty* FF, 15 November 1897, p. 283

p. 54 *usually receiving it* Young-Bruehl, *Anna Freud*, p. 42

p. 54 *sanatorium with fever* The Psychopathology of Everyday Life, SE VI, p. 180

p. 54 *of her recovery* The Psychopathology of Everyday Life, SE VI, p. 169

p. 55 *towards the convalescent* The Psychopathology of Everyday Life, SE VI, p. 169

p. 55 *suspect peritonitis* LC, Freud to Abraham, 19 January 1908

p. 55 *more beautiful* Letters, Freud to Mathilde Freud, 19 March 1908, p. 281

p. 55 *the master's daughter* Letters, Freud to Martha, 20 January 1886, p. 209

p. 55 *shabby chandelier* Binswanger, 'My First Three Visits with Freud', p. 361

p. 55 *Freud's daughters* FJung, 144J, 4 June 1909, p. 229

p. 56 *engagement to Mathilde* J II, p. 61; *Correspondance I*, Ferenczi to Freud, 30 October 1909, p. 98

p. 56 *serious operation* LC, Freud to Pfister, 17 March 1910

p. 56 *be with her* *FJ*, Freud to Jones, 3 and 7 September 1912
p. 56 *two weeks later* *Letters*, Freud to Martha, 20 September 1912, p. 300
p. 56 *egoism à deux* Freud to Anna von Vest, 14 November 1922, in Goldmann, 'Eine kur aus der Frühzeit', p. 325
p. 56 *child, so much* *Letters*, Freud to Kata and Lajos Levy, 11 May 1923, p. 349
p. 56 *daughter after her* Personal communication, Paul Roazen, 7 October 1991
p. 56 *can give them* Gay, p. 590; *SFC*, Freud to Sam Freud, 1 December 1931
p. 56 *marvellous normal way* *SFC*, Freud to Sam Freud, Manchester, 6 December 1929
p. 56 *hand-woven clothes* Young-Bruehl, *Anna Freud*, p. 42
p. 56 *misanthropic man* Freud said of Robert on one occasion: 'A world that was run on Robert's lines would be a world not worth living in.' (Personal communication, Victor Ross, 13 October 1991)
p. 56 *in the 1960s* Personal communication, Victor Ross, 13 October 1991
p. 57 *on her head* *FF*, 17 May 1896, pp. 186–7
p. 57 *radiant, determined* *Letters*, Freud to Max Halberstadt, 7 July 1912, p. 296
p. 57 *a loving woman* *Letters*, Freud to Max Halberstadt, 24 July 1912, p. 299
p. 57 *Yes and Amen* *Letters*, Freud to Max Halberstadt, 7 July 1912, p. 296
p. 57 *marriage ceremony* *Letters*, Freud to Max Halberstadt, 7 July 1912, p. 297
p. 57 *intelligent husband* *Letters*, Freud to Max Halberstadt, 7 July 1912, p. 297
p. 57 *weak human being* *LC*, Freud to Mathilde, 24 July 1912, quoted in Gay, p. 309
p. 58 *so imperturbable* *Letters*, Freud to Sophie, 20 July 1912, p. 298
p. 58 *the needlework* *Letters*, Freud to Sophie, 20 July 1912, p. 298
p. 58 *all by herself* *FLou*, 30 July 1915, p. 32
p. 58 *being depressed* Young-Bruehl, *Anna Freud*, p. 63
p. 58 *Rudi Kaufmann* Young-Bruehl, *Anna Freud*, p. 467 n. 93
p. 59 *wonders of sexuality!* Freud to Ferenczi, 11 March 1914, *LC*, quoted in Gay, p. 310n
p. 59 *first child analyst* *FA*, Freud to Abraham, 22 September 1914, p. 197
p. 59 *pregnant again* Gay, p. 391, citing interview with Lampl de Groot, 24 October 1985
p. 59 *of course permissible* *Letters*, Freud to Amalie Freud, 26 January 1920, p. 332
p. 59 *not get over* *LC*, Freud to Ferenczi, 4 February 1920, quoted in Gay, p. 393
p. 59 *follow only later* *Letters*, Freud to Pfister, 27 January 1920, p. 333
p. 59 *well prepared* Freud to Binswanger, 15 October 1926, quoted in Binswanger, *Erinnerungen*, pp. 94–5, and in Gay, p. 422
p. 59 *my own life* Freud to Binswanger, 15 October 1926, quoted in Binswanger, *Erinnerungen*, pp. 94–5, and in Gay, p. 422
p. 60 *game of fort/da* *Beyond the Pleasure Principle*, *SE* XVIII, pp. 14–18; see Derrida, 'Spéculer – sur Freud'
p. 60 *his watch-chain* H.D., *Tribute to Freud*, p. 128
p. 60 *the daughter's line?* Derrida, 'Spéculer – sur Freud', pp. 322–3

3: The First Patients pp. 63–116
p. 63 *across the country* Micale, 'Hysteria and its Historiography: A Review of Past and Present Writings', p. 332
p. 63 *Great Confinement* Foucault, *Madness and Civilization*
p. 63 *female adulterers* Guillain, *J.-M., Charcot*, p. 41
p. 63 *were housed* Harris, 'Introduction' to Charcot, p. xvi
p. 63 *and the hysterics* Marie, 'Discours' cited in Trillat, *Histoire de l'hystérie*, pp. 130–1
p. 63 *in both sexes* Mai and Merskey, 'Briquet's *Treatise on Hysteria*'; Mai and Merskey, 'Briquet's concept of hysteria'; Merskey, *The Analysis of Hysteria*
p. 63 *the wandering womb* For the general history of hysteria, see Veith, *Hysteria*; Ellenberger, *The Discovery of the Unconscious*, pp. 141–5; Krohn, *Hysteria*; Trillat, *Histoire de l'hystérie*
p. 64 *becoming medicalized* Goldstein, 'The Hysteria Diagnosis'
p. 64 *of clinical neurology* Foucault, Collège de France, 6 February 1974, quoted in Lagrange, 'Versions de la psychanalyse dans le texte de Foucault', pp. 262–3
p. 64 *sobbing, tears and laughter* Trillat, *Histoire de l'hystérie*, p. 135

p. 64 *stigmata of hysteria* Micale, 'Hysteria and its Historiography: The Future Perspective', pp. 80–4

p. 64 *the Middle Ages* Goldstein, 'The Hysteria Diagnosis'

p. 64 *phenomena at all* Micale, 'Hysteria and its Historiography: The Future Perspective', p. 84

p. 65 *17.8 per cent* Goldstein, *Console and Classify*, p. 322

p. 65 *nervousness and insanity* Micale, 'Hysteria and its Historiography: The Future Perspective', p. 41

p. 65 *general internal medicine* Trillat, *Histoire de l'hystérie*, pp. 121–5

p. 65 *anaesthetic surgery* Ellenberger, *The Discovery of the Unconscious*, pp. 110–331; Gauld, *A history of hypnosis*; Winter, 'Ethereal Epidemics'

p. 65 *newly created laboratories* Trillat, *Histoire de l'hystérie*, pp. 138–42; Micale, 'Hysteria and its Historiography: A Review of Past and Present Writings', p. 335

p. 65 *photographic studios* Didi-Huberman, *Invention de l'hystérie*

p. 65 *nineteenth century* Trillat, *Histoire de l'hystérie*, p. 141

p. 65 *First World War* Menzaghi, Millot and Pillot, *Evolution de la conception de l'hystérie de 1870 à 1930*, discussed in Micale, 'Hysteria and its Historiography: The Future Perspective', pp. 57 ff.; see also Salow, 'Where Has all the Hysteria Gone?', and Shorter, *From Paralysis to Fatigue*, pp. 186 ff. and pp. 267 ff.

p. 65 *through the town* Jones, *Free Associations*, pp. 114–15

p. 66 *self-indulgent patient* Smith-Rosenberg, 'The Hysterical Woman', pp. 208–12

p. 66 *their hysterical patients* Carter, *Hysteria*, is the classic, and most intriguingly ambiguous, example; see commentaries by Micale, 'Hysteria and its Historiography: A Review of Past and Present Writings', pp. 238–42, and Showalter, *The Female Malady*, pp. 132, 154

p. 67 *back of the house* See Showalter, *The Female Malady*, pp. 121–44

p. 67 *a healthy woman* Smith-Rosenberg, 'The Hysterical Woman', p. 208

p. 67 *her deviant role* Smith-Rosenberg, 'The Hysterical Woman', p. 211

p. 67 *effective in childhood* 'Dora', *SE* VII, pp. 44–5

p. 68 *life's great struggles* Channing, *Bed Case*, p. 22, cited in Smith-Rosenberg, 'The Hysterical Woman', pp. 210–11

p. 68 *autonomy and powerlessness* Showalter, *The Female Malady*, p. 173

p. 68 *hysterical protest* Showalter, *The Female Malady*, p. 161

p. 68 *the outer world* Hunter, 'Hysteria, Psychoanalysis and Feminism: The Case of Anna O.', p. 485

p. 68 *a proto-feminist* Gallop, 'Nurse Freud', quoted in Showalter, *The Female Malady*, p. 160

p. 68 *biological irresponsibility* Mort, *Dangerous Sexualities*, pp. 117 ff.

p. 69 *language of words* Goldstein, *Console and Classify*, p. 325

p. 69 *bourgeois value system* Goldstein, *Console and Classify*, pp. 325–6

p. 69 *his later work* See the well-known story of the comparative development of the landlord's daughter and her proletarian playmate in *Introductory Lectures on Psychoanalysis*, *SE* XVI, pp. 352–4

p. 69 *psychological gentrification* Micale, 'Hysteria and its Historiography: The Future Perspective', p. 91

p. 69 *to both transformations* Forrester, *Language and the Origins of Psychoanalysis*, Chapter 1

p. 69 *brought to awareness* Ellenberger, 'La psychiatrie et son histoire inconnue'; Showalter, *The Female Malady*, p. 143

p. 70 *emergencies of life* Channing, *Bed Case*, p. 22

p. 70 *patients themselves do* *Studies*, *SE* II, p. 260

p. 71 *unimportant one* *Studies*, *SE* II, p. 99

p. 71 *medical charisma* Forrester, 'Contracting the Disease of Love'; see also Swaan, 'On the Sociogenesis of the Psychoanalytic Situation'

p. 72 *to be overcome* 'Editor's introduction', *Studies*, *SE* II, p. xvi

p. 72 *time for work* *FF*, 4 February 1888, pp. 18–19

p. 72 *with Elisabeth von R*   Gedo *et al.*, *Studies on Hysteria*, pp. 185–6; but see Hölzer and Kächele, 'Die Entwicklung der freien Assoziation durch Sigmund Freud', and Zilboorg, 'Some Sidelights on Free Association'

p. 72 *life never emerged*   Breuer, 'Fräulein Anna O.', *Studies*, *SE* II, pp. 21–2

p. 72 *other than himself*   *Letters*, Freud to J.J. Putnam, 8 July 1915, p. 315: 'I was never Breuer's assistant, never saw his famous first case, and only learned of it years later from Breuer's report.'

p. 73 *this first patient*   Forrester, 'The True Story of Anna O.', pp. 28–9

p. 73 *the early 1840s*   Hirschmüller, *Breuer*, p. 99

p. 74 *studying law*   Stewart, 'Analytic Biography of Anna O.', in Rosenbaum and Muroff eds, *Anna O.*, pp. 47–51; see also Freeman, *The Story of Anna O.*, p. 74

p. 74 *of the illness*   *Studies*, *SE* II, p. 24

p. 74 *The symptoms*   For recent rediagnoses of Bertha's strange collection of symptoms, see Hollender, 'The Case of Anna O: A Reformulation', Hurst, 'What Was Wrong with Anna O.?', Orr-Andrawes, 'The Case of Anna O.: A Neuropsychiatric Perspective', Rosenbaum and Muroff, *Anna O.*

p. 74 *as well, disappeared*   *Studies*, *SE* II, p. 25

p. 74 *spoke only English*   The fact that Bertha briefly lost the power to formulate sentences in any language has been used by Hunter to argue, in a quasi-Lacanian fashion, that she was regressing in non-linguistic protest at her suffocating and monotonous existence (Hunter, 'Hysteria, Psychoanalysis and Feminism: The Case of Anna O.')

p. 74 *mind completely clear*   *Studies*, *SE* II, pp. 27–8

p. 75 *utterance to them*   *Studies*, *SE* II, pp. 29–30

p. 75 *feeling my hands*   *Studies*, *SE* II, p. 30

p. 75 *helped her greatly*   *Studies*, *SE* II, p. 31

p. 75 *her imagination*   *Studies*, *SE* II, p. 32

p. 76 *winter of 1881–2*   *Studies*, *SE* II, p. 33

p. 76 *permanently removed*   *Studies*, *SE* II, p. 35

p. 76 *her in writing*   *Studies*, *SE* II, p. 37

p. 76 *unpublished manuscript*   Quoted in Ellenberger, 'The Story of "Anna O."', p. 276. This important note indicates that Breuer was fully aware that any deceit he practised on Bertha would repeat the deception her family practised on her, in concealing her father's death from her – a deception which had precipitated a sudden worsening of her condition after she had achieved a considerable improvement in the period when she believed herself and her father to be in parallel sickrooms in the house. It also becomes clearer from Ellenberger's account than it is in Breuer's published version that Breuer had very skilfully taken over her father's position in her emotional world, and that force rather than deception would preserve this.

p. 77 *agitated state*   Hirschmüller, *Breuer*, pp. 293–4

p. 77 *tangible relief*   Letter dated 27 August 1882, reproduced in Hirschmüller, *Breuer*, p. 301. For comparison, see Hirschmüller, 'Eine bisher unbekannte Krankengeschichte Sigmund Freuds und Josef Breuers'

p. 77 *theoretical course*   Hirschmüller, *Breuer*, p. 114

p. 77 *or other troubles*   Robert Binswanger to Breuer, 13 January 1884, quoted in Hirschmüller, *Breuer*, p. 116

p. 77 *and of Freud's*   *Letters*, Freud to Martha, 19 April 1884, p. 121

p. 77 *Inzersdorf in 1887*   Hirschmüller, *Breuer*, p. 116

p. 78 *the moral sense*   Quoted in Jensen, 'Anna O.', p. 279

p. 78 *to eliminate entirely*   Jacobus, 'Taking Liberties with Words', pp. 209–10

p. 79 *to be helpers*   Kaplan, *Jewish Feminist Movement*, p. 36, citing *Blätter des Jüdischen Frauenbundes*, July 1936, p. 12. See also the useful preface by Yolande Tisseron in Pappenheim, *Le travail de Sisyphe*

p. 79 *against white slavery*   Cora Berliner, one of *JFB*'s vice-presidents, on Bertha, quoted in Kaplan, *Jewish Feminist Movement*, p. 36; see also Jensen, *Streifzüge durch das Leben von Anna O./Bertha Pappenheim*

p. 79 *a friendly face* Bertha Pappenheim, Poem, about 1911, reproduced in Hirschmüller, *Breuer*, p. 308

p. 79 *remained untouched* Kaplan, *Jewish Feminist Movement*, p. 39, citing *Blätter des Jüdischen Frauenbundes*, July 1936, p. 16

p. 79 *natural mothers* Edinger, *Bertha Pappenheim – Freud's Anna O.* p. 60; see also Hirschmüller, *Breuer*, p. 124

p. 80 *the father* Jacobus, 'Taking Liberties with Words', p. 208

p. 80 *successful hysteric* Israël, *L'hystérique, le sexe et le médecin*, pp. 197 ff.

p. 80 *published in 1895* Hirschmüller, cited in Reeves, 'Breuer, Freud and the Case of Anna O.', p. 206

p. 80 *two-edged sword* Edinger, *Bertha Pappenheim: Leben und Schriften*, p. 12, quoted in Jensen, 'Anna O.', p. 289

p. 80 *they were married* *Letters*, Freud to Martha, 13 July 1883, p. 56

p. 81 *two daughters* Swales, 'Freud, Breuer and the Blessed Virgin', p. 26

p. 81 *the early 1880s* Hirschmüller, *Breuer*, p. 158; Swales, 'Freud, his Teacher and the Birth of Psychoanalysis', p. 42. On other influences on the development of Freud's concept of catharsis, see Macmillan, 'Delboeuf and Janet'

p. 81 *marriage around 1880* Swales, 'Freud, Breuer and the Blessed Virgin', pp. 25–6. Freud reported to Martha having met Emma Pappenheim in the street in Vienna in September 1883 (*Letters*, Freud to Martha, 4 September 1883, p. 69)

p. 81 *in the evenings* Private communication, Paul Homburger, cited in Karpe, 'The Rescue Complex', p. 10

p. 81 *child is coming!* *Letters*, Freud to Stefan Zweig, 2 June 1932, pp. 408–9

p. 81 *in a sanatorium* *Letters*, Freud to Stefan Zweig, 2 June 1932, pp. 408–9

p. 82 *love with her* *LC*, Freud to Martha, 31 October 1883

p. 82 *sleep last night* *LC*, Martha to Freud, 2 November 1883

p. 82 *isn't that so?* *LC*, Freud to Martha, 4 November 1883

p. 82 *let it drop* *Letters*, Freud to Stefan Zweig, 2 June 1932, pp. 408–9

p. 82 *been in love* *Studies on Hysteria*, SE II, pp. 21–2

p. 83 *by that relationship* Breuer's 1882 case notes, quoted in Hirschmüller, *Breuer*, p. 108

p. 83 *that frightens her* *Studies on Hysteria*, SE II, p. 246

p. 83 *patients are concerned* *Studies on Hysteria*, SE II, p. 246 n. 1. In the conversation with Breuer quoted below in the letter from Freud to Martha, Breuer asked Freud to repeat certain things to her only after he was married, an injunction that foreshadows Breuer's graphic description of the veil of secrecy drawn by senior doctors over the subject of sexuality. Freud's response to this injunction is also a foreshadowing: in claiming that he can already say anything to his wife, he implicitly refuses to obey any such injunction to secrecy, a position he will vigorously defend in the Dora case history as necessary in any scientific study (see *SE* VII, p. 9). In the story Freud recounted later (*SE* XIV, p. 13), Breuer expressed himself as follows: 'These things are always *secrets d'alcôve*!', and when asked by the young Freud what he meant, explained what the word '*alcôve*' (marriage-bed) meant – again, Breuer took this topic to be one in which the dialectic of the knowledge of experience and the ignorance of innocence was paramount. Freud's conception was altogether differently oriented.

p. 83 *deeper connections* *Letters*, Freud to Stefan Zweig, 2 June 1932, p. 409

p. 83 *in June 1882* *Studies*, SE II, p. 33 (translation modified); '*Dieses Wiederdurchleben des verflossenen Jahres dauerte fort bis zum definitiven Abschluß der Krankheit im Juni 1882*'

p. 83 *7 June 1881* Reeves, 'Breuer, Freud and the Case of Anna O.', p. 209. For other speculations on the significance of the loss of children in the dramatic breaking off of the treatment, see Pollock, 'The Possible Significance of Childhood Object Loss'

p. 84 *his own daughter* Ellenberger, 'The Story of "Anna O."', p. 273: 'The approximate time of Dora's conception (June 1881) would rather coincide with the date of Bertha's transfer to the country-house [7 June 1881], but there is no evidence that Breuer interrupted the treatment at this time.'

p. 84 *as the father* We should always bear in mind that there were other doctors whose name began with B whose baby it might have been, in particular Dr Breslauer at the Inzersdorf Sanatorium, who treated Bertha over the next four years.

p. 84 *his wife Cordelia* Letters, Freud to Martha, 13 July 1883, pp. 55–6

p. 84 *sexual nature* See *Studies on Hysteria*, SE II, pp. 40–1 n. 1, in which Freud's description of an 'untoward event' (*SE* XIV, p. 12) is referred to.

p. 84 *transference love* An Autobiographical Study, SE XX, p. 26

p. 84 *universal* 'On the History of the Psychoanalytic Movement', SE XIV, p. 12

p. 85 *to abandon hypnotism* An Autobiographical Study, SE XX, p. 27

p. 85 *affects one deeply* Letters, Freud to Martha, 27 January 1886, pp. 211–12

p. 85 *made his fortune* FF, 14 October 1900, p. 427

p. 85 *in one person* Hirschmüller, Breuer, p. 34

p. 85 *a healing influence* Hirschmüller, Breuer, p. 19

p. 85 *to do good* FF, 16 January 1898, p. 294

p. 85 *so much badness* J I, p. 183, quoting Freud to Martha, 6 June 1883

p. 86 *little woman* FF, 3 December 1895, p. 153, trans. modified

p. 86 *excludes her* Jacobus, 'Taking Liberties with Words', pp. 223–4

p. 86 *fore-runner of psycho-analysis* Ferenczi, 'The Principle of Relaxation and Neocatharsis', p. 109

p. 86 *boys' own story* See Israël, L'hystérique, le sexe et le médecin, p. 205

p. 86 *his teacher* FF, 8 February 1897, p. 229

p. 86 *prima donna* FF, 12 July 1892, p. 32

p. 87 *autumn of 1893* Studies, SE II, p. 69

p. 87 *Sophie (née Gomperz)* Following Swales, 'Freud, his Teacher and the Birth of Psychoanalysis', for much of the information on Anna von Lieben

p. 87 *possibly have them* Kupper and Rollman-Branch, 'Freud and Schnitzler – Doppelgänger', p. 416

p. 88 *ideal human being* FS, 7 March 1875, p. 95

p. 88 *Helmholtz school* See McGrath, Freud's Discovery of Psychoanalysis, pp. 111 ff.; Eissler, 'Creativity and Adolescence', p. 479

p. 88 *beliefs and desires* Bernfeld, 'Freud's Scientific Beginnings', p. 245

p. 88 *on 8 February* Hirschmüller, Breuer, p. 94

p. 88 *and February 1880* Hirschmüller, Breuer, p. 92

p. 88 *genuineness of hypnosis* An Autobiographical Study, SE XX, p. 16. It is thus plausible that it was Brentano who informed Freud of Heidenhain's work.

p. 89 *Anna alongside Freud* It is possible that Rudolf Chrobak, another of Freud's much needed medical patrons and supporters, recommended Freud to the von Liebens.

p. 89 *'Preliminary Communication'* Studies, SE II, p. 178

p. 89 *technique almost daily* There is some doubt about whether Freud visited Paris in 1888; nor is it certain that he accompanied Anna.

p. 89 *went to Nancy* It is curious that he was at Fanny Moser's castle on 19 July 1889: did he take Fanny or Anna to Nancy? It seems likely he took Anna, but dropped in to visit Fanny on the way.

p. 89 *do with her* An Autobiographical Study, SE XX, p. 17; trans. modified

p. 89 *with amnesia* An Autobiographical Study, SE XX, pp. 17–18

p. 89 *payment of old debts* Studies, SE II, p. 69 n. 1

p. 90 *physical expression* Studies, SE II, p. 70 n. 1

p. 90 *hysterical symptoms* Studies, SE II, p. 76 n. 1

p. 90 *at an end* Studies, SE II, p. 178

p. 90 *conflict and defence* Studies, SE II, pp. 178–9

p. 90 *of great perfection* Studies, SE II, p. 180. Indeed, it was the presence of her posthumously published book of poems in Freud's library that enabled Swales to establish her identity.

p. 90 *sink away forever* von Lieben, Anna, Gedichte, pp. 155–6, quoted in Swales, 'Freud, his Teacher and the Birth of Psychoanalysis', p. 42. The date of composition is not known, but it seems likely that she wrote it during or after her treatment, maybe even on reading her case history in *Studies on Hysteria* (given the poem's title).

p. 91 *strong innervations*   *Studies*, *SE* II, p. 181

p. 91 *hint at transference*   *An Autobiographical Study*, *SE* XX, p. 27; this passage is quoted at the end of the section on Bertha Pappenheim, pp. 84–5 above

p. 92 *non-marriageability*   Ellenberger, 'L'histoire d'"Emmy von N."', p. 528; see also de Boor and Moersch, 'Emmy von N. – eine Hysterie?', and Meissner, 'Studies on Hysteria – Frau Emmy von N.'

p. 92 *people their name*   Andersson, 'A Supplement to Freud's Case History of "Frau Emmy v. N."', p. 10

p. 92 *to value little*   *Studies*, *SE* II, p. 54

p. 92 *turned to Freud*   Note the mysterious letter (*Letters*, Freud to Breuer, 3 May 1889, pp. 236–7), responding to some unstated criticisms of Breuer's in a letter which almost certainly arrived on 1 May, the day Freud started treating Fanny – could it have been connected with the transfer of Fanny from Breuer to Freud?

p. 93 *for her recovery*   *Studies*, *SE* II, p. 48

p. 93 *education and intelligence*   *Studies*, *SE* II, p. 49

p. 93 *store of memories*   *Studies*, *SE* II, p. 99

p. 93 *seventeen and fifteen*   Note that in the case history Freud changed the ages of the two daughters by one year, probably so as to avoid identification of Frau Emmy von N. as Fanny Moser.

p. 93 *the slightest objection*   *Studies*, *SE* II, p. 50

p. 94 *with her correspondence*   *Studies*, *SE* II, p. 51

p. 94 *of the family*   See Forrester, *Language and the Origins of Psychoanalysis*, pp. 10–11, and Smith-Rosenberg, 'The Hysterical Woman', p. 211

p. 94 *guided by chance*   *Studies*, *SE* II, p. 56

p. 94 *against any constraint*   *Studies*, *SE* II, p. 62 n. 1

p. 95 *fell in with this*   *Studies*, *SE* II, p. 63

p. 95 *to produce material*   *Studies*, *SE* II, p. 76

p. 95 *very grave*   *Studies*, *SE* II, p. 81

p. 95 *your masterly doctor!*   Assoun, *Freud et la femme*, p. 51

p. 95 *docile and submissive*   *Studies*, *SE* II, p. 82

p. 95 *you say so*   *Studies*, *SE* II, p. 82

p. 95 *laid upon her*   *Studies*, *SE* II, p. 99

p. 95 *immediate and lasting*   *Studies*, *SE* II, p. 83

p. 96 *wiping away*   *Studies*, *SE* II, p. 53

p. 96 *even under hypnosis*   *Studies*, *SE* II, pp. 58–9

p. 96 *need reproach himself*   *Studies*, *SE* II, p. 65

p. 96 *of her fear*   *Studies*, *SE* II, p. 73

p. 96 *tended to Fanny*   Cf. *Jokes*, *SE* VIII, pp. 98ff.

p. 96 *pointed out to Freud*   *Studies*, *SE* II, pp. 79–80

p. 97 *me in astonishment*   *Studies*, *SE* II, pp. 84–5

p. 97 *temperance movement*   Andersson, 'A Supplement to Freud's Case History of "Frau Emmy v. N."' p. 5

p. 97 *prerogative in writing*   *Studies*, *SE* II, p. 85

p. 97 *characteristics of love*   'Psychical Treatment', *SE* VII, p. 296

p. 97 *smile of pity*   *Studies*, *SE* II, p. 105 n. 1

p. 98 *father's fortune*   *Studies*, *SE* II, p. 105 n. 1; emphasis added

p. 98 *of these affairs*   Andersson, 'A Supplement to Freud's Case History of "Frau Emmy v. N."' p. 11, also in Else Pappenheim, 'Freud and Gilles de la Tourette', p. 267, and in Ellenberger, 'L'histoire d'"Emmy von N."', p. 530

p. 98 *severely neurotic woman*   *Studies*, *SE* II, pp. 66–7

p. 98 *was her doctor*   *Studies*, *SE* II, p. 102

p. 98 *with the profession*   *Studies*, *SE* II, pp. 83–4

p. 98 *lady as well*   *Studies*, *SE* II, pp. 103–4

p. 99 *helplessness of a woman*   *Studies*, *SE* II, p. 102

p. 99 *patients themselves do*   *Studies*, *SE* II, p. 260

p. 99 *a new marriage* Studies, *SE* II, p. 103

p. 99 *sexual abstinence* Studies, *SE* II, p. 88

p. 100 *financial difficulties* Studies, *SE* II, p. 105 n. 1

p. 100 *character-change* Studies, *SE* II, p. 77

p. 100 *occurred in the girl* Studies, *SE* II, p. 83

p. 100 *undermine her health* Studies, *SE* II, p. 85

p. 100 *pride of her mother* Anderson, 'A Supplement to Freud's Case History of "Frau Emmy v. N."', p. 12

p. 101 *Freud's advice* Ellenberger, 'L'histoire d'"Emmy von N."', p. 531

p. 101 *in other cases* Ellenberger, 'L'histoire d'"Emmy von N."', p. 538

p. 101 *was married* Studies, *SE* II, p. 105 n. 1

p. 101 *of her life* Andersson, 'A Supplement to Freud's Case History of "Frau Emmy v. N."', pp. 14–15

p. 101 *compulsion to repeat* Studies, *SE* II, p. 105 n. 1 ; Freud notes that he pieced this together years later

p. 102 *as their lovers* *FF*, Draft H, 24 January 1895, p. 110

p. 102 *in her mind* Studies, *SE* II, p. 61

p. 102 *instance of amnesia* Studies, *SE* II, p. 61 n. 1

p. 102 *conflicts of her life* Andersson, 'A Supplement to Freud's Case History of "Frau Emmy v. N."', pp. 14–15

p. 103 *daughter, Aurelia Kronich* We owe the identification of Katharina as Aurelia to Peter Swales, and the information on her life and family to Swales, 'Freud, Katharina and the First "Wild Analysis"'; Gerhardt Fichtner and Albert Hirschmüller, 'Freuds "Katharina"', and Ellenberger's researches.

p. 103 *nice case for me* *FF*, 20 August 1893, p. 54

p. 104 *mountain to another* Studies, *SE* II, p. 134 n. 2

p. 104 *world of sexuality* Studies, *SE* II, p. 127

p. 104 *not have seen* Studies, *SE* II, p. 127

p. 104 *in my head* Studies, *SE* II, p. 128

p. 104 *explain the case* Studies, *SE* II, p. 129

p. 105 *fourteen years old* Studies, *SE* II, p. 129

p. 105 *Not at the time* Studies, *SE* II, p. 130

p. 105 *lightened and exalted* Studies, *SE* II, p. 131

p. 105 *what I thought* Studies, *SE* II, p. 131 ; see Breuer and Freud, *Studien*, pp. 105–6

p. 105 *bottom of everything* 'auf der Grund der Dinge gekommen ist'; Strachey gives 'a fundamental position has been reached'

p. 105 *natural as shameful* Studies, *SE* II, p. 132; Breuer and Freud, *Studien*, p. 106; trans. modified

p. 105 *they were divorced* Studies, *SE* II, p. 127

p. 105 *say that too* Studies, *SE* II, p. 132

p. 106 *her own father* Studies, *SE* II, p. 134 n. 2; Strachey mistranslated this as 'sexual attempts on the part of her own father'; Swales was the first to point out this mistranslation.

p. 106 *of sexual life* Studies, *SE* II, p. 133

p. 107 *show-business family* Swales, 'Katharina', p. 153 n. 38

p. 107 *Alpine-folkloric make-believe* Swales, 'Katharina', p. 124

p. 107 *left in 1903* Made more improbable by the fact that the Freud family spent the summer of 1903 at Königsee, not far from Salzburg, and a long way from the Rax; Freud wrote to Anna von Vest from there on 20 July and again on 28 August, and was back in Vienna by 20 September, when he wrote to her again.

p. 108 *longing for love* Studies, *SE* II, p. 143

p. 108 *pretence treatment* Studies, *SE* II, p. 138

p. 108 *trunk bent backward* Studies, *SE* II, p. 137; trans. modified following Gay, p. 71

p. 108 *highly intelligent person* Studies, *SE* II, p. 136

p. 108 *undertaken by me* Studies, *SE* II, p. 139

p. 109 *ambitious plans* Studies, *SE* II, p. 140

p. 109 *of her family* Studies, *SE* II, p. 140
p. 109 *invalid of the family* Studies, *SE* II, p. 142
p. 109 *her own pains* Studies, *SE* II, pp. 143–4
p. 110 *in the right* Studies, *SE* II, pp. 144–5
p. 110 *disorder which you bemoan* Lacan, 'Intervention on Transference', p. 65
p. 110 *after a party* Studies, *SE* II, p. 145
p. 110 *her first love* Studies, *SE* II, p. 146
p. 110 *or shortly before* Studies, *SE* II, pp. 146–7
p. 111 *decisive explanation* Studies, *SE* II, p. 155
p. 111 *began to melt* Studies, *SE* II, p. 155
p. 111 *brother-in-law of hers* Studies, *SE* II, p. 156
p. 111 *be his wife* Studies, *SE* II, p. 156
p. 111 *whole moral being* Studies, *SE* II, p. 157
p. 111 *in herself instead* Studies, *SE* II, p. 157
p. 112 *no other interpretation* Studies, *SE* II, p. 157
p. 112 *each other splendidly* Studies, *SE* II, p. 158
p. 112 *mere sisterly affection* Studies, *SE* II, p. 158
p. 112 *her present circumstances* Studies, *SE* II, p. 158
p. 112 *would come true* Studies, *SE* II, p. 159
p. 112 *would come right* Studies, *SE* II, p. 160
p. 112 *unknown to me* Studies, *SE* II, p. 160; this passage is the end of this most 'written' of
        the case histories, with its suspense-filled denouement and happy ending.
p. 113 *pugnacity and reserve* Studies, *SE* II, p. 161
p. 113 *wasn't really so* Gay, p. 72
p. 113 *few years later* Freud treated Ilona in the latter part of 1892 (see Gay, p. 72), and
        probably wrote up the case in May 1894 (see Schur, *Freud*, pp. 50–4, who interprets
        Freud's reference to a case history, 'among my most difficult pieces of work', as being
        to Ilona Weiss's (see *FF*, 21 May 1894, p. 74)).
p. 113 *Memory yields* 'Notes upon a Case of Obsessional Neurosis,' *SE* X, p. 184
p. 113 *of such baseness* 'Notes upon a Case of Obsessional Neurosis', *SE* X, p. 183
p. 113 *undertaken by me* Studies, *SE* II, p. 139
p. 113 *tale of trouble* Studies, *SE* II, p. 116
p. 114 *cure in his patients* Gay, p. 72, implies that Lucy R. was treated after Elisabeth von R.,
        whom he dates to the autumn of 1892; this implies that Lucy R.'s treatment took place
        right at the end of 1892.
p. 114 *broken this promise* Studies, *SE* II, p. 115
p. 115 *towards anyone else* Studies, *SE* II, p. 117
p. 115 *crushed her hopes* Studies, *SE* II, p. 120
p. 115 *what one wishes* Studies, *SE* II, p. 121, trans. modified; Breuer and Freud, *Studien*, p. 97:
        'Man kann ja bei sich denken und empfinden, was man will.'
p. 115 *in her place* 'Some Character Types Met with in Psychoanalytic Work', *SE* XIV, p. 331
p. 116 *through a misunderstanding* Studies, *SE* II, p. 260; Breuer and Freud, *Studien*, p. 208: '*ein
        überreifes, liebebedürftiges Mädchen, dessen Neigung zu rasch durch ein Missverständnis erweckt wird.*'

4: The Dream of Psychoanalysis pp. 117–45

p. 117 *not been clean* The Interpretation of Dreams, *SE* IV, p. 107. The ellipses in the dream text
        are Freud's.
p. 118 *to other factors* The Interpretation of Dreams, *SE* IV, p. 118
p. 118 *professional fault* Cf. Freud's important use of this strategy of turning the self-defence
        inside out, like a coat with a lining, in his discussion of *Dora*, and also Lacan's discussion
        of the importance of this. One might say that this mirror of self-justification is a major
        theme of identification.
p. 119 *of his hip* The Interpretation of Dreams, *SE* IV, p. 112
p. 119 *primal scene of psychoanalysis* Assoun, *Freud et la femme*, p. 56
p. 119 *meaning of dreams* Schur, 'Some Additional "Day-Residues"'; Masson, *The Assault on Truth*

p. 119 *emanated from her nose* See Hartman, 'A Reappraisal of the Emma Episode and the Specimen Dream'

p. 119 *a surgeon, Rosanes* It is typical of the close-knit nature of Freud's circle and his medical practice, which is so important to an understanding of the dream of Irma's injection, that Freud was to take Rosanes's wife into treatment with him a few years later.

p. 119 *the strong sex* FF, 8 March 1895, p. 117

p. 119 *at all abnormal* FF, 8 March 1895, p. 117

p. 119 *operation had caused* FF, 11 April 1895, p. 124

p. 120 *undesired accident* FF, 13 March 1895, p. 119

p. 120 *someone to remember* See Castoriadis, *Crossroads in the Labyrinth*, pp. 67ff.

p. 121 *very high opinion* The Interpretation of Dreams, SE IV, p. 110

p. 121 *my own wife* The Interpretation of Dreams, SE IV, p. 110

p. 121 *the German text* The Interpretation of Dreams, SE IV, p. 110; Stud II, p. 130

p. 121 *most part broken* Studies on Hysteria, SE II, pp. 294–5; Stud Erg, p. 87

p. 121 *accepted my solution* The Interpretation of Dreams, SE IV, p. 111

p. 121 *yielded sooner* The Interpretation of Dreams, SE IV, p. 111

p. 121 *without outside help* The Interpretation of Dreams, SE IV, p. 110

p. 121 *of neither party* The Interpretation of Dreams, SE IV, p. 109

p. 121 *almost two years* Letters, Freud to Martha, 20 January 1886, p. 209

p. 121 *one dishonest word* Letters, Freud to Martha, 20 January 1886, p. 209

p. 122 *up her secret* Studies on Hysteria, SE II, p. 138. This passage forms part of a discussion of the difference between cases in which the patient is aware of the origin and precipitating cause of her illness, and those in which she is not: those in which the cause is a secret, and those in which it is a foreign body. It is clear that Freud based this distinction, which he hinted was a false one in a footnote on the following page, on an adapted quote from Goethe: '*Das Mäskchen da weissagt verborgnen Sinn.*' That is, the girl-mask reveals a hidden sense, where girl and mask become one word. This pun thus embodies the conviction that it is a feminine secret Freud is penetrating into, that the woman is the secret meaning he is unmasking.

p. 123 *young widow* The Interpretation of Dreams, SE IV, pp. 116–17

p. 123 *of the habit* The Interpretation of Dreams, SE IV, p. 116

p. 123 *problem of sex* 'On the Grounds for Detaching ...', SE III, p. 99

p. 123 *anxiety neurosis* 'On the Grounds for Detaching ...', SE III, p. 100

p. 123 *abstinent women* 'On the Grounds for Detaching ...', SE III, pp. 100–1

p. 123 *a similar sense* 'On the Grounds for Detaching ...', SE III, p. 111

p. 124 *domestic misfortune* 'On the History of the Psycho-analytic Movement', SE XIV, p. 14

p. 124 *penis normalis* 'On the History of the Psycho-analytic Movement', SE XIV, pp. 14–15; see the excellent discussion of the larger questions concerning the counter-transferential foundation of analysis, or the desire of the analyst, in Cottet, *Freud et le désir du psychanalyste*

p. 124 *patient's family* The Interpretation of Dreams, SE IV, p. 106. From his earliest days, Freud had been treating patients he knew well, sometimes intimately; his successful case of hypnotic treatment of 1893 was a woman he had known since childhood (SE I, p. 119).

p. 124 *infection in the patient* FA, Abraham to Freud, 8 January 1908, p. 18

p. 124 *intimate things, naturally* FA, Freud to Abraham, 9 January 1908, p. 20; Freud's emphasis and exclamation mark

p. 125 *at this point* The Interpretation of Dreams, SE IV, p. 113; trans. modified

p. 125 *Mathilde Breuer* The exact identity of Irma was recognized as a matter of some importance, although subject to much confusion and faulty conjecture, especially by those anxious to subsume the Irma dream within the reality of the Emma episode (Clark, Schur, Masson, Krull). There has, however, never been any doubt about her identity. Anzieu's surmise in 1959 that Irma was Anna, together with a note published by James Strachey in the version of the *Project* in SE (SE I, p. 341 n. 3), would have made it clear that Irma was Anna Hammerschlag, even before the publication of selections from the Freud–Abraham correspondence in 1965. Strachey records that in Freud's manuscript of the *Project*, the patient is called A. and the doctor R.: A. is Anna, and R. is Rie.

p. 125 *my school days* Letters, Freud to Martha, 10 January 1884, pp. 102–3
p. 125 *paternally solicitous* 'Obituary of Professor S. Hammerschlag', *SE* IX, p. 255
p. 125 *as his son* J I, p. 179
p. 125 *admirable girl* Letters, Freud to Martha, 10 January 1884, p. 102
p. 125 *congratulatory postcard* Letters, Freud to Martha, 23 June 1885, p. 167
p. 125 *within a year* J I, p. 179
p. 125 *schoolteacher* Young-Bruehl, *Anna Freud*, p. 46
p. 125 *in Neustiftgasse* Hirschmüller, *Breuer*, p. 31 n. 191, p. 337
p. 125 *and my family* The Interpretation of Dreams, *SE* IV, p. 106
p. 125 *inhabited by Freud* Anzieu, *Freud's Self-Analysis*, p. 29
p. 126 *out of Dickens* Letters, Freud to Martha, 15 April 1884, pp. 118–19
p. 126 *letter mocking it* J I, p. 154
p. 126 *four-day-old lady* Letters, Freud to Emmeline and Minna Bernays, 21 October 1887, p. 235
p. 126 *than intelligence* Studies on Hysteria, *SE* II, p. 164. The attribution is Swales's 'Freud, Martha Bernays and the Language of Flowers', pp. 34–5n
p. 126 *final illnesses* Studies on Hysteria, *SE* II, pp. 162–4
p. 126 *I greatly value* The Interpretation of Dreams, *SE* V, p. 422
p. 126 *keep a secret* The Interpretation of Dreams, *SE* V, p. 482
p. 126 *call for suppression* The Interpretation of Dreams, *SE* V, p. 484
p. 126 *lost come back* The Interpretation of Dreams, *SE* V, p. 486
p. 127 *path to immortality?* The Interpretation of Dreams, *SE* V, p. 487
p. 127 *non vixit dream* FF, 7 November 1899, p. 383
p. 127 *led to her death* The Interpretation of Dreams, *SE* IV, p. 111; Voswinckel, 'The Case of Mathilde S.', and Hirschmüller, 'Freuds "Mathilde"'
p. 127 *for a tooth* The Interpretation of Dreams, *SE* IV, p. 112
p. 127 *way to recovery* J I, p. 167
p. 128 *close to the hospital* Hirschmüller, *Breuer*, p. 22
p. 128 *reserved woman* Hirschmüller, *Breuer*, p. 30
p. 128 *her own father* Letters, Freud to Martha, 13 July 1883, p. 56
p. 128 *a beautiful sign* Letters, Freud to Martha, 29 May 1884, p. 127
p. 128 *in April 1886* J I, p. 157
p. 128 *Breuerisation* FF, 11 March 1900, p. 402
p. 128 *most deferential thanks* J III, p. 130, citing Freud to Mathilde Breuer, 13 May 1926; see Hirschmüller, '"Balsam auf eine schmerzende Wunde"'
p. 129 *trauma in childhood* 'Further Remarks on the Neuro-Psychoses of Defence', *SE* III, p. 166. At the end of this passage, Freud appends a note that addresses the question: 'Why is it only ideas with a *sexual* content that can be repressed?' His lengthy answer introduces the concept of deferred action and the importance of the 'retardation of pubertal maturity as compared with the psychical functions'.
p. 129 *accompanied by pleasure* FF, 8 October 1895, p. 141
p. 129 *sexual shocks* FF, 15 October 1895, p. 143. The fact that Freud is spelling this out to Fliess implies both that he had not told him this in September when they met, and that it was not seen as implicit in the case history Freud had included in the *Project* he had recently sent him (the case of Emma).
p. 129 *obsessional neurosis* FF, 8 December 1895, p. 154
p. 129 *of the events* FF, 3 January 1897, p. 219
p. 129 *repudiated perversion* FF, 6 December 1896, p. 212
p. 129 *by anyone later* FF, 6 December 1896, p. 213
p. 129 *oral sexual system* FF, 11 January 1897, p. 222
p. 130 *urine, faeces, blood* FF, 14 January 1897, p. 224

p. 130 *from a phonograph*   *FF*, 24 January 1897, p. 226

p. 130 *only subsequently*   *FF*, 6 April 1897, p. 234

p. 130 *masturbation fantasies*   *FF*, 2 May 1897, p. 239. Freud was to employ this argument in one of his 'mature' works, the case history of the Rat Man, precisely in the context of deciding whether his 'memories' of infancy pertain to real events or not. It thus became a canonical rule for the interpretation of certain fantasies: 'in his phantasies about his infancy the individual as he grows up *endeavours to efface the recollection of his auto-erotic activities*; and this he does by exalting their memory-traces to the level of object-love, just as a real historian will view the past in the light of the present. This explains why these phantasies abound in seductions and assaults, where the facts will have been confined to auto-erotic activities and the caresses and punishments that stimulated them.' (*SE* X, pp. 206–7 n. 1)

p. 130 *should die*   *FF*, Draft N, 31 May 1897, p. 250

p. 130 *then come together*   *FF*, Draft N, 31 May 1897, p. 251; see Levin, *Freud's Early Theories*, p. 226

p. 130 *protective fictions*   *FF*, 2 May 1897, p. 239

p. 130 *a prior defence*   *FF*, 25 May 1897, p. 247

p. 130 *genuine memories*   *FF*, 7 July 1897, p. 255

p. 131 *fulfilment of a wish*   *FF*, Draft N, 31 May 1897, p. 251

p. 131 *memory of the maid*   *FF*, 20 June 1898, p. 317

p. 131 *theme of the parents*   *FF*, 21 September 1897, pp. 264–5

p. 131 *have at present*   *FF*, 15 October 1897, p. 270

p. 131 *whole problem*   *FF*, 3 October 1897, p. 268

p. 132 *going on living*   *FF*, 3 October 1897, pp. 268–9

p. 132 *washed herself*   *FF*, 4 October 1897, p. 269

p. 132 *lack of cleanliness*   *The Interpretation of Dreams*, *SE* IV, pp. 239, 247

p. 132 *one's childhood*   *The Psychopathology of Everyday Life*, *SE* VI, p. 178; see Anzieu, *Freud's Self-Analysis*, p. 246

p. 133 *the old woman*   *The Psychopathology of Everyday Life*, *SE* VI, p. 178

p. 133 *her the injection*   *FF*, 9 June 1901, pp. 441–2

p. 133 *his present one*   *FF*, 15 October 1897, p. 272

p. 133 *mental life springs*   *FF*, 19 February 1899, p. 345

p. 134 *went on sleeping!*   *FF*, 4 March 1895, p. 114. This example was included in *The Interpretation of Dreams* (*SE* IV, p. 125); Kaufmann later became a leading Viennese cardiologist, to whom Freud referred patients, amongst them Loë Kann (see *FJ*, 10 July 1913) and his own daughter Sophie.

p. 134 *threatening idea*   'The Neuro-Psychoses of Defence (I)', *SE* III, p. 47

p. 134 *would bring him*   *FF*, Draft H, 24 January 1895, p. 110

p. 134 *for her bridegroom*   'The Neuro-Psychoses of Defence (I)', *SE* III, p. 60

p. 134 *apparatus at work*   *The Interpretation of Dreams*, *SE* IV, p. 567

p. 134 *several occasions*   See Anzieu, *Freud's Self-Analysis*, pp. 221–9; Strachey's notes to the excerpts from the Fliess correspondence, in *SE* I, pp. 256 n. 3, 276 n. 3; Levin, *Freud's Early Theories of the Neuroses*, pp. 220 ff.

p. 134 *sympton-formation*   *FF*, Draft N, 31 May 1897, p. 251; see Levin, *Freud's Early Theories*, p. 226

p. 135 *mental life springs*   *FF*, 19 February 1899, p. 345

p. 135 *logical context*   *Studies*, *SE* II, pp. 302–3

p. 136 *theoretical schema*   See Holt, *Freud Reappraised*, esp. Chapter 7 'Drive or Wish?', pp. 171–96; Ricoeur, *Freud and Philosophy*, pp. 88–114

p. 136 *individual's development*   *Project*, *SE* I, p. 356

p. 137 *rearousing my affection*   *FF*, 17 May 1896, p. 186

p. 137 *the term 'wish'*   Note that he had not as yet settled on the term '*Wunsch*'; he utilized the strange composite term '*Sehnsuchtsabsicht*'. But in a letter dated 4 June 1896, he settles on the 'wish' terminology, confirming that wishes are the key to her symptoms: 'Her story is becoming even clearer; there is no doubt that her hemorrhages were due to wishes, she has had several similar incidents, among them actual simulations.' (*FF*, pp. 191–2)

p. 137 *knife or otherwise* *FF*, 17 January 1897, pp. 224–5

p. 137 *in this way* *FF*, 24 January 1897, p. 227

p. 138 *doing very well* *FF*, 12 December 1897, p. 286

p. 138 *bourgeois family* Masson, *The Assault on Truth*, Appendix A, pp. 233–4

p. 138 *light of the world* *LC*, Freud to Emma Eckstein, 17 April 1904

p. 139 *in particular Minna* Swales, 'Freud, Minna Bernays and the Conquest of Rome', p. 15; see also *LC*, Freud to Emma Eckstein, 16 January 1902

p. 139 *pains as organic* Masson, *The Assault on Truth*, Appendix A, pp. 248–9, letter from Freud to Emma Eckstein, 30 November 1905

p. 139 *like to say* Masson, *The Assault on Truth*, Appendix A, p. 249, letter from Freud to Emma Eckstein, 30 November 1905

p. 140 *need for love* 'Observations on Transference-Love', *SE* XII, pp. 166–7

p. 140 *university in 1900* *FF*, 16 May 1900, p. 414; see also *J* II, p. 289

p. 140 *Freud's courses* *LC* B21, List of students attending Freud's courses 1886–1919

p. 140 *cure her neurosis* Masson, *The Assault on Truth*, Appendix A, p. 250

p. 140 *encyclopaedic knowledge* *Civilization and its Discontents*, *SE* XXI, pp. 72–3

p. 141 *holiday activities* *LC*, Freud to Emma Eckstein, 4 August 1906

p. 141 *pregnant condition* Freud intimates in a footnote that the navel of the dream, the place where he doesn't even *wish* to look further, is the element concerning his wife's condition. See Elms, 'Freud, Irma, Martha'.

p. 141 *Dr Sigm. Freud* *FF*, 12 June 1900, p. 417. As the editor notes, such a plaque was indeed placed there on 6 May 1977.

p. 141 *inside his cloak* Young-Bruehl, *Anna Freud*, pp. 452–3

p. 142 *ever-recurring doubts* *FF*, 31 May 1897, p. 249; see Langs, 'Freud's Irma Dream', p. 611: 'There is a correlation between Freud's repudiation of the seduction hypothesis and his discovery or invention of transference. In both instances, Freud denied the reality of seduction, both by the parents and by the analyst.'

p. 142 *of their neuroses* Anzieu, *Freud's Self-Analysis*, p. 224

p. 143 *upon the hysteric* Irigaray, *Speculum*, p. 41, quoted in Gallop, *Feminism and Psychoanalysis*, p. 38; emphasis in the original

p. 143 *conform to his truths* Assoun, *Freud et la femme*, p. 55

p. 143 *a man's life* *The Interpretation of Dreams*, *SE* IV, p. 204

p. 143 *a woman's breast* *The Interpretation of Dreams*, *SE* IV, p. 204

p. 143 *made of earth* *The Interpretation of Dreams*, *SE* IV, p. 205

p. 143 *death inevitable* *The Interpretation of Dreams*, *SE* IV, p. 207

p. 143 *pair of spectacles* *On Dreams*, *SE* V, pp. 636–7

p. 144 *relations with her* *On Dreams*, *SE* V, p. 637

p. 144 *costs nothing* *On Dreams*, *SE* V, pp. 638–9, 655; emphasis in the original; see Anzieu, *Freud's Self-Analysis*, pp. 531 ff.

p. 144 *follower in Vienna* *FF*, 16 October 1895, p. 145

p. 145 *path to immortality* *The Interpretation of Dreams*, *SE* V, p. 487

5: Dora: An Exemplary Failure pp. 146–67

p. 146 *taedium vitae* 'Dora', *SE* VII, p. 27

p. 146 *force of women* Cixous and Clément, *La jeune née*, p. 283

p. 146 *resistant heroine* Kahane, 'Introduction: Part Two', in Bernheimer and Kahane, *In Dora's Case*, p. 25

p. 146 *history of woman* Kahane, 'Introduction: Part Two', in Bernheimer and Kahane, *In Dora's Case*, p. 31

p. 146 *women's language* Cixous and Clément as rendered by Moi, 'Representation of Patriarchy', p. 192

p. 146 *a power relation* Ramas, 'Freud's Dora, Dora's Hysteria', in Bernheimer and Kahane, *In Dora's Case*, p. 151

p. 146 *have been used* Cixous in Cixous and Clément, *The Newly Born Woman*, pp. 153–4

p. 146 *that is astounding* Cixous in Cixous and Clément, *The Newly Born Woman*, pp. 153–4

p. 146 *wayward wandering* Foucault, 'Introduction', p. 77

p. 147 *political vote* Rose, 'Psychopolitics II', p. 24

p. 147 *declaration of defeat* Cixous and Clément, as rendered by Moi, 'Representation of Patriarchy', p. 192

p. 147 *adorable, white body* 'Dora', *SE* VII, p. 61

p. 147 *silent body* Rose, in Bernheimer and Kahane, *In Dora's Case*, p. 129

p. 147 *whom Dora adores* Jacobus, 'Dora and the Pregnant Madonna', pp. 141–2

p. 147 *textile trade* Decker, *Freud, Dora, and Vienna 1900*, pp. 42 ff.

p. 147 *lived unpretentiously* Decker, *Freud, Dora, and Vienna 1900*, p. 44

p. 147 *shrewdness and obstinacy* 'Dora', *SE* VII, p. 26

p. 147 *infected with syphilis* Decker, *Freud, Dora, and Vienna 1900*, p. 43, and Ramas, 'Freud's Dora, Dora's Hysteria', p. 160

p. 148 *of my childhood* Otto Bauer to Karl Kautsky, 20 June 1922, Letter 521, Kautsky Archives, International Institute for Social History, Amsterdam, cited in Rogow, 'Dora's Brother', p. 245

p. 148 *paternal aunt* 'Dora', *SE* VII, p. 75

p. 148 *this knowledge led* 'Dora', *SE* VII, p. 20

p. 148 *her family* Leichter, *Otto Bauer*, p. 23, quoted in Loewenberg, 'Otto Bauer', p. 190

p. 148 *nursed Philipp* Decker, *Freud, Dora, and Vienna 1900*, p. 65

p. 148 *later described her* 'Dora', *SE* VII, p. 32

p. 148 *almost a mother* 'Dora', *SE* VII, p. 25

p. 149 *her to reason* 'Dora', *SE* VII, p. 26

p. 149 *unlock the door* 'Dora', *SE* VII, p. 115

p. 149 *elucidating symptoms* 'Dora', *SE* VII, p. 10; for a speculative challenge to this project of Freud's, see McCaffrey, *Freud and Dora*

p. 150 *to her honour* 'Dora', *SE* VII, p. 26

p. 150 *during the treatment* 'Dora', *SE* VII, p. 28

p. 150 *upon her lips* 'Dora', *SE* VII, p. 28

p. 150 *is by disgust* 'Dora', *SE* VII, p. 29

p. 150 *a grown woman* Marcus in Bernheimer and Kahane, *In Dora's Case*, p. 78

p. 150 *of female sexuality* Marcus in Bernheimer and Kahane, *In Dora's Case*, p. 82

p. 150 *sexuality, openness, and candor* Marcus in Bernheimer and Kahane, *In Dora's Case*, p. 78; for a different view of Freud's response to 'adolescent' sexuality, see Glenn, 'Freud's Adolescent Patients'

p. 151 *in her memory* 'Dora', *SE* VII, p. 32

p. 151 *elbow-room* 'Dora', *SE* VII, p. 33

p. 151 *adulterous situation* Cixous in Cixous and Clément, *The Newly Born Woman*, pp. 149–50; see also Marcus in Bernheimer and Kahane, *In Dora's Case*, p. 59

p. 151 *affection for him* 'Dora', *SE* VII, p. 34

p. 152 *love with Herr K* 'Dora', *SE* VII, p. 37

p. 152 *lake was inexplicable* 'Dora', *SE* VII, pp. 38 n. 2 and 46 ff.

p. 152 *save her pride* 'Dora', *SE* VII, p. 58

p. 152 *jealous wife* 'Dora', *SE* VII, p. 56

p. 152 *love with him* 'Dora', *SE* VII, p. 56

p. 152 *by Lacan* Lacan, 'Intervention on Transference', p. 67

p. 152 *followed by others* Jacobus, 'Dora and the Pregnant Madonna', p. 181; Moi, 'Representation of Patriarchy', pp. 190–2; Sprengnether in Bernheimer and Kahane, *In Dora's Case*, p. 258

p. 152 *medical discretion* 'Dora', *SE* VII, p. 8

p. 152 *psychological problem* 'Dora', *SE* VII, p. 61

p. 152 *sexual matters* 'Dora', *SE* VII, p. 26

p. 153 *not be disturbed* 'Dora', *SE* VII, p. 62

p. 153 *deeper sense unconscious* 'Dora', *SE* VII, p. 62

p. 153 *to the man* 'Dora', *SE* VII, p. 73

p. 153 *for a stranger* 'Dora', *SE* VII, p. 86

p. 153 *governess viewed it* 'Dora', *SE* VII, p. 84

p. 154 *in another way* 'Dora', *SE* VII, pp. 99–100

p. 154 *from masturbation* Decker, *Freud, Dora, and Vienna 1900*, p. 116

p. 154 *a big book* 'Dora', *SE* VII, p. 100

p. 154 *phantasy of childbirth* 'Dora', *SE* VII, p. 103

p. 154 p. 154 *Tell me* 'Dora', *SE* VII, p. 105

p. 154 *of my wife* 'Dora', *SE* VII, pp. 98, 106

p. 154 *jealousy and revenge* 'Dora', *SE* VII, p. 106

p. 154 *was too much* 'Dora', *SE* VII, p. 106

p. 154 *renew his proposal* 'Dora', *SE* VII, p. 107

p. 155 *the appendicitis* 'Dora', *SE* VII, p. 108

p. 155 *and not marry* 'Dora', *SE* VII, p. 110 n. 1

p. 155 *on her part* 'Dora', *SE* VII, p. 109

p. 155 *of the physician?* 'Dora', *SE* VII, p. 120

p. 155 *for no doubts* 'Dora', *SE* VII, p. 109

p. 155 *her internal difficulties* 'Dora', *SE* VII, pp. 109–10

p. 155 *the short treatment* 'Dora', *SE* VII, p. 13

p. 156 *Ida's father* 'Dora', *SE* VII, p. 118

p. 156 *of Herr K.* 'Dora', *SE* VII, p. 119

p. 156 *after her recovery* 'Dora', *SE* VII, p. 119

p. 156 *impotent, invalid father* Kahane, 'Introduction: Part Two', in Bernheimer and Kahane,
    In Dora's Case, p. 27; Sprengnether, *In Dora's Case*, p. 258

p. 156 *omission* 'Dora', *SE* VII, p. 120 n. 1

p. 156 *in my technique* 'Dora', *SE* VII, p. 120 n. 1

p. 156 *further complication* 'Dora', *SE* VII, p. 59

p. 156 *her mental life* 'Dora', *SE* VII, p. 120 n. 1

p. 156 *accusations against her* 'Dora', *SE* VII, p. 120 n. 1

p. 157 *yield to the man* 'Dora', *SE* VII, p. 73

p. 157 *possibly feminine* *FF*, 7 May 1900, p. 412

p. 157 *concept of bisexuality* Swales, 'Freud, Fliess and Fratricide'

p. 157 *conversations about sexuality* Hertz in Bernheimer and Kahane, *In Dora's Case*, p. 234;
    Bernheimer, 'Introduction' to Bernheimer and Kahane, *In Dora's Case*, pp. 17–18;
    Swales, 'Are We Getting the Freud We Deserve?'

p. 157 *prepossessing appearance* 'Dora', *SE* VII, p. 29 n. 3

p. 157 *hardness of his theory* See Muslin and Gill, 'Transference in the Dora Case', p. 322

p. 157 *psychoanalytical science* Glenn, 'Freud's Adolescent Patients', 'Freud, Dora and the
    Maid'

p. 158 *be quite unavailing* 'Dora', *SE* VII, p. 8

p. 158 *private delectation* 'Dora', *SE* VII, p. 9

p. 158 *method must afford* 'Dora', *SE* VII, p. 49

p. 158 *dry and direct* 'Dora', *SE* VII, p. 48

p. 158 *technical names* 'Dora', *SE* VII, p. 48

p. 158 *Mr X's conversation!* 'Dora', *SE* VII, p. 49

p. 158 *these oral exchanges* Hertz in Bernheimer and Kahane, *In Dora's Case*, p. 229

p. 158 *eroticism of conversation* Forrester, 'The Untold Pleasures of Psychoanalysis', p. 57

p. 158 *between two women* Hertz in Bernheimer and Kahane, *In Dora's Case*, p. 234

p. 159 *on this subject* 'Dora', *SE* VII, p. 31

p. 159 *use the phrase* 'Dora', *SE* VII, p. 49

p. 159 *what Freud knew* Hertz in Bernheimer and Kahane, *In Dora's Case*, p. 234

p. 159 *her governess* 'Dora', *SE* VII, p. 36n

p. 159 *fantasy of childbirth* 'Dora', *SE* VII, p. 103

p. 159 *direct technical names* 'Dora', *SE* VII, p. 48

p. 159 *as any other* Forrester, 'The Untold Pleasures of Psychoanalysis', p. 59

p. 160 *testimony demonstrates*   See the case of homosexuality discussed in Chapter 6, pp. 182–9, and his remarks to H. D., discussed in Chapter 13, pp. 387–93

p. 160 *with his interpretations*   Marcus in Bernheimer and Kahane, *In Dora's Case*, p. 85; Gay, p. 251

p. 160 *endless reproachfulness*   Marcus, in Bernheimer and Kahane, *In Dora's Case*, p. 90

p. 160 *two governesses figure*   See Cixous and Clément, *La jeune née*, p. 276

p. 160 *advanced views*   'Dora', *SE* VII, p. 36

p. 160 *governess to leave*   'Dora', *SE* VII, pp. 60–1

p. 160 *to her parents*   'Dora', *SE* VII, p. 36 n. 1

p. 160 *a whole year*   'Dora', *SE* VII, p. 35

p. 160 *general hypocrisy*   Cixous in Cixous and Clément, *The Newly Born Woman*, pp. 149–50

p. 161 *kind by herself*   'Dora', *SE* VII, p. 95

p. 161 *no longer required*   Gallop, 'Keys to Dora', in Bernheimer and Kahane, *In Dora's Case*, p. 210

p. 161 *their own names!*   *The Psychopathology of Everyday Life*, *SE* VI, p. 241

p. 161 *treatment as well*   *The Psychopathology of Everyday Life*, *SE* VI, p. 241

p. 161 *daughter's self-abasement*   *FF*, Draft L, 2 May 1897, p. 241; trans. modified

p. 161 *in sexual matters*   *FF*, 4 October 1897, p. 269

p. 162 *for her father*   *Studies*, *SE* II, p. 170; passage amended to correct Freud's substitution of 'uncle' for 'father'. in the first edition

p. 162 *governess, the maid*   Gallop, 'Keys to Dora', in Bernheimer and Kahane, *In Dora's Case*, p. 213

p. 162 *of the hysteric*   Assoun, *Freud et la femme*, p. 183

p. 162 *I ever saw*   *FJ*, Freud to Jones, 1 January 1913

p. 162 *dependent on them*   'Female Sexuality', *SE* XXI, p. 232

p. 162 *and the governess*   Jacobus, '*Dora* and the Pregnant Madonna', p. 189

p. 162 *between these women*   Jacobus, '*Dora* and the Pregnant Madonna', pp. 190–2

p. 163 *with the family*   'Dora', *SE* VII, p. 121

p. 163 *without serious injury*   'Dora', *SE* VII, p. 121

p. 163 *for her troubles*   'Dora', *SE* VII, p. 122

p. 164 *collection of pick-locks*   *FF*, 14 October 1900, p. 427

p. 164 *written so far*   *FF*, 25 January 1901, p. 433

p. 164 *its planned publication*   *J* II, pp. 286–7, pieces together a story – which remains hypothetical – concerning its refusal by one editor and doubts expressed by another about its propriety. The point of our argument is that, whatever Freud's reasons for withdrawing it from publication in 1901 (which were probably, but not certainly, bound up with medical discretion and propriety), something happened in early 1905 to change his view of the case history's impropriety.

p. 164 *have grown faint*   'Dora', *SE* VII, p. 8

p. 164 *realities of life*   'Dora', *SE* VII, p. 122

p. 164 *their help entirely*   'Dora', *SE* VII, p. 22

p. 164 *a back seat*   *Secret Symmetry*, Freud to Sabina Spielrein, August 1912, p. 117

p. 164 *his own music*   Bernheimer and Kahane, *In Dora's Case*, p. 33

p. 165 *and his memory*   Bernheimer and Kahane, *In Dora's Case*, p. 34

p. 165 *demanding and ungiving*   Deutsch in Bernheimer and Kahane, *In Dora's Case*, pp. 37–8

p. 165 *he could love*   'Dora', *SE* VII, p. 54

p. 165 *quiet and well-behaved*   'Dora', *SE* VII, p. 82 n. 1

p. 165 *morally obligated*   Decker, *Freud, Dora, and Vienna 1900*, p. 59

p. 165 *of the prostate*   Decker, *Freud, Dora, and Vienna 1900*, p. 159

p. 166 *do not wish happiness*   Loewenberg, 'Otto Bauer', p. 196, quoting Leichter's biography of Bauer, p. 371 n. 13, and an interview with Leichter of 1972

p. 166 *the Allied Powers*   Bottomore and Goode, *Austro-Marxism*, p. 288

p. 166 *jaws of victory*   Rogow, 'Dora's Brother', p. 239

p. 166 *as an adult*   Decker, *Freud, Dora, and Vienna 1900*, pp. 55, 177

p. 166 *place of honour*   Loewenberg, 'Otto Bauer', p. 192

p. 166 *to her mother* Deutsch in Bernheimer and Kahane, *In Dora's Case*, pp. 37–8

p. 166 *as little Hans* See Gallup, *A History of the Salzburg Festival*, and Kaut, *Die Salzburger Festspiele 1920–1981*

p. 167 *distinctly unreliable* Personal communication, Anthony Stadlen, who interviewed Deutsch's informant

p. 167 *pause for thought* Decker, *Freud, Dora, and Vienna 1900*, p. 175, citing Leichter, p. 23. A delightful and perspicacious fictional version of 'Dora's' later response to Freud is to be found in Mannoni, 'Fiction I. Viennoise', in *Fictions freudiennes*, pp. 11–22.

6: Early Friends, Early Cases, Early Followers pp. 171–203

p. 171 *doing without it* Freud, 'Interview with Adelbert Albrecht', p. 23

p. 171 *sometime around 1900* See Gay, p. 103n, from Marie Bonaparte's notes for her incomplete Freud biography

p. 171 *no princess* Hartman, 'A Reappraisal of the Emma Episode', p. 567

p. 171 *without any patients* Wagner-Jauregg, *Lebenserrinerungen*, p. 72, quoted in Swales, 'Freud, his Teacher and the Birth of Psychoanalysis', p. 4

p. 171 *have confidence* *J* I, p. 196; letter to Martha dated roughly November 1882

p. 171 *Fleischl circle* Hirschmüller, *Breuer*, p. 32

p. 171 *a certain notoriety* Bertin, *La femme à Vienne*, p. 54

p. 171 *on a cure* Swales, 'Freud, his Teacher and the Birth of Psychoanalysis', p. 27 and n. 24; unpublished letter of 14 April 1888

p. 171 *and respect* Swales, 'Freud, his Teacher and the Birth of Psychoanalysis', p. 27 and n. 25

p. 172 *at least October 1889* Fichtner, *Freuds Patienten*, # 232

p. 172 *urban life* Swales, 'Freud, his Teacher and the Birth of Psychoanalysis', p. 28, quoting Kann, *Theodor Gomperz*, pp. 169–70

p. 172 *pupil Freud* Kann, *Theodor Gomperz*, p. 170; see also Vogel, 'The Case of Elise Gomperz'; Gelfand, '"Mon cher docteur Freud"'; Gelfand, 'Charcot's Response to Freud's Rebellion'

p. 172 *a few hours* Kann, *Theodor Gomperz*, letter from Theodor to Heinrich Gomperz, 23 October 1892, p. 234

p. 172 *so little tried* Kann, *Theodor Gomperz*, letter from Theodor to Heinrich Gomperz, 13 November 1892, p. 234

p. 172 *of a poison* Kann, *Theodor Gomperz*, letter from Theodor to Elise Gomperz, 8 January 1893, p. 235

p. 173 *for hallucination* Kann, *Theodor Gomperz*, letter from Theodor to Elise Gomperz, 7 April 1893, p. 236

p. 173 *hypnotic treatments* Kann, *Theodor Gomperz*, letter from Theodor to Heinrich Gomperz, 13 February 1894, p. 251

p. 173 *eight years later* *FF*, 16 May 1897, p. 244: the patient, 'cousin Elise v. G.', mentioned here as terminating her treatment may well be Elise Gomperz, which would mean her treatment had lasted eleven years, off and on.

p. 173 *your inner life* *Letters*, Freud to Heinrich Gomperz, 15 November 1899, p. 249

p. 173 *had indicated* *FF*, 26 November 1899, p. 389

p. 173 *everything already* *FF*, 19 November 1899, p. 387 n. 3

p. 173 *track of already* *FF*, Heinrich Gomperz to Freud, 5 May 1931, p. 388 n. 3

p. 174 *her friend Elise Gomperz* Kann, *Theodor Gomperz*, Theodor to Elise Gomperz, 28 September 1898, p. 301

p. 174 *had cured her* *FF*, 11 March 1902, p. 456

p. 174 *I've done it!* *J* I, p. 374

p. 174 *Ringstrasse buildings* Swales, 'Freud, Katharina, and the first "Wild analysis"', p. 148 n. 23

p. 174 *in August 1901* *FF*, 7 August 1901, p. 446; see also Goldmann, 'Eine Kur aus der Frühzeit der Psychoanalyse', p. 307

p. 174 *under the tree* *J* II, p. 433

p. 174 *Freud soon sold* Swales, 'Freud, Katharina, and the first "Wild analysis"', p. 148 n. 23

p. 174 *his reputation*   Eissler, 'A Possible Endangerment of Psychoanalysis', p. 19

p. 174 *disgusting man*   '*ein ekelhafter Kerl*'. Koestler, *Arrow in the Blue*, pp. 32–3. For a general overview, see Kubes, '"Moderne Nervositäten" und die Anfänge der Psychoanalyse'

p. 175 *parents' door*   *LC*, SF Archive B16; see Goldmann, 'Eine Kur aus der Frühzeit der Psychoanalyse'

p. 175 *his patients*   For a good l. er example of such a friendship with a patient, see Freud's correspondence with Frau A. Goetzel, from 1918–37, *LC* B8 – a correspondence at the rate of roughly one letter a year. In their letters, Freud and Frau Goetzel resolved amicably her struggle with the desire for more analysis, which, classically, revolved around the question of a baby.

p. 175 *one Anna*   Freud to Anna von Vest, 26 March 1925, quoted in Molnar, *Diary*, p. 180

p. 176 *of her life*   'Analysis Terminable and Interminable', *SE* XXIII, p. 222

p. 176 *treatment by him*   *Introductory Lectures*, *SE* XVI, pp. 459–60

p. 176 *else to do*   Gay, Anna Freud to Freud, 20 July 1922, p. 438

p. 176 *patient no more*   *FF*, Draft H, 24 January 1895, pp. 107–10

p. 177 *unmistakeable fashion*   *FF*, Draft H, *SE* I, p. 210

p. 177 *is the secret*   *FF*, Draft H, *SE* I, pp. 210–12

p. 177 *of self-reproach*   'Further Remarks on the Neuro-Psychoses of Defence', *SE* III, p. 184

p. 178 *new reality*   'The Loss of Reality in Neurosis and Psychosis', *SE* XIX, pp. 183–5

p. 178 *own thoughts*   *FF*, 19 September 1901, p. 450

p. 178 *thought of doing*   'Some Neurotic Mechanisms in Jealousy, Paranoia and Homosexuality', *SE* XVIII, p. 226

p. 178 *impulses against them*   'Some Neurotic Mechanisms in Jealousy, Paranoia and Homosexuality', *SE* XVIII, p. 226; see also *The Psychopathology of Everyday Life*, *SE* VI, pp. 255–7

p. 179 *the primary form*   *FJung*, 22F, between 14 and 20 April 1907, p. 38; the closeness of fit between this scene and the case of paranoia written up in 1915, though investigated 'some years ago', encourages the speculation that Freud's letter to Jung was written just after he had examined the girl complaining of being persecuted by her lover. If this were the case, one might have to reconsider whether the impulse to revise his theory of paranoia in favour of the homosexual hypothesis was solely due to the examination of male paranoia.

p. 179 *homosexual component*   *FJung*, 70F, 17 February 1908, p. 121

p. 179 *paranoiac fails*   Freud to Ferenczi, 6 October 1910, quoted in Gay, p. 275

p. 179 *husband's sisters*   *FJung*, 70F, 17 February 1908, p. 121; see also a letter written a few days earlier to Ferenczi, quoted in *J* II, p. 488; now available in Freud–Ferenczi, *Correspondence*, pp. 6–9

p. 179 *brothers and sisters*   'Further Remarks on the Neuro-Psychoses of Defence', *SE* III, p. 176

p. 180 *of a woman*   'A Case of Paranoia', *SE* XIV, p. 265

p. 180 *two scenes*   See Rosolato, 'Paranoïa et scène primitive'

p. 180 *but a woman*   'A Case of Paranoia', *SE* XIV, p. 267

p. 181 *of her mother*   'A Case of Paranoia', *SE* XIV, pp. 267–8

p. 181 *and persecutor*   'A Case of Paranoia', *SE* XIV, p. 268

p. 181 *in her clitoris*   'A Case of Paranoia', *SE* XIV, p. 270; see Schor, 'Female Paranoia'

p. 181 *the interposition*   Assoun, *Freud et la femme*, p. 144 n. 5

p. 182 *analyst in Ipswich*   *J* II, pp. 477–8

p. 182 *noticed in him*   Riviere, 'An Intimate Impression', p. 210

p. 182 *completely indifferent*   'Homosexuality in a Woman', *SE* XVIII, p. 163

p. 183 *weeks or months*   'Homosexuality in a Woman', *SE* XVIII, p. 152

p. 183 *without a gap*   'Homosexuality in a Woman', *SE* XVIII, p. 147

p. 183 *of the analysis*   'Homosexuality in a Woman', *SE* XVIII, p. 152

p. 184 *never attempted*   'Homosexuality in a Woman', *SE* XVIII, p. 151

p. 184 *validity for it*   'Homosexuality in a Woman', *SE* XVIII, p. 156

p. 184 *her father*   'Homosexuality in a Woman', *SE* XVIII, p. 157

p. 185 *of her love* 'Homosexuality in a Woman', *SE* XVIII, pp. 157–8

p. 185 *possess a penis* 'Femininity', *SE* XXII, p. 130

p. 185 *man in love* 'Homosexuality in a Woman', *SE* XVIII, pp. 155 and 169

p. 185 *on her mother* 'Homosexuality in a Woman', *SE* XVIII, p. 168

p. 185 *against her father* 'Homosexuality in a Woman', *SE* XVIII, p. 159

p. 186 *a woman doctor* 'Homosexuality in a Woman', *SE* XVIII, p. 164

p. 187 *of her mother* Jacobus, 'Russian tactics', p. 2; Merck, 'The Train of Thought', pp. 35–46

p. 187 *sex-glands* *Three Essays*, *SE* VII, p. 215

p. 187 *hope of motherhood* 'Homosexuality in a Woman', *SE* XVIII, p. 172

p. 188 *the alien invader* *J* III, p. 188

p. 189 *give him pleasure* *J* II, p. 189

p. 189 *comments on it* *FJung*, 25F, 23 May 1907, p. 46; *FJung*, 26J, 24 May 1907, p. 49; *FJung*, 27F, 26 May 1907, p. 51

p. 190 *contradicting it* 'Gradiva', *SE* IX, p. 21

p. 190 *completely as possible* 'Gradiva', *SE* IX, p. 22

p. 190 *behind the delusion* 'Gradiva', *SE* IX, p. 70

p. 190 *her 'patient'* 'Gradiva', *SE* IX, p. 29

p. 190 *Norbert Hanold* 'Gradiva', *SE* IX, p. 27

p. 190 *the ruins* 'Gradiva', *SE* IX, p. 40

p. 190 *his writings* See 'Ratman', *SE* X, p. 176; *Civilization and its Discontents*, *SE* XXI, pp. 70–1; see also Gamwell, 'Freud's Antiquities Collection'; Donald Kuspit, 'A Mighty Metaphor'; Schmidt-Dengler, 'Decadence and Antiquity'; Suzanne Bernfeld, 'Freud and Archaeology'

p. 190 *even possible* 'Gradiva', *SE* IX, p. 87

p. 190 *female readers* 'Gradiva', *SE* IX, p. 87

p. 191 *the doctor* 'Gradiva', *SE* IX, p. 90

p. 191 *love to him* 'Gradiva', *SE* IX, p. 88

p. 192 *task before us* 'Gradiva', *SE* IX, p. 90

p. 192 *complicated technique* 'Gradiva', *SE* IX, p. 89

p. 192 *patient's demands* Assoun, *Freud et la femme*, p. 87

p. 192 *Libido on her* *LC*, Freud to Ferenczi, 23 June 1912; Freud–Ferenczi, *Correspondence*, p. 407

p. 193 *superstition* 'Gradiva', *SE* IX, p. 7

p. 193 *important correlation* *Introductory Lectures*, *SE* XVI, p. 397

p. 193 *true originator* See Kofman, *The Enigma of Woman*, p. 76, and Jacobus, '*Dora* and the Pregnant Madonna', pp. 192–3

p. 193 *collection of pick-locks* *FF*, 14 October 1900, p. 427

p. 193 *old confessional* Wexler, *Emma Goldman*, pp. 85 and 295 n. 3 (quote from latter note). The quote from Goldman about Freud's lectures is from a letter to Berkman, 20 February 1929, in Drinnon and Drinnon, *Nowhere at Home*, p. 146

p. 193 *from the back* Kerr, *A Most Dangerous Method*, p. 268

p. 193 *against the door* *Five Lectures on Psycho-analysis*, *SE* XI, p. 25

p. 193 *from 1906 to 1910* *LC* B21, List of students attending Freud's courses 1886–1919

p. 194 *on principle* *Minutes II*, 13 April 1910; see Gay, p. 503

p. 194 *student movement* Hilferding, *Finance Capital*, p. 3

p. 194 *fantasy life* *Minutes III*, 2 November 1910, p. 47

p. 194 *mother love* *Minutes III*, 11 January 1911, p. 114

p. 194 *for the mother* *Minutes III*, 11 January 1911, p. 115

p. 195 *next child* *Minutes III*, 11 January 1911, p. 115

p. 195 *play in it* *Minutes III*, 11 January 1911, p. 118

p. 195 *original and independent* *Minutes III*, 11 January 1911, p. 118

p. 195 *sexual cravings* *Minutes III*, 11 January 1911, p. 119

p. 195 *are possible* *Minutes III*, 9 November 1910, p. 56

p. 196 *with her sister* *Minutes III*, 22 March 1911, p. 202

p. 196 *resigned then* *Minutes III*, 11 October 1911, p. 283

p. 196 *quiet, withdrawn* Deutsch, *Confrontations with Myself,* p. 136

p. 196 *our psychoanalysis* F*Jung,* 289F, 28 December 1911, p. 474

p. 196 *deal of good* F*A,* Freud to Abraham, 22 September 1914, p. 197

p. 196 *psychoanalytical periodicals Introductory Lectures, SE* XV, p. 142; 'A Childhood Recollection from *Dichtung und Wahrheit', SE* XVII, pp. 154–5; 'History of the Psychoanalytic Movement', *SE* XIV, p. 46

p. 197 *same context An Autobiographical Study, SE* XX, pp. 69–70

p. 197 *in that field* See Hug-Hellmuth, 'On the Technique of Child-Analysis', 1920, a paper first presented at the Sixth International Psychoanalytic Congress in The Hague, collected in MacLean and Rappen, *Hermine Hug-Hellmuth,* pp. 138–53

p. 197 *daily circumstances* Anna Freud, 'Four Lectures on Child Analysis', p. 35

p. 197 *training as teachers* MacLean and Rappen, *Hermine Hug-Hellmuth,* p. 5, quoting the Kriegsarchiv Vienna – Quall. K 1174

p. 198 *less-loved followers* See Jones, *Free Associations,* p. 169, where Jones calls him 'morose' and 'pathetic'; cf F*Jung,* 77F, 5 March 1908, p. 130: 'I hear that Sadger, that congenital fanatic of orthodoxy, who happens by mere accident to believe in psychoanalysis rather than in the law given by God on Sinai-Horeb....'

p. 198 *they were lovers* MacLean and Rappen, *Hermine Hug-Hellmuth,* p. 7

p. 198 *you're a man* Bertin, *La femme à Vienne,* p. 274

p. 198 *to delinquency* MacLean and Rappen, *Hermine Hug-Hellmuth,* pp. 270–1

p. 198 *of lesbianism Les premiers psychanalystes. IV 1912–18,* session of 8 November 1916, p. 341 (protocols for 1914–18 absent from English edn of *Minutes*)

p. 198 *for education* MacLean and Rappen, *Hermine Hug-Hellmuth,* p. 120

p. 200 *aesthetic values* MacLean and Rappen, *Hermine Hug-Hellmuth,* p. 138

p. 200 *you for it* 'Letter to Dr Hermine von Hug-Hellmuth', *SE* XIV, p. 341

p. 201 *written by him* Hearnshaw, *Cyril Burt,* pp. 242–7

p. 201 *psychoanalytic literature* Deutsch, *Confrontations with Myself,* p. 136

p. 201 *child analysis* Klein, unpublished autobiography, quoted by Phyllis Grosskurth, *Melanie Klein,* p. 93

p. 202 *friends emerged* MacLean and Rappen, *Hermine Hug-Hellmuth,* pp. 40–1

p. 202 *demand for analysis* Gunn and Guyomard, *A Young Girl's Diary,* Editors' introduction

p. 202 *Helene Deutsch* Deutsch, *Confrontations with Myself,* p. 137

p. 202 *psychoanalytic publications* MacLean and Rappen, *Hermine Hug-Hellmuth,* quoted pp. 42–3; see also Huber, 'Die erste Kinderanalytikerin'

7: Sabina Spielrein and Loë Kann: Two Analytic Triangles pp. 204–39

p. 204 *paths in therapy* Jung, *Memories, Dreams, Reflections,* p. 145

p. 205 *anima to him Secret Symmetry,* p. 190. For other, more speculative commentaries on the significance of Spielrein for Jung's development, see Bouttes, *Jung. La puissance d'une illusion;* Holl, *Der Fisch aus der Tiefe,* pp. 71–81

p. 205 *to cure her* Bettelheim, *Secret Symmetry,* p. xxxviii

p. 205 *to exclude biology* Spielrein, 'Beiträge', p. 57

p. 206 *with its education* Spielrein, 'Beiträge', p. 60

p. 206 *of anxiety started* Spielrein, 'Beiträge', p. 58

p. 206 *the seducer* Spielrein, 'Beiträge', p. 59

p. 206 *sign of loathing* Jung, 'The Freudian theory of Hysteria', *CW* IV, p. 21

p. 206 *1 June 1905 Secret Symmetry,* pp. 137–41

p. 207 *interested her husband Secret Symmetry,* Spielrein to Freud, 13 June 1909, pp. 101–2

p. 207 *as their husbands* Brill, *Lectures on Psychoanalytic Psychiatry,* p. 27, cited in Kerr, *A Most Dangerous Method,* p. 187. Note: pagination to Kerr's study is to the unpublished doctoral dissertation with the same title, New York University, 1989

p. 207 *before their eyes* F*Jung,* 28J, 30 May 1907, p. 55

p. 207 *crude transference* F*Jung,* 31J, 12 June 1907, p. 63

p. 208 *who can believe Secret Symmetry, Diary,* September 1910, p. 17

p. 208 *the medallion Secret Symmetry, Diary,* September 1910 [?], p. 8

p. 208   *a great deal*   *Secret Symmetry, Diary*, 11 September 1910, p. 11

p. 208   *friendship to Freud*   Bettelheim, 'Commentary', p. xxiii; Swales, 'What Jung *Didn't* Say',
p. 3

p. 208   *to see Freud*   Kerr, *A Most Dangerous Method*, pp. 61–2; Swales, 'What Jung *Didn't* Say',
p. 6

p. 208   *Russian peculiarities*   *Secret symmetry*, Jung's letter quoted by Spielrein to Freud, 13 June
1909, p. 101

p. 208   *of this story*   *FJung*, 4J, 23 October 1906, p. 7

p. 209   *for a while*   Kerr, *A Most Dangerous Method*, p. 119

p. 209   *marked sexual excitement*   Kerr, *A Most Dangerous Method*, pp. 105–6, citing Jung, 'The
Psychology of Dementia Praecox', *CW* III, p. 46

p. 209   *sexual-phallic wishes*   *FJung*, 35J, 6 July 1907, pp. 72–3; see Kerr, *A Most Dangerous Method*,
p. 156

p. 209   *Jewess complex*   *FJung*, 4 June 1909, p. 229

p. 209   *although she was not*   See Ellenberger, 'The Story of Helene Preiswerk'; Kerr, *A Most
Dangerous Method*, p. 42; *Secret Symmetry*, Spielrein to Freud, 20 June 1909, p. 105

p. 209   *a Jewish girl*   Kerr, *A Most Dangerous Method*, p. 42; Jung & F. Riklin, *The Associations of
Normal Subjects* (1904), *CW* II, p. 86

p. 209   *and in Jung*   *Secret Symmetry*, Spielrein to Freud, 20 June 1909, p. 104; see also *Secret
Symmetry, Diary* 19 October 1910, p. 30, and *Secret Symmetry*, letter from Spielrein to
Freud, around 1909, p. 106

p. 210   *Eugen Bleuler*   See Jung, 1925 Seminar, personal communication, John Kerr, 6 November
1991

p. 210   *about himself*   *Secret Symmetry*, p. 107; Carotenuto dates this to 'around 1909', but Kerr,
A Most Dangerous Method, p. 209, is surely correct in locating this in the Gross period
of May 1908

p. 210   *of the child*   Spielrein, 'Extraits inédits d'un journal', pp. 166–7

p. 210   *desired from him*   *Secret Symmetry*, Spielrein to Jung, 26/27 January 1918, p. 82

p. 210   *create a hero*   *Secret Symmetry*, Spielrein to Jung, 19 January 1918, p. 80

p. 210   *my baby son*   *Secret Symmetry, Diary*, 9 October 1910, p. 21

p. 211   *own wish-child*   Spielrein, 'Die Destruktion', p. 495. We would also like to thank John
Kerr for making available to us a draft translation of 'Die Destruktion'.

p. 211   *instinct to become*   Spielrein, 'Die Destruktion', p. 495

p. 211   *to be annihilated*   Spielrein, 'Extraits inédits d'un journal', p. 156

p. 211   *an illicit affair*   Opinions as to whether it was consummated differ. Carotenuto leaves
the question open; Bettelheim concludes it was; Kerr thinks it plausible that they
stopped short of intercourse and sums up succinctly the problem of interpreting the
textual evidence Spielrein has left us by noting how 'a certain maidenly modesty
intervenes in her account like a dogged literary chaperone trying to avoid the worst'
(Kerr, *A Most Dangerous Method*, p. 250); Swales (private communication, 7 August 1991)
was 'as good as convinced, much against my disposition to believe such, that in fact
the relation of Jung and Spielrein was never sexually consummated (at least, with
anything more than kisses)'.

p. 211   *your saucy letters*   Spielrein, *Tagebuch einer heimlich Symmetrie*, p. 189

p. 211   *freedom and independence*   Spielrein, *Tagebuch einer heimlich Symmetrie*, p. 189

p. 211   *banality of habit*   *Secret Symmetry*, p. 167

p. 211   *freedom, not ties*   Spielrein, *Tagebuch einer heimlich Symmetrie*, p. 189

p. 211   *lie only once*   Spielrein, *Tagebuch einer heimlich Symmetrie*, p. 196

p. 211   *who am ill*   *Secret Symmetry*, p. 169

p. 211   *in February 1909*   Kerr, 'The Devil's Elixirs', p. 4

p. 212   *You struck me!*   *Secret Symmetry*, pp. 96–7, 12 June 1909 (not sent until the end of the
month)

p. 212   *Emma Jung*   In a rather downcast plea for help in a letter to Freud of 24 November
1911 (*FJung* p. 467), Emma Jung implied that her 'main complex' was the fact that the
'women are all of course in love with him'.

p. 212 *as they wish* Letter from Jung to Spielrein's mother, quoted by Spielrein in her letter to Freud, 11 June 1909, *Secret Symmetry*, p. 94

p. 212 *ideal salvaged*   *Secret Symmetry, Diary,* 19 October 1910, p. 28

p. 212 *angel of deliverance*   *Secret Symmetry,* Spielrein to Freud, 12 June 1909, p. 97

p. 212 *my polygamous components*   F*Jung,* 133J, 7 March 1909, p. 207

p. 212 *on their account*   F*Jung,* 134F, 9 March 1909, p. 210

p. 213 *a narrow escape* English in the original

p. 213 *blessing in disguise* English in the original

p. 213 *changes amazingly*   F*Jung,* 145F, 7 June 1909, pp. 230–1

p. 213 *guess the situation*   F*Jung* 147F, 18 June 1909, pp. 234–5

p. 213 *of third persons*   *Secret Symmetry,* Freud to Spielrein, 8 June 1909, p. 114

p. 213 *laboratory explosions*   F*Jung,* 147F, 18 June 1909, p. 235

p. 213 *brotherly love*   F*Jung,* 146J, 12 June 1909, p. 232

p. 213 *understand this*   *Secret Symmetry,* Spielrein to Freud, 10 June 1909, p. 93

p. 213 *and nicest way*   F*Jung,* 148J, 21 June 1909, p. 236

p. 214 *as my father*   F*Jung,* 148J, 21 June 1909, p. 236

p. 214 *in high regard*   *Secret Symmetry,* Freud to Spielrein, 24 June 1909, p. 115

p. 214 *confesses her passion* 'Observations on Transference-Love', *SE* XII, p. 170; see Stein, 'Nouvelles observations sur l'amour de transfert 1', p. 17

p. 214 *greatest spectacles*   F*Jung,* 145F, 7 June 1909, pp. 230–1

p. 214 *planning my seduction*   F*Jung,* 144J, 4 June 1909, p. 228

p. 214 *dumplings for arguments* 'Observations on Transference-Love', *SE* XII, pp. 166–7

p. 215 *by Dr Jung*   *Secret Symmetry,* Spielrein to Freud, 11 June 1909, p. 93

p. 215 *best of friends*   *Secret Symmetry, Diary,* 11 September 1910, p. 12

p. 215 *continue living*   *Secret Symmetry,* Jung to Spielrein, 1 September 1919, p. 190

p. 216 *death instinct*   *Secret Symmetry, Diary,* September 1910?, p. 20; see also *Secret Symmetry, Diary,* 9 November 1910, p. 33. It is interesting that Jung referred to her hypothesis of the 'death instinct' before she had published the paper, which did not, in fact, use the phrase – although she did use it in the oral version of the paper delivered to the Vienna Psycho-Analytical Society

p. 216 *work in common* Cifali, 'Une femme dans la psychanalyse', p. 255

p. 216 *after all*   *Secret Symmetry, Diary,* 26 November 1910, p. 35

p. 216 *death and sexuality*   *Minutes III,* 15 November 1911, pp. 310–13

p. 216 *Ilya Mechnikov*   *Minutes III,* 29 November 1911, p. 329

p. 216 *Freud and Tausk* Cifali, 'Une femme dans la psychanalyse', p. 258

p. 217 *such a mood?* Spielrein, 'Die Destruktion', p. 467

p. 217 *pleasure equally* Spielrein, 'Die Destruktion', p. 472

p. 217 *so like oneself* Spielrein, 'Die Destruktion', p. 477

p. 217 *of the species* Spielrein, 'Die Destruktion', p. 475

p. 217 *sexual instinct* Kerr, 'Freud, Jung and Sabina Spielrein', p. 26

p. 217 *resistance in everyone*   *Secret Symmetry,* pp. 107–8; Carotenuto dates this to around 1909, but Kerr, *A Most Dangerous Method,* p. 209, is surely correct in locating the thought in the 'Gross period' of May 1908 – it is implicit in the *Journal* – and the writing of this passage as June 1909

p. 218 *of the self* Spielrein, 'Die Destruktion', p. 480

p. 218 *in self-destruction* Spielrein, 'Die Destruktion', p. 486

p. 218 *negative component* Spielrein, 'Die Destruktion', pp. 490–2

p. 218 *love and hate* Bleuler, 'Vortrag über Ambivalenz', p. 266; see Laplanche and Pontalis, *The Language of Psychoanalysis,* p. 28, and Spielrein, 'Die Destruktion', p. 465

p. 218 *abnormally ambivalent*   F*Jung,* 306F, 21 March 1912, p. 494

p. 218 *in 1952*   *Symbols of Transformation, CW* V, p. 328 n. 38

p. 218 *it is sexual* Kerr, 'Freud, Jung and Sabina Spielrein', p. 29

p. 219 *Ψa fara da se*   F*Jung,* 286F, 30 November 1911, p. 469, also quoted in *J* II, p. 501

p. 219 *reality his mother*   F*Jung,* 288F, 17 December 1911, p. 473

p. 219 *very demanding*   F*Jung,* 288F, 17 December 1911, p. 473

p. 219   *it from me*   Spielrein, *Tagebuch einer heimlich Symmetrie*, 25 March 1912, p. 208

p. 219   *for the public*   Spielrein, *Tagebuch einer heimlich Symmetrie*, 25 March 1912, p. 208

p. 219   *facts of life*   Spielrein, 'Beiträge', p. 57

p. 220   *leave me cold*   *Secret Symmetry, Diary*, 22 February 1912, p. 43

p. 220   *as "destructive"*   *Beyond the Pleasure Principle, SE* XVIII, p. 55 n. 1

p. 220   *involved with her*   Sonu Shamdasani points out (personal communication) that the prospective function is already present in his dissertation.

p. 220   *intimate matters*   *FJung*, 311F, 21 April 1912, p. 499

p. 220   *influence on me*   *Secret Symmetry*, Spielrein to Jung, 6 January 1918, p. 71

p. 221   *Siegfried dream*   *Secret Symmetry*, Spielrein to Jung, 6 January 1918, p. 77

p. 221   *To be continued*   *Secret Symmetry*, 11 July 1912, p. 43

p. 221   *At night – "Freud"*   *Secret Symmetry*, 11 July 1912, p. 44

p. 221   *a back seat*   *Secret Symmetry*, Freud to Spielrein, August 1912, p. 117

p. 221   *my prejudices*   *Secret Symmetry*, Freud to Spielrein, August 1912, p. 117

p. 221   *Siegfried dreams*   *Secret Symmetry*, Spielrein to Jung, 6 January 1918, p. 77

p. 222   *hatred he merits*   *Secret Symmetry*, 8 May 1913, p. 120

p. 222   *stalwart Zionist*   *Secret Symmetry*, Freud to Spielrein, 28 August 1913, p. 120

p. 222   *his time comes*   *Secret Symmetry*, 29 September 1913, p. 121

p. 222   *go to Switzerland*   Personal communication, John Kerr, November 1991

p. 222   *something useful*   *Secret Symmetry*, prob. 26–27 January 1918, p. 87

p. 222   *works into Russian*   Kerr, 'Spielrein's Later Career', p. 34

p. 222   *through this process*   *Secret Symmetry*, 27–28? January 1918, p. 85

p. 222   *with devotion*   Spielrein, *Tagebuch einer heimlich Symmetrie*, Jung to Spielrein, 3 April 1919, p. 222

p. 223   *daughter's life*   *Secret Symmetry*, Spielrein to Jung, prob. 26–27 January 1918, p. 87

p. 223   *Don Juan*   Spielrein, 'Briefmarkentraum', p. 243

p. 223   *psychoanalysis in 1913*   Cifali, 'Le fameux couteau de Lichtenberg'; Cifali, 'Théodore Flournoy, la découverte de l'inconscient'; Flournoy, *Théodore et Léopold*

p. 223   *as his assistant*   Cifali, 'Entre Genève et Paris: Vienne' p. 125n

p. 224   *time to Paris*   Roudinesco, *La bataille de cent ans*, I, p. 332

p. 224   *all my complexes*   *Secret Symmetry*, p. 144

p. 224   *walked out*   Personal communication, John Kerr, November 1991

p. 224   *Congress of 1922*   Freud, 'Lettres à Raymond de Saussure', Freud to Raymond de Saussure, 3 July 1922, p. 192

p. 224   *of the World*   Piaget, *The Child's Conception of the World*, p. 409

p. 224   *of Piaget*   Vygotsky, *Thought and Language*, pp. 11–24

p. 224   *a younger man*   Spielrein, 'Rêve et vision'

p. 225   *24 March 1919*   *FJ*, Jones to Freud, 25 March 1919

p. 225   *probably in 1922*   *FJ*, Freud to Jones, 9 December 1921; see Roazen, *Freud and his Followers*, pp. 408, 415

p. 225   *lay analysis*   Freud, 'Lettres à Raymond de Saussure', Freud to Raymond de Saussure, 21 February 1928, p. 197

p. 225   *wont to do*   *Secret Symmetry*, 9 February 1923, p. 127

p. 225   *of children*   *Secret Symmetry*, p. 207; info. from Lampl de Groot

p. 225   *suggestive influence*   Spielrein, 'Referat zur Psychoanalyse' (in Russian, 1929), in Spielrein,

p. 225   *Ausgewählte Schriften*, pp. 205–12, cited in Cifali, 'Une femme dans la psychanalyse', pp. 258–9

p. 225   *the twentieth century*   Kerr, 'Spielrein's Later Career', p. 55; see also Palmier, 'la psychanalyse en Union Soviétique', pp. 220–6

p. 226   *synagogue and shot*   McGuire, 'Postscript', in *Secret Symmetry*, p. xi

p. 226   *of a woman*   *FJ*, Freud to Jones, 8 June 1913

p. 226   *analysis with him*   We would like to thank Harvard University Press for making available to us the edition of the Freud–Jones correspondence before publication, and the Freud Museum, London, for making available Loë Kann's letters to Freud.

p. 227   *Wilfred Trotter*   Brome, *Ernest Jones*, p. 37

p. 227 *patient of mine*   *FJ*, Jones to Freud, 28 June 1910
p. 227 *furnished house*   *FJ*, Jones to Freud, 10 December 1908
p. 227 *developed prudery*   *FJ*, Jones to Freud, 11 February 1911
p. 227 *do her good*   *FJ*, Jones to Freud, 11 February 1911
p. 227 *hid from Freud*   Compare his letters to Putnam, in which he mentions paying the patient $500, with his letter of 11 February 1911 to Freud.
p. 228 *by detectives*   *FJ*, Jones to Freud, 11 February 1911
p. 228 *dangerous work*   *FJ*, Jones to Freud, 8 March 1911
p. 228 *years later*   *FJ*, Freud to Jones, 2 June 1914; Freud regularly wrote to Jones in English, except at times of stress and illness, particularly after 1923; where indicated, therefore, passages from Freud to Jones were written by Freud in English – which has not been 'corrected'.
p. 228 *by anyone else*   *FJ*, Jones to Freud, 17 October 1911
p. 228 *of the dangers*   *FJ*, Freud to Jones, 14 January 1912
p. 228 *inner circle*   *FJ*, Jones to Freud, 30 July 1912
p. 228 *of psychoanalysis*   see *J* II, pp. 172ff.; the story of the secret committee thus constituted is told in Grosskurth, *The Secret Ring*
p. 229 *Libido on her*   *LC*, Freud to Ferenczi, 23 June 1912
p. 229 *highest value*   *FJ*, Freud to Jones, 28 October 1912
p. 229 *[Jones's] letters*   *FJ*, Freud to Jones, 28 October 1912
p. 229 *her personality*   *FJ*, Jones to Freud, 13 November 1912
p. 229 *from the soul*   *FJ*, Freud to Jones, 15 November 1912
p. 229 *when a child*   *FJ*, Freud to Jones, 15 November 1912
p. 229 *of its fires*   *FJ*, Jones to Freud, 17 November 1912
p. 229 *well she is*   *FJ*, Freud to Jones, 26 December 1912
p. 230 *[Christmas Eve]*   *FJ*, Freud to Jones, 26 December 1912
p. 230 *time and practice*   *FJ*, Jones to Freud, 29 December 1912
p. 230 *the mistress*   *FJ*, Freud to Jones, 1 January 1913; the phrase 'she nursing her' probably signifies that Loë was nursing her nurse Lina
p. 230 *desire intercourse*   *FJ*, Jones to Freud, 29 December 1912
p. 230 *dangerous experiment*   *FJ*, Freud to Jones, 10 February 1913
p. 230 *or feminine*   *FM*, Loë to Freud, 24 January 1913
p. 231 *Till then*   *FM*, Loë to Freud, 24 January 1913
p. 231 *love isn't lacking*   *FM*, Loë to Freud, 24 January 1913
p. 231 *her anaesthasia*   Phrase in brackets written out on the left-hand side of the page.
p. 231 *is causing me*   *FJ*, Jones to Freud, 30 January 1913
p. 231 *mean and treacherous*   *FJ*, Freud to Jones, 10 February 1913
p. 231 *is unavoidable*   *FJ*, Freud to Jones, 10 February 1913
p. 231 *every other aim*   *FJ*, Freud to Jones, 10 February 1913; emphasis added
p. 232 *an illness*   '"Civilized" Sexual Morality', *SE* IX, p. 195
p. 232 *of his life*   *Introductory Lectures*, *SE* XVI, pp. 459–60
p. 232 *sometimes the same*   *FM*, Loë to Freud, 26 March 1913
p. 232 *of my friends*   *FJ*, Freud to Jones, 9 April 1913
p. 232 *his wife anymore*   *LC*, Freud to Ferenczi, 4 May 1913
p. 233 *her and Davy*   *FM*, Loë to Freud, 14 May 1913
p. 233 *earliest wish-fancies*   *FJ*, Freud to Jones, 8 June 1913
p. 233 *dearest to me*   *FJ*, Jones to Freud, 11 June 1913
p. 233 *(E. J.) in on*   *LC*, Freud to Ferenczi, 9 July 1913
p. 233 *fond of her*   *FJ*, Freud to Jones, 10 July 1913
p. 233 *a young life*   *FJ*, Jones to Freud, 18 August 1913
p. 233 *when she loves*   *FJ*, Jones to Freud, 18 August 1913
p. 234 *can't be helped*   *FM*, Loë to Freud, 1 September 1913
p. 234 *taste for life*   *FM*, Loë to Freud, prob. 2 September 1913
p. 234 *as you see*   *FM*, Loë to Freud, 8 October 1913

p. 234 *our relations*   *FJ*, Freud to Jones, 4 December 1913
p. 234 *into the matter*   *FJ*, Freud to Jones, 16 January 1914
p. 235 *mother relation*   *FJ*, Freud to Jones, 8 February 1914
p. 235 *within her soul*   *FJ*, Freud to Jones, 25 March 1914
p. 235 *penises, no doubt*   On Freud's later view of little girls' rage at the mother when enemas are administered, see 'Female Sexuality', *SE* XXI, p. 238, where Freud follows Mack Brunswick in likening 'the outbreak of anger after an enema to an orgasm following genital excitation'.
p. 235 *this right*   *FJ*, Jones to Freud, 8 April 1914
p. 236 *more satisfying* . 'Femininity', *SE* XXII, pp. 132–3
p. 236 *it is true*   *FJ*, Jones to Freud, 25 May 1914
p. 236 *feelings of such*   Freud omitted to write the word that the syntax demands.
p. 236 *her only self*   *FJ*, Freud to Jones, 2 June 1914
p. 237 *me over it*   *FJ*, Jones to Freud, 27 July 1914
p. 237 *of my action*   *J* II, p. 456
p. 237 *certainly true*   *J* II, p. 477
p. 237 *she wonderful*   *FJ*, Jones to Freud, 3 August 1914
p. 238 *being bombed*   *FM*, Loë to Freud, 20 August 1919
p. 238 *you and Annerl*   *FM*, Loë to Freud, 20 August 1919
p. 238 *ton métier*   *FM*, Loë to Freud, 20 August 1919
p. 238 *start analysis*   *FM*, Loë to Freud, 13 July 1912
p. 238 *there permanently*   *FJ*, Jones to Freud, 8 December 1919
p. 238 *inlaid with ivory*   *FM*, Loë to Freud, undated, but prob. August/September 1919
p. 238 *your memory*   *FM*, Loë to Freud, undated, but prob. August/September 1919
p. 239 *bumble bees*   *FM*, Loë to Freud and Anna Freud, 10 September 1920
p. 239 *have no news*   *FJ*, Jones to Freud, 30 November 1921
p. 239 *here goes*   *FM*, Loë to Freud, 1923?, letter dated as February or March by snowdrops enclosed with it; although late April, which is when Loë could first have heard of Freud's illness, is rather late for snowdrops in England; yet 1924 is rather late to be writing as if the news of Freud's serious illness were still fresh.
p. 239 *us have it*   *FM*, Loë to Freud, 1923?, letter dated as February or March by snowdrops enclosed with it
p. 239 *witness HJ*   *FM*, Loë to Freud, 1923?, letter dated as February or March by snowdrops enclosed with it
p. 239 *of a woman*   *FJ*, Freud to Jones, 8 June 1913
p. 239 *had recently died*   Brome, *Ernest Jones*, p. 211

8: Lou Andreas-Salomé: 'The Fortunate Animal' pp. 240–71
p. 240 *could not attain*   Freud to Arnold Zweig, 11 May 1934, quoted by *J* III, p. 489; for a detailed study of the relationship between Freud and Nietzsche's thought, see Assoun, *Freud et Nietzsche*
p. 240 *who ever lived*   *J* II, p. 385
p. 241 *politely but firmly*   *FJung*, 291J, 2 January 1912, and 293F, 10 January 1912, pp. 477–80
p. 241 *of psychoanalysis*   *FA*, Freud to Abraham, 28 April 1912, p. 115
p. 242 *happier sex*   See, for example '*Der Mensch als Weib*' (The Human Being as Woman) (1899) and '*Die Erotik*' (1910), in *Die Erotik*
p. 242 *very girlish child*   Pfeiffer, *Friedrich Nietzsche, Paul Rée, Lou Andreas-Salomé*, letter to Peter Gast, 13 July 1882, p. 159
p. 242 *without selfishness*   Letter from Anna Freud to E. Pfeiffer, quoted by Livingstone, *Lou Andreas-Salomé*, p. 11. Livingstone is in many respects the best, certainly the most literary, of Lou's biographers and we are indebted to her insights. Moscovici's 'Preface' to *L'amour du narcissisme* was also invaluable. See also Binion, *Frau Lou*; Koepcke, *Lou Andreas-Salomé*

p. 242 *on their side* Pfeiffer, *Rainer Maria Rilke-Lou Andreas-Salomé Briefwechsel*, letter of 29 July 1913, p. 568

p. 242 *Thank-you* Andreas-Salomé, *Lebensrückblick*, pp. 68–9

p. 243 *which we repose* Andreas-Salomé, 'Zum Typus Weib', p. 11

p. 243 *in the world* Andreas-Salomé, *Lebensrückblick*, p. 51

p. 244 *frozen tears* Andreas-Salomé, *Lebensrückblick*, p. 16

p. 245 *always awaited* Andreas-Salomé, *Lebensrückblick*, p. 32

p. 248 *give that up* Andreas-Salomé, *Lebensrückblick*, p. 97

p. 248 *of his life* Pfeiffer, *Friedrich Nietzsche, Paul Rée, Lou Andreas-Salomé*, p. 219

p. 248 *they'd learnt* Pfeiffer, *Friedrich Nietzsche, Paul Rée, Lou Andreas-Salomé*, p. 229

p. 249 *Eternal-Masculine* Pfeiffer, *Friedrich Nietzsche, Paul Rée, Lou Andreas-Salomé*, letter to Heinrich von Stein, a mutual friend, 15 October 1885, p. 362

p. 250 *most dignified way* FLou, Freud to Lou, 8 May 1932, p. 198

p. 253 *amongst women* Quoted in Welsch and Wiesner, *Lou Andreas-Salomé*, p. 74

p. 253 *own perception* From the Pfeiffer Archive, quoted in Welsch and Wiesner, *Lou Andreas-Salomé*, p. 74

p. 253 *man and body* Andreas-Salomé, *Lebensrückblick*, p. 173

p. 253 *commentators* See, for example, Peters, *My Sister, My Spouse*

p. 253 *been played out* 'Lou Andreas-Salomé: Obituary', *SE* XXIII, p. 297

p. 254 *wholly myself* Pfeiffer, *Rainer Maria Rilke-Lou Andreas-Salomé Briefwechsel*, letter of 26 February 1901, known as *Letzter Zuruf* [last call], p. 54

p. 256 *formal analysis* For an insight into Lou's reasons here, see her discussion of the artist in section four of 'Narzissmus als Doppelrichtung', pp. 379–86

p. 257 *Christmas present* Freud Journal, p. 90

p. 257 *in the totality* Freud Journal, p. 90

p. 258 *psychic difficulties* Andreas-Salomé, *Lebensrückblick*, p. 191

p. 258 *ambiguous deformations* 'Le 6 mai 1926, soixante-dixième anniversaire de Freud', in Andreas-Salomé, *L'amour du narcissisme*, p. 181

p. 259 *of true egoism* Freud Journal, p. 89

p. 260 *once possessed* 'On Narcissism: An Introduction', *SE* XIV, pp. 88–90

p. 260 *of inferiority* Riviere, 'Review of Sigmund Freud, *New Introductory Lectures on Psycho-Analysis*', in Riviere, *Collected Papers*, p. 128

p. 260 *to be happy* Freud Journal, p. 118

p. 260 *to unhappiness* Kofman, *The Enigma of Woman*, p. 52

p. 260 *losing itself* Freud Journal, p. 118

p. 260 *and vice versa* Freud Journal, p. 41

p. 260 *reserved for you* Freud Journal, p. 44

p. 261 *not yet exist* Freud Journal, p. 48

p. 261 *the pathological* Andreas-Salomé, *Lebensrückblick*, quoted in notes by Pfeiffer, p. 284

p. 261 *working tirelessly* Freud Journal, p. 37

p. 261 *be overestimated* FLou, 14 July 1929, p. 180

p. 261 *such an office* FLou, 29 June 1914, p. 17

p. 262 *bestow grace* Reprinted in Andreas-Salomé, *L'amour du narcissisme*, p. 185

p. 262 *and so forth* Freud Journal, pp. 97–8

p. 262 *faulty reasoning* From an entry in Lou's unpublished diary, 14 March 1913, quoted by Welsch and Wiesner, *Lou Andreas-Salomé*, p. 249

p. 262 *should be perfect* Jokes, *SE* VIII, p. 61

p. 263 *his own doing* Freud Journal, pp. 166–7

p. 263 *Brother-animal. You* Freud Journal, pp. 167–8

p. 264 *living tissue* FLou, 22 November 1917, p. 67

p. 264 *their existence* FLou, 25 May 1916, p. 45

p. 264 *of the male* FLou, 30 January 1919, p. 89

p. 265 *expressible in words* FLou, 22 November 1917, pp. 67–8

p. 265 *opinions together* FLou, 3 March 1930, p. 185

p. 265 *final truths* FLou, c. 10 July 1931, pp. 195–6

p. 266 *feminine love*   Cf. Andreas-Salomé, 'Zum Typus Weib'

p. 266 *every homecoming*   FLou, 6 May 1922, p. 115

p. 267 *my warning*   FLou, 5 August 1923, pp. 124–5

p. 267 *what they've got*   Pfeiffer, *Rainer Maria Rilke-Lou Andreas-Salomé Briefwechsel*, letter to Rilke, 16 March 1924, p. 464

p. 267 *great listener*   Peters, *My Sister, My Spouse*, p. 283, no source given

p. 268 *warmly and freely*   FLou, soon after 15 February 1925, p. 151

p. 268 *have been saved*   See Livingstone, *Lou Andreas-Salomé*, pp. 173–4, from unpublished diary of 1917

p. 268 *an altruist*   Andreas-Salomé, 'Zum Typus Weib', p. 8

p. 268 *needlessly active*   Andreas-Salomé, 'Zum Typus Weib', p. 8

p. 269 *it on lease*   *Three Essays*, SE VII, p. 187, footnote added 1920

p. 269 *graphically puts it*   Andreas-Salomé, '"Anal" und "Sexual"', p. 249

p. 270 *of the whole*   Andreas-Salomé, 'Narzissmus als Doppelrichtung', pp. 365–7

p. 271 *in a woman*   Andreas-Salomé, *Lebensrückblick*, p. 41

p. 271 *arm around her*   Andreas-Salomé, *Lebensrückblick*, p. 213

p. 271 *really lives it*   Anna Freud to Lou Andreas-Salomé, 11 December 1932, quoted in Young-Bruehl, *Anna Freud*, p. 230

9: Anna Freud: The Dutiful Daughter pp. 272–306

p. 273 *and left alone*   From a letter to Muriel Gardiner in the Hampstead Bulletin, 6 January 1983, quoted in Young-Bruehl, *Anna Freud*, p. 37

p. 273 *get lost*   Anna Freud, 'On Losing and Being Lost', *Writings* IV, p. 311

p. 273 *of my practice*   FF, 8 December 1895, p. 154

p. 274 *unwelcome verdict*   *The Interpretation of Dreams*, SE IV, p. 130

p. 274 *have made her*   FLou, Freud to Lou, 16 May 1935, pp. 208–9

p. 274 *asking after you*   FM, Anna to Sigmund, 24 September 1913

p. 275 *do you good*   FM, Sigmund to Anna, 13 December 1912

p. 276 *from yourself*   FM, Sigmund to Anna, 5 January 1913

p. 276 *throw oneself into*   FM, Sigmund to Anna, 2 February 1913

p. 277 *my) consent*   FM, Sigmund to Anna, 16 July 1914

p. 277 *a week later*   FM, Sigmund to Anna, 22 July 1914

p. 277 *dutiful and teasing*   FM, Anna to Sigmund, 26 July 1914

p. 277 *sometime or other*   FLou, 13 March 1922, p. 113

p. 278 *it has crawled*   Freud to Lou, 13 May 1924, quoted by Gay, p. 441, excised from letter of that date in *FLou*

p. 278 *me with it*   Freud to Lou, 10 May 1925, quoted by Gay, p. 441, excised from letter of that date in *FLou*

p. 278 *long cherished*   Young-Bruehl, *Anna Freud*, p. 96

p. 278 *judged correctly*   FM, Anna to Sigmund, 7 July 1921

p. 278 *a lesser man*   Kardiner, *My Analysis with Freud*, p. 77

p. 279 *for learning*   FJ, Freud to Jones, 22 July 1914

p. 279 *sometime in 1918*   Gay, p. 435

p. 279 *partner him in it*   Young-Bruehl, *Anna Freud*, p. 111, and Gay, who refers to the analysis only as 'quasi-analytical conversations', p. 437

p. 280 *recurrent theme*   FM, Anna to Sigmund, 24 July 1919

p. 280 *very agitating*   FM, Anna to Sigmund, 6 August 1915

p. 280 *back to reality*   Anna Freud, 'Beating Fantasies and Daydreams', *Early Papers*, p. 157

p. 280 *the sexual act*   'A Child Is Being Beaten', SE XVII, p. 199

p. 280 *efficient work*   'A Child Is Being Beaten', SE XVII, p. 167

p. 281 *remain the latter*   Freud to Eitingon, 6 March 1926, quoted by Gay, p. 442

p. 281 *herself very tired*   Freud to Ferenczi, 25 March 1927, quoted by Young-Bruehl, *Anna Freud*, p. 189

p. 281 *place of another*   Freud to Lou, 11 May 1927, quoted by Gay, p. 541

p. 281 *for the summer*   Binswanger, *Sigmund Freud: Reminiscences of a Friendship*, p. 88

p. 283 *an unhappy virgin*   Freud to Lou, 11 May 1927, quoted by Gay, p. 540, letter excised in published correspondence

p. 284 *self analysis*   Freud to Dorothy Burlingham, 29 May 1938, quoted by Young-Bruehl, *Anna Freud*, p. 238

p. 284 *able to do so*   Dorothy Burlingham to Edith Jackson, 20 June 1938, quoted in Burlingham, *The Last Tiffany*, p. 266

p. 285 *the treatment*   Burlingham, 'Child Analysis and the Mother', in *Psychoanalytic Studies*, pp. 6–7

p. 285 *the supernatural*   'Child Analysis and the Mother', in *Psychoanalytic Studies* p. 8; see also Freud, 'Dreams and Occultism', *SE* XXII, p. 56

p. 285 *obscure and uncertain*   'Analysis of a Phobia in a Four-Year-Old Boy', *SE* X, p. 64

p. 286 *other factors*   Anna Freud, *Introduction to the Technique of Child Analysis, Writings I*, pp. 37–40

p. 287 *on the subject*   See Hug-Hellmuth, 'On the Technique of Child Analysis', in MacLean and Rappen, *Hermine Hug-Hellmuth*, pp. 138–53

p. 287 *more experience*   Anna Freud to Lou, 16 February 1928, quoted by Young-Bruehl, *Anna Freud*, pp. 163–4

p. 288 *she is right*   Freud to Eitingon, 21 November 1926, quoted by Young-Bruehl, *Anna Freud*, p. 163

p. 288 *independent work*   FLou, 11 May 1927, quoted by Gay, p. 541, excised in published correspondence

p. 288 *year of life*   Melanie Klein, 'Symposium on Child Analysis', p. 357. For an interesting discussion of the differences between Anna Freud and Melanie Klein, see Rose, 'Psychopolitics II'.

p. 289 *adult neurotic*   Anna Freud, *Introduction to the Technique of Child Analysis, Writings I*, p. 44

p. 289 *to progress*   Anna Freud, *Introduction to the Technique of Child Analysis, Writings I*, pp. 166–7

p. 289 *as they are*   Peters, *Her Father's Daughter*, p. 85

p. 290 *demands of pedagogy*   LC, Freud to Maggie Heller, Corr. 1910–14

p. 290 *dreaded retributions*   Riviere, 'Symposium on Child Analysis', pp. 376–7; also in Riviere, *Collected Papers*, p. 87

p. 290 *this in detail*   FJ, Jones to Freud, 16 May 1927

p. 290 *is in error*   FJ, Freud to Jones, 31 May 1927

p. 291 *child before him*   Sharpe, 'Contribution', p. 384

p. 291 *primitive urges*   FJ, Freud to Jones, 23 September 1927. For an extended discussion of this episode, see Steiner, 'Some Thoughts about Tradition and Change'

p. 291 *secret sentimentalist*   Bloomsbury/Freud, letter dated 14 December 1924, p. 146

p. 292 *upbringing and education*   Anna Freud, *The Psychoanalytic Treatment of Children*, p. 55

p. 292 *still, analysed*   Anna Freud, 'Tribute to Dorothy Burlingham', p. 76

p. 293 *Psychoanalytic Educator*   Burlingham, *Psychoanalytic Studies*, p. 78

p. 293 *psychic things*   Dorothy Burlingham, 'Memorabilia', quoted by Burlingham, *The Last Tiffany*, p. 217

p. 294 *its integrity*   Anna Freud, *The Ego and the Mechanisms of Defence*, p. 4

p. 294 *his love objects*   Anna Freud, *The Ego and the Mechanisms of Defence*, p. 133

p. 295 *the defences*   Sterba, *Reminiscences of a Viennese Psychoanalyst*, p. 130

p. 296 *that she does*   Burlingham, *The Last Tiffany*, Dorothy to Bob Burlingham, 19 April 1940, p. 273

p. 296 *die in freedom*   J III, p. 240, Freud to Ernst Freud, 12 May 1938

p. 297 *ghosts and bogeymen*   Anna Freud, *Reports on the Hampstead Nurseries 1939–1945, Writings III*, p. 169

p. 297 *'shocked' children*   Anna Freud, *Reports on the Hampstead Nurseries 1939–1945, Writings III*, p. 169

p. 297 *hard to bear*   Anna Freud, *Reports on the Hampstead Nurseries 1939–1945, Writings III*, p. 189

p. 298 *better than she*   Melanie Klein to Ernest Jones, quoted by Young-Bruehl, *Anna Freud*, p. 265

p. 299 *particular the future*   *Freud–Klein Controversies*, letter from James Strachey to Edward Glover, 23 April 1940, pp. 32–3

p. 299 *scheme of things*   *Freud–Klein Controversies*, p. 418

p. 299 *described by Freud*   *Freud–Klein Controversies*, pp. 420–1

p. 300 *of the infant*   *Freud–Klein Controversies*, pp. 422–3

p. 300 *instinct theory*   *Freud–Klein Controversies*, p. 424

p. 301 *alone and 'lost'*   Young-Bruehl, *Anna Freud*, p. 286, from AF folder on losing and being lost

p. 302 *come their way*   Letter from Dorothy to Bob and Rigmor Burlingham, 20 September 1942, quoted in Burlingham, *The Last Tiffany*, pp. 283–4

p. 303 *problem child oneself*   Young-Bruehl, *Anna Freud*, p. 340, letter from Anna Freud to Milton Senn, 16 February 1952

p. 304 *needs resignation*   T. Reik, 'Freud in Conversation', *LC*, B46, p. 6

p. 304 *already caught up*   Elster, *Solomonic Judgements*, Chapter III: 'Solomonic Judgements: against the best interests of the child', pp. 123–74, esp. pp. 126 ff.

p. 305 *weak a weapon*   Young-Bruehl, *Anna Freud*, p. 413, Anna Freud to Ralph Greenson, 20 January 1963

p. 305 *lost this way*   Young-Bruehl, *Anna Freud*, p. 457; see also Sophie Freud, *My Three Mothers and Other Passions*

p. 305 *for so long*   Young-Bruehl, *Anna Freud*, p. 450

10: Helene Deutsch: As If A Modern Woman pp. 307–28

p. 308 *of the species*   See Beauvoir, Greer, Millett, Caplan *et al.*

p. 308 *what is biological*   *LC*, Box 15, letter from Freud to Carl Muller-Braunschweig, 21 July 1935

p. 308 *of the world*   Deutsch, *Confrontations with Myself*, p. 63

p. 309 *normal sexuality*   Deutsch, *The Psychology of Women*, I, p. 195

p. 309 *this relation*   Deutsch, *The Psychology of Women*, I, p. 196

p. 309 *until I married*   Deutsch, *Confrontations with Myself*, p. 80

p. 310 *veiled case history*   Deutsch, 'On the pathological lie'

p. 311 *identification possible*   Deutsch, *Confrontations with Myself*, p. 28

p. 311 *fulfilment of love*   Deutsch, *The Psychology of Women*, I, pp. 158–9

p. 312 *respectable profession*   Deutsch, *Confrontations with Myself*, p. 96

p. 312 *own ego-ideal*   Deutsch, *Confrontations with Myself*, p. 103

p. 313 *of the question*   Deutsch, *Confrontations with Myself*, p. 104

p. 313 *feeling of liberation*   Deutsch, *Confrontations with Myself*, p. 107

p. 314 *against Freud*   Quoted by Roazen, *Helene Deutsch*, p. 111. We are indebted to this biography for many of the details of Deutsch's life.

p. 317 *she had rejected*   Deutsch, *The Psychology of Women*, II, pp. 146–9

p. 317 *my little son*   Deutsch, *Confrontations with Myself*, p. 125

p. 318 *her as well*   Roazen, *Helene Deutsch*, p. 146

p. 318 *lastly Freud*   Deutsch, *Confrontations with Myself*, p. 131

p. 319 *oedipal fantasy*   Deutsch, *Confrontations with Myself*, p. 132

p. 319 *cleverest son*   Deutsch, *Confrontations with Myself*, p. 132

p. 321 *set of genitals*   Deutsch, *Confrontations with Myself*, p. 134

p. 321 *and tormented*   Roazen, *Helene Deutsch*, p. 197

p. 323 *feminine disciple*   J. Simpson, *New York Herald Tribune*, 3 August 1930

p. 324 *the Institute*   See *Int J Psa 6*, 1925, p. 528

p. 324 *regular drilling*   Quoted by Roazen, *Helene Deutsch*, p. 250, from her paper of 1935 on the 'Principles and Practices of the Vienna Society'

p. 324 *his personality*   Roazen, *Helene Deutsch*, p. 248

p. 324 *transference agencies*   Roazen, *Helene Deutsch*, letter to Felix Deutsch from Italy, 5 April 1926, p. 261

p. 325 *mass neurosis*   Roazen, *Helene Deutsch*, letter to Felix Deutsch from Boston, 18 October 1935, p. 288; 'Obituary: Helene Deutsch', *Int J Psa 63* 1982, pp. 491–2

p. 325 *to psychoanalysis*   Deutsch, *Confrontations with Myself*, p. 179

p. 325 *bisexual disposition*   'Femininity', *SE* XXII, p. 116

p. 325 *women from men*   But contrast Deutsch's own analysis in Deutsch, *The Psychology of Women*, I, pp. 180–7

p. 326 *of these attempts*   Deutsch, *The Psychology of Women*, I, p. 16

p. 327 *perfect woman*   See Rosen, 'Hélène Deutsch', p. 55

p. 327 *warmth of motherliness*   Deutsch, *The Psychology of Women*, II, p. 430

p. 328 *profession for women*   Deutsch, *Confrontations with Myself*, p. 209

11: Marie Bonaparte and Freud's French Court pp. 329–51

p. 330 *Plato's ideas*   Bertin, Marie Bonaparte to Freud, 7 January 1937, pp. 196–7

p. 330 *of the dead*   Bonaparte, 'A Defence of Biography', p. 239

p. 331 *have a liaison*   *Journal d'analyse*, 16 November 1925, quoted Bertin, p. 155

p. 331 *her realism*   *Journal d'analyse*, 15 February 1927, quoted Bertin, p. 170

p. 331 *quite helpless*   *Journal d'analyse*, 30 April 1932, quoted Bertin, p. 185

p. 331 *phallic woman*   Bonaparte, *Five Copy-Books*, I, p. 39

p. 332 *legs and skirts*   Bonaparte, *Five Copy-Books*, I, p. 39

p. 334 *most analysts do*   Bertin, quoting from *The Psychoanalytic Movement Project*, p. 84, The Oral History Archive, Columbia University, p. 247

p. 335 *the oppressed*   Bertin, p. 54

p. 335 *So did Proust*   Proust, *Remembrance of Things Past*, II, p. 507

p. 335 *we want children*   Bertin, p. 94

p. 335 *I would pick*   Bertin, p. 76

p. 335 *necessary malady*   See 'Tristesse feminine', unpublished manuscript, 1913, quoted by Bertin, p. 111

p. 336 *the longest*   Bertin, p. 111

p. 336 *wasn't wrong*   *Journal d'analyse*, undated, quoted by Bertin, p. 132

p. 338 *in their bodies*   Bonaparte, 'Considérations sur les causes anatomiques', p. 770

p. 338 *without his penis*   Bonaparte, 'Considérations sur les causes anatomiques', p. 776

p. 338 *treatment of her*   Bourguignon, 'Correspondance Sigmund Freud–René Laforgue', Laforgue to Freud, 9 April 1925, p. 260

p. 339 *be indicated*   Bourguignon, 'Correspondance Sigmund Freud–René Laforgue', p. 267

p. 339 *the same case*   Bourguignon, 'Correspondance Sigmund Freud–René Laforgue', p. 268

p. 339 *masculine female*   Gay, Freud to Eitingon, 30 October 1925, p. 542

p. 339 *made on me*   Bourguignon, 'Correspondance Sigmund Freud–René Laforgue', Freud to Laforgue, 15 November 1925, p. 273

p. 340 *orgastic normality*   Bertin, p. 157

p. 340 *imperceptible fragment*   Bertin, p. 153

p. 340 *not so very*   *Journal d'analyse*, 24 February 1926, quoted by Bertin, p. 156

p. 340 *marriage problem*   *J* III, p. 209, Freud to Marie Bonaparte, 27 September 1936

p. 340 *Marie declares*   Bonaparte, *Five Copy-Books*, I, pp. 49ff.

p. 342 *fatal sex act*   Bonaparte, *Five Copy-Books*, I, p. 63; see also 'Notes on the Analytical Discovery of a Primal Scene'

p. 342 *duplicates of him*   Bonaparte, *Five Copy-Books*, I, p. 213

p. 342 *He's right*   *Journal d'analyse*, quoted in *New York Times*, 12 November 1985, Sec. C. 3

p. 343 *doctoral degrees*   Bertin, p. 161

p. 343 *master them*   Bertin, p. 171

p. 343 *frightens me*   Bertin, p. 175

p. 343 *anatomical factor* 'Femininity', *SE* XXII, p. 132
p. 343 *case completely* 'Female Sexuality', *SE* XXI, pp. 226–7
p. 343 *in question* 'Female Sexuality', *SE* XXI, p. 226
p. 344 *organic evolution* Bonaparte, *Female Sexuality*, p. 8
p. 344 *who wishes it* Bonaparte, *Psychanalyse et biologie*, p. 119; see also her earlier 'Passivity, Masochism and Femininity'
p. 344 *feminine organism* Bonaparte, *Female Sexuality*, p. 7
p. 345 *almost a man* Bertin, p. 248
p. 345 *nor analysand* Though Monk, *Ludwig Wittgenstein*, p. 16, maintains she was analysed by Freud
p. 345 *an equal degree* Wittgenstein, *Lectures and Conversations*, p. 43
p. 345 *special status* Monk, *Ludwig Wittgenstein*, p. 16
p. 345 *of Athene* *J* III, p. 243, Freud to Marie Bonaparte, 8 June 1938
p. 346 *on the executive* *FJ*, Freud to Jones, 23 August 1933
p. 346 *the King* Bertin, letter to Loewenstein, 2 July 1945, p. 222
p. 347 *personal interference* Bertin, letter to Loewenstein, 2 July 1945, p. 222
p. 347 *ridiculous subjection* Miller, *La scission*, Lacan to Loewenstein, 14 July 1953, p. 123
p. 347 *abnormal and unjust* Bertin, p. 247
p. 347 *particular talent* Roudinesco, *Jacques Lacan & Co.*, p. 251
p. 347 *is grilling* Lacan, 'Seminar on *The Purloined Letter*', p. 67
p. 348 *scientific creation* Bonaparte, *Five Copy-Books*, II, p. 46
p. 348 *a little happier* Bertin, p. 253
p. 348 *on 8 November* See *Minutes: Les premiers psychanalystes*, p. 340 (protocols for 1914–18 absent from English edition)
p. 348 *in Psycho-Analysis* See Grosskurth, *The Secret Ring*, p. 96. Grosskurth also notes that in a letter to Ferenczi, Freud referred to Sokolnicka as 'an intelligent but "repulsive person"', who could not accept that she was growing old' (6 June 1920). This inability to face old age may have been one of the determining motives in her suicide at the age of fifty.
p. 350 *at twenty-two* Choisy, *Sigmund Freud*, p. 7
p. 350 *of the name* Roudinesco, *Jacques Lacan & Co.*, p. 197, and Mijolla, 'La psychanalyse en France', pp. 42–6; Mijolla, personal communication, 5 July 1992
p. 351 *sacramental pardon* Roudinesco, *Jacques Lacan & Co.*, p. 197

12: Joan Riviere and Alix Strachey: Translating Psychoanalysis pp. 352–71
p. 352 *Brunswick Square* On Sinclair, see Beauman, *A Very Great Profession*, Chapter 6 'Psycho-analysis', pp. 147 ff.; Showalter, *The Female Malady*, pp. 195–201
p. 352 *analysis in 1920* Wahl, 'Ella Freeman Sharpe', pp. 265–71
p. 353 *Miss Terry* *FJ*, Jones to Freud, 30 September 1927
p. 353 *collaborators achieved* Segal, 'Foreword', in Riviere, *Collected Papers*, p. xiii. We are indebted to this finely edited collection, and to Athol Hughes' acute biographical portrait of Riviere in her introduction.
p. 353 *so remarked on* See Monro, 'Contribution', and Segal, 'Foreword', in Riviere, *Collected Papers*
p. 353 *somehow impressive* Strachey, 'Contribution', p. 238
p. 353 *Joan of Freud* Strachey, 'Contribution', p. 238
p. 354 *especially the women* *FJ*, Jones to Freud, 21 January 1922
p. 354 *beneath her feet* *FJ*, Jones to Freud, 22 May 1922
p. 354 *clear-headed* *FJ*, Freud to Jones, 23 March 1922
p. 354 *a powerful helpmate* *FJ*, Freud to Jones, 6 April 1922
p. 354 *concentrated acid* *FJ*, Freud to Jones, 11/12 May 1922
p. 354 *unusually intelligent* *FJ*, Jones to Freud, 21 January 1922
p. 354 *prose writing* Strachey, 'Contribution', p. 229
p. 354 *for analysis* *FJ*, Jones to Freud, 21 January 1922
p. 354 *Freud in 1922* Riviere's analysis with Freud lasted from January to December 1922,

with a break from July to September. She returned to Vienna for six weeks in 1924 for further analysis; (letter from Athol Hughes to the authors, 27 January 1992)

p. 354 *'wounded' state* Brome, *Ernest Jones*, Riviere to Jones, 30 October 1918, p. 116

p. 355 *human nature* Jones, *Free Associations*, p. 247

p. 355 *in my power* FJ, Jones to Freud, 21 January 1922

p. 355 *to the past* FJ, Freud to Jones, 5 February 1922

p. 355 *to a close* FJ, Freud to Jones, 23 March 1922

p. 356 *special circumstances* FJ, Jones to Freud, 1 April 1922

p. 356 *her greatness* FJ, Jones to Freud, 22 May 1922

p. 356 *modification* FJ, Jones to Freud, 22 May 1922

p. 357 *in German* FJ, Freud to Jones, 4 June 1922

p. 358 *as to ours* FJ, Freud to Jones, 4 June 1922

p. 358 *clinical facts* *The Ego and the Id*, SE XIX, p. 49

p. 358 *ego and super-ego* See *The Ego and the Id*, SE XIX, pp. 49 and 52; the latter passage concerns the manner in which the ego of the hysteric 'turned the same weapon against its harsh taskmaster' by repressing the super-ego. It is interesting that Jones's initial diagnosis of Riviere is not that distant from Freud's later one: 'It is a case of typical hysteria, almost the only symptoms being sexual anaesthesia and unorganized Angst, with a few inhibitions of a general nature. Most of her neurosis goes into marked character reactions, which is one reason why I was not able to cure her.' (FJ, Jones to Freud, 21 January 1922)

p. 358 *regards indefinitely* FJ, Freud to Jones, 4 June 1922

p. 358 *well together* FJ, Jones to Freud, 22 December 1922

p. 358 *terms with myself* FJ, Jones to Freud, 9 February 1924

p. 358 *her judgments* Segal, 'Foreword', in Riviere, *Collected Papers*, p. xii

p. 359 *Child Analysis* *Int J Psa* 8 1927, pp. 370–7, also in Riviere, *Collected Papers*, pp. 80–7

p. 359 *way with them* Riviere, *Collected Papers*, p. 83

p. 359 *largely consists* Riviere, *Collected Papers*, pp. 83–4

p. 359 *sexual desires* Riviere, *Collected Papers*, p. 85

p. 360 *critical comment* FJ, Freud to Jones, 9 October 1927

p. 360 *the picture* FJ, Jones to Freud, 18 October 1927

p. 360 *phantastic half* 'The phantastic half' is in English in the original

p. 360 *article again* Riviere, *Collected Papers*, p. 87

p. 361 *estranged* FJ, Freud to Jones, 22 October 1927

p. 361 *jealous of Riviere* Grosskurth, *Melanie Klein*, Anna Freud to Jones, 14 February 1954, p. 207n

p. 361 *object (projection)* Riviere, *Collected Papers*, p. 286

p. 361 *personal hostilities* *Freud-Klein Controversies*, pp. 112–19

p. 362 *reconciling them* Riviere, *Collected Papers*, pp. 165–6

p. 362 *mortal, too* Riviere, *Collected Papers*, p. 209

p. 362 *outside himself* Riviere, *Collected Papers*, p. 211

p. 362 *operation in 1924* Riviere, *Collected Papers*, pp. 210–11

p. 363 *type psychologically* Riviere, *Collected Papers*, p. 91

p. 363 *feminine activities* Riviere, *Collected Papers*, p. 94

p. 364 *the same thing* Riviere, *Collected Papers*, p. 94

p. 364 *gives rise to* Riviere, *Collected Papers*, p. 101

p. 365 *be realized* Riviere, *Collected Papers*, p. 144

p. 365 *early as 1913* Steiner, 'To explain our point of view'

p. 365 *Second World War years* 'General Preface', SE I, p. xix

p. 365 *colony of Nutley* Bloomsbury/Freud, pp. 8 ff. We are indebted to the fine introduction and epilogue of this book for much of the biographical material on Alix Strachey.

p. 366 *anorexic condition* Bloomsbury/Freud, p. 12

p. 366 *she was bored* *The Diary of Virginia Woolf*, I, pp. 60–1

p. 367 *in Piccadilly* *The Diary of Virginia Woolf*, I, p. 63

p. 367 *moral generations* *The Diary of Virginia Woolf*, I, p. 176

p. 367 *absolute boy* Bloomsbury/*Freud*, James to Lytton Strachey, 12 September 1910, p. 23
p. 367 *murder and rape* Bloomsbury/*Freud*, p. 25
p. 367 *an analyst* Bloomsbury/*Freud*, Freud to James Strachey, 4 June 1920, p. 29
p. 367 *us at once* Bloomsbury/*Freud*, James to Lytton Strachey, 6 November 1920, p. 6
p. 367 *for life* Bloomsbury/*Freud*, James to Lytton Strachey, 6 November 1920, p. 29
p. 368 *best analyst* Bloomsbury/*Freud*, Alix to James Strachey, 29 April 1925, p. 252
p. 368 *to practise* Bloomsbury/*Freud*, James to Lytton Strachey, 22 June 1922, p. 30
p. 368 *very valuable* FJ, Freud to Jones, 25 June 1922
p. 368 *be marriage* *The Diaries of Virginia Woolf*, II, p. 135
p. 368 *my attention* 'Dora', *SE* VII, p. 13 n. 1
p. 369 *they hate her* Bloomsbury/*Freud*, Alix to James Strachey, 21 May 1925, p. 188
p. 369 *with the paper* Bloomsbury/*Freud*, Alix to James Strachey, 11 January 1925, p. 179
p. 369 *degree of coherence* Bloomsbury/*Freud*, Alix to James Strachey, 5 March 1925, p. 226
p. 369 *fail to do* Bloomsbury/*Freud*, Alix to James Strachey, 9 May 1925, p. 260
p. 370 *latter's four* *Freud-Klein Controversies*, pp. 193–5
p. 370 *dominate and guide* Strachey, *The Unconscious Motives of War*, p. 183
p. 370 *well-being* Strachey, *The Unconscious Motives of War*, p. 222
p. 371 *destructive energy* Strachey, *The Unconscious Motives of War*, p. 266

13: The Friendship of Women pp. 372–93
p. 373 *taking this step* 'Analysis Terminable and Interminable,' *SE* XXIII, p. 249
p. 373 *Freud habit* Roazen, *Freud and his Followers*, pp. 415–30 passim
p. 374 *highly elusive* FM, Freud to Lampl de Groot, 23 October 1932
p. 374 *according to Anna Freud* Cf. Young-Bruehl, *Anna Freud*, Anna Freud to Eitingon, 7 November 1928, p. 482
p. 375 *extremely jealous* Roazen, *Helene Deutsch*, p. 251
p. 375 *patient and Freud* Brunswick, 'Supplement', *Reader*, p. 103
p. 375 *is of importance* Brunswick, 'Supplement', *Reader*, p. 102
p. 375 *pre-Oedipal phase* See Brunswick, 'The Analysis of a Case of Paranoia'
p. 375 *situation at all* 'Femininity', *SE* XXII, p. 130
p. 376 *as its object* Brunswick, 'Pre-Oedipal Phase', *Reader*, pp. 235–6
p. 376 *possessing the mother* Brunswick, 'Pre-Oedipal Phase', *Reader*, p. 244; see also Zanardi,
p. 376 *Essential Papers*, p. 19
p. 376 *for a baby* Brunswick, 'Pre-Oedipal Phase', *Reader*, p. 245; see Laplanche and Pontalis, *The Language of Psycho-analysis*, p. 335
p. 377 *to be analysed* Gardiner, *Code Name 'Mary'*, p. 32
p. 377 *by the Wolf Man* Gardiner, *The Wolfman by the Wolfman*
p. 378 *have been yours* Gardiner, *Code Name 'Mary'*, p. 179
p. 378 *of the combatants* H.D., *Tribute to Freud*, p. 192
p. 378 *analyses with Freud* Roazen, *Freud and his Followers*, p. 331
p. 379 *an actress* Young-Bruehl, *Anna Freud*, p. 52
p. 379 *Jung and Bleuler* *Minutes III*, pp. xvi and xvii
p. 379 *are you?* Young-Bruehl, *Anna Freud*, pp. 40–1
p. 380 *friendship for you* LC, Freud to Kata Levy, 16 August 1920, quoted by Gay, p. 440
p. 380 *in hard currency* LC, Freud to Kata Levy, 28 November 1920, quoted by Gay, p. 388
p. 380 *the older sister* Young-Bruehl, *Anna Freud*, p. 195
p. 380 *doesn't speak French* J III, p. 108
p. 381 *Fifth Avenue* Interview with Victor Ross, 13 September 1991
p. 381 *emigrate to Britain* Letter in Victor Ross's collection dated 19 December 1937
p. 381 *enjoy themselves* Interview with Victor Ross, 13 October 1991
p. 381 *intimate one* FM, letters transcribed by P. Heller, now published in Heller, 'Briefe'
p. 382 *share with you* Letter possibly of September 1927? in *FM* transcribed and dated by P. Heller .
p. 382 *the guiding forces* Burlingham, *The Last Tiffany*, p. 185

p. 382 *culture and music* Burlingham, *The Last Tiffany*, p. 183

p. 382 *to an animal* *LC*, Freud to Eva Rosenfeld, 1 September 1929

p. 382 *rightfully yours* Young-Bruehl, *Anna Freud*, Anna Freud to Eva Rosenfeld, June 1929, p. 136

p. 382 *about her condition* Ross Collection, Anna Freud to Eva Rosenfeld, 30 September 1929, quoted in Burlingham, *The Last Tiffany*, p. 194

p. 382 *a viable universe* Heller, 'Briefe', p. 442

p. 382 *loved so much* Heller, 'Briefe', p. 442

p. 383 *particularly for you* *LC*, Freud to Eva Rosenfeld, 15 August 1937

p. 384 *obstacles at least* Susan Isaacs to Clifford Scott, 13 January 1939, Grosskurth, *Melanie Klein*, p. 244

p. 384 *personal friendship* Interview with Pearl King, quoted by Grosskurth, *Melanie Klein*, p. 361

p. 384 *to Anna Freud* Grosskurth, *Melanie Klein*, p. 361

p. 384 *wanted to be?* Grosskurth, *Melanie Klein*, p. 361

p. 384 *disciples or opponents* Interview with Victor Ross, 13 October 1991

p. 384 *patients and friends* See Dr Paula Heimann and Dr M. B. Conran in Records of Scientific Meeting of British Society, 5 October 1977, in Institute of Psycho-Analysis, London

p. 384 *defeated her* Interview with Victor Ross, 13 September 1991

p. 385 *treatment of patients* *FM*, Freud to Jeanne Lampl de Groot, 11 September 1921

p. 385 *humane and generous* Quoted from interview with Jeanne Lampl de Groot, Gay, p. 464

p. 385 *at that time* Young-Bruehl, *Anna Freud*, p. 99

p. 386 *principally by men* Lampl de Groot, 'Oedipus Complex', *Reader*, p. 182

p. 386 *oedipus attitude* Lampl de Groot, 'Oedipus Complex', *Reader*, p. 194

p. 386 *in 1931* 'Female Sexuality', *SE* XXI, pp. 226–7

p. 386 *correspondence with her* *FM*, Freud to Lampl de Groot, 17 April 1932

p. 386 *in the dark* *FM*, Freud to Lampl de Groot, 24 April 1932: '*tappe ich wieder ganz im Dunkeln*'

p. 386 *of the formulations* Lampl de Groot, *Man and Mind*, p. 12

p. 387 *to love me* H.D., *Tribute to Freud*, p. 16

p. 387 *vers libre relationship* H.D. to Kenneth Macpherson, 1 April 1933, quoted by Friedman, 'A Most Luscious *Vers Libre* Relationship', p. 319

p. 387 *war-shattered people* H.D., *Tribute to Freud*, p. 93

p. 387 *of my contemporaries* H.D., *Tribute to Freud*, p. 13

p. 388 *over all others* H.D. to Kenneth Macpherson, 13 and 14 June 1933, quoted in Friedman, *Psyche Reborn*, pp. 19–20

p. 388 *he CAN be* H.D. to Kenneth Macpherson 14 and 15 March 1933, quoted in Friedman, *Psyche Reborn*, p. 19

p. 389 *literary history* Friedman, *Psyche Reborn*; Duplessis, H.D.; Buck, 'Freud and H.D.'; Gubar, 'The Echoing Spell of H.D.'s Trilogy'

p. 390 *for my mother* H.D., *Tribute to Freud*, p. 176

p. 390 *wonder-making* H.D. to Bryher, 23 March 1933, quoted in Friedman, *Psyche Reborn*, p. 132

p. 391 *so very masculine* H.D., *Tribute to Freud*, pp. 145–6

p. 391 *so is love* H.D., *Tribute to Freud*, p. 194

p. 391 *'biologically' happy* H.D., *Tribute to Freud*, p. 152

p. 391 *not always right* H.D., *Tribute to Freud*, p. 101

p. 392 *it isn't always* Quoted in Friedman, *Psyche Reborn*, p. 167

p. 392 *till day-break* Cited by Friedman, *Psyche Reborn*, p. 121. In a letter (H.D. to Bryer, 1 November 1935), H.D. also says she did not want her analysis spoiled by being made public, so she had refused to allow the poem to be published by Robert Herring in *Life and Letters Today* (Friedman, *Psyche Reborn*, p. 303 n. 45).

p. 392 *watch over you* *FM*, H.D. to Freud, 6 May 1939

p. 393 *humanity so much* Bryher, *The Heart to Artemis*, p. 246

p. 393 *spiritualist work* Friedman, *Psyche Reborn*, p. 175

14: Freud's Femininity: Theoretical Investigations pp. 397–429

p. 397 *of course defenceless* 'Femininity', *SE* XXII, p. 132

p. 398 *patients themselves do* *Studies on Hysteria, SE* II, p. 260

p. 398 *the female sex* 'Hysteria', *SE* I, p. 51

p. 398 *the marriage bed* *Studies on Hysteria, SE* II, p. 246

p. 398 *their husbands' neuroses* Assoun, *Freud et la femme*, pp. 101–3

p. 398 *women workers without* Bernheimer, 'Introduction: Part One', in Bernheimer and Kahane, *In Dora's Case*, p. 13

p. 399 *these scenes flourish* Assoun, *Freud et la femme*, p. 182

p. 399 *sick, hypocrites nowadays* 'Sexuality in the Aetiology of the Neuroses', *SE* III, p. 266

p. 399 *Ida Bauer*) Assoun, *Freud et la femme*, p. 182

p. 399 *a passive nature* *FF*, 1 January 1896, p. 169

p. 399 *one in girls* *FF*, 1 January 1896, p. 164

p. 399 *inclined to hysteria* *FF*, 1 January 1896, p. 169

p. 399 *repudiated perversion* *FF*, 6 December 1896, p. 212

p. 399 *away in disgust* *FF*, 14 November 1897, p. 280

p. 399 *the feminine one* *FF*, 14 November 1897, p. 281

p. 399 *for rejecting it* 'A Child Is Being Beaten', *SE* XVII, pp. 200–2

p. 400 *by reflex action* *FF*, 14 November 1897, pp. 280–1

p. 400 *female cycles* *FF*, 6 December 1896, p. 212; see Sulloway, *Freud*, on the development of Fliess's theories and their impact on Freud

p. 401 *understanding of sexuality* *Three Essays, SE* VII, pp. 147–8

p. 401 *feminine really mean* See Kofman, *The Enigma of Woman*, p. 123, who uses the term 'keeps us from simply *deciding*' where we use the term 'postponing'.

p. 401 *individuals are involved* *FF*, 1 August 1899, p. 364

p. 401 *the contrary meaning* 'Hysterical Phantasies in their Relation to Bisexuality', *SE* IX, pp. 165–6

p. 401 *sexual attraction proceeds* *Three Essays, SE* VII, p. 135

p. 401 *instinct tends* *Three Essays, SE* VII, p. 136

p. 401 *its object's attractions* *Three Essays, SE* VII, p. 148

p. 401 *the most prominent* *Three Essays, SE* VII, p. 162

p. 402 *the digestive tract* *Three Essays, SE* VII, p. 150

p. 402 *overriding this disgust* *Three Essays, SE* VII, p. 152

p. 402 *in the perversions* *Three Essays, SE* VII, p. 162

p. 402 *one unified act* Mitchell, *Psychoanalysis and Feminism*, p. 17; Davidson, 'How To Do the History of Psychoanalysis'

p. 402 *a chemical nature* *Three Essays, SE* VII, p. 144 n. 1 (actually at foot of p. 146)

p. 402 *negative of perversions* *Three Essays, SE* VII, p. 165

p. 403 *shaping of human life* *Three Essays, SE* VII, p. 219

p. 403 *topic, in 1932* 'Femininity', *SE* XXII, p. 117

p. 403 *or a woman* *Three Essays, SE* VII, p. 219

p. 403 *own sexual processes* *Three Essays, SE* VII, p. 220

p. 403 *new leading zone* *Three Essays, SE* VII, p. 221

p. 403 *essence of femininity* *Three Essays, SE* VII, p. 221

p. 404 *in other zones* *Three Essays, SE* VII, p. 221

p. 404 *relation of love* *Three Essays, SE* VII, p. 222

p. 404 *in later life* *Three Essays, SE* VII, p. 182

p. 404 *complete sexual object* *Three Essays, SE* VII, p. 223

p. 404 *of sexual love* *Three Essays SE* VII, p. 224

p. 404 *towards her father* *Three Essays, SE* VII, p. 227

p. 405 *in the unconscious* *Leonardo, SE* XI, pp. 115–17

p. 405 *to sexual satisfaction* *The Interpretation of Dreams, SE* IV, p. 257

p. 405 *females for himself* *Totem and Taboo, SE* XIII, p. 141

p. 406 *facts of life* For instance, Horney wrote in 1933: '[rape] fantasies, dreams and anxiety of this type usually betray quite unmistakably an instinctive knowledge of the actual

sexual processes.' ('The Denial of the Vagina', *Feminine Psychology*, p. 154; all references
to Horney's papers are to this edition)

p. 406 *into sexual problems* 'The Sexual Theories of Children', *SE* IX, pp. 211–12

p. 406 *of a penis* 'The Sexual Theories of Children', *SE* IX, p. 215

p. 406 *themselves unfairly treated* 'The Sexual Theories of Children' *SE* IX, p. 218

p. 406 *for the girl* Laplanche, *Problématiques II*, p. 81

p. 407 *birth to children* 'The Sexual Theories of Children', *SE* IX, p. 219

p. 407 *of the parts* See 'Wolfman', *SE* XVII, pp. 36–44; also 'Psychical Consequences', *SE* XIX, p. 250

p. 407 *with the father* Assoun, *Freud et la femme*, p. 155

p. 407 *on the mother* 'Special Type of Object-Choice Made by Men', *SE* XI, p. 169

p. 408 *an incestuous one* 'Universal Tendency to Debasement', *SE* XI, p. 186

p. 408 *their sexual object* 'Universal Tendency to Debasement', *SE* XI, p. 186

p. 408 *of orgasmic pretense* Masters and Johnson, *Human Sexual Response*, p. 137

p. 409 *eventually be traced* Forrester, *Language and the Origins of Psychoanalysis*, pp. 84–95

p. 409 *between the sexes* Mitchell, 'Introduction – I', p. 10

p. 409 *heterosexual attraction* Mitchell, 'Introduction – I', p. 10

p. 409 *mother loved them* *Three Essays*, *SE* VII, p. 145 n. 1 (added 1910)

p. 410 *its former nature* 'On Narcissism', *SE* XIV, p. 91

p. 411 *who nurses him* 'On Narcissism', *SE* XIV, p. 88

p. 411 *themselves once possessed* 'On Narcissism', *SE* XIV, pp. 88–90

p. 411 *of object choice* 'Instincts and their Vicissitudes', *SE* XIV, pp. 128ff.

p. 411 *this very narcissism* Kofman, *The Enigma of Woman*, p. 57

p. 411 *once loved himself* Kofman, *The Enigma of Woman*, p. 58

p. 411 *gift = baby* 'On Transformations of Instinct as Exemplified in Anal Erotism', *SE* XVII, pp. 129–30

p. 412 *pure sexual form* 'The Economic Problem of Masochism', *SE* XIX, pp. 163–4

p. 412 *to a baby* 'The Economic Problem of Masochism', *SE* XIX, p. 162

p. 412 *passive narcissism* 'The Dissolution of the Oedipus Complex', *SE* XIX, p. 176

p. 413 *later adult sexuality* 'The Infantile Genital Organization', *SE* XIX, p. 142

p. 413 *opposition active-passive* 'The Infantile Genital Organization', *SE* XIX, p. 145

p. 413 *loss of love* 'The Dissolution of the Oedipus Complex', *SE* XIX, p. 178

p. 413 *is never fulfilled* 'The Dissolution of the Oedipus Complex', *SE* XIX, pp. 178–9

p. 413 *catastrophic downfall* The word '*Untergang*', translated by Strachey as 'dissolution', is also
to be found in the title of a very influential German-language work of this period,
Spengler's *The Decline [Untergang] of the West*.

p. 414 *the object's love* *Inhibitions, Symptoms and Anxiety*, *SE* XX, pp. 142–3

p. 414 *certainly not that* Mitchell, 'Introduction – I', pp. 18–19

p. 414 *nevertheless be different* 'Psychical Consequences', *SE* XIX, p. 249

p. 414 *as an object?* 'Psychical Consequences', *SE* XIX, p. 251

p. 414 *child by him* 'Psychical Consequences', *SE* XIX, p. 251

p. 415 *to have it* 'Psychical Consequences', *SE* XIX, p. 252

p. 415 *were a man* 'Psychical Consequences', *SE* XIX, p. 253

p. 415 *than of men* 'Psychical Consequences', *SE* XIX, p. 254

p. 415 *lack of a penis* 'Psychical Consequences', *SE* XIX, p. 254

p. 415 *her of a penis* See Young-Bruehl, *Freud on Women*, 'Introduction', pp. 31 ff., for an
argument that emphasizes the importance of 'A Child Is Being Beaten' in the
development of Freud's views

p. 415 *than of men* 'Psychical Consequences', *SE* XIX, p. 255

p. 415 *development of femininity* 'Psychical Consequences', *SE* XIX, p. 255

p. 415 *her penis-envy* 'Psychical Consequences', *SE* XIX, p. 256

p. 415 *a little woman* 'Psychical Consequences', *SE* XIX, p. 256; emphasis in original

p. 415 *hope of revenge* As we have seen, Freud's 'The Psychogenesis of a Case of Homosexuality
in a Woman' had included many of the elements of this new account of femininity,
but these elements were being considerably reshuffled. The female homosexual retired

in favour of her *mother*, not the little boy, and she hoped for revenge on her *father*, not on her *mother*, for depriving her of the partial object.

p. 416 *suitable mother-substitute* 'Female Sexuality', *SE* XXI, p. 226
p. 416 *with their father* 'Psychical Consequences', *SE* XIX, p. 251
p. 416 *with their mother* 'Female Sexuality', *SE* XXI, p. 231
p. 417 *were built up* 'Mourning and Melancholia', *SE* XIV, p. 249; *The Ego and the Id*, *SE* XIX, pp. 28–9
p. 417 *object (the mother)* *The Ego and the Id*, *SE* XIX, p. 30
p. 417 *of her mourning* Assoun, *Freud et la femme*, p. 147
p. 417 *then forbade it* 'Female Sexuality', *SE* XXI, p. 234
p. 417 *was so intense* 'Female Sexuality', *SE* XXI, p. 234
p. 417 *occasions for aggression* 'Female Sexuality', *SE* XXI, p. 234
p. 417 *to their mother* 'Femininity', *SE* XXII, p. 124
p. 417 *it once again* Kofman, *The Enigma of Woman*, pp. 167–9
p. 418 *at a disadvantage* 'Femininity', *SE* XXII, p. 124
p. 418 *accompanied by hostility* 'Femininity', *SE* XXII, p. 121; the importance to Freud of this point, since his major problem was to explain the turning away from the mother, can be gauged from him singling out Jeanne Lampl de Groot, his faithful analysand, follower and friend, for criticism because she had not mentioned this hostility (see 'Female Sexuality', *SE* XXI, p. 241).
p. 418 *all through life* 'Femininity', *SE* XXII, p. 121
p. 418 *phallic father instead* Assoun, *Freud et la femme*, p. 120
p. 418 *has been denied* *An Outline of Psycho-analysis*, *SE* XXIII, p. 193
p. 418 *boy and mother* Rosen, 'Hélène Deutsch', p. 45
p. 418 *the new baby* 'Female Sexuality', *SE* XXI, p. 239
p. 418 *the little man* 'Femininity', *SE* XXII, p. 118; see Chasseguet-Smirgel, 'Introduction', in her collection, *Female Sexuality*, pp. 4–5
p. 418 *disavowing it* 'Fetishism', *SE* XXI, pp. 153–6
p. 418 *attain a woman* Assoun, *Freud et la femme*, pp. 156–7
p. 419 *female sexual function* 'On Transformations of Instinct as Exemplified in Anal Erotism', *SE* XVII, pp. 129–30
p. 419 *mother to him* 'Femininity', *SE* XXII, pp. 133–4
p. 419 *and women inhabit* Kofman, *The Enigma of Woman*, p. 134
p. 420 *with unhesitating certainty* 'Femininity', *SE* XXII, p. 113
p. 420 *a biological sense* *Three Essays*, *SE* VII, p. 219 n. 1
p. 420 *stronger object-cathexes* 'Femininity', *SE* XXII, p. 117
p. 420 *can be disregarded* 'Femininity', *SE* XXII, p. 117
p. 421 *be in men* 'Psychical Consequences', *SE* XIX, p. 257
p. 421 *average feminine character* 'Femininity', *SE* XXII, p. 129
p. 422 *wife in maturity* *Letters*, Freud to Martha, 15 November 1883, pp. 90–1
p. 422 *of the market* Assoun, *Freud et la femme*, p. 174
p. 423 *to have abortions* Timms, 'The "Child-Woman"', p. 88
p. 423 *lag behind men* *Minutes I*, 15 May 1907, p. 199 (response to Wittels on 'Female Physicians')
p. 423 *of sexual life* *Civilization and its Discontents*, *SE* XXI, pp. 103–4
p. 423 *outside these organizations* *Group Psychology and the Analysis of the Ego*, *SE* XVIII, p. 141
p. 423 *interests of humanity* 'Schreber', *SE* XII, p. 61
p. 423 *attitude towards it* *Civilization and its Discontents*, *SE* XXI, pp. 103–4
p. 424 *interests of mankind* '"Civilized" Sexual Morality', *SE* IX, p. 195
p. 424 *pressures of Thanatos* Assoun, *Freud et la femme*, p. 193
p. 424 *death instinct* *The Ego and the Id*, *SE* XIX, p. 53
p. 424 *animal kingdom* *Civilization and its Discontents*, *SE* XXI, p. 106n
p. 425 *penis-envying girl* Kofman, *The Enigma of Woman*, pp. 185, 209; 'Femininity', *SE* XXII, p. 127
p. 425 *activity directed inward* Deutsch, *The Psychology of Women*, I, p. 141
p. 425 *birth to a baby* 'The Economic Problem of Masochism', *SE* XIX, p. 162; one should

not underestimate the importance for Deutsch's work of this conception of passivity as constituted by the characteristically female acts of being castrated, being raped and giving birth (see 'The Significance of Masochism in the Mental Life of Women' [1930]).

p. 425 *wholly masculine character* Three Essays, SE VII, p. 219

p. 425 *functions at all* Laqueur, Making Sex, p. 240

p. 425 *of an anaesthetic* Laqueur, Making Sex, p. 237; Kinsey, Female, p. 580; Beauvoir, The Second Sex, p. 394

p. 426 *feminine vagina* 'Femininity', SE XXII, p. 118

p. 426 *aptly put it* Three Essays, SE VII, p. 187n (added 1920); see also 'The Disposition to Obsessional Neurosis', SE XII, p. 322, and Three Essays, SE VII, p. 198 (added 1915)

p. 426 *Deutsch in 1924* Deutsch, 'The Psychology of Women in Relation to the Function of Reproduction'

p. 426 *Jones in 1927* Jones, 'Early Development of Female Sexuality', p. 443

p. 426 *Klein in 1928* Klein, 'The Early Stages', pp. 192–3

p. 426 *normal hysteric* Laqueur, Making Sex, pp. 242–3

p. 426 *to the vagina* 'Femininity', SE XXII, p. 118

p. 427 *passive instinctual impulses* 'Femininity', SE XXII, p. 128

p. 427 *ground for femininity* 'Femininity', SE XXII, p. 128

p. 427 *a feminine one* 'Femininity', SE XXII, p. 129

p. 427 *of her love* 'Homosexuality in a Woman', SE XVIII, pp. 157–8

p. 427 *towards that object* 'Homosexuality in a Woman', SE XVIII, p. 154

p. 428 *possesses a penis* 'Analysis Terminable and Interminable', SE XXIII, p. 251

p. 428 *best possible fruition* Kofman, The Enigma of Woman, pp. 193–4; see also Bowlby, 'Still Crazy After All These Years', p. 49

p. 428 *riddle of sex* 'Analysis Terminable and Interminable', SE XXIII, p. 252

p. 428 *what femininity is* Bowlby, 'Still Crazy After All These Years', p. 49. Cf. also Granoff, La pensée et le féminin

p. 428 *his life's work* His recognition of the importance of Adler's concept of 'masculine protest', despite his dispute about the usefulness of the term, is also perhaps a way of finally settling his accounts with his ex-disciple, who had died a few months earlier; see J III, pp. 222–3

p. 428 *castration anxiety* 'Analysis Terminable and Interminable', SE XXIII, p. 252 n. 1

p. 429 *sexual activities* 'On the History of the Psycho-analytic Movement', SE XIV, pp. 54–5

15: The Dispute Over Woman pp. 430–54

p. 430 *never resolved* Cf. Gay, p. 515

p. 431 *born or made* Jones, 'Early Female Sexuality', p. 495

p. 431 *such an observation* 'Femininity', SE XXII, pp. 115–16

p. 431 *Freud's positions clearly* Mitchell, Psychoanalysis and Feminism, pp. 130–1; Mitchell, 'Introduction – I', p. 1; see Gallop, 'Moving Backwards or Forwards', p. 35

p. 431 *anatomy and physiology* LC, B15, dated 21 July 1935, Wien XIX Strasserg. 47; no German original, only typescript translation; for alternative translation see Psychiatry 34 1971, p. 329, reprinted in Young-Bruehl, Freud on Women, pp. 340–1

p. 432 *and the physical* Three Essays, SE VII, p. 168

p. 432 *a male one* LC, B15, dated 21 July 1935, Wien XIX Strasserg. 47; no German original, only typescript translation; for alternative translation see Psychiatry 34 1971, p. 329, reprinted in Young-Bruehl, Freud on Women, pp. 340–1

p. 432 *feminine personality* Deutsch, The Psychology of Women, I, p. 226, also cited in Webster, 'Helene Deutsch', p. 558

p. 432 *down to constitution* Letters, Freud to Else Voigtländer, 1 October 1911, pp. 292–4; see Forrester, The Seductions of Psychoanalysis, pp. 205 ff. and notes

p. 434 *and onanism* Horney, 'The Flight from Womanhood', p. 63

p. 434 *penis-envy stage* Jones, 'Early Development of Female Sexuality', p. 444

p. 434 *biological science* Horney, 'On the Genesis of the Castration Complex', p. 38

p. 434 *processes in children* Horney, 'On the Genesis of the Castration Complex', p. 39

p. 434 *female development*   Horney, 'On the Genesis of the Castration Complex', p. 42

p. 434 *of the child*   Horney, 'On the Genesis of the Castration Complex', p. 47

p. 434 *castration complex*   Horney, 'On the Genesis of the Castration Complex', p. 51

p. 434 *to the father*   Horney, 'On the Genesis of the Castration Complex', p. 49

p. 435 *sexual differences*   Mitchell, 'Introduction – I', pp. 22–3

p. 435 *vagina denied*   Horney, 'The Denial of the Vagina', p. 160; see also Zanardi, *Essential Papers*, p. 16

p. 435 *of its existence*   Horney, 'The Denial of the Vagina', p. 160

p. 435 *feminine wishes*   Horney, 'The Flight from Womanhood', p. 66

p. 435 *herself inadequate*   Horney, 'The Flight from Womanhood', p. 67

p. 435 *attraction of the sexes*   Horney, 'The Flight from Womanhood', p. 68

p. 436 *the father occur*   Horney, 'The Flight from Womanhood', p. 68

p. 436 *into sexual life*   'Female Sexuality', *SE* XXI, p. 238

p. 437 *breasts and suckling*   Horney, 'The Flight from Womanhood', pp. 60–1

p. 437 *of the girl*   Horney, 'The Flight from Womanhood', p. 57; see Gay, p. 520; for an extended argument following Horney's approach, see Heath, 'Difference'

p. 437 *sexual constitution*   Jones, 'The Phallic Phase', p. 472; Horney and Jones both use this reading of Freud's theory of children's sexual theories to imply that the sexual interests of analysts may be at stake in the debate on femininity.

p. 437 *Horney was claiming*   At times; her arguments are wayward on this point.

p. 437 *to no decision*   'Female Sexuality', *SE* XXI, p. 230 and n. 1

p. 437 *Vienna's Helene Deutsch*   Quinn, *A Mind of her Own*, pp. 196 ff.; Sayers, *Mothering Psychoanalysis*, pp. 88 ff.

p. 438 *function of reproduction*   Horney, 'The Flight from Womanhood', p. 59

p. 438 *source of knowledge*   Deutsch, 'The Psychology of Women', *Reader*, p. 166

p. 438 *the vagina*   Deutsch, 'The Psychology of Women', *Reader*, p. 167

p. 438 *developmental sequence*   Rosen, 'Hélène Deutsch', p. 48

p. 438 *function of suckling*   Deutsch, 'The Psychology of Women', *Reader*, p. 169

p. 438 *secretion and contraction*   Deutsch, ' The Psychology of Women', *Reader*, p. 169

p. 439 *for the girl*   Rosen, 'Hélène Deutsch', p. 50

p. 439 *become a woman*   Deutsch, 'The Psychology of Women', *Reader*, p. 171

p. 439 *beginning of parturition*   Deutsch, 'The Psychology of Women', *Reader*, pp. 171–2

p. 439 *are separated*   Deutsch, 'The Psychology of Women', *Reader*, p. 173. Note how Horney, having previously ridiculed the notion of parturition as the acme of sexual pleasure ('Review of Deutsch (1925)', *Int J Psa 7* 1926, pp. 92–100), managed to weave Deutsch's conception of parturition as part of the sexual act into her own account of the guilt-ridden primary fantasies of the girl: 'this [warding off of dangerous fantasies] would also throw a new light on the unconscious pleasurable feelings that, as various authors have maintained, occur at parturition, or alternatively, on the dread of childbirth. For (just because of the disproportion between the vagina and the baby and because of the pain to which this gives rise) parturition would be calculated to a far greater extent than subsequent sexual intercourse to stand to the unconscious for a realization of those early incest fantasies, a realization to which no guilt is attached.' (Horney, 'The Flight from Womanhood', p. 66)

p. 440 *becomes the penis*   Deutsch, 'The Psychology of Women', *Reader*, p. 178

p. 440 *at the beginning*   Deutsch, 'The Psychology of Women', *Reader*, p. 179

p. 440 *penis certifies that*   Rosen, 'Hélène Deutsch', pp. 55–6

p. 440 *mother-daughter relation*   Deutsch, 'On Female Homosexuality', *Reader*, p. 225; Rosen, 'Hélène Deutsch', pp. 51–2; Sayers, *Mothering Psychoanalysis*, pp. 52–3; see also Thompson and Webster

p. 441 *Deutsch's work*   See Zanardi, *Essential Papers*, pp. 15–16

p. 441 *passivity and masochism*   Deutsch, *The Psychology of Women*, I, p. x

p. 441 *lay analysis*   Jones, 'Discussion on Lay Analysis', pp. 185 ff.

p. 441 *child analysis*   Jones, 'Symposium on Child-Analysis', pp. 389–90

p. 442 *Horney and Klein*   Jones, 'The Phallic Phase', p. 468

p. 442 *into sexual problems* 'The Sexual Theories of Children', *SE* IX, pp. 211–12
p. 442 *he could penetrate* Jones, 'The Phallic Phase', p. 458
p. 442 *castration in men?* Jones, 'Early Development', p. 438
p. 442 *the object's love* Inhibitions, *Symptoms and Anxiety*, *SE* XX, pp. 142–3
p. 442 *same thing, aphanisis* Jones, 'Early Development', p. 440
p. 442 *created He them* Jones, 'The Phallic Phase', p. 484
p. 443 *female organ* Jones, 'Early Development', p. 443
p. 443 *penis of her own* Jones, 'Early Development', p. 444
p. 443 *que le roi* Jones, 'The Phallic Phase', p. 474
p. 443 *father's penis* Jones, 'The Phallic Phase', p. 480
p. 443 *Oedipus complex proper* Jones, 'The Phallic Phase', p. 463
p. 444 *true developmental stage* Jones, 'Early Development', pp. 450–1
p. 444 *of some importance* *FJ*, Jones to Freud, 10 January 1932
p. 444 *forgotten the father* *FJ*, Jones to Freud, 10 January 1932
p. 444 *you then indicated* *FJ*, Jones to Freud, 10 January 1932
p. 444 *my latest experiences* *FJ*, Freud to Jones, 23 January 1932
p. 445 *to be so* *FJ*, Freud to Jones, 23 January 1932
p. 445 *komplexbedingt* *FJ*, Jones to Freud, 12 February 1932
p. 445 *complex reaction* Jones, 'The Phallic Phase', pp. 465–6
p. 445 *penetrative impulses* Jones, 'The Phallic Phase', p. 462
p. 445 *sexual development* Jones, 'The Phallic Phase', p. 466
p. 445 *reach the vagina* Jones, ' The Phallic Phase', p. 466
p. 445 *of parental coitus* Jones, 'The Phallic Phase', p. 472
p. 446 *persists in them* Jones, 'The Phallic Phase', p. 479
p. 446 *child-bearing organs* Jones, 'The Phallic Phase', p. 479
p. 446 *outwards takes place* Jones, 'Early Female Sexuality', p. 489
p. 446 *their own genitals* Jones, 'The Phallic Phase', p. 482
p. 446 *have been damaged* Jones, 'The Phallic Phase', p. 476
p. 446 *in the mother* Jones, 'The Phallic Phase', p. 481
p. 446 *Controversial Discussions* Steiner, 'Some Thoughts about Tradition and Change'
p. 446 *into a child* Jones, 'Early Female Sexuality', pp. 491–2
p. 446 *reserve my judgement* *FJ*, Freud to Jones, 22 February 1928; see also Steiner, 'Some Thoughts about Tradition and Change', p. 36, and Gay, p. 501
p. 447 *an oral act* Klein, 'The Psychological Principles of Early Analysis', *Writings I*, p. 129 n. 1
p. 447 *the primal scene* Klein, 'The Psychological Principles of Early Analysis', *Writings I*, p. 138
p. 447 *in her mother* Jones, 'The Phallic Phase', p. 473
p. 447 *the adult woman* Jones, 'The Phallic Phase', p. 473
p. 447 *of her own* Jones, 'The Phallic Phase', pp. 473–4
p. 447 *phallocentric* Jones, 'Early Development', p. 438
p. 448 *born or made* Jones, 'Early Female Sexuality', p. 495
p. 448 *written 'Freudian'* Note the interestingly Freudian definition of feminist given by Lampl de Groot, 'Oedipus Complex', *Reader*, p. 187: 'she was pronounced feminist, denying the difference between man and woman; thus she had gone right back to the first, negative phase of the Oedipus complex.'
p. 448 *The Ego and the Id* The Ego and the Id, *SE* XIX, pp. 33–4
p. 448 *to her mother* 'Female Sexuality', *SE* XXI, p. 225
p. 448 *oedipus attitude* Lampl de Groot, 'Oedipus Complex', *Reader*, p. 186
p. 448 *clitoral onanism* Lampl de Groot, 'Oedipus Complex', *Reader*, p. 187
p. 449 *secondary formation* 'Psychical Consequences', *SE* XIX, p. 256
p. 449 *life of women* Lampl de Groot, 'Oedipus Complex', *Reader*, p. 190; see Mitchell,
p. 449 *Psychoanalysis and Feminism*, p. 129
p. 449 *herself be loved* Lampl de Groot, 'Oedipus Complex', *Reader*, p. 187
p. 449 *mother and child* Brunswick, 'Pre-Oedipal Phase', *Reader*, p. 232

p. 449 *a little boy* Brunswick, 'Pre-Oedipal Phase', *Reader*, p. 233; see 'Introduction', p. 24, in Chasseguet-Smirgel, *Female Sexuality*

p. 449 *of the boy* Brunswick, 'Pre-Oedipal Phase', *Reader*, p. 232

p. 450 *as its object* Brunswick, 'Pre-Oedipal Phase', *Reader*, pp. 235–6

p. 450 *nuclear passivity* Brunswick, 'Pre-Oedipal Phase', *Reader*, p. 251

p. 450 *phallic but omnipotent* 'Introduction', p. 25, in Chasseguet-Smirgel, *Female Sexuality*

p. 450 *to the mother* Brunswick, 'Pre-Oedipal Phase', *Reader*, p. 251

p. 450 *active mother* Brunswick, 'Pre-Oedipal Phase', *Reader*, p. 244

p. 450 *win the mother* Brunswick, 'Pre-Oedipal Phase', *Reader*, p. 245

p. 450 *extend considerably* Lacan, 'The Meaning of the Phallus'

p. 451 *man in coitus* Brunswick, 'Pre-Oedipal Phase', *Reader*, p. 245

p. 451 *with the man* Brunswick, 'Pre-Oedipal Phase', *Reader*, p. 250

p. 452 *fidelity to Freud* *Freud–Klein Controversies*

p. 452 *clearly it was* See 'Explanatory Notes', Klein, *Writings I*, p. 426

p. 452 *early identification* Klein, 'Early Stages', *Writings I*, p. 189

p. 452 *in the mother* Klein, 'Early Stages', *Writings I*, p. 190

p. 452 *mother alike* Klein, 'Early Stages', *Writings I*, p. 190

p. 453 *to her mother* 'Female Sexuality', *SE* XXI, p. 242

p. 453 *figure at all* See Laplanche and Pontalis, *The Language of Psycho-analysis*, p. 329

p. 453 *internal organs* Klein, 'Early Stages', *Writings I*, pp. 194–5

p. 453 *to the genital* Klein, 'Early Stages', *Writings I*, p. 192

p. 454 *to the 1970s* For a textbook version of object-relations theory as it was imported into the USA, see Greenberg and Mitchell, *Object Relations in Psychoanalytic Theory*; see also Hughes, *Reshaping the Psychoanalytic Domain*

p. 454 *to its mother* For a subtle study of the development of ideas about mothers and children and their place in society, and the place of psychoanalysis in this transformation, see Riley, *War in the Nursery*, esp. pp. 80–108

p. 454 *was introduced* Phillips, 'Playing Mothers', p. 3

p. 454 *understand psychoanalysis* Phillips, 'Playing Mothers', p. 5

16: Feminism and Psychoanalysis pp. 455–74

p. 455 *sexual politics* Millett, *Sexual Politics*, p. 178

p. 456 *volcanic ash* Friedan, *The Feminine Mystique*, pp. 114–15

p. 456 *is in men* 'Psychical Consequences', *SE* XIX, p. 257

p. 457 *mature, and normal* Lydon, 'The Politics of Orgasm', p. 199

p. 457 *female's pelvis* Masters and Johnson, *Human Sexual Response*, p. 60

p. 458 *power and prestige* Millett, *Sexual Politics*, pp. 180–3

p. 458 *male oppression model* Hartman and Banner, *Clio's Consciousness Raised*, p. vii

p. 458 *any political action* Riley, '*Am I that Name?*'

p. 459 *expunged without mercy* Rosalind Coward, 'Preface to the British Edition', in Snitow, Stansell and Thompson, *Desire*, pp. xiii–xiv

p. 459 *oppressive practices* See Vance, 'Epilogue', in Vance, *Pleasure and Danger*, pp. 431–9

p. 459 *modern society* Mitchell, *Women's Estate*, pp. 162 ff.

p. 460 *purports to cure* Firestone, *The Dialectic of Sex*, esp. pp. 43–4

p. 460 *unto the death* Bowlby, 'Still Crazy After All These Years', pp. 42–3

p. 460 *theory manqué* Rubin, 'The Traffic in Women', p. 185

p. 460 *social subordination* Rubin, 'The Traffic in Women', p. 157

p. 460 *human activity* Rubin, 'The Traffic in Women', p. 159; another important and influential contribution was Mulvey, 'Visual Pleasure and Narrative Cinema'

p. 460 *to neglect it* Mitchell, *Psychoanalysis and Feminism*, p. xv

p. 461 *her emotional life* Beauvoir, *The Second Sex*, p. 69

p. 461 *original femininity* See the sustained development of the relation between psychoanalysis and feminism in the journal *m/f*, articles from which are reprinted in Adams and Cowie, *The Woman in Question*

p. 461 *as a victim* Wood, 'The Fashionable Diseases'

p. 462 *relations to psychoanalysis*   Roudinesco, *Jacques Lacan & Co.*; Turkle, *Psychoanalytic Politics*; Wilden, *The Language of the Self*

p. 462 *rebuild the family*   Mitchell, *Psychoanalysis and Feminism*, pp. 227 ff.

p. 463 *and a premise*   *Moses and Monotheism*, *SE* XXIII, p. 114

p. 463 *symbolic order*   Lacan, *Séminaire IV*, p. 742; the most systematic account of the Lacanian revision of Freud's theory is Safouan, *La sexualité féminine*

p. 464 *in primary narcissism*   Kristeva, *Histoires d'amours*; see also Kristeva, 'Freud and Love'

p. 464 *to have it*   'Psychical Consequences', *SE* XIX, p. 252

p. 464 *on incestuous desires*   Mitchell, 'Introduction – I', p. 17

p. 464 *symbolic debt*   Lacan, *Séminaire IV*, p. 851

p. 464 *of psychic life*   Rose, 'Femininity and its Discontents', p. 91

p. 465 *violating penis*   Irigaray, 'This Sex Which Is Not One', in *This Sex Which Is Not One*, p. 24

p. 465 *relation to language*   See Irigaray, *Speculum*, and *This Sex Which Is Not One*

p. 465 *his prerogatives*   Irigaray, 'Psychoanalytic Theory: Another Look' (1973), in *This Sex Which Is Not One*, p. 67

p. 465 *interpretation itself*   Derrida, 'Le facteur de la vérité'

p. 465 *trivializing of women*   Heath, 'Difference'; Macey, *Lacan in Contexts*, Chapter 6 'The Dark Continent', pp. 177–209

p. 465 *is never secure*   Gallop, 'Writing Erratic Desire', in *Feminism and Psychoanalysis*, pp. 96–7; Gallop, 'Phallus/Penis: Same Difference', in *Thinking Through the Body*, pp. 124–33

p. 465 *enemies of feminism*   Gallop, 'Phallus/Penis: Same Difference', in *Thinking Through the Body*, p. 125

p. 466 *out of hand*   Chodorow, *Feminism and Psychoanalytic Theory*, p. 4. The plethora of collections and accounts of the relation between psychoanalysis and women bears out her point: see Alpert, *Psychoanalysis and Women*; Anzieu, *La femme sans qualité*; Brun, *La maternité et le féminin*; Feldstein and Roof, *Feminism and psychoanalysis*; Stimpson and Person, *Women: Sex and Sexuality*; Walsh, *The Psychology of Women*; Zanardi, *Essential Papers*.

p. 466 *new feminism*   Cf. Wilson, 'Psychoanalysis: Psychic Law and Order'; Sayers, 'Psychoanalysis and Personal Politics'; Rose, 'Sexuality and its Discontents'

p. 466 *absent-mindedly, provides*   Dinnerstein, *The Mermaid and the Minotaur*, p. xi

p. 466 *forever limited*   Chodorow, *Feminism and Psychoanalytic Theory*, p. 3

p. 466 *passivity and activity*   Chodorow, *The Reproduction of Mothering*, p. 158

p. 466 *different presences*   Chodorow, *The Reproduction of Mothering*, p. 157

p. 466 *division of labor*   Chodorow, *The Reproduction of Mothering*, p. 3

p. 466 *come to mother?*   Chodorow, *The Reproduction of Mothering*, p. 4

p. 466 *women in men*   Chodorow, *The Reproduction of Mothering*, pp. 218–19

p. 467 *drives and genitalia*   Chodorow, *The Reproduction of Mothering*, p. 157

p. 467 *am a female*   Stoller, 'The Sense of Femaleness', p. 54

p. 467 *they are females*   Stoller, 'The Sense of Femaleness', p. 48

p. 468 *preoedipal phenomenon*   Chodorow, *The Reproduction of Mothering*, p. 158

p. 468 *of both genders*   Chodorow, 'Gender, Relation and Difference', p. 111

p. 468 *male dominance*   Chodorow, *Feminism and Psychoanalytic Theory*, p. 6

p. 468 *be in men*   'Psychical Consequences', *SE* XIX, p. 257

p. 469 *justice of boys*   Gilligan, *In a Different Voice*

p. 469 *pre-Oedipal mother*   Gilligan, 'Remapping the Moral Domain', p. 483

p. 469 *finds maternal care*   Winnicott, 'The Theory of the Parent–Infant Relationship'

p. 469 *the dyadic trap*   Benjamin, Jessica, 'Interview', in Baruch and Serrano, *Women Analyze Women*, p. 322; see also Benjamin, *Bonds of Love*

p. 470 *universal battlefield*   Cixous, 'Sorties', in *The Newly Born Woman*, pp. 63–4

p. 471 *analysis of the patient*   Micale, 'Hysteria and its Historiography', p. 331

p. 472 *disciplinary project*   Felman, 'To Open the Question', pp. 3–7; cf. Feldstein and Sussman, *Psychoanalysis and...*

p. 472 *to be raped*   Brownmiller, *Against our Will*, p. 346; see Forrester, 'Rape, Seduction and Psychoanalysis', pp. 62–89

p. 472 *of such abuse*   Rush, 'Freud and the Sexual Abuse of Children'; *The Best Kept Secret*
p. 472 *seduction in childhood*   Masson, *The Assault on Truth*
p. 472 *therapy industry*   Miller, *The Drama of the Gifted Child*; *For Your Own Good*; *Du Sollst Nicht Merken*
p. 473 *maintenance of civilization*   *J* III, p. 484, Freud to Marie Bonaparte, 30 April 1932
p. 473 *not possible there*   Wortis, *Fragments of my Analysis*, p. 150
p. 474 *wife in maturity*   *Letters*, Freud to Martha, 15 November 1883, pp. 90–1
p. 474 *don't think so*   Segal, 'Interview', in Baruch and Serrano, *Women Analyze Women*, p. 249

The Summing Up pp. 475–92

p. 476 *Ferenczi and Freud*   See *The Correspondence of Sigmund Freud and Sándor Ferenczi, Volume 1, 1908–1914*, eds Eva Brabant, Ernst Falzeder and Patrizia Giampieri-Deutsch, trans. Peter T. Hoffer, with an introduction by André Haynal (Cambridge, Mass.: Belknap Press of Harvard University Press, 1994) and *The Correspondence of Sigmund Freud and Sándor Ferenczi, Volume 2, 1914–1919*, eds Ernst Falzeder and Eva Brabant, with the collaboration of Patrizia Giampieri-Deutsch, under the supervision of André Haynal, transcribed by Ingeborg Meyer-Palmedo, trans. Peter T. Hoffer, with an introduction by Axel Hoffer (Cambridge, Mass.: Belknap Press of Harvard University Press, 1996). On the quadrille, see John Forrester, 'Casualties of Truth' in Forrester, John, *Dispatches from the Freud Wars* (Cambridge, Mass. and London: Harvard University Press, 1997), pp. 44–106
p. 477 *countless lives*   Frederick Crews, 'The Unknown Freud', *New York Review of Books*, 18 November 1993, pp. 55–66, reprinted in Crews, Frederick and His Critics, *The Memory Wars: Freud's Legacy in Dispute* (New York: NYRev, Inc., 1995)
p. 477 *What does woman want?*   Undated letter to Marie Bonaparte, quoted *J* II (UK), p. 468/(US), p. 421. This is the only source for this much-quoted phrase
p. 478 *heart of analysis*   See John Forrester, 'Who is in Analysis with Whom?' in Forrester, *The Seductions of Psychoanalysis. Freud, Lacan and Derrida*, pp. 221–42, esp. p. 240
p. 479 *'tele-'*   Forrester, *The Seductions of Psychoanalysis. Freud, Lacan and Derrida*, pp. 235–7, and Jacques Derrida, 'Télépathie', *Cahiers Confrontation, 10*, Autumn 1983, pp. 201–30, reprinted in Derrida, Jacques, *Psyché. Inventions de l'autre* (Paris: Galilée, 1987), pp. 237–70
p. 479 *very many*   H.D., *Tribute to Freud*, pp. 146–7
p. 480 *as a category*   See the important new account of the place of hysteria in psychoanalytic and psychiatric thought in Juliet Mitchell, *Mad Men and Medusas* (London: Allen Lane, The Penguin Press, 2000)
p. 480 *psychiatric classification*   See *Diagnostic and Statistical Manual of Mental Disorders*, 3rd edn (Washington: American Psychiatric Association, 1987); useful accounts of this transformation can be found in Alan Young, *The Harmony of Illusions: An Ethnography of Post-Traumatic Stress Syndrome* (Princeton: Princeton University Press, 1994); S. Kirk and H. Kutchins, *The Selling of DSM: The Rhetoric of Science in Psychiatry* (New York: Aldine de Gruyter, 1992) and the excellent M. Wilson, 'DSM III and the Transformation of American Psychiatry: A History', *American Journal of Psychiatry, 150* (1993), pp. 399–410
p. 480 *companies have decided*   See, for example, Elaine Showalter, *Hystories: Hysterical Epidemics and Modern Culture* (London: Picador, 1997)
p. 480 *other modes*   Elisabeth Young-Bruehl, *Subject to Biography: Psychoanalysis, Feminism, and Writing Women's Lives* (Cambridge, Mass. and London: Harvard University Press, 1998), p. 209
p. 480 *personal puritanism*   Young-Bruehl, *Subject to Biography*, p. 210
p. 484 *really guilty*   'Psycho-analysis and the Establishment of the Facts in Legal Proceedings', *SE* IX, p. 113
p. 485 *female patients*   Judith Lewis Herman, *Trauma and Recovery: From Domestic Abuse to Political Terror* (London: HarperCollins, 1992), p. 14
p. 485 *outrage and humiliation*   Herman, *Trauma and Recovery*, p. 14
p. 485 *women's reality*   Herman, *Trauma and Recovery*, p. 14
p. 485 *life decisions*   Herman, *Trauma and Recovery*, p. 135
p. 485 *sense of justice*   Herman, *Trauma and Recovery*, p. 135

p. 486 *to the police*   Christopher Bollas and David Sundelson, *The New Informants: Betrayal of Confidentiality in Psychoanalysis and Psychotherapy* (London: Karnac, 1995)

p. 486 *dire consequences*   Bollas and Sundelson, *The New Informants*, p. 76

p. 486 *this restriction*   'On Beginning the Treatment', *SE* XII, p. 136n

p. 486 *any such regard*   'On Beginning the Treatment', *SE* XII, p. 136n

p. 487 *clinical psychology*   Mark Pendergrast, *Victims of Memory: Incest Accusations and Shattered Lives* (London: HarperCollins, 1996)

p. 487 *into their own hands*   See Rachel P. Maines, *The Technology of Orgasm: 'Hysteria,' The Sexual Vibrator and Women's Sexual Satisfaction* (Baltimore, MD: Johns Hopkins University Press, Studies in the History of Technology, 1998) and Bruno Latour, *Science in Action: How to Follow Scientists and Engineers Through Society* (Milton Keynes: Open University Press, 1987)

p. 488 *'genuine' love*   'Observations on Transference-Love', *SE* XII, p. 168

p. 488 *doing without it*   Interview with Adelbert Albrecht, *Boston Transcript*, 11 September 1909, reprinted in Ruitenbeek, *Freud As We Knew Him*, pp. 22–7, this passage from p. 23

p. 489 *normal people*   Joseph Weizenbaum, *Computer Power and Human Reason: From Judgement to Calculation* (1976; Harmondsworth: Penguin, 1984), p. 6

p. 490 *psychotherapist*   Sherry Turkle, *Life on the Screen: Identity in the Age of the Internet* (New York: Simon & Schuster, 1995), pp. 102–24, esp. p. 112

p. 490 *these problems*   Turkle, *Life on the Screen*, p. 113

p. 490 *to Eternity*   Shakespeare, Sonnet 77

p. 491 *several of them*   Turkle, *Life on the Screen*, p. 229

p. 491 *that disturbed*   Turkle, *Life on the Screen*, p. 230

p. 492 *wonder drug*   Peter D. Kramer, *Listening to Prozac* (1993; London: Fourth Estate, 1994), p. 265n, pp. 366–7

BIBLIOGRAPHY

Apart from primary sources, we are indebted to the major biographical studies of Freud by Jones, Schur, Clark and Gay, and to the fine historical work of Ellenberger, Fichtner, Hirschmüller and Swales. Amongst the wide range of more detailed studies of individuals, certain works have been particularly useful: Anzieu (Freud's self-analysis), Bertin (Bonaparte), Grosskurth (Klein), Livingstone and Pfeiffer (Andreas-Salomé), Roazen (Deutsch), Roudinesco (Bonaparte) and Young-Bruehl (Anna Freud). Of studies of the psychoanalytic debate on femininity, we found excellent the works by Mitchell, Kofman and Assoun.

Works are listed alphabetically by author's name; where a number of works by one author are cited, they are listed alphabetically by title.

Abraham, Karl, 'Manifestations of the Female Castration Complex', in *Selected Papers of Karl Abraham*, trans. Douglas Bryan and Alix Strachey (London: The Hogarth Press and the Institute of Psycho-analysis, 1927), pp. 338–69

Abraham, R., 'Freud's Mother Conflict and the Formulation of the Oedipal Father', *Psychoanalytic Review 69* 1982, pp. 441–53

Adams, Parveen, and Cowie, Elizabeth, *The Woman in Question* (London and New York: Verso, 1990)

Alpert, Judith (ed.), *Psychoanalysis and Women: Contemporary Reappraisals* (New York: Analytic Press, 1986)

Andersson, Ola, 'A supplement to Freud's Case History of "Frau Emmy v. N." in *Studies on Hysteria* 1895', *Scandinavian Psychoanalytic Review.2* 1979, pp. 5–15

Andreas-Salomé, Lou, *L'Amour du narcissisme*, trans. Isabelle Hildenbrand, with a preface by Marie Moscovici (Paris: Editions Gallimard, 1980)

'"Anal" und "Sexual"', *Imago 4* 1916, pp. 249–73

Die Erotik: Vier Aufsätze (1910); new edn with an appendix by Ernst Pfeiffer. (Munich: Matthes & Seitz, 1979)

Fenitschka. Eine Ausschweifung (Stuttgart, 1898)

The Freud Journal, trans. Stanley A. Leavy, with an introduction by Mary-Kay Wilmers (London: Quartet, 1987)

Henrik Ibsens Frauen-Gestalten nach seinen sechs Familiendramen, ed. and trans. as *Ibsen's Heroines*, with an introduction by Siegfried Mandel (Redding Ridge, Conn.: Black Swan Books, 1985)

Lebensrückblick, Grundriss einiger Lebenserinnerungen, ed. E. Pfeiffer (Zurich: Max Niemans Verlag and Wiesbaden: Insel-Verlag, 1951); trans. as *Ma Vie*, by D. Miermont and B. Vergne (Paris: PUF, 1977)

Ma. Ein Porträt (Stuttgart, 1901)

Mein Dank an Freud: Offener Brief an Professor Sigmund Freud zu seinem 75 Geburtstag (Vienna: Internationaler Psychoanalytische Verlag, 1931); trans. as *Lettre ouverte à Freud* by Dominique Miermont, with the collaboration of Anne Lagny and with a preface by Marie Moscovici (Paris: Lieu Commun, 1983)

'Narzissmus als Doppelrichtung [Narcissism as Dual Orientation]' *Imago 7* 1921, pp. 361–86

Ruth (Stuttgart, 1895)

'Zum Typus Weib', *Imago 3* 1914, pp. 1–14

Anzieu, Annie, *La femme sans qualité, Esquisse psychanalytique de la féminité* (Paris: Dunod, 1989)

Anzieu, Didier, *L'Auto-analyse de Freud.* (Paris: PUF, 1975); trans. as *Freud's Self-Analysis* by Peter Graham (London: The Hogarth Press and the Institute of Psycho-analysis, 1986)

Assoun, Paul-Laurent, *Freud et la femme* (Paris: Calmann-Levy, 1983)

Freud et Nietzsche (Paris: PUF, 1980)

Le pervers et la femme (Paris: PUF, 1990)

Balmary, Marie, *Psychoanalyzing Psychoanalysis: Freud and the Hidden Fault of the Father*, trans., with an introduction, by Ned Lukacher (Baltimore: Johns Hopkins University Press, 1982)

Baruch, E.H., and Serrano, L.J., *Women Analyze Women, in France, England and the United States* (New York and London: New York University Press, 1988)

Beauman, Nicola, *A Very Great Profession: The Woman's Novel, 1914–1939* (London: Virago, 1983)

Beauvoir, Simone de, *The Second Sex* (1949), trans. H.M. Parshley (London: Jonathan Cape, 1953; Harmondsworth, Middx: Penguin, 1972)

Benjamin, Jessica, *Bonds of Love: Psychoanalysis, Feminism and the Problem of Domination* (London: Virago, 1988)

Bernays, Anna Freud, 'My brother, Sigmund Freud', in Ruitenbeek, Hendrik M., *Freud As We Knew Him*, pp. 140–7

Bernfeld, Siegfried, 'Freud's Scientific Beginnings', *American Imago 6* 1949, pp. 163–96; reprinted in Ruitenbeek, Hendrik M., *Freud As We Knew Him*, pp. 222–48

Bernfeld, Suzanne Cassirer, 'Freud and Archaeology', *American Imago 8* 1951, pp. 107–28

Bernheimer, C., and Kahane, C. (eds), *In Dora's Case* (New York: Columbia University Press; London: Virago, 1985)

Berthelsen, Detlef, *Alltag bei Familie Freud. Die Erinnerungen der Paula Fichtl* (Hamburg: Hoffmann & Campe, 1987; revised edn, Munich: Deutscher Taschenbuch Verlag GMBH & Co., 1989)

Bertin, Celia, *Marie Bonaparte: A Life* (New York: Harcourt Brace Jovanovich, 1982; London, Melbourne, New York: Quartet, 1983)

La Femme à Vienne au temps de Freud (Paris: Editions Stock/Laurence Pernoud, 1989)

Bettelheim, Bruno, *Recollections and Reflections* (London: Thames & Hudson, 1990)

'Commentary', in *Secret Symmetry*, pp. xv–xxxix

Binion, Ralph, *Frau Lou: Nietzsche's Wayward Disciple* (Princeton: Princeton University Press, 1968)

Binswanger, Ludwig, *Sigmund Freud: Reminiscenses of a Friendship*, trans. Norbert Guteman (New York: Grune & Stratton, 1957)

'My First Three Visits with Freud in Vienna', in Ruitenbeek, Hendrik M., *Freud As We Knew Him*, pp. 360–8

Bleuler, Eugen, 'Die Ambivalenz', *Festgabe der med. Fakultät Zurich 3* 1914, pp. 93–106

'Vortrag über Ambivalenz', *Zentrallblatt für Psychoanalyse 1* 1910, p. 266

Bonaparte, Marie, *Cinq cahiers écrits par une petite fille entre sept ans et demi et dix ans et leur commentaire*, I (Paris, 1939); II (London, 1948); III & IV (London, 1951); trans. as *Five Copy-Books* by Nancy Procter-Gregg (London: Imago, 1950–3)

'Considérations sur les causes anatomiques de la frigidité chez la femme', *Journal Médicale de Bruxelles*, 27 April 1924, pp. 768–78 (written under the pseudonym A.E. Narjani)

'A Defence of Biography', *Int J Psa 20* 1939, pp. 231–40

'Les deux frigidités de la femme', *Bulletin de la Société de Sexologie 1* 1933 May 5, p. 8

Female Sexuality (New York: International Universities Press, 1953)

'L'identification d'une fille à sa mère morte', *Revue francaise psychanalyse 2* 1928, pp. 541–65

The Life and Works of Edgar Allan Poe: A Psychoanalytic Interpretation (London: Imago, 1949)

Myths of War, trans. J. Rodker (London: Imago, 1947)

'Notes on the Analytical Discovery of a Primal Scene', *Psychoanalytic Study of the Child 1* 1946, pp. 119–25

'Notes sur l'excision', *Revue francaise psychanalyse 12* 1948, pp. 213–31; trans. as 'Notes on Excision', *Psychoanalysis and the Social Sciences 2* 1950, pp. 67–84

'Passivity, Masochism and Femininity', *Int J Psa 16* 1935, pp. 325–33

Psychanalyse et biologie (Paris: PUF, 1952)

Boor, Clemens de, and Moersch, Emma, 'Emmy von N. – eine Hysterie?', *Psyche 34* 1980, pp. 265–79

Bottomore, Tom, and Goode, Patrick (eds), *Austro-Marxism* (Oxford: Clarendon Press, 1978)

Bourguignon, André (ed.), 'Correspondance Sigmund Freud–René Laforgue, Memorial d'une rencontre', *Nouvelle Revue de Psychanalyse No. 15: Mémoires*, Spring 1977, pp. 235–314

Bouttes, Jean-Louis, *Jung. La puissance d'une illusion* (Paris: Seuil, 1990)

Bowlby, Rachel, 'Still Crazy After All These Years', in Brennan, Teresa (ed.), *Between Feminism and Psychoanalysis*, pp. 40–59

Boyer, John W., 'Freud, Marriage and Late Viennese Liberalism: A Commentary from 1905', *Journal of Modern History 50* 1978, pp. 72–102

Brennan, Teresa (ed.), *Between Feminism and Psychoanalysis* (London: Routledge, 1989)

Breuer, Josef, and Freud, Sigmund, *Studien über Hysterie* (1895; Frankfurt: Fischer Taschenbuch, 1970; for English trans. see *SE* II)

Briehl, Marie H., 'Helene Deutsch', in Alexander, Franz, Eisenstein, Samuel, and Grotjahn, Martin (eds), *Psychoanalytic Pioneers* (New York: Basic Books, 1966), pp. 282–98

Brill, A.A., *Lectures on Psychoanalytic Psychiatry* (New York: Norton, 1938)

Brinker-Gabler, Gisela, *Zur Psychologie der Frau. Die Frau in der Gesellschaft: Frühe Texte* (Frankfurt: Fischer Taschenbuch, 1978)

Brome, Vincent, *Ernest Jones: Freud's Alter Ego* (London: Caliban, 1982)

Brownmiller, Susan, *Against Our Will: Men, Women and Rape* (New York: Simon & Schuster, 1975; Bantam, 1976)

Brun, Danièle, *La maternité et le féminin* (Paris: Denoel 'L'espace analytique', 1990)

Brunswick, Ruth Mack, 'The Analysis of a Case of Paranoia', *Journal of Nervous and Mental Diseases 70* 1929, pp. 1–22, 155–79

'The Pre-Oedipal Phase of the Libido Development' (1940); reprinted in *Reader*, pp. 231–52

'A Supplement to Freud's "History of an Infantile Neurosis"' (1928); reprinted in *Reader*, pp. 65–103, and also in Gardiner, Muriel, *The Wolfman by the Wolfman*, pp. 286–331

Bryher, Winifred, *The Heart to Artemis: A Writer's Memoirs.* (New York: Harcourt, Brace and World, 1962; London: Collins, 1963)

Buck, C., 'Freud and H.D. – Bisexuality and Feminine Discourse', *m/f 8* 1983, pp. 52–65

Buckley, N., *Women Psychoanalysts and the Theory of Feminine Development: A Study of Helene Deutsch, Karen Horney and Marie Bonaparte*, PhD dissertation (Ann Arbor: University of Michigan, 1982. Xerox Microfilms)

Burlingham, Dorothy, *Psychoanalytic Studies of the Sighted and the Blind* (New York: International Universities Press, 1972)

Burlingham, Michael John, *The Last Tiffany* (New York: Atheneum, 1989)

Caplan, Paula J., 'The Myth of Woman's Masochism', *The American Psychologist 39* 1984, pp. 130–9

Carotenuto, Aldo, *A Secret Symmetry: Sabina Spielrein between Jung and Freud* (1980; trans. Arno Pomerans, John Shepley and Krishna Winston, 1982; 2nd edn with additional material, London: Routledge & Kegan Paul, 1984)

Tagebuch einer heimlichen Symmetrie. Sabina Spielrein zwischen Jung und Freud (Freiburg i.B.: Kore, 1986)

Carter, Robert Brudenell, *On the Pathology and Treatment of Hysteria*, (London: John Churchill, 1853; reprint, W. F. Bynum [ed.], London: Routledge & Kegan Paul, forthcoming)

Castoriadis, Cornelius, *Crossroads in the Labyrinth*, (Hassocks, Sussex: Harvester, 1984)

Channing, Walter, *Bed Case: Its History and Treatment* (Boston: Ticknor and Fields, 1860)

Chasseguet-Smirgel, J. (ed.), *Female Sexuality: New Psychoanalytic Views* (1964; Ann Arbor: University of Michigan Press, 1970)

Chodorow, Nancy, *Feminism and Psychoanalytic Theory* (Cambridge: Polity, 1989)

'Gender, Relation and Difference in Psychoanalytic Perspective', in Chodorow, *Feminism and Psychoanalytic Theory*, pp. 99–113

'Psychoanalyse und Psychoanalytikerinnen. Der Beitrag der Frauen zur psychoanalytischen Bewegung und Theorie', *Psyche 41* 1987, pp. 800–31

The Reproduction of Mothering (Berkeley: University of California Press, 1978)

'Seventies Questions for Thirties Women: Gender and Generation in a Study of Early Women Psychoanalysts', in Chodorow, *Feminism and Psychoanalytic Theory*, pp. 199–218

'Varieties of Leadership among Early Women Psychoanalysts', in Dickstein, Leah, and Nadelson, Carol (eds), *Women Physicians in Leadership Roles* (New York: American Psychiatric Press, 1986), pp. 47–54

Choisy, Maryse, *Sigmund Freud: A New Appraisal* (London: Peter Owen, 1963)

Cifali, Mireille, 'Entre Genève et Paris: Vienne', *Le Bloc-Notes de la Psychanalyse No. 2* 1982, pp. 91–130

'Théodore Flournoy, la découverte de l'inconscient', *Le Bloc-Notes de la Psychanalyse No. 3* 1983, pp. 111–31

'Le fameux couteau de Lichtenberg', *Le Bloc-Notes de la Psychanalyse No. 4* 1984, pp. 171–90 ·

'Charles Bally et les psychanalystes', *Le Bloc-Notes de la Psychanalyse No. 6* 1986, pp. 131–53

'Une femme dans la psychanalyse. Sabina Spielrein, un autre portrait', *Le Bloc-Notes de la Psychanalyse No. 8* 1988, pp. 253–65

Cixous, Hélène, and Clement, Cathérine, *La jeune née*, (Paris: Editions 10/18, 1975); trans. as *The Newly Born Woman* by Betsy Wing, with a foreword by Sandra M. Gilbert, Theory and History of Literature, vol. 24 (Minneapolis: University of Minnesota Press; Manchester: Manchester University Press, 1986)

Clark, Ronald W., *Freud: The Man and the Cause* (London: Jonathan Cape/Weidenfeld & Nicolson, 1980)

Coleman, Elizabeth, 'From "Dear Lou" to "Code Name Mary": A Glorious Tradition', October 1985, paper deposited at Freud Museum, London

Cottet, Serge, *Freud et le désir du psychanalyste* (Paris: Navarin, 1982)

Davidson, Arnold I., 'How To Do the History of Psychoanalysis: A Reading of Freud's *Three Essays on the Theory of Sexuality*', in Meltzer, Françoise (ed.), *The Trial(s) of Psychoanalysis*. (Chicago and London: Chicago University Press, 1988), pp. 39–64

Davis, F.B., 'Three letters from Sigmund Freud to André Breton', *Journal of the American Psychoanalytical Association 21* 1973, pp. 127–34

Decker, Hannah S., 'Freud and Dora: Constraints on Medical Progress', *Journal of Social History 14* 1981, pp. 445–64

Freud, Dora, and Vienna 1900 (New York: Free Press, 1991)

Derrida, Jacques, 'Le facteur de la vérité', in Derrida Jacques, *La Carte Postale* (Paris: Flammarion, 1980), pp. 441–524; trans. *The Post Card: From Socrates to Freud and Beyond* by Alan Bass (Chicago: Chicago University Press, 1987), pp. 411–96

'Spéculer – sur Freud', in Derrida, *La Carte Postale* (Paris: Flammarion, 1980), pp. 277–437; trans. *The Post Card: From Socrates to Freud and Beyond* by Alan Bass (Chicago: Chicago University Press, 1987), pp. 257–409

Deutsch, Felix, 'A Footnote to Freud's "Fragment of an Analysis of a Case of Hysteria"', *Psychoanalytic Quarterly 26* 1957, pp. 159–67; reprinted in Bernheimer, C., and Kahane, C. (eds), *In Dora's Case*, pp. 35–43

Deutsch, Helene, *Confrontations with Myself* (New York: Norton, 1973)

'On Female Homosexuality' (1932); reprinted in *Reader*

Neuroses and Character Types (New York: International Universities Press, 1965)

'On the Pathological Lie' (1921); reprinted in *Journal of the American Academy of Psychoanalysis 10* 1982, pp. 369–86

Psychoanalyse der weibliche Sexualfunktionen (Vienna: Internationaler Psychoanalytische Verlag, 1925); ed. and trans. as *Psychoanalysis of the Female Sexual Function* by Paul Roazen (London: Karnac, 1991)

'The Psychology of Women in Relation to the Function of Reproduction', *Int J Psa 6* 1925, pp. 405–18; reprinted in *Reader*

The Psychology of Women, 2 vols (London: Research Press, 1946)

'The Significance of Masochism in the Mental Life of Women (Part I: "Feminine" Masochism and its Relation to Frigidity)', *Int J Psa 11* 1930, pp. 48–61

The Therapeutic Process, the Self, and Female Psychology: Collected Psychoanalytic Papers, ed. with an introduction by Paul Roazen (New Brunswick and London: Transaction, 1992)

Didi-Huberman, Georges, *Invention de l'hystérie. Charcot et l'iconographie photographique de la Salpêtrière* (Paris: Editions Macula, 1982)

Dinnerstein, Dorothy, *The Mermaid and the Minotaur: Sexual Arrangements and Human Malaise* (New York: Harper & Row, 1976)

Drinnon, Richard and Anna Maria (eds), *Nowhere at Home: Letters from Exile of Emma Goldman and Alexander Berkman* (New York: Schocken, 1975)

Duplessis, Rachel Blau, *H.D.: The Career of that Struggle* (Bloomington, IN.: Indiana University Press, 1986)

Edinger, Dora, *Bertha Pappenheim – Freud's Anna O.* (Highland Park, Ill.: Congregation Solel, 1968)

Bertha Pappenheim: Leben und Schriften (Frankfurt: Ner Tamid, 1963)

Eissler, K.R., 'Creativity and Adolescence: The Effect of Trauma on Freud's Adolescence', *The Psychoanalytic Study of the Child 33* 1978, pp. 461–517

'A Possible Endangerment of Psychoanalysis in the United States', *International Review of Psycho-Analysis 6* 1979, pp. 15–21

Ellenberger, Henri F., *The Discovery of the Unconscious: The History and Evolution of Dynamic Psychiatry* (London: Allen Lane, 1970)

'L'histoire d'"Emmy von N."', *L'Evolution psychiatrique 42* 1977, pp. 519–40

'La psychiatrie et son histoire inconnue', *L'Union Médicale du Canada 90* 1961, pp. 281–9

'The Story of "Anna O.": A Critical Review with New Data', *Journal of the History of the Behavioral Sciences 8* 1972, pp. 267–79

'The Story of Helene Preiswerk: A Critical Study with New Documents', *History of Psychiatry 2* 1991, pp. 41–52

Elms, Alan C., 'Freud, Irma, Martha: Sex and Marriage in the "Dream of Irma's Injection"', *Psychoanalytic Review 67* 1980, pp. 83–109

Elster, Jon, *Solomonic Judgements: Studies in the Limitations of Rationality* (Cambridge: CUP, 1989)

Feldstein, R., and Roof, J. (eds), *Feminism and Psychoanalysis* (Ithaca, NY: Cornell University Press, 1989)

and Sussman, H. (eds), *Psychoanalysis and ...* (New York and London: Routledge, 1990)

Felman, Shoshana, 'To Open the Question', in Felman, Shoshana (ed.), *Yale French Studies Nos. 55/56; Literature and Psychoanalysis. The Question of Reading: Otherwise* (New Haven and London: Yale University Press, 1977), pp. 3–7

Ferenczi, Sándor, 'The Principle of Relaxation and Neocatharsis' (1929), in Ferenczi, *Final Contributions to the Problems and Methods of Psycho-analysis*, ed. Michael Balint, trans. Eric Mosbacher and others (London: The Hogarth Press and the Institute of Psycho-analysis, 1955); original German text: 'Relaxationsprinzip und Neokatharsis', in *Bausteine zur Psychoanalyse*, 2nd edn, vol. III (Bern: Hans Huber, 1964)

Fichtner, Gerhard, *Freuds Patienten* (Tübingen: Institut für Geschichte der Medizin, December 1979), mimeo. (*LC* B33)

and Hirschmüller, A., 'Freuds "Katharina" – Hintergrund, Entstehungsgeschichte und Bedeutung einer frühen psychoanalytischen Krankengeschichte', *Psyche 39* 1985, pp. 220–40

Firestone, Shulamith, *The Dialectic of Sex: The Case for Feminist Revolution* (New York: Bantam, 1970)

Fliess, Robert (ed.), *The Psycho-Analytic Reader* (London: The Hogarth Press, 1950)

Flournoy, Olivier, *Théodore et Léopold. De Théodore Flournoy à la psychanalyse. Suivi d'une correspondance entre Théodore Flournoy et Hélène Smith* (Neuchâtel: Editions de La Baconnière, 1986)

Forrester, John, *Language and the Origins of Psychoanalysis* (London: Macmillan; New York: Columbia University Press, 1980)

The Seductions of Psychoanalysis: Freud, Lacan and Derrida (Cambridge: CUP, 1990)

'Contracting the Disease of Love: Authority and Freedom in the Origins of Psychoanalysis', in Forrester, *The Seductions of Psychoanalysis*, pp. 30–47

'Rape, Seduction and Psychoanalysis', in Forrester, *The Seductions of Psychoanalysis*, pp. 62–89

'The True Story of Anna O.', in Forrester *The Seductions of Psychoanalysis*, pp. 17–29

'The Untold Pleasures of Psychoanalysis', in Forrester, *The Seductions of Psychoanalysis*, pp. 48–61

Foucault, Michel, 'Introduction', Ludwig Binswanger, *Le Rêve et l'Existence*, trans. Jacqueline Verdeaux (Paris: Desclée de Brouwer, 1954)

Madness and Civilization: A History of Insanity in the Age of Reason (London: Tavistock, 1965), an abridged translation of *Folie et déraison. Histoire de la folie à l'âge classique* (Paris: Plon, 1961)

Freeman, Lucy, *The Story of Anna O.* (New York: Walker, 1972)

and Strean, Herbert S., *Freud and Women* (New York: Frederick Ungar, 1981)

Freud, Anna, *The Writings of Anna Freud, Volumes I-VIII* (New York: International Universities Press, 1966–81)

'About Losing and Being Lost', in *Indications for Child Analysis and other Papers, 1945–56. Writings Vol. IV* (New York: International Universities Press, 1968), pp. 302–16

'Beating Fantasies and Daydreams' (1922), in *Introduction to Psychoanalysis. Lectures for Child Analysts and Teachers, 1922–35. Early writings. Writings Vol. I* (New York: International Universities Press, 1974)

The Ego and the Mechanisms of Defence. Writings Vol. II, revised edn (New York: International Universities Press, 1966)

Infants Without Families. Reports on the Hampstead Nurseries 1939–1945. Writings Vol. III (New York: International Universities Press, 1973)

The Psychoanalytic Treatment of Children, trans. Nancy Procter-Gregg (London: Imago, 1946)

'Tribute to Dorothy Burlingham', *Bulletin of the Hampstead Clinic 3* 1980, p. 76

Freud, Ernst, Freud, Lucie, and Grubrich-Simitis, Ilse (eds), *Sigmund Freud: His Life in Words and Pictures*, with a biographical sketch by K. R. Eissler, trans. Christine Trollope (London: André Deutsch, 1978)

Freud, Esti D., 'Mrs Sigmund Freud', *Jewish Spectator 45* 1980, pp. 29–31

Freud, Martin, *Glory Reflected* (London: Angus & Robertson, 1957)

'Who Was Freud?', in Fraenkel Josef, (ed.), *The Jews of Austria: Essays on their Life, History and Destruction* (London: Vallentine Mitchell, 1967), pp. 197–211

Freud, Sigmund, 'Address Delivered in the Goethe House at Frankfurt'. *SE* XXI

'Address to the Society of B'nai B'rith' (1926), *SE* XX

'Analysis Terminable and Interminable' (1937), *SE* XXIII

'An Autobiographical Study' (1925), *SE* XX

Beyond the Pleasure Principle (1920), *SE* XVIII

'A Case of Paranoia Running Counter to the Psycho-analytical Theory of the Disease' (1915), *SE* XIV

'A Case of Successful Treatment by Hypnotism' (1892–3), *SE* I

'Some Character Types Met with in Psychoanalytic Work' (1916), *SE* XIV

'A Child Is Being Beaten: A Contribution to the Study of the Origin of Sexual Perversion' (1919), *SE* XVII

'A Childhood Recollection from *Dichtung und Wahrheit*' (1917), *SE* XVII

Civilization and its Discontents (1930), *SE* XXI

'"Civilized" Sexual Morality and Modern Nervous Illness" (1908), *SE* IX

The Complete Letters of Sigmund Freud to Wilhelm Fliess: 1887–1904, ed. J. M. Masson (Cambridge, Mass.: Harvard University Press, 1984)

'Delusions and Dreams in Jensen's *Gradiva*' (1907), *SE*, IX

'The Disposition to Obsessional Neurosis' (1913), *SE* XII
'The Dissolution of the Oedipus Complex' (1924), *SE* XIX
'On Dreams' (1901), *SE* V
'The Economic Problem of Masochism' (1924), *SE* XIX
The Ego and the Id (1923), *SE* XIX
'Female Sexuality' (1931), *SE* XXI
'Femininity' (1932), *SE* XXII
'Fetishism' (1927), *SE* XXI
Five Lectures on Psycho-analysis (1910), *SE* XI
'A Fragment of the Analysis of a Case of Hysteria' (1905), *SE* VII
'From the History of an Infantile Neurosis' [Wolfman] (1918), *SE* XVII
'Further Remarks on the Neuro-Psychoses of Defence' (1896), *SE* III
'On the Grounds for Detaching a Particular Syndrome from Neurasthenia under the Description "Anxiety Neurosis"' (1895), *SE* III
Group Psychology and the Analysis of the Ego (1921), *SE* XVIII
'On the History of the Psychoanalytic Movement' (1914), *SE* XIV
'Hysteria' (1888), *SE* I
'Hysterical Phantasies in their Relation to Bisexuality' (1908), *SE* IX
Die infantile Cerebrallähmung, II Theil, II Abt. of Nothnagel's *Specielle Pathologie und Therapie 9* (Vienna, 1897)
'The Infantile Genital Organization' (1923), *SE* XIX
Inhibitions, Symptoms and Anxiety (1926), *SE* XX
'Instincts and their Vicissitudes' (1915), *SE* XIV
The Interpretation of Dreams (1900), *SE* IV & V
'Interview with Adelbert Albrecht', *Boston Transcript*, 11 September 1909; reprinted in Ruitenbeek, Hendrik M., *Freud As We Knew Him*, pp. 22–7
Introductory Lectures on Psycho-analysis (1916–17), *SE* XV & XVI
Jokes and their Relation to the Unconscious (1905), *SE* VIII
'Zur Kenntniss der cerebralen Diplegien des Kindesalters (im Anschluss an die Little'sche Krankheit' Heft III, Neue Folge, *Beiträge zur Kinderheilkunde*, ed. Max Kassowitz (Vienna, 1893)
'Leonardo da Vinci and a Memory of his Childhood' (1910), *SE* XI
'Letter to the Burgomaster of Pribor' (1931), *SE* XXI
'Letter to Dr Hermine von Hug-Hellmuth' (1919 [1915]), *SE* XIV
Letters of Sigmund Freud, 1873–1939, ed. Ernst L. Freud, trans. Tania and James Stern (London: The Hogarth Press, 1970)
The Letters of Sigmund Freud to Eduard Silberstein, 1871–1881, ed. Walter Boehlich, trans. Arnold J. Pomerans (Cambridge, Mass.: Harvard University Press, 1990)
'Lettres à Raymond de Saussure', *Le Bloc-Notes de la Psychanalyse No. 6* 1986, pp. 191–8
'The Loss of Reality in Neurosis and Psychosis' (1924), *SE* XIX
Moses and Monotheism (1939), *SE* XXIII
'Mourning and Melancholia' (1917), *SE* XIV
'Obituary: Lou Andreas-Salomé' (1937), *SE* XXIII
'On Narcissism: An Introduction' (1914), *SE* XIV
'The Neuro-Psychoses of Defence (I)' (1894), *SE* III
'Notes upon a Case of Obsessional Neurosis' (1909), [Ratman] *SE* X
'Obituary of Professor S. Hammerschlag' (1904), *SE* IX
'Observations on Transference-Love' (1915), *SE* XII
'On the Psychical Consequences of the Anatomical Sex-Distinction' (1925), *SE* XIX
An Outline of Psycho-analysis (1938), *SE* XXIII
'Psychical Treatment' (1890), *SE* VII
'Psycho-analytic Notes on an Autobiographical Account of a Case of Paranoia (Dementia Paranoides)' (1911) [*Schreber*], *SE* XII
'The Psychogenesis of a Case of Homosexuality in a Woman' (1920), *SE* XVIII
The Psychopathology of Everyday Life (1901), *SE* VI

The Question of Lay Analysis (1926), *SE* XX

'Screen Memories' (1899), *SE* III

'The Sexual Theories of Children' (1908), *SE* IX

'Sexuality in the Aetiology of the Neuroses' (1898), *SE* III

'Some Neurotic Mechanisms in Jealousy, Paranoia and Homosexuality' (1922), *SE* XVIII

'A Special Type of Object-Choice Made by Men' (1910), *SE* XI

The Standard Edition of the Complete Psychological Works of Sigmund Freud, 24 vols, ed. by James Strachey in collaboration with Anna Freud, assisted by Alix Strachey and Alan Tyson (London: The Hogarth Press and the Institute of Psycho-analysis, 1953–74)

Studienausgabe, 10 vols with an unnumbered *Ergänzungsband* (abbreviated as *Erg*) (Frankfurt: Fischer Verlag, 1969–75)

'The Theme of the Three Caskets' (1913), *SE* XII

Three Essays on the Theory of Sexuality (1905), *SE* VII

Totem and Taboo (1912–13), *SE* XIII

'On Transformations of Instinct as Exemplified in Anal Erotism' (1917), *SE* XVII

'On the Universal Tendency to Debasement in the Sphere of Love' (1912), *SE* XI

and Abraham, Karl, *A Psycho-analytic Dialogue: The Letters of Sigmund Freud and Karl Abraham, 1907–1926*, eds Hilda C. Abraham and Ernst L. Freud (London: The Hogarth Press and the Institute of Psycho-analysis, 1965)

and Breuer, Josef, *Studies on Hysteria* (1895), *SE* II

and Ferenczi, Sándor, *Correspondence, 1908–1914*, eds Eva Brabant, Ernst Falzeder and Patrizia Giampieri-Deutsch (Paris: Calmann-Lévy, 1992)

and Jones, *The Complete Correspondence of Sigmund Freud and Ernest Jones, 1908–1939*, ed. R. Andrew Paskauskas (Cambridge, Mass., and London: Harvard University Press, 1993)

and Jung, C.G, *The Freud/Jung Letters*, ed. William McGuire, trans. R. Manheim and R. F. C. Hull (Princeton: Princeton University Press, 1974)

and Pfister, Oskar, *Psycho-analysis and Faith: The Letters of Sigmund Freud and Oskar Pfister*, ed. Heinrich Meng and Ernst L. Freud, trans. Eric Mosbacher (London: The Hogarth Press and the Institute of Psycho-analysis, 1963)

Freud, Sophie, *My Three Mothers and other Passions* (New York: New York Universities Press, 1988)

Friedan, Betty, *The Feminine Mystique* (New York: Norton, 1963; New York: Dell, 1964)

Friedman, Susan Stanford, *Psyche Reborn: The Emergence of H.D.* (Bloomington, IN.: Indiana University Press, 1981)

'A Most Luscious *Vers Libre* Relationship: H.D. and Freud', *Annual of Psychoanalysis 14* 1986, pp. 319–43

Gallop, Jane, *Feminism and Psychoanalysis: The Daughter's Seduction*, (London: Macmillan, 1982)

'Moving Backwards or Forwards', in Brennan, Teresa (ed.), *Between Feminism and Psychoanalysis* pp. 27–39

'Nurse Freud: Class Struggle in the Family', unpublished paper, Miami University, 1983

Thinking Through the Body (New York: Columbia University Press, 1988), pp. 124–33

Gallup, Stephen, *A History of the Salzburg Festival* (London: Weidenfeld & Nicolson, 1987)

Gamwell, Lynn, 'Freud's Antiquities Collection', in Gamwell, Lynn, and Wells, Richard (eds), *Sigmund Freud and Art*, pp. 21–32

and Wells, Richard (eds), *Sigmund Freud and Art: His Personal Collection of Antiquities*, with an introduction by Peter Gay (London: Freud Museum/State University of New York, Binghamton, 1989)

Gardiner, Muriel, *The Wolfman by the Wolfman* (New York: Basic Books, 1971)

Code Name 'Mary': Memoirs of an American Woman in the Austrian Underground (New Haven and London: Yale University Press., 1987), with a foreword by Anna Freud

Gauld, Alan, *A History of Hypnosis* (Cambridge: CUP, forthcoming)

Gay, Peter, *Freud: A Life for our Time* (London: Dent, 1988)

Reading Freud: Explorations and Entertainments (New York and London: Yale University Press, 1990)

'Sigmund and Minna? The Biographer as Voyeur', *New York Times Book Review*, 29 January 1989, p. 44

'Six Names in Search of an Interpretation: A Contribution to the Debate over Freud's Jewishness', (1982); reprinted in Gay, *Reading Freud: Explorations and Entertainments*, pp. 54–73

'The Dog that Did not Bark in the Night', in Gay, *Reading Freud: Explorations and Entertainments*, pp. 164–79

Gedo, John E., 'On the Origins of the Theban Plague: Assessments of Freud's Character', in Stepansky, Paul E., *Freud. Appraisals and Reappraisals. Contributions to Freud Studies. Vol. 1* (New Jersey: The Analytic Press, 1986), pp. 241–59

and Shabshin, Melvin, Sadow, Leo, and Schlessinger, Nathan, '*Studies on Hysteria*: A Methodological Evaluation' (1964), in Gedo, J.E., and Pollock, G.H. (eds), *Freud: The Fusion of Science and Humanism: The Intellectual History of Psychoanalysis* (New York: International Universities Press, 1976), pp. 167–86

and Wolf, E.S. 'The "Ich" Letters', in Gedo, J.E., and Pollock, G.H. (eds), *Freud: The Fusion of Science and Humanism: The Intellectual History of Psychoanalysis* (New York: International Universities Press, 1976), pp. 71–86

Gelfand, Toby, '"Mon cher docteur Freud": Charcot's Unpublished Correspondence to Freud, 1888–1893. Annotation, Translation, and Commentary', *Bulletin of the History of Medicine 62* 1988, pp. 563–88

'Charcot's Response to Freud's Rebellion', *Journal of the History of Ideas 50* 1989, pp. 293–307

Gilligan, Carol, *In a Different Voice: Psychological Theory and Women's Development* (Cambridge, Mass. and London: Harvard University Press, 1982)

'Remapping the Moral Domain: New Images of the Self in Relationship', in Zanardi, Claudia (ed.), *Essential Papers on the Psychology of Women*, pp. 480–95

Glenn, Jules, 'Freud's Adolescent Patients: Katharina, Dora and the "Homosexual Woman"' in Kanzer, Mark, and Glenn, Jules (eds), *Freud and his Patients* (New York and London: Jacob Aronson, 1980), pp. 23–47

'Freud, Dora and the Maid: A Study of Countertransference', *Journal of the American Psychoanalytic Association 34* 1986, pp. 591–606

Glover, Edward, 'Psychoanalysis in England', in Alexander, Franz, Eisenstein, Samuel and Grotjahn, Martin (eds), *Psychoanalytic Pioneers* (New York: Basic Books, 1966)

Goldmann, S., 'Eine Kur aus der Frühzeit der Psychoanalyse: Kommentar zu Freuds Briefen an Anna v. Vest', *Jahrbuch der Psychoanalyse 17* 1985, pp. 296–337

Goldstein, Jan, 'The Hysteria Diagnosis and the Politics of Anticlericalism in Late Nineteenth-Century France', *Journal of Modern History 104* 1982, pp. 209–39

Console and Classify: The French Psychiatric Profession in the Nineteenth Century (Cambridge: CUP, 1987)

Granoff, Wladimir, *La pensée et le féminin* (Paris: Editions de Minuit, 1976)

Greenberg, Jay R., and Mitchell, Stephen A., *Object Relations in Psychoanalytic Theory* (Cambridge, Mass.: Harvard University Press, 1983)

Greer, Germaine, *The Female Eunuch* (London: MacGibbon & Kee, 1970; London: Paladin, 1971)

Grigg, Kenneth A., '"All Roads Lead to Rome": The Role of the Nursemaid in Freud's Dreams', *Journal of the American Psychoanalytic Association 21* 1973, pp. 108–26

Grinstein, A., *Sigmund Freud's Dreams*, 2nd edn (New York: International Universities Press, 1980)

Grosskurth, Phyllis, *Melanie Klein: Her World and Her Work* (London: Hodder & Stoughton, 1986)

The Secret Ring: Freud's Inner Circle and the Politics of Psychoanalysis (New York: Addison-Wellesley; London: Jonathan Cape, 1991)

Grotjahn, Martin, 'Sigmund Freud and the Art of Letter Writing' (1967), in Ruitenbeek, Hendrik M., *Freud As We Knew Him*, pp. 433–46

Gubar, Susan, 'The Echoing Spell of H.D.'s Trilogy', in Gilbert, Sandra, and Gubar, Susan,

Shakespeare's Sisters: Feminist Essays on Women Poets (Bloomington, IN.: Indiana University Press, 1979), pp. 200–18

Guillain, Georges, *J.-M. Charcot 1825–1893: His Life – His Work*, trans. Pearce Bailey (London: Pitman Medical, 1959)

Gunn, D., and Guyomard, P. (eds), *A Young Girl's Diary* (London: Unwin Hyman, 1990), with a preface by Sigmund Freud

Hardin, Harry T., 'On the Vicissitudes of Freud's Early Mothering. I: Early Environment and Loss; II: Alienation from his Biological Mother; III: Freiberg, Screen Memories, and Loss', *Psychoanalytic Quarterly 56* 1987, pp. 628–44; *57* 1988, pp. 72–86 and pp. 209–23

Harris, Ruth, 'Introduction' to Charcot, J.-M., *Clinical Lectures on Diseases of the Nervous System* (1889; London and New York: Tavistock/Routledge, 1991), pp. ix-lxviii

Hartman, Frank R., 'A Reappraisal of the Emma Episode and the Specimen Dream', *Journal of the American Psychoanalytic Association 31* 1983, pp. 555–85

Hartman, Mary S., and Banner, Lois (eds), *Clio's Consciousness Raised: New Perspectives on the History of Women* (New York: Harper Colophon, 1974)

H.D., *Her* (1927); (New York: New Directions, 1981)
  Palimpsest (1925–6); (Carbondale, Ill.: Southern Illinois University Press, 1968)
  Tribute to Freud (Manchester: Carcanet, revised edn, 1985)

Hearnshaw, L.S., *Cyril Burt Psychologist* (London: Hodder & Stoughton, 1979)

Heath, Stephen, 'Difference', *Screen 19* 1978, pp. 51–112

Heller, Judith Bernays, 'Freud's Mother and Father', in Ruitenbeek, Hendrik M., *Freud as We Knew Him*, pp. 334–40

Heller, Peter, 'Briefe Anna Freuds an Eva Rosenfeld', *Psyche 5* 1991, pp. 434–47
  A Child Analysis with Anna Freud, trans. Salome Burckhardt and Mary Weigand (Madison, Conn.: International Universities Press, 1990)

Hertz, Neil, 'Dora's Secrets, Freud's Techniques', *Diacritics 13* Spring 1983, pp. 65–76; reprinted in Bernheimer, C., and Kahane, C. (eds), *In Dora's Case*, pp. 221–42

Hilferding, Rudolf, *Finance Capital: A Study of the Latest Phase of Capitalist Development*, ed. and with an introduction by Tom Bottomore, from trans. by Morris Watnick and Sam Gordon (London: Routledge & Kegan Paul, 1981)

Hirsch, M., *The Mother/Daughter Plot: Narrative, Psychoanalysis, Feminism* (Bloomington, IN.: Indiana University Press, 1989)

Hirschmüller, Albrecht, '"Balsam auf eine schmerzende Wunde" – Zwei bisher unbekannte Briefe Sigmund Freuds über sein Verhältnis zu Josef Breuer', *Psyche 41* 1987, p. 58
  'Eine bisher unbekannte Krankengeschichte Sigmund Freuds und Josef Breuers aus der Entstehungszeit der "Studien über Hysterie"', *Jahrbuch der Psychoanalyse 10* 1978, pp. 136–68
  Freuds Begegnung mit der Psychiatrie. Von der Hirnmythologie zur Neurosenlehre (Tübingen: Edition Diskord, 1991)
  'Freud's Mathilde: Ein weiterer Tagesrest zum Irma Traum', *Jahrbuch der Psychoanalyse 24* 1989, pp. 128–59
  Physiologie und Psychoanalyse in Leben und Werk Josef Breuers [*Jahrbuch der Psychoanalyse*, Suppl. 4] (Bern: Hans Huber, 1978); trans. as *The Life and Work of Josef Breuer: Physiology and Psychoanalysis* (New York and London: New York University Press, 1989)

Holl, Adolf, *Der Fisch aus der Tiefe, oder Die Freuden der Keuschheit* (Reinbek bei Hamburg: Rowohlt, 1990)

Hollender, M.H., 'The Case of Anna O: A Reformulation', *American Journal of Psychiatry 137* 1980, pp. 797–800

Holt, R.B., *Freud Reappraised: A Fresh Look at Psychoanalytic Theory* (New York and London: Guilford Press, 1989)

Hölzer, Michael, and Kächele, Horst, 'Die Entwicklung der freien Assoziation durch Sigmund Freud', *Jahrbuch der Psychoanalyse 22* 1987, pp. 184–217

Horney, Karen, 'The Denial of the Vagina', *Int J Psa 14* 1933, pp. 57–70; reprinted in Horney, *Feminine Psychology*, pp. 147–61

'The Dread of Woman', *Int J Psa 13* 1932, pp. 348–60; reprinted in Horney, *Feminine Psychology*, pp. 133–46

Feminine Psychology, ed. Harold Kelman (New York: Norton, 1973)

'The Flight from Womanhood: The Masculinity Complex in Women, as Viewed by Men and by Women', *Int J Psa 7* 1926, pp. 324–39; reprinted in Horney, *Feminine Psychology*, pp. 54–70

'On the Genesis of the Castration Complex in Women', *Int J Psa 5* 1924, pp. 50–65; reprinted in Horney, *Feminine Psychology*, pp. 37–53

Huber, Wolfgang, 'Die erste Kinderanalytikerin', in *Psychoanalyse als Herausforderung: Festschrift Caruso* (Vienna: Verlag Verband der Wissenschaftlichen Gesellschaften Osterreichs [VWGO], 1980), pp. 125–33

Hug-Hellmuth, Hermine, *Aus dem Seelenleben des Kindes. Eine psychoanalytische Studie* (Leipzig and Vienna: Deuticke, 1913); trans. as *A Study of the Mental Life of the Child* by J.J. Putnam and Mabel Stevens (Washington: Nervous and Mental Disease Publishing Co., 1919)

'On the Technique of Child-Analysis', *Int J Psa 2* 1921, pp. 287–305

Hughes, Judith M., *Reshaping the Psychoanalytic Domain: The Work of Melanie Klein, W.R.D. Fairbairn, and D.W. Winnicott* (Berkeley, Los Angeles, and London: University of California Press, 1989)

Hunter, Dianne, 'Hysteria, Psychoanalysis and Feminism: The Case of Anna O.', *Feminist Studies 9* 1983, pp. 465–88

Hurst, Lindsay C., 'What Was Wrong with Anna O.?', *Journal of the Royal Society of Medicine 75* 1982, pp. 129–31

Irigaray, Luce, *Speculum* (Paris: Editions de Minuit, 1974; trans. Ithaca, NY: Cornell University Press, 1985)

This Sex Which Is Not One, trans. Catherine Porter with Carolyn Burke (Ithaca, NY: Cornell University Press, 1985)

Israël, Lucien, *L'hystérique, le sexe et le médecin* (Paris: Masson, 1985)

Jacobus, Mary, '*Dora* and the Pregnant Madonna', in Jacobus, *Reading Woman* (London: Methuen, 1986), pp. 137–93

'Russian Tactics: Freud's "Case of Homosexuality in a Woman"', paper delivered to Session on 'Psychoanalysis and the Passions', Conference on 'Passions, Persons, Powers', University of California at Berkeley, 30 April–3 May 1992

'Taking Liberties with Words', in Jacobus, *Reading Woman* (London: Methuen, 1986), pp. 205–28

Jensen, Ellen, 'Anna O., a Study of her Later Life', *Psychoanalytic Quarterly 39* 1970, pp. 269–93

Streifzüge durch das Leben von Anna O./Bertha Pappenheim: Ein Fall für die Psychiatrie – Ein Leben für die Philanthropie (Frankfurt: ZTV, 1984)

Jones, Ernest, 'Discussion on Lay Analysis', *Int J Psa 8* 1927, pp. 185 ff.

'Early Development of Female Sexuality', *Int J Psa 8* 1927, pp. 459–72; reprinted in Jones, *Papers on Psycho-analysis*, pp. 438–51

'Early Female Sexuality', *Int J Psa 16* 1935, pp. 263–73; reprinted in Jones, *Papers on Psycho-analysis*, pp. 485–95

Free Associations: Memories of a Psycho-Analyst (1959), with a new introduction by Mervyn Jones (New Brunswick and London: Transaction, 1990)

Papers on Psycho-analysis, 5th edn (London: Baillière, Tindall & Cox, 1950)

'The Phallic Phase', *Int J Psa 14* 1933, pp. 1–33; reprinted in Jones, *Papers on Psycho-analysis*, pp. 452–84

Sigmund Freud: Life and Work, vols I–III (London: The Hogarth Press, 1953–7; 2nd edn of vol. I, 1954)

'Symposium on Child-Analysis', *Int J Psa 8* 1927, pp. 389–90

Jung, C.G., *The Collected Works of C.G.Jung*, eds Sir Herbert Read, Michael Fordham and Gerhard Adler, trans. R.F.C. Hull (London: Routledge & Kegan Paul, vol. III, 1960; vol. IV, 1961)

Memories, Dreams, Reflections, recorded by Aniela Jaffé, trans. Richard and Clara Winston (New York: Pantheon, 1963)

'The Psychology of Dementia Praecox' (1907); English edn first published in Jung, *The Collected Works, Vol. III*, pp. 1–151

and Riklin F., *The Associations of Normal Subjects* (1904), in Jung, *Collected Works. Vol. II. Experimental Researches*, trans. Leopold Stein in collaboration with Diana Riviere (London: Routledge & Kegan Paul, 1973), pp. 3–196

Kann, R.A., *Theodor Gomperz: Ein Gelehrtenleben im Bürgertum der Franz-Josefs-Zeit* (Vienna: Österreichschen Akademie der Wissenschaften, 1974)

Kaplan, Marion, *The Jewish Feminist Movement in Germany: The Campaign of the Jüdischer Frauenbund, 1904–1938* (Westport, Conn., and London: Greenwood, 1979)

Kardiner, Abram, *My Analysis with Freud: Reminiscences* (New York: Norton, 1977)

Karpe, Richard, 'The Rescue Complex in Anna O's Final Identity', *Psychoanalytic Quarterly 30* 1961, pp. 1–24

Kaut, Josef, *Die Salzburger Festspiele 1920–1981* (Salzburg und Wien: Residenz Verlag, 1982)

Kerr, John, *A Most Dangerous Method: The Story of Jung, Freud and Sabina Spielrein* (New York: Knopf, 1993)

'The Devil's Elixirs: Jung's "Theology" and the Dissolution of "Freud's Poisoning Complex"', *Psychoanalytic Review 75* 1988, pp. 1–33

'Freud, Jung and Sabina Spielrein', unpublished ms.

'Spielrein's Later Career', unpublished ms.

King, Pearl, and Steiner, Riccardo (eds), *The Freud-Klein Controversies 1941–45* (London and New York: Tavistock/Routledge, 1990)

Kinsey, Alfred C., Pomeroy, Wardell B., Martin, Clyde E., and Gebhard, Paul H., *Sexual Behavior in the Human Female* (Philadelphia and London: W.B. Saunders Company, 1953)

Klein, Melanie, *The Writings of Melanie Klein*, under the general editorship of Roger Money-Kyrle, in collaboration with Betty Joseph, Edna O'Shaughnessy and Hanna Segal, 4 vols (London: The Hogarth Press and the Institute of Psycho-analysis, 1975)

'Symposium on Child Analysis', *Int J Psa 8* 1927, p. 357; also in *Writings 1*, pp. 139–69

'The Early Stages of the Oedipus Complex', *Writings 1*, pp. 186–98

Koepcke, Cordula, *Lou Andreas-Salomé: Leben, Persönlichkeit, Werk; eine Biographie* (Frankfurt: Insel, 1986)

Koestler, Arthur, *Arrow in the Blue* (London: Hutchinson, 1952; Danube edn, 1969)

Kofman, Sarah, *The Enigma of Woman. Woman in Freud's Writings*, trans. Catherine Porter (Ithaca, NY: Cornell University Press, 1985)

Kris, Ernst, 'Introduction', *The Origins of Psycho-analysis: Letters to Wilhelm Fliess, Drafts and Notes, 1887–1902*, ed. Marie Bonaparte, Anna Freud, Ernst Kris, trans. Eric Mosbacher and James Strachey (London: Imago, 1954)

Kristeva, Julia, *Histoires d'amours* (Paris: Denoel, 1983)

'Freud and Love: Treatment and its Discontents', in Moi, Toril (ed.), *The Kristeva Reader* (Oxford: Blackwell, 1986), pp. 238–71

Krohn, Alan, *Hysteria: The Elusive Neurosis*, Psychological Issues Monograph 45/46 (New York: International Universities Press, 1978)

Krüll, Marianne, *Freud and his Father* (1979); trans. Arnold J. Pomerans (New York and London: Norton, 1986)

Kubes, Ursula, '"Moderne Nervositäten" und die Anfänge der Psychoanalyse' in Kadrnoska, Franz (ed.), *Aufbruch und Untergang. Österreichische Kultur zwischen 1918 und 1938* (Vienna: Europa Verlag, 1981), pp. 267–80

Kupper, Herbert I., and Rollman-Branch, Hilda S., 'Freud and Schnitzler – *Doppelgänger*', *Journal of the American Psychoanalytic Association 7* 1959, pp. 109 ff; reprinted in Ruitenbeek, Hendrik M., *Freud As We Knew Him*, pp. 412–27

Kuspit, Donald, 'A Mighty Metaphor: The Analogy of Archaeology and Psychoanalysis', in Gamwell, Lynn, and Wells, Richard (eds), *Sigmund Freud and Art*, pp. 133–52

Lacan, Jacques, 'Intervention on Transference' (1951), in Mitchell, Juliet, and Rose, Jacqueline (eds), *Feminine Sexuality ...*, pp. 61–73

'The Meaning of the Phallus' (1958), in Mitchell, Juliet, and Rose, Jacqueline (eds), *Feminine Sexuality ...*, pp. 75–85

Le Séminaire. Livre IV. La relation d'objet et les structures freudiennes. 1956–1957, Comptes rendus by J.-B. Pontalis, *Bulletin de Psychologie 10* 1956–7, pp. 426–30, 602–5, 742–3, 851–4; *11* 1957–8, pp. 31–4

'Seminar on *The Purloined Letter*', trans. Jeffrey Mehlman, *Yale French Studies 48* 1972, pp. 39–72

Laforgue, René, 'Personal Memories of Freud', in Ruitenbeek, Hendrik M., *Freud As We Knew Him*, pp. 341–9

Lagrange, Jacques, 'Versions de la psychanalyse dans le texte de Foucault', *Psychanalyse à l'Université 12* no. 45, January 1987, pp. 99–120, and no. 46, April 1987, pp. 259–80

Lampl de Groot, Jeanne, 'The Evolution of the Oedipus Complex in Women', *Int J Psa 9* 1928, pp. 332–45; reprinted in *Reader*
Man and Mind: Collected Papers (New York: International Universities Press, 1985)
'Masochismus und Narzissmus', *Int. Zeitschrift für ärztliche Psychoanalyse 23* 1937, pp. 479–89; translated in *Man and Mind*
'Problems of Femininity', *Psychoanalytic Quarterly 2* 1933, pp. 489–518; reprinted in *Man and Mind*

Langs, Robert, 'Freud's Irma Dream and the Origins of Psychoanalysis', *Psychoanalytic Review 71* 1984, pp. 591–617

Laplanche, Jean, *Problématiques II. Castrations Symbolisations* (Paris: PUF, 1980)
and Pontalis, J.-B., *The Language of Psychoanalysis*, trans. Donald Nicholson-Smith (London: The Hogarth Press and the Institute of Psycho-analysis, 1973)

Laqueur, Thomas, *Making Sex: Body and Gender from the Greeks to Freud* (Cambridge, Mass. and London: Harvard University Press, 1990)

Leichter, Otto, *Otto Bauer: Tragödie oder Triumph* (Vienna: Europa Verlag, 1970)

Le Rider, Jacques, *Modernité viennoise et crises de l'identité* (Paris: PUF, 1990)

Lerman, H., *A Mote in Freud's Eye: From Psychoanalysis to the Psychology of Women* (New York: Springer, 1986)

Levin, Kenneth, *Freud's Early Theories of the Neuroses* (Hassocks, Sussex: Harvester, 1978)

Livingstone, Angela, *Lou Andreas-Salomé: Her Life and Writings* (London: Gordon Fraser Gallery, 1984)

Loewenberg, P., 'Otto Bauer, Freud's "Dora" Case, and the Crises of the First Austrian Republic', in Loewenberg, P., *Decoding the Past: The Psychohistorical Approach* (New York: Knopf, 1983), pp. 161–204

Lydon, Susan, 'The Politics of Orgasm', in Morgan, Robin (ed.), *Sisterhood Is Powerful*, pp. 197–205

McCaffrey, P., *Freud and Dora: The Artful Dream* (New Brunswick, NJ: Rutgers University Press, 1984)

Macey, David, *Lacan in Contexts* (London: Verso, 1988)

McGovern, C., 'Psychiatry, Psychoanalysis and Women in America: A Historical Note', *Psychoanalytic Review 71* 1984, pp. 541–52

McGrath, William J., *Freud's Discovery of Psychoanalysis: The Politics of Hysteria* (Ithaca, NY, and London: Cornell University Press, 1986)

MacLean, George, and Rappen, Ulrich, *Hermine Hug-Hellmuth: Her Life and Work* (London and New York: Routledge, 1991)

Macmillan, M.B., 'Delboeuf and Janet as Influences in Freud's Treatment of Emmy von N.', *Journal of the History of the Behavioral Sciences 20* 1984, pp. 340–58

Mai, François, and Merskey, Harold, 'Briquet's *Treatise on Hysteria*: A Synopsis and Commentary', *General Archives of Psychiatry 37* 1980, pp. 1401–5
'Briquet's Concept of Hysteria: An Historical Perspective', *Canadian Journal of Psychiatry 26* 1981, pp. 57–63

Malcolm, Janet, *In the Freud Archives* (London: Jonathan Cape, 1984)

Man, Paul de, 'Excuses (*Confessions*)', in *Allegories of Reading: Figural Language in Rousseau, Nietzsche, Rilke, and Proust* (New Haven and London: Yale University Press, 1979), pp. 278–301

Mannoni, Octave, *Fictions freudiennes* (Paris: Seuil, 1978)

Marcus, Steven, 'Freud and Dora: Story, History, Case History', *Partisan Review 41* 1974, pp. 12–23, 89–108; reprinted in Marcus, *Freud and the Culture of Psychoanalysis* (London: Allen & Unwin, 1984), pp. 42–86, and in abbreviated form in Bernheimer, C., and Kahane, C. (eds), *In Dora's Case*, pp. 56–91

Marie, Pierre, 'Discours à l'occasion du centenaire de Charcot', *Revue neurologique 1* 1925, pp. 731–45

Masson, J.M., *The Assault on Truth: Freud's Suppression of the Seduction Theory,* (London: Faber & Faber, 1984)

Masters, William H., and Johnson, Virginia E., *Human Sexual Response* (Boston: Little, Brown, 1966; New York: Bantam paperback, 1980)

Meisel, Perry, and Kendrick, Walter (eds), *Bloomsbury/Freud: The Letters of James and Alix Strachey 1924–1925* (London: Chatto & Windus, 1986)

Meisel-Hess, Grete, *Die Sexuelle Krise. Eine Socialpsychologische Untersuchung* (Jena: Eugen Diederichs, 1909)

Meissner, W.W., 'Studies on Hysteria – Frau Emmy von N.', *Bulletin Menninger Clinic 45* 1981, pp. 1–19

Menzaghi, Frédérique, Millot, Annie, and Pillot, Michèle, *Evolution de la conception de l'hystérie de 1870 à 1930,* 2 vols (Maîtrise de psychologie clinique, University of Nancy II, 1987)

Merck, Mandy, 'The Train of Thought in Freud's "Case of Homosexuality in a Woman"', *m/f 11/12* 1986, pp. 35–46

Merskey, Harold, *The Analysis of Hysteria* (London: Baillière Tindall, 1979)

Micale, Mark, 'Hysteria and its Historiography: A Review of Past and Present Writings I & II', *History of Science 27* 1989, pp. 223–61, 319–51

'Hysteria and its Historiography: The Future Perspective', *History of Psychiatry 1* 1990, pp. 33–124

Mijolla, Alain de, 'La psychanalyse en France (1893–1965)', in Roland Jaccard (ed.), *Histoire de la Psychanalyse*, vol. II (Paris: Hachette, 1982), pp. 5–118

Miller, Alice, *The Drama of the Gifted Child and the Search for the True Self* (1979; London: Faber & Faber, 1983)

For Your Own Good: Hidden Cruelty in Child-Rearing and the Roots of Violence (1980; London: Faber & Faber, 1983)

Du Sollst Nicht Merken. Variationen über das Paradies-Thema (Frankfurt: Suhrkamp Verlag, 1981)

Miller, J.-A. (ed.), *La scission* (Paris: Bibliothèque d'Ornicar?, 1976)

Miller, Jean Baker (ed.), *Psychoanalysis and Women* (Harmondsworth, Middx: Penguin, 1973)

Millett, Kate, *Sexual Politics* (1969; London: Rupert Hart-Davis, 1971)

Minutes of the Vienna Psychoanalytical Society, ed. Herman Nunberg and Ernst Federn, trans. M. Nunberg, 4 vols (New York: International Universities Press, 1962–76); *Les premiers psychanalystes. Minutes de la Société psychanalytique de Vienne, IV 1912–18* (Paris: Gallimard, 1984)

Mitchell, Juliet, 'Introduction – I', in Mitchell, Juliet, and Rose, Jacqueline (eds), *Feminine Sexuality: Jacques Lacan and the Ecole Freudienne*, trans. Jacqueline Rose (London: Macmillan, 1982); reprinted in Mitchell, Juliet, *Women: The Longest Revolution*, pp. 249–77

Psychoanalysis and Feminism (London: Allen Lane, 1974)

Women: The Longest Revolution. Essays on Feminism, Literature and Psychoanalysis (London: Virago, 1984)

Women's Estate (Harmondsworth, Middx: Penguin, 1971)

Moi, Toril, 'Representation of Patriarchy: Sexuality and Epistemology in Freud's Dora', *Feminist Review 9* Autumn 1981, pp. 60–74; reprinted in Bernheimer C., and Kahane, C. (eds) *In Dora's Case*, pp. 181–99

Molnar, Michael (ed.), *The Diary of Sigmund Freud, 1929–39* (London: The Hogarth Press; New York: Charles Scribner and Son, 1992)

Monk, Ray, *Ludwig Wittgenstein: The Duty of Genius* (London: Jonathan Cape, 1990)

Monro, Lois, 'Contribution to the Memorial Meeting of the British Psycho-Analytical Society, London, 3 October 1962', *Int J Psa 44* 1963, pp. 228–35

Morgan, Robin (ed.), *Sisterhood Is Powerful: An Anthology of Writings from the Women's Liberation Movement* (New York: Vintage, 1970)

Mort, Frank, *Dangerous Sexualities: Medico-Moral Politics in England since 1830* (London: Routledge & Kegan Paul, 1987)

Mulvey, Laura, 'Visual Pleasure and Narrative Cinema', *Screen 16* no. 3, 1975 pp. 6–18

Muslin, Hyman, and Merton, Gill, 'Transference in the Dora Case', *Journal of the American Psycho-analytic Association 26* 1978, pp. 311–28

Olivier, Christiane, *Les enfants de Jocaste. L'empreinte de la mère* (Paris: Denoël/Gonthier, 1980)

Orr-Andrawes, Alison, 'The Case of Anna O.: A Neuropsychiatric Perspective', *Journal of the American Psycho-analytic Association 35* 1987, pp. 387–419

Palmier, Jean-Michel, 'La psychanalyse en Union Soviétique', in Roland Jaccard (ed.), *Histoire de la Psychanalyse*, vol. II (Paris: Hachette, 1982), pp. 213–69

Pappenheim, Bertha, *Le travail de Sisyphe* (1924), trans. Jacques Legrand, with a preface by Yolande Tisseron (Paris: Des femmes, 1986)

Pappenheim, Else, 'Freud and Gilles de la Tourette: Diagnostic Speculations on "Frau Emmy von N."' *International Review of Psycho-analysis 7* 1980, pp. 265–77

Peters, H.F., *My Sister, My Spouse: A Biography of Lou Andreas-Salomé* (New York: Norton, 1962)

Peters, Uwe, *Anna Freud: Her Father's Daughter* (New York: Schocken, 1985)

Pfeiffer, E. (ed.), *Friedrich Nietzsche, Paul Rée, Lou Andreas-Salomé: Die Dokumente ihrer Begegnung,* (Frankfurt: Insel, 1970)

Rainer Maria Rilke–Lou Andreas-Salomé. Briefwechsel 1897–1926, (Frankfurt: Insel, 1975)

Phillips, Adam, 'Playing Mothers: Between Pedagogy and Transference', *Nouvelle Revue de Psychanalyse* Spring 1991; typescript in English

Piaget, Jean, *The Child's Conception of the World*, trans. Joan and Andrew Tomlinson (London: Paladin, 1973)

Pollock, George H., 'The Possible Significance of Childhood Object Loss in the Josef Breuer–Bertha Pappenheim (Anna O.)–Sigmund Freud Relationship', *Journal of the American Psychoanalytic Association 16* 1968, pp. 711–39

Pontalis, J.-B., 'Les vases communicants (Freud et Breton)', *Nouvelle Revue de Psychanalyse 8* 1973, pp. 12–26

Proust, Marcel, *Remembrance of Things Past*, vol. II, trans. C.K. Scott Moncrieff and Terence Kilmartin (Harmondsworth, Middx: Penguin, 1983)

Putnam, J.J., 'Bemerkungen über einer Krankheitsfall mit Griselda-Phantasien', *Internationale Zeitschrift für Ärztliche Psychoanalyse 1* 1913, pp. 205–18, trans. Katherine Jones in Putnam, *Addresses on Psycho-analysis*, with a preface by Sigmund Freud (London, New York and Vienna: International Psycho-analytic Press, 1921), pp. 75–93

Quinn, Susan, *A Mind of her Own: The Life of Karen Horney* (New York: Summit Books, 1987; London: Macmillan, 1988)

Ramas, Maria, 'Freud's Dora, Dora's Hysteria', in Newton, Judith L., Ryan, Mary P., and Walkowitz, Judith R. (eds), *Sex and Class in Women's History* (London: Routledge & Kegan Paul, 1983), pp. 72–113; reprinted in Bernheimer, C., and Kahane, C. (eds), *In Dora's Case*, pp. 149–80

Reeves, Christopher, 'Breuer, Freud and the Case of Anna O.: A Re-examination', *Journal of Child Psychotherapy 8* 1982, pp. 203–14

Ricoeur, Paul, *Freud and Philosophy* (New Haven: Yale University Press, 1970)

Riley, Denise, *War in the Nursery: Theories of the Child and Mother* (London: Virago, 1983)

'Am I that Name?': Feminism and the Category of 'Women' in History (Minneapolis: University of Minnesota Press, 1988)

Riviere, Joan, *The Inner World and Joan Riviere. Collected Papers: 1920–1958*, ed. with a biographical chapter by Athol Hughes and a foreword by Hanna Segal (London and New York: Karnac, 1991)

'Symposium on Child Analysis', *Int J Psa 8* 1927, pp. 370–7

'An Intimate Impression' (1939), in *Collected Papers*, pp. 208–12

Roazen, Paul, *Brother Animal: The Story of Freud and Tausk* (Harmondsworth, Middx: Penguin, 1973)

Freud and his Followers (New York: Knopf; London: Allen Lane, 1975)

Helene Deutsch: A Psychoanalyst's Life (New York: Anchor Press Doubleday, 1985)

Rogow, Arnold A., 'A Further Footnote to Freud's "Fragment of an Analysis of a Case of Hysteria"', *Journal of the American Psychoanalytic Association 26* 1978, pp. 331–56

'Dora's Brother', *International Review of Psycho-analysis 6* 1979, pp. 239–59

Rose, Jacqueline, 'Dora – A Fragment of an Analysis', *m/f 2* 1978, pp. 5–21; reprinted in Rose, Jacqueline, *Sexuality in the Field of Vision*, pp. 27–48, and Bernheimer, C., and Kahane, C. (eds), *In Dora's Case*, pp. 128–48

'Femininity and its Discontents', reprinted in Rose, *Sexuality in the Field of Vision*, pp. 83–103

Sexuality in the Field of Vision (London: Verso, 1986)

'Psychopolitics II: Controversial Discussions: Anna Freud and Melanie Klein', unpublished paper

Rosen, Nicole Kress, 'Hélène Deutsch, une théorie de la femme', *Ornicar? 15* 1978, pp. 41–57

Rosenbaum, Max, and Muroff, Melvin (eds), *Anna O: Fourteen Contemporary Reinterpretations* (New York and London: Free Press, 1984)

Rosenfeld, Eva M., 'Dream and Vision: Some Remarks on Freud's Egyptian Bird Dream', *Int J Psa 37* 1956, pp. 97–105

Rosolato, Guy, 'Paranoïa et scène primitive', in Rosolato, Guy, *Essais sur le Symbolique* (Paris: Gallimard, 1969), pp. 199–241

Roudinesco, Elisabeth, *La Bataille de Cent Ans. L'Histoire de la psychanalyse en France, Vol. I. 1886–1925* (Paris: Editions Ramsey, 1983; reprinted by Seuil, 1986)

La Bataille de Cent Ans. L'Histoire de la psychanalyse en France. Vol. 2. 1925–1985 (Paris: Seuil, 1986); trans. as *Jacques Lacan & Co.*, by Jeffrey Mehlman (London: Free Association Books, 1990)

Rousseau, J.-J., *Oeuvres complètes. Les confessions, autres textes autobiographiques*, ed. Bernard Gagnebin and Marcel Raymond (Paris: Gallimard, Pléiade, 1959), vol. 1

Rubin, Gayle, 'The Traffic in Women: Notes on the "Political Economy" of Sex', in Reiter, Rayna R. (ed.), *Toward an Anthropology of Women* (New York and London: Monthly Review Press, 1975), pp. 157–210

Rubins, Jack L., *Karen Horney: Gentle Rebel of Psychoanalysis* (London: Weidenfeld & Nicolson, 1979)

Ruitenbeek, Hendrik M. (ed.), *Freud as We Knew Him* (Detroit, Mich.: Wayne State University Press, 1973)

Rush, Florence, 'Freud and the Sexual Abuse of Children', *Chrysalis 1* 1977, pp. 31–45

The Best Kept Secret: Sexual Abuse of Children (Englewood Cliffs, NJ: Prentice-Hall, 1980)

Safouan, Moustapha, *La sexualité féminine dans la doctrine freudienne* (Paris: Seuil, 1976)

Sajner, Josef, 'Sigmund Freuds Beziehungen zu seinem Geburtsort Freiberg (Pribor) und zu Mähren', *Clio Medica 3* 1968, pp. 167–80

Salow, Roberta, 'Where Has all the Hysteria Gone?', *Psychoanalytic Review 66* 1979–80, pp. 463–78

Sayers, Janet, 'Psychoanalysis and Personal Politics: A Response to Elizabeth Wilson', *Feminist Review 10* 1982, pp. 91–5

Mothering Psychoanalysis: Helene Deutsch, Karen Horney, Anna Freud and Melanie Klein (London: Hamish Hamilton, 1991)

Schlesier, Renate, *Konstruktionen der Weiblichkeit bei Sigmund Freud. Zum Problem von Entmythologisierung und Remythologisierung in der psychoanalytischen Theorie* (Frankfurt: Europäische Verlagsanstalt, 1981)

Schmidt-Dengler, W. 'Decadence and Antiquity: The Educational Preconditions of Jung Wien', in Nielsen, E. (ed.), *Focus on Vienna 1900: Change and Continuity in Literature, Music, Art, and Intellectual History* (Munich: Wilhelm Fink Verlag, 1982)

Schor, Naomi, 'Female Paranoia: The Case for Psychoanalytic Feminist Criticism', *Yale French Studies 62* 1981, pp. 204–19

Schuker, E., 'Creative Productivity in Women Analysts', *Journal of the American Academy of Psychoanalysis 13* 1985, pp. 51–75

Schur, Max, 'Some Additional "Day Residues" of the Specimen Dream of Psychoanalysis', in Loewenstein, Rudolph M., Newman, Lottie M., Schur, Max, and Solnit, Albert J. (eds),

Psychoanalysis. A General Psychology: Essays in Honor of Heinz Hartmann (New York: International Universities Press, 1966), pp. 45–85

Freud: Living and Dying (London: The Hogarth Press and the Institute of Psycho-analysis, 1972)

Seifert, Edith, '*Was will das Weib?*'. *Zu Begehren und Lust bei Freud und Lacan* (Weinheim and Berlin: Quadriga, 1987)

Sharpe, Ella Freeman, 'Contribution to a Symposium on Child-Analysis', *Int J Psa 8* 1927, pp. 380–4

Shorter, Edward, *From Paralysis to Fatigue. A History of Psychosomatic Illness in the Modern Era* (New York: Free Press, 1992)

Showalter, Elaine, *The Female Malady: Women, Madness and English Culture, 1830–1980* (New York: Pantheon, 1985; London: Virago, 1987)

Smith-Rosenberg, Carroll, 'The Hysterical Woman: Sex Roles and Role Conflict in Nineteenth-Century America' (1972), in Smith-Rosenberg, *Disorderly Conduct: Visions of Gender in Victorian America* (New York: Knopf, 1985; Oxford: Oxford University Press., 1985), pp. 197–216

Snitow, Ann, Stansell, Christine, and Thompson, Sharon (eds), *Desire: The Politics of Sexuality* (London: Virago, 1983)

Spiegel, R., 'Freud and the Women in his World', *Journal of the American Academy of Psychoanalysis 5* 1977, pp. 377–402

Spielrein, Sabina, *Ausgewählte Schriften*, (Berlin: Brinkmann & Bose, 1986)

'Beiträge zur Kenntnis der Kindlichen Seele', *Zentralblatt für Psychoanalyse und Psychotherapie 3* 1912, pp. 57–72

'Briefmarkentraum', *Internationale Zeitschrift für ärztliche Psychoanalyse 8* 1922, p. 243

'Die Destruktion als Ursache des Werdens' *Jahrbuch für psychoanalytische und psychopathologische Forschungen 4* 1912, pp. 465–503

'Extraits inédits d'un journal', trans. Jeanne Moll, *Le Bloc-Notes de la Psychanalyse 3* 1983, pp. 147–70

'Qui est l'auteur du crime?' *Journal de Genève*, 15 January 1922; reprinted in *Le Bloc-Notes de la Psychanalyse No. 2* 1982, pp. 141–6

'Rêve et vision des étoiles filantes', *Int J Psa 4* 1923, pp. 129–32

Tagebuch einer heimlich Symmetrie. Sabina Spielrein zwischen Jung und Freud, ed. A. Carotenuto (Freiburg i.B.: Kore, 1986)

'Uber den psychologischen Inhalt eines Falles von Schizophrenie (Dementia Praecox)', *Jahrbuch für psychoanalytische und psychopathologische Forschungen 3* 1911, pp. 329–400

Spivak, G.C., 'Displacement and the Discourse of Women', in Krupnick, M. (ed.), *Displacement, Derrida and After* (Bloomington IN.: Indiana University Press, 1983)

Sprengnether, Madelon, 'Enforcing Oedipus: Freud and Dora', in Bernheimer C., and Kahane, C. (eds), *In Dora's Case*, pp. 254–75

The Spectral Mother: Freud, Feminism and Psychoanalysis, (Ithaca, NY, and London: Cornell University Press, 1990)

Spurling, Laurence (ed.), *Sigmund Freud. Critical Assessments*, 4 vols (London and New York: Routledge, 1989)

Stein, Conrad, 'Nouvelles observations sur l'amour de transfert 1', unpublished paper, 1989

Steiner, Riccardo, 'Some Thoughts about Tradition and Change Arising from an Examination of the British Psychoanalytical Society's *Controversial Discussions', International Review of Psycho-analysis 12* 1985, pp. 27–71

'"To Explain our Point of View to English Readers in English Words"', *International Review of Psycho-analysis 18* 1991, pp. 351–92

Stekel, Wilhelm, *The Autobiography of Wilhelm Stekel: The Life Story of a Pioneer Psychoanalyst*, ed. E. Gutheil (New York: Liveright, 1950)

Sterba, Richard, *Reminiscences of a Viennese Psychoanalyst* (Detroit: Wayne State University Press, 1982)

Stimpson, C., and Person, E. (eds), *Women: Sex and Sexuality* (Chicago and London: Chicago University Press, 1980)

Stoller, R.J., 'The Sense of femaleness', *Psychoanalytic Quarterly 37* 1968, pp. 42–55

Stolorow, R.D., and Atwood, G.E., 'A Defensive-Restitutive Function of Freud's Theory of Psychosexual Development', *Psychoanalytic Review 65* 1978, pp. 361–78

Stone, Irving, *The Passions of the Mind* (London: Cassell, 1971)

Strachey, Alix, *The Unconscious Motives of War*, (London: Unwin Brothers, 1957)

Strachey, James, 'Contribution to the Memorial Meeting of the British Psycho-Analytical Society, London, 3 October 1962', *Int J Psa 44* 1963, pp. 228–35

Sulloway, Frank, *Freud: Biologist of the Mind* (London: Burnett Books, 1979)

Swaan, A. de, 'On the Sociogenesis of the Psychoanalytic Situation', *Psychoanalysis & Contemporary Thought 3* 1980, pp. 381–413

Swales, Peter, 'Freud, Minna Bernays and the Conquest of Rome: New Light on the Origins of Psychoanalysis', *The New American Review 1* 1982, pp. 1–23

'Freud, Johann Weier, and the Status of Seduction; the Role of the Witch in the Conception of Fantasy' (1982), in Spurling, Laurence (ed.), *Sigmund Freud. Critical Assessments*, vol. I, pp. 530–56

'Freud, Fliess and Fratricide; the Role of Fliess in Freud's Conception of Paranoia' (1982), in Spurling, Laurence (ed.), *Sigmund Freud. Critical Assessments*, vol. I, pp. 330–56

'A Fascination with Witches', *The Sciences*, vol. 22, No. 8, November 1982, pp. 21–5

'Freud, Krafft-Ebing and the Witches: The Role of Krafft-Ebing in Freud's Flight into Fantasy' (1983), in Spurling, Laurence (ed.), *Sigmund Freud. Critical Assessments*, vol. I, pp. 357–63

'Freud, Martha Bernays and the Language of Flowers, Masturbation, Cocaine, and the Inflation of Fantasy', privately printed, 1983

Freud, Cocaine, and Sexual Chemistry: The Role of Cocaine in Freud's Conception of the Libido' (1983), in Spurling, Laurence (ed.), *Sigmund Freud. Critical Assessments*, vol. I, pp. 273–301

'Freud, his Teacher and the Birth of Psychoanalysis', in Stepansky, Paul E. (ed.), *Freud. Appraisals and Reappraisals. Contributions to Freud Studies. Vol. I* (New Jersey: The Analytic Press, 1986), pp. 3–82

'Freud, Breuer and the Blessed Virgin', privately printed, 1986

'Freud, Katharina and the First "Wild analysis"', in Stepansky, Paul (ed.), *Freud. Appraisals and Reappraisals. Contributions to Freud Studies. Vol. 3* (New Jersey: The Analytic Press, 1988), pp. 79–164

'Are We Getting the Freud We Deserve?', talk given to Cambridge Group for the History of Psychiatry, Psychoanalysis and Allied Sciences, University of Cambridge, 7 February 1990

'What Jung *Didn't* Say', in Papadopoulos, Renos (ed.), *Jung* (London: Routledge, forthcoming)

Swan, J., '*Mater* and Nannie: Freud's Two Mothers and the Discovery of the Oedipus Complex', *American Imago 31* 1974, pp. 1–64

Székely-Kovács, Olga, and Berény, Robert, *Karikaturen vom achten Internationalen Psychoanalytischen Kongress, Salzburg, Ostern 1924* (Privatdruck, Leipzig, Vienna, Zürich: Internationaler Psychoanalytischer Verlag, 1924)

Thompson, N.L., 'Helene Deutsch – A Life in Theory', *Psychoanalytic Quarterly 56* 1987, pp. 317–53

Timms, Edward, 'The "Child-Woman": Kraus, Freud, Wittels, and Irma Karczewska', *Austrian Studies 1* 1990, pp. 87–107

Trillat, Etienne, *Histoire de l'hystérie* (Paris: Editions Seghers, 1986)

Turkle, Sherry, *Psychoanalytic Politics: Jacques Lacan and Freud's French Revolution* (London: Burnett Books, in association with André Deutsch, 1979)

Vance, Carole S. (ed.), *Pleasure and Danger: Exploring Female Sexuality* (London: Routledge & Kegan Paul, 1984)

Veith, Ilza, *Hysteria: The History of a Disease* (Chicago: Chicago University Press, 1965)

Vogel, L.Z., 'The Case of Elise Gomperz', *American Journal of Psychoanalysis 46* 1986, pp. 230–8

Voswinckel, Peter, 'The Case of Mathilde S.: Acute Porphyria. A Hitherto Unknown Clinical

Record of Sigmund Freud. On the Occasion of the 100th Anniversary of Sulfonal BAYER', *Arzt und Krankenhaus 41* 1988, pp. 177–85

Vranich, S.B., 'Sigmund Freud and the "Case History of Berganza": Freud's Psychoanalytical Beginnings', *Psychoanalytic Review 63* 1976, pp. 73–82

Vygotsky, Lev Semenovich, *Thought and Language* (1934), trans. Eugenia Hanfmann and Gertrude Vakar (Cambridge, Mass.: MIT Press, 1962)

Wagner-Jauregg, J., *Lebenserinnerungen* (Vienna: Springer, 1950)

Wahl, Charles William, 'Ella Freeman Sharpe, 1875–1947', in Alexander, Franz, Eisenstein, Samuel, and Grotjahn, Martin (eds), *Psychoanalytic Pioneers* (New York and London: Basic 1966), pp. 265–71

Walsh, Mary Roth (ed.), *The Psychology of Women: Ongoing Debates* (New Haven and London: Yale University Press, 1987)

Wanner, Oskar, 'Der Moser vom "Charlottenfels"', *Schweizer Archiv für Neurologie, Neurochirurgie und Psychiatrie 131* No. 1 1982, pp. 55–68

Webster, Brenda, 'Helene Deutsch: A New Look', *Signs 10* 1985, pp. 553–71

Welsch, Ursula, and Wiesner, Michaela, *Lou Andreas-Salomé: vom 'Lebensurgrund' zur Psychoanalyse* (Munich: Verlag Internationale Psychoanalyse, 1988)

Weskott, Marcia, *The Feminist Legacy of Karen Horney* (New Haven and London: Yale University Press, 1986)

Wexler, Alice, *Emma Goldman. An Intimate Life* (London: Virago, 1984)

Whyte, Lancelot, *Focus and Diversions* (New York: Braziller, 1963)

Wilden, Anthony, *The Language of the Self* (Baltimore: Johns Hopkins University Press, 1968); reprinted as *Speech and Language in Psychoanalysis* (Baltimore: John Hopkins University Press, 1975)

Wilson, Elizabeth, 'Psychoanalysis: Psychic Law and Order', *Feminist Review 8* 1981, pp. 63–78

Winnicott, D.W., 'The Theory of the Parent–Infant Relationship' (1960), in Winnicott, D.W., *The Maturational Processes and the Facilitating Environment* (London: The Hogarth Press and the Institute of Psycho-analysis, 1979), pp. 37–55

Winter, Alison, 'Ethereal Epidemics: Mesmerism and the Introduction of Inhalation Anaesthesia to Early Victorian London', *Social History of Medicine 4* 1991, pp. 1–33

Wittgenstein, Ludwig, *Lectures and Conversations on Aesthetics, Psychology and Religious Belief*, ed. Cyril Barrett (Oxford: Basil Blackwell, 1970)

Wood, Ann Douglas, 'The Fashionable Diseases: Women's Complaints and their Treatment in Nineteenth-Century America', in Hartman, Mary S., and Banner, Lois (eds), *Clio's Consciousness Raised*, pp. 25–52

Woolf, Virginia, *The Diary of Virginia Woolf*, ed. Anne Olivier Bell, 5 vols (Harmondsworth, Middx: Penguin, 1979–85)

Wortis, Joseph, *Fragments of an Analysis with Freud*, (New York: Simon & Schuster, 1954)

Young-Bruehl, Elisabeth, *Anna Freud* (London: Macmillan, 1988)

  (ed.), *Freud on Women* (London: The Hogarth Press, 1990)

Zanardi, Claudia, *Essential Papers on the Psychology of Women* (New York and London: New York University Press, 1990)

Zilboorg, Gregory, 'Some Sidelights on Free Association', *Int J Psa 33* 1952, pp. 489–95

Index